THE ORIGINS OF MEDIEVAL ARCHITECTURE

THE ORIGINS OF MEDIEVAL ARCHITECTURE

Building in Europe, A.D. 600–900

Charles B. McClendon

YALE UNIVERSITY PRESS
NEW HAVEN AND LONDON

Designed by Kate Gallimore

Printed in China

Library of Congress Cataloging-in-Publication Data
McClendon, Charles B.
The origins of medieval architecture : building in Europe, A.D 600-900 / Charles B. McClendon.
p. cm.
Includes bibliographical references and index.
ISBN 0-300-10688-2 (cl : alk. paper)
1. Architecture, Medieval—Europe. 2. Architecture, Early Christian. 3. Architecture, Carolingian. 4. Church architecture—Europe. I. Title.
NA5453.M38 2005
723'.1—dc22
2004023967

Illustration on p. ii: Lorsch, abbey gateway, detail of exterior (fig.99).
Illustration on p. vi: Corvey, abbey church, facade of westwork (fig. 189).
Illustration on p. xii: Cologne, St. Pantaleon, abbey church, exterior view of westwork (fig. 204).

For illustrations 60, 135, 145-48, 157, 161, 163, 166, 171-72, 174, 177-78, 186, 188, 197, 200, 206 hatching indicates preserved foundations and black indicates remains of raising walls.

To the Memory of Richard Krautheimer

CONTENTS

Milan
Ravenna
Split
Rome
Constantinople
Antioch
Jerusalem
Bethlehem

ACKNOWLEDGMENTS

This book has been long in the making and during this process I have benefited from the assistance of many individuals and institutions. The project began under the auspices of a fellowship from the John Simon Guggenheim Memorial Foundation. Since then expenses for travel and assembling illustrations have been supplemented in part by grants from Yale University and Brandeis University. The text, in turn, was completed during a recent sabbatical leave from Brandeis University.

Four eminent scholars, Sible de Blaauw, Peter Fergusson, James Morganstern, and Thomas Noble, kindly read the manuscript in its entirety and provided expert advice about improvements. Others who provided important information include: Susan Boynton, Walter Cahn, William Clark, Deborah Deliyannis, Joseph Dyer, Judson Emerick, Margot Fassler, Caroline Goodson, Richard Gem, Peter Jeffrey, Dale Kinney, John Mitchell, Carol Neuman de Vegvar, Jerome Pollitt, Alexander Purves, Eric Rice, Valentino Pace, Christian Sapin, and Matthew Tash. The architectural drawings, except where otherwise noted, were produced by a series of talented young architects: John Blood, James Cronenberg, Keith Hudson, and Michael Rey. Jennifer Stern and Joy Vlachos at Brandeis and Helen Chillman at Yale helped with procuring photographs. Of the many libraries I have consulted, those at Yale have been particularly accommodating.

Two great historians of medieval architecture, Jean Bony and Walter Horn, offered encouragement during the initial phase of my research. Richard Krautheimer served as a mentor in every sense of the word and it is with gratitude that I dedicate this book to his memory.

At Yale University Press, I wish to thank Gillian Malpass for her enthusiastic support and her recognition of the importance of a study about a seemingly obscure topic. Kate Gallimore deserves special thanks for both her skill as a designer and her patience in dealing with an author often distracted by other matters. Joyce Ippolito assisted with copyediting and Fred Kameny created the index.

My wife, Judith Calvert, provided constant support and encouragement, as did our daughters, Gwyneth and Emma, who became stunning young women while this book was being prepared. They have made the enterprise worthwhile.

(Facing page) Roman Empire under Justinian, ca. A.D. 565.

Lindisfarne
Yeavering
Hexham
Jarrow
Wearmouth
Ripon
York
London
Canterbury
Paris
Jouarre
Tours
Poitiers
Vienne
Toulouse
Santa Comba de Bande
Braga
San Juan de Baños
San Pedro de la Nave
Toledo
Cividale
Brescia
Pavia
Ravenna
Spoleto
Rome
Benevento

Western Europe, ca. A.D. 700.

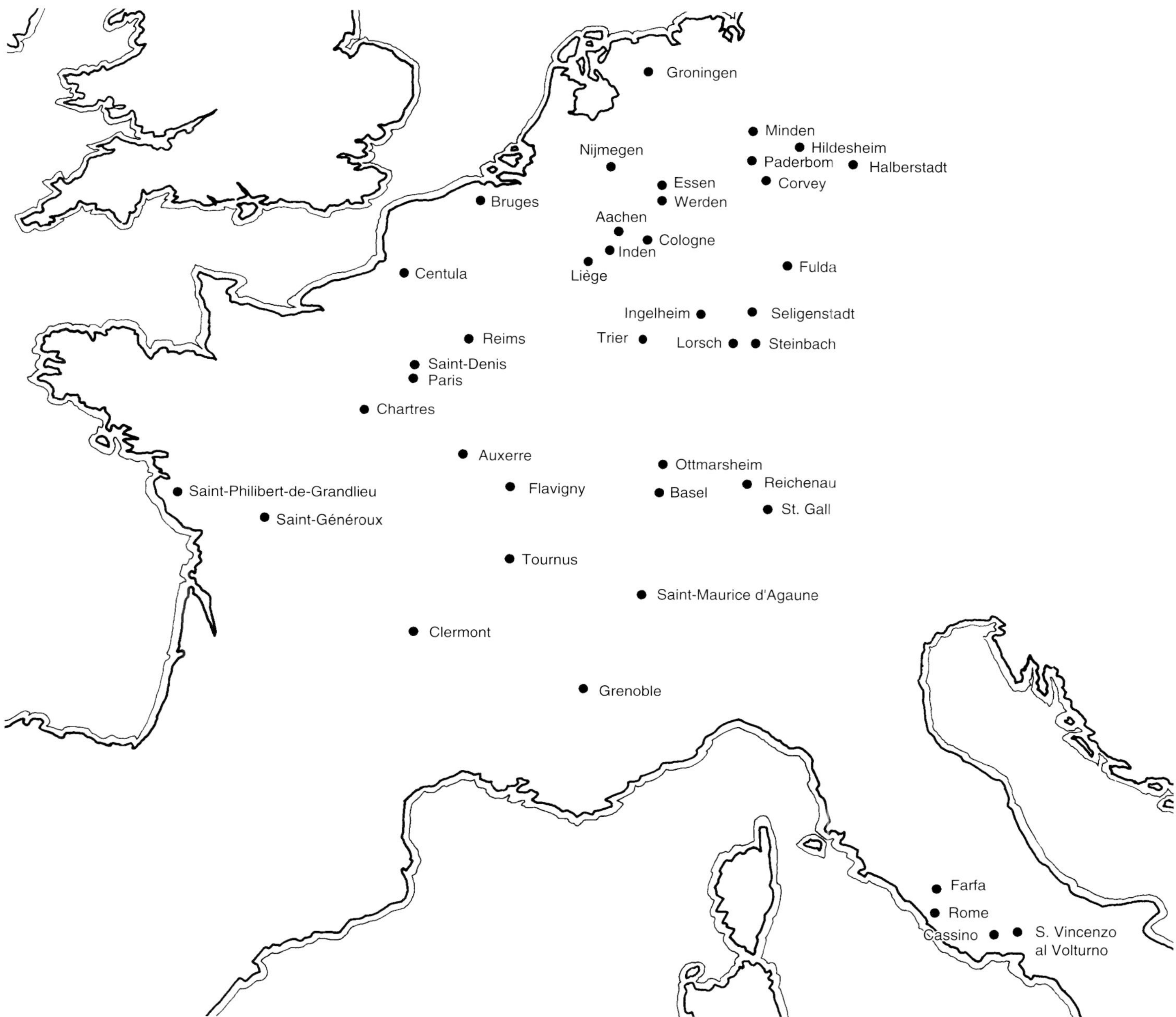
Groningen
Minden
Hildesheim
Nijmegen
Paderborn
Halberstadt
Essen
Corvey
Bruges
Werden
Aachen
Cologne
Inden
Fulda
Centula
Liège
Ingelheim
Seligenstadt
Reims
Trier
Lorsch
Steinbach
Saint-Denis
Paris
Chartres
Auxerre
Ottmarsheim
Reichenau
Saint-Philibert-de-Grandlieu
Flavigny
Basel
St. Gall
Saint-Généroux
Tournus
Saint-Maurice d'Agaune
Clermont
Grenoble
Farfa
Rome
Cassino
S. Vincenzo
al Volturno

Western Europe, ca. A.D. 750–1000.

Introduction

This study concerns the architectural transition from late antiquity to the Middle Ages in the Latin West. Although the great Romanesque and Gothic churches of Europe have long been the subject of detailed study by historians of architecture, the major buildings of the early Middle Ages have received comparatively little attention. No doubt, the smaller scale and often fragmentary nature of these remains have tended to discourage research, but this has meant that the significance of the architectural achievements of this earlier period has gone largely unappreciated. And yet, many of the features generally considered to be hallmarks of Romanesque and Gothic architecture, such as towered facades, colonnaded ambulatories, subterranean crypts, and interior vaulting, to name but a few, all find their origins in the early Middle Ages.

Put more succinctly, this study examines the innovations in architecture that transformed the Early Christian basilica into the medieval church in both form and function. But more than that, it tries to see the buildings of the early Middle Ages on their own terms, as the architectural expressions of an emerging Europe following the decline of the Roman Empire. The documentary evidence for many of the most important monuments is surprisingly rich and varied. In addition, the rapid growth in recent years of medieval archaeology has provided a new wealth of information for many individual sites. A concerted effort, therefore, has been made to use both written records and archaeological data, whenever possible, in order to place these buildings in their proper historical and cultural context. It should also be pointed out that until now this material has been dealt with only in regional and highly specialized studies written in a variety of languages. Despite the fundamental importance of the subject, no study focusing on the architecture of this period is readily available in English. In short, the need for such a study seemed clear.

No single event, of course, marked the end of antiquity and the beginning of the Middle Ages. Many different dates, all equally valid, have been proposed by various scholars depending upon their individual perspective, but no general consensus on the matter has ever been reached or ever will be. It was, instead, a gradual process covering many centuries whereby the social, political, and religious framework of the Roman Empire was transformed into a new, medieval mold. Nevertheless, the chronological framework of the book is far from arbitrary. Following the death of the Emperor Justinian in 565 the last remnants of the western half of the Roman Empire collapsed and were replaced by a mosaic of Germanic kingdoms. By the end of the eighth century, however, most of Europe was united under the rule of the Frankish king, Charlemagne, who, on Christmas Day 800, was proclaimed "Emperor of the Romans" by the pope and those assembled in St. Peter's basilica in Rome. The political unity of this empire ended soon after Charlemagne's death in 814, but members of the Carolingian dynasty continued to dominate Europe for another century until a combination of factors, including regional warfare, ever-increasing attacks by the Vikings from the North and the Muslims from the South, and the rise of a new landed aristocracy brought it to an end. This period in the history of western Europe (from the sixth to the tenth centuries) could be characterized, therefore, as having been shaped by the traumas of invasion and collapse at both the beginning and the end. Yet within this tumultuous time medieval architecture was born.

In architectural terms, the death of Justinian marked the end of any hope of imperial support for major building in the West. In contrast, the Germanic tribes ruling Europe by the end of the sixth century had no permanent building tradition of their own. They turned instead to the rich architectural legacy of late antiquity for inspiration. We know, for example, that during the reign of Charlemagne (768–814) the Early Christian basilicas of Rome and Ravenna served as primary models for several of the most important churches built north of the Alps. Above all, however, it was the spread of new forms resulting from experiments in design and construction that gave the architecture of the period its vitality. The development of the annular crypt in Rome around 600, for instance, may be seen as a specific response to the growing importance of the cult of relics that would have important ramifications for centuries to come. Similarly, the innovative character of late Carolingian architecture from ca. 840 to 900—a fact rarely noted—may be seen to have prepared the way for the emergence of Romanesque architecture in the later tenth and eleventh centuries. Another theme of this study, among others, is the role of monasticism in the development of medieval architecture and the formulation of the medieval cloister. In other words, I argue that a period that is all too often ignored, or at best passed over with little comment, was, in fact, of fundamental importance to the history of architecture in Europe.

A study of this kind must inevitably concentrate on church building. This is not to suggest that domestic architecture was without significance, but the simple fact remains that most houses during this period were built of wood, which means they have perished with little trace aside from the arrangement of postholes. As more archaeological information is gathered, it may well be possible, indeed necessary, to give greater attention to secular building. For now, what evidence we have suggests that domestic architecture was essentially conservative; the primary resources and creative energy of the time were focused, not surprisingly, on the glorification of the Church. Nevertheless, the two categories of domestic and ecclesiastical architecture should not be viewed as mutually exclusive. In the realm of monastic architecture, for example, the famous Plan of St. Gall, drawn up around 830, is a tour de force in planning on a grand scale integrating religious and utilitarian structures to serve the purpose of economic self-sufficiency. In addition, excavations of the imperial palaces at Aachen, Ingelheim, and Paderborn, together with more limited information about the papal palaces of Rome, provide us with a rare insight into the daily lives and political aspirations of the leaders of Europe in the ninth century.

Not long ago a project of this scope would have been hampered by a dearth of information about specific sites; however, the publication of comprehensive, multivolume compendia, such as *Vorromanische Kirchenbauten*, dealing with German-speaking lands, H. M. Taylor's *Anglo-Saxon Architecture*, dealing with pre-Norman England, and *Les premiers monuments chrétiens de la France*, together with numerous archaeological reports and regional studies, makes the undertaking feasible. This book is, therefore, intended both as an introduction to anyone interested in medieval architecture and as a guide to more specialized literature for those pursuing further research.

The book is divided into two parts. The first part covers the years from roughly 600 to 750, a period commonly known as the "Dark Ages," but one that was, in fact, a period of dynamic change that produced buildings of both lasting beauty and great significance through a new assimilation of seemingly antithetical "barbarian" and "classical" attitudes toward architecture and its decoration. The second part, covering the next century and a half, from 750 to ca. 900, is concerned with the architecture of the Carolingian Empire, which sponsored building on a grand scale not seen since the reign of Justinian. Indeed, the period around 800 has often been referred to as a "Renaissance" in arts and letters whereby Charlemagne and his successors saw themselves as the legitimate heirs of their ancient Roman forebears. And this concept was expressed in architecture in tangible and often eloquent terms, on both the public and private level, which helped to make the achievements of late antiquity more accessible to the later Middle Ages. The last section, an epilogue, suggests ways in which the achievements of these three centuries set important precedents and thereby helped to reshape the future of medieval architecture.

The following pages do not pretend to provide the final word on the subject nor is the approach comprehensive. The choice of monuments, by necessity, is highly selective, and is only meant to highlight major developments of the period. Current theory in the methodology of art historical research often stresses the fallacy of truly objective scholarship. As products of our own time with a biased outlook, it is argued, we can never recover fully the original intent of artists, builders, and patrons of the remote past. This may be true, but I do not believe that the goal of trying to understand the past should be abandoned, however difficult the task may be. One can only hope to arrive at a reasonable assessment of the information available at a given time. Historical analysis is a process of interpretation and constant revision. If this work stimulates interest and promotes further investigations, whether all my conclusions are accepted, then it will have served its purpose.

PART ONE THE "DARK AGES"

CHAPTER I

The Legacy of Late Antiquity

In 565, the Emperor Justinian died and with him the dream of a reunified Roman Empire. His generals had won back much of the territory in the western Mediterranean that had been overrun by Ostrogoths, Visigoths, and Vandals in the preceding century, but within a few years of Justinian's death Byzantine control of most of these lands was lost again, never to be recovered. Italy, for example, was invaded in 568 by yet another barbarian people, the Lombards, and soon much of the country was in their hands. In Spain, the Visigoths initiated a counter-offensive, regaining Cordoba in 584 and the rest of the Iberian peninsula within another generation. Only North Africa remained under firm imperial control, despite incursions by the local Berbers, but it too fell to Islam in the following century. To be sure, a vestige of Byzantine rule was maintained in Italy around Naples into the ninth century and, in the person of the exarch, in the area immediately surrounding Ravenna until as late as 751. Rome, as part of the exarchate, continued to recognize the authority of the Greek emperor in distant Constantinople, but in reality, the city was governed by the pope, who took on more and more of the administrative duties once carried out by imperial appointees. In other words, Justinian's military victories only forestalled, but did not prevent, the ultimate collapse of imperial rule in the West. His death, then, marked the end of an age.[1]

The same holds true for architecture as well. Justinian's program of reconquest had a devastating effect on the general economy of the empire through the imposition of heavy taxes to support the armies and through the ravages of warfare, especially in Italy. In addition, a great plague swept through Europe and Byzantium in 542 precipitating a decline in the population of cities and rural settlements alike.[2] Thus, the public and private funds that had sustained the grandiose scale and luxurious decoration of many Early Christian churches in the past were no longer available. Above all, the imperial coffers that had played such a vital role in the patronage of architecture in major cities in western Europe were now closed. Hereafter, monumental building programs became increasingly rare in the West as the financial and technological resources available to patrons and builders became more and more limited.[3]

Still, the architectural achievements of late antiquity were not forgotten. Every town of any size, after all, possessed one or more churches built during the Early Christian period, structures that for the most part continued to be used and maintained well into the Middle Ages. In addition, these churches were often associated with prominent figures of the past who had been instrumental in the establishment and defense of Christianity in the region, such as local bishops who may have served as early patrons or holy martyrs who lay buried nearby.[4] Most important, however, the churches of the fourth, fifth, and early sixth centuries provided the fundamental vocabulary of forms from which early medieval architecture emerged.

The rich architectural legacy of late antiquity was the product of two and a half centuries of experimentation. Each building represented an individual solution to the demands of a particular site, one or more patrons, local building traditions, and current liturgical practices. These complex developments have already received detailed study and need not be repeated here.[5] Instead, we need only review some of the most important trends that had an enduring impact on the Latin West. For example, within the wide range of possible solutions, Early Christian monuments may be classified under two basic types: the longitudinal basilica and the centrally planned church, whether round, polygonal, or even cruciform. This formal dichotomy can be traced to the reign of Constantine when Christian architecture first took on a monumental character.

Christian architecture may be said to have begun with the conversion of the Emperor Constantine in 312. Initially, Christianity appealed primarily to the lower echelons of society and its followers had neither the means nor the desire to develop a public architecture of their own. Christians, therefore, met in private houses or apartments to celebrate the eucharist and the initiation rite of

1 Rome, Temple of Fortuna Virilis, exterior view.

baptism took place wherever there was water. As the religion spread and became more rooted in the middle classes older dwellings were sometimes modified and enlarged to accommodate the growing Christian communities, especially in urban centers.[6] Nevertheless, conspicuous projects were ill advised for a religion that was held in suspicion by the Roman state and whose adherents were periodically persecuted. This situation changed dramatically, however, when under Constantine Christianity not only was made legal but was now favored by the emperor himself. A form of architecture had to be devised that could be deemed worthy of imperial largesse and representative of Christianity's newly elevated status in late antique society.

The traditional Greco-Roman temple with its high podium, colonnaded porch, and small cella could not serve this new purpose for obvious reasons (fig. 1). Paganism was still very much alive in the early fourth century—it was not totally banned until 391—and any reference to it in the architecture of a church would have been highly objectionable to both Christians and non-Christians alike.[7] Moreover, the design of the pagan temple was functionally inappropriate, for it served to house the cult statue of a particular god or goddess while public ceremonies took place at an altar located outside in the open air. The Early Christians, on the other hand, forbade the worship of graven images in keeping with the second commandment; they needed instead a large interior space in order to permit observation of and participation in the celebration of the mass, which involved, among other things, the reading of scripture, and both the consecration of bread and wine at a table (or altar) and their distribution to the faithful.

In response to these needs, Constantine and his builders turned to a more purely utilitarian class of Roman architecture, the basilica. This simple, rectangular hall in many variations—a central nave with or without aisles and an apse or tribunal at one or both of the short ends—had served a wide range of functions throughout the Roman world from marketplaces to law courts, from army drill halls to audience halls.[8] It was a type of building, then, that was ideally suited for large assemblies. Moreover, shortly before marching on Rome in 312, Constantine had used the basilican scheme on a monumental scale for his audience hall (aisleless with exterior blind arcading to buttress walls over 50 m high) in the provincial capital at Trier in northern Gaul (fig. 2).[9] The basilican hall, set along a strict longitudinal axis with an apse at one end, could therefore be seen to carry implicit imperial connotations making it appropriate both for the patronage of the new Christian emperor and as the setting for the worship of Christ, the king of kings. It seems almost inevitable, therefore, that this basic scheme should have been employed for the Lateran basilica, the first of several churches in Rome sponsored by Constantine.

Begun perhaps as early as 313, the Lateran was designed to serve as the residential church or cathedral of the bishop of Rome—the term cathedral being derived from the *cathedra*, or bishop's throne, which stood in the apse. Although remodeled extensively in the seventeenth century and partially rebuilt in the nineteenth century, much of the foundations and raising walls are still preserved from Constantine's day, showing it to have been 75 m long × 55 m wide composed of a nave flanked by double aisles to hold Rome's burgeoning Christian population (fig. 3A).[10] The nave was terminated in the west by an apse while the outer aisles ended in tranverse alcoves, their original purpose unknown. Soon after, between ca. 320 and 329, an even larger Christian basilica (119 m long, over 350 Roman feet) was built to house the venerated tomb of St. Peter, located in a cemetery on the western outskirts of town (fig. 3B). The basic formula of a nave, double aisles, and western apse was used once again, but a new element, the transept, was introduced to set off the tomb, marked by a marble-reveted block-like memorial, which, in turn, was enframed by spiral columns and bronze railings and set directly in front of the apse. The T-shaped basilica was to become one of the most popular designs in ecclesiastical architecture in the Middle Ages, but in the early fourth century it represented a totally new invention.[11]

2 Trier, Basilica of Constantine, exterior view.

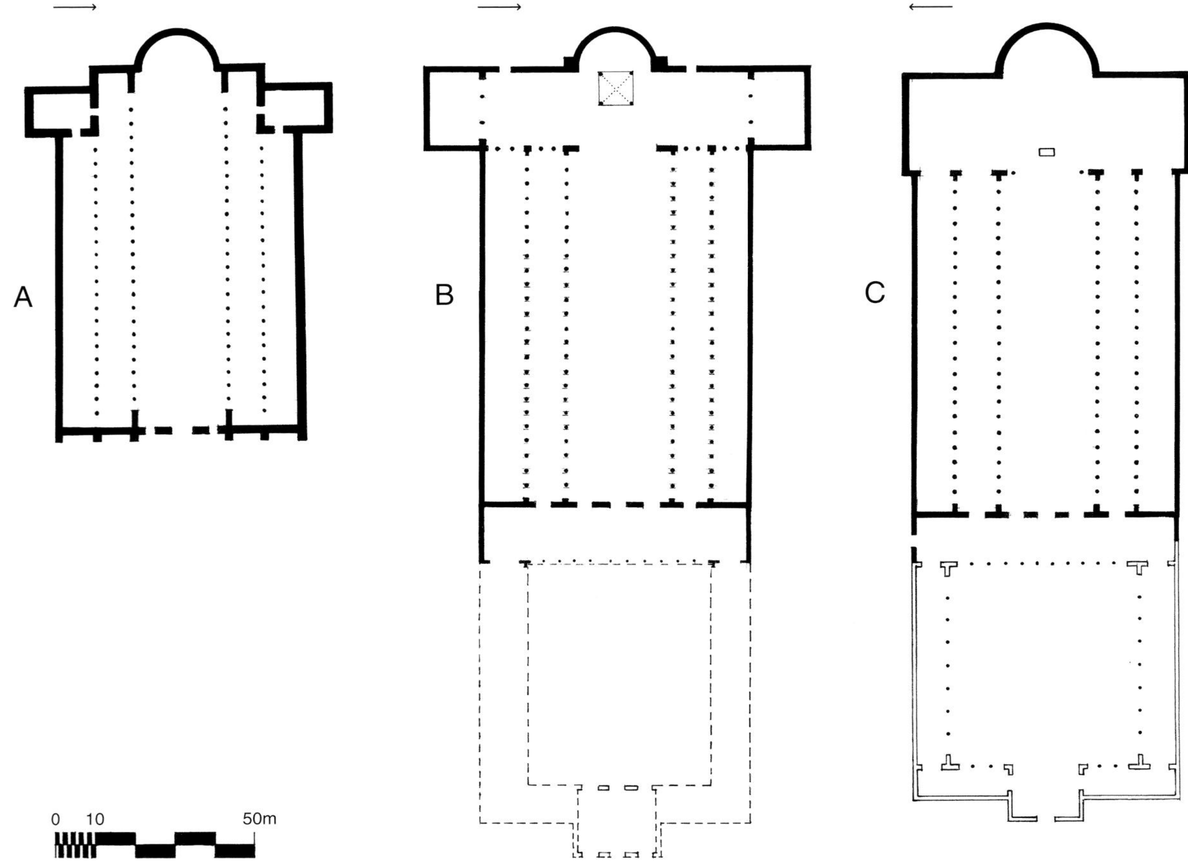

3 A Rome, Lateran Basilica, plan. B Rome, St. Peter's, plan. C Rome, St. Paul's-outside-the-Walls, plan.

Both the Lateran and St. Peter's made extensive use of *spolia,* that is to say architectural elements taken from older buildings, such as columns, capitals, and sections of architraves of varying sizes, styles, and even color. Although some effort was made to pair matching elements in the nave and aisle colonnades, the overall impression must have been one of both visual richness and striking diversity (fig. 4). The reasons for this amazing jumble are not fully known. Certainly, it represents a love of color and decorative exuberance for their own sake. Too, the reuse of older material presumably helped to speed the completion of the two churches. But there also seems to have been a reverence for, or admiration of, artifacts from the past in an attitude comparable to the use of *spolia* on the Arch of Constantine, dedicated in 315, where reliefs of Trajan, Hadrian, and Marcus Aurelius are juxtaposed to the narrative frieze of Constantine's own day. In this way, reminders of Rome's former glory were used to announce the dawn of a new "golden age," that of Constantine.[12] To the medieval observer, however, the basilicas in Rome of the Lateran and of St. Peter stood as symbols of Constantine's conversion and the triumph of the Church. Indeed, an inscription over the arch leading into the transept at St. Peter's proclaimed "Constantine, victor, built this hall."[13] At the same time, the Vatican basilica was the site of the tomb of the Prince of the Apostles. As such, it played a special role in the bishop of Rome's claim to primacy in the hierarchy of the Church. And for the West in general, St. Peter's became a primary goal of pilgrimage.

Other less elaborate basilicas, lacking transepts and often supported by masonry piers instead of columns, were also built around the time of Constantine's reign to commemorate the burial sites of other Roman martyrs (Lawrence, Agnese, Marcellinus and Peter, and Sebastian) located in cemeteries to the east and south of the city.[14] In the North, at Trier, Constantine also sponsored the construction of a vast cathedral complex composed of two aisled basilicas set side by side.[15] Centrally planned churches, on the other hand, did not appear until relatively late in Constantine's reign and only then in the eastern Mediterranean, when in 324 Constantine became master of the eastern half of the empire and his concerns turned away from the West.

In 327, Constantine left Rome never to return. Instead, he established a new permanent capital in the city of Byzantium on the Bosphorus, which he proclaimed as the "Nova Roma"; with time, however, it became known as Constantinopolis, "the city of Constantine." In that same year, Constantine initiated construction at Antioch of a cathedral adjoining the imperial palace. Nothing remains of the building, but the main outline of its design is known from contemporary descriptions. Eusebius, Constantine's biographer, tells us that it was eight-sided with a gilded roof, hence the name "Golden Octagon." In addition, he states that the core of the building was enveloped by a colonnaded aisle supporting a gallery that undulated in the form of eight exedrae. The specific sources for this design are unknown, but the centralized plan with billowing niches recalls pavilions common in imperial palace complexes from the time of Hadrian's villa at Tivoli in the early second century A.D. to the early fourth century when Constantine built the so-called Temple of Minerva Medica in Rome's Licinian Gardens.[16]

Constantine's primary patronage, however, was directed toward the Holy Lands and his new capital in Asia Minor. By 333, a church was built over the purported grotto of Christ's Nativity at Bethlehem. A short, squat basilica with twin side aisles (30 m long), one-third the size of St. Peter's in Rome, served as the site of assembly for the celebration of the eucharist, while an octagon rose at the east end of the hall enclosing the grotto (fig. 5). At about the same time, an even more monumental complex was erected to commemorate the site of Christ's Passion on the Hill of Golgotha in Jerusalem. Again, a relatively short, double-aisled basilica was employed, although this time with galleries. Some twenty meters to the west, however, across an open courtyard, a vast rotunda (33 m in diameter) with a flat facade, presumably to receive a colonnaded porch, marked the venerated site of Christ's tomb and resurrection (in Greek, Anastasis) (fig. 6). To be sure, the Anastasis Rotunda was not yet constructed by the formal consecration in 336; at least Eusebius, who attended the event, does not appear to refer to it in his rather convoluted description of the complex. But the rotunda was clearly in use by mid-century and may well have been planned before Constantine's death in 337 and completed not long after during the reign of his son, Constantius II. In any case, the sheer magnitude of the project would seem to require imperial patronage at every stage.[17]

It is therefore important to note that, at both Bethlehem and Jerusalem, Constantine's builders turned to traditional forms in imperial architecture to serve as models for these memorials (*martyria*) of Christ's life and death. The aisleless octagon of the church of the Nativity, for example, recalled not so much the aforementioned cathedral in Antioch as the great mausolea of Constantine's immediate predecessors, that of the Emperor Diocletian at Split, on the Adriatic coast in present-day Croatia, and that of Maximian in Milan in north Italy (fig. 7).[18] The rotunda of the Holy Sepulchre, on the other hand, was derived, it would seem, from another, closely related, source. It may be no mere

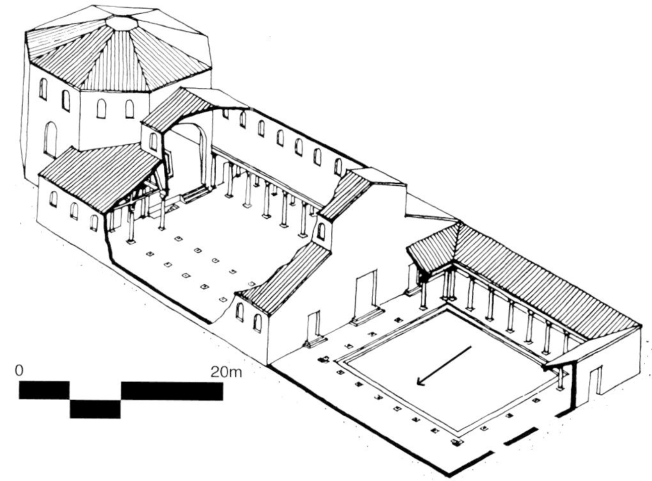

5 Bethlehem, Church of the Nativity, reconstruction.

4 Rome, Lateran Basilica, painted interior view, partly reconstructed, of ca. 1650 by F. Gagliardi.

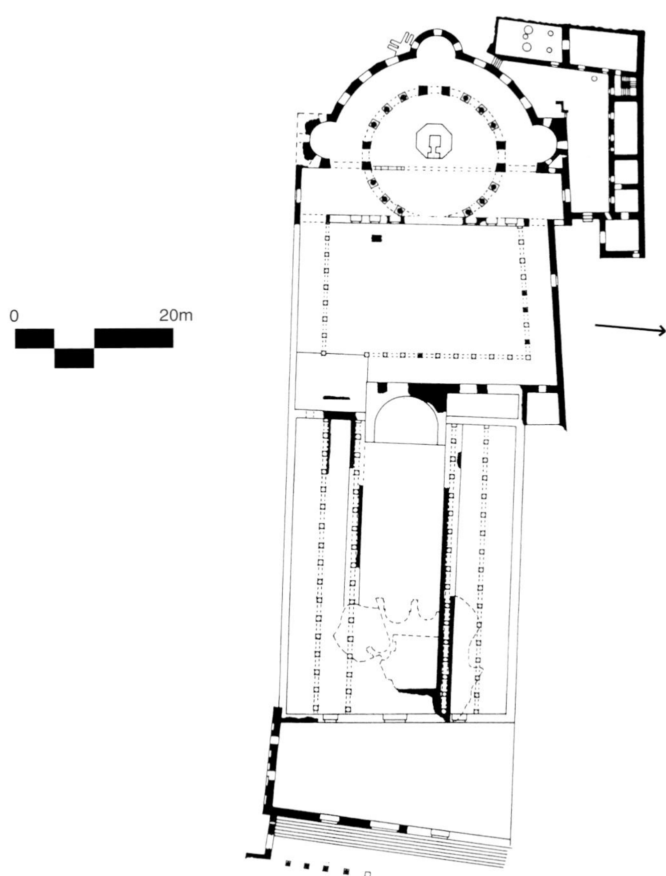

6 Jerusalem, Basilica and Anastasis Rotunda, plan.

coincidence that the colossal size (over 100 Roman feet in diameter) and general design of the rotunda (domed with a flat, columnar facade), as uncovered by excavations, should correspond to that of the Pantheon in Rome (fig. 8). Certainly, the Anastasis Rotunda in Jerusalem was far less structurally daring than the Pantheon, having been built of cut stone, in keeping with local building tradition, instead of brick-faced concrete, and covered by a timber roof rather than a concrete dome. Nonetheless, the implication is that the greatest building of imperial Rome was seen fit as a model for the structure housing the tomb of the king of heaven, which Constantine, in a letter of 325/26 to the bishop of Jerusalem, called "the most wondrous place in the world." After all, the Pantheon had already inspired a series of imperial mausolea in Rome in the third and early fourth centuries, and the Anastasis Rotunda could be seen as a culmination of this process.[19]

In Constantinople, Constantine's building activities were no less ambitious. Although virtually nothing remains today of the city's transformation into an imperial capital in the fourth century, Constantine's pronouncements make it clear that his new city was to bear all the accoutrements of an ancient capital: a palace complex, colonnaded thoroughfares, fora with monumental fountains and statues, a Senate house, and fortification walls. In order to obtain materials for this program, pagan temples and secular structures throughout the eastern Mediterranean were stripped of columns, statues, and other architectural ornament. But the Nova Roma was to be above all a Christian capital. Thus, a cathedral was begun adjoining the imperial palace on the site of its Justinianic successor, the great Hagia Sophia; indications are that it was a basilica extremely long and

7 Split, Mausoleum of Diocletian, exterior view.

broad with a colonnaded forecourt.[20] More innovative was the church of the Holy Apostles, also replaced later by Justinian, but originally built either by Constantine or by his son and successor Constantius II. In any event, the church was cross-shaped with, at its center, the high altar, which in 356 and 357 received relics of SS. Timothy, Luke and the apostle Andrew. Whatever the true meaning of the arrangement, the Holy Apostles' church in Constantinople represented an important stage in the development of the centrally planned church in that for the first time the central focus of the aforementioned martyria was combined with a congregational hall.[21]

In Rome, nevertheless, the longitudinal basilica remained the preferred scheme for church building. This is not to say that centralized plans were unknown. A domed rotunda was built around 350 as the mausoleum for Constantine's daughter Constantina, later known as S. Costanza (fig. 9), and ca. 400, a similar structure was built by the Emperor Honorius adjoining the south arm of the transept of St. Peter's to serve as his dynastic tomb. But such designs were used exclusively for imperial mausolea and not for churches; only much later were these rotundas transformed into places of Christian worship.[22] Not until the middle of the fifth century was a centrally planned church built in Rome, derived from a long tradition of cylindrical structures including the Anastasis Rotunda in Jerusalem and, ultimately, the Pantheon. It was dedicated to St. Stephen (hence the name S. Stefano Rotondo), a non-Roman saint and deacon of the church in Jerusalem who became the first Christian martyr. Otherwise, the major churches of Rome such as S. Sabina and S. Maria Maggiore, to name but the prime examples, were aisled basilicas.[23]

The church of St. Paul's-outside-the-Walls was even built in direct imitation of the basilica of St. Peter's on the Vatican Hill (fig. 3c).[24] Here the T-shaped plan that had been devised to mark the tomb of the Prince of the Apostles was used to house the tomb of the Apostle of the Gentiles. Through imperial patronage, the tombs of the two Apostolic martyrs of Rome received churches of similar size and shape. In 384 or 386, the emperors Valentian II, Theodosius, and Arcadius commanded the prefect of Rome to consult with the bishop of Rome, the clergy, and the congregation about the project. Thus any divergence from the Petrine scheme (the broader apse, deeper and shorter transept, and the location of the saint's tomb just inside the transept near the head of the nave) must have been the result of careful deliberations. The plan may represent a critique of St. Peter's, but differences may just as well be due to specific topographical considerations, such as the location of the martyr's tomb, the path of nearby roads, and the proximity of the Tiber River. In any event,

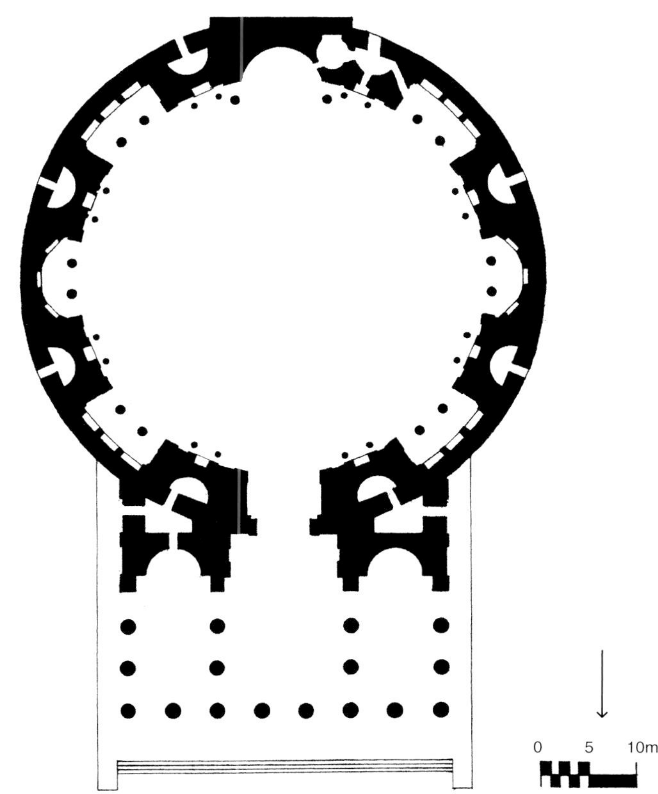

8 Rome, Pantheon, plan.

St. Paul's stood virtually intact until 1823 when it was severely damaged in a fire and subsequently almost totally rebuilt, and drawings and engravings depicting the interior of the church before the fire provide a sense of the monumental scale and decorative richness that embodied all of Rome's great basilicas (fig. 10).

While Rome remained faithful to the basilican scheme established under Constantine in the early fourth century, the provincial capitals in the West of Trier and Milan, and later Ravenna, seem to have been more open to the later architectural experiments during Constantine's reign in the eastern Mediterranean. Around 380, for example, the Emperor Gratian sponsored the substantial remodeling of the north basilica of the cathedral complex at Trier, built first under Constantine.[25] The nave colonnade was strengthened with intermittent piers in order to support galleries over the aisles, an eastern motif, while the eastern half of the basilica was replaced by a massive quadratic structure, composed of four corner towers supporting a central lantern with a wooden roof. The motivation behind this change seems to have been the importation of the purported cloak worn by Christ at Calvary. Thus, the

9 Rome, S. Costanza, interior view.

10 Rome, St. Paul's-outside-the-Walls, interior view ca. 1750 by G.B. Piranesi.

centralized scheme devised for martyria in the Greek east was here adapted to fit the original basilican layout in order to provide a suitable setting for a relic of Christ.

In Milan, at approximately the same time, a variation on this design was used for the vast centrally planned church now known as S. Lorenzo (figs. 11–12).[26] The church is well preserved despite substantial remodelings in later centuries. The present dome, for example, set on a high octagonal drum, belongs to a rebuilding campaign of the sixteenth century. Originally, the central space was covered either by a timber, pyramidal roof as at Trier or by a groin vault of light material, such as cane or hollow ceramic tubes. Be that as it may, S. Lorenzo represents a far more sophisticated version of the Trier monument; whereas the central complex at Trier was ponderous and blocky, the church of S. Lorenzo is a subtle orchestration of rectilinear and curvilinear forms, whereby the central space expands gently outward through four colonnaded exedrae. Indeed, S. Lorenzo may be seen as one of the great monuments of late antiquity. As such it is both a direct descendant of Hadrian's pavilion, the so-called Piazza d'Oro, at his villa in Tivoli and a precursor of Justinian's Hagia Sophia in Constantinople. The original dedication and specific function of the church of S. Lorenzo remain unknown, however. Even the date of construction is controversial. Nevertheless, its monumental scale, delicate detailing, and fine masonry together with its location near the site of the imperial palace all strongly suggest that the church was built under imperial patronage.

Two centrally planned structures are appended to the main church of S. Lorenzo. Bonded with the eastern exedra stands a small chapel, octagonal on the outside but cruciform on the inside, with a central groin vault supported by applied columns set in the corners. Adjoining the exedra to the south is a much larger octagonal structure with eight interior niches in the form of semicircles alternating with squares all supporting a cloister vault, that is to say a dome in eight sections. It was once thought that this subsidiary structure served as a baptistery but there are no traces of a font.[27] In view of the imperial connotations of the main church, and the building's close resemblance to imperial mausolea, it seems more likely that it was built as a dynastic tomb for the emperors when they resided in Milan. For our purposes, however, the precise date of the complex of S. Lorenzo is less important than the recognition that it demonstrates the variety of centralized designs available to builders in the late fourth or early fifth century.

In 374, Ambrose, a local lawyer and magistrate, was elected bishop of Milan by public acclamation. Over the next twenty-three years, Ambrose proved to be not only an able administrator but a champion of orthodoxy and episcopal power even when at variance with imperial policy. Through the sheer force of his personality and the influence of his teaching (Augustine of Hippo was one of his pupils), he transformed the see of Milan into the most influential ecclesiastical center in Europe. His impact on church architecture was equally profound. The three churches built under Ambrose, today known as S. Ambrogio, S. Nazaro, and S. Simpliciano, were remarkable for their day and exerted a lasting influence on the architecture of the region.[28] Technically speaking, their masonry is far cruder than that of S. Lorenzo, suggesting that the financial resources at Ambrose's disposal were limited. But this negative factor does not hide their sophisticated design. The Basilica Ambrosiana, perhaps the first and least innovative in the series, was located in a cemetery outside the city walls to the southwest and designated by Ambrose as his final resting place. Only the foundations of this church are preserved below the present Romanesque structure, but they suffice to show that it was a basilica approximately the same size as its Romanesque successor with side aisles and a single apse to the east. The church may have had galleries above the side aisles like the remodelled cathedral in Trier and ultimately following eastern Mediterranean precedents, but this remains unproven.

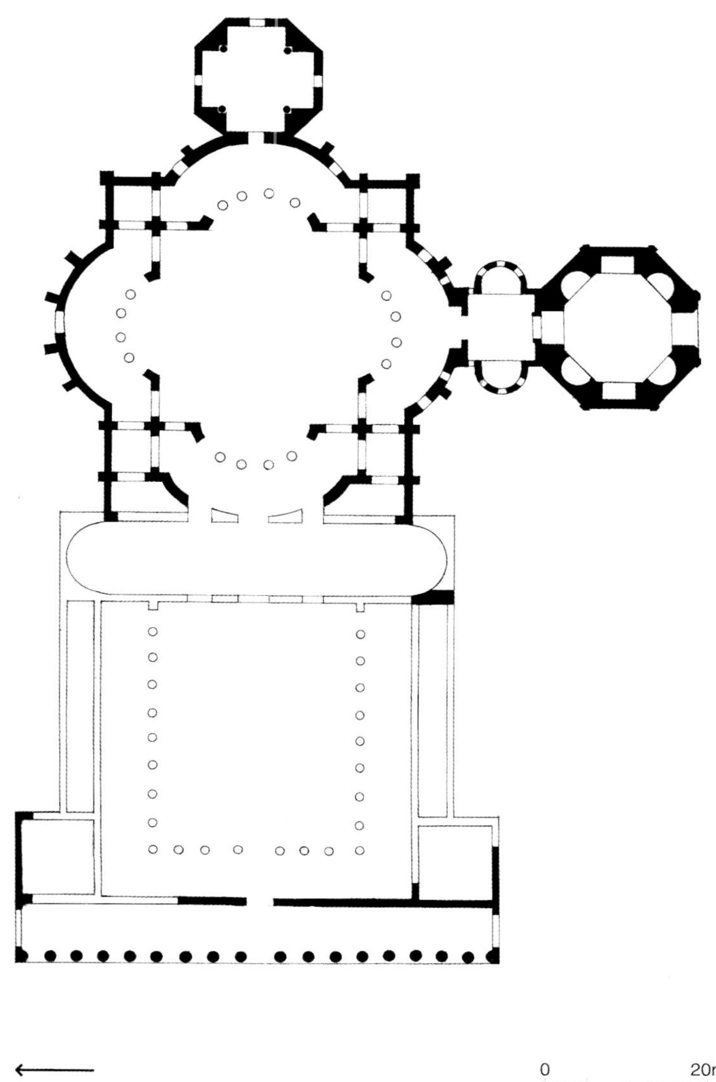

11 Milan, S. Lorenzo, plan.

Far more remarkable was the church of the Holy Apostles begun in 382. Also located outside the city walls, this time to the southeast along the road ultimately leading to Rome, the Holy Apostles' church was laid out in the

12 Milan, S. Lorenzo, exterior view.

form of a cross with the western arm slightly longer than the others (fig. 13A). The design and dedication of the church strongly suggest that it was built in imitation of Constantine's church of the Holy Apostles in Constantinople. Indeed, in 386 relics of the apostles Thomas, John, and Andrew were deposited below the altar in the crossing, relics which may have been obtained from the Byzantine capital. In 395, Ambrose placed the body of a local martyr, St. Nazarius or S. Nazaro, in the eastern apse at which time he composed an inscription, still partially preserved, explaining the meaning of the church's cruciform design: "The temple has the form of the victory of Christ . . . where the cross raises its sacred head ending in a semicircle is now the house of Nazaro. He (was) a victor . . . the cross his palm and the cross his resting place." Here then, for the first time, we have clear evidence of an iconography of architecture whereby the form of the church held a specific symbolic meaning. The cruciform design was deemed appropriate for the site of the martyr's grave and conveyed a universal message of salvation to the faithful.[29]

Late in his life, Ambrose may have initiated construction of another church, again outside the walls but this time to the north, closely modelled after the Basilica Apostolorum and dedicated originally to the Virgin but now known as S. Simpliciano. Unlike the church of S. Nazaro, which was heavily remodelled in the Romanesque period, the church of S. Simpliciano stands virtually intact, recently freed from later masonry and plaster coatings.[30] Although clearly dependent upon S. Nazaro for its cruciform design, S. Simpliciano displays important differences as well. Like S. Nazaro, the church remains aisleless (piers subdividing the nave were added in the early Middle Ages), but the northern and southern arms of the cross are now much broader and no longer screened off from the nave by a pair of columns (fig. 13B). The nave, too, is broader and was originally surrounded by a low outer corridor, perhaps to allow access to the cross arms without entering the nave. The eastern apse and forechoir are also stunted in comparison to S. Nazaro due in part to the fact that the relics, those of minor martyrs from the Trentino region of Italy, were placed in an adjoining chapel, itself a miniature version of the main church. Most remarkable, however, is the exterior articulation of the rising walls which are accented with a series of projecting pilasters and blind arches (fig. 14). Such a wall system served to sustain the soaring height of the aisleless structure in a manner reminiscent of Constantine's basilica in Trier, no doubt reflecting the close cultural and architectural ties which existed between Milan and the Rhineland in the fourth century. Together, therefore, S. Nazaro and S. Simpliciano provided two variations of the cruciform design.

Once established, the cruciform church became extremely popular in north Italy and the Alpine region in the fifth through the tenth centuries (figs. 13C–E). Some churches, such as the recently excavated church of S. Lorenzo in Aosta, dating from the fifth century, followed more closely the model of S. Nazaro by retaining cross arms of approximately equal length, while others such as SS. Peter and Paul in Como and S. Stefano in Verona preferred the broader proportions, albeit on a smaller scale, of S. Simpliciano.[31] In this way, Milan, through the active patronage of St. Ambrose, served as a gateway for the transmission of architectural forms from the eastern Mediterranean to western Europe. At the same time, these building types became associated with Milan and the age of Ambrose for centuries to come.

The most influential of the Milanese architectural developments, however, was the formulation of the octagonal bapistery. In 1943 and again in the early 1960s, excavations in the heart of the city revealed the remains of the Early Christian cathedral on the site, dedicated in the Middle Ages to S. Tecla, a female saint from Asia Minor (fig. 15).[32] The plan of the church (the remains of a second and even earlier cathedral known to have stood in the vicinity have never been found) was a basilica with a nave flanked by twin aisles and terminated by a non-projecting transept further subdivided by a continuation of the nave and aisle colonnades. Immediately to the east of the cathedral stood a baptistery, recognizable as such by its central font, that was octagonal on the outside and articulated on the inside by alternating square and semicircular niches. Such a plan, minus the font, is identical to that of S. Aquilino, adjoining

13 A Milan, S. Nazaro, plan; B Milan, S. Simpliciano, plan; C Verona, S. Stefano, plan; D Aosta, S. Lorenzo, plan; E Como, SS. Peter and Paul, plan.

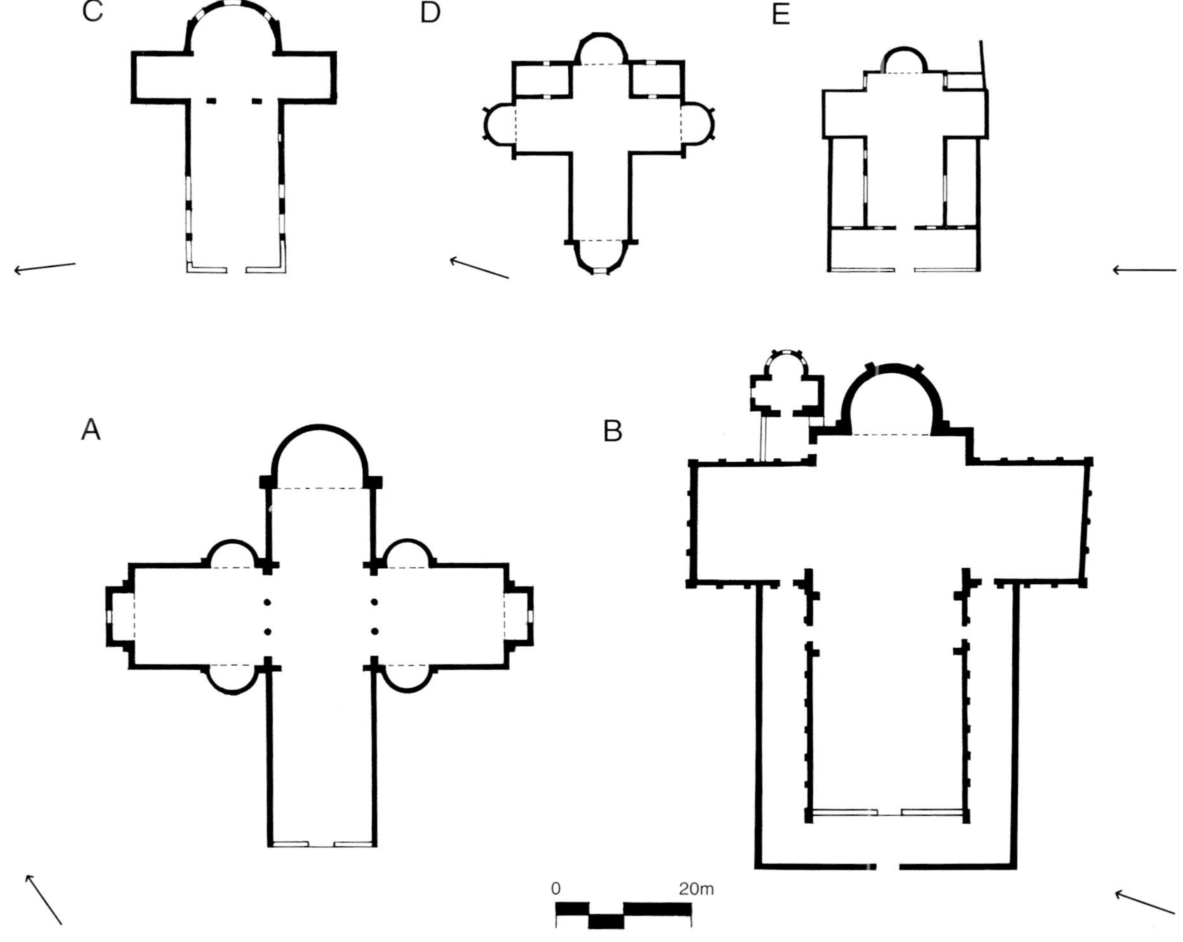

14 Milan, S. Simpliciano, exterior detail.

the church of S. Lorenzo, and to the now-destroyed mausoleum of the Emperor Maximian (d. 312), which also stood outside Milan's city walls. In short, the baptistery of Milan took on the form of imperial mausolea in the area.

For the Early Christians, baptism was not only a symbolic cleansing of sin but a ritualistic reenactment of the death and resurrection of Christ as expressed by St. Paul in his letter to the Romans (6:3–4): "We are buried with Christ by baptism into his death; as Christ was raised from the dead by the glory of the Father so we too walk in the newness of life." Ambrose reiterated this concept of baptism in his writings and, in one instance, referred to the font as "like a tomb."[33] The baptistery of Milan may, in fact, predate the reign of Ambrose; certainly the cathedral was complete by 355 when a synod met there. Nevertheless, Ambrose is generally credited with having composed an inscription for the interior of the baptistery, which read: "Eight-niched soars this temple for sacred rites / Eight corners has its font / Right it is to build this baptismal hall about the sacred number eight / For here the people are reborn." For Ambrose, or whoever composed the verse, the plan of the baptistery, like that of S. Nazaro, bore a symbolic meaning. For Ambrose and other Early Christian authors, the number eight represented eternity and continual rebirth for it is the day of Christ's resurrection.[34] One could argue that because the inscription seems to stress rebirth and not death, the octagonal form of the baptistery need not be interpreted as referring to a mausoleum.[35] And yet, as St. Paul explained, one cannot be reborn without first experiencing death. Indeed, the inscription goes on to make clear that absolution is achieved through baptism because Christ defeated death.[36] Moreover, the fact that an octagonal design was also used to mark the grotto of Christ's birth in Bethlehem further indicates that the concepts of death and rebirth were integrally connected in the minds of the Early Christians.

More important for us is to recognize that like the cruciform church, the octagonal baptistery, once established in Milan, spread throughout north Italy and into southern France.[37] Again, the basic formula appeared in many variations, depending particularly upon whether or not the niches were allowed to project on the outside. In every case, however, the octagonal core was preserved and its presence can only be explained by the authority of Ambrose and the see of Milan in its architectural formulation of the Pauline doctrine of baptism. Even Rome did not remain unaffected. This would seem to explain why the baptistery of the Lateran was remodelled by Pope Sixtus III (432–40) (fig. 16). Although resting on circular foundations, it is now generally agreed that the current octagonal exterior elevation dates to the Constantinian period. The outline of the Lateran baptistery, therefore, antedates that of the Milan baptistery and would seem to have set a precedent for the Ambrosian formulation. The octagonal mausoleum, however, while common in Milan,

15 Milan, Cathedral and Baptistery, plan.

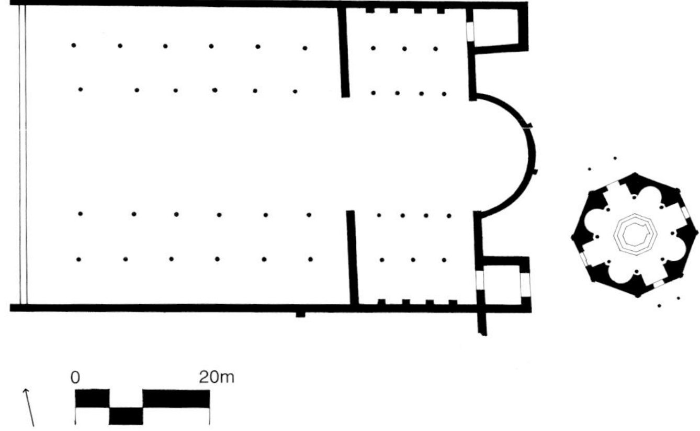

16 Rome, Lateran Baptistery, interior view.

was rare, if not unknown, in Rome. As we have just seen, imperial mausolea in and around Rome were invariably cylindrical. It seems more likely that the octagonal configuration in Rome, which lacks the peripheral wall niches found in the Milan baptistery and related mausolea, was derived instead from similarly shaped spaces in bath complexes. A century later, Sixtus III felt the need to alter the original arrangement by moving monumental porphyry columns from the inner walls to the center in order to form an octagonal ring of columns about a vast baptismal font, which, in turn, created an ambular passage and a central dome perched on a drum with ample clerestory windows in the manner of imperial mausolea in Rome, like S. Costanza, thus making the sepulchral association more apparent to Roman eyes. Here, too, the pope devised a lengthy inscription, still to be seen along the marble cornice supported by the porphyry columns, which proclaims the sacred font to be the "fountain of life" (*fons vitae*), echoing the concept ascribed to St. Ambrose.[38] This transformation is best explained, it seems to me, by the influence of St. Ambrose. Nonetheless, by whatever means, the octagonal baptistery became pervasive throughout the western Mediterranean in the Early Christian period.

Major building activity in Trier and Milan came to an end with new incursions by Germanic barbarians along the empire's northern border. The two cities that had risen to

17 Ravenna, Orthodox Baptistery, exterior view.

such prominence earlier in the fourth century, because of their proximity to the frontier, were by the end of the century vulnerable to attack. In 395, the capital of the province of Gaul was moved from Trier in the north to Arles near the Mediterranean coast at the mouth of the Rhône River. A few years later, in 402, the Emperor Honorius transferred his court from Milan to Ravenna on the Adriatic coast of Italy thereby gaining a direct link by sea with Constantinople. The Goths soon appeared in the Po Valley, but they were persuaded, through bribery, to leave Milan unharmed; instead, they headed south to Rome, which they sacked in 410. While the former *caput mundi* was besieged, the imperial court remained secure, protected by the impenetrable marshes that surrounded Ravenna. Here, over the next one hundred and fifty years, a once-provincial town was transformed through the construction of churches and palaces into the capital of the West. Despite later remodelings, many of these buildings are extremely well preserved affording the visitor to Ravenna today the unique opportunity to appreciate the variety and sophistication of Early Christian architecture as a whole.[39]

Not surprisingly, the earliest preserved buildings in Ravenna, even those dating from shortly before the arrival of the imperial court, display strong Milanese influence. The so-called Orthodox Baptistery, for example, built around 400, uses the aforementioned octagonal plan, albeit in a slightly modified version (fig. 17).[40] That is to say, in comparison with the Milan baptistery, the semi-circular niches project boldly on the exterior, while the square-ended niches have been reduced to shallow recesses without any exterior expression. Nevertheless, like the many other variants of the scheme, the Pauline symbolism of baptism as death and rebirth is equally clear at Ravenna. As originally built, the Orthodox Baptistery was timber roofed; not until fifty years later, under Bishop Neon, did it receive a dome constructed of hollow, interlocking ceramic tubes, a construction method for lightweight vaulting developed in North Africa and Italy in the late third and early fourth centuries. Today, the interior of the baptistery still glows with the light reflected from the luxurious marble revetment and mosaic decoration. The new dome in particular received an elaborate mosaic composition of three concentric rings filled with representations of altars and empty thrones, the apostles carrying their crowns of martyrdom, and finally, the Baptism of Christ. This last scene, set at the apex of the vault against a gold background and framed by an imitation egg-and-dart molding, resembles an oculus, like that of the Pantheon, so that Christ's Baptism is presented as a celestial vision to the neophyte, who reenacts the same rite in the font directly below.[41]

An equally sophisticated integration of architecture and mosaic decoration is found in the so-called Mausoleum of Galla Placidia, built around 425 (fig. 18).[42] Galla Placidia was the sister of the Emperor Honorius and reigned in her own right following her brother's death and as regent for her son, Valentinian III, from 425 to 450. The term "mausoleum" for the building that bears her name is a misnomer, however, for Galla Placidia and other members of her family were most likely buried in the rotunda built for Honorius around 400 adjoining the south transept arm of St. Peter's in Rome; the occupants of the three large sarcophagi found inside the Ravenna building remain unidentified.[43] The links to Milan are immediately apparent. Most

18 Ravenna, so-called Mausoleum of Galla Placidia, exterior view.

striking are the exterior blind arcades, reminiscent of S. Simpliciano and ultimately Constantine's basilica at Trier, used here, however, to sustain interior vaulting (the cross arms are barrel-vaulted, while the center is covered by a domical vault on pendentives). Milanese, too, are the thick bricks set in thin beds of white mortar. Now freestanding, the mausoleum originally joined one end of the porch of a church dedicated to the Holy Cross, hence S. Croce, which was laid out in an aisleless cross plan—again analogous to churches in Milan—of which only the foundations are preserved. A comparison could thus be made to the cruciform chapels found in Milan adjoining the churches S. Lorenzo and S. Simpliciano.

The chapel was dedicated to St. Lawrence, who is represented in a mosaic in the lunette of the cross arm in line with and opposite from the main entrance. The entire interior is sumptuously decorated with figural and abstract mosaic decoration. Over the entrance doorway Christ, "the way and the truth," is represented as a shepherd with his flock, but dressed in regal garb and holding a gold cross.[44] The barrel vaults are covered with star-shaped patterns on a blue ground and the central dome bears a celestial vision with a gold cross at its summit surrounded by gold stars and the symbols of the four evangelists in the pendentives. Cruciform in plan, with the cross as a prominent decorative motif, and attached to a cruciform church dedicated to the Holy Cross, mosaic decoration and architectural design combine to provide the specific Christian meaning of this monument.

If the Orthodox Baptistery and the mausoleum of Galla Placidia reveal their debt to Milan, the basilican churches of Ravenna tended to incorporate features originating in the eastern Mediterranean. The church of St. John the Evangelist, for example, another building patronized by Galla Placidia, has a polygonal apse, a feature usually associated with Constantinople, and a continuous arcade of round-arched windows similar to contemporary churches in Greece (fig. 19). Flanking the apse, moreover, are two chambers that project eastward from the aisles in a manner resembling not only the mid-fourth-century cathedral in Milan but numerous fifth-century churches in southeastern Asia Minor and northern Syria.[45] Other details, such as

19 Ravenna, St. John the Evangelist, exterior view of east end.

the use of impost blocks, in the form of inverted truncated pyramids, surmounting the capitals of the nave arcade also point to mainland Greece as a primary source of influence. Ravenna in the first half of the fifth century may therefore be seen as a point of convergence where western (i.e., Milanese) and eastern trends in church building design merged to produce a local style of its own.

These same building patterns continued with little change even after the Ostrogoths became the overlords of Italy in the second half of the fifth century. The last Roman emperor of the West, Romulus Augustulus, was deposed in 476. In 490, Theodoric became the leader of the Ostrogoths in large part through the aegis of the emperor in Constantinople. Having grown up in Constantinople as a political hostage, Theodoric was well accustomed to the refinements of urban life in the late Roman world, despite his Germanic origin. Indeed, taking the titles "patrician of the Romans" and "prince of Italy," he sought to restore many elements of Rome and Ravenna that had fallen into disrepair.[46] The Ostrogoths, though Christians, were considered to be heretics, however, having been converted in the mid-fourth century by a Greek missionary named Ulfilas who was an Arian. Arianism, which derived its name from an early proponent, a certain Arius, maintained that Christ was similar to the Father but not equally divine. This flew in the face of the orthodox doctrine of the Trinity which held that Christ was consubstantial with the Father. Nevertheless, the Ostrogoths did not try to impose their Arian beliefs on the general populace and the two factions seem to have lived in relative harmony. This did not mean, however, that they worshipped in the same churches. Indeed, among Theodoric's first priorities was to build a cathedral complex for the Arians of which the baptistery still survives. And yet, the architectural formulas of the past were continued. The Arian baptistery, for example, follows the octagonal plan and elevation of the earlier Orthodox baptistery; even the mosaic decoration in the dome is basically the same, despite some subtle stylistic and compositional differences. Similarly, the church of S. Apollinare Nuovo, which he originally built as his palace church dedicated to the Savior, follows the outlines of buildings fifty years earlier. The apse, round on the inside, is polygonal on the exterior. Also on the outside, the windows of the aisles and clerestory of the nave are framed by blind arcades. And the capitals of the nave arcade are surmounted by high impost blocks.

Still, the Ostrogoths remained heretics in the eyes of the Western Church, and their hold on Italy did not long outlast Theodoric's death in 526, the year before Justinian ascended the imperial throne. Early in his reign, Justinian made a special effort to reestablish good relations with the bishop of Rome and when his troops entered Ravenna in 540 they were looked upon by many as "Catholic" liberators. Reminders of Ostrogothic rule were systematically obliterated. In S. Apollinare Nuovo, for example, mosaic representations of Theodoric and his court were reset and replaced by a procession of male and female martyrs and the church was rededicated to St. Martin, a western holy man.[47] At the same time, building projects initiated during Ostrogothic rule were brought to completion with the help of men and materials from the eastern Mediterranean.

The churches of S. Vitale in Ravenna and S. Apollinare in the nearby port town of Classe, for example, were both begun around 531 with the assistance of a local financier, Julius Argentarius, but they were not dedicated until 547 and 549 respectively, several years after the Byzantine reconquest. They therefore represent primary examples of Justinianic architecture in Ravenna. The sophisticated design of S. Vitale, in particular, can only be explained by the impact of architectural developments in Constantinople in the 530s (figs. 20–22).[48] The double shell construction centered about an octagonal core supporting a dome is comparable to that of SS. Sergius and Bacchus completed shortly before 536. But there are differences, too. Unlike the Constantinopolitan churches, the exterior is clearly octagonal and the dome rises on a high drum. The overall effect is one of verticality and clarity as opposed to the low proportions and more hidden massing of SS. Sergius and Bacchus. Moreover, the emphasis on the exterior of great expanses of flat wall pierced by large but simple round-arched windows with recessed surrounds is purely Ravennate in character.

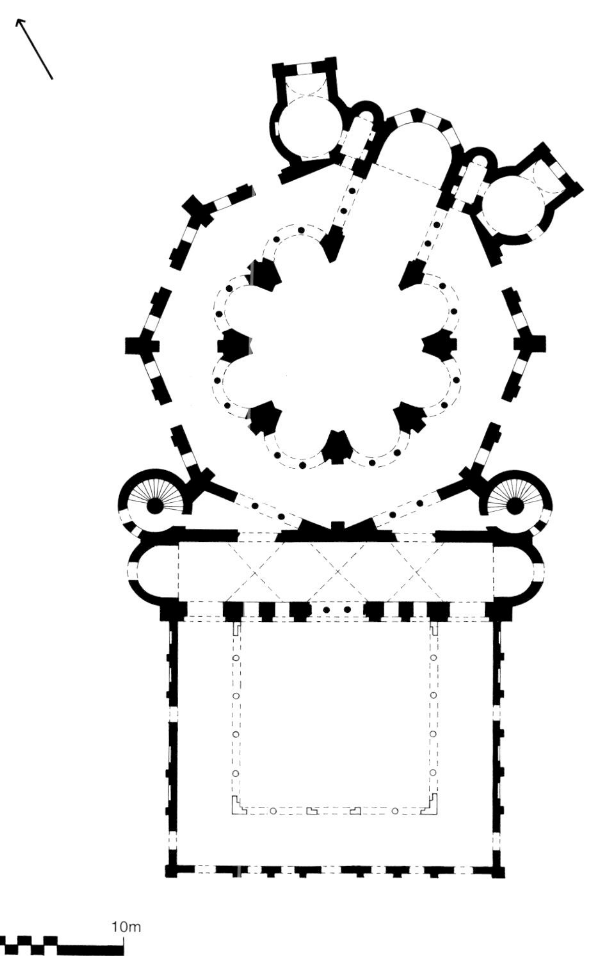

20 Ravenna, S. Vitale, plan.

The church of S. Apollinare in Classe, on the other hand, is far more conservative in design (fig. 23).[49] Indeed, aside from its slightly larger size, there is little to distinguish it from St. John the Evangelist, built over a century earlier. The polygonal apse flanked by projecting rooms, the narthex terminated at each end by stunted towers, and exterior blind arcading are all still present. Current imperial patronage is manifest, however, in the high quality of the brick masonry and the decorative details, such as the imported veined-marble shafts and delicate wind-blown capitals of the nave arcade, and the luxurious mosaic decoration in the apse.

The churches of S. Vitale in Ravenna and S. Apollinare in Classe may be said to represent the culmination of the architectural trends that began in the age of Constantine. The formal dichotomy, noted earlier, between the longitudinal basilica and the centrally planned church was still very much present in the middle of the sixth century. But

22 Ravenna, S. Vitale, exterior view.

21 *(facing page)* Ravenna, S. Vitale, interior view.

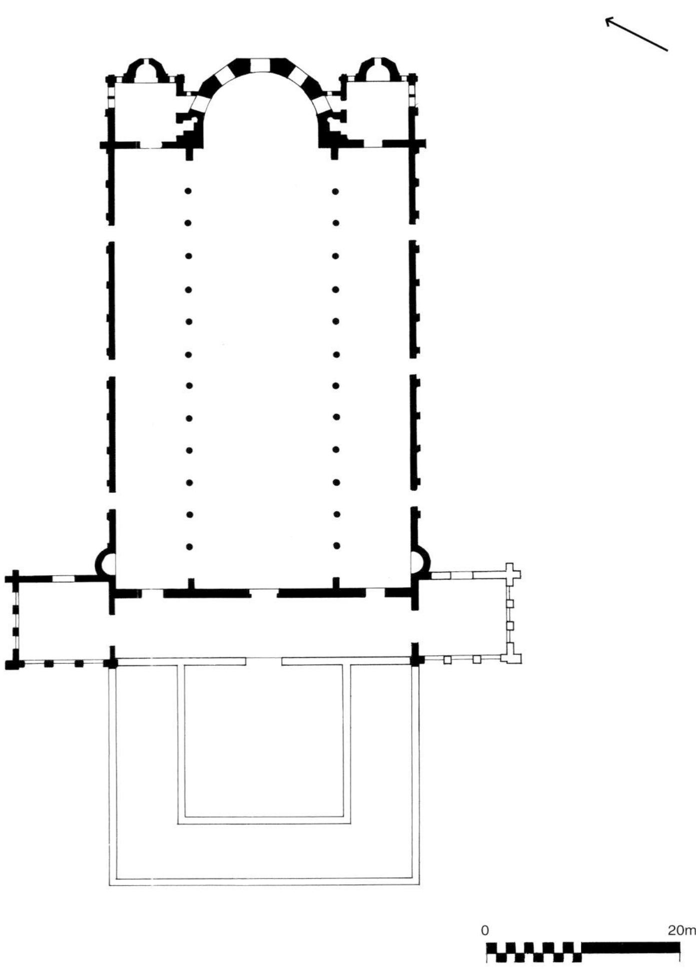

23 Ravenna, S. Apollinare in Classe, plan.

with the collapse of Justinian's empire, these two church types would follow very different lines of development. The aisled basilica, in part because of its association with Rome, became the standard plan for all churches in the West throughout the Middle Ages with few exceptions. In the Byzantine East, on the other hand, the centrally planned, domed church became the norm, following the example of Justinianic churches in Constantinople. Thus, the reign of Justinian marked an architectural as well as a political watershed for western Europe.

Early Christian writers, however, rarely commented upon the design of a church (as opposed to that of a baptistery); instead they invariably stressed the general impression of its size, interior decoration, and, above all, the quality of reflected light. Eusebius in the early fourth century, for example, described the basilica of the Holy Sepulchre as "gleaming with flashes of light," while for Prudentius, around 400, the basilica of St. Peter in Rome was "a golden dwelling" and the light inside the basilica of St. Paul was "golden like the sun's radiance at its rising." In the middle of the sixth century, Procopius described the vast domed interior of Hagia Sophia in terms that would have been equally appropriate for S. Vitale in Ravenna: "You might say that the space is not illuminated by the sun from the outside, but that the radiance is generated from within, so great an abundance of light bathes this shrine all round."[50] The extensive use of marble revetment, mosaic decoration, and gilded coffering served to transform the interior of the church into a series of shimmering surfaces of color and light seemingly without material substance. This aesthetic was rooted in Roman architecture dating back to the late third and early fourth centuries. In Constantine's audience hall at Trier, for example, the holes of the clamps that once held the plaques of marble veneer in place are still clearly visible today throughout the vast expanses of the flat interior walls. The use of such luxurious materials was deemed particularly fitting for churches patronized by the emperor, as Constantine made clear in his letter to the Bishop of Jerusalem concerning the basilica at Golgotha where he urged the use of precious marbles and gold coffering. But in purely Christian, metaphysical terms, the effect of reflected light could also be seen as symbolic of Christ himself, the *lux nova* or "new light."[51]

The design and decoration of Early Christian churches provided the models that early medieval builders and patrons would try to emulate. In addition, the monuments themselves were associated with great figures of the past. Churches of the major cities in Italy and Gaul, for example, were able to boast connections of particular renown: in both Trier and Rome, the Emperor Constantine and in the latter the apostles Peter and Paul; in Milan, the bishop and church father, St. Ambrose; and in Ravenna, the Empress Galla Placidia, the Ostrogothic king, Theodoric, and the Emperor Justinian. It was from this rich legacy of late antiquity in terms of design, construction, decoration, and historical association that early medieval architecture emerged.

CHAPTER 2

The Roman Response to the Cult of Relics

In a letter dated 594, Pope Gregory the Great wrote that "the bodies of the apostles Saint Peter and Saint Paul glitter with such great miracles and awe in their churches that one cannot even go to pray there without considerable fear."[1] Although perhaps difficult for us to comprehend today, for Gregory and his contemporaries the miraculous power that emanated from a martyr's tomb was very real; to be near the burial site was to be in the presence of the saint, which could be both an exhilarating and a terrifying experience. The graves of the holy were considered to be "the *loci* where Heaven and Earth had met," as the historian Peter Brown has so eloquently expressed it.[2]

The cult of relics was yet another important aspect of the legacy of late antiquity. Indeed, many of the great basilicas discussed in the last chapter were built to honor the resting place of a particular saint. Such churches rose in the cemeteries that surrounded every late Roman town, since burial within city limits was strictly forbidden under Roman law. The city of Rome itself was especially rich in such holy treasures. Not only did it possess the tombs of the apostles Peter and Paul, but it was a veritable storehouse of the remains of numerous other martyrs of the early Church. In the Early Christian period, churches in Rome associated with a martyr's grave tended to follow one of two distinct building types depending upon whether the venerated tomb was in a catacomb chamber below ground or within a crowded *necropolis* at ground level. Examples of the first type, such as the basilicas of S. Lorenzo-fuori-le-mura, S. Agnese, and SS. Marcellinus and Peter, consisted of a nave and aisles divided by masonry piers or columns and terminated by a U-shaped ambulatory and were built near the entrances to catacombs (fig. 24). On the other hand, St. Peter's and St. Paul's, as examples of the second type, were columnar basilicas with double aisles terminated by an apse and an intermediate transept that housed the apostolic tomb encased within a marble shrine (fig. 25). They were, therefore, *basilicae ad corpus*, meaning that they stood directly over the martyr's grave.[3]

Basilicas of both types served not only as sites for the celebration of the mass but also as covered cemeteries where the faithful could be buried *ad sanctos* or "near the saints," to use the phrase current at the time. Wealthy members of the Christian community constructed individual mausolea attached to the outer walls of the basilicas or were buried in tombs set along the inner aisle walls, while those of lesser financial means and social status were interred under the floor. These funerary halls were not the sites of regular masses and they had no permanent clergy. Instead, they served as the site for the celebration of the anniversary of the saint and for individual funerary banquets (*refrigeria*) held by family and friends on the deceased's "birthday" (*dies natalis*), which referred to the day the loved one had died and was believed to have been "born" into a new life. In this way, the tomb of the saint played a vital role in the religious life of the Christian community as a whole.[4]

By the end of the sixth century, however, when Gregory the Great wrote his vivid account of the terrifying aura associated with the bodies of Peter and Paul, the cult of relics and the architectural response to it were in the process of changing in ways that would have profound implications for centuries to come. Funerary banquets had by then long fallen out of favor. Indeed, as early as the late fourth century such eminent churchmen as bishops Ambrose of Milan and Augustine of Hippo had discouraged the celebration of *refrigeria* in their dioceses, citing the rowdy behavior that often accompanied such feasting. In the course of the fifth and sixth centuries the practice seems to have died out altogether. Thus, while the *basilicae ad corpus* in Rome of St. Peter's and St. Paul's retained their importance as cult centers, those funerary basilicas that did not contain a martyr's tomb lost their *raison d'être* and most were subsequently abandoned.[5]

The sixth and seventh centuries also saw the rapid growth of pilgrimage, especially to Rome, to visit the graves of the martyrs. To accommodate this ever-increasing

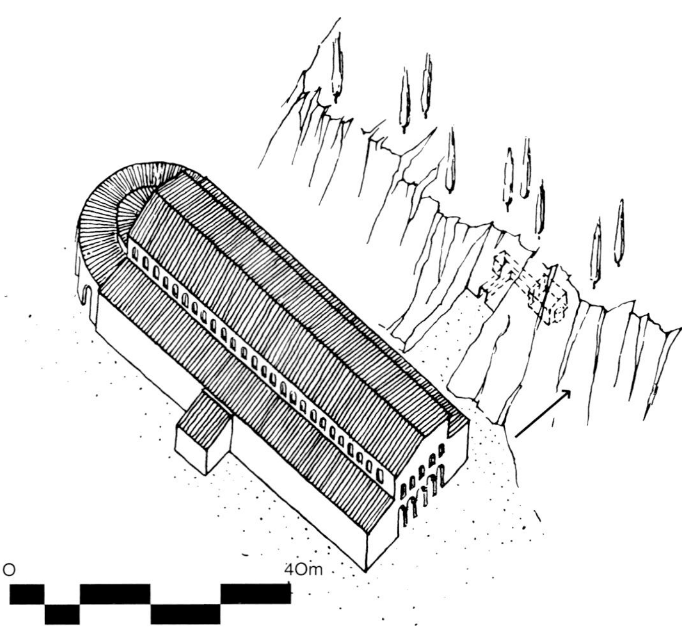

24 Rome, S. Lorenzo fuori-le-mura, basilica and underground memoria, ca. 330. Isometric reconstruction.

25 Rome, St. Peter's, reconstruction of the fourth-century shrine.

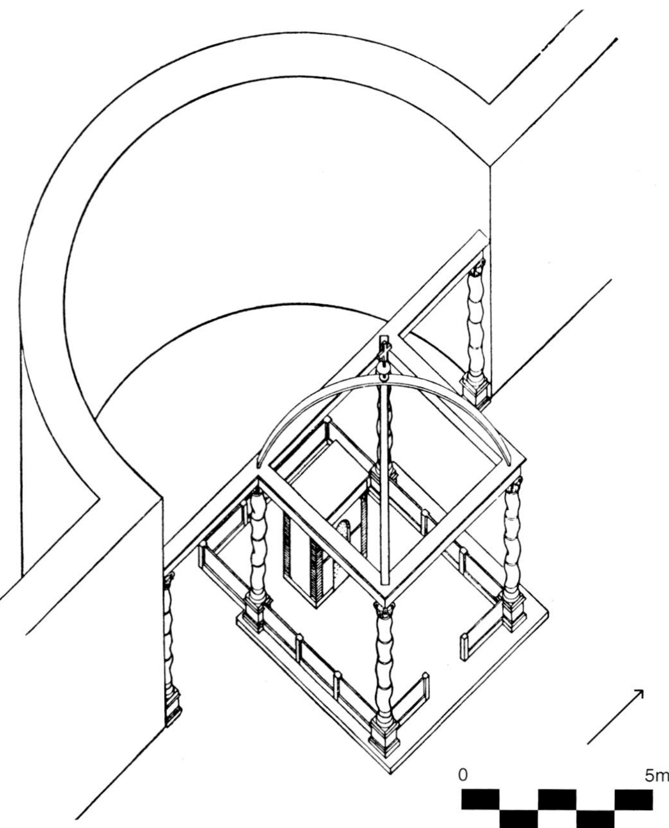

stream of visitors wishing to have tangible and visible contact with the sacred tombs, hostels were set up near the churches of St. Peter, St. Paul, and S. Lorenzo fuori-le-mura. Guide books were written to direct the pilgrims to the holy sites along the roads and among the cemeteries outside the city walls. At times the directions could be amazingly specific, even to the point of providing the number of steps at an entrance to a catacomb.[6] Not surprisingly, this influx of pilgrims brought about a growing concern for congestion near the tombs of the saints; new ways had to be found to make them more accessible.

With the growth in pilgrimage also came an increasing demand for relics throughout Christendom. Indeed, the aforementioned letter of Gregory the Great was written as a reply to a request from Constantina, wife of the Byzantine Emperor Maurice, for nothing less than the head of St. Paul. Despite the singular importance of the head of the apostle (Paul was decapitated), the fact that the Byzantine empress requested a relic from Rome should not be surprising. First of all, the empress was sponsoring the construction of a church in Constantinople dedicated to St. Paul. And second, moving the bodies of saints had long been an accepted practice in the eastern Mediterranean. The first recorded instance is the translation of the body of St. Babylos from the city of Antioch to the nearby suburb of Daphne in the early 350s.[7] Not long after, in 359, the relics of SS. Luke, Timothy, and Andrew were placed in the crossing of the church of the Holy Apostles in Constantinople, built by Constantine in the 330s.[8] Even in the Latin West, where the attitude of the Church was generally more conservative in such matters, Bishop Ambrose of Milan, in 386, ceremoniously interred relics of the apostles Andrew and Thomas and the evangelist John in his Basilica Apostolorum, presumably following the example of Constantine's church of the same name in Constantinople; the relics may even have come from the Byzantine capital.[9] A decade later, in 395, the remains of a Milanese martyr, Nazarius, were discovered by Ambrose near the same church and deposited in the apse.[10]

Ambrose used the cult of relics as a powerful weapon in his fight against Arianism and the celebration of *refrigeria*, but he also gave the veneration of relics a new ritualistic focus. In 383, for example, he placed the bodies of two local martyrs, Gervasius and Protasius, below the altar of the newly constructed church bearing his name, Basilica Ambrosiana, which occupied the same site as the present Romanesque church known as S. Ambrogio. Interestingly enough, Ambrose's original intention had been to have his own tomb placed below the altar, in order to mark the spot where he had officiated mass. When it came time to dedicate the church, however, the congregation protested.

According to Ambrose, they cried out to him to "dedicate the basilica as they do in Rome." To which Ambrose replied that he would do so *if* he found the relics of martyrs.[11] Thus pressured by his flock, Ambrose ordered an excavation in a nearby cemetery "in the presence of the awe-stricken clergy." The bodies of two saints were discovered—"the bones were all intact and there was much blood"—and within two days they were transferred to the new basilica and set below the altar, which in Ambrose's view was "a place owed to martyrs." In this way, the cult of relics was joined with the celebration of the eucharist, so that, as Ambrose explains: "He who has suffered for all [Christ] is placed above the altar; they who have been redeemed by His passion are below the altar."[12] Theological justification for this arrangement was not difficult to find. Indeed, it seemed to be prefigured in the vision of the souls of martyrs below the altar of heaven described in Revelation 6:9: "I saw underneath the altar the souls of those who had been slaughtered for God's word and for the testimony they bore."

Yet in spite of the reference by the Milanese congregation to Roman precedent, the actions of Ambrose in moving the bodies of the saints were, in fact, directly contrary to current practice in Rome. Gregory the Great again makes this clear in his letter to Constantina. "It is not the custom of the Romans," he writes, "to presume to touch the body when they give the relics of the saints." Instead, he explains that a piece of cloth, called a *brandeum*, is placed in a box near the body of the saint and it is this "contact" relic that is deposited in a church about to be dedicated. Gregory assures the empress that such *brandea* are capable of the same powerful effects as sacred bodies and he reiterates that in the West "it is intolerable and sacrilegious for anyone by any happenstance to desire to touch the bodies of the saints." Anyone foolish enough to do so would not go unpunished. Gregory underscores this point by recounting several lurid stories in which those who touched the body of a saint died instantly or within a few days. He also questions the Greek claim to having disturbed the remains of saints; only two years before, he recalls, Greek monks had been caught exhuming bodies in a Roman cemetery with the intention of taking them to Greece and passing them off as holy relics. Gregory concludes by saying that the empress will have to be satisfied with *brandea* and filings from the chains that once held St. Peter in prison.[13]

Not surprisingly, some modern scholars have suggested that in this instance Gregory exaggerated the extent of the Roman ban on disturbing the bodies of saints in order to protect one of Rome's most valued relics. But detailed studies of the matter by John McCulloh have shown that Gregory's attitude toward the cult of relics, as expressed in his letter to Constantina, represents a valid statement of Roman practice and papal policy up to that time.[14] And it is this attitude toward the cult of relics that helps to explain one of Rome's major contributions to medieval architecture: the union of the altar, martyr's tomb, and crypt. It was not so much that the individual components of this formulation were new, indeed they were not; it was instead the particular manner in which they were combined in Rome that proved to be of such importance for the early Middle Ages.

We have already seen, for example, that in the late fourth century Ambrose placed the bodies of SS. Protasius and Gervasius in the Basilica Ambrosiana "below the altar." It may well be that the term *sub altare* should not be taken literally. According to Ambrose the saints took the place he had reserved for his own tomb, and Friedrich W. Deichmann has pointed out that comparable episcopal tombs in Ravenna were never set directly under but rather next to or in front of the altar, marking the spot where the bishop had celebrated mass.[15] Thus, the physical union of altar and tomb at the Basilica Ambrosiana may have been only approximate. Nevertheless, the symbolic union of the celebration of the eucharist and the martyrs' tombs was clear.

A similar broad interpretation must be assumed in Jerome's letter to Vigilantius, dated 406, in which reference is made to "the bishop of Rome who offers sacrifice over the bones of Peter and Paul and who treats their tombs as the altar of Christ."[16] Jerome is presumably describing the situation in Rome as of 386 when he departed Rome for the Holy Lands, a date that coincides exactly with the actions of Ambrose in Milan. Excavations undertaken below the high altar of St. Peter's basilica in the 1940s, however, found no evidence that a permanent altar stood over the apostolic tomb in the Early Christian period (fig. 25). Instead, it seems that a temporary altar, perhaps of wood sheathed in gold, was set up either inside the 5 × 6.5 m precinct in front of the tomb or, just as likely, at the head of the nave on those rare occasions when mass was celebrated at St. Peter's.[17]

Crypts, too, were, on occasion, incorporated into Early Christian churches. The term *cripta* or *crypta*, it should be noted, was used in the Early Christian period to describe almost any kind of underground burial chamber, including the corridors and rooms of catacombs, regardless of its form[18] and we have already seen that in Rome funerary basilicas were sometimes placed near entrances to the catacombs but never over them. Evidence for the placement of "crypts" in Early Christian churches elsewhere in Europe is less precise, because it is based almost exclusively

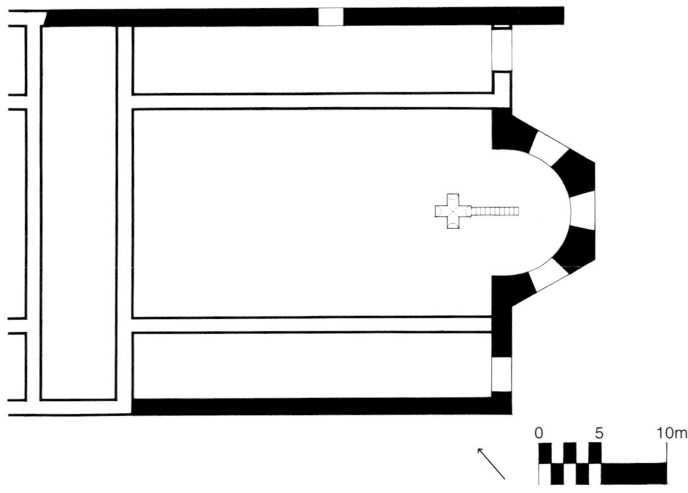

26 Constantinople, St. Mary in Chalkopratiae, ground plan.

on literary references that are open to varied interpretations. The historian and bishop Gregory of Tours (539–94), for example, mentions the presence of crypts in or near several churches in Gaul in a number of his writings without making any reference to an altar.[19] In one instance, however, he uses the same term as Ambrose, *sub altare*, to describe the location of a crypt containing the body of St. Irenaeus in the church of St. John at Lyon; however, limited archaeological investigations undertaken in the 1940s and 1950s revealed that this arrangement resulted from the conversion of a second-century pagan mausoleum, with an underground burial chamber, into a church in the fifth century.[20] In the church of St. Peter at Bordeaux, on the other hand, Gregory of Tours states that the altar was elevated on a platform (*pulpita*) above an area containing the relics of saints and built "in the manner of a crypt" (*in modum cryptae*); but here, unfortunately, we have no archaeological information to confirm this statement nor do we know the design of the crypt or the church.[21] On the whole, however, the Franks in Gaul seem to have preferred to display visibly the sarcophagus of the saint, or a stone marking the tomb, in the apse behind the altar, as was the case in Gregory's own church of St. Martin at Tours.[22]

In North Africa, archaeological fieldwork has been far more extensive, and crypts of various types have been uncovered in chapels or *martyria* attached to the sides or apses of churches but not in association with the main altar. In addition, the cathedral of Orléansville (El-Asnam), when excavated in 1840, was found to have a small crypt below the elevated floor of an eastern apse, belonging perhaps to the first church on the site dedicated in 324, but the location of the main altar, as indicated by a floor mosaic, was in the nave. Similarly, at Carthage, somewhat later in the fourth century, an approximately square (3.70 × 3.60 m), vaulted crypt stood in the middle of the nave of a church (Damous El Karita) situated in a cemetery outside the city. But again, the burial chamber did not mark the location of the main altar, which, in this instance, was placed in the eastern apse.[23]

In the eastern Mediterranean, however, one can find very sophisticated and well-preserved examples of crypts associated with altars in churches dating to the Early Christian period. The remains of two churches built in the mid-fifth century in Constantinople, that of St. John Studios and St. Mary in the Chalkopratiae, possess small cruciform crypts reached by a single flight of stairs and set immediately in front of the apse below where the altar presumably stood (fig. 26).[24] A similar arrangement from approximately the same time is found in the chancel area of St. Demetrios at Salonica.[25] Here a cruciform crypt was set below the altar in front of the apse with a short stairway leading south. In addition, the entire east end of the church was built atop the remains of several vaulted rooms of an ancient Roman bath where St. Demetrius was believed to have been imprisoned and martyred; stairways to either side of the sanctuary led down to this subterranean area.[26] Elsewhere in Macedonia, at Stobi in present-day Yugoslavia, the episcopal basilica, in a phase dating to the mid-fifth century, exhibited a somewhat different arrangement. Instead of a cruciform crypt, there was a "sunken apse" at a level ca. 1.75 m below the floor of the chancel and ringed by a semi-circular colonnade or ambulatory passage ca. 1 m wide.[27] It seems clear, then, that by the middle of the fifth century, in the eastern Mediterranean in particular, a variety of crypt designs had appeared in association with altars in church architecture. None of these examples, however, has been shown to have contained a saint's tomb. The cruciform crypts of Constantinople and Salonica seem to have been for privileged, presumably clerical, burial *sub altare* in the manner of Ambrose. At Stobi, the crypt may have been a cult site with holy objects, such as an icon, but no martyr's grave.

With these precedents in mind, let us return to the situation in Rome. It is important to note that when and if the bodies of saints were involved in any of the aforementioned examples, whether in the Latin West or the Greek East, they were brought to the church and its altar, a procedure that was clearly against Roman practice. Thus, if in Rome the holy tomb could not come to the altar, the altar had to come to the tomb. And that is precisely what happened in the late sixth and early seventh centuries.

The first manifestation of this important change came under Pope Pelagius II (579–90), who sponsored the building of a new church dedicated to St. Lawrence some 30 m

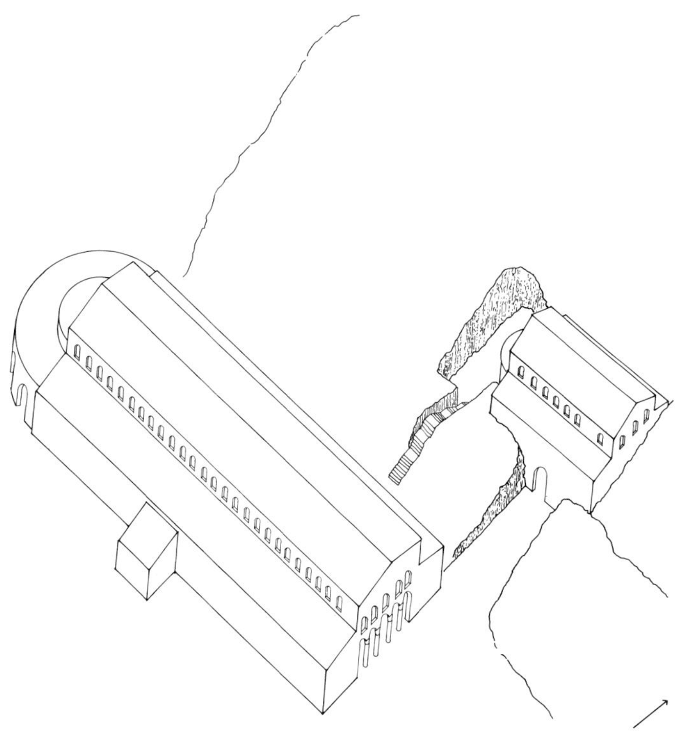

the venerated tomb of St. Lawrence, which stood in the middle of the nave. The present altar, a large marble-covered block, marking the tomb dates from the late eleventh or the early twelfth century and we have no specific information about the appearance of the tomb in Pelagius's day, not even whether or not it protruded above the floor level of the nave. The original relationship between the tomb and the altar, therefore, remains uncertain. The altar may have surmounted the tomb or, in keeping with earlier *basilicae ad corpus*, it may have stood nearby. In any event, the tomb was now made readily accessible and visible to a sizeable congregation assembled both in the aisles and in the galleries surrounding the nave.

The sixth-century church of S. Lorenzo, minus its western apse, was converted into the chancel of a much larger

27 *(left)* Rome, S. Lorenzo fuori-le-mura, covered cemetery and Pope Pelagius' basilica.

28 *(below)* Rome, S. Lorenzo fuori-le-mura, reconstruction of Pelagius' basilica in the late sixth century. The precise location of the saint's tomb remains conjectural.

to the north of the old funerary basilica in order to enclose the tomb of the martyr situated underground in the nearby catacombs (fig. 27).[28] The construction of the new church of S. Lorenzo, in spite of its small scale—it was 60 m shorter than its predecessor—involved a formidable earth-moving operation so that the new church could be embedded in the hillside at the level of the martyr's tomb in the catacombs. The resultant design, a basilica with galleries, was new to Rome. To be sure, it had been used extensively in the eastern Mediterranean, as witness the aforementioned churches of St. John Studios and St. Mary in Chalkopratiae in Constantinople among others, but in Rome this design was used less for stylistic reasons than for purely practical ones.

To be precise, the galleried basilica was ideally suited to the uneven terrain surrounding Lawrence's tomb for it allowed the faithful to enter the building on two different levels; there was one entrance at ground level along the south side of the church, while the galleries enveloping the interior of the church were entered from the crest of the hillside through two doors in the west wall. The nave was terminated by an apse ca. 10 m in diameter behind which stood an irregular, rectangular space cut out of the living rock of the hillside containing a cataract grave of an unknown martyr (fig. 28). This *retro sanctos* was visible from the nave through several windows in the lower zone of the apse. The main focus of the church, however, was clearly

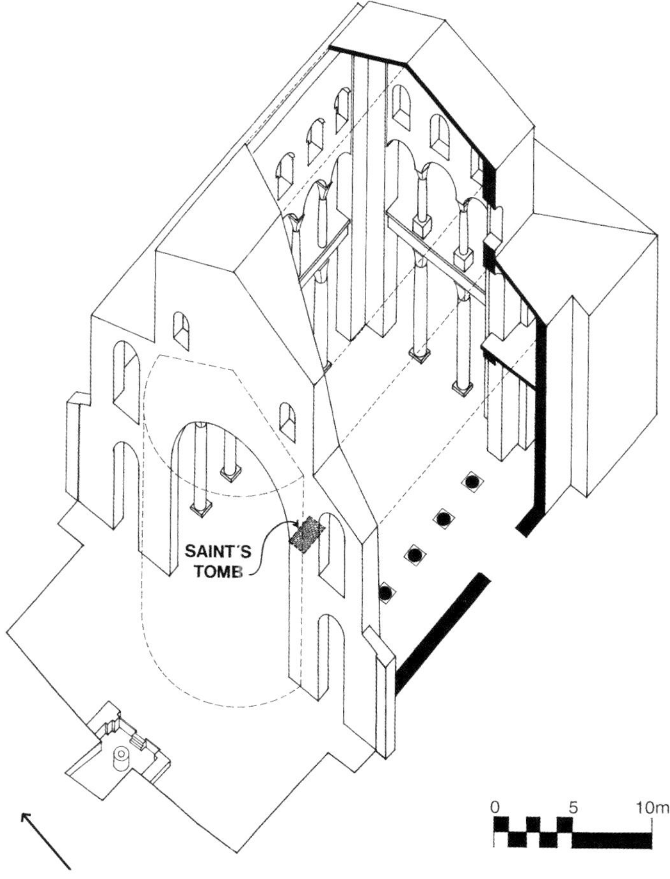

church in the thirteenth century and as such it is one of the most beautiful medieval monuments to be seen in Rome today (fig. 29). Its Roman *spolia* of fluted and spiral columns, Corinthian capitals, and a variety of elegantly and deeply carved entablatures dramatically catch the light that streams from the ample fenestration in the clerestory and south aisle. And it is this quality of spaciousness and light that is singled out for special praise in a mosaic inscription seen on the triumphal arch, the opening lines of which proclaim that "brightness enters this once hidden place (of the tomb)" and that "a larger hall (*largior aula*) now receives the people."[29] The construction of S. Lorenzo under Pelagius II provided a new model for the *basilica ad corpus*, specifically adapted to the topographical requirements of the catacombs. And not long after, two, albeit less elegant, churches were built, one over the tomb of St. Hermes (S. Ermete) in a catacomb along the Via Salaria and the other over the tombs of the martyrs Nereus and Achilleus in the catacomb of Domitilla on the Via Ardeatina. In both cases, however, the tombs of the saints stood underneath the apse and thus below the altar.[30]

Gregory the Great was the immediate successor of Pelagius II. Generally regarded as the first pope of the Middle Ages, Gregory has won renown as an effective administrator, as the author of the collection of saints' lives known as the *Dialogues*, among other writings, and for initiating the conversion of England, but he is considerably less well known as a patron of architecture.[31] Indeed, in contemporary sources, he is not credited with the construction of a single church during his pontificate. And yet, his impact on the development of medieval architecture was profound. As secretary to Pelagius II, Gregory was well aware of his predecessor's work at S. Lorenzo. In fact, he refers to Pelagius's "improvements not far from the body of Saint Lawrence" in his letter to Constantina. As to Gregory's own building activities, however, the *Liber Pontificalis* states only that he "arranged so that mass could be celebrated above the body of St. Peter."[32] But what exactly is the meaning of this passage?

First of all, we must remember that the tomb of Peter could not be moved. Instead, the aforementioned excavations below the high altar at St. Peter's revealed that the floor of the original apse was raised 1.5 m—a relatively easy operation—so that a permanent altar could be placed directly over the Constantinian memorial containing the tomb (fig. 30). Stairs, eight to ten in number, presumably led up to the new apse platform and spiral columns were rearranged to form a screen in front. In this way, Gregory was able to unify directly the altar and apostolic tomb for the first time.[33]

But Gregory, like Pelagius II, also wanted to make the tomb itself more accessible to the public than it had been

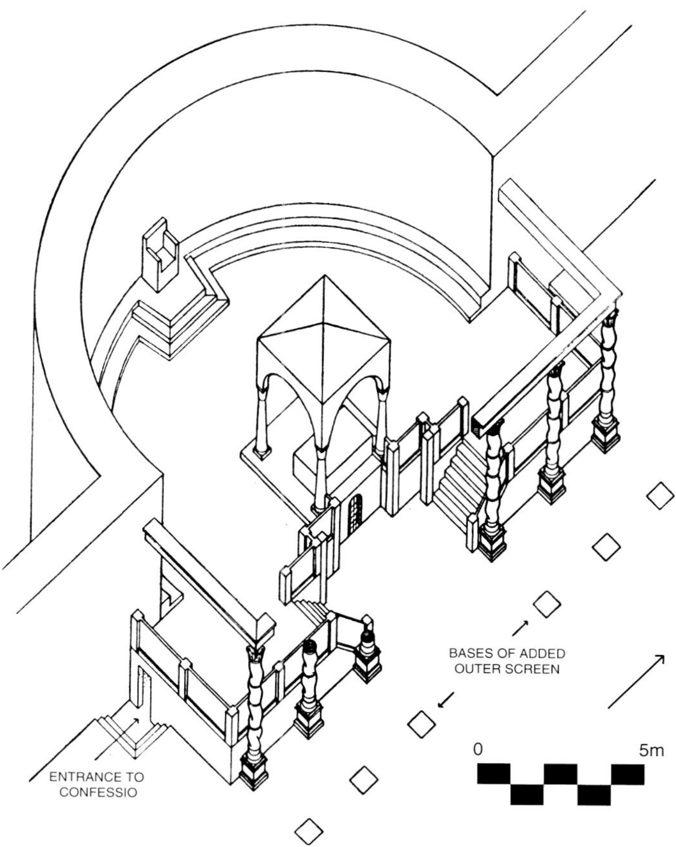

30 Rome, St. Peter's, reconstruction of the shrine with raised presbytery and annular crypt as in ca. 600. Outer screen of columns added in the eighth century.

in the past. The problem confronting any pilgrim to St. Peter's was vividly described by Gregory of Tours, writing around 590, at the time Gregory the Great became pope:

> His [St. Peter's] sepulchre, which is placed under the altar [*sub altare*], is very rarely entered. However, if anyone wishes to pray the gates by which the spot is enclosed are opened, and he enters above the sepulchre; then he opens a little window there and puts his head inside, and makes his requests according to his needs. Nor is the result delayed, if only his petition be a just one. If he desires to carry away with him some blessed memorial, he throws inside a small handkerchief which has been carefully weighted and then, watching and fasting, he prays most fervently that the apostle may give a favorable answer to his devotion. Wonderful to say, if the man's faith prevails, the handkerchief when drawn up from the tomb is so filled with divine virtue that it weighs much more than it did before; and then he who has pulled it up knows that he has obtained the favor he sought.[34]

29 *(facing page)* Rome, S. Lorenzo fuori-le-mura, Pelagius' basilica, interior, looking east.

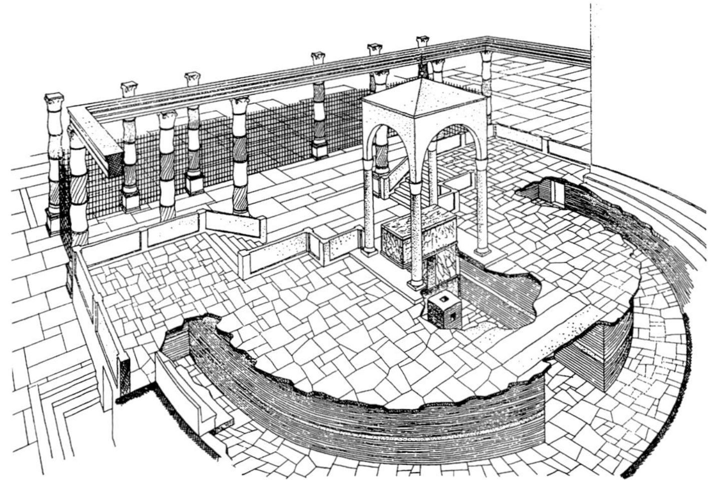

31 Rome, St. Peter's, isometric reconstruction of the annular crypt.

In order to avoid the gymnastics described in this passage, a corridor was devised to allow pilgrims to approach the tomb in a more orderly fashion. The tomb, as we have seen, lay immediately in front of the apse. The passageway could not have been constructed in front of the tomb and altar without blocking the view of the congregation from the nave and aisles. By necessity, therefore, the crypt passage had to follow the curvature of the apse resulting in a semi-circular corridor which was then met at its apex by a perpendicular corridor leading directly to the tomb (fig. 31). Those visiting the tomb of Peter were now able to descend a short flight of stairs to the left or right, pass by the tomb and then exit out the other side. It was a simple yet ingenious solution to what we would call today a major traffic flow problem.[35] In fact, numerous graffiti scratched into the walls of the crypt attest to the popularity of the site.[36] Still, the crypt's design called for order and control. Access, no doubt, would have had to have been limited by necessity. The vast majority of pilgrims must have remained content to view the oil lamp burning above the tomb through the small window or *fenestella* situated directly below the altar.

But Gregory's efforts were not restricted to St. Peter's, because the *Liber Pontificalis* also says that "he did the same at St. Paul's."[37] Excavations comparable to those at St. Peter's have never been carried out at St. Paul's, therefore information about the disposition of Paul's tomb in late antiquity and the early Middle Ages is far more limited. Nevertheless, a careful study of descriptions and drawings of the tomb area made before and soon after the Early Christian basilica was destroyed by fire in 1823, especially those of Onofrio Panvinio and P. Ugonio in the late sixteenth century, provides the basic elements of Gregory's remodeling.[38]

Here again, an altar was placed on an elevated platform directly over the tomb. The platform created an approximately square (11 × 12 m) precinct or presbytery around the altar, delineated by a series of twenty colonnettes bearing a wooden architrave, with a curved east side to accommodate the papal throne (fig. 32). The principal entrance to the crypt, still in use in the sixteenth century, was a stairway approaching the tomb from the east in line with the apse of the church. The precise design of the crypt is not known, but it must have consisted of more than one corridor. Panvinio and Ugonio state only that a small room or "oratory" below the presbytery opened onto the tomb. Panvinio, however, adds that there were two walled-up doors in the crypt which originally communicated with another subterranean passage, believed to be an ancient cemetery, extending below the south arm of the transept.[39] In a reexamination of the evidence, Francesco Tolotti has pointed out that it is difficult to imagine how Panvinio could have seen two doors to the same corridor if they were both already sealed. He suggests that, instead of being set one behind the other, the two doors in question faced

32 Rome, St. Paul's-outside-the-Walls, plan of apse and transept showing hypothetical reconstruction of crypt added by Pope Gregory the Great.

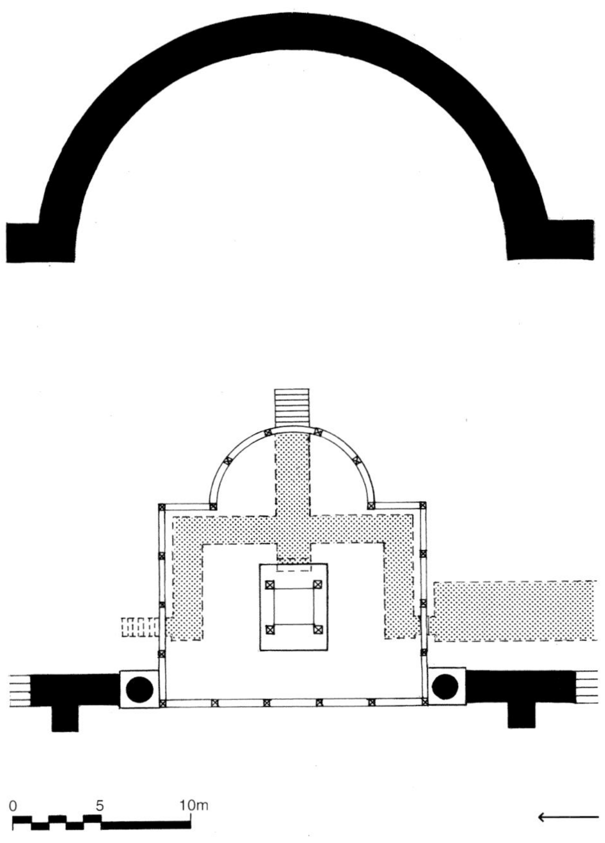

one another and therefore led to two separate corridors of the crypt branching off in opposite directions in a roughly symmetrical composition.[40] The fact that the tomb of St. Paul did not stand near the apse, as at St. Peter's, but just inside the transept at the head of the nave meant that a series of straight, *not* curved, corridors could be devised. Thus, according to this reconstruction, the crypt at St. Paul's represented a variation on the design of the crypt at St. Peter's.

The pattern of movement through the crypt at St. Paul's is less apparent than at the Vatican. It seems reasonable to assume that pilgrims would have exited through the south corridor of the crypt and out via a stairway that presumably stood at the end of the cemetery passage, but where would they have entered the crypt? The only known stairway extended in the direction of the eastern apse, an area reserved for the clergy, which suggests that this crypt entrance, too, was reserved for Church officials, in an arrangement similar to the placement of stairs to crypts in Constantinopolitan churches. Could there originally have been a second stairway leading to the postulated north corridor of the crypt? Surely, this narrow corridor would not have led to a dead end. More important, a north entrance would have allowed highly efficient and easily controllable circulation of the tomb area by large numbers of worshippers without restricting access by the clergy, but this is merely a hypothesis.

Although many of the details of Gregory's modifications at St. Paul's must remain conjectural, the date can be calculated with considerable precision, for in his letter to Constantina, he mentions that in his desire "to improve" the area around the tomb of St. Paul, it had been necessary "to dig to some depth near his sepulchre."[41] Assuming this statement refers to the construction of the crypt, the work must have been carried out between 590, when Gregory became pope, and 594, when the letter was written. The date of the crypt at St. Peter's, however, is less certain. The fact that Gregory does not mention it in the letter would suggest that the remodeling of St. Peter's belongs to the period after 594 and before his death in 604. But this need not have been the case, for Gregory's reference to the work at St. Paul's, as well as to Pelagius's rebuilding of S. Lorenzo, comes in the context of his admonition against disturbing the resting places of saints. To be more specific, he recounts that a man, who presumed to lift some bones found in the course of digging near St. Paul's grave, died suddenly, even though these remains had no connection with the apostle's tomb. If no such tragic event took place during the construction of the crypt at St. Peter's, Gregory would have had no reason to mention it to Constantina. Moreover, it seems unlikely that Gregory would have given precedence to making "improvements" at the tomb of St. Paul before doing so at the tomb of St. Peter, Rome's primary pilgrimage site. I would suggest, therefore, that both projects were carried out early in Gregory's pontificate.

Whether or not Gregory's actions at St. Peter's and St. Paul's were affected by the use of crypts in churches outside Italy remains an open question. There is no evidence that he had firsthand knowledge of the aforementioned examples in Gaul and North Africa. He was, however, Pelagius II's representative (*apocrisiarius*) at the imperial court in Constantinople from 579 to 586. We may also assume that he visited Salonica, for it was an important stopover on the Via Egnatia, which served as the main travel route between Italy and Constantinople.[42] Thus, in spite of his criticism of the Greek attitude toward relics in his letter to Constantina, Gregory may have been influenced, at least to some degree, by the placement of crypts below altars in churches in the eastern Mediterranean. Be that as it may, Gregory's remodeling of St. Peter's and of St. Paul's was a specifically "Roman" response to the cult of relics, because, in keeping with Roman practice, the tombs of the apostles remained untouched. Above all, the designs of the two crypts should be seen as variations on the same theme, which was the desire to unite the altar and apostolic tomb while, at the same time, providing access to the relics for an ever-growing number of pilgrims.

Architectural projects related to papal concern for the cult of relics did not end with Gregory the Great. In 609 (or 613), for example, the Pantheon was dedicated by Pope Boniface IV to the Virgin Mary and the martyrs (*S. Maria ad martyres*) (fig. 8). One of the great monuments of ancient Rome, the building had remained imperial property until it was given over to the papacy by the Emperor Phocas, who resided in Constantinople. Interestingly enough, this marked the first time that a pagan temple in Rome was converted to Christian use. Even more significant is the fact that the temple which had been built originally to honor "all the gods" was now dedicated to the Virgin Mary and "all saints." Still, the relics used in the consecration of the building were certainly *brandea*; the popular story that Boniface IV brought cartloads of martyrs' bones to the Pantheon from the catacombs is pure legend. Moreover, the Christianization of the Pantheon was a relatively easy task requiring no substantial physical changes aside from the setting up of an altar in the main niche.[43]

The far more innovative building programs of Pelagius II and Gregory the Great were taken up again by Honorius I (625–38). His new church of S. Agnese, for example, followed the lines of the Pelagian church of S. Lorenzo.[44] Here a galleried basilica, decorated with Roman *spolia*, was set in the hillside directly over the tomb of St. Agnes, which was located a considerable distance from the

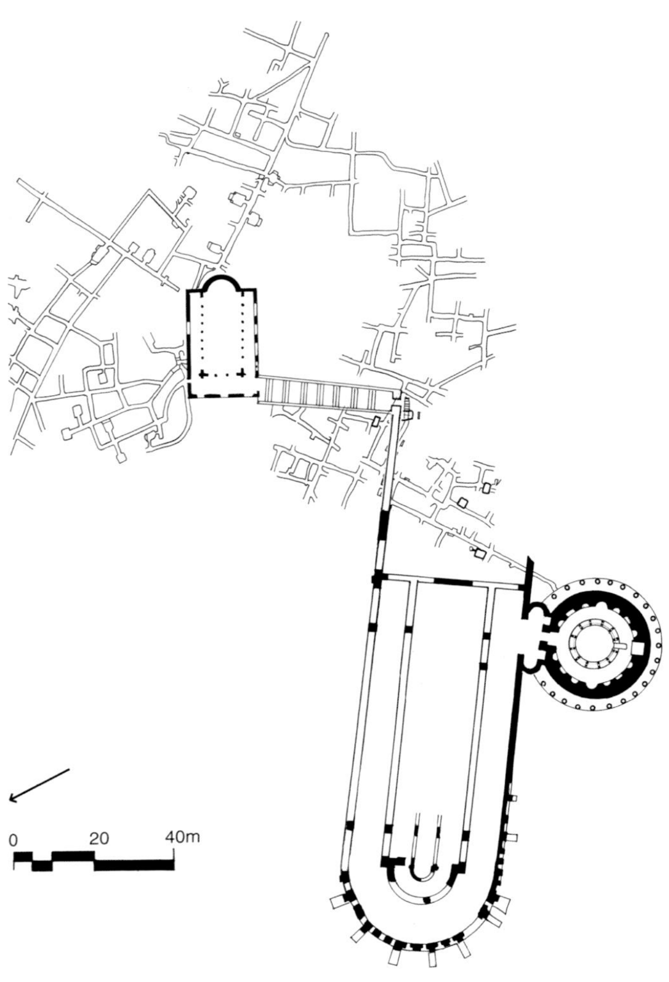

33 Rome, S. Agnese, fourth-century basilica (lower right) and seventh-century basilica (upper left).

34 Rome, S. Agnese, seventh-century basilica, ground plan and section.

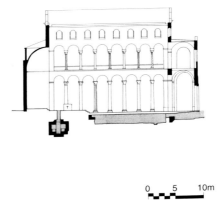

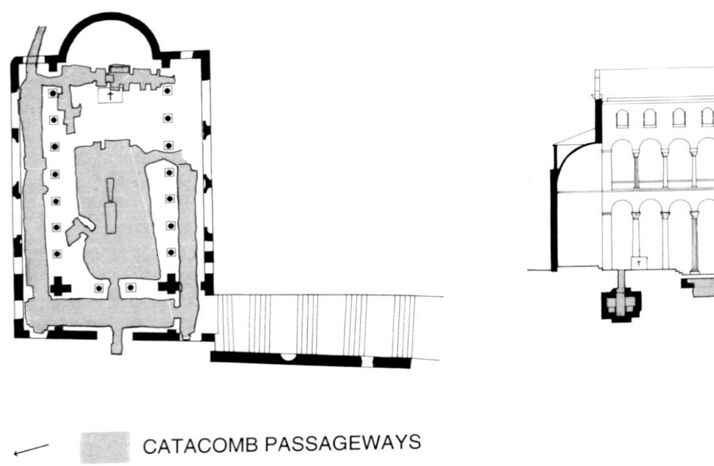

abandoned funerary hall built in the fourth century (fig. 33). But this time, unlike at S. Lorenzo, the catacomb passage containing the tomb of the martyr was left untouched so that it served as a subterranean crypt below the altar of the new church (fig. 34). In this way, Honorius was able to combine the architectural innovations of both Pelagius II and Gregory. His recognition of the building achievements of the latter was made even more evident at S. Pancrazio, also built above a catacomb, where both the plan and crypt design of Old St. Peter's were revived to create a basilica with a broad transept and an annular crypt housing the martyr's tomb (fig. 35).[45]

Taken together, then, Pelagius II, Gregory the Great, and Honorius I transformed the architectural setting of the tombs of some of Rome's most venerated saints. It was this aspect of Rome, as the city of the holy martyrs, that drew pilgrims from all over Europe and, not surprisingly, the two earliest surviving pilgrims' guides appear to have been written during the pontificate of Honorius I.[46] More important for us, however, the unification of the altar, tomb, and crypt as formulated in the age of Gregory the Great offered a new model for the veneration of relics in church architecture.

The annular crypt in particular became especially popular, because of its association with St. Peter's. Pope Gregory III (731–41), for example, inserted an annular crypt in the apse of the church of S. Crisogono, located in the Trastevere section of Rome (fig. 36).[47] This revival of the annular crypt may represent an expression of Gregory III's personal devotion to the memory of his renowned namesake, as seen

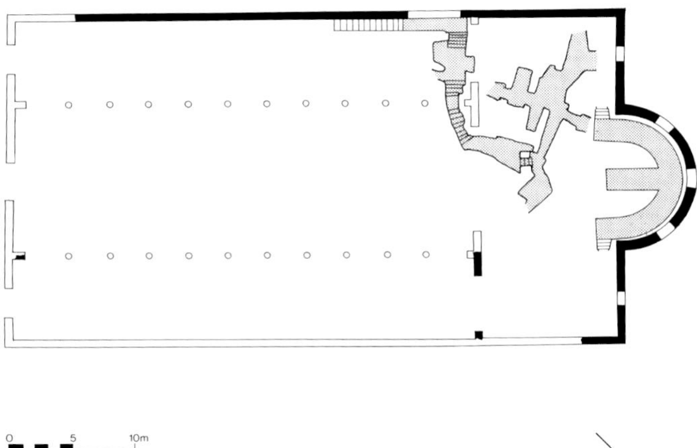

35 Rome, S. Pancrazio, ground plan with annular crypt, early seventh century.

also in his gift to St. Peter's of six twisted columns—originally a gift of the exarch in Ravenna—which he had set up in front of the chancel in line and parallel to the six older columns that had been rearranged by Gregory I when the crypt at St. Peter's was first built.[48] As we shall see in the second part of this book, the use of the annular crypt spread from Rome to religious centers north of the Alps in the later eighth and early ninth centuries as a result of a new political and cultural alliance between the papacy and the Franks.

But the spread of the annular crypt was encouraged by other factors as well. For one thing, the concept of the *basilica ad corpus* diminished in importance as the Roman ban on the transferal of corporal relics was gradually relaxed. This change in attitude came about for several reasons. From the middle of the seventh to the middle of the eighth centuries, the majority of the popes were no longer Roman by birth but foreigners, coming first from Dalmatia and later from the Greek East. As we have already noted, the eastern Mediterranean had long tolerated, indeed promoted, the movement of corporal relics. Thus, Pope John IV (640–42) brought remains of martyrs from his homeland in Dalmatia to the chapel of S. Venanzio adjoining the Lateran baptistery. The next pope, Theodore I (642–49), a Palestinian by birth, translated the relics of SS. Primus and Felicianus from the catacombs along the Via Nomentana outside Rome to the church of S. Stefano Rotondo inside the city on the Celian Hill.[49]

Also contributing to this change in attitude toward the treatment of martyrs' relics was the gradual abandonment of the catacombs. With the dramatic decline in the population of Rome in the course of the early Middle Ages (the result of many factors), it became increasingly difficult to maintain the suburban cemeteries and to protect the sacred tombs from vandalism.[50] Such concerns, for example, prompted the translation of the relics of S. Petronilla, the purported daughter of St. Peter, at the request of Pepin, King of the Franks, in 754, from the catacomb of Domitilla on the Via Ardeatina to a mausoleum rotondo, built ca. 400, adjoining the south transept of St. Peter's basilica.[51] To be sure, some popes, such as Hadrian I (772–95) and Leo III (795–816), tried to repair and restore the suburban basilicas and catacombs.[52] Nevertheless, their successor, Paschal I (817–24), felt it necessary to transfer "many remains of saints lying in ruined cemeteries so as to save them from neglect," and these he deposited in the annular crypt of the newly constructed church of S. Prassede.[53] In this case, both the plan of the church and its crypt were modelled after that of St. Peter's. In other words, the Roman model *par excellence* was seen as the most appropriate resting place for the protection and veneration of Rome's precious relics.

At the same time, the popes began to realize the political potential of the gift of corporal relics. Beginning with the pontificates of Paul I (757–67) and Stephen III (768–72), the remains of numerous martyrs, usually of relatively minor saints, were dispersed throughout northern Europe, thus solidifying Rome's influence in both secular and ecclesiastical matters.[54] By the early Middle Ages, Rome had long relinquished its title as the capital of an empire, but what it had lost in political power it gained as the repository of the graves of the martyrs and, above all, as the site of the tombs of St. Peter and St. Paul. As the holy city of the West, Rome was the natural focus of the cult of

36 Rome, S. Crisogono, reconstruction with annular crypt inserted 731–41.

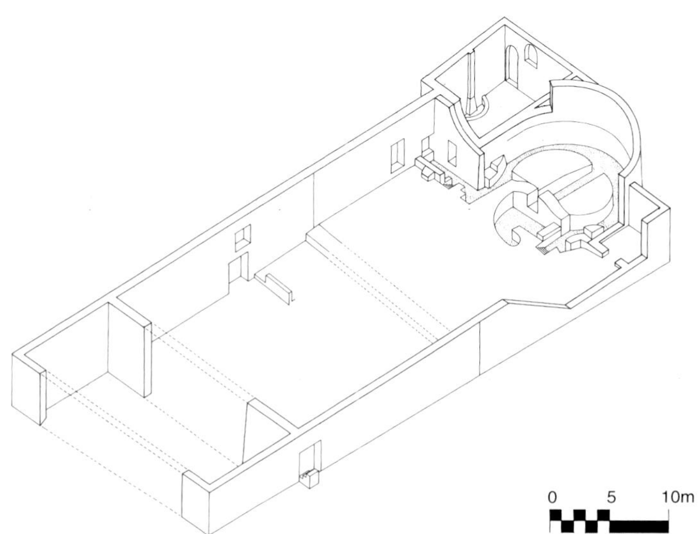

relics, a situation which, as we have seen, was carefully promoted and nurtured in the late sixth and early seventh centuries through the construction of tomb churches (*basilicae ad corpus*) and crypts. And it is this Roman response to the cult of relics, providing a new formulation for the unification of the altar and saint's tomb, that would eventually transform the nature and meaning of church architecture in medieval Europe.[55]

CHAPTER 3

Romanitas *and the Barbarian West*

By the end of the sixth century, all semblance of a unified empire in the West had vanished. Europe, instead, was a mosaic of Germanic kingdoms including, above all, Frankish Gaul, Visigothic Spain, Lombard Italy, and Anglo-Saxon England. The transformation of the Western Roman Empire that had begun with the incursions of the Goths and the Vandals at the end of the fourth century was now complete. Europe, it used to be said, had entered the so-called Dark Ages.

The reality of the situation, however, was far more complex. Although Europe was now ruled by Germanic overlords, much of late Roman culture had survived. In fact, the indigenous romanized inhabitants far outnumbered the new barbarian settlers. The towns and cities, founded under Roman rule, as essential components of classical civilization, seem to have remained relatively intact, albeit with their populations much reduced and their urban fabric deteriorating. Politically, too, many Germanic chieftains sought legitimacy by adopting the trappings of Roman authority embodied in the codification of laws and symbols of power. This was particularly true of the Visigoths and the Franks, who settled in present-day France and Spain respectively in the fifth and sixth centuries, for they had already been in contact with Roman culture along the Rhenish and Danube borders long before. Moreover, the Church was Roman and its bishops were, to a large extent, descendants of the old Roman landed aristocracy, who consciously tried to sustain the vestiges of classical culture wherever possible within the towns where they resided. And all indications are that in the course of the sixth and seventh centuries both the Franks in Gaul and the Visigoths on the other side of the Pyrénées were largely Latin speaking. Thus when referring to the barbarization of the West, one should also keep in mind the simultaneous and reciprocal process of the romanization of the barbarians.[1]

The blending of barbarian and Roman is particularly evident in the art and architecture of the period. Originating as nomadic people, the Germanic tribes had from the beginning focused their creative energies on portable objects, especially regalia and ceremonial weapons, of glittering gold and silver studded with precious stones in the form of brooches, belt buckles, helmets, swords, and shields that were symbols of power and status. Many of the forms and decorative motifs used in such metalwork were ultimately classical in origin, but they were transformed by fragmenting and reassembling the old motifs in order to create a new and abstract vocabulary of dynamic, undulating patterns that retained only the faintest resemblance to their Roman prototypes.[2]

The Roman ingredient in architecture was far more obvious. The Franks, Anglo-Saxons, Visigoths, and Lombards had no permanent building tradition of their own. Instead, they built huts, halls, and barricades in the perishable materials of wood, earth, and thatch.[3] The very concept of building in stone or brick and mortar was Roman in origin and a structure built with such materials was deemed a potent symbol of "Romanness" or *romanitas*. In early medieval Europe, the remnants of the Roman past were everywhere to be seen. Even in Britain, the most remote and least romanized of the western provinces of the empire, baths, temples, fora, and fortification walls stood, albeit often in ruins and largely abandoned, as perhaps the most eloquent and impressive reminders of the Roman past. Not surprisingly, therefore, permanent architecture was promoted by the Church, centered in Rome.

The Visigoths, like the Ostrogoths and the Vandals, had already converted to Christianity before invading the empire, but they were Arian, part of a sect that denied the divine nature of Christ, which made them heretics in the eyes of the largely Catholic West. It was therefore considered a major triumph for the Church of Rome when Clovis, leader of the still-pagan Franks, was baptized as an orthodox Christian around the year 500. By the end of the century, the Visigoths followed suit and joined the Catholic faith. For the Anglo-Saxons it was a very different course of events. They, too, had migrated to the West by the middle of the fifth century but they seem to have come from northern Europe (present-day Denmark and northern Germany) first as mercenaries, invited by the Roman Britains in order to defend the island along its northern and western borders from attack by the indigenous non-romanized and pagan Picts and Celts. Soon more Angles, Saxons, and Jutes arrived not to defend Britain but to occupy and settle it. The Anglo-Saxons, as these Germanic peoples may be called collectively, however, had had relatively little experience dealing with the Romans, and they were pagan. Indeed, their conversion to Christianity was considered one of the major accomplishments of the pontificate of Gregory the Great (590–604). The Lombards were the last of the major Germanic tribes to appear in western Europe, entering the plains of northern Italy in 568. Although many were pagan, their leaders, like the Goths before them, were Arian and their conversion to Catholicism was also a major concern of Gregory the Great. The Lombards, however, were, by some accounts, among the more ferocious of the barbarian tribes and certainly, at least initially, the most antagonistic toward Byzantium in large part because of their geographic proximity to the eastern Mediterranean and the persistence of the exarchate in Ravenna.[4]

Nevertheless, the early churches built for and by the newly Christianized Germanic rulers of Europe may be said to bespeak a common language of style with Latin roots but adapted to fit barbaric tastes, resulting in something very new. At once, decorative richness and regional diversity became hallmarks of this architecture. In order to understand this process, it will be necessary to examine each regional or tribal entity in turn—Visigoths, Franks, and Lombards. The Anglo-Saxons, for reasons that will become evident, are treated separately in the next chapter. As we shall see, the melding of barbarian and Roman provided the basis for the first architecture that may be truly termed "medieval."

A prime example of the early stages of this development is the enigmatic monument in Toulouse known as La Daurade.[5] Although destroyed in the middle of the eighteenth century, earlier records—including plans, elevation drawings and written descriptions of varying accuracy—indicate that the building was originally a decagon to which a nave was added considerably later to the west, thereby destroying one-third of the central plan (fig. 37). The interior was composed of three tiers of superimposed niches decorated with gleaming mosaics depicting narrative scenes from the infancy of Christ along with more static images of Christ in Majesty, as well as standing figures of apostles, saints and Old Testament prophets. All that is left today of this building, however, is an array of delicately carved columns, covered by vine scrolls and other decorative vegetation, that once framed the niches and are now to be seen in several different museums. The general building type seems clear in its resemblance to the oval, multi-niched plan of the late fourth-century martyrium in Cologne, later dedicated to St. Gereon, but originally dedicated to a variety of saints and referred to by Gregory of Tours in the late sixth century as *ad sanctos aureos* ("at the golden saints") because of its golden mosaic decoration (fig. 38).[6] Nonetheless, neither the precise function nor date of La Daurade is certain. It may be the church in Toulouse mentioned also by Gregory of Tours as dedicated to the Virgin Mary; certainly by the twelfth century the church was known as *Sancta Maria deaurata* ("the golden Saint Mary") or simply La Daurade ("the golden church") because of its glistening interior.[7] It could therefore be considered as one of a series of centralized churches dedicated to the Virgin, including the Pantheon in Rome, which, as we have seen, was consecrated to the Mother of God in the early seventh century.[8] Some scholars, however, believe that La Daurade was built as a royal chapel or mausoleum for the Visigothic kings who used Toulouse as their capital from 418 to 507, and the interior decoration has been likened to the elaborate, and roughly contemporary, figural mosaics sponsored by the Ostrogothic king, Theodoric, in Ravenna. After all, the eastern and western branches of the Goths were related and closely allied, sharing also a common belief in the Christian heresy of Arianism. Other scholars contend, however, that, if the church was indeed dedicated to the Virgin, La Daurade must have been built, instead, to serve the Catholic Franks after they drove the Visigoths out of the area in the early sixth century, since Arians did not assign an elevated status to Mary. In either case, whether Visigothic or Frankish, mausoleum or church, La Daurade testifies to the conscious desire on the part of the new barbarian rulers of Europe to emulate late antique forms. This must have been achieved by employing local Gallo-Roman masons and artisans steeped in the traditions of Early Christian art and architecture, but that would not always be the case.

Visigoths had already begun to settle in the Iberian peninsula during the fifth century, but defeat by the Franks under Clovis at Vouillé near Poitiers in 507 forced those remaining to migrate south of the Pyrénées, leaving only Septimania along the Mediterranean coast as a lasting Visigothic outpost in otherwise Frankish Gaul. By the middle of the sixth century, Visigoths had gained control of most of Spain and established the centrally located city of Toledo as their royal capital.[9] Byzantine reconquest under Justinian was limited to the southeastern coast, and by 624 the last remnants of this occupation had been expelled. Thereafter, Visigothic rule remained unchallenged until the

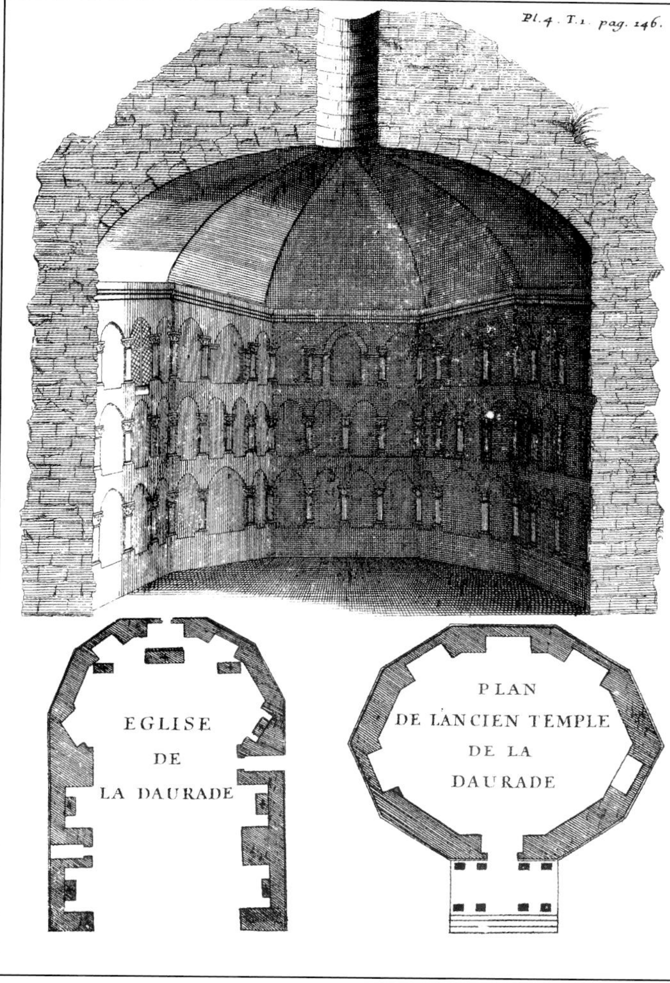

37 Toulouse, La Daurade, section and plan, eighteenth-century engraving (Dom J. Martin, *La religion des Gaulois tirée des plus pures sources de L'Antiquité*, Paris, 1727, vol. I, pl. 4).

appearance of Muslim forces across the Straits of Gibraltar in 711. In the meantime, however, after ineffective attempts to promote Arianism, Visigothic overlords had converted to orthodox Christianity, announced first by King Reccared in 587 and proclaimed at the Third Council of Toledo two years later. At the latter occasion Latin was also named as the official language of the kingdom, in lieu of the ruling elite's native Gothic tongue, thereby bringing the Visigothic minority closer to the indigenous Catholic Hispano-Roman population. The king served as the head of a new national Church, and rulers from Reccared to Recceswinth (d. 672) furthered the complex process of unification on many levels. In its new alliance with the state, the Church became an increasingly important intellectual institution in the course of the later sixth and seventh centuries as exemplified by the polymath and archbishop Isidore of Seville (ca. 560–636), whose many works, but especially his *Twenty Books of Etymologies*, offered a rich compilation of ancient sources that served as a cornerstone of scholarly erudition throughout the Middle Ages.[10] It is against this background of political and religious unity, together with the resurgence of Latin learning under Isidore and his contemporaries, that the achievements of Visigothic architecture in Spain can best be understood.

Before the arrival of the Visigoths, church building in Spain had followed the general trends of Latin Christendom in its predilection for the aisled basilica. Unique in western Europe, however, was the appearance in southern Spain around 500 or shortly thereafter of a basilican scheme with an apse at both ends of the nave, an arrangement influenced perhaps from similar designs in North Africa. The exact purpose of the counter-apse plan in Spain remains unclear, but it did not continue into the

38 Cologne, St. Gereon, plan.

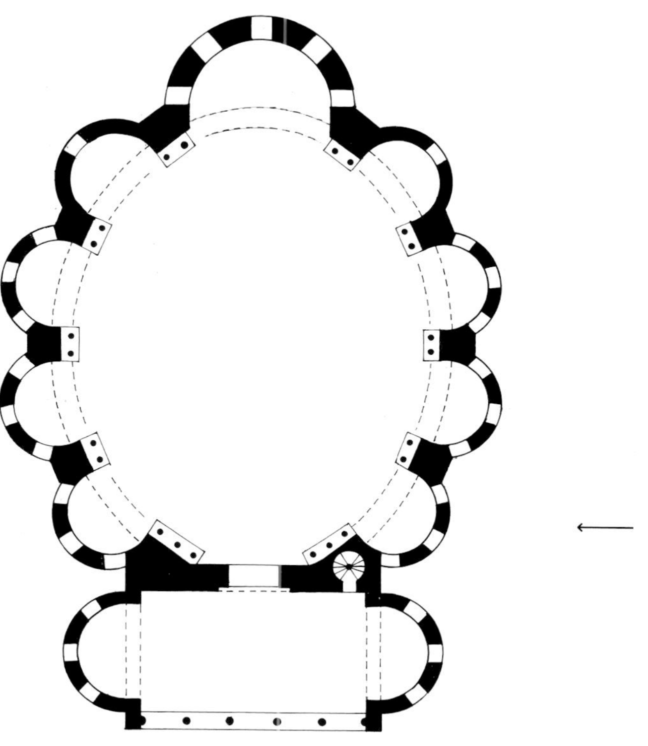

seventh century.[11] By this time the main monuments of Visigothic patronage were in the north and central highlands of the peninsula, which marked the focus of Visigothic power with its capital in Toledo. Of particular importance are a small number of churches dating from the second half of the seventh and the beginning of the eighth centuries. Among the most striking characteristics of these buildings is their fine-cut stone masonry, representing a technique not seen in Spain since the late fourth century.[12] During the interim churches had been built of mortared rubble. The reasons behind this reappearance of cut stone and the possible source, or sources, of influence have been much debated. Some scholars have suggested links with neighboring North Africa where the technique was prevalent, while others have pointed instead to the Near East, especially Syria, a region noted for its imposing churches of finely hewn limestone. Yet both areas were well within the Byzantine sphere and the use in Spain of the same mode of construction for churches could be seen to correspond to the well-documented imitation of Byzantine coins, regalia, and court ceremony by Visigothic rulers.[13] Contact with the Greek East had become especially close through Justinian's reconquest of the southeastern coast and even after the departure of Byzantine troops means of communication were plentiful. Nonetheless, a more immediate source was also available. The preference for ashlar blocks could also be understood as a conscious attempt to emulate the abundant remains of ancient Roman structures, from aqueducts to civic buildings, found both in urban centers and throughout the countryside in an effort to instill a potent element of *romanitas* in churches patronized by Visigothic rulers, who in their new-found orthodoxy saw themselves as successors to western Roman emperors. They even went so far as to assume the ancient imperial name "Flavius."[14] In the end, however, trying to make such fine distinctions about the possible sources of influence may be going too far. It should be remembered, after all, that the term "Byzantine" is a modern construct without meaning in the Middle Ages. The rulers in Constantinople saw themselves as "Roman" and their capital as the "New Rome," and they were recognized as such by their contemporaries throughout Europe, including Spain. Isidore of Seville, for example, consistently refers to the emperors in Constantinople and their armed forces as "Roman" in his *History of the Kings of the Goths*, which he may have written at the suggestion of the Visigothic king Sisebut (611–20). Differentiations between what we would categorize as Roman as opposed to Byzantine had little or no meaning in the time period that concerns us. Both periods offered equally valid models for creating an aura of *romanitas*, and the Visigoths freely appropriated them to define their own political self-awareness and perceived, or desired, position of prominence within western Christendom. Thus the influence at work here would best be termed "Romano-Byzantine."[15]

In spite of a dearth of contemporary documentation related to these churches, their relative chronology is confirmed by a close affiliation with San Juan de Baños, which bears a dated inscription over the interior arch leading to the apse. The plaque states, in part, that the church was "built, dedicated, and endowed" by King Recceswinth in 661.[16] Although only portions of the original fabric are preserved, this church exhibits many of the distinctive characteristics of this group. In addition to the use of large cut stones, the east end apse is rectangular in form rather than semicircular and covered by a barrel vault. There are also broad friezes at various levels of stylized vegetal and geometric patterns carved in low relief. These bands frame the arch leading into the apse, extend from impost blocks immediately below the arch, and surround the interior apse wall. They also surmount the clerestory windows of the nave, producing decorative patterns that seem to tie the interior of the building together. Equally striking is the horseshoe shape of the arch leading into the apse and its corresponding barrel vault. The horseshoe-shaped arch, defined by a curvature of anything over a true half-circle of 180 degrees, was not new to Spain. It appeared occasionally, at least in plan, in the design of apses as early as the fourth century; it may have appeared in earlier elevations as well, but they are not preserved. It also appeared occasionally in the Greek East, as seen, for example, in the apse arch and several windows of the so-called east church at Alahan Monastir in Cilicia from shortly before 500 and it was not unknown in Frankish Gaul.[17] Even so, the prominent use of the horseshoe arch at San Juan de Baños foreshadows its prime importance in Spain during the Visigothic period and later in both Christian and Islamic architecture. And like the bands of relief sculpture, its dynamic form adds a decorative exuberance to the building's otherwise massive sobriety.

As reconstructed, San Juan de Baños in its original design, and as later rebuilt, was basilican in form with a short row of rather squat columns dividing the nave and single aisles. But more centralized plans appeared at this time as well. The most telling example is the cruciform chapel of San Fructuoso de Montelios near the northwestern town of Braga (figs. 39–40).[18] According to tradition it was constructed to serve as the burial place of St. Fructuosus (d. 665), a holy man of noble Visigothic lineage, who was a renowned monastic leader and was named bishop of Braga in 656 by King Recceswinth. In truth, the funerary function of this structure, while plausible, is unproven; nonetheless, the distinctive ashlar masonry is indicative of its seventh-century date. Much of the building

39 Braga, San Fructuoso, exterior view.

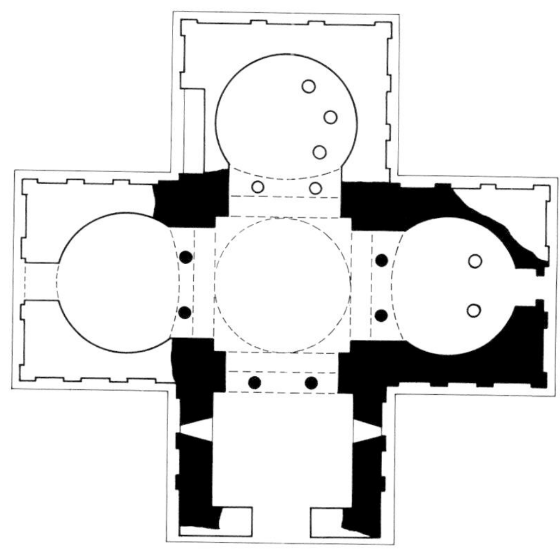

40 Braga, San Fructuoso, plan.

has been rebuilt over time. It was considerably altered in the eighteenth century and extensively restored in the 1930s, with some work still ongoing. Nonetheless, foundations certify its cruciform design, while most of the western entrance cross arm and much of the southern cross arm elevations are original along with their shallow exterior niches capped by alternating gables and arches. The rest of the exterior elevation has been restored to copy these remains. The overall cruciform design, shallow niches, and low central crossing tower resemble closely the so-called Mausoleum of Galla Placidia in Ravenna from the first half of the fifth century discussed in chapter one (fig. 18). The relationship, however striking the similarities, was certainly not direct given the separation in time of more than two centuries and in distance between Italy and Spain, not to mention a dramatic difference in building materials between brick and mortar on the one hand and mortarless cut stone on the other. Even so, San Fructuoso no doubt attempts to emulate the generic form of cruciform churches and chapels that, as previously discussed, had their ultimate origins in the eastern Mediterranean. There may, of course, have been intermediary prototypes in Spain as well, but, if so, they are not preserved. It has also been suggested that an association with the Greek East may have been consciously promoted by St. Fructuosus himself for his burial place because he had fervently wished to make a pilgrimage to the Holy Lands, a goal that was blocked by the king, who did not wish him to leave the country.[19] Be that as it may, the chapel of San Fructuoso exemplifies, perhaps more clearly than any other monument in Spain, the desire of the Visigoths to instill their architecture with a sense of *romanitas* through design, mode of construction, and even reuse of ancient columns and capitals on the interior.[20] Once again, however, Roman and early Byzantine forms have been instilled with a new and vibrant aesthetic through the use of the horseshoe arch both in the plan of the three apses and the interior elevation of the four arches about the crossing. Here the relief sculpture is more restrained than San Juan de Baños and predominantly vegetal in nature; still, a distinct horizontal decorative band is formed by linking up with capitals and impost blocks. There is also a sense of experimentation with the interior vaulting. Although now largely rebuilt, sufficient traces remain to suggest that the western arm was covered by a barrel vault while the low crossing tower, now heightened, and three horseshoe-shaped apses bore domical vaults of some kind, although not necessarily in the manner seen today. Certainly the immense thickness of the walls indicates that the interior was meant to be vaulted throughout. Moreover, unlike the interior of the Ravennate structure

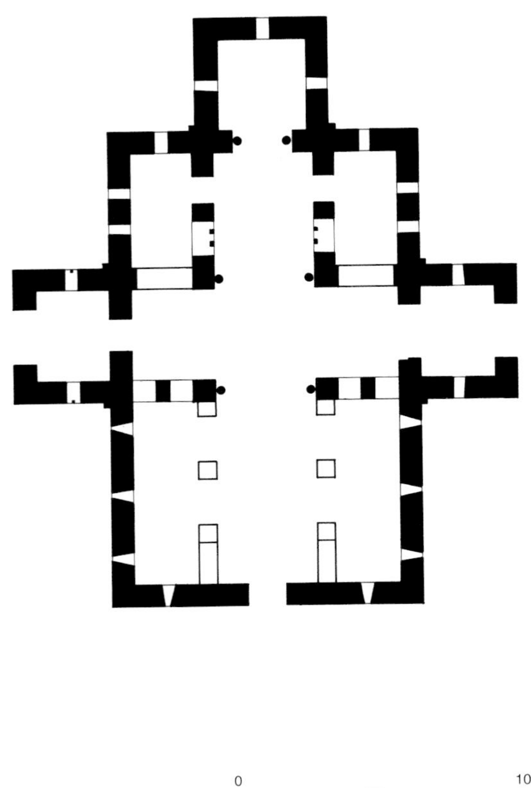

41 and 42 San Pedro de la Nave, exterior view and plan.

associated with Galla Placidia, the four arms of the cruciform design are screened off from the crossing by paired columns, so that even here a sense of distinct interior compartmentalization is apparent. On the exterior, the niches are far too shallow to have served any structural purpose. They are there only for decoration and to heighten the building's affiliation with the Romano-Byzantine past.

Other churches, such as Santa Comba de Bande, are worthy of mention, too, but the high point of this development was unquestionably reached at San Pedro de la Nave (figs. 41–42).[21] Again, there is no documentation for this building before the tenth century. Moreover, the structure was disassembled and carefully rebuilt stone by stone on a new site a few kilometers away in 1930 in order to rescue it from the flood waters of a newly built dam. In this process, however, the character of its original ashlar masonry was preserved with minimal alteration. In design, San Pedro de la Nave represents a combination of a basilican and a cruciform scheme. Like San Juan de Baños, it has a clear nave and aisles, in this case divided by piers instead of columns from a later medieval rebuilding, and a now-familiar rectilinear east end. But like San Fructuoso, it also possesses a distinct central crossing, surmounted by a low tower, from which extend four corridors at right angles to one another: to the west is the nave, to the east a choir area in front of the sanctuary, and to the north and south are short pockets of space connected to projecting porch-like vestibules that mimic the eastern apse in their roughly square form. Similarly, short rectangular passageways to either side of the choir echo the shape of the aisles to the west. Each of these spatial compartments is clearly distinguished on the exterior by different roof levels beginning with the high point of the prominent central lantern tower above the crossing to the nave and choir to the areas flanking the choir (sacristies or chapels most likely) and the aisles to, at the lowest level, the northern and southern vestibules. Only the true interior height of the apse is masked by a roof line that continues the ridge of the nave and choir, thus creating a false attic-like space, the exact function of which is unknown, above the sanctuary. This tight fusion of compartmentalized spaces was accented on the interior by a variety of vaulting types, while chancel screens once segregated the east end, delegated to the clergy, from the west end, accessible to the laity. Like other churches in this group, the interior is dimly lit from the outside by a limited number of extremely small windows (fig. 42). At San Pedro de la Nave, only a single round-arched window penetrates each of the three thick walls of the square apse, while the outer aisle walls are allowed only a few narrow slits to offer daylight. The result is a rather murky, if not gloomy, interior whereby the apse appears far more distant from the nave and aisles than its intimate scale might suggest (fig. 43). The open views, free-flowing spaces, and light-filled interiors of Early Christian churches have been transformed here into a highly compartmentalized environment of dark recesses and extremely limited sources of sunlight. Such a dramatic change cannot have been accidental. Although the precise reasons must remain open to speculation, the end result seems to be the creation of a setting that stresses the mystery of the eucharist as celebrated by the clergy in the sanctuary and as observed with only partial views by the laity in the aisles.[22]

In place of gleaming mosaics and marble revetment, the massive walls of San Pedro de la Nave, like other Visigothic churches of the period, are enlivened by an array of carved reliefs in both geometric and vegetal patterns. In the apse such carved friezes frame the windows, extend from impost blocks, and form a horizontal band at the springing of the barrel vault. Most striking are the impost blocks, capitals, and even the bases of the column shafts attached to the four crossing piers (fig. 44). In some places undulating vine scrolls betray their ultimately classical origins, while more stylized ones with banded stems and pecking birds in strict profile on the crossing impost blocks suggest influence

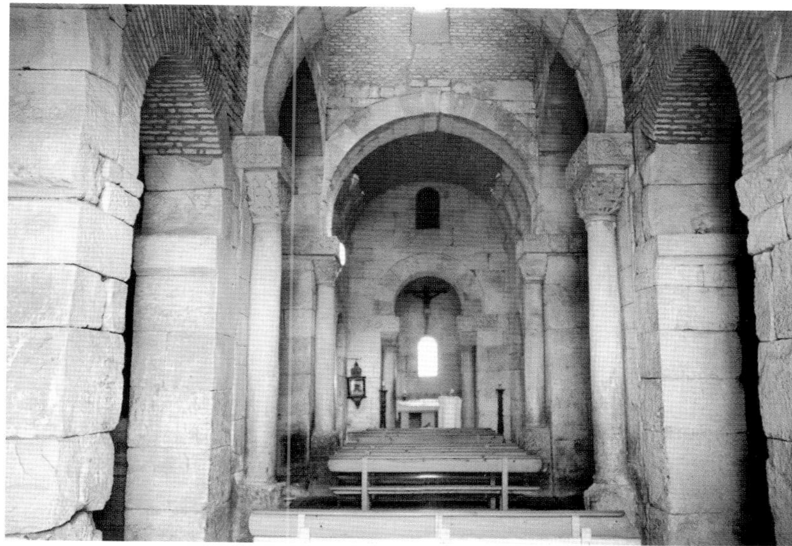

43 San Pedro de la Nave, interior view looking east.

from Sasanian art. Similar motifs, through trade with Persia of luxury items such as textiles and metalwork, had by the sixth century migrated into carved ornament throughout the Byzantine world from Ravenna to Constantinople.[23] Indeed, the closest comparison to the carving at San Pedro de la Nave is the openwork patterns of a bronze belt buckle of the seventh century found in Spain, which is either a Byzantine import or an accomplished Visigothic imitation of one.[24] No exact comparisons, however, can be found for the figural compositions of the two westernmost capitals

44 San Pedro de la Nave, crossing capital with relief of Daniel in the Lions' Den.

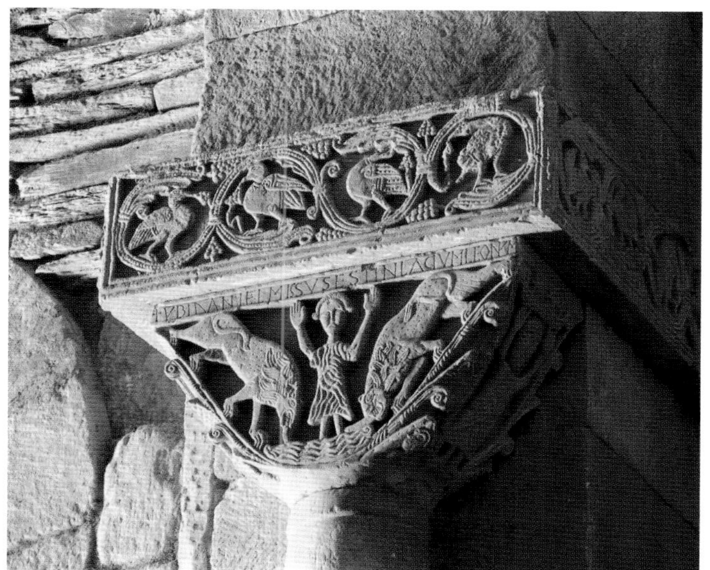

bearing images, labelled by Latin inscriptions, of Daniel in the Lions' Den and the Sacrifice of Isaac. Although both subjects are not uncommon in Early Christian art, going back to the Roman catacombs of the third century and sarcophagi throughout the Mediterranean world, there are no precedents for their appearance in architectural sculpture. In fact, these carvings are so remarkable that some scholars in the past have been tempted to attribute these capitals to the Romanesque era of the eleventh and twelfth centuries when so-called historiated capitals were common, especially in certain areas of Spain and France. But the flat, cookie-cutter technique of the carving of the capitals at San Pedro de la Nave, along with a total absence of the use of the drill, common both in Roman antiquity and during the Romanesque period, demonstrate that these reliefs are part of the original structure. Once again, examples of indigenous metalwork offer the closest parallels.[25] No doubt their placement at the entrance to the crossing, the point of demarcation between the clergy and the laity, is not without significance. Surely they are meant to symbolize the sacrifice of Christ and promise of salvation through the teachings of the Church and the holy rites performed at the altar within this structure.

Although figural carving was not completely unknown in the Early Christian and Byzantine world, as witness, for example, the relief sculpture of the so-called west basilica at Alahan, there is nothing preserved quite like the rich array of ornament here.[26] Both the design and decoration of San Pedro de la Nave were inspired by ancient Roman, Early Christian, and Byzantine precedents, but like Visigothic Spain itself the resultant synthesis was something new: dark yet decorative, massive yet small in scale, tightly fused yet clearly compartmentalized, basilican and cruciform, to name but a few of its most important, and seemingly contradictory, characteristics. The slightly later church of Quintanilla de las Viñas, with its stratified friezes of strikingly sophisticated vine scroll ornament on the exterior and flat and highly schematized figural reliefs of angels with Christ and other holy figures on the interior, shows that the fusion of architecture and relief sculpture achieved at San Pedro de la Nave continued into the early eighth century.[27] Further development, however, was cut short by the dramatic success of the Muslim invasion in 711. Within two years Toledo fell. Only the northwestern province of Asturias remained as an outpost of Christianity on the Iberian peninsula. The monuments just discussed were for a time abandoned, but not destroyed, and they lay in areas that were far enough north to be soon recovered by the Christians. The glories of Visigothic Toledo, on the other hand, were lost forever and one can only assume that much of what we see in the churches of these outlying regions represents, in fact, a somewhat rustic reflection of the aesthetics of the royal court and the Church hierarchy in the capital. Even so, the creative impulse of this handful of preserved buildings should not be overlooked, nor were the lessons they offer completely lost to later generations. The horseshoe-shaped arch, for example, would become ubiquitous for both Christian and Muslim Spain for the next several centuries. Nevertheless, the appropriation of the past to serve the present together with the combination of austere geometric form and decorative exuberance would remain unique to the Visigothic period.

At approximately the same time, a similar process had been taking place in Frankish Gaul. The desire to adopt the trappings of *romanitas* is evident in Frankish art and architecture from an early date. As we have already seen, La Daurade in Toulouse, if indeed it was built around 507, exemplifies the Frankish ability to appropriate, or at least sponsor, late antique forms. Such conscious use of distinctively Roman elements is already apparent in the luxurious burial treasure of Childeric, the father of Clovis, who died ca. 482. His tomb, containing a vast array of bejewelled regalia and weapons, was discovered in Tournai in 1653. Although much of the hoard was stolen in 1831, detailed engravings of many of the most prominent objects, published shortly after their discovery, document the presence of a gold signet ring bearing the Latin inscription CHILDERICI REGIS ("belonging to King Childeric") and a schematic, frontal portrait of the king with long hair, wearing Roman military dress and carrying a lance over one shoulder. Both the notion of a ring, used to seal written documents, and the language of the inscription itself are Roman in origin. Moreover, the image of the king clearly imitates the armor and spear-bearing gesture of fourth- and fifth-century imperial coins of which several were found in Childeric's tomb. Such items were no doubt intended to legitimize Childeric among the Gallo-Roman inhabitants of the regions he conquered; even the luxurious gold and inlaid garnet ornament on numerous objects, such as a sword handle and belt buckle, may have been largely Byzantine in origin. Soon thereafter, garnet jewelry would be produced locally, as evidenced by numerous wealthy, although far less elaborate, burials of German elites. The contents of the Childeric's tomb, therefore, seems to reflect the fact that he enhanced his position of prominence in northern Gaul by cooperating with local Roman military officials to curtail the advances of other barbaric peoples such as the Visigoths and the Saxons.[28] In short, he was a creature of a world in transition. His reign initiated a new era of Frankish dominance in northern Europe, and the term, Merovingian, which is commonly applied to this period until the rise of the Carolingian dynasty in the mid-eighth century, comes from Merovech, a semi-legendary figure identified as the father of Childeric by Gregory of Tours and other early medieval chroniclers. And it was, in turn, under Childeric's son,

Clovis, that Frankish control expanded throughout Gaul in the course of which the Visigoths were defeated at Vouillé. Clovis had, in the meantime, converted to orthodox Christianity which helped to endear him to the local population and the Gallo-Roman church hierarchy.

The reign of Clovis became directly linked to Roman rule when, in 508, the emperor in Constantinople, Anastasius, bestowed upon the Frankish king the office of consul, in part because the Byzantines were forming an alliance against the Ostrogoths in Italy. Clovis celebrated this honor, along with his recent victory at Vouillé, at the shrine of St. Martin in Tours, where he stood before the saint's tomb dressed in a purple tunic and military mantle and crowned himself with a diadem.[29] The setting for this display of power was a basilica built over a generation earlier under the auspices of Bishop Perpetuus of Tours (458–88). Only the basic dimensions of the church (approximately 48 m long × 18 m wide × 13.5 m high), along with the number of columns (120), windows (52), and doorways (8), are known from a sixth-century description. An entrance tower of some kind and another tower or dome over the main altar are suggested by the wording of inscriptions that are known to have appeared both inside and outside the building.[30] Regardless of its specific design, the structure certainly must have impressed the triumphant ruler. In fact, soon after, Clovis sponsored the construction of a church dedicated to the Holy Apostles to serve as his burial place in Paris, which he established as the permanent capital for his realm. The building was destroyed by the Vikings in the late ninth century, but documentary sources tell us that it was preceded by an atrium and was decorated inside by scenes of patriarchs, prophets, and martyrs in mosaic in the tradition of Early Christian churches.[31] Not surprisingly, by the end of the sixth century, Gregory of Tours refers to Clovis as a "new Constantine," and this epithet must have been applied already in the king's own lifetime.[32] Indeed, not only his religious conversion but also the founding of a capital and the construction of a dynastic burial church dedicated to the Holy Apostles were in clear imitation of the first Christian emperor.

Preserved architectural monuments, as opposed to those known only from brief literary descriptions, are few. The originally aisleless church of Saint-Pierre in Vienne seems to date to the late fifth or early sixth century and may help us envision on a somewhat smaller scale the church of St. Martin at Tours (fig. 45). Certainly, the interior wall articulation of superimposed rows of shallow niches flanked by engaged colonnettes is strikingly similar to that of La Daurade and the double range of these niches at Vienne may help to account for the extraordinarily large number of columns reported for the church at Tours.[33] But these churches, like their contemporaries in Theodoric's Ravenna, belong to the legacy of late antiquity, as discussed

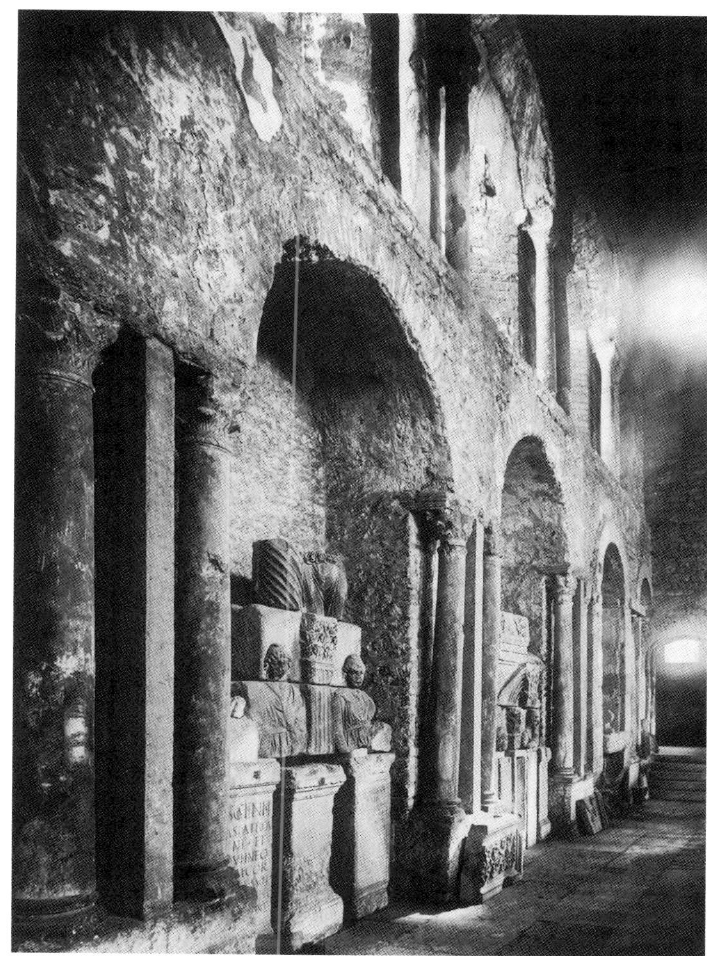

45 Vienne, Saint-Pierre, interior view.

in the first chapter, and they must have been built by Gallo-Romans and not Franks. As with the Visigoths, we must look to the latter part of the seventh century for the first tangible evidence of an architecture with qualities that may be considered distinctly Frankish.

The baptistery of Saint-Jean at Poitiers is perhaps the best- known and certainly the best-preserved monument of early medieval France, but the exact circumstances of its construction are far from certain. The structure, situated 100 m south of the cathedral, is dominated by a rectangular hall (12.3 m long × 8.25 m wide) set along a roughly east–west axis (fig. 46). The baptistery has been an object of study since the early nineteenth century and portions of the building have been restored and rebuilt several times since then; the current two small, semicircular apses to the east and west, for example, are creations of the mid-1800s. In the process much archaeological information has been lost. Preliminary results of new, ongoing investigations have underscored the complexity of the situation by identifying at least seven stages before a major intervention

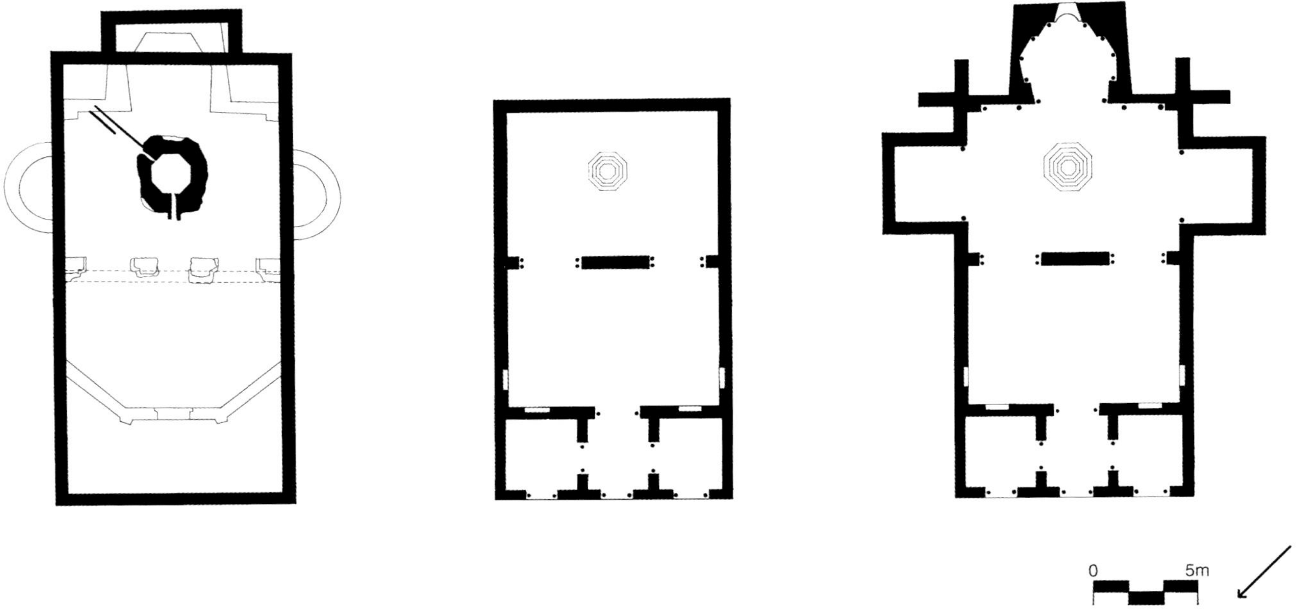

46 and 47 Poitiers, Baptistery of Saint-Jean, exterior view and plan with various phases: (left) overlay, original state in black, present clear; (center) ca. 700; (right) ca. 1000.

around 1100, when the interior was decorated with elaborate, Romanesque wall paintings, portions of which can still be seen today. Although the dating remains problematic, the general sequence of developments may be summarized as follows (fig. 47).[34] The structure began in the Early Christian period as a large undivided rectangular space with the octagonal font as its central focus. Over time, annexes, first rectangular, then semi-circular, were added to the north and south and the east end was extended, while the interior was separated into two main halls and a tripartite entryway introduced. The exterior walls were also patched and rebuilt on several occasions, employing first an irregular masonry of very small stonework (*petit appareil*), which was followed by a more regular system of noticeably larger blocks. In the process, the elevation of the easternmost hall was raised producing a prominent counter north–south axis crowned by decorative pediments. In a subsequent phase, perhaps attributable to the tenth or early eleventh century, the lower portions of round-arched windows were walled up to create oculi. It seems that a fire prompted the Romanesque remodeling mentioned above.

The precise chronology of the imposing eastern rectangular hall of the building remains, as yet, undetermined, but the exterior wall articulation, especially in its upper ranges, offers important clues to the time of its construction (figs. 46 and 48). The masonry, where it has not been restored, consists of an *opus mixtum*, composed of moderate-sized limestone blocks alternating with single courses of brick. This technique resembles the *opus listatum* of many late Roman buildings in Gaul, but the elongated shape of the stones along with the undulating nature of the courses indicates a much later date, as does the accompanying decorative elements inserted in the masonry. Particularly striking are a series of stubby pilasters with crude Corinthian capitals supporting a string course atop which are three small pediments, alternating triangular and round-arched in shape. Within these recesses are plaques carved in shallow relief with crosses surrounded by vegetal ornament. In the main gable above, marked by a more formal cornice with stone brackets, are more triangular forms. Of special interest are the two containing rosettes composed of inlaid terra-cotta tiles, because these designs are virtually identical to compass-drawn patterns common in Frankish manuscripts from around 700, such as a title page from a sacramentary produced at the monastery of Luxeuil (fig. 49). Similarly, the relief carvings, especially the plaque in the

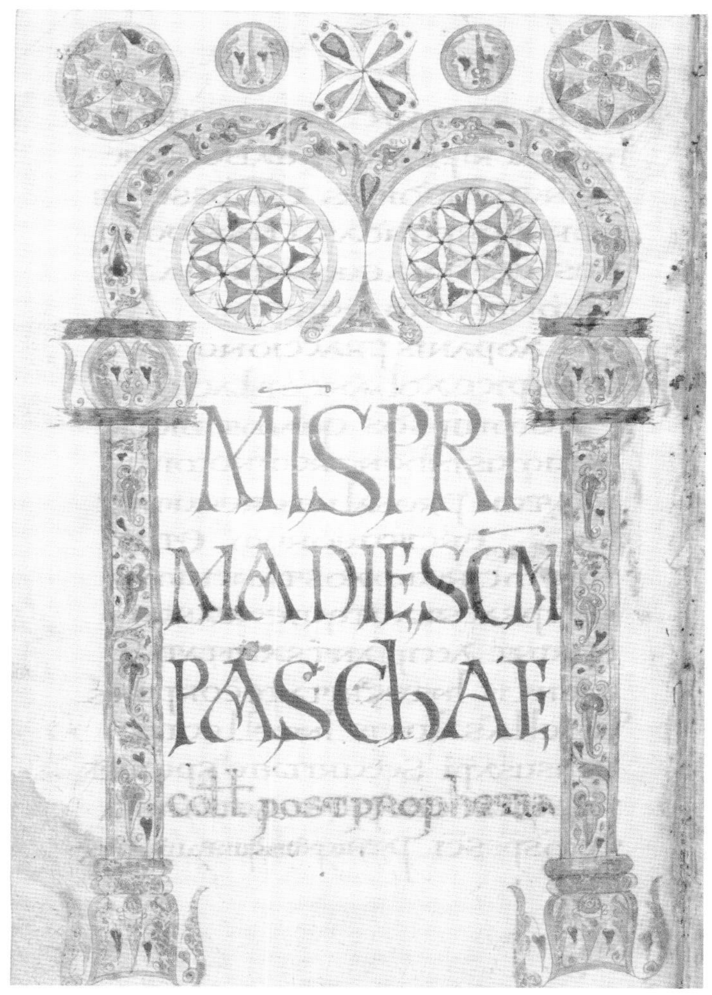

48 *(top)* Poitiers, Baptistery of Saint-Jean, detail of exterior.

49 *(right)* Luxeuil, Sacramentary (Biblioteca Apostolica Vaticana, Reg. lat. 317, fol. 169v).

center of the gable, resemble closely an array of carved slabs, some for sarcophagi, from the surrounding area, usually dated to the seventh century.[35] The engaged columns on the interior are reused Roman *spolia* while their capitals, all variations on the Corinthian order and far more elegant than the exterior pilasters, were most likely imported from marble quarries in the Pyrénées, where extremely high quality sculpture continued to be produced throughout the seventh century until halted by Muslim incursions from Spain in the early 700s.[36] In sum, the ensemble at St. Jean at Poitiers seems to exhibit a continued reverence for late antique forms in combination with more colorful and abstract patterns. To be sure, some elements, especially the exterior pilasters and their capitals, could simply be dismissed as evidence of a decline in technical skill, but that is not the case for the capitals on the inside. More important is the overall effect, resulting from an integration of classical and, for want of a better word, "barbarian" taste. Such a lively display of surface pattern has nothing to do with structural logic; instead it is there, I suspect, to convey a sense of authority through association with the ancient past and splendor through decorative richness. As discussed in chapter one, baptisteries were major civic monuments in late antiquity and symbols of episcopal power, and they remained so in the early Middle Ages. It is therefore interesting to note that carved slabs in the north and south gables of the baptistery are extremely similar to those from the nearby abbey of Mazerolles, which is known to have been rebuilt by the bishop of Poitiers, Ansoald (674–96).[37] Just such a patron could well have been responsible for this rebuilding phase of the baptistery in Poitiers.

A similar fusion of disparate elements is found on a more modest and private scale just outside the city. On the other side of the river, Le Clain, lies an elevated plain known as "les Dunes," which has served as a cemetery area since antiquity; therefore, since its discovery in 1879, a small funerary chapel within this area has been referred to as the "Hypogée des Dunes."[38] More specifically, a lengthy carved inscription *in situ* tells us that this structure was built for the tomb of Abbot Mellebaude, an individual otherwise unknown, although the profuse decoration seems to reflect his elevated status. The rectilinear design and barrel-vaulted interior are ultimately Roman in origin and correspond to numerous other semi-subterranean burial chambers, including the many private *memoriae* and *cryptae* mentioned in the writings of Gregory of Tours, as discussed in the previous chapter. Roman, too, is the practice of plastering the interior walls and painting their borders with brightly colored bands, now much faded but carefully recorded at the time of discovery, along with a lengthy Latin inscription in ochre uncials commemorating the transferal of relics. The presence of relics and remnants of a stone altar, plastered and decorated with a painted cross, attest to the fact that the structure served as an oratory or chapel as well as a burial chamber. The stone steps and doorway leading to the chapel are carved in low relief using a familiar Early Christian repertoire of motifs, such as vine scrolls, fish, and rosettes; however, the image of three intertwined snakes on the third step from the bottom has very different roots. Such animal ornament is barbarian in origin and has its closest comparison in Frankish metalwork of the sixth and seventh centuries, while the interlace pattern formed by the bodies of the snakes is a common form of decoration for letters and borders in Merovingian manuscripts of the late seventh and early eighth centuries. It also brings to mind a relief found at Hornhausen, in present-day Germany, with interlocked serpentine creatures; once considered to be a Frankish funerary stele, it is now understood to be part of a series of chancel screens from a church in the eastern part of the Frankish realm around 700.[39] In both cases, these carvings are believed to have served an apotropaic function to ward off evil spirits and, I suspect, to signify the triumph of Christianity over paganism as well.

A related funerary monument, the crypt of Saint-Paul at Jouarre, some 60 km east of Paris, is more overtly classicizing in its decorative features (fig. 50).[40] It, too, is a semi-underground vaulted chamber but much larger and subdivided into bays by two rows of three columns on high pedestals. Although the groin vaulting was no doubt added in the later Middle Ages, the columns are *in situ*. Their shafts seem to be ancient *spolia*, while the capitals, like those on the interior of the Poitiers baptistery, are clearly products of the Pyrénées, datable to the seventh century. The extremely high craftsmanship of these capitals can only partially be explained as a continuation of ancient techniques, because, although four of the capitals are traditional in form (fig. 51), two others are far more imaginative, manipulating the basic design of the Corinthian and Composite type by introducing a tall band of fluting crowned by a broad egg-and-dart molding (fig. 52). Only a simultaneous respect for classical tradition and a distance from the original models could have produced such remarkable results. The crypt is the earliest preserved remnant of a double monastery, that is, an abbey for both monks and nuns, founded in the early seventh century by Ado, a member of the Frankish royal court. It once housed three churches of which that of St. Paul (not the apostle but the hermit in Egypt who was an early founder of monasticism) was built within the communal cemetery to house the remains of the monastery's earliest leaders, including Abbess Theodechilde (d. after 662), a cousin of Ado, and her brother, Agilbert, who retired to Jouarre in

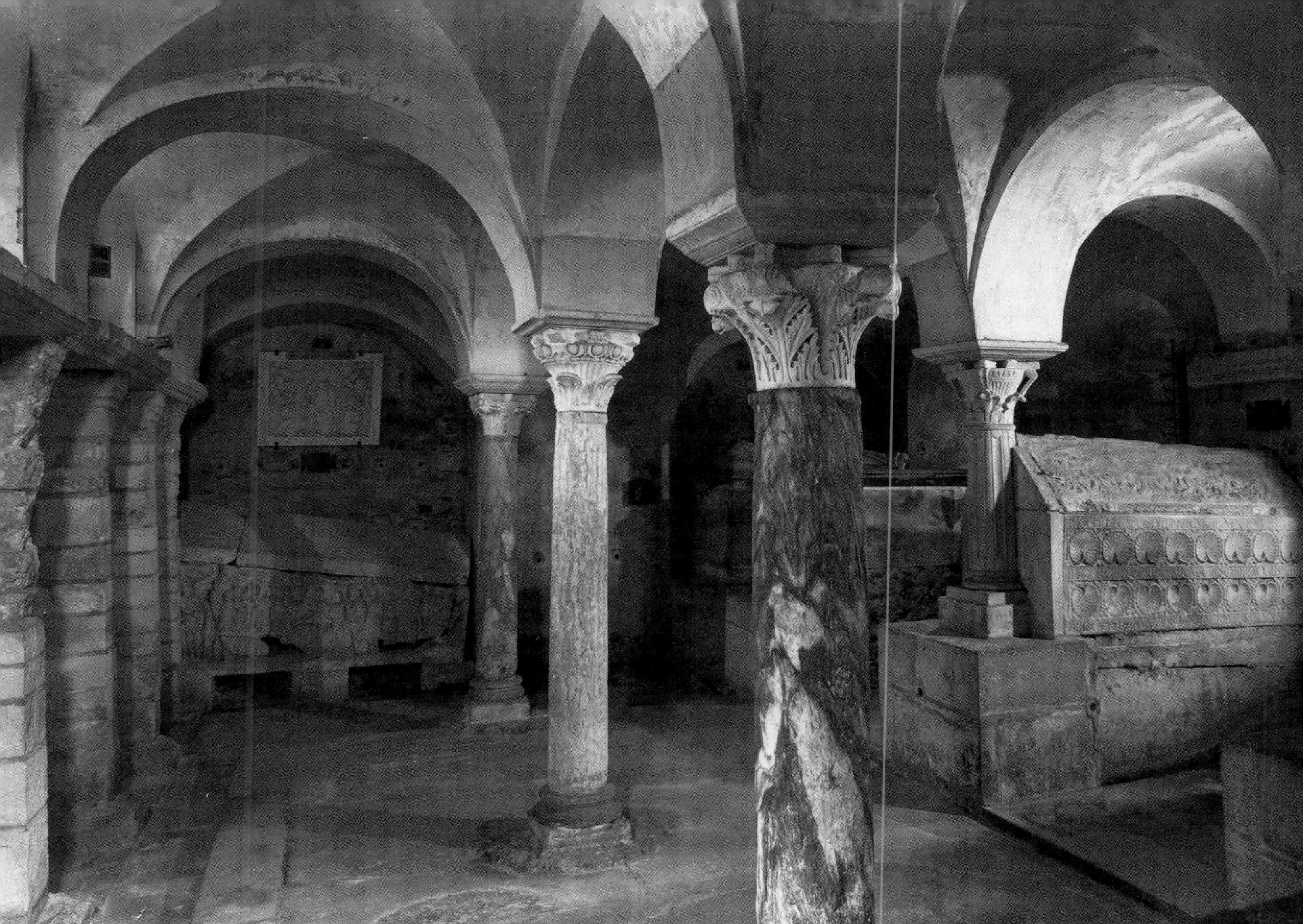

50 Jouarre, Saint-Paul, crypt, interior view.

the 680s after a distinguished career as a missionary bishop in England and subsequently bishop of Paris. Each has a magnificent stone sarcophagus displayed in the crypt; that of Theodechilde, identified by a lengthy and extremely elegant inscription, with two registers of delicately carved conch shells and the other, traditionally ascribed to Agilbert, bears remarkable figural representations on two sides of Christ in Majesty and the Last Judgment respectively.

A prominent feature of the crypt is its west wall, which unlike the rest of the crypt is constructed of decorative masonry in three distinct registers composed, from bottom to top, of squares, diamond or lozenge patterns, and octagons (fig. 53). Although this wall is often referred to as *opus reticulatum*, only the middle register bears any resemblance to the ancient Roman masonry technique, but even here any direct connection seems unlikely. *Opus reticulatum* was devised in Italy in the first century B.C. to provide a purely utilitarian facing for concrete walls, but it was very rarely used in Gaul due to differences in local materials and building practices. Instead a wall facing of small squared stones in horizontal courses, usually termed *petit appareil,* was preferred. This does not mean that work at Jouarre could not have been inspired, at least in part, by ancient Roman models. Decorative patterns, for example, are prominently displayed, in the masonry of the early third-century walls of Le Mans, but the stripes, V-shapes and other patterns are created by using roughly squared stones and bricks always in horizontal courses.[41] Moreover, the walls at Le Mans are highly colorful (black, gray, white, and brick red) whereas the masonry at Jouarre is uniformly monochrome. If anything, the masonry in the crypt is more finely done, albeit on a much smaller scale, than the ancient example, with a far greater range of geometric

51 and 52 Jouarre, crypt, capitals.

shapes. Indeed, the meticulous workmanship of the Jouarre masonry calls to mind the intricacies of Frankish cloisonné metalwork. To be sure, the comparison is not exact, but the mindset may have been much the same. That is to say, like the inlaid jewels of seventh- and eighth-century reliquaries, this delicate masonry was meant to honor the crypt's sacred contents.

Again, the date of this construction is not certain, although it clearly represents a later remodeling, indicated by the pinkish color of its mortar as opposed to the yellowish hue of the crypt's first phase. But how much later is it? Recent attempts to date it to around the year 800 or later in comparison with the Lorsch *Torhalle*, a well-known monument of the Carolingian period (see chapter five, fig. 97), are not convincing, because, upon closer inspection, the two monuments are in fact very different.[42] Among other things, the *Torhalle* is a freestanding structure above ground with a highly colorful exterior surface decoration and it uses hexagonal star patterns in place of Jouarre's distinctive octagons. There may be some indirect relationship, such as a common inspiration from Roman models, but certainly the two monuments are not directly linked. In the end, it seems more reasonable to accept the opinion of the most recent investigators of Jouarre who assign the initial construction of the crypt to the last third of the seventh century and the decorative masonry wall to a rebuilding "a few decades later" perhaps as a buttressing element in conjunction with making the burial chamber more accessible to visitors.[43] In any event, the buildings at Poitiers and the crypt at Jouarre seem to be roughly contemporary and represent in their design, construction, and decoration the further melding of Gallo-Roman and Frankish traditions, resulting in a synthesis that is uniquely early medieval.

By 568, when the Lombards swept into the Po River valley from the Danube region via the Alpine passes, the Franks had long controlled much of Gaul and the Visigoths were well established in Spain. Italy, on the other hand, was still suffering from famine and plague in the wake of the long and bitter decades of fighting between the Byzantine forces of Justinian and the Ostrogoths in the so-called Gothic Wars. As a result the peninsula lay largely defenseless and its inhabitants offered little resistance to the newest invaders; soon only certain areas remained under Byzantine jurisdiction: Sicily, portions of south Italy, and the territory immediately around Venice and Ravenna, as well as a strip of land connecting the latter with Rome. Lombard relations with Rome and the papacy were often tense, since the city was technically a duchy overseen by the imperial exarch, or viceroy, residing in Ravenna. At first the Lombards and their leaders remained aloof from their subjects, a division that was exacerbated by the fact that most Lombards were either pagan or Arian Christians. Conversion to orthodoxy was slow and sporadic; it would take a hundred years before Lombard rulers were uniformly Catholic. Still, like the other Germanic overlords of Europe, the Lombard elite quickly appropriated Roman symbols of power.[44]

Already by the end of the sixth century, Lombard kings bore the title "Flavius" in an effort, like the Visigoths, to legitimize their rule.[45] Such pretensions are seen clearly in a gilded bronze relief discovered near Lucca in the nineteenth century and now in the Bargello museum in Florence. It was originally designed to fit the brow of a helmet and shows in the center King Agilulf (590–616), identified by name in an accompanying inscription, enthroned and flanked by armed guards and winged victories, much in the manner of portrayals of late antique emperors as can be found on the famous silver plate or *missorium*, now in Madrid, of Theodosius I. Not that this could be mistaken for a Roman work. The rendering of the figures is too rudimentary and the letters of the inscription are crudely punched. More important, the king's personal appearance is totally contrary to imperial custom but very much in keeping with Lombard tradition. He has long hair and a full, pointed beard (hence the origin of the term Lombard derived from *longobard* or "long beard"); he also wears trousers and holds a sword across his lap. In other words, the Bargello relief illustrates perfectly the blending of a Roman and barbarian visual vocabulary of sovereignty.[46] Agilulf showed that he was adept at using ritual as well as imagery to promote his reign when in 604, in order to guarantee a smooth succession, he presented his son, Adaloald, as co-ruler in the circus at Milan in the same way new Byzantine emperors were acclaimed in the hippodrome in Constantinople.[47] As the setting of this ceremony suggests, Lombard rulers, like their Ostrogothic predecessors, resided in cities and sought to maintain at least the basic elements of the urban fabric, including roads, fortification walls, and bridge, albeit on a modest scale.[48]

Although there is ample documentary evidence of the patronage of church building as well, there is precious little physical evidence available. For instance, Agilulf's wife, Theodolinda, a Catholic princess from Bavaria, is reported to have built in Monza a church dedicated to John the Baptist, which was decorated "with many ornaments of gold and silver," but nothing is known about the design of the building itself.[49] We have a bit more information about

53 Jouarre, Saint-Paul, crypt, west wall.

a church sponsored by Queen Rodelinda (672–88) in a cemetery outside the city walls of Pavia, which by then had become the capital of the kingdom. Referred to as S. Maria ad Pertica (or St. Mary "at the poles" because of a local landmark), it served as a burial place for Lombard royalty. Although the church was demolished in 1815, a section and plan made before this destruction show that it was centrally planned with a small dome atop a drum pierced by windows and supported by six columns. The hexagonal core was enveloped by a surrounding aisle with a series of flat-ended niches in its outer wall. Clearly, the church was

54 Spoleto, Tempietto del Clitunno, exterior view.

derived from late antique funerary chapels and *martyria*, such as S. Costanza in Rome or St. Gereon in more distant Cologne (figs. 33? and 38).[50] Still, as with Visigothic Spain, standing monuments lie far from the royal capital. Lombard rule was far less centralized than that of the Franks or even the Visigoths. While royal authority presided over much of north Italy and present-day Tuscany, dukes in two vast regions, one around Spoleto in central Italy and the other around Benevento in the south, enjoyed semi-autonomous rule. It is in the principal cities of these two duchies that one finds remarkably well-preserved examples of Lombard architecture at its finest.

The Tempietto del Clitunno is situated 13 km north of Spoleto astride the modern course of the ancient Via Flaminia, the major thoroughfare linking Rome with the Adriatic (fig. 54).[51] Its name, "little temple of the Clitunno," comes from its diminutive size (ca. 11 m long × 4.5 m wide), its temple-like facade, and its location on a hillside overlooking the plain of what was once the Clitumnus River, praised in antiquity by many classical authors.[52] The structure is composed of a small aisleless nave with a narrow porch perched atop a high podium and reached originally by stairs to left and right, only one of which has been rebuilt in much altered form. Although the walls of the nave are rubble, they support a barrel vault (5 m high) of neatly coursed rough-hewn blocks abutted front and back (that is east and west) by ashlars, *spolia* mostly, of travertine (figs. 54–55). The porch is similarly vaulted. Since it is situated on a steep slope, the base of the apse is buried in the hillside with only its conch and a surmounting gable above ground, while the elaborate west facade of podium, columnar screen, and pediment rise some nine meters above ground level. Particularly striking is the decorative use of *spolia* pilasters, columns, and their capitals, producing a visual

55 *(facing page)* Spoleto, Tempietto del Clitunno, interior view.

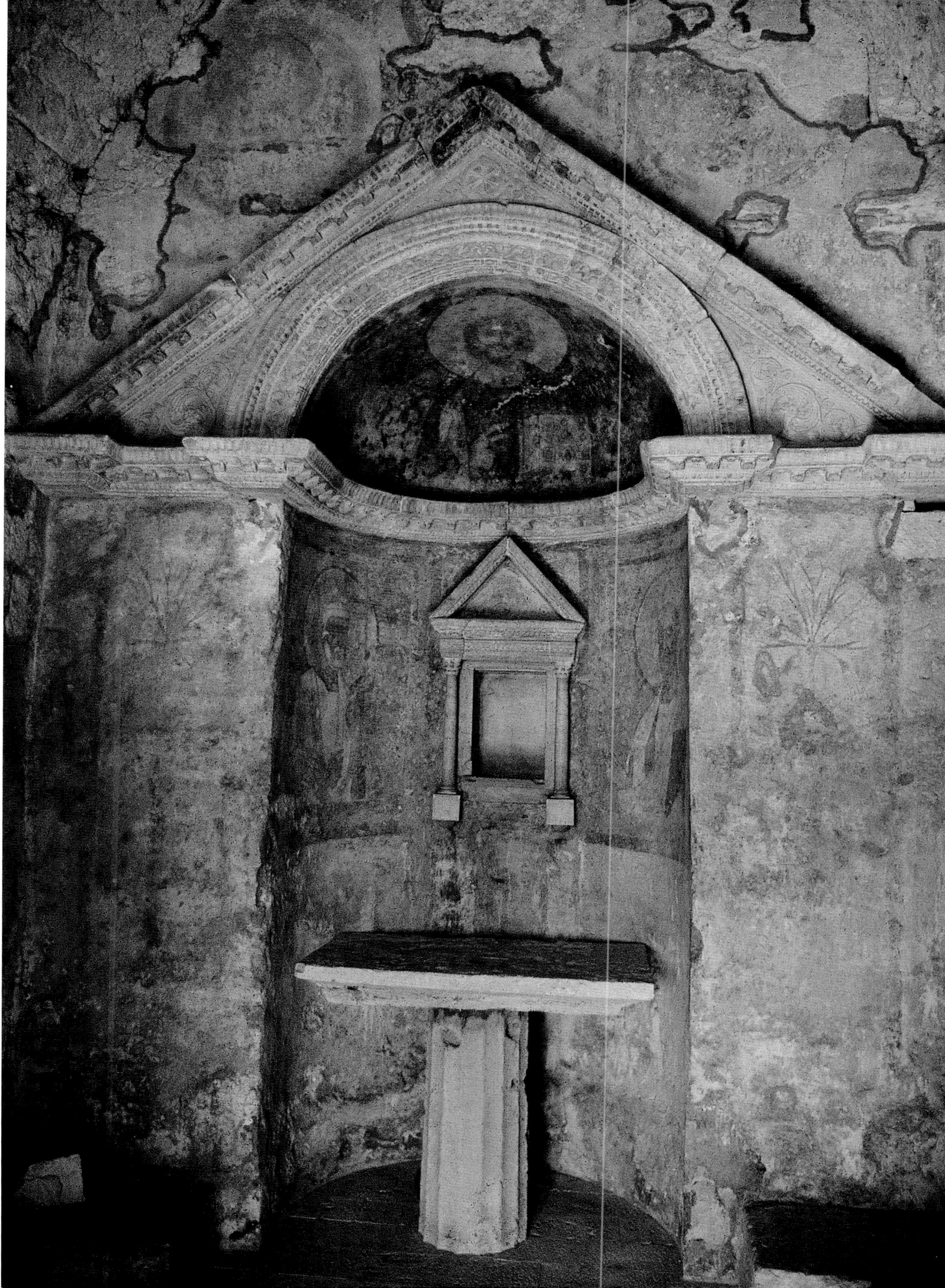

alternation of fluted, spiral, and scaled shafts in an A-B-C-C-B-A sequence, crowned by a carved pediment bearing a delicate vine scroll from which emerges a leafy cross (fig. 56). A single loop at the top of the cross transforms it into the chi-rho monogram of Christ as well. A similar relief is found at the opposite, east end of the building.

The frieze of the west facade is adorned with a monumental inscription, bracketed by crosses, of bold, finely cut capital letters reading: SCS DEUS ANGELORUM QUI FECIT RESURRECTIONEM (Holy God of the angels who rose from the dead). Fragments of complementary inscriptions, originally displayed above the entry stairs, have been found nearby. A similar high technical skill is apparent in the carved and painted decoration of the interior. The apse of the rear wall is crowned by a delicately carved marble ornament of horizontal and raking cornices linked by an archivolt framing the curve of the apse (fig. 54). In the center of the apse wall is a shallow niche with pediment, entablature, and colonnettes that echo the larger composition of the nave end wall and the exterior of the west facade; its purpose remains unknown, although it may have served as a reliquary or an ambry for preservation of the consecrated host. The accompanying wall paintings are no less skilled. Framing the aforementioned tabernacle are three-quarter busts of St. Peter on the left, recognizable by the attribute of keys as well as his short white hair and beard, and on the right St. Paul with a book in his left hand, and a frontal bust of Christ blessing in the apse above. The wall space above and to either side of the apse bears traces of painted vine scrolls and busts of angels.

The seeming blend of pagan and Christian elements at the Tempietto has intrigued students of architecture since the fifteenth century and has inspired the admiration of such eminent figures of the Italian Renaissance as Alberti, Antonio da Sangallo the Younger, and Palladio, all of whom thought the building to be the result of the conversion of an ancient Roman temple into a church. But this was clearly not the case. Despite the extensive, although not exclusive, use of ancient *spolia*, the building is inherently Christian and not pagan. One would never find such a decorative appliqué of classical orders in a pagan temple, and the relief panels with the chi-rho cross are integral to the structure of the building. Yet there is no documentary reference to the building before the end of the Middle Ages and we are thus left with the structure itself to provide a date. But when would such an assemblage have been made? Proposed dates have ranged from the fourth to the twelfth centuries, but the years around 700 seem the most likely, based on archaeological, stylistic, and historical factors. To begin with, carbon-14 tests of mortar samples from the nave provide a broad but defined chronological range of construction between 603 and 743.[53] The style and iconography of the interior wall paintings, which are of course integral to the structure, concur with these dating perimeters, for the isolated nature and composition of the portraits of Peter, Paul, and Christ resemble the famous early icons from the seventh and early eighth centuries preserved in the monastery of St. Catherine at Mount Sinai. Rome at this time was greatly influenced by Byzantine artistic developments perhaps in part because many of the popes were in fact Greek. Indeed, by far the closest stylistic comparison to the portraits of saints at the Tempietto is found among the elaborate frescoes in the church S. Maria Antiqua in Rome, sponsored by Pope John VII (705–707).[54] Both depict holy figures in three-quarter poses with a striking combination of subtle modelling and heavy outline.

Even so, we do not know the specific function of the Tempietto. It may have served as a funerary chapel for a dignitary or as a local shrine of some kind. Whatever the original purpose, I do not think it accidental that the building resembles, at least in miniature, an ancient Roman temple with its high podium and pedimented, columnar facade (fig. 1). Yet such a reference would have been unthinkable in the Early Christian period when its direct association with paganism was still very much alive. Indeed, there is no known Early Christian building that resembles the Tempietto. Thus while the facade seems to flaunt its Romanness and thereby a desire on the part of the Lombards to evoke the ancient past, it also reveals its distance from that past. We do not know the patron of the building, but it must have been someone with sufficient rank to sequester an abundance of high-quality material from Roman ruins in the region. Under the Ostrogoths such use would have required the authorization of the king, but here it must have received the approval, if not the direct involvement, of the Lombard Duke of Spoleto.

With this in mind, it is interesting to note that the period around 700 was one of rapprochement between the Duchy of Spoleto and the papacy. Since 680, as the result of a political treaty and the resolution of religious disputes, the Lombards had been at peace with Byzantium, which, in turn, allowed relations with Rome to improve markedly.[55] By 705, Duke Faroaldus II (ca. 703–20) was in direct and extremely cordial correspondence with Pope John VII. In reciprocal letters, concerning support for the abbey of Farfa in the Sabine Hills, they refer to one another with expressions of the highest esteem.[56] Given such documented contact, it seems reasonable to assume that artists, both painters and sculptors, could easily have come from Rome to Spoleto by way of the via Flaminia. At the same time, the building materials and presumably the masons were local. The Tempietto del Clitunno may thus be seen as a synthesis of ancient and contemporary Roman, quasi-

56 *(facing page)* Spoleto, Tempietto del Clitunno, facade.

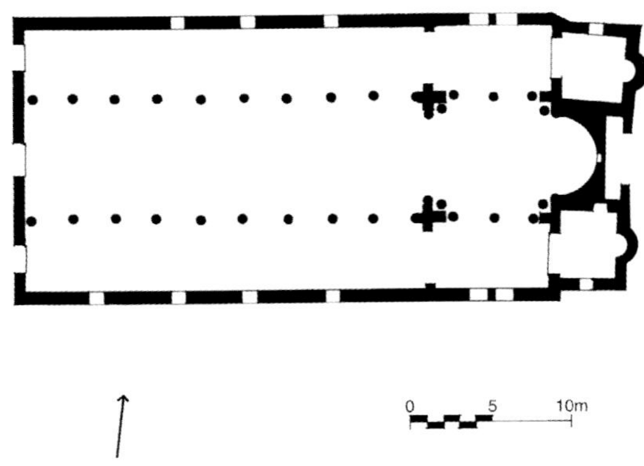

57 Spoleto, S. Salvatore, plan.

Byzantine, elements, that reflects the political position of the Lombards as the heirs of ancient Rome and, in their new-found orthodoxy, the allies of papal Rome. It is a monument proclaiming at once the Christianization of the Romans and the romanization of the Lombards.

The same circumstances help to explain another and equally alluring building just outside Spoleto, the church of S. Salvatore.[57] In contrast to the Tempietto, S. Salvatore is a large basilican structure with a nave, single aisles, and an apse flanked by square projecting chapels (fig. 57). Between the apse and the nave is a square crossing marked by angled piers with columns set in the corners and surmounted by a low lantern tower and cupola. The close connection with the Tempietto is not in the design but in the style of the decorative sculpture. Here, too, there is an extensive use of ancient Roman *spolia* columns and capitals, although in this case Doric, subtly combined with newly carved elements. Indeed, an extremely well-trained eye is required to distinguish between the two. Like the Tempietto, it is an assemblage that is highly deceptive. The same is true of the imposing facade, which presents a massive flat plane relieved only by richly carved ornament around the three doors at ground level and three large windows above. Some of the carved elements are antique but most are new. Each of the lintels above the portals, for example, bear a chi-rho cross flanked by luscious vine scrolls in a manner strikingly similar to the pediments of the Tempietto. Over three decades ago, Jean Hubert compared the classicizing window frames, alternating gabled and round-arched, of the west facade of S. Salvatore to the pilasters and decorative niches on the exterior of the baptistery at Poitiers (figs. 46 and 58).[58] Accepting the traditional fourth-to-fifth-century date of S. Salvatore, Hubert used this comparison to demonstrate the degenerate nature, and hence the later date, of the building in Poitiers. Now, it seems evident that the two structures are in fact contemporary. The differentiating factor was not a difference in time but in place. Whereas the Franks in central western Gaul attempted to evoke an antique facade *ex novo*, the Lombards in central Italy were able to take advantage of an abundance of ancient *spolia* in marble and travertine and the availability of sculptors who were remarkably conversant with classical ornament and thus able to blend new and old carving in an almost seamless manner. Carola Jäggi, in the most detailed study of S. Salvatore to date, conjectures that such artists must have come from the eastern Mediterranean by way of Ravenna or Rome.[59] Certainly, the plan of the church with eastern side chapels suggests a connection with Ravenna in its similarities to St. John the Evangelist and S. Apollinare in Classe (figs. 56 and 23). And, as already noted, Byzantine influence was particularly strong in Rome in the seventh and early eighth centuries, as reflected in the art of the period, especially under Pope John VII. To be sure, the square crossing finds no comparison in either city, although it was used occasionally in the provinces of Byzantium and, as we have already seen, was a prominent feature of some Visigothic churches around 700.[60] Nonetheless, S. Salvatore, like the Tempietto, remains unique. In the end, this seems to reflect the place and time of their creation in a Lombard duchy almost equidistant between Ravenna and Rome around the year 700.

Not long after, the autonomy of such duchies began to change. In 729, the dukes of Spoleto and Benevento were forced to swear fealty to the Lombard king in Pavia and a decade later both duchies were under direct royal control. In 758, after a struggle for royal succession, the new ruler, Desiderius, in order to consolidate his power throughout Italy, appointed an ally, Arichis II, as duke of Benevento to whom he offered the hand of his daughter, Adelperga, in marriage. Soon after, perhaps in order to strengthen his own position among his subjects, the new duke initiated an ambitious building campaign, including two palaces, one in Benevento and the other in Salerno, and several monasteries throughout the duchy. For one such establishment in Benevento he sponsored construction of the church of S. Sofia.[61] The name, Holy Wisdom, recalls the great church of Hagia Sophia in Constantinople, and a late eighth-century source states explicitly that Arechis built S. Sofia "in imitation of that [church, i.e. Hagia Sophia] of Justinian."[62] Scholars differ, however, as to how close the design of the church actually approximates its great prototype.

A restoration campaign in the early 1950s removed results of several later remodelings, including extensive Baroque decoration, and revealed much of the original structure in the process. The masonry consists of an *opus mixtum*, composed of a single course of stone blocks alternating with two of brick, in a pattern that is also found in portions of S. Salvatore in Spoleto, and is no doubt inspired in both cases by late antique *opus listatum* (fig. 59). More

58 *(facing page)* Spoleto, S. Salvatore, facade.

59 Benevento, S. Sofia, exterior view.

startling is the plan, which, based on the outline of the foundations and segments of preserved masonry, was discovered to be star-shaped. Instead of the curves of a round or oval plan, as one might expect, the north and south exterior walls were found to zigzag at sharp angles (figs. 59 and 60). The entrance, as now, was at the west end, and the east end terminated with three modest-sized apses, the central one being the largest. The interior is divided into double enveloping aisles with the center marked by six sizable granite columns and marble Corinthian capitals, all *spolia*. The outer ring of supports, however, is made up of ten masonry piers, the two westernmost having been replaced by columns in the later Middle Ages. The current vaulting and central tower are not original and different reconstructions have been proposed. Nonetheless, it seems likely that the hexagonal core would have been covered by a small dome atop a drum with windows; otherwise, the interior would have been without any direct lighting (fig. 61). Moreover, this configuration bears a striking resemblance to the lost church of S. Maria ad Pertica, discussed earlier. Such a royal foundation would have been a more readily available model and no doubt exerted an influence. Even so, S. Sofia shares many basic features with its Constantinopolitan counterpart, including a central plan, a domed interior, three apses (at Hagia Sophia a central apse is flanked by a semicircular array of columns surmounted by a half-dome), and an array of both columns and piers. In an age without detailed architectural drawings, only a few elements were needed to connect a building with its model.[63] Literary descriptions of Hagia Sophia, known to have been in circulation in the eighth century, are either vague or open to broad interpretation. In a popular travelogue of holy places in the eastern Mediterranean, for example, the pilgrim and priest Arculf, when referring to Hagia Sophia, mentions only "a single dome . . . borne upon great arches," while the famous passage in the account of Justinian's building projects by the sixth-century historian Procopius is extremely convoluted.[64] In other words, although S. Sofia is far from an exact copy of Hagia Sophia in either form or scale, its basic centralized design seems to have been sufficiently similar to have allowed Arichis to associate himself with one of the empire's greatest rulers and builders, whose achievements were still being acclaimed at the time. Indeed, Paul the

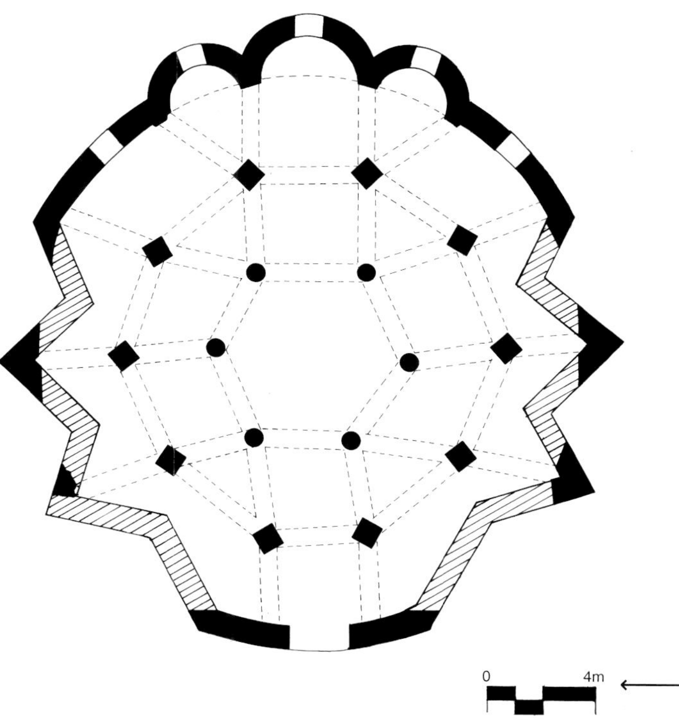

60 Benevento, S. Sofia, plan.

Deacon, a Lombard, praises Justinian for restoring the Roman state and promoting orthodoxy in his *Historia Romana*, an ambitious chronicle written around 773 and dedicated to Adelperga, the wife of Arichis II.[65] Interestingly enough, this was a time when Byzantine control in central Italy had dramatically receded. Already in 751, the Lombard king Aistulf, had taken over Ravenna, while the Byzantines were too preoccupied in the eastern Mediterranean with numerous urgent matters, including wars with Islam and the Iconoclastic controversy, to intervene. Although they continued to rule Sicily and the southernmost regions of the Italian peninsula, the pope turned instead to the Franks for assistance against the Lombards and their involvement in Italian politics ultimately led to the downfall of the Lombard kingdom in 774. In the meantime, however, Arichis II was able, with considerable diplomatic skill, to maintain relative independence until his death in 787.[66]

The Lombard achievement in art and architecture was not lost with the arrival of the Franks. In fact, a strong case can be made that the new Frankish rulers and their retinues were greatly impressed by what they saw when they came to Italy and that many aspects of the so-called Carolingian Renaissance have Lombard roots.[67] Some of this will be discussed in later chapters. For now it is worth noting that two important early medieval monuments in Italy often assigned to Lombard patronage may in fact be Carolingian in date. The date of the preserved church of S. Salvatore in Brescia, with its triple-apsed plan and exterior blind arcading, remains disputed. Some believe it to be the monastic church, founded originally by Desiderius and his queen in the middle of the eighth century, while others see it as a ninth-century replacement of a substantially smaller and differently designed structure.[68] And the small, cubic groin-vaulted chapel of S. Maria in Valle at Cividale, with elegant stucco ornament of vine scrolls and standing female saints, may well date from the end of the eighth century or the beginning of the ninth instead of a generation or two earlier.[69] Regardless, both buildings should be seen as evidence of the continuation of the sophistication of Lombard art in Italy even if under Frankish patronage.

Although the melding of Roman and Germanic traditions was a complex and gradual process, the previous discussion suggests that the period around the year 700 was of particular importance for the development of church architecture in western Europe. The reasons for this are no doubt many and varied. The building boom of late antiquity had ended in the sixth century and it was no longer possible to hire artisans trained in the traditions of Early Christian art and architecture, as seems to have been the case with La Daurade in Toulouse. By the late seventh century, political, social, and religious distinctions between the conquerors and the conquered were increasingly blurred, if not irrelevant, and this same fusion is apparent in the buildings studied here. They seem to be the products of local

61 Benevento, S. Sofia, section with hypothetical dome reconstruction.

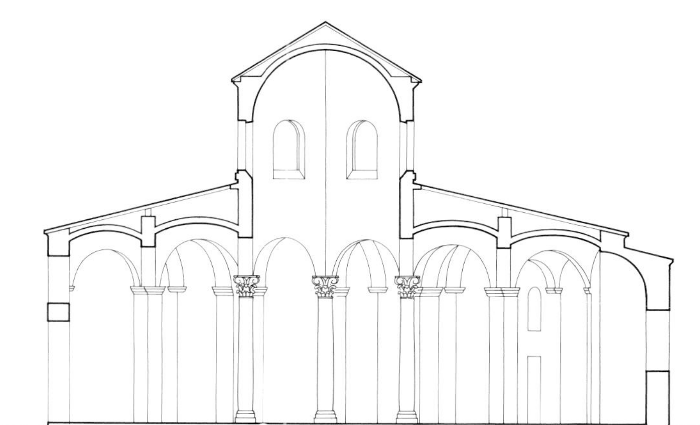

artisans with occasional direct or indirect outside influences, especially via Byzantium. The results are at once both consciously tied to the past and distinct from it. Some might argue that we are simply dealing with the result of accidents of preservation, but it seems unlikely that such would be the case in three distinctly separate regions. And, as we shall see in the next chapter, a similar situation can be observed in Anglo-Saxon England. Instead, there seems to have been a widespread and more or less simultaneous period of synthesis of classical and barbarian forms, with regional variations, across the face of Europe around 700. The Visigoths, Franks, and Lombards enthusiastically appropriated or perpetuated many elements from the late antique past—classical orders, centrally planned and basilican schemes, and various types of ornament (both sculpture and painting, and sometimes even mosaic)—in order to perpetuate the notion of themselves as heirs to that legacy, but in the process new approaches to the manipulation of space and the application of surface ornament were introduced. This synthesis, in turn, would provide a new basis for further developments to come. In short, the European architecture of the romanized barbarians around 700 should be seen as the first architecture of a new era, which we call the Middle Ages.

CHAPTER 4

The Christianization of Anglo-Saxon England

Wonderful is this stone wall, wrecked by fate.
The city buildings crumble, the bold work of giants
   decay.
Roofs have caved in, towers collapsed,
Barred gates have gone, gateways have gaping mouths,
   hoar
frost clings to mortar.[1]

Thus begins *The Ruin*, one of the oldest poems in the English language. Although not written down until the eighth century, these words may be taken to reflect the attitude of the Germanic peoples newly arrived in the Roman Empire's most northern province. For the Anglo-Saxons, the buildings of Roman civilization were objects of awe, mystery, and bewilderment; they were "the bold work of giants."

The process by which Roman Britain was transformed into Anglo-Saxon England remains a topic of considerable debate. Certainly, it was not the result of a single organized invasion but rather of a gradual process involving migration and settlement over more than a century. As the western empire disintegrated in the early fifth century, Roman troops were withdrawn to serve on the continent. Britain was left to her own defense. The hiring of Germanic mercenaries was a normal part of Roman military practice in late antiquity and thus it may have been that warriors from Germanic tribes in northern Europe were invited to assist in defending the island's northern and western borders from attack by the indigenous, non-romanized Celtic peoples. But if so, the barbarian mercenaries soon came to reject British rule and, reinforced by a constant flow of new immigrants, they began to control more and more of the island.

The new invaders were members of various Germanic tribes from along the coastlands of the North and the Baltic seas. The majority were Angles and Saxons, referred to collectively as the Anglo-Saxons for convenience's sake. The monk and scholar Bede in his famous work the *Ecclesiastical History of the English People*, written in the early eighth century, uses the term "English people" (*gens Anglorum*) to describe the Germanic inhabitants of Britain as a whole, regardless of their diverse backgrounds.[2]

In their continental homeland on the fringe of the known world, the Anglo-Saxons had experienced relatively little contact with Roman civilization and in spite of the wonder and amazement expressed in *The Ruin*, they seem to have had little use for the architectural remains of Roman rule. Indeed, on the whole, the Anglo-Saxons seem to have avoided urban centers and villas, preferring instead to settle on rural sites.[3] Similarly, they had no experience of building in the permanent materials of brick and stone. Like other Germanic tribes, they preferred to build in wood, which, because of its perishability, has left little trace aside from the arrangement of postholes that can be recovered only through very careful excavation. From such archaeological information, we know that the Anglo-Saxons preferred small rectangular buildings, some with floors or storage areas sunk below ground level, to serve a variety of functions from houses to workshops to barns. In addition to post-built huts, most major Anglo-Saxon settlements contained at least one hall, measuring 10 m or more in length (fig. 62); those built on a particularly grand scale were presumably used for assembly and possibly as a residence for tribal leaders. There can be no doubt that the carpenter's art could produce structures of considerable size and beauty, ones that could rival the "high, wide-gabled" royal hall, named *Heorot*, in the Old English saga *Beowulf*,[4] but the fact remains that any reconstruction of the superstructure of such timber buildings remains largely conjectural. Our knowledge, then, of architecture in Anglo-Saxon England during its first century and a half is still extremely limited.[5]

The situation changes dramatically, however, with the coming of Christianity, because the technique of building in stone or brick and mortar was introduced by Christian missionaries sent by Pope Gregory the Great at the end of

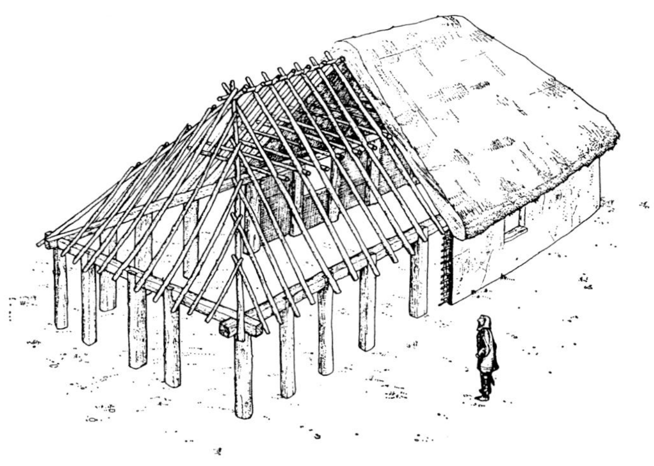

62 Hypothetical reconstruction of an early Anglo-Saxon post-built hall at Chalton, Hampshire.

the sixth century. Indeed, a significant portion of the beginning of Bede's *Ecclesiastical History* is devoted to this mission and to the role Gregory the Great played in it. Bede reports that upon seeing a group of fair-skinned, handsome youths for sale as slaves in a marketplace in Rome, Gregory asked who they were. He was told that they were heathens from the island of Britain and were called 'Angles'. In Latin, as in English, there is an obvious play on the words 'Angles' or *Angli* and 'angels' or *angeli*, because Gregory is said to have responded that the name was appropriate for those with such "angelic" faces. He decided then and there, according to Bede, to remove the land of the Angles from the grip of the devil and to convert it to Christ.[6] Although this famous story of Gregory's first encounter with the Anglo-Saxons is surely apocryphal, it probably contains a kernel of truth.

For whatever reasons—no doubt there were many—in 596, Gregory dispatched forty monks from the monastery of St. Andrew in Rome to convert the Anglo-Saxons. When the party reached southern Gaul, there was talk of turning back for fear of the possible dangers that lay ahead and Augustine, who had served as prior of the monastery in Rome, was selected to return to Rome to consult with Pope Gregory. Augustine was subsequently consecrated abbot of the group by the pope and instructed to proceed to England. The letters of introduction he carried with him, addressed to bishops in various towns in Gaul, allow us to reconstruct the route they followed: Lérins, Marseilles, Aix-en-Provence, Arles, Vienne, Lyons, Autun, and Tours. At this point, the recorded letters break off, but we may assume that the group continued on to a northern port from which to cross the Channel.[7]

They landed on the island of Thanet, off the coast of Kent. Of the various Anglo-Saxon kingdoms, Kent, ruled by Ethelbert from his capital at Canterbury, was a particularly advantageous place from which to initiate a Christianizing mission. Ethelbert was, it seems, the most powerful ruler in England at the time and although pagan he was well acquainted with the new faith through his wife, Bertha, a Frankish princess, who was a Christian. In fact, Bertha and a Frankish priest in her entourage were allowed to worship in a church which, according to Bede, lay "on the east side of town" and "had been built in honor of St. Martin during the Roman occupation of Britain."[8] While the church may well have been Roman, the dedication to St. Martin, the patron saint of the Franks, was most likely a more recent occurrence, resulting from Bertha's presence at the Anglo-Saxon court. A church with the same dedication stands today about half a mile to the east of Canterbury and its chancel, composed of flints and brick fragments, is usually assigned to this early period (fig. 63).[9] Be that as it may, Bede tells us that upon their arrival at Canterbury the missionaries led by Augustine were allowed to use the church of St. Martin; they were also given a dwelling (*mansio*) in the city itself.[10]

Perhaps as early as the middle of 597, King Ethelbert converted to Christianity and was baptized, at which time the mission was given more permanent quarters within the city walls. Augustine had by now been designated a bishop by the pope and Bede tells us that, in a manner reminiscent of the church of St. Martin, Augustine renovated an old church to serve as his cathedral "which he was informed had been built long ago by Roman Christians."[11] The church was dedicated to Christ following the example of the Lateran basilica in Rome and most other cathedrals in Italy and it is upon this same site that the present Christ Church Cathedral stands today (fig. 63). Recent excavations below the present nave have, in fact, uncovered what may be remnants of the western termination of the original church.[12] Not enough is left to reconstruct its appearance in any detail, but there are more substantial remains of other churches in Canterbury that date to Augustine's time.

Augustine was both a bishop and an abbot, and so, after having established the cathedral, he proceeded to found a monastery. The site chosen lay a short distance outside the city to the east, between the Roman fortification walls and St. Martin's church, and adjacent to a major Roman road lined with burials (fig. 63). The main abbey church was dedicated to SS. Peter and Paul, another clear reference to Rome. Like the cathedral, St. Augustine's abbey has been enlarged and rebuilt many times over the centuries, particularly in the middle and at the end of the eleventh century; however, the site was abandoned as a result of the dissolution of monasteries by Henry VIII in the early sixteenth century, which made it available for excavation in more

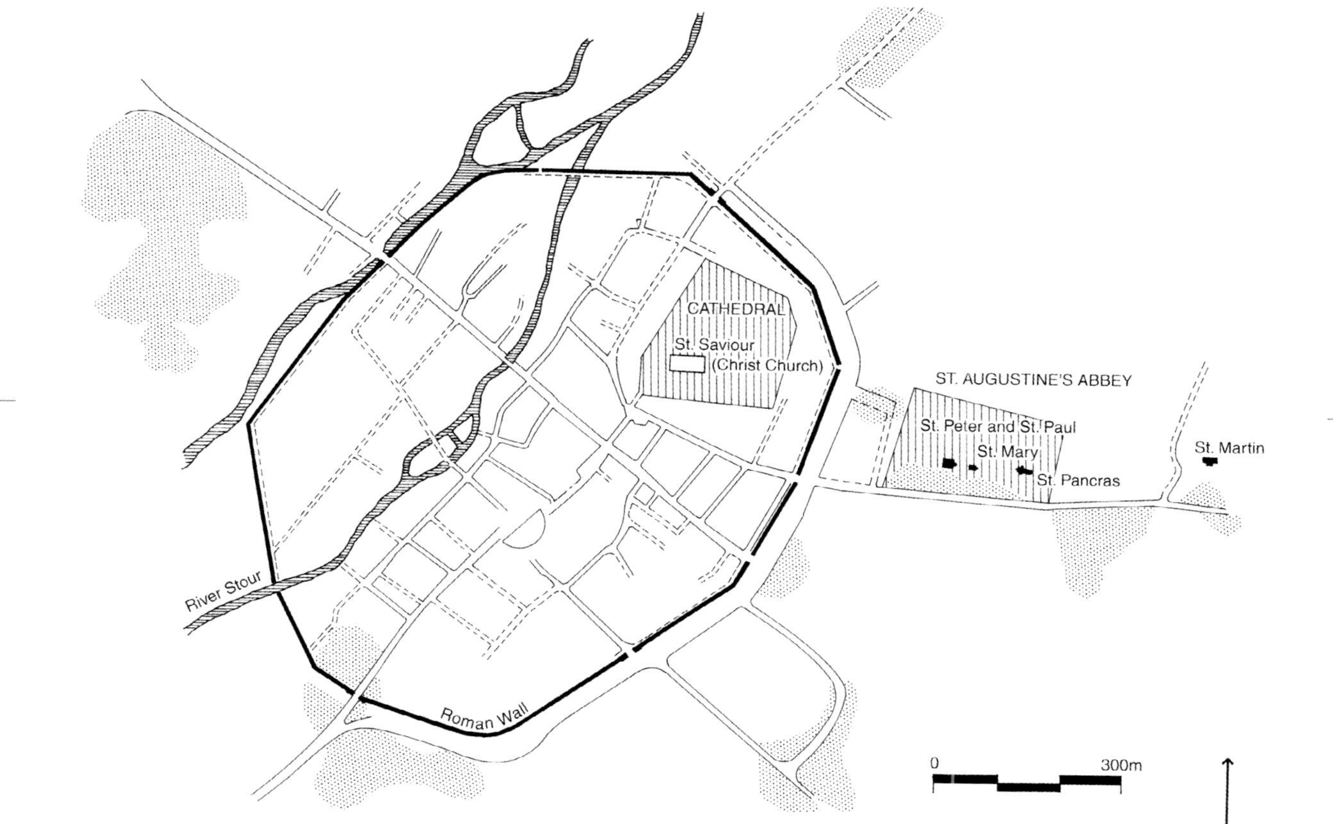

63 Map of Anglo-Saxon Canterbury.

recent times. The first extensive excavations took place early in the twentieth century and work since World War II has helped to clarify and add to the earlier findings.[13] The remains of three small churches are visible today, set along a roughly axial, east–west alignment (fig. 64). The vestiges of the westernmost church, that of SS. Peter and Paul, are indeed fragmentary but they are sufficient to provide its basic outline (fig. 65).[14] The church was small with a rectangular nave measuring on the interior approximately 13 × 7.5 m. All traces of the east end are gone, but the foundations of the entrance at the west end, composed of a central doorway leading to a narthex, are well preserved. The nave was also flanked to the north and south by subsidiary rooms referred to by Bede as *porticus*, which may be loosely translated as "porches." Bede, moreover, explains the function of this design in two related passages that deserve to be quoted in full:

> It was here [the church of SS. Peter and Paul] that the bodies of Augustine and all the archbishops of Canterbury and of the kings of Kent were to rest. . . . When Augustine, the beloved of God, died [A.D. 604], his body was laid to rest just outside the church . . . since the church was not yet completed or consecrated. But as soon as it was dedicated, his body was brought inside and buried in the north porch [*porticus*] with great honor. This is also the last resting-place of all succeeding archbishops except Theodore and Bertwald, whose bodies lie inside the church, no space remaining in the porch. Almost in the center of the chapel stands an altar dedicated in honor of blessed Pope Gregory, at which a priest of the place says solemn mass in their memory each Saturday.[15]

Here Bede tells us many things. We learn, for example, that the north *porticus* served as the burial place for the archbishops of Canterbury until there was no more space available, at which time burial took place in the nave. Excavators, in fact, found the remains of three tombs set along the inner north wall of the north *porticus*. The identity of the tombs is provided by an eyewitness account of the removal of the bodies in 1091 to the newly constructed Norman church.[16] Elsewhere, Bede also says that the south *porticus* was dedicated to St. Martin and that in 616 it received the body of King Ethelbert and later his queen, Bertha.[17] Thus, the north and south *porticus* functioned both as side chapels and sites for interment. The extramural location of the abbey, as opposed to the cathedral situated

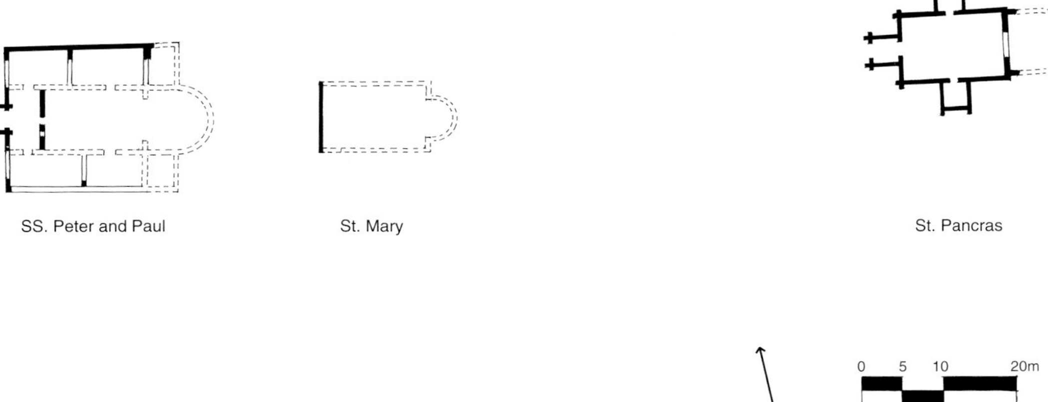

64 Canterbury, Abbey of St. Augustine, site plan, seventh century.

inside the city walls, made it an obvious site for the burial of the archbishops of Canterbury, and the placement of tombs in the abbey church itself followed the long-standing practice of burial *ad sanctos* in Rome and elsewhere on the continent.[18]

In 620, Ethelbert's successor, King Eadwald, built the church of St. Mary, of which only the base of the west wall remains, a few feet to the east of the apse of the church of SS. Peter and Paul.[19] Another 200 feet further east stand the vestiges of the church of St. Pancras, which is similar in size and design to that of SS. Peter and Paul (fig. 64). Of the three churches at Canterbury that of St. Pancras is by far the best preserved with several courses of its brick walls still extant (fig. 66). The exact date of the church is unknown—it is not mentioned by Bede—but excavations in the 1970s revealed a building sequence that is in general agreement with the historical situation described in Bede's narrative.[20] The church was built in two phases. The first consisted of a rectangular nave, roughly the same size as that of the church of SS. Peter and Paul, with a stilted apse all built of reused Roman brick in regular courses with a yellow mortar. At the base of the outer south wall of the nave was found a coin "of the House of Constantine I."

65 Canterbury, SS. Peter and Paul, plan showing locations of tombs of archbishops in the seventh century.

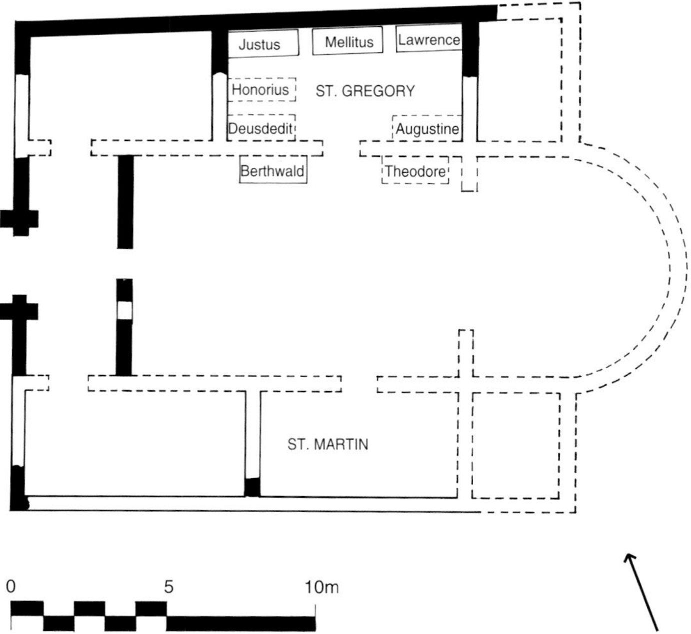

The second phase took place after some 22 cm of soil had accumulated in the nave. The earlier walls were reduced to the height of only a few courses and rebuilt with a white mortar and Roman bricks that were rarely complete. At this time, external *porticus* were added along the north and south sides as well as an entrance porch to the west. The remains of an altar in the south *porticus* are still clearly visible. In addition, walls flanking the original chancel arch were built up to support a triple arcade of which the base and lower part of one of the columns still survive *in situ*. Associated with this second phase were found a number of burials just south of the church of which the earliest "appear to belong to the late 7th or early 8th century."

This archaeological information indicates that the core of the church was originally built in the fourth century following the conversion of Constantine and the spread of Christianity to Britain. In other words, like the fabric of the church of St. Martin, the earliest portions of St. Pancras's were built during the Roman occupation. The church was presumably abandoned sometime in the late fourth or early fifth century and lay in disrepair until it was rebuilt in the second half of the seventh century following

66 Canterbury, St. Pancras, view of remains looking southeast, south wall of entrance porch (foreground) and south porch (center background).

the model of SS. Peter and Paul with north and south *porticus*. More recently, however, some scholars have questioned the early date of phase one, because they find construction of an apsed church in Britain unlikely before the mission of Augustine. They prefer to assign it to the second quarter of the seventh century and to date the second phase a century later.[21]

Although the date of this rebuilding must remain approximate, it is interesting to note that in 668 Pope Vitalian reportedly sent to England Roman relics, including those of St. Pancras. Admittedly, this reference comes in a letter recorded by Bede from the pope to Oswiu, the ruler, not of Kent, but of the northern Anglo-Saxon kingdom of Northumbria.[22] Still, the letter was written in connection with Oswiu's involvement in the selection of a new archbishop of Canterbury, a matter of such concern to the welfare of the newly established Church in England that the king of Northumbria and Egbert, the king of Kent, are said to have taken counsel together. In other words, this gift of relics may be interpreted as a diplomatic gesture on the part of the pope during a time of crisis in the see of Canterbury.[23] It seems unlikely, therefore, that under these circumstances Pope Vitalian would have failed to make a comparable gift to the king of Kent even though no record of it has come down to us. Furthermore, we do know that in 669 the same King Egbert sponsored the construction of a church at nearby Reculver that was very similar in plan to that of phase two of St. Pancras, i.e., an aisleless nave, lateral *porticus*, and a triple arcade in front of the apse (in this case, polygonal). Regardless of whether the church of St. Pancras was rebuilt around 668 or sometime later, the fact that it was dedicated to the same saint for whom Pope Honorius I (625–38) built the church of S. Pancrazio (discussed in chapter two) serves to underscore yet again Canterbury's strong allegiance to Rome.

Thus, the remains of the three churches at Canterbury should be seen as tangible expressions of the Roman mission to England. The very material employed in their construction, reused Roman brick, was not only found in abundance among the city's ancient ruins, but it was also

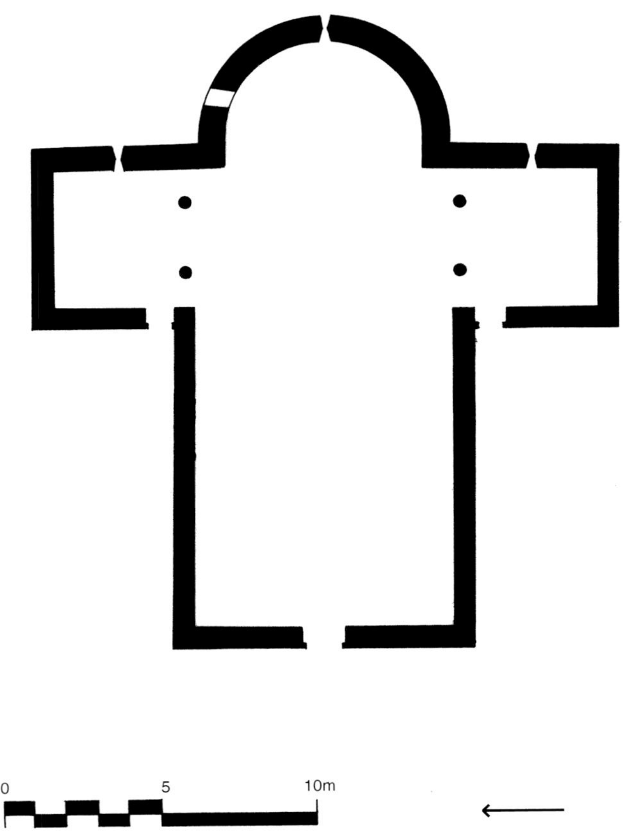

67 Arezzo, environs of, S. Paolo (known as S. Polo), plan, fifth–sixth century.

the building material with which Augustine and his entourage would have been familiar in their native land. Indeed, we must assume that skilled masons from Italy, if not Rome itself, either formed part of the original mission or, more likely, were sent later by Pope Gregory I and his successors as needed.

The design of the churches, too, bespeaks an Italian origin. More specifically, the plan composed of an aisleless nave with flanking *porticus*, such as one finds in the churches at Canterbury, is ultimately derived, I suggest, from the cruciform churches of North Italy, described in chapter one. Beginning with the Church of the Holy Apostles built by Bishop Ambrose of Milan in the late fourth century, the cruciform design spread throughout north Italy and into the Alpine regions in the course of the next century, the churches becoming ever smaller and less elaborate in the process (fig. 13A–D). Moreover, by the sixth and seventh centuries, the design had been reduced to a simple rectangular nave with a semicircular apse to the east and block-like wings projecting to the north and south as seen, for example, in two churches, both dedicated to SS. Peter and Paul, one at Como in the foothills of the Alps just north of Milan and the other at Romainmôtier in western Switzerland (fig. 13E). This reduced version of the cruciform church also appeared as far south as Tuscany as revealed in 1969 by excavations of the small church of S. Paolo (known locally as S. Polo) near Arezzo, and here the derivation from the Church of the Holy Apostles in Milan is made emphatic by the inclusion of paired columns screening the projecting alcoves from the nave (fig. 67).[24]

There is as yet no conclusive evidence that this church type appeared in Rome during this time. It is particularly unfortunate that we have no specific information about the plan of the monastery of St. Andrew founded by Gregory the Great on his family estate on the Celian Hill, to which Augustine and his companions belonged before being sent on their mission to England. It is intriguing to note, nonetheless, that a famous plan of Old St. Peter's, made by the Vatican archivist, Tiberio Alfarano, in the late sixteenth century, shows the small abbey church of St. Martin, located immediately to the left or south of the apse of the Constantinian basilica, with a short, broad nave and side alcoves not unlike the church of SS. Peter and Paul in Canterbury (fig. 68). The exact date of this church is not known but it was presumably already in existence before

68 Rome, basilica of St. Peter's, sixteenth-century plan by Alfarano, detail.

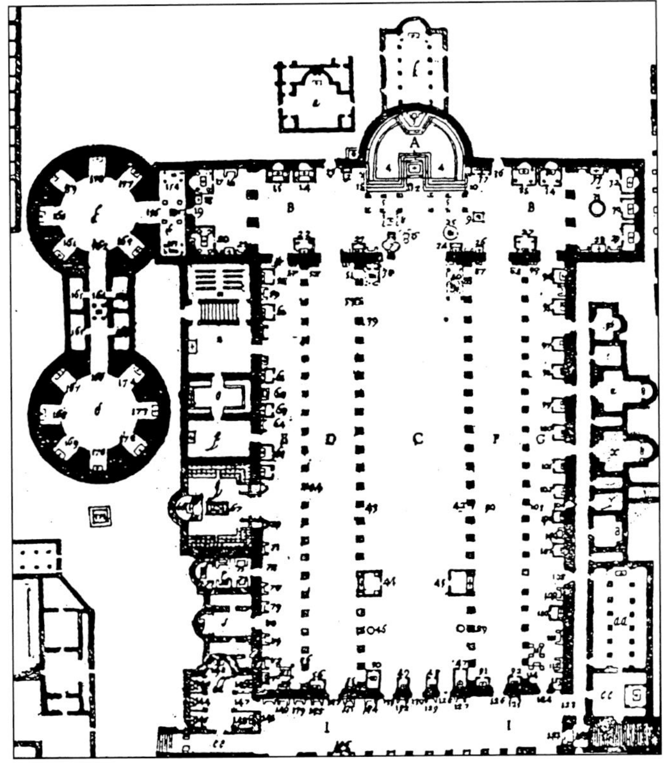

680 when a monk by the name of John, who was both abbot of St. Martin's and archcantor of St. Peter's, is reported by Bede to have travelled to England in order to teach Roman chant and liturgical practices in monastic houses in Northumbria.[25] Could not a similar link have been established earlier in the same century between St. Martin's at the Vatican and the abbey of Augustine in Canterbury? One thinks, for example, of Bede's reference to Gregory the Great's sending of "several colleagues and clergy" from Rome to Canterbury in order to help Augustine with his mission, together with "everything necessary for the worship and service of the Church."[26] Through such an exchange, the design of the *porticus* church, as it appeared in Canterbury, could have been imported directly from Rome, but this is merely a hypothesis. Although the overall reliability of the plan is well attested, it should be pointed out that the church of St. Martin, as well as most other features near the apse of St. Peter's, was no longer visible in Alfarano's day, having been demolished and covered over by the foundations and rising walls of the crossing of the new Renaissance basilica, begun in 1506. The depiction of St. Martin may have been based on earlier records which are now no longer extant, but this cannot be proven.[27] Even so, it seems safe to say that this church type developed out of an Italian building tradition.[28]

In the course of the first half of the seventh century, the Roman church established a firm foothold in Kent through the work of Augustine and his successors but its position in England as a whole remained precarious. Indeed, representatives sent from Canterbury to establish bishoprics in London and York were forced to flee from hostile inhabitants and rulers who were either reluctant to convert to Christianity or having done so reverted to paganism.[29] There was, however, another missionary movement on the island, one that was centered in the north and led not by Roman but by Irish monks.

It is an irony of history that in the course of the fifth century, at the same time Roman Britain was succumbing to the pagan Anglo-Saxons, Ireland was being converted to Christianity by the famous but enigmatic St. Patrick and other Christians from western Britain. The Church that took shape in Ireland, however, was very different from that of Britain and the continent. Ireland had never formed part of the Roman Empire and its indigenous Celtic peoples lived in a predominantly rural society without cities, the very essence of the classical culture in which the structure of the Christian Church had developed. Although bishops, as elsewhere, played an essential role in the functioning of the Irish Church, it was monasticism, based upon isolation and self-sufficiency, that proved to be particularly suited for this non-urban environment. Monastic communities were

69 Church Island, estuary of Valencia River, County Kerry, Ireland, seventh–eighth century, reconstruction.

built on the scheme of prehistoric ring-forts, consisting of roughly circular walls of dry stone masonry or earthen ramparts that enclosed a group of round, so-called beehive, huts. In the densely forested eastern half of the island, these huts were built of wood with thatched roofs, but along the rocky treeless landscape of the rugged western coast they were made instead of unhewn stones roofed by means of corbel vaulting, one of the most ancient of vaulting techniques. The only rectilinear structure was the oratory or chapel (fig. 69). As the early churches of Canterbury reflected their Roman roots, so the early Irish monasteries expressed their dependence upon the prehistoric, non-Roman past of the Celts.[30]

Once Christianized, the Irish became fervent missionaries often setting out in small boats to traverse the North and Irish Seas as far as Iceland and Scotland. In 565, St. Columba, one of the great figures of the early Irish Church, left the northern coast of Ireland and settled with a band of twelve monks on a tiny island, known today as Iona, just off the western coast of Scotland. The outline of the enclosing ramparts of this early monastery may still be seen on the site today.[31] In 597, the very year that Augustine arrived in Canterbury, Columba died, leaving Iona firmly established as the center from which the process of converting the Picts, who lived north of Hadrian's Wall, could continue. The fame of Columba and his monastery spread quickly. As a young man, King Oswald of Northumbria came to study at Iona and in 635 he invited a group of its monks, headed by Aidan, to establish a monastery in his own realm. The site selected was another island, this time off the eastern coast of England, which is known today as Lindisfarne or simply Holy Isle. There are no visible remains of this early monastic settlement, but Bede tells us that Aidan's successor Finan built a church on the island of Lindisfarne "according to the Irish manner" (*more Scottorum*) which he defines as construction

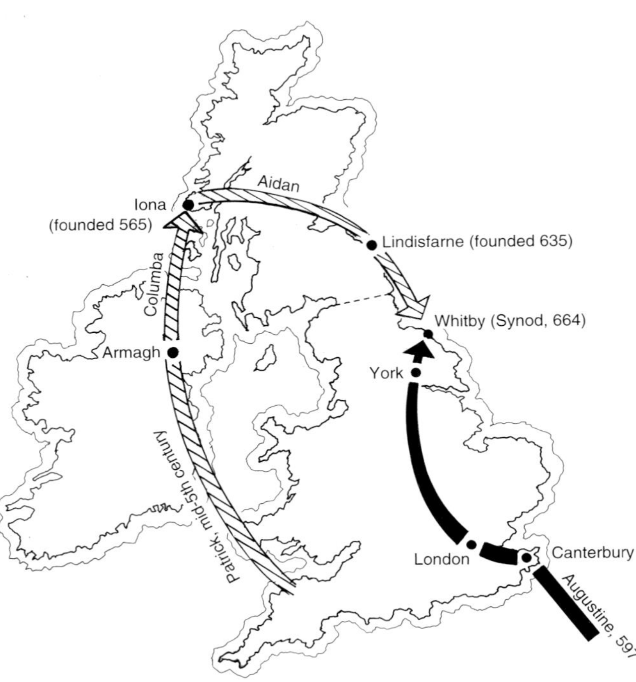

70 Map, missionary movements in the British Isles, fifth–seventh centuries. Irish/Celtic Church (hatched arrow), Roman Church (solid arrow).

"not of stone but entirely of cut oak and roofed with reeds."[32]

From the benefit of historical hindsight, it seems inevitable that the two Churches in England, that of the Irish in the north and of Rome in the south, should clash (fig. 70). While both professed orthodox Christianity based upon the same basic teachings, there were many differences in religious attitude and practice. Irish monks, for example, tended to pursue a much more ascetic life than their Roman counterparts. The tonsure, the physical symbol of their monastic vows, took the form of shaving the front half of the head rather than just the crown. Most important, however, Iona and its affiliate monasteries followed an older system for calculating the date of Easter, one that had been brought to Ireland in the fifth century, while the Roman church had changed to a different system in more recent times. This meant that the holiest day in the Christian calendar could be celebrated at different times depending upon which system was followed.[33] The discrepancy was acutely felt in Northumbria where missionaries from both traditions were active.

In 664, therefore, the king of Northumbria, Oswiu, called a synod at Whitby to decide which system his realm would follow. Colman, bishop and abbot of Lindisfarne, represented the Irish Church, while Agilbert, another local bishop but a Frank by birth, stood for the Church of Rome. Agilbert's knowledge of the local language was limited, however, and so he selected as his spokesman a Northumbrian by the name of Wilfrid, who had received his early training at Lindisfarne but who was known as an expert on matters concerning the Church of Rome. The outcome of the Synod of Whitby was predictable. As Bede tells it, after hearing both sides, the king turned to Colman and asked, "Which is the greater in the kingdom of Heaven, Columba or the apostle Peter?" Colman had to admit the primacy of Peter, whereupon Oswiu responded, "He [Peter] is the keeper of the door and the keys. I will not enter into strife or controversy with him."[34]

Such were the auspicious beginnings of the tumultuous career of Wilfrid, who became one of the most influential and controversial churchmen of his day; outspoken and difficult to deal with, he remained an impassioned advocate of Rome until his death in 709. Already in 653, at age nineteen, he had embarked on the first of three pilgrimages to Rome, establishing a precedent that was to be emulated by many of his countrymen for centuries to come. Indeed, throughout the early Middle Ages, the Anglo-Saxons were regarded as perhaps the most fervent and frequent pilgrims to Rome from northern Europe.[35]

Wilfrid plays a minor role in Bede's narrative, but his *Life*, written by a follower named Eddius Stephanus between 710 and 720, provides considerable information that is pertinent to this study.[36] Upon arriving in Rome in 655, for example, after having spent two years in Lyons, Wilfrid went first to "the oratory dedicated to St. Andrew," which must refer to the rotunda of St. Andrew that stood next to St. Peter's basilica, the primary goal of any pilgrim, and not to the monastery of Gregory the Great on the Celian Hill, as is usually assumed. We also learn that "he passed many months in daily visits to the shrines of the saints; he then set off . . . armed with the holy relics he had collected in Rome."[37] After his return to England, he was granted two tracts of land by the king of Northumbria, first at Ripon and then later at Hexham, where he established monasteries that followed the Rule of St. Benedict, the Italian church father whose biography had been written by Pope Gregory the Great.[38] In the 670s, Wilfrid built churches on both sites that were derived from those he had seen in Rome as made clear, first of all, by their dedications to St. Peter at Ripon and to St. Andrew at Hexham.

The best-preserved features of the two churches are their crypts (fig. 71). As discussed in chapter two, the subterranean crypt was a feature that had first appeared in Rome under Gregory the Great and no doubt this association was known to Wilfrid as it was to Bede who states that the "blessed Pope Gregory decreed that Mass should be said over the tombs of the holy Apostles Peter and Paul in their churches."[39] Indeed, the angular passageways of the

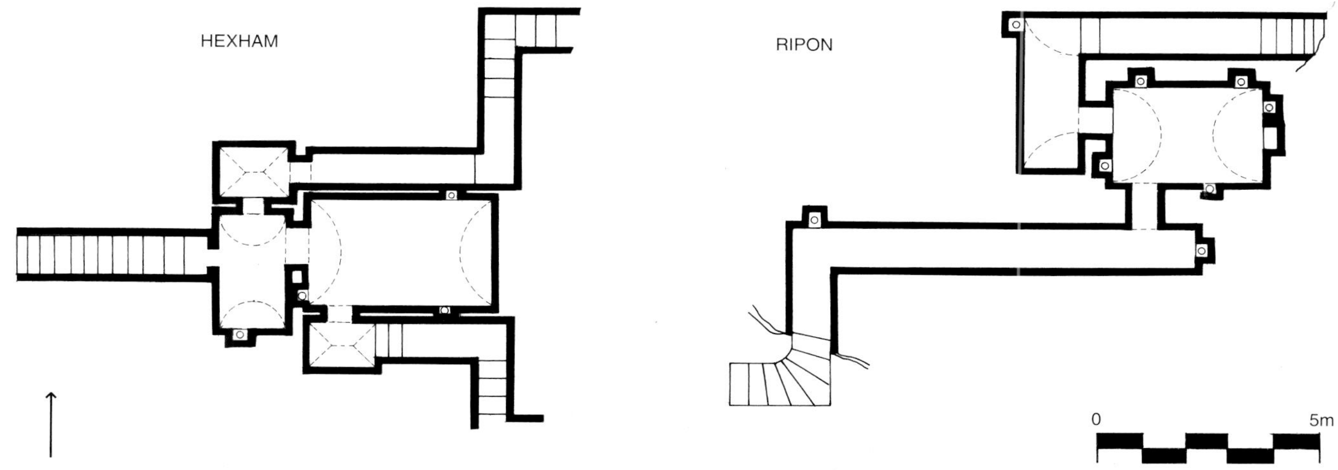

71 Hexham, St. Andrew, and Ripon, St. Peter, plans of crypts, seventh century.

crypts at Ripon and especially Hexham show a striking resemblance to the crypt arrangement at St. Paul's-outside-the-Walls (fig. 32). Presumably, the designs of the crypts at Ripon and Hexham were meant to resemble the dark, winding corridors of the catacombs as well, such as those that underlie the church of S. Agnese, built by Honorius I (625–38) (fig. 34). In other words, it would seem that Wilfrid's crypts represent a conscious attempt to emulate one of the most recent architectural developments in Rome. To be sure, the plans of these crypts are not exact copies of their Roman counterparts. After all, Wilfrid had not been in Rome for twenty years at the time of their construction, and comparisons have also been made to subterranean burial chambers in Gaul, such as the "Hypogée des Dunes" in Poitiers, discussed in the previous chapter, which may have inspired the form of the central relic space.[40] Nevertheless, I would contend that the Roman element is predominant and not limited to the design of the crypts, for the building material is also Roman, not brick as at Canterbury, but cut stone taken from Hadrian's Wall and related Roman sites. In the case of the church of St. Andrew, where Roman tool marks and fragmentary Latin inscriptions are clearly visible in the crypt, the stones probably came from the nearby station of Corbridge (*Corstopitum*), on the other side of the Tyne River directly opposite Hexham (fig. 72).

As with the crypts in Rome, those of Ripon and Hexham were built to honor holy relics, most likely those Wilfrid brought back from Rome, and to accommodate the faithful coming to see them. And yet, although inspired by precedents in Rome, the spatial arrangements in these two Northumbrian churches represent unique and original solutions to the problem. In both cases, the relics were presumably kept in the central, barrel-vaulted chamber (fig. 73). At Ripon the north stairway leads to a vestibule set directly in front of the reliquary chamber to the west, while the stairway to the south is connected directly to the chamber without an intervening vestibule. Thus, unlike the Roman crypts, the intended direction of movement seems to be clearly indicated. At Ripon the pilgrims probably entered by the north stairway and gathered in the vestibule; they would then have been allowed to enter the central room containing the relics, one by one or perhaps in groups of two or three, after which they would have been ushered out by the passageway leading to the south stairway.

The crypt at Hexham is obviously later in date and more complex than the one at Ripon. Here two smaller compartments have been added at the points where the corridor of the north stairway joins the vestibule and the corridor leading to the south stairway leaves the central chamber. It is interesting to note, too, that spatial units have been roofed in different ways: the central chamber and vestibule are barrel vaulted (at Ripon the vestibule has a half-barrel vault); the two smaller rooms or "subsidiary" vestibules have gable roofs; and, the corridors leading to the stairs have flat stone slabs for a covering. Again, the north stairs may have been the entrance and the south stairway the exit. On the other hand, a third stairway to the west may have allowed visitors to approach the reliquary chamber more directly and gaze in without actually entering it, after which they would have left by the north passage.

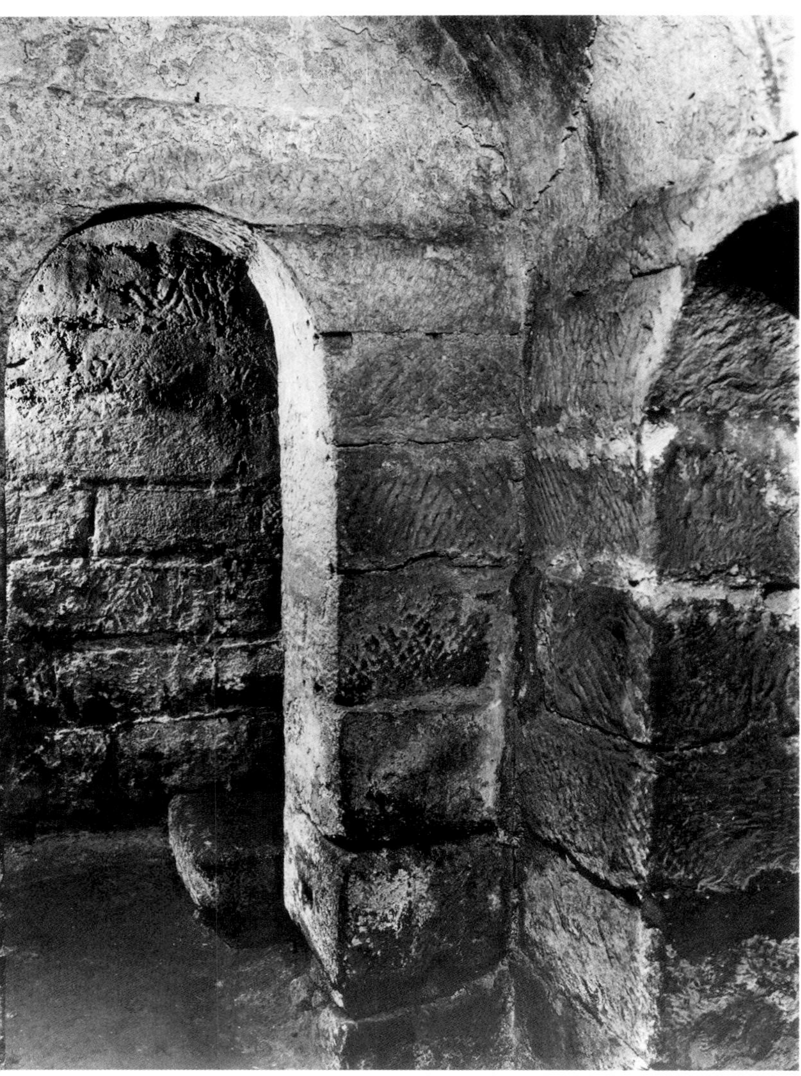

72 Hexham, St. Andrew, crypt, view of entrance vestibule looking north, seventh century.

Moreover, a liturgical procession would have been able to negotiate these western stairs far more easily than the narrow, winding corridors to the north and south, while the south stairs may have been reserved for the clergy or a porter. Regardless of how people actually moved through them, the crypts of Ripon and Hexham are among the most impressive remains of early medieval architecture in England and they bespeak, it seems to me, the very character and outlook of their patron.

The plan and elevation of the churches themselves are another matter. Very little is known about the design of Ripon; the present church dates from the thirteenth century. At Hexham, limited excavations were undertaken at the beginning of the twentieth century when the present nave was built. Yet the records of this investigation are incomplete and what little information has been made available is open to interpretation. Nor have subsequent probings resolved the matter. Indeed, several reviews of the matter have concluded that little of what has been assigned to the Anglo-Saxon period by scholars in the past can be accepted with any confidence.[41] Thus, any reconstruction of the plan of Wilfrid's church of St. Andrew at Hexham seems futile until more reliable archaeological evidence is found. One must therefore turn to literary sources for assistance and here it becomes clear that the spirit of Rome must have played a major role in the design. Eddius Stephanus, the contemporary biographer of Wilfrid, describes the church as follows:

> At Hexham he [Wilfrid] built a church in honor of St. Andrew the apostle. I am unable to describe adequately in words the foundations set deep in the earth with chambers of beautifully dressed stone, and, above ground, the vast structure supported by various columns and with numerous side aisles, and adorned with walls of remarkable height and length, surrounded by various winding passages and spiral staircases leading up and down; for our holy bishop, taught by the Spirit of God, contrived to carry out this work; nor have we heard of any other church built in like manner on this side of the Alps.[42]

73 Hexham, St. Andrew, crypt, view of central chamber looking east (altar and crucifix are modern).

74 Rome, S. Agnese, nave (apse mosaic, although restored, dates to the early seventh century; the rest of the decoration, aside from the columns and capitals, are later embellishments).

Eddius no doubt exaggerates the size and beauty of the edifice in order to enhance the fame of his hero, Wilfrid. Nonetheless, in spite of the hyperbole, there are details that surely were not invented. He stresses, for example, the fine cut-stone masonry of the crypt, which is a feature we are able to verify and one that was truly remarkable in Eddius's time. He also indicates that the church had galleries, reached by spiral staircases, and he is emphatic about the entire structure being supported by "various columns." He concludes by saying there was nothing like it "this side of the Alps," which is a clear reference to Rome. Eddius's observations are supported and enlarged upon by later writers. Prior Richard, a twelfth-century chronicler of Hexham, refers to the same basic elements of a crypt, aisles, galleries, and columns.[43] He adds that the building was divided into three storeys and that people could walk about the building without being seen from below, obviously a reference to continuous galleries with high parapets or balustrades.[44]

But are there, in fact, churches in Rome that fit this description? When the church at Hexham is taken as a whole, the answer is no; however, when the features mentioned by Eddius and Prior Richard are taken individually or in combination, the comparison to various monuments in Rome is telling. First of all, consideration should be restricted to those churches with crypts that were complete at the time of Wilfrid's visit to Rome in 655. They are the churches of St. Peter, St. Paul, S. Pancrazio, and S. Agnese. As already noted, St. Paul's-outside-the-Walls offers the closest comparison to the design of the crypt at Hexham (fig. 32). That Wilfrid had a particular regard for St. Paul's is shown by the fact that on his deathbed he instructed that gifts from his estate be given to two churches in Rome, that dedicated to the Virgin Mary and that of St. Paul.[45] However, the presence of continuous galleries supported by columns of various kinds points to S. Agnese, one of only two galleried basilicas in Rome (the other being S. Lorenzo, which lacked a crypt) (fig. 74). And finally, the foundations of a small apsed chapel directly to the east of the crypt at Hexham, one of the few undisputed features found by earlier excavators, brings to mind the location of the basilica Probi, built originally as a private mausoleum circa A.D. 400, just outside the apse of St. Peter's (fig. 74).[46]

It would seem, then, that the church of St. Andrew at Hexham was a composite of features from the primary pilgrimage churches in Rome and surely this was no accident. Eddius credits Wilfrid with having devised the church at Hexham. In doing so, it seems reasonable to assume that Wilfrid consciously selected aspects of the churches he had visited in Rome two decades before. These features, it should be pointed out again, represented the most recent architectural developments in Rome; Hexham, in short, was very up-to-date. Moreover, the models used were associated not only with St. Peter, the brother of Andrew, and St. Paul, the doctor of the Church, but with Pope Gregory the Great who had brought Christianity to the Anglo-Saxons. Thus, the church at Hexham was meant to be a "Roman" church on Northumbrian soil: Roman in design, built of Roman material, housing Roman relics, to serve Benedictine monasticism; and, to further the cause of Roman liturgical practice. It seems that Eddius was right when he wrote that there was nothing like it "this side of the Alps."

And yet, it should be noted that nothing quite like it existed in Rome either. To be sure, Roman features were used, but in so doing they had to be translated into a local building idiom. Wilfrid, like Augustine at Canterbury, used ancient Roman material to construct his church. But in the north of England, as witness Hadrian's Wall, the Romans had preferred to build not in brick, as at Canterbury and in Rome, but in stone. Thus, in the very fabric of the walls of the church of St. Andrew at Hexham, Northumbria's Roman past was fused with the image of Rome's present. Still, it should be remembered that in Wilfrid's day there were no masons in England, or in Rome for that matter, who were experienced in building in stone.[47] This was not the case in Frankish Gaul, as we saw in the last chapter, and Wilfrid's ties to the Franks were very close. In fact, he had spent several years in Gaul, first on his journey to Rome in 653 when he stayed in Lyons for two years and later, immediately following the Synod of Whitby, when he crossed the channel to be consecrated bishop by his friend and mentor Agilbert, who was then the bishop of Paris.[48] It seems more than likely, therefore, that Wilfrid turned to Gaul for the skilled labor needed to build his church.[49] As we shall see, this would not be the only instance of Gallic masons at work in Northumbria in the late seventh century.

Eddius, however, credits Wilfrid with having designed the building and one cannot help but wonder how Wilfrid conveyed his architectural ideas and memories of Rome to

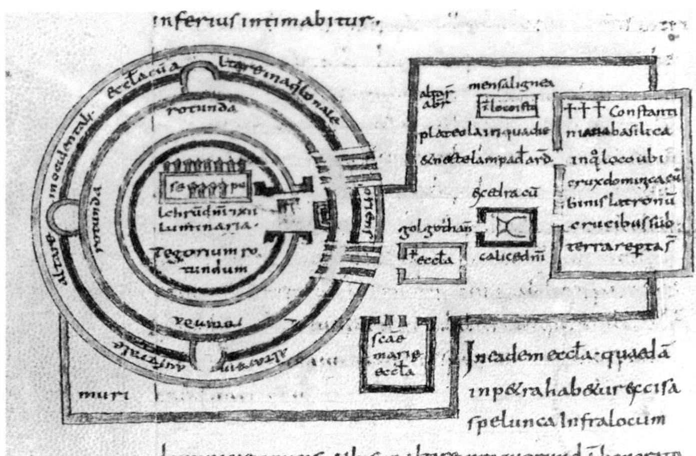

75 Jerusalem, Church of the Holy Sepuchre, Anastasis rotunda, copy of plan ca. 670 by Arculf, tenth century (Vienna, Österreichische Nationalbibliothek, cod.458, fol. 4v).

those foreign masons. The most likely answer is provided by the example of Wilfrid's contemporary Arculf, a Frankish bishop who made a pilgrimage to the Holy Lands in the 670s. On his return trip to Gaul, Arculf's ship was blown off course to western Britain. He sought refuge in the Columban monastery of Iona, then ruled by the abbot Adomnan (679–704). Adomnan subsequently wrote a book about the Holy Lands, *De locis sanctis*, which was based largely on Arculf's account of his travels. Of interest to us is the fact that in order to describe the churches he had seen in Jerusalem, Arculf is said to have drawn their plans on wax tablets using a stylus, a long-established method of making preliminary notes in order to save costly vellum in an age before the invention of paper.[50] We can get some idea of what these drawings looked like by turning to preserved early medieval copies of Adomnan's book that contain, interspersed within the text, relatively simple line drawings, such as that of the Holy Sepulchre, which, in spite of their schematic nature, have been shown by recent archaeological investigations to be remarkably accurate renderings (fig. 75).[51] Surely this was not an isolated example and we may assume that Wilfrid used a similar procedure in order to see his image of Rome become a reality in his native land.

After completing the church of St. Andrew at Hexham, Wilfrid was not again in a position to sponsor a major building project until very late in life, for in 678 he was removed from office by the Archbishop of Canterbury and his diocese was subdivided and given over to other bishops. Feeling wronged, Wilfrid appealed to the pope—he was the first English churchman to do so—and set out on his second journey to Rome to present his case in person. Although he received a favorable judgment in Rome, Wilfrid's career in England remained troubled. He even lost the lands of Ripon and Hexham for a time and was forced to live in exile in Mercia. In 703 Wilfrid was excommunicated and he again appealed to Rome where in 704 he was exonerated of all charges. During the return journey, Eddius relates that Wilfrid fell ill, at which time he had a vision of the archangel Michael who reprimanded him for having built churches in honor of SS. Peter and Andrew but not the Virgin Mary. "You have to put this right," Wilfrid was told, "and dedicate a church in her honor."[52] Wilfrid recovered and returned to his native land to live his last years in relative peace.

He did not, however, forget the archangel's admonition. Eddius does not describe the church of the Virgin built by Wilfrid at Hexham, but Prior Richard does, saying that "it is nearly round and built like a tower and it has wings [*porticus*] on four sides."[53] Another twelfth-century writer, Aelred of Rievaulx, also says that it was a rotunda with four *porticus* and adds that these "porches" were set around the building in accordance with "the four regions of the earth"; we would say "the four points of the compass."[54]

This description has long baffled scholars; no reconstruction has ever been attempted and no satisfactory source for this design has ever been suggested. Yet in the context of the churches in Rome that Wilfrid knew in the early Middle Ages, the prototype is immediately clear. It is S. Stefano Rotondo, built by Pope Simplicius (468–83).[55] Not only does it present a cylindrical plan with a "tower-like," central core, but originally it had four wings or chapels projecting on the cross axes (fig. 76). To be sure, S. Stefano Rotondo embodied an extremely complex design of concentric rings of columns and curved walkways that was rooted in late antique villa and pavilion architecture and could hardly have been reproduced in Anglo-Saxon England without considerable simplification, but its remarkable combination of rotonda and cross plan is so similar to the descriptions of Wilfrid's church of St. Mary at Hexham that a direct link between the two buildings must be assumed. It is therefore interesting to note that under Pope Theodore I (642–49), S. Stefano Rotondo was the first church inside the city of Rome to receive relics transferred from the catacombs and Wilfrid must have visited the church for that reason during his last trip to Rome when, according to Eddius, he "went round the shrines of the saints with his friends, collecting, as was his habit, holy relics, each labelled with the saint's name."[56]

During his travels in Italy, Wilfrid may also have seen the church of S. Angelo on the outskirts of Perugia which is a reduced version of S. Stefano Rotondo (fig. 77). Probably built in the sixth or early seventh century, with a solid outer wall and no enveloping courtyards, it is just the kind of simplified copy of S. Stefano Rotondo that we would expect to find at Hexham: a tall, cylindrical core with

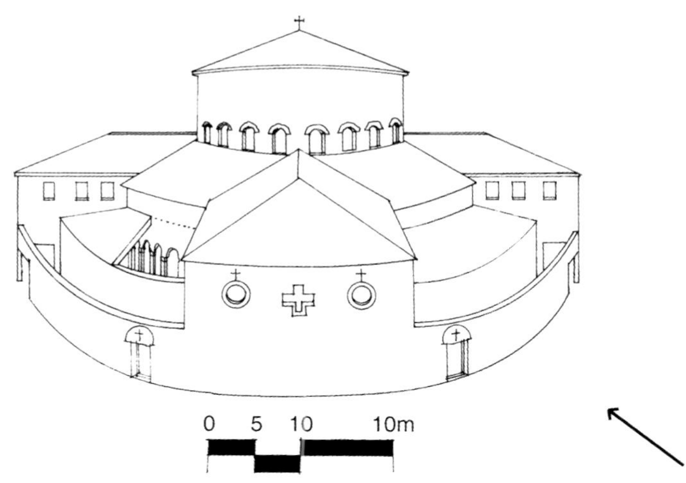

76 Rome, S. Stefano Rotondo, reconstruction of exterior elevation, fifth century.

77 Perugia, S. Angelo, plan, sixth century.

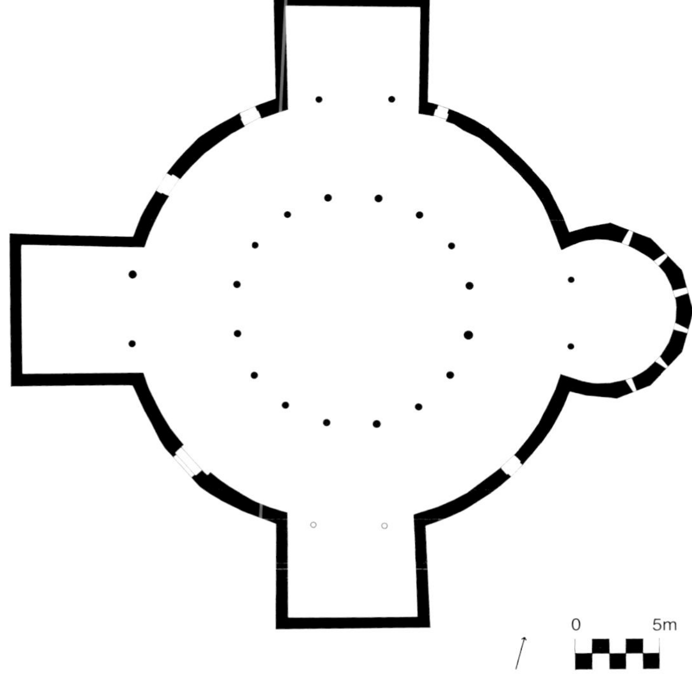

clerestory windows and a wooden roof supported by columns (or perhaps piers); an enveloping, continuous outer aisle; and four chapel wings or *porticus* projecting on the cross axes, screened from the aisle by paired columns.[57] Again, Wilfrid would have been able to convey his ideas for the plan of his church to the masons by tracing its outline on wax tablets.

But why did Wilfrid choose such an unusual design, one that was rare even in Rome? Why did he not build a longitudinal basilica as he had done in the past? Here, I think, the dedication of the church is of vital importance. On his deathbed, Wilfrid asked that gifts be offered not only to St. Paul's but also to "the church (in Rome) dedicated to St. Mary the Mother of the Lord."[58] It is usually assumed that Wilfrid was referring to S. Maria Maggiore, a sumptuously decorated basilica built under Pope Sixtus III (432–40) and located not far from S. Stefano Rotondo.[59] But in Wilfrid's day there was one other major church in Rome dedicated to the Virgin, the Pantheon. The awesome domed rotunda, built by the Emperor Hadrian in the early second century A.D. and dedicated to all the gods, was, and still is, regarded as perhaps the greatest building of the ancient world. As late as the mid-fourth century, for example, the building so impressed the (Christian) Emperor Constantius II that it was called "a city unto itself." As we have already seen, the Pantheon remained imperial property until 609, when the Emperor Phocas gave the building to Pope Boniface IV, who then dedicated the former pagan temple "of all the gods" to the Virgin Mary and all the saints (*Sancta Maria ad martyres*), an event that is prominently mentioned by Bede in his *Ecclesiastical History* and was no doubt known to Wilfrid.[60] In fact, the Pantheon was the first pagan temple in Rome to be converted into a church, which helps to explain why it has remained so well preserved throughout the Middle Ages.

Obviously, the Pantheon's revolutionary construction of brick-faced concrete was far beyond the capacity of any early medieval builder to emulate, but the basic features of its design—a circular plan, dome, and axial niches screened off from the central space by paired columns—were all to be found in a more easily adaptable form in the churches of S. Stefano Rotondo in Rome and S. Angelo in Perugia. Indeed, a strong case can be made for seeing the Pantheon in its Christian guise as the primary model for all subsequent centrally planned churches in the West dedicated to the Virgin, an association that was expressed in its more popular name in the Middle Ages, S. Maria Rotonda.[61] In sum, while Wilfrid's church of St. Mary at Hexham may have looked more like S. Stefano Rotondo in Rome or S. Angelo in Perugia, the ultimate source of its design and the primary association intended was, I submit, the Pantheon in Rome.

At Hexham, then, Wilfrid expressed his devotion to Rome in very specific and tangible terms through the design and construction of the churches of St. Andrew and St. Mary. Indeed, if my analysis is correct, his churches represented composites of specific features associated with the major pilgrimage churches in the Eternal City. Hexham, in turn, became a center of pilgrimage for the Anglo-Saxons. The apostle Andrew, likewise, became the patron saint of the region and Wilfrid's cult also spread. And yet, architecturally, Hexham seems to have exerted a limited influence. The very elements that made the churches at Hexham so unique in England also made them difficult to emulate. They were perhaps too bold, too grandiose, too uncompromisingly Roman—qualities personified by Wilfrid himself—to be easily adopted elsewhere. The immediate future lay with a more modest vision of building. Hexham, nevertheless, remained a spiritual touchstone for Northumbria and all of England for the rest of the Middle Ages. Indeed, as late as the twelfth century, William of Malmesbury, a contemporary of Prior Richard and Aelred of Rievaulx, wrote that "those who have visited Italy say that at Hexham they see the glories of Rome."[62] These are sentiments with which Wilfrid would have wholeheartedly agreed.

Wilfrid's building activities at Ripon and Hexham should be seen in the broader context of a remarkable flowering of arts and letters in Northumbria in the late seventh and early eighth centuries, inspired by the importation of manuscripts, artisans, and works of art from the continent and especially Rome. In fact, the period from the Synod of Whitby in 664 to roughly 750 may be termed a "Northumbrian Renaissance." The richly illuminated manuscripts of the Book of Durrow, the Lindisfarne Gospels, and the Codex Amiatinus, together with the subtle carving of the monumental stone crosses at Ruthwell, Bewcastle, and Hexham form the backdrop to this movement.[63] The prime example of this phenomenon, however, is the monk and scholar the Venerable Bede (673–735), the greatest historian of his age, whose pure Latin prose exhibits a profound debt to classical civilization as derived from the volumes of the substantial library that he had at his disposal. From the age of seven, Bede lived within the confines of the twin monasteries of Wearmouth and Jarrow, situated but thirty miles east of Hexham and founded by a contemporary of Wilfrid's named Benedict Biscop. The circumstances surrounding the establishment of these two monasteries are recounted in considerable and loving detail in another of Bede's writings, *The Lives of the Abbots of Wearmouth and Jarrow*.[64]

Benedict Biscop was a Northumbrian nobleman who at age twenty-five renounced the life of a soldier to enter the service of the Church. Soon after, in 653, he came in contact with his slightly younger countryman Wilfrid and served as the latter's companion on what proved to be the first of many journeys to Rome for both men. Indeed, by the time of his death in 689, Biscop made six journeys to Rome. After his second visit to Rome in 665, Biscop spent two years at the island monastery of Lérins, off the southern coast of present-day France, where he became a monk and assumed the name Benedict, presumably in honor of St. Benedict, the author of the famous monastic Rule. In 667, Biscop yearned to see the city of Peter and Paul once more, but his pilgrimage was cut short by the pope, who ordered the now forty-year-old Northumbrian to serve as the guide and translator for the newly appointed archbishop of Canterbury, Theodore, who was a Greek-speaking native of Tarsus in Asia Minor. After delivering his charge at Canterbury in 669, Biscop spent the next two years there as abbot of the monastery of SS. Peter and Paul, founded by Augustine. In 671 Biscop set out again for Rome returning this time laden with what Bede describes as "a large number of books on all branches of sacred knowledge."[65] Upon returning to his native land, in 673, Ecfrith, the king of Northumbria, gave Biscop a substantial piece of land situated at the mouth of the Wear River, known today as Monkwearmouth (or simply Wearmouth), in order to establish a monastery in honor of St. Peter.

A year after work on the monastery was begun, Bede tells us that Biscop crossed the channel to Gaul in order to bring back masons (*cementarii*) able to build a stone church "according to the Roman manner (*iuxta morem Romanorum*) which he loved so much."[66] Here the term "Roman manner" seems to refer more to Biscop's desire for a church built of stone rather than to any particular aspect of design, and it should be compared to Bede's reference in the *Ecclesiastical History* to a church at Lindisfarne being built "according to the Irish manner," which he defines as being "not of stone but of cut oak and roofed with reeds." Biscop, therefore, consciously turned away from local building tradition, be it Irish or Anglo-Saxon, preferring instead to emulate the more permanent construction methods of churches he had seen on the continent. Similarly, as the new church neared completion, less than a year after the foundations had been laid, Biscop sent messengers to Gaul to fetch glass-makers, "who were at this time unknown in Britain," to glaze the windows of the church.[67] Bede goes on to say that these foreign craftsmen not only carried out their work at Wearmouth but they taught the English the art of glass-making.

Biscop was equally concerned with procuring liturgical objects from Gaul. Some items, however, could only be obtained in Rome and so Biscop set out on his fifth trip to the Eternal City, probably around 676. He returned laden more than ever with "spiritual goods," which Bede categorizes as books, relics, Roman liturgical practices, a papal privilege for the monastery, and icons; it was also on this occasion that Biscop brought with him the archcantor John from the monastery of St. Martin adjoining St. Peter's in Rome.[68] The icons, or panel paintings, depicted a variety of subjects and were placed throughout the church. Those portraying the Virgin Mary and the twelve apostles (presumably a group of thirteen individual icons), were, according to Bede, fixed to a wooden beam that stretched from wall to wall across the "middle of the roof." This arrangement must have resembled a simplified version of a rood screen or iconostasis dividing the nave and sanctuary, and if it did, it is one of the earliest references to such a feature in church architecture.[69] Other images, depicting scenes from the Gospels and the Book of Revelation, were displayed along the north and south walls of the church. Thus Bede provides a remarkably detailed image of both the construction and decoration of the church at Wearmouth. Portions of the original church preserved on the site today agree well with Bede's description and more recent information about the monastery as a whole has been provided by extensive excavations conducted in the

78 Monkwearmouth, monastery of St. Peter, reconstruction plan of excavations showing early features.

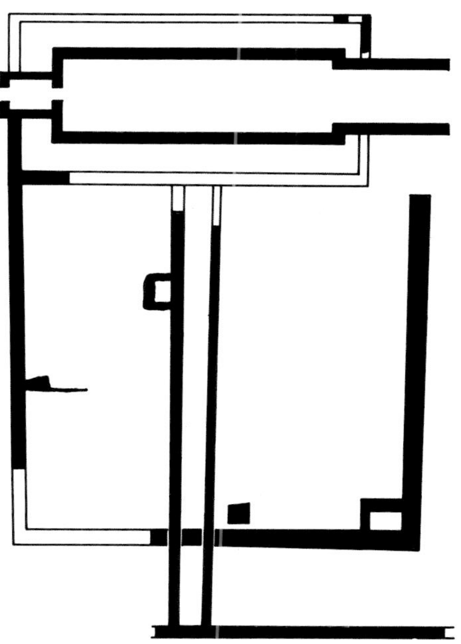

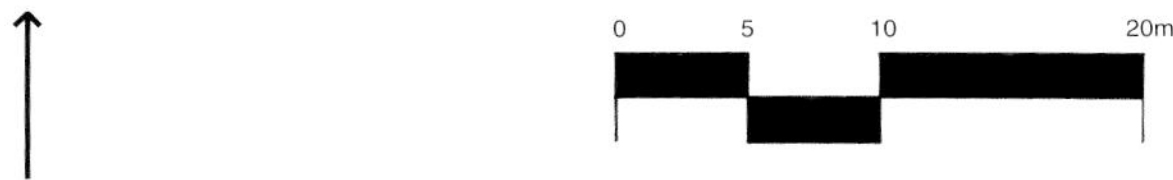

80 Monkwearmouth, St. Peter, archway at base of western tower, detail of right jamb.

1960s and the early 1970s.[70] The church was largely rebuilt in subsequent centuries but the present nave rests on earlier foundations that indicate a simple, rectangular plan approximately 20 m long and only 5.5 m wide with a narrower chancel, the termination of which has yet to be found (fig. 78). There also may have been an aisle or separate corridor along the south side and perhaps one to the north as well. The entire west wall is preserved in its original state, however, reaching at its apex a height of some 10 m and pierced by two small windows and a central, round-arched doorway. The most impressive feature of the church is its western tower (fig. 79). At first this tower stood only two storeys high with a single arched opening on axis in the ground floor and surmounted by a simple gable, the outline of which is still visible as a masonry scar. The upper storeys of the tower block the windows of the west wall of the nave and were therefore added later, most likely when the monastery was refounded in the late eleventh century. But the lower two storeys of the tower do not bond with the west wall of the nave either and the original position of the nave doorway was modified slightly to align it with the central arch of the tower. In other words, the base of the tower was also constructed after the nave was already built, which has led some scholars to question its early date. Bede, on the other hand, seems to refer to this feature when he states that the body of Abbot Eosterwine, who died in 685, lay in the entrance porch (*porticus ingressus*) until it was moved inside the church in 716.[71] One could argue, therefore, that the base of the tower was built as an entrance porch sometime during the ten-year period between the completion of the church around 675 and the death of Eosterwine in 685. But can we assume that the present structure actually corresponds to Bede's reference? I think we can, but only after a careful analysis of its decorative details.

Perhaps the most striking features are the paired, squat shafts, their surfaces incised by a series of parallel grooves, supporting the central archway (fig. 80).[72] Virtually identical shafts are preserved at the abbey church of Nouaillé near Poitiers, founded in 678 (fig. 81), and at the church of

81 Nouaillé, baluster shaft from late seventh century, reused in Romanesque crypt of present abbey church, drawing.

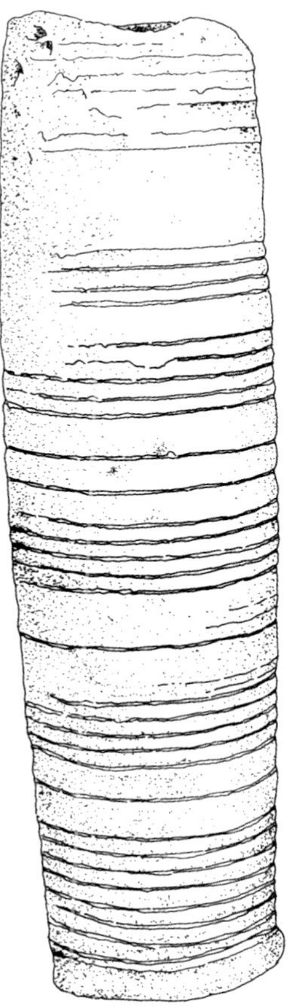

79 *(facing page)* Monkwearmouth, St. Peter, exterior west wall and tower base.

82 Monkwearmouth, St. Peter, archway at base of western tower, detail of right jamb, drawing based on fig. 80.

Notre-Dame at Evrecy in Normandy, the site of another monastery also thought to have been founded in the second half of the seventh century.[73] Somewhat cruder examples, from around the same time, can be seen in the famous Hypogée des Dunes at Poitiers, discussed in the previous chapter. The obvious conclusion is that these so-called baluster shafts at Wearmouth are the work of the masons Biscop brought from Gaul.

But why were these baluster shafts included at all? They serve no real structural purpose; a solid wall could easily have been built at this point; indeed it would have been expected. It is interesting to note, therefore, that applied orders were a common feature of late antique and Early Christian architecture, especially in southern Gaul. Furthermore, we know that on his fourth journey to Rome, made just before founding Wearmouth, Biscop stopped in Vienne, in the Dauphiné,[74] where he must have seen the fifth-century church of Saint-Pierre with its two superimposed rows of columns applied along the inner face of the originally aisleless nave. In Rome, Biscop would have seen applied columns supporting the triumphal arch of the church of St. Paul's-outside-the-Walls and decorating the monumental Arch of Constantine, among other monuments. It seems reasonable to assume, therefore, that the use of applied shafts at Wearmouth related to Biscop's desire, as recorded by Bede, to build a church "according to the Roman manner which he loved so much."

But there is a more personal level of meaning to be appreciated here. The baluster shafts at Wearmouth are not reused Roman *spolia* as at Vienne or in Rome, but objects carved on the spot while being turned on a lathe. It is therefore important to note that Bede singles out the artistry of the lathe worker for special praise in his commentary on the *Song of Songs* because "he (the lathe worker) needs no external pattern . . . to guide his work."[75] Bede's admiration for this craft must have come from personal observation. To be sure, Bede need not be referring to the baluster shafts at Wearmouth—he was only seven years old when he entered the monastery in 680—but similar shafts were used at the church at Jarrow, dedicated five years later, and lathe carving probably continued thereafter at both sites. Most important, Bede's remarks help to explain the appeal of this particular feature in a Northumbrian monastery in the late seventh century.

Situated just below the baluster shafts, however, are low reliefs that are purely Anglo-Saxon in character (fig. 82). Although badly eroded today, one can still make out the outline of two intertwined serpentine beasts with intersecting bird-like beaks. This motif is so close to the animal ornament in the Book of Durrow (especially the carpet page on folio 192v), generally assigned to a scriptorium in Northumbria or perhaps at Iona around the year 675 (fig. 83),[76] and to details of metalwork from the famous Sutton Hoo ship burial (especially the purse lid and shoulder clasps), dated by coins to 625–50 (fig. 84),[77] that a date in the last quarter of the seventh century for the Wearmouth reliefs may be readily assumed. In other words, these reliefs must represent the translation of a decorative motif from the native medium of metalwork into the newly imported technique of building in stone. Here again, foreign and local artisans must have worked side by side. It is worth noting, too, that a motif originating in the artistic tradition of the barbarian, pre-Christian past of the Anglo-Saxons was now seen as an appropriate decoration for both a Gospel book and the entrance to a church, most likely in order to ward off evil spirits. They are akin to the serpentine reliefs at Poitiers and Hornhausen, cited in the previous chapter, and may also have symbolized the indigenous beliefs over which Christianity had triumphed.[78]

In sum, the independently determined dates of the closest comparisons to both the baluster shafts and the relief carvings at Wearmouth coincide with the period between the founding of the monastery and the death of Abbot

83 The Book of Durrow, carpet page with animal interlace, ca. 675 (Dublin, Trinity College Library, MS 57 fol. 192v),

Eosterwine. This, it seems to me, substantiates a date for the western porch of roughly 675 to 685 and further indicates that its decoration represents a merging of artistic trends that were current at the time in both Anglo-Saxon England and Frankish Gaul. Thus, one portion of the church of St. Peter at Wearmouth, when considered in detail, becomes a microcosm of the creative forces at work in this crucial, early stage of Anglo-Saxon architecture.

In 680, six years after the founding of Wearmouth, Biscop was given another, somewhat smaller, parcel of land by the king of Northumbria in order to establish another monastery approximately five miles away.[79] The site was located along the banks of the Don River, near where it merged with the Tyne River, some thirty miles downstream from Hexham. On April 23, 685, the abbey church was dedicated, this time to St. Paul.[80] Much of the original building seems to have stood until the late eighteenth century, when the church was demolished and rebuilt. The nave of the present church, however, resulted from a second rebuilding in the mid-nineteenth century following the design of Gilbert Scott, but it seems to rest, more or less, on the original foundations.

Not surprisingly, survey drawings made just before the demolition of the original church in 1769 and more recent archaeological investigations show that the church of St. Paul was very similar in both scale and elevation to the church of St. Peter at Wearmouth (fig. 85).[81] According to the eighteenth-century drawings, it even had a two-storeyed western entrance porch, of which no trace is visible today. There were also, apparently, a rectilinear chancel to the east and narrow aisles along the northern and southern flanks of the church. The only visible remains of the original structure are the numerous baluster shafts that line the inside of a modern vestibule. Some were presumably used to decorate doorways, as at Wearmouth, while others, it has been suggested, formed part of a choir screen.

The only visible remnant of a more substantive kind attributable to the time of the foundation of Jarrow, or

84 The Sutton Hoo ship burial, deatil of one of the shoulder clasps, 625–50.

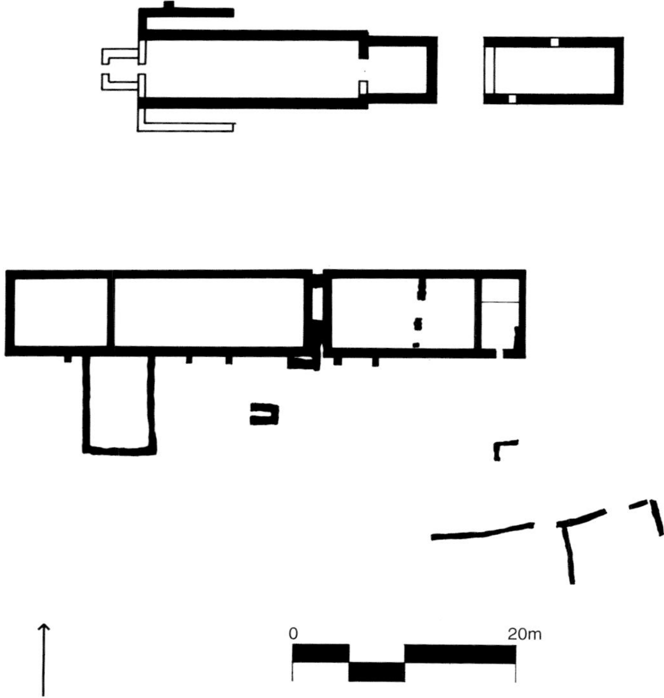

85 Jarrow, monastery of St. Paul, reconstruction plan of excavations, late seventh–eighth century.

soon after, is the structure that serves as the chancel of the present church; originally it was a separate building, presumably a subsidiary church, and was only later joined to the main church by a tower, still standing, that was probably built in the eleventh century (fig. 85). The south wall is by far the best-preserved portion of this small church-*cum*-chancel. The pattern of quoining resembles that of the church at Wearmouth. The masonry itself, however, is far more regular, being composed of coursed, roughly squared stones instead of the coursed rubble at Wearmouth (fig. 86). The reason for this difference may be due more to the source of the stone than to any advance in technical skill, for the presence of Roman tool marks suggests that the building material came from Hadrian's Wall and its adjacent structures, which met the sea but a short distance from Jarrow on the other side of the Tyne River. Thus, like the porch and west wall of the church at Wearmouth, this building may be seen as a result of the influence of Biscop's Gallic masons. Influence from Wilfrid's constructions at Ripon and Hexham is also possible. Interesting, too, are the tiny windows framed by vertical and horizontal stones capped by a curious-looking, monolithic arch; it is a feature that will appear again. And the small glazed oculus in the left window may well be original—the wintry blasts of this northern clime permitted only the smallest of apertures.

We can get a very good idea of what the churches at Wearmouth and Jarrow looked like in their entirety by turning to the parish church of St. John at Escomb near the banks of the Wear River about twelve miles south of Biscop's twin monasteries. Indeed, the small church at Escomb is the best-preserved church in England from this early period (fig. 87). There is no documentary evidence to provide an exact date for the church, but its mode of construction and design clearly indicate that it must be contemporary with the neighboring abbey churches of Wearmouth and Jarrow. Its plan is simple, composed of two rectilinear blocks: a nave, measuring on the inside 13.24 m long × 4.42 m wide, and a square chancel, measuring 3.07 m long by 3.11 m wide. Both the size and proportions of the church at Escomb compare to those at Wearmouth and Jarrow, and its masonry is also very similar. Again, the building material consists of reused Roman blocks. Not only are the characteristic tool marks evident throughout, but one stone on the exterior north wall of the nave bears a fragmentary inscription, reset upside down, that reads: *VI LEG*. The sixth legion (*VI Victrix*) is known to have been stationed in the area from the early second century. Most likely, the building material at Escomb was taken from the nearby Roman fort at Binchester (*Vinovium*). The fact that these stones are notably larger than those employed at Jarrow, again indicates only that they came from a different source.

The fine quality of the masonry is equally evident on the interior (fig. 88). Particularly impressive is the tall, narrow arch leading to the chancel. The large stone blocks of the arch have been set in alternating horizontal and vertical positions in a technique that has come to be known as "Escomb fashion." The arch itself is constructed of finely cut voussoirs with radial joints and the imposts have elegant champfered profiles comparable to those found in Roman forts along Hadrian's Wall. It may even be that the chancel arch is Roman work that has been dismantled and re-erected at Escomb.[82] Like the east church at Jarrow, the interior of St. John's at Escomb was originally lit by small single-splayed windows; the large round-arched window in the east wall of the chancel is a later addition. The two windows in the north wall of the nave have straight monolithic lintels, whereas the lintels of the windows in the south wall are composed of two stones that have been cut to form a small arch. The sills and jambs of these windows also have incised grooves to hold wooden shutters or frames for glass panels.

The original location of the main entrance to the church is not known. Excavations along the exterior of the church demonstrated that the present entrance porch, on the south side, does not rest on earlier foundations and is thus a later addition.[83] This archaeological work did, however, uncover the foundations of two *porticus*, one adjoining

86 *(facing page)* Jarrow, St. Paul, detail of exterior south wall of chancel, late seventh century.

87 Escomb, St. John, exterior, late seventh–eighth century.

the west wall of the nave and the other attached to the north wall of the chancel. The latter communicated with the chancel through a small doorway, still clearly visible, which is now blocked up. The western *porticus* may have opened onto the nave, as the analogous *porticus* at Wearmouth and Jarrow would suggest, but the corresponding masonry in the nave's west wall has been much disturbed in subsequent centuries, leaving no trace of a doorway. Like the western porch at Wearmouth, the porches at Escomb do not bond with the adjacent walls of the nave and chancel, but their masonry is so similar to that of the body of the church that they must be roughly contemporary with it. Traces of a gable in the exterior west wall of the nave indicate that the western *porticus* was two-storeyed, similar to the western porches at both Wearmouth and Jarrow. The specific function of the subsidiary chambers is not known.

The churches at Wearmouth, Jarrow, and Escomb form a recognizable group, modest in scale, rectilinear in plan, with tall, narrow proportions, and built of stone, of which the latter two contain reused Roman masonry. Above all, one is struck by the austere simplicity of these buildings, but their present state can be deceiving. We know, for example, that the churches at Wearmouth and Jarrow were originally plastered both inside and out and painted white. The baluster shafts and relief sculpture also seem to have been painted. Certainly the windows were filled with stained glass. Indeed, more than one thousand fragments of colored glass, some with bits of lead still adhering to them, were found in the excavations at Jarrow.[84] Most can be reconstructed to form simple geometric patterns, but some pieces were cut to form curved edges suggesting that figural decoration may also have been employed (fig. 89). No evidence of paint was found on the glass; thus, if human figures were represented, they were devoid of any facial features or details of drapery. Fragments of colored window glass were also discovered at Wearmouth and in association with the north *porticus* at Escomb.[85] In addition to stained-glass windows, sacred vessels and rich vestments adorned the altar, while colorful icons were hung throughout the

88 *(facing page)* Escomb, St. John, interior, late seventh–eighth century.

89 Jarrow, St. Paul's monastery, reconstruction of excavated window glass (Bede's World, Jarrow).

churches. With the completion of the church of St. Paul at Jarrow in 685, Biscop set out on yet another and this time final journey to Rome in order to obtain sacred objects similar to those he had acquired for Wearmouth. He returned with more books and icons. This time the icons included a series of panels illustrating concordances between the Old and New Testaments, such as a representation of Isaac carrying the wood for his sacrifice paired with Christ carrying the cross, which were hung in the church and elsewhere in the monastery.[86]

Thus, in both construction and decoration, the monastic churches at Wearmouth and Jarrow reflected Biscop's desire for "Romanness." To be sure, Biscop, as Bede tells us, recruited the masons and glaziers from Gaul, but this was largely for the sake of convenience. Gaul was simply close at hand. But there, too, as we have seen, architecture had retained a distinct air of *romanitas*. The building material was taken from the ruins of ancient Roman stations and fortifications in the area. Bede, interestingly enough, does not assign the construction of the great defensive wall of north Britain to the time of Hadrian in the early second century but to the early fifth century when Roman garrisons were preparing to withdraw from the island.[87] In other words, for Bede, and presumably his contemporaries, Hadrian's Wall was a "Christian" monument marking the final phase of Roman rule. It is worth noting, too, that the dimensions Bede gives for the Wall apply only to the short stretch from present-day Newcastle to Wallsend that was the section closest to Jarrow.[88] It was presumably from this general area that the building material for Jarrow was obtained.

Stained-glass windows were another Roman feature. Certainly, Biscop must have seen stained-glass windows in churches in Gaul, but there are also clear literary references to windows of colored glass in churches in Rome of the period.[89] The icons, too, were a direct link with Rome. Biscop may have seen religious panel paintings for the first time in Canterbury; Bede, for example, says that Augustine met the King of Kent for the first time while carrying "the image of our Lord and Savior painted on a board (*tabula*)."[90] But for both Augustine and Biscop the source of these panel paintings was Rome. It should also be pointed out that the importance of icons in Christian worship was a relatively recent phenomenon. Indeed, as Ernst Kitzinger has shown, the cult of images, as manifested in icons, began to intensify in the second half of the sixth century ultimately leading to the Iconoclastic controversy of the eighth century. It seems to be no mere coincidence that the earliest icons preserved in Rome are generally dated to the late sixth and early seventh centuries.[91]

At the same time, the "Roman manner" at Wearmouth and Jarrow was subtly combined with local traditions. The relief carving of the intertwined beasts on the entrance porch at Wearmouth is derived from Anglo-Saxon metalwork. The baluster shafts, too, while perhaps ultimately inspired by Roman models, take on distinctly unclassical proportions. Even the highly stylized human figures of the stained glass, assuming the reconstruction is correct, seem to recall more the jeweller's craft of the Sutton Hoo purse lid and shoulder clasps than any example of Mediterranean art.[92] Most important, the rectilinear design of Biscop's churches comes directly out of a wood-building tradition. This is demonstrated by the meticulous excavations of the royal Saxon villa of Yeavering in Northumbria, some 45 miles north of Jarrow, where the outline of a woodframed church—virtually identical in both size and plan to the

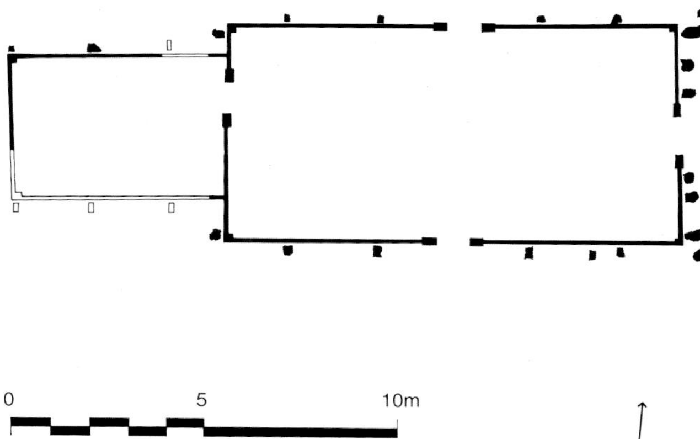

90 Yeavering, royal villa, plan of woodframe church, mid-seventh century.

rectilinear churches at Wearmouth, Jarrow, and Escomb—was uncovered, dating most likely to the second quarter of the seventh century (fig. 90). The design of the Yeavering church, in turn, is clearly derived from the tradition of the Anglo-Saxon long hall, of which a particularly splendid example was found on the same site.[93] Thus, Biscop's churches should be seen as direct translations into stone of an indigenous wooden building type.

This synthesis of foreign and local, of Roman and Anglo-Saxon, traditions needs to be contrasted with Wilfrid's more blatant allusions to Rome at Hexham. Whereas at Wearmouth and Jarrow, the Roman features (cut-stone masonry, applied orders, stained-glass windows, and icons, not to mention the dedications of the churches) served as a veneer to local building forms, at Hexham, Wilfrid's churches seem to have been more thoroughly Roman in both form and construction. To be sure, both men were strong advocates of the Roman Church, but where Wilfrid was uncompromising and combative in all aspects of religious life, Biscop, as portrayed by Bede, seems to have been far more diplomatic in his ability to compromise. One is reminded in particular of the episode in which Bede tells how Biscop explained on his deathbed that the rule for his monasteries had been derived from the best of monastic life he had observed in the seventeen different abbeys during his many journeys abroad.[94] Without wishing to stress the point too much, it seems to me that the personalities of each man are reflected in the buildings they sponsored.

Wearmouth and Jarrow continued to thrive after Benedict Biscop's death in 689. Indeed, by the early eighth century the two monasteries are reported by Bede to have had a combined population of around 600 brethren.[95] Only the core of the two monasteries has, as yet, been excavated, which makes it difficult to imagine how such a large monastic community was accommodated on the two sites. Wearmouth was the mother house and the larger of the two monasteries, but no subsidiary buildings, aside from the covered walkway, have been uncovered. No doubt their remains lie still unearthed beyond the zone of excavations. At Jarrow, on the other hand, the foundations of two rectangular buildings were found on an east–west axis set parallel to and some 10m to the south of the churches (figs. 85 and 91). This arrangement of buildings on axial alignments seems to be characteristic of Anglo-Saxon monasteries and should be contrasted with the more circular disposition of Irish monasteries.

The function of these two buildings (fig. 85) is not known, but the director of the excavations, Rosemary Cramp, has interpreted them as a refectory, to the west, and an assembly hall, to the east, based upon the artifacts found in association with each unit.[96] Like the churches they were built of stone and covered by plaster on the interior and exterior. The windows of the refectory were glazed with colored glass and the floor was composed of *opus signinum*, that is concrete mixed with crushed brick, an ancient Roman technique of waterproofing a surface. The same technique was used in the separate chamber at the east end of the assembly hall, which also contained fragments of plain and colored glass. In the center of the floor of the refectory was found a stone shaft, elaborately carved with interlace and vine scrolls, that may have served as the base for a lectern. In the assembly hall, a podium was found against the east wall.

South of these two buildings, the ground was found to have been terraced as it sloped toward the Don River. In this area were found traces of cultivation and wattle huts used as workshops. At the southernmost point on the site,

91 Jarrow, St. Paul's monastery, reconstruction drawing.

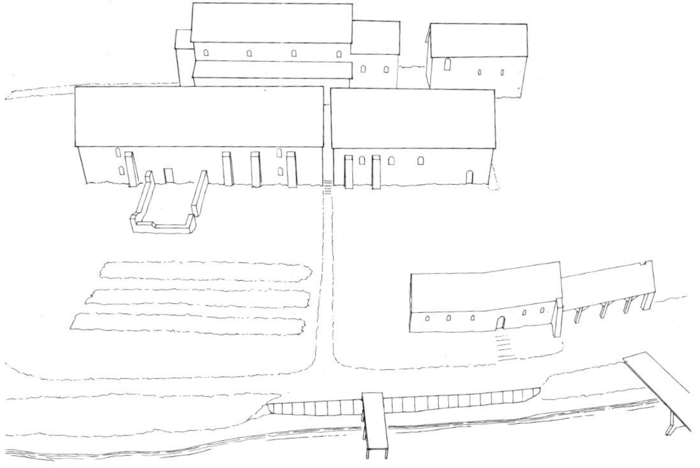

on the banks of the river, part of a stone structure was uncovered. Although not fully excavated, it is clear that this building was originally impressive in appearance. The walls, constructed of large reused Roman blocks, were covered with painted plaster and it is here that the vast majority of fragments of colored glass were found (fig. 89). At some later stage, it was used as an area for glassmaking as evidenced by pieces of fused glass, millefiori rods, a crucible, and bronze implements. In short, despite the restricted area of the excavations, sufficient evidence has been recovered to show how the monastery functioned as a largely self-sufficient entity.

It was within this central precinct that monastic life at Jarrow revolved. It was a highly disciplined existence of order and routine, centered about a daily round of communal prayer, what the Rule of St. Benedict terms the *opus dei* or "work of God." It can be estimated that each monk spent a total of approximately four hours per day worshiping in the church, divided up into eight intervals beginning at around two in the morning and ending at sunset. An equal amount of time was spent in reading and meditation, while up to six hours were spent in manual labor. Thus, a visitor to Jarrow in the eighth century would have found the monastery to be a place of almost constant work and prayer: the churches, resounding with the clear voices of Roman chant, as the focal point of religious worship; the workshops busy with the making of glass, metal implements, and other essential goods; the gardens being tended; and the assembly hall being used, at least in part, for scribal activities, reading, and teaching. It was presumably in the assembly hall, or in a building nearby, that the grandiose Codex Amiatinus was made;[97] certainly it was here that Bede taught the wisdom of his age. Indeed, through his pupils and through his writings, Bede helped to transform Wearmouth and Jarrow, and other religious houses in Northumbria, into the leading centers of learning in Europe in the eighth century. From England, missionaries such as Willibrord and Boniface carried these ideals of religious life to the heathen fringes of the Frankish kingdom on the continent. And by the end of the eighth century, the Anglo-Saxon scholar and teacher Alcuin, trained at York in the tradition of Bede, served at Charlemagne's court at Aachen. In this way, the intellectual, artistic, and architectural achievements of Northumbria in the seventh and eighth centuries had a profound effect on the development of early medieval Europe as a whole.[98]

The brilliance of the Northumbrian Renaissance, however, was soon extinguished. On January 8, 793, the monastery of Lindisfarne was "miserably destroyed with plunder and slaughter" by Viking raiders from Scandinavia. The following year, the Norsemen attacked Jarrow.[99] In 802, Iona was plundered for the first time and after a second sack in 806, most, if not all, of the monks abandoned the island and returned to Ireland.[100] Wearmouth and Jarrow continued to exist well into the ninth century (the last coins found on the site date from the middle of the century), but by 875, they, too, were finally abandoned.

Through the process of Christianization, Anglo-Saxon England came into ever closer contact with the rest of western Europe. And yet, in spite of the devotion to Rome and the dependency upon foreign craftsmanship, architecture in England during this period (from the arrival of Augustine at Canterbury to the first incursions of the Norsemen) retained a distinct character of its own. Indeed, it is this unique synthesis of continental and insular traditions that makes the churches of Anglo-Saxon England so important for an understanding of the origins of medieval architecture. But at the very moment when the British Isles were feeling the brunt of the Viking terror, mainland Europe was experiencing a resurgence under the vigorous rule of Charlemagne. It is to the architectural achievements of this new era that I shall now turn.

PART TWO THE CAROLINGIAN ERA

CHAPTER 5

Symbols of the New Alliance

In 750, two envoys from Pippin III, the *major domus* or mayor of the Frankish palace, arrived in Rome in order to pose an urgent question to Pope Zacharias: "Is it right for one who has no power to continue to bear the title of king?"[1] For more than a century, the Merovingian dynasty of the Franks had been in decline, during which time members of the landed aristocracy usurped more and more royal authority through the office of the so-called 'mayor of the palace'. Under such auspices, Pippin's father, Charles Martel, "the Hammer," led the forces that defeated Muslim raiders near Poitiers in 733, while the king, Theuderic IV, remained at court far from the scene of battle. After Charles's death in 741, the *Regnum Francorum* was divided between his two sons, Carloman, who ruled the eastern lands known as Austrasia, and Pippin, who was given control of the western and southern regions of Neustria, Burgundy, and Provence. In 747, however, Carloman retired to the monastery of Montecassino in south Italy, and Pippin was left to rule alone, albeit in the king's name. In other words, in 750, the pope was being asked to give his blessing to a proposed *coup d'état*.

The pope's positive response (". . . he who has the power should also be called king") must have come as no surprise to the Frankish envoys; it was, after all, a seemingly clear-cut issue of identifying title with power (*potestas*), an association with ample precedent in both Germanic and Roman law. What is surprising, though, is that the pope was consulted at all. In so doing, Pippin evidently sought to legitimize his right to rule through papal sanction in order to compensate for his lack of royal blood. By the end of 751, the last member of the Merovingian line, Childeric III, was deposed and sent to a monastery. Pippin, in turn, was elected king of the Franks and consecrated by a group of bishops assembled at Soissons. On this occasion Pippin was also anointed. This practice, which was known in Visigothic Spain and Ireland but not in Francia, placed the new ruler in the tradition of the exalted kings of the Old Testament and demonstrated that his position was sanctified by the Church thereby adding a new dimension to the aura of Frankish kingship.[2]

At the same time, the pope must have welcomed the opportunity to intervene in the affairs of the Franks in the hope that they would prove useful against the growing threat of the Lombards. Indeed, in the summer of 751 had come the alarming news that the exarchate of Ravenna, the last vestige of Byzantine rule in Italy, had fallen to the Lombards. And a year later, led by their king, Aistulf, the Lombards besieged Rome. In 752, Pope Zacharias died and was succeeded by Stephen II, who was able to negotiate a temporary truce. The new pope sought first the help of the emperor in Constantinople, but when it became apparent that no military assistance would be forthcoming, his thoughts turned to the Franks and their new leader. Already a century and a half before, the Byzantine emperor Maurice and Pope Gregory the Great had tried to persuade the Franks to intervene when the Lombards first appeared in north Italy but to no avail; subsequent appeals were no more successful. In the past the Franks had been reluctant to attack another Germanic tribe beyond their own borders, but now the situation was more urgent than ever and, more importantly, the new Frankish king was in the papacy's debt. Thus, in 753, Stephen II left Rome in order to appeal in person to Pippin.

Once over the Alps (the Lombard king did not dare deter the pope's journey for fear of Frankish reprisals), Pope Stephen II was met by Pippin's son Charles, later to be known as Charles the Great (*Karolus Magnus*) or Charlemagne, and he was escorted to the royal villa at Ponthion near Châlons-sur-Marne, where he arrived on January 6, 754. Upon meeting the pope, Pippin is reported to have bowed in supplication and led the pontiff's horse by the reins. In the negotiations that followed, Pippin agreed to undertake to wrest the exarchate of Ravenna from the Lombards and to restore the territories of the "Roman republic" to the pope, even though this land previously was considered to be under the sole jurisdiction of the emperor. In return, Stephen II repeated the coronation of Pippin and his two sons as kings of the Franks, this time at the abbey church of Saint-Denis, near Paris. Pippin was anointed by the pope and named, along with his sons, "Patrician of the Romans" (*patricius Romanorum*), a title heretofore borne by the exarch of Ravenna and bestowed only by the emperor.[3] It may also have been during this period that the famous forgery, the so-called Donation of Constantine (*Constitutum Constantini*), was formulated, wherein it was claimed that in the early fourth century the Emperor Constantine had endowed Pope Sylvester I and his successors with jurisdiction over Rome, Italy, and the entire western half of the empire. The document bears all the marks of being the work of members of the Lateran staff following older traditions, both oral and written. Whatever the exact circumstances of its creation, the Donation helped to justify papal temporal rule. It may also have solidified and given legal status to the new political alliance between the Franks and the papacy.[4]

It is against this background that one must understand the first major architectural campaign of the new Carolingian dynasty, the rebuilding of the abbey church of Saint-Denis. Indeed, Pippin III has been called "the man of Saint-Denis."[5] He had been educated there; his father, Charles Martel, was buried there. He chose one of the emissaries to Pope Zacharias, Fulrad, to be the abbot of Saint-Denis soon after 750. It was at Saint-Denis that Pope Stephen II anointed Pippin and his sons as kings of the Franks in 754. And it was there that Pippin chose to be buried, as is stated in a diploma issued shortly before his death in 768.[6]

The church that served as the setting for the papal ceremony of 754 had been built more than a century before by King Dagobert (629–39) and its size and design must have seemed inadequate for such an occasion. For whatever reason, a new and larger abbey church was built and consecrated in the presence of Charlemagne on February 25, 775.[7] The date when construction began is less certain. Ninth-century documents state that on the occasion of the royal anointing on July 25, 754, Pope Stephen II also dedicated an altar to SS. Peter and Paul described as having been located "in front of the tomb" (*ante sepulchrum*) of St. Denis.[8] There is, however, no evidence to suggest that this dedication involved or was meant to initiate the rebuilding of the church, as has been assumed by many scholars. Indeed, a description of the Carolingian church, written in 799, states that it was erected on Pippin's command but only "after his death" by his sons Charles and Carloman.[9] The ninth-century *Miracula sancti Dionysii,* on the other hand, says that the building was begun by Pippin and finished by Charlemagne; it, however, is considered to be a less reliable source. In sum, the new church seems to have been built between 768 and 775.[10]

Although the Carolingian church of Saint-Denis was replaced in the twelfth and thirteenth centuries by the present Gothic structure, we are able to gain some idea of its salient features from a variety of different sources. The aforementioned description of the church from the late eighth century is brief but provides some important information. There are also the writings of Abbot Suger, who in describing the building of the new Gothic church in the 1130s and 1140s makes mention of parts of the eighth-century church.[11] And finally there is the archaeological record derived from restoration work carried out by Viollet-le-Duc in the middle of the nineteenth century and from a series of limited excavations directed by Sumner Crosby in the late 1930s, 1940s, and 1960s and by Jules Formigé in the 1950s. These investigations have been recently reexamined, summarized, and partially reinterpreted by Michaël Wyss.[12]

Much of the eighth-century church was destroyed in the Gothic rebuilding; only relatively small portions of the Carolingian church have been recovered through excavations and what little has been found is open to varying interpretations (fig. 92). The basic dimensions of the main body of the church, however, are certain. The total width of the nave and aisles, including the width of the walls, was little more than 20 m; the width of the nave was approximately 10 m from the center of the columns of the flanking colonnades, and the width of the aisles simply half that measurement. Crosby also found the remains of the southwest corner of a projecting transept. The total length of the transept was approximately 28 m, including the thickness of the walls and assuming a matching transept arm existed to the north. The width (or depth) of the transept is less clear. Formigé claims to have uncovered part of the east wall of the south transept arm at the point where it joined the apse and, therefore, reconstructs the transept with an interior width of 11 m. Crosby, however, was unable to confirm Formigé's finding and believes instead that the east wall of the transept was completely enveloped in the Gothic foundations. Crosby prefers to envision the transept as only 8 m wide, but this would make the apse extremely stilted and the transept unusually narrow. Wyss, instead, sides with Formigé but agrees with Crosby that the original foundations were enveloped by later construction. Thus, the exact width of the transept remains open to conjecture, although its length is not in dispute.

The nave and aisles were divided by eight columns set on carved, roughly square, bases. The bases vary greatly in height, so that the column shafts must have been of different dimensions in a manner similar to the use of ancient *spolia* in churches in Rome. Indeed, it has been suggested

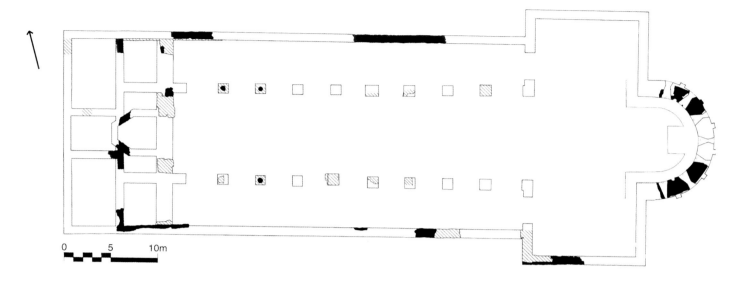

92 Saint-Denis, reconstructed plan of abbey church, 768–75, with western extension, late eighth century.

that columns and bases from the Merovingian church were deliberately reused to add to the new building's legitimacy.[13] Similarly, the shallow relief carving varies from base to base, ranging from stylized birds and abstract patterns, similar to motifs in Merovingian metalwork and book illumination, to elegant vine scrolls with grape bunches, reflecting an interest in the delicate naturalism of classical art (fig. 93). As to the latter example, one is reminded of the carved reliefs of the Tempietto del Clitunno, from the early eighth century, or of the columns of La Daurade and the Aquitanian school of sculpture in late antiquity, discussed in chapter three. In addition to the nave colonnades, the interior of Saint-Denis was further interrupted by what Suger describes as "a certain obstruction which cut as a dark wall through the center of the church (*medium ecclesiae*)."[14] Most likely, he is referring to a transverse wall dividing the nave from the transept similar to one preserved from the tenth or early eleventh century in the priory church of Saint-Généroux (fig. 94).

Among the best-preserved remains are the eastern and western extremities; together they provide an overall length of a little over 60 m. At the east end there are the foundations of a broad semicircular apse (9.40 m wide) pierced by a series of deeply splayed windows (1.05 m wide × 0.70 m high) of which portions of six are preserved (fig. 95); a seventh window at the apex of the apse was destroyed when an outer crypt was built in the ninth century. The windows were so wide on the inside (over a meter) that central mullions were needed for support. The windows, of course, allowed light to enter a crypt where the remains of St. Denis were venerated; there are also preserved two shallow niches that held lamps to provide further illumination. In addition, the crypt was once richly decorated, as is shown by traces of painted plaster, imitating marble revetment, found in the splays of the windows.

The innermost walls of the crypt passage were removed by Viollet-le-Duc in the middle of the nineteenth century, but plans made earlier in the same century show that the crypt was semicircular with what appears to have been a broad perpendicular corridor at its apex, similar in design to the annular crypts in Rome discussed in chapter two.[15] The exact position and number of steps of the crypt's entrances are not known.

93 Saint-Denis, abbey church, column base (Musée Lapidaire, Saint Denis).

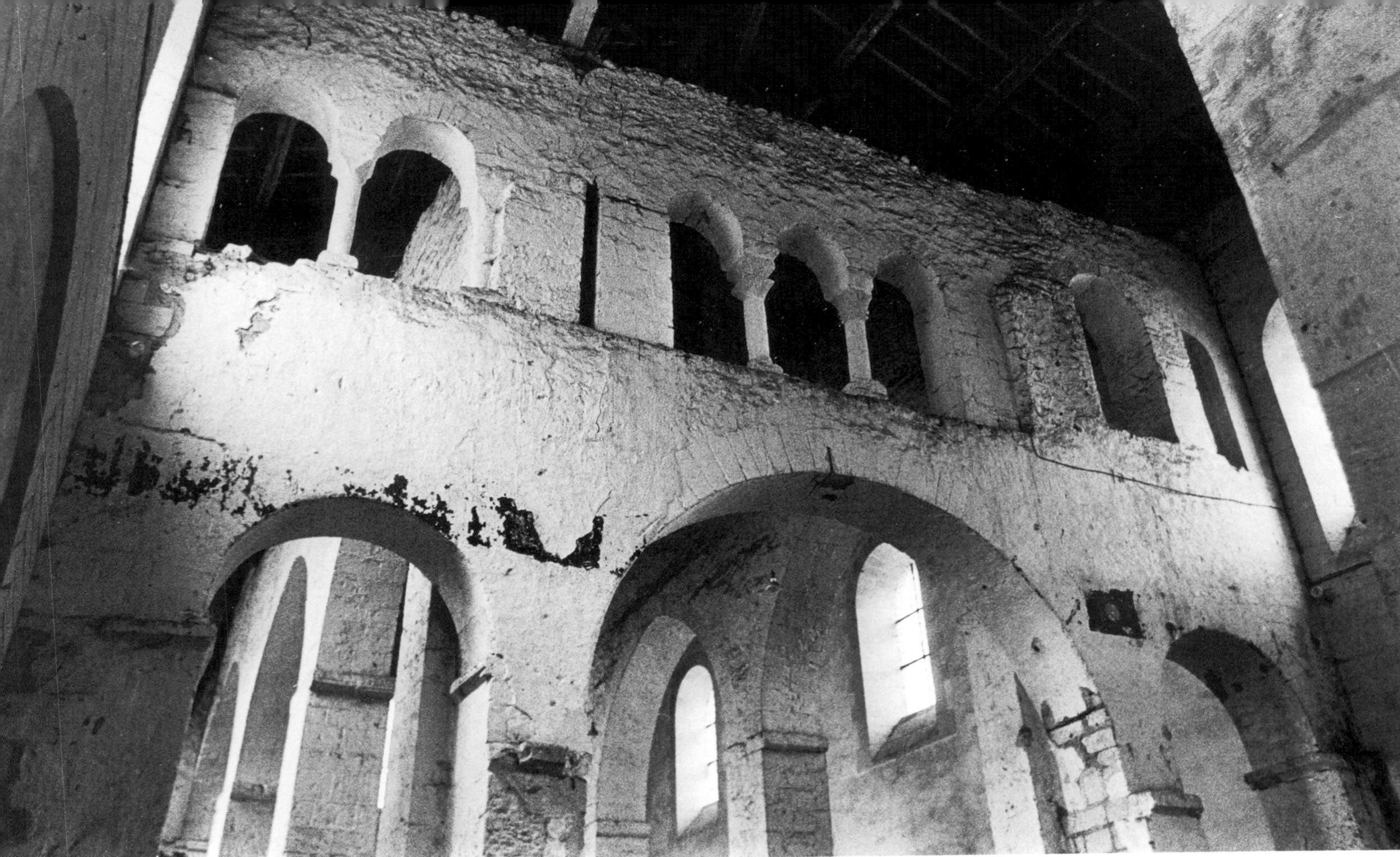

94 Saint-Généroux, priory church, transverse wall separating nave and transept, tenth century.

The remains of the west facade are even more fragmentary than those of the east end. Abbot Suger, the patron of the great Gothic structure of the mid-twelfth century, described the entrance of the old church as a "narrow hall squeezed in on either side by twin towers neither high nor very sturdy."[16] He also explained that in demolishing the old facade "we tore down a certain addition asserted to have been made by Charlemagne on a very honorable occasion (for his father, . . . Pippin, had commanded that he be buried, for the sins of his father Charles Martel, outside at the entrance with the doors, face downward and not recumbent)."[17] Crosby uncovered what seem to be the partial foundations of this arrangement and attempted to reconstruct an admittedly hypothetical plan. Most recently, Wyss, together with Werner Jacobsen, has carefully reexamined the evidence and identified several pre-Gothic phases, which may be summarized as follows:[18] The church built under Abbot Fulrad originally had a relatively simple narthex composed of three compartments, corresponding in widths to the nave and aisles. Pippin was, therefore, buried "outside the entrance" of this structure. The "addition" of Charlemagne, mentioned by Suger, represented a slightly later remodeling and extension of the west end. In the center of the westernmost wall, Crosby found the lower courses of two short walls set at oblique angles from the facade, which he and, subsequently, other scholars interpreted as the remains of a polygonal apse. Wyss and Jacobsen point out, however, that this feature lies below the ground level of the Carolingian entrance and was too insubstantial to support an apse. They believe, instead, that it formed part of Pippin's tomb, which may have been refashioned to accept the body of the king's wife, Bertrada, who died in 783. Details of the elevation of the tomb and the rest of the west end are far less certain, but there seem to have been at least six unequal compartments and possibly towers of some kind. The "twin towers" seen by Suger, on the other hand, may have resulted from a remodeling in the eleventh century along the same lines as its Carolingian predecessor. This collaborative study of the west end of Saint-Denis is apparently an ongoing effort, and while this primary report is certainly the best analysis of the meager remains presented thus far, one hopes that in time more archaeological data will become available so that a truly reliable reconstruction can be made.

Nonetheless, from this information a general picture of the abbey church emerges. It was a basilica with a nave and aisles divided by *spolia* columns; to the east, a projecting transept was followed by a semicircular apse housing an annular crypt; and to the west, at least by the late eighth century, stood a monumental entryway, probably with low twin towers, incorporating at its core a polygonal tomb structure. In addition, the description of 799 refers to exterior "porticoes," presumably an atrium adjoining the west facade, and to a *casabula*, usually interpreted to mean a crossing tower, surmounting the roof of the church. The latter was presumably the tower from which bells were hung, according to ninth-century sources.[19] Still, the exact form of the tower and its relationship to the transept remain unknown.

Although the 799 description is extremely useful in its reference to certain features not revealed by the excavations, it is difficult, if not impossible, to reconcile the dimensions of the church provided in this late eighth-century account with the archaeological findings.[20] The description states, for example, that the total length of the church was 245 (Carolingian) feet, or 81.56 m, which is some 20 m longer than the excavated church. To be sure, the presence of an atrium could explain the church's extra length; but the width of the church is given as 103 feet, or 34.29 m, whereas we know that the nave was little more than 20 m wide and that the transept was no more than 28 m in length. The description also states that the interior of the church contained 50 "major" and 35 "minor" columns, whereas only 16 bases are known to have stood in the nave, of which 4 were found in situ. In order to accommodate so many columns, one would have to imagine either galleries, for which there is no evidence, or tiers of applied shafts in the manner of the church of St. Pierre in Vienne. Even so, it seems virtually impossible to account for an additional 59 "major" and 37 "minor" columns that are said to have stood in the atrium. Similarly, the stated height of the nave, 75 feet (25 m), would mean that the church had an extraordinarily steep and unprecedented 1 : 2.5 ratio of the width of the nave to its height. In addition, the roof covering the nave is said to have been 30 feet (9.9 m) high and the crossing tower, another 33 feet (10.98 m) high. The foundations that would have been needed to sustain a crossing tower of stone have not been found, although they may have been enveloped or displaced by the later Gothic foundations; it seems more likely that a tower of such height had to have been built of wood, which, in turn, would have made a masonry crossing unnecessary. In any event, the total height for the church of 140 feet (46.6 m) must be assumed to be an exaggeration.

95 Saint-Denis, abbey church, view of annular crypt and apse wall looking east.

Even so, the major source of influence for the design of the church is clear. The presence of an annular crypt, a projecting transept, and an atrium can only refer to Rome. As noted in chapter two, St. Peter's in Rome was the first church to receive an annular crypt, ca. 600, and thereafter it became the model for the use of annular crypts at S. Pancrazio (625–38) and S. Crisogono (731–41). Saint-Denis, in turn, seems to have been the first church north of the Alps to use an annular crypt. Not only did the emulation of St. Peter's reflect the new alliance with the papacy, but it also expressed the desire to associate the martyred bishop of Paris and apostle of the Gauls, St. Denis, with the martyred bishop and apostle of the Romans, St. Peter. The Frankish devotion to St. Peter was strengthened by other factors as well. Pope Stephen II (752–57), for example, gave the abbot of Saint-Denis, Fulrad, two residences in Rome near the basilica of St. Peter's.[21] Moreover, in 757, at the request of Pippin, Pope Paul I translated the purported relics of the daughter of St. Peter, Petronilla, from the catacombs of S. Domitilla to the imperial mausoleum, built by the Emperor Honorius ca. 400, adjoining the end of the south transept arm of St. Peter's.[22] Thereafter, this rotunda became known not only as S. Petronilla but as the "chapel of the kings of the Franks" (*capella regum Francorum*) until it was torn down in the early sixteenth century to make way for the new, Renaissance church of St. Peter.[23]

No doubt, the transept at Saint-Denis could also be seen as a reference to St. Peter's, but its broad proportions (assuming the reconstruction is correct) and the fact that it projected only slightly from the body of the church find a closer parallel in another church in Rome, St. Paul's-outside-the-Walls. This comparison is all the more intriguing when one considers that St. Denis was believed to have been the same person as Dionysius the Areopagite, the disciple of Paul mentioned in the Acts of the Apostles. This identification of St. Denis is usually dated to the abbacy of Hilduin (814–40), but it must have been current as early as 758 when Pope Paul I sent Pippin copies of the writings thought to be by the Areopagite but which were in truth the work of a Greek theologian, the Pseudo-Dionysius, living around 500.[24]

The size of the church of Saint-Denis, however, does not begin to approach the monumental scale of St. Peter's and St. Paul's in Rome. It is therefore interesting to note that Saint-Denis is almost exactly the same size as S. Pancrazio, the largest church built in Rome between the sixth and the ninth centuries and the first to be modelled after St. Peter's, with its annular crypt, and after St. Paul's-outside-the-Walls, with its broad transept (fig. 35). In other words, the church of S. Pancrazio offered a reduced, and therefore more easily imitated, version of a basilica that contained the most salient features of the two great apostolic basilicas. Thus, the design of the church of Saint-Denis expressed associations with Rome on many levels, associations that were already established in 754 by Stephen II's dedication of an altar, in front of the tomb of St. Denis, to SS. Peter and Paul.

Although the Roman elements are unmistakable, the church of Saint-Denis was not a slavish copy of one or more Roman models. The church seems to have been built using the slightly longer Carolingian foot instead of the Roman foot. More important, the presence of a crossing tower at the east end and the addition of a two-tower facade to the west find no precedents in Rome. They must be seen as specifically northern elements that were incorporated into an otherwise Roman design. It is this synthesis of northern and Roman features that makes the abbey church of Saint-Denis such a potent symbol of the new Carolingian era.

When Charlemagne attended the consecration of the new abbey church of Saint-Denis in 775, he was not only the sole ruler of the Franks (his brother Carloman having died in 771) and patrician of the Romans, but he was also, as of 774, the king of the Lombards. The alliance with the Franks did not, at first, prove to be of great benefit to the papacy. After initial forays into north Italy in 754 and 756, Pippin had been content to maintain a tenuous *modus vivendi* with the Lombards and after his death in 768, rivalry between his two sons, Charlemagne and Carloman, prevented the Franks from presenting a united front in support of Rome. Charlemagne, in fact, married a daughter of the Lombard king, Desiderius, in 770, but within a year, Charlemagne repudiated her and thereby ended any possibility of an alliance with the Lombards. A year later Carloman died and in February, 772, a newly elected pope, Hadrian I (772–95), ascended the throne of Peter. When the Lombards besieged Rome in the winter of 772–73, Hadrian appealed to Charlemagne for help and after Desiderius refused to negotiate with the Franks, Charlemagne marched into the Po Valley.

By the spring of 774, Lombard resistance had all but collapsed and Charlemagne, leaving the Lombard capital of Pavia under siege, surprised the pope by deciding to make his first pilgrimage to Rome in order to be there for Easter on April 3. Charlemagne was accorded all the honors due a "patrician of the Romans." He was greeted by church officials thirty miles outside of Rome and then again at the foot of Monte Mario, the first milestone, by a military assembly and children waving banners. From there Charlemagne continued on foot in the manner of a pilgrim to St. Peter's, where he ascended the stairs leading to the atrium of the basilica, reportedly kissing each step as he went out of reverence for the Prince of the Apostles. At the gateway to the atrium at the top of the stairs, the pope embraced him and led him into the basilica as the choir sang "Blessed is he who comes in the name of the Lord." Once inside, Charlemagne descended into the crypt in order to pray before the tomb of Peter.

During his visit, Charlemagne resided not in the former imperial palace on the Palatine Hill, but near St. Peter's in the manner of other Frankish visitors, such as Fulrad, before him. Pope Hadrian took the opportunity, in extended negotiations, to persuade Charlemagne to carry out the territorial donations promised by his father to Stephen II. After having spent several days in Rome attending papal masses in the city's principal churches, Charlemagne returned to north Italy and on June 7, he entered Pavia and assumed the title *rex Francorum et Langobardorum atque patricius Romanorum*. Thus, exactly twenty years after Stephen II had visited the Frankish court, Pippin's son wore the iron crown of the Lombards.

Among Charlemagne's first actions upon his return to the north after conquering the Lombards was to attend the consecration of a new church at the royal abbey of Lorsch near Worms on September 1, 774. The monastery of Lorsch had been founded exactly ten years earlier through the donation of a small villa by a local count, Cancor, and his mother, Williswinths, and with a relative, Chrodegang, the archbishop of Metz, serving as the first abbot. Chrodegang was a major figure at the Frankish court and he had played a prominent role in establishing the alliance of the Franks with the papacy. He had, for example, accompanied Pope Stephen II from Rome to see Pippin III and thereafter had been a driving force in the adoption of Roman liturgical usage in the Frankish church. Not surprisingly, therefore, the monastery of Lorsch was originally dedicated to SS. Peter and Paul. In 765, however, Chrodegang was able to obtain the remains of St. Nazarius from Pope Paul I, marking the first time corporal relics were allowed to leave the city,[25] giving tangible expression to the favored status the Franks enjoyed with Rome on an ecclesiastical as well as a political level. Interestingly enough, these were the remains of the same Nazarius whose body had been discovered in Milan by St. Ambrose in 395 and subsequently housed in the church of the Holy Apostles.[26] How the remains of this Milanese saint got to Rome we do not know, but a recorded inscription indicates that they were venerated in a cemetery outside the city as early as 404.[27] Be that as it may, with the arrival of the relics of St. Nazarius Lorsch soon became a center of pilgrimage and in 767, work began on a new and larger monastic complex on a nearby site to accommodate the rapidly growing monastery. In 772, Charlemagne declared Lorsch a royal abbey placing it under his protection and recognizing the abbey's land holdings and immunity from episcopal intervention and the right of the monks to elect their own abbot. On September 1, 774, with Charlemagne in attendance, the relics of St. Nazarius were ceremoniously transferred to the apse of the new church.

The small church on the site today dates from the twelfth century and any attempt to reconstruct the eighth-century church of St. Nazarius is fraught with difficulties. First of all, the nature of the site itself, a sandy hillock, meant that masonry foundations in the manner of Saint-Denis could not be used; instead, a platform of mortared rubble was laid to support the church, making the exact position of internal divisions impossible to ascertain. Secondly, although the Carolingian church has been the focus of numerous excavation campaigns, these investigations were all carried out in the nineteenth and early twentieth centuries, the most recent being those directed by Friedrich Behn in the 1920s and 1930s, using methods that were far from ideal by today's standards.[28] A new and systematic archaeological investigation of the site is sorely needed. In the meantime, one is left with incomplete reports, a few murky photographs, and a handful of drawings that are all subject to varying interpretations. Yet, in spite of these problems, the basic outline of the church seems evident.

It consisted of a basilica approximately 35 m long and 21 m wide (fig. 96). According to Behn's reconstruction, the nave was broad (ca. 11 m) and flanked by single, narrow aisles, but these dimensions are far from certain. A funerary chapel that was added in the late ninth century apparently obliterated all traces of the eastern termination of the church, although Behn claims to have seen the outline of a shallow rectangular apse. There is no evidence of a transept. At the west end, however, massive foundations indicate a tripartite, multistoried facade composed of a central, block-like unit projecting some 5 m to the west and flanking stairtowers, presumably low like those adjoining the west facade at Saint-Denis. This portion of the church must have been very imposing, for in an account of the fire that destroyed the Carolingian church in 1090, it is referred to as a "fortress" (*castellum*).[29] Indeed, the west end of Lorsch may well have been an early form of westwork, a major feature of later Carolingian architecture that will be discussed in subsequent chapters. Unlike Saint-Denis, the design of the church of St. Nazarius seems to have had no direct references to Rome except for the fact that it was preceded by an atrium 25 m long; the west wall of the atrium was obliterated by another two-tower entranceway added sometime before 1090, most likely in the early eleventh century.

In front of this atrium, Behn found traces of a second courtyard, longer and broader and framed on the north and south by porticoes. The western terminations of these porticoes were never uncovered, but they presumably extended

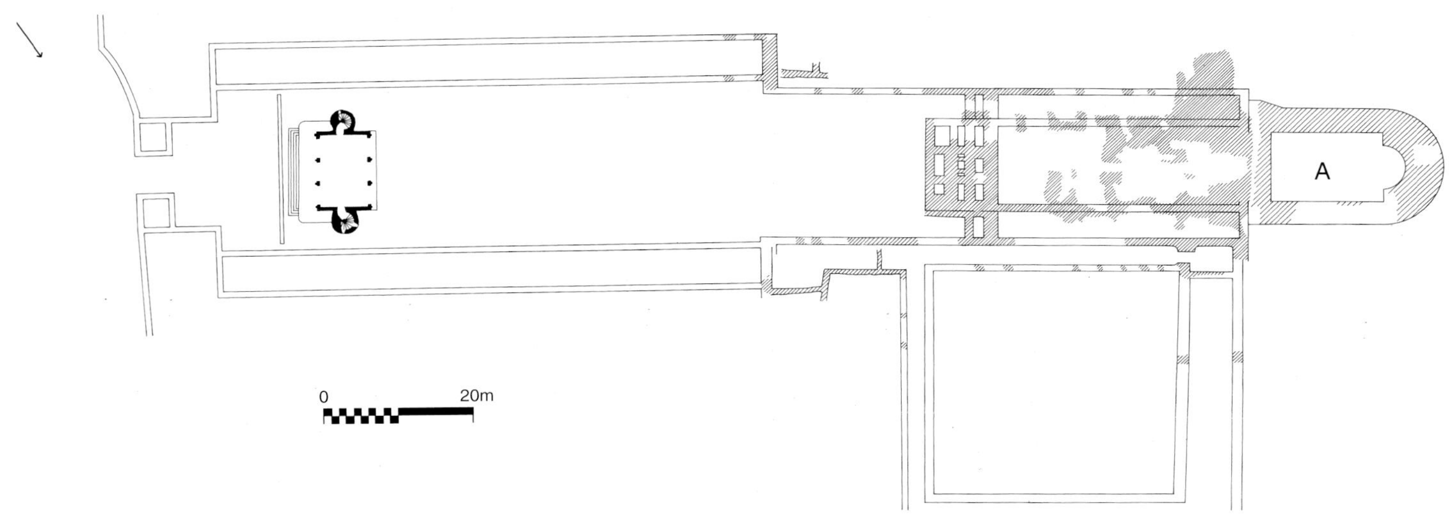

96 Lorsch, abbey church of St. Nazarius, plan, forecourt and cloister, ca. 800, structure "A" added ca. 876.

the full 75 m to the enclosure wall of the monastery. In what was originally the western end of this colonnaded courtyard stands the famous Lorsch *Torhalle* or gateway, one of the best-preserved and most striking monuments of the early Middle Ages (fig. 97).

The gateway forms a rectangular block (10.88 m long, 7.50 m deep, and 7.06 m high) divided into two storeys; the high-pitched roof was added in the eighteenth century. The ground floor consists of three arched openings of equal height supported by rectangular piers with engaged columns. The interior of the ground floor is undecorated and covered by a groin vault. The upper storey is made up of a rectangular hall illuminated by three windows piercing the broad east and west sides and painted on the inside with an illusionistic architectural order composed of a checkerboard dado, freestanding columns with ionic capitals, and a broad entablature (fig. 98). This upper storey was reached by spiral staircases enclosed within the stunted towers attached to the gateway's narrower north and south ends. The south stair tower is original. The one to the north was rebuilt in the nineteenth century, but its foundations bond with those of the gateway demonstrating that both stair towers should be considered integral parts of the original design.

The piers of the ground floor are articulated on the outside by engaged columns bearing composite capitals topped by a single, narrow palmette frieze carved in low relief (fig. 99). The second storey, in turn, is subdivided by a series of fluted pilasters with ionic capitals crowned by blind gabled arches. The elevation ends with a simple cornice of rough-hewn corbels. The most notable feature of the gateway is, of course, its colorful exterior decoration. All of the carved architectural details are of reddish sandstone, except for the capitals which are carved in a grayish-white limestone, and set against an inlay of complex geometric patterns. The spandrels of the arches, for example, are filled with rectangles and squares alternating red and white. A thin horizontal course of red sandstone is then set just above the apex of the three arches followed by a narrow band of inlaid squares set diagonally to form criss-cross diamond patterns. The entire upper storey is covered, in turn, by an array of hexagonal lozenges framed by triangles to form star patterns. In all, the east and west facades of the Lorsch gateway present a tour de force in color and line.

This colorful display has been likened to the use of precious stones in barbarian metalwork, but in truth the entire decorative vocabulary is Roman, or at least pseudo-Roman. The geometric patterns of the stone inlay, for example, have often been compared to the supposed imitation of ancient Roman *opus reticulatum* in the crypt at Jouarre (fig. 53). And indeed, at both Jouarre and Lorsch

97 Lorsch, abbey gateway, exterior, west side.

98 Lorsch, abbey gateway, painted decoration of interior upper wall.

the stones are pyramidal in section and embedded in a rubble masonry core, like *opus reticulatum*, but they are also much larger than any ancient examples of this type of masonry. Although the decorative stonework at Jouarre is an interesting precedent for Lorsch, it should be remembered, as noted in chapter three, that the stone patterning in each monument is very different as is their location: the wall at Poitiers is part of a subterranean crypt whereas at Lorsch the wall is visible above ground offering a vibrant public display. One source for Lorsch, therefore, would seem to be the decorative use of brick and stone in late Roman architecture, particularly in northern Europe, as seen in the so-called *Römerturm* in Cologne (fig. 100), dating from the third century,[30] and portions of the Constantinian Baths at Trier (fig. 101). Yet the use of hexagons and triangles to form star patterns (like those in the second storey) is, as far as I know, without precedent in ancient Roman decorative masonry. This pattern is found, instead, in late antique *opus sectile* floors (fig. 102). Thus, a motif derived from ancient Roman pavements seems to have been used at Lorsch for an exterior elevation, which further serves to underscore the originality of the gateway's design. In other words, ancient construction techniques and decorative motifs were combined, and thereby transformed, in order to serve a nonclassical aesthetic concerned primarily with surface pattern.

Similar remarks may be made about the carved decoration. On one level the capitals and frieze represent a remarkable attempt at copying ancient models in an almost antiquarian manner. This is particularly true of the composite capitals on the ground floor (fig. 103). The characteristic features of this capital type, the two tiers of acanthus leaves, the egg-and-dart molding, the foliated volutes, and the abacus are all correctly proportioned according to ancient precedent. And although the capitals are not carved in the round, they project significantly from the wall, producing a sense of weight and substance. On closer inspection, though, one would hardly confuse the medieval capitals with their ancient prototypes (fig. 104). The acanthus leaves, for instance, in comparison to ancient examples seem rigid and brittle. Nor do they emerge naturally from the base of the capital but appear, instead, to have been pasted on one at a time. Similarly, the egg-and-dart molding is little more than a shallow band of linear patterns; in fact, the dart motif is missing altogether. The frieze, too, is derived from ancient models but the leaf ornament is highly stylized with its low relief achieved through angled cuts, resembling the chip-carving technique used in metalwork.

The ionic capitals of the second storey are even more fanciful in their thoroughly unclassical, trapezoidal shape and in the use of two superimposed bands of an egg-and-dart-like molding below the volutes. Moreover, the capitals, like the pilasters, are completely flat, as if created by a cookie cutter instead of a hammer and chisel, with no sense of weight or volume (fig. 99). Likewise, the gabled arches above serve no structural function as they zigzag between the ionic capitals and the cornice following the triangular patterns of the stone inlay patterns behind them. They seem more appropriate to a building of wood than to one of stone and mortar. In all, the carved architectural members—the engaged columns, capitals, pilasters, and central frieze—form a mere appliqué that seems to float in front of the busy network of the geometric patterns of the stone enlay. To be sure, in comparison to the crude exterior decoration of the baptistery of Saint-Jean at Poitiers, a century earlier (fig. 48), the Lorsch gateway is remarkable in its studied classicism. And yet it should be stressed that this careful rendering of ancient forms serves only to create a decorative veneer without any structural logic. It is, nonetheless, a valiant attempt to incorporate elements of ancient architecture into a more decorative, medieval mode.

In spite of its renown, the function and date of the Lorsch gateway remain a topic of scholarly debate. Indeed, there is extensive literature on the subject. The various interpretations can, however, be categorized under four major headings: 1. a chapel dedicated to St. Michael; 2. a royal audience hall (*aula regia*); 3. a triumphal arch; 4. a copy of the gatehouse of St. Peter's in Rome.[31]

The first and oldest of these interpretations assumes that the dedication of the upper chamber to St. Michael in the fourteenth century with its accompanying late Gothic fresco decoration derives from an older tradition. The comparison has been made to the late eighth-century monastery of Saint-Riquier which is known from

99 *(facing page)* Lorsch, abbey gateway, detail of exterior.

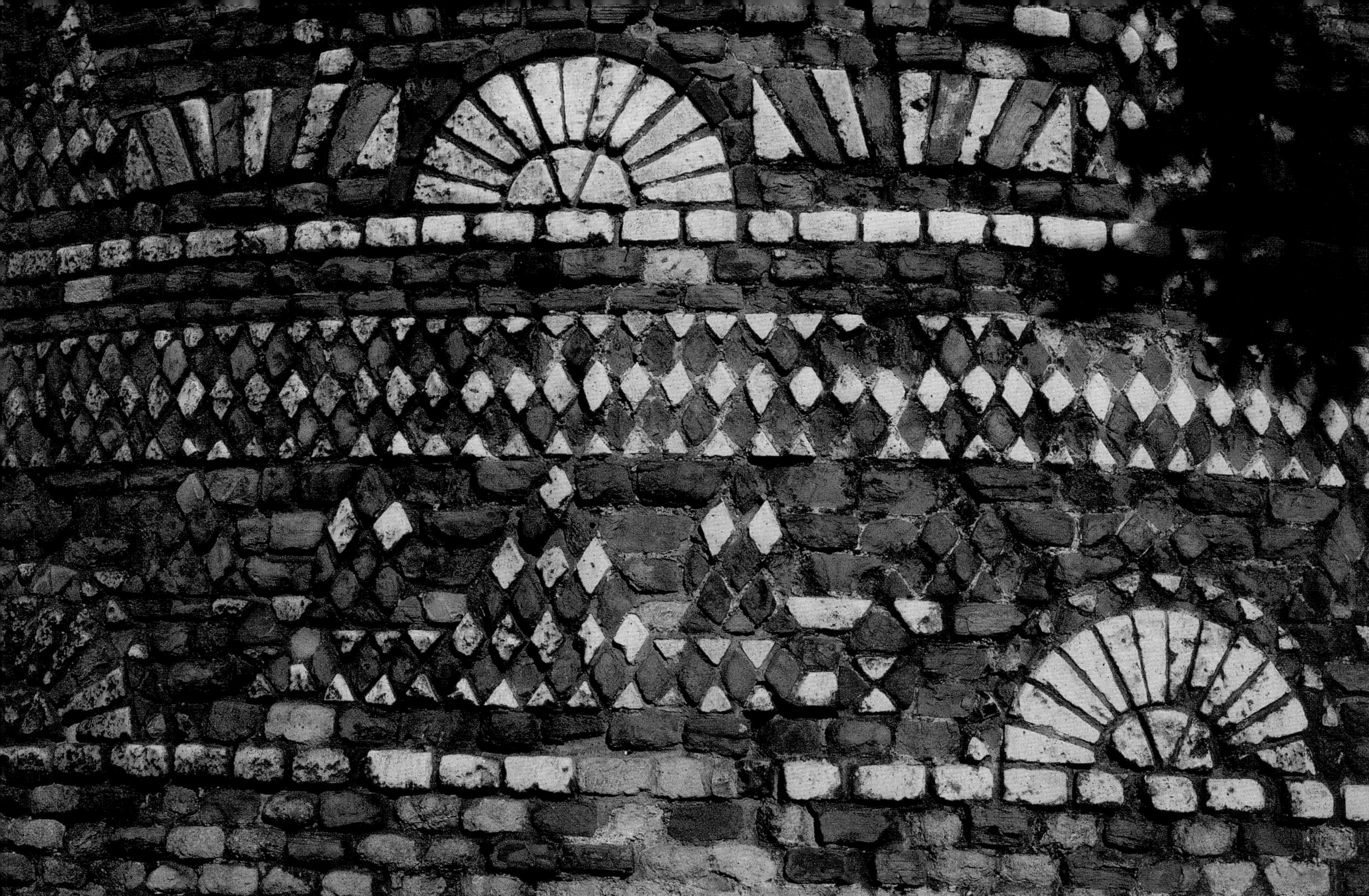

100 Cologne, detail of the "Römerturm," part of Roman fortification wall, third century.

contemporary documents to have had chapels dedicated to the archangels above three gateways leading to the atrium of the abbey church. The discovery by Behn in the late 1920s that the *Torhalle* was originally free-standing and that the upper chamber was originally decorated by a painted ionic order without any recognizable religious imagery seemed, however, to indicate the secular nature of the structure (fig. 98). Another prototype for the upper chamber was therefore sought in the Germanic tradition of the so-called *königshalle,* described in a variety of early medieval literary sources as normally being reached by a flight of one or more stairs, meaning it was on an upper storey, but there were no preserved examples of royal halls from this period to which to compare the Lorsch *Torhalle*. More recent archaeological studies of Carolingian palaces at Aachen and Paderborn, as discussed in the next chapter, demonstrate that formal reception halls were many times larger than the Lorsch *Torhalle,* that they were not set above archways, and that they were directly linked to a larger palace complex.

The third interpretation, that of a triumphal arch, has much to recommend it. Like a Roman triumphal arch, the Lorsch *Torhalle* is slightly raised on a platform and free-standing. Many, though not all, Roman triumphal arches have three archways decorated by applied orders and a small, vaulted chamber in the attic zone. It is possible to be even more precise. As Richard Krautheimer pointed out in a now classic article on the Carolingian revival of Early Christian architecture,[32] only two of the triumphal arches preserved from Roman antiquity in the West—and therefore accessible to Carolingian builders and patrons—have triple-arched openings, those of Septimius Severus and Constantine, both in Rome. Of these two, only the arch of the first Christian emperor, Constantine, would have had any particular significance for the early Middle Ages (fig. 105). Indeed, the term *arcu(s) triumph(is)* appears only in the inscription of the Arch of Constantine, where victory is attributed to *instinctu divinitatis,* an admittedly ambiguous phrase implying an impersonal deity, but one easily open to interpretation as referring to the divine intervention of the

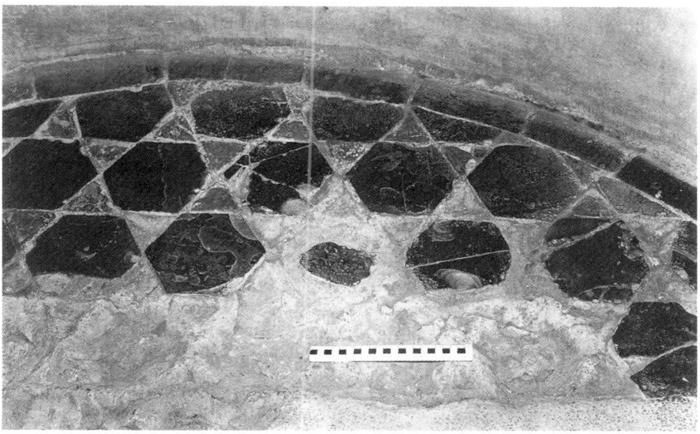

102 Riva San Vitale, baptistery, interior, detail of *opus sectile* floor, early fifth century.

101 Trier, detail of Constantinian Baths, early fourth century.

Christian God. Moreover, Charlemagne was often called by contemporaries the "new Constantine," *novus Constantinus*.[33]

Of the first three theories, then, clearly the third, that of the triumphal arch, seems to be the most satisfactory. And yet a basic problem still remains: If the *Torhalle* is meant to be a "copy" of the Arch of Constantine, why does it not look more like it? The lack of figural sculpture can be explained by the absence of such a tradition on a monumental scale anywhere in Europe at the time. But why are all of the arches the same height and width? Why, too, unlike ancient precedent, is the upper storey almost as high as the ground floor? And why is the upper chamber timber-roofed, unlike the vaulted attic chambers of triumphal arches? It could be argued, of course, that medieval copies invariably differed significantly from their models and that only one or two elements were necessary to make the reference to the prototype apparent to an observer in the early Middle Ages.[34] Even so, one still cannot help but wonder if there was not some intermediary between the Arch of Constantine and the Lorsch gateway that would explain these discrepancies. Here, the fourth and last interpretation, i.e., a copy of the gatehouse of St. Peter's basilica in Rome, becomes especially intriguing.

The gatehouse of St. Peter's stood at the top of a long flight of stairs as the primary entrance to the atrium of the basilica until it was demolished in the early seventeenth century to make way for the facade of the present church.[35] It is, however, recorded in several Renaissance drawings, such as a view of the Vatican complex around 1533 by Martin van Heemskerck (fig. 106), and it is mentioned in a number of written sources. The gatehouse formed a tall rectangular block pierced by three arched openings in the ground floor, the outlines of which are clearly visible in the Heemskerck drawings; the rectilinear doorways and their moldings were added by Pope Nicholas

103 Lorsch, abbey gateway, detail of west side.

104 Rome, Arch of Septimius Severus, detail, early third century.

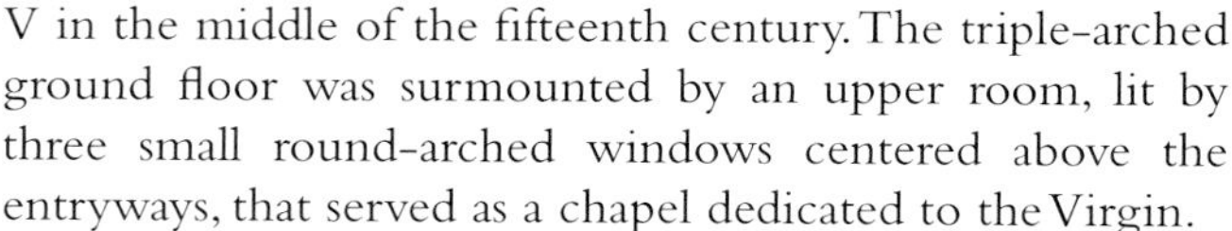

V in the middle of the fifteenth century. The triple-arched ground floor was surmounted by an upper room, lit by three small round-arched windows centered above the entryways, that served as a chapel dedicated to the Virgin.

By the early sixteenth century, when Heemskerck made his drawing, the gatehouse was framed by several other multistoried buildings, including the monumental benediction loggia of the fifteenth and early sixteenth centuries to the right (or north), but this may not have always been the case. One can, for example, make out in Heemskerck's drawing a vertical break between the gatehouse and the adjoining building of the same height to the left (or south). Its original relationship to the porticoes of the atrium is difficult to ascertain, but in Alfarano's famous plan of 1590, which we have seen before, it is apparent that the gatehouse was not integrated with the eastern range of the atrium colonnades and, if the flanking structures are removed, seems to have projected significantly from it (fig. 107). In other words, although it was not freestanding, the gatehouse may have originally stood in relative isolation with only the back or western side connected to the atrium. Certainly, the gatehouse must have risen high above the surrounding structures in the early Middle Ages, for by the middle of the eighth century, when it is first specifically mentioned in any documents, it is referred to as the "tower of the Virgin Mary at the stairway" (*turris sanctae Mariae ad Grada*).[36]

We also know that by the eighth century, if not earlier, the interior of the triple-arched ground floor was vaulted and the chapel of the Virgin above was timber-roofed. It is also likely, although it is not proven, that the exterior of the ground floor of the entryway was articulated by applied columns, presumably *spolia* as elsewhere in the basilica. It is certain, however, that the exterior east wall of the upper storey was decorated with a figural mosaic during the reign of Pope Paul I (757–67), portions of which may still be seen in the Heemskerck drawing (fig. 107).[37] In other words, the gatehouse received this glittering surface decoration shortly

105 Rome, Arch of Constantine, A.D. 315.

before the visit of Charlemagne in 774 and it is here, it should be remembered, that Pope Hadrian I officially received the Frankish king. Thereafter, the designation of the gatehouse as the official site for the reception of royalty by the pope is attested time again from the eighth through the twelfth centuries.[38]

The date of the construction of the gatehouse of St. Peter's is not known; the middle of the eighth century, when it is first mentioned in connection with the facade mosaic, may be taken only as a *terminus ante quem*. Still, the fact that the gatehouse stood on the central axis of the basilica and at the eastern end of the massive platform built to support the entire Vatican complex, suggests that it belonged to the original Constantinian project of the early fourth century. Indeed, similar tripartite entranceways to atria seem to have existed at the early-fourth-century cathedral of Trier, also built by Constantine, and at St. Paul's-outside-the-Walls in Rome, which, as we have seen, was built under the Emperor Theodosius at the end of the fourth century in direct imitation of St. Peter's. The gateways of these churches, all built under imperial patronage, find an important precedent in the monumental entranceway to the forum of Trajan in Rome which took the form of a triumphal arch, albeit with only one arched opening following the design that was prevalent in the early second century.[39] In like manner, the gatehouse at St. Peter's may have been built in imitation of Constantine's tripartite triumphal arch in the heart of Rome. In this way, as was the case with Trajan's forum, the entrance would have proclaimed the emperor's association with the entire building complex.

There is, admittedly, no evidence to suggest that the gateway at St. Peter's was ever interpreted specifically as a triumphal arch in the early Middle Ages—the terms most commonly used to describe it were simply "tower" (*turris*) or "gateway" (*fores*)—but it should not be forgotten that the Petrine complex as a whole, including the gateway, was associated in the Middle Ages with Constantine. Thus, it

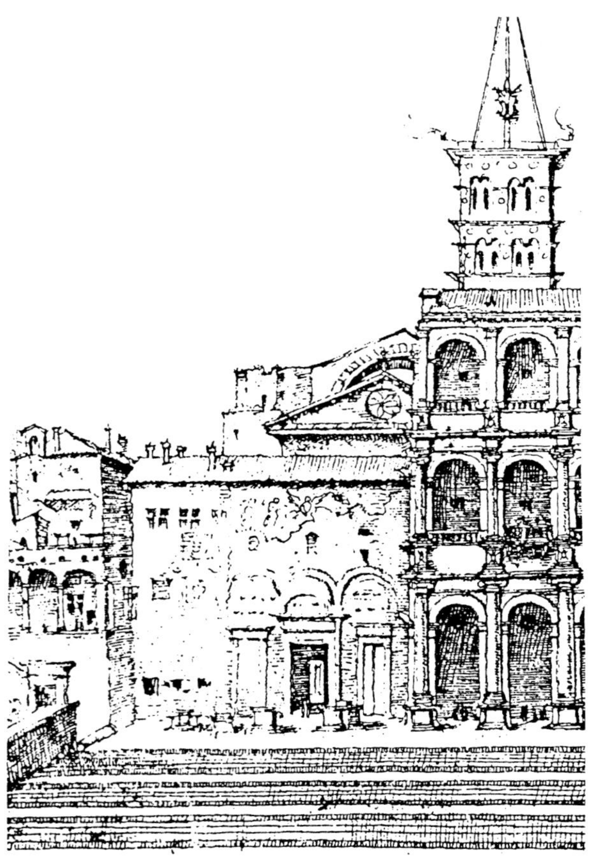

may well be that at St. Peter's the concept of a church gateway and triumphal arch were consciously combined. Indeed, it would seem that all the basic elements of the first three interpretations of the Lorsch *Torhalle*—as a chapel, as a royal audience hall, and as a triumphal arch—were already embodied in the gatehouse of St. Peter's, making it a particularly fitting model for a ceremonial entranceway to the royal abbey of the "new Constantine." There are, however, problems with this suggestion. The fundamental difference remains that the gatehouse was never freestanding like the *Torhalle*. Moreover, the *Liber Pontificalis* indicates that already in 772, Pope Hadrian I had installed bronze doors, brought from Perugia, in the gateway, which would have presumably required the remodeling and partial blocking of at least one, if not more, of the archways.[40] Thus, if the gateway played a role in the formulation of the Lorsch *Torhalle*, which I still think is likely, it must have been a secondary one to that of a triumphal arch.

106 Rome, Old St. Peter's, view of atrium facade, gatehouse in center, detail of drawing by Martin van Heemskerck, ca. 1533.

107 Rome, Old St. Peter's, atrium plan: detail of Alfarano's plan (left); hypothetical reconstruction of atrium and gatehouse plan in the eighth century (right).

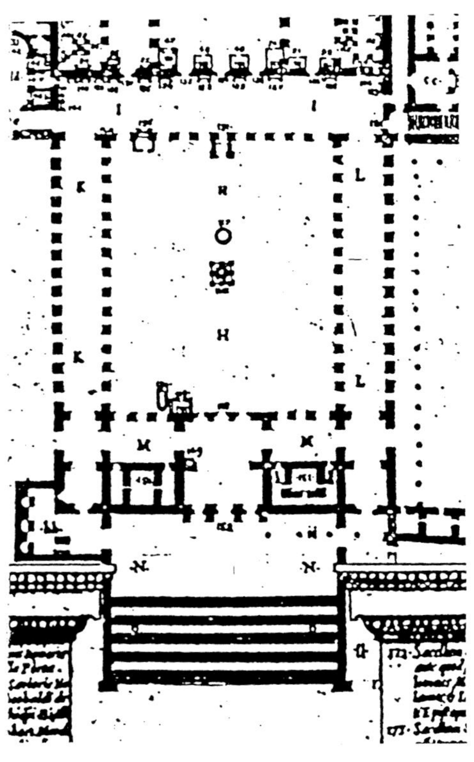

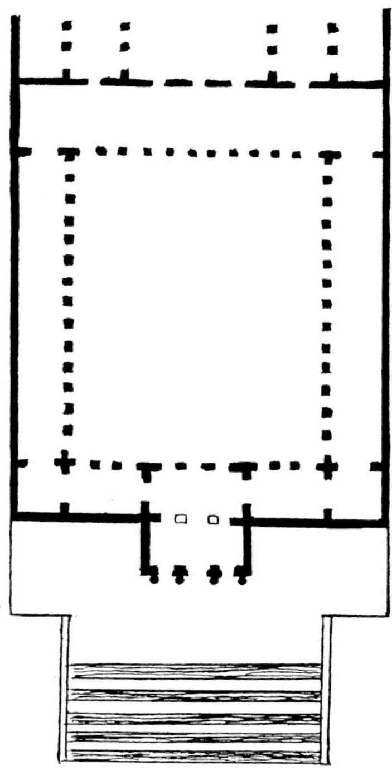

The precise date of the Lorsch *Torhalle* is also debated. Josef Fleckenstein, for example, has suggested that, as a triumphal arch, the *Torhalle* could only have been built after the year 800, when Charlemagne assumed the title of emperor of the Romans.[41] Yet, it should be emphasized that the tradition of building triumphal arches had been dead in the West for centuries and it remains to be seen whether such monuments were so strictly categorized in the early Middle Ages. Already by A.D. 500, strict protocol had broken down to such an extent that the Ostrogothic king of Italy, Theodoric, was received in Rome with imperial honors, including being allowed to address the senate and to enter the palace on the Palatine "triumphantly with the people," where he then resided during his visit.[42] One senator at the time went so far as to style Theodoric as "Augustus," even though there was no constitutional basis for such a claim.[43] More to the point, Charlemagne himself was referred to as the *novus Constantinus* by Pope Hadrian I as early as 778 and this epithet was used with increasing frequency in reference to the Frankish king as the eighth century drew to a close.[44] Thus, the events of 800 need not have played a role in the construction of the *Torhalle*.

Werner Jacobsen, on the other hand, has proposed a much later date, around 880.[45] According to him, the *Torhalle* was built in conjunction with the burial chapel, now lost, of Louis the German (d. 876) and his son, Louis the Younger (d. 782), attached to the east end of the abbey church. In this instance, too, it would have served as a commemorative monument, derived from the Roman triumphal arch, to mark the entrance to the dynastic burial place of the eastern Franks. In support of his late-ninth-century date for the gateway, Jacobsen asserts that the classicizing composite capitals could only have been produced in the early ninth century. He suggests that they must have been reused for the gateway from an unknown earlier monument on the site; whereas the ionic pilaster capitals of the second storey are, in his view, original and comparable to those of miniature ionic pilasters that decorate the sides of a sarcophagus found in the royal burial chapel. Ruth Meyer, in turn, has rejected Jacobsen's thesis and reaffirmed the traditional dating of around 774 in a recent monumental study of Carolingian architectural sculpture.[46] She points out that the ionic capitals on the gateway and the sarcophagus are only generically similar and that they differ in important details, such as a distinctive double egg-and-dart-like molding on the *Torhalle* versions. She acknowledges that four of the composite capitals on the gateway are precocious in their classicism and distinct from the Corinthian pilaster capitals of the abbey church, built between 767 and 774 (figs. 103 and 108), but she notes that other composite capitals of the same group, together with the palmette molding immediately above, do in fact resemble the extremely shallow relief and curvilinear leaf patterns found in the church, which also find a close comparison in the aforementioned contemporary column base from Saint-Denis (fig. 94). She therefore sees the decoration of the gateway as an amalgam of stylistic traits combining more traditional elements with new classicizing tendencies.

By the late eighth century, as is discussed in the next chapter, carvers at Charlemagne's chapel at Aachen not only imitated the form and decoration of an ancient Corinthian capital, but they seem to have revived the late Roman technique of the running drill in order to make deep grooves and sharply undercut serrated edges in the acanthus leaves (figs. 104 and 109). In fact, the imitation of antique models was so successful at Aachen that it is sometimes difficult to distinguish the medieval copies from the Roman *spolia*.[47] The Lorsch capitals are less successful in this regard and lack the vivacious naturalism of the Aachen examples; they seem dry and brittle in comparison. I do not wish to suggest that Carolingian architectural sculpture followed a strict evolutionary development, but, for these and other reasons, a date for the Lorsch *Torhalle* in the last quarter of the eighth century, sometime between the completion of the abbey church and the work at Aachen, seems the most likely.

In my view, the events of 774 were decisive from both a formal and an iconographic point of view. September 1, 774, marked Charlemagne's first and only visit to Lorsch. Early in the same year, Charlemagne had been received at St. Peter's as *patricius Romanorum* and crowned in Pavia as *rex Langobardorum*, whereupon he returned to the north from Italy "in great triumph" (*cum magno triumphis*).[48] Moreover, Charlemagne's successes in Italy presumably held special significance for the monastic community of Lorsch not only because Lorsch was a royal abbey but also because St. Nazarius, whose relics rested in the abbey church, was closely associated both with Rome and with Milan in the heart of Lombardy. And yet, the Lorsch *Torhalle* must have been built as a commemorative monument. The three-month period between Charlemagne's coronation as king of the Lombards and his visit to the abbey seems too short a time for such a complex structure as the Lorsch gateway to have been completed. Even more important, Charlemagne's visit to Lorsch does not seem to have been planned in advance. Indeed, a brief, but contemporary, account in the Lorsch Chronicle states that Charlemagne was invited to attend the consecration of the abbey church by the abbot of Lorsch only after the king had stopped upon his return from Italy at nearby Speyer.[49] One is left with the distinct impression that Charlemagne's appearance at Lorsch was a last-minute arrangement. If so,

108 Lorsch, pilaster capital from abbey church, dedicated 774 (Lapidarium Lorsch).

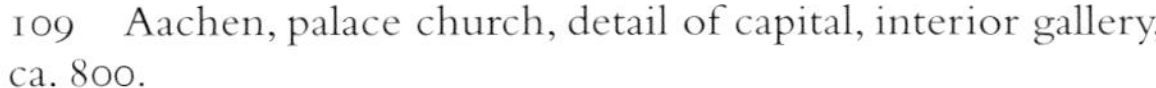

109 Aachen, palace church, detail of capital, interior gallery, ca. 800.

the *Torhalle* must have been erected after 774. A more appropriate occasion, it seems to me, would have been a major anniversary of the dedication of the abbey church.

In February, 784, a new abbot was named to Lorsch, Richbod, who had been a student of Alcuin at the royal court at Aachen and was noted as a scholar of classical authors.[50] Furthermore, as abbot, he is known to have been an important patron of building at Lorsch. While no specific mention is made of the *Torhalle*, the Lorsch Chronicle does credit Richbod with having rebuilt the abbey's wooden cloister in stone, of which only the foundations have been found, as well as installing a marble pavement, now lost, about the high altar of the church, which is one of the first examples of the revival of this late antique tradition during the Carolingian period.[51] Could not the present *Torhalle*, too, have been built to replace a gateway of wood that had been hastily constructed for the king's visit in 774? And could not its decoration be derived in part from the new *opus sectile* floor? This is only a hypothesis, but it is worth noting that September 1, 784, six months after Richbod's election as abbot, marked the tenth anniversary of Charlemagne's visit to Lorsch and the dedication of the abbey church. In 794, on the other hand, the twentieth anniversary of the event, Richbod was both abbot of Lorsch and, since 791, archbishop of Trier, a city with strong Constantinian associations. In fact, Trier cathedral itself, as already mentioned, was constructed under Constantine's patronage. I would therefore suggest that the Lorsch *Torhalle* was built around either 784 or 794.

In either case, the gateway would represent a transitional monument between the earlier and later phases of Charlemagne's reign and the corresponding increase in the specificity of reference to ancient models. If one were to look for a parallel in the development of Carolingian book illumination, it could be found in the famous evangelistary produced by the scribe Godescalc between 781 and 783,

110 Godescalc Evangelistary, Christ, 781–83 (Paris, Bibliothèque Nationale, Nouv.Acq.Lat.1203, fol. 3r).

for here one finds full-page portraits of Christ and the four evangelists that achieve a similar synthesis of three-dimensional classical forms, based on late antique and more recent Italian models, and two-dimensional surface decoration, reflecting a native taste for ornament and pattern (fig. 110). This valiant attempt on the part of a Frankish artist to incorporate the lessons of Mediterranean art has been called a "daring experiment."[52] The same may be said of the Lorsch *Torhalle*.

In its evocation of the gateway of St. Peter's in Rome and of the Arch of Constantine, the *Torhalle* seems to have been erected as a monument to Charlemagne's victory in Italy and his patronage of this royal abbey. Thus, like the abbey church of Saint-Denis, the Lorsch gateway symbolized the new alliance between the Franks and Rome. Equally important, its studied classicizing details and overall decorative exuberance place it on the threshold of the Carolingian Renaissance.

CHAPTER 6

Aachen and Rome: The Poles of an Empire

Late in November 800, Charlemagne visited Rome for the fourth, and what would prove to be the last, time. He came at the behest of Pope Leo III to restore order. More than a year earlier, the pope had been assaulted in the street by a small band of disgruntled nobles and forced to flee the city, whereupon he traveled north of the Alps to seek the aid of Rome's protector, the Frankish king. Leo was honorably received by Charlemagne and subsequently accompanied back to Rome by a strong Frankish escort. Now, as he had promised, Charlemagne, in his role as patrician of the Romans, appeared to preside over an assembly of church leaders to decide the fate of the rebels. On December 23, Leo was declared innocent of any wrongdoing and his attackers were condemned to exile.

Two days later, on Christmas Day, Charlemagne attended mass at the basilica of St. Peter. As the king rose from prayer before the confessio of the apostle's tomb, Pope Leo III placed a crown on Charlemagne's head and, together with the assembled congregation, acclaimed him, "Charles, most pious Augustus, crowned by God, great and peace-loving emperor, life and victory!"[1] In this manner, Charlemagne, already the king of the Franks and of the Lombards, became the Emperor of the Romans. Scholars have long debated the motivating forces which led up to this event and opinions differ as to whether Charlemagne was surprised by the pope's actions, but whatever the exact circumstances, the imperial coronation of Charlemagne transformed, or at least redefined, the political landscape of Europe. What had previously been two separate kingdoms under one ruler was now united under the guise of a single empire with its political power centered in the north and its source of legitimacy, as defined by the Donation of Constantine, in Rome. This dichotomy of rule was reflected, moreover, in the ambitious architectural projects undertaken just before and after the year 800 by Charlemagne in his new capital at Aachen (in French, Aix-la-Chapelle) and by the pope in Rome.

In order to appreciate the significance of Charlemagne's building activities at Aachen, it should first be noted that the Frankish monarchy was by nature an itinerant institution. That is to say, the king traveled constantly throughout his realm from one royal estate to another. He would stay at each for weeks or months at a time, declaring law, dispensing justice, and awarding favors. In other words, wherever the king resided, however temporarily, there was the center of government.

Charlemagne continued the practice of his predecessors and maintained a vast network of palaces concentrated along the Meuse, Mosel, and central Rhine river valleys. Indeed, he is recorded as having sponsored the rebuilding or new construction of no less than sixty-five royal villas during his forty-six-year reign as compared to only twenty-nine for all the previous Frankish kings combined.[2] As the setting for assemblies, religious ceremonies, preparations for military campaigns, and the pleasures of the hunt and feasting such establishments were composed of reception and dining halls, living quarters, guest facilities, a church or chapel and lodgings for the clergy, quarters for soldiers, stables, a treasury, and other rooms devoted solely to recordkeeping and other administrative purposes, not to mention housing and working areas for numerous servants. In short, the Carolingian palace was a fundamental and virtually self-sufficient instrument of rule. Unfortunately, little is known about the physical layout of most of Charlemagne's palaces; however, detailed excavations at two sites—Paderborn and Ingelheim—have provided a unique insight into the variety and complexity of Carolingian architecture in this secular sphere during the time leading up to the work at Aachen.[3]

Paderborn, located 90 miles northeast of Cologne, was one of Charlemagne's northernmost residences and as such it served as an important staging area for the protracted wars against the Saxons and their enforced conversion to Christianity during the last three decades of the eighth

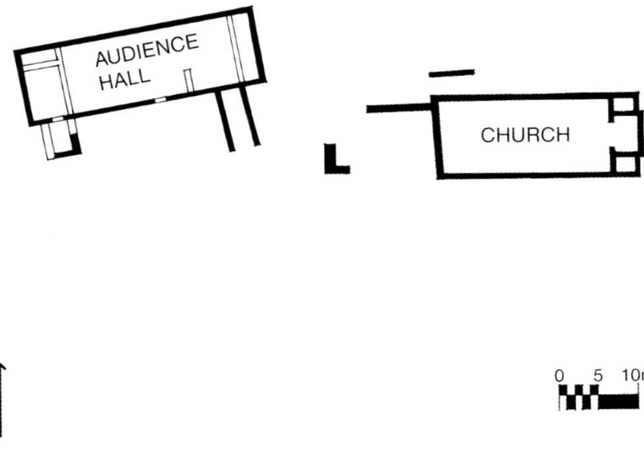

111 Paderborn, royal palace, plan.

century.[4] Construction of the palace complex must have been well under way by 777 when Charlemagne is recorded as having presided over an assembly of nobles, a synod of church leaders, and the consecration of a church on the site. Another major council was held at Paderborn in 785, and it was there that Pope Leo III sought the king's help in 799.

The core of the complex was revealed through excavations in the 1960s (fig. 111).[5] Built atop the charred remains of a Saxon settlement, the Carolingian palace was centered about a rectangular audience hall measuring 10.30 m wide by 30.90 m long and preceded by a large, irregular courtyard. An aisleless church stood a short distance to the east, while to the northeast were found the foundations of several smaller buildings of undetermined function. Two distinct layers of burning indicate that the palace was twice destroyed by Saxon rebels, probably in 778 and 794, but in each instance the main structures were rebuilt on the earlier foundations with only minor changes. During the first rebuilding, for example, the open courtyard was flanked by narrow corridors running north–south, while perimeter walls of either a modest atrium or perhaps a timber-roofed western extension of some kind were added to the front of the church. During the second rebuilding, a new and much larger church was laid out, traces of which have been found below the present cathedral, and along the east wall of the central courtyard a low masonry podium preceded by six steps was set up and covered by a wooden canopy, as indicated by surrounding postholes, in an arrangement which has been interpreted as the platform for an outdoor throne.

What is most striking about the Paderborn complex, however, is its apparent fusion of Germanic and Roman building traits. The design of the audience hall, with its long and narrow proportions, aisleless interior, and lateral entrance, belongs to the centuries-old tradition of the Germanic long hall, which was still very much alive in the region in the eighth century as witness the remains of a Saxon village uncovered at nearby Warendorf.[6] And yet the audience hall's construction in mortared rubble, instead of wood, plastered on the interior and painted, at least in its last phase, with Latin inscriptions and a delicate rinceaux frieze, and its position within a courtyard, instead of being freestanding, resemble the arrangement of innumerable rustic villas that once studded the upper Rhine Valley in late Roman times.[7] It is tempting to see this formal dichotomy as a conscious expression of Charlemagne's dual role in his Saxon mission as Germanic chieftain and Christian ruler, as conqueror of the heathens and patrician of the Romans. Nevertheless, whether compared to Germanic or Roman models, the buildings at Paderborn were in this early phase relatively modest in scale and unpretentious in form. Even the early-ninth-century extension of the west wall of the audience hall in order to add a small apse, perhaps to provide a new setting for the throne, seems awkward and out of place.

The palace of Ingelheim, situated on the banks of the Rhine River just outside of Mainz, involved by contrast a far more ambitious scheme.[8] Construction was begun at least ten years after that at Paderborn, for it is first mentioned as a palace in 787 and work probably continued until 807, the year of Charlemagne's last lengthy stay. It was also a favored residence of his son and successor, Louis the Pious (d. 840), and portions of the palace may have been constructed during his reign as well. In any event, the most striking feature at Ingelheim in comparison to Paderborn was the east wall of the complex that formed a great semicircle, measuring 45 m in diameter (fig. 112). Lined with a colonnade on the inside, this curved walkway ultimately derived from the U-shaped porticoes that commonly

112 Ingelheim, royal palace, axonometric reconstruction.

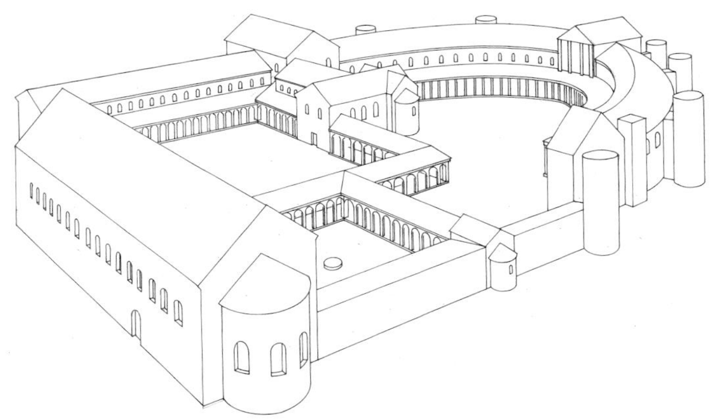

113 Montmaurin, ancient Roman villa, model.

formed part of ancient villas throughout the western Roman Empire, best known from excavations of such luxurious late antique estates as Piazza Armerina in Sicily, Montmaurin in southwestern Gaul, and Teting in the Mosel Valley not far from Trier (fig. 113).[9] Indeed, the similarity is so striking that when Ingelheim was first investigated at the beginning of the twentieth century, it was assumed that the Carolingian palace occupied the remains of an ancient Roman villa, but more recent excavations have found only traces of an earlier Frankish farmhouse of modest dimensions. The layout of Ingelheim, in fact, is not a simple copy of a late antique model but rather an adaptation designed to meet the needs of a Carolingian palace. In late antiquity, for example, the curved walkways of Roman villas were usually open to the outside in order to serve as the primary reception area, funneling visitors toward a main entrance or vestibule as at Montmaurin or linking a series of separate rooms or building axes as at Piazza Armerina and Teting. At Ingelheim the arrangement was reversed. The curved portico was still used to link various parts of the villa (in this case the northern and southern ranges), but it faced inward and was entered from the outside only by a single gateway at its apex. The Carolingian villa was therefore a far more closed scheme and fortified, at least along its eastern perimeter, by a series of cylindrical towers placed at 25 m intervals, which gave the entrance the impression of a walled city. It should be remembered that late antique fortification walls with similar cylindrical towers still stood surrounding nearby urban settlements along the Rhine, such as Mainz and Cologne, and were at the time among the most prominent vestiges of the Roman past.[10]

Indeed, the closest comparison to the curved entryway at Ingelheim seems to be an exedra of similar dimensions that formed one side of the ancient Roman forum in Cologne. As recently excavated and reconstructed, it was composed of a semicircular corridor with columns along the inside and projecting rectilinear towers, as opposed to cylindrical ones, on the exterior. Moreover, the forum in Cologne seems to have been at least partially standing in the eighth century and may have been referred to as the "Forum Iulii" in contemporary sources. Thus, a major imperial monument of the region seems to have been used as a direct model.[11] Another model may have come from the city of Rome itself, for the Baths of Constantine seem to have been entered via a gateway at the apex of a grand semicircular precinct wall (100 m in diameter), if one can trust drawings made in the sixteenth century when the complex was still standing.[12] This comparison is all the more intriguing because imperial baths were often referred to as palaces in early medieval guide books to the city.[13] Ancient literary sources may also have played an important role in the design of Ingelheim; Roman villas with curved porticoes, for instance, are described in the letters of Pliny the Younger from the first century A.D. and the poems of Sidonius Apollinaris five hundred years later; both works were found in manuscripts known to have been in monastic libraries during the Carolingian period.[14] Whatever the source, the formal language at Ingelheim was clearly Roman. It therefore comes as no surprise to find a ninth-century source boast that marble columns were brought from Rome and Ravenna for use at Ingelheim.[15]

The audience hall at Ingelheim was equally impressive and considerably larger (14.50 × 38.20 m) than that at Paderborn. Terminated by a semicircular apse (9.80 m in diameter) framing the raised platform for the king's throne, the model here was clearly not the Germanic long hall but late antique audience halls such as the ones at Piazza Armerina and Constantine's basilica at Trier. Opposite the apse, the audience hall, or aula, was preceded by a forecourt and a triple entrance, perhaps arched, although this remains conjectural. Full details of the elevation are not known, but a poem by Ermoldus Nigellus, composed around 826, describes the lavish wall paintings that once decorated the interior, representing the deeds of famous rulers from the mythical past to the present, including Romulus and Remus, Alexander the Great, Hannibal, various Roman emperors including Constantine and Theodosius, and culminating in the apse with the victorious leaders of the Franks: Charles Martel, Pippin, and finally Charlemagne, as the conqueror of the Saxons.[16] In this way the architectural setting and the fresco decoration combined to present the Carolingian view of the direct link of Frankish kingship with that of antiquity.

The apparent hybrid nature of the complex at Paderborn as compared to the overt Roman pretensions of the palace at Ingelheim was no doubt related to its different

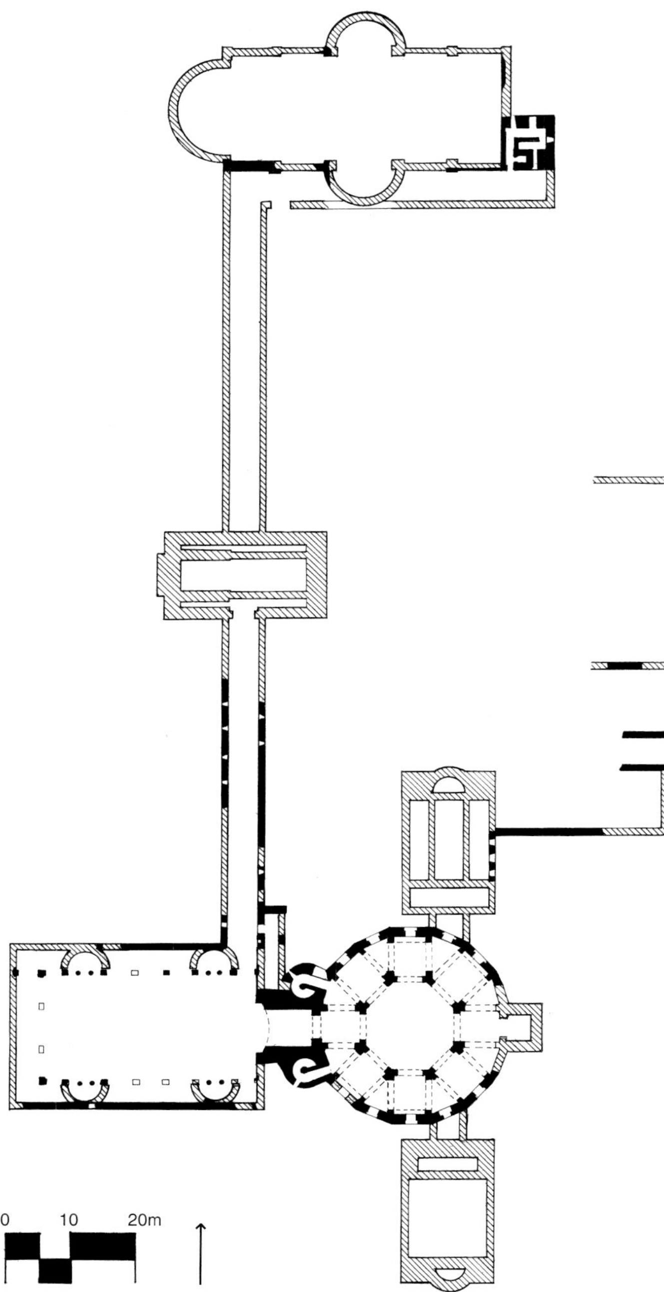

114 Aachen, palace complex, plan.

function. Paderborn was a strategic base for ongoing military campaigns along the eastern frontier far from the more Romanized areas of the Rhineland, whereas Ingelheim served primarily as a summer palace in the heartland of the Frankish kingdom near the ancient Roman city of Mainz. But the ten or more years separating the initial construction of the two palaces are also significant, it seems to me. By the end of the eighth century Charlemagne and his builders must have felt a growing desire to emulate ancient models of the most lavish kind in order to provide an appropriate setting for the dominant ruler of western Europe, one who was seen by those around him as the heir to the Roman emperors. The dramatic change in palace architecture between Paderborn and Ingelheim provides the background for the work at Aachen where similar concerns for architecture and politics were expressed on an even more grandiose scale. Most important, however, Aachen was built to serve not as a temporary residence but as a more permanent capital.[17]

The reasons for Charlemagne's selection of the site seem obvious enough. Aachen had originated as a modest Roman settlement at the juncture of several important roads linking northern Gaul and the Rhineland, and its central position within the Frankish realm offered distinct strategic advantages. Moreover, it was the natural source of numerous hot sulphur springs (hence the Latin name Aquae or Aquis), and partial remains of no less than three Roman bath complexes, built between the first and the third centuries A.D., have been uncovered in the center of the city. Although Roman Aquis suffered destruction at the end of the fourth century when the eastern frontier of the Roman Empire collapsed in the wake of Germanic invasions, the salutary properties of the waters encouraged continued habitation, albeit on a reduced scale. It was the thermal springs above all else that attracted Charlemagne to the site, because it was there, according to his biographer Einhard, that the king "loved to exercise himself in the water whenever he could."[18] He found such activity therapeutic, especially as he grew older, and a welcome diversion during the region's long winters. Already in 765, Pippin III, Charlemagne's father, had chosen to winter at a villa in Aachen, and Charlemagne followed suit, spending Christmas there four years later and again in 787. By 794, construction of the new palace was sufficiently advanced to allow Charlemagne to use it regularly. Indeed, with only rare exceptions, he spent all or part of each winter in Aachen until his death in 814.[19]

Thanks to archaeological investigations carried out intermittently over the past hundred years the basic layout of the core of the palace complex is well known (fig. 114).[20] A centrally planned royal chapel, still extant, was flanked at the east end by two basilican structures and approached from the west through a monumental atrium. Some 125 m to the north stood an audience hall, its foundations still embedded within the present town hall, set on a parallel axis to that of the church but with its main apse in the west rather than the east. The aula and atrium of the church were in turn connected by a narrow two-storeyed walkway, portions of which were still visible as recently as 1898, that was intersected midway by a massive rectangular gatehouse. Around this ceremonial core of stone and mortar stood the more strictly utilitarian structures of the king's private living quarters, accommodations for courtiers, clergy, and servants, as well as other subsidiary buildings (workrooms, stables, and the like), presumably all built of wood, for no trace of them remains.

In antiquity, like most Roman towns, Aachen had been laid out in four sections created by the perpendicular intersection of two main thoroughfares as is still evident in the street patterns in the heart of the modern city. The alignment of the Carolingian palace, however, was shifted approximately 40 degrees in order to place the royal chapel on a strict east–west axis. Yet in spite of this deviation from the earlier Roman scheme, the Carolingian layout was equally rigid in its emphasis on interlocking perpendicular axes. Indeed, Leo Hugot has gone so far as to propose that the entire plan was centered about a square with sides of 360 Carolingian feet (in this case, the Carolingian or Drusian foot equals 33.3 cm) subdivided into sixteen squares of 84 feet per side.[21] The basic unit of measure according to this system would have been a 7-foot rod. Much has been written about the possible symbolic meaning of these dimensions, especially their Christological associations as multiples of three, seven, and twelve, and there can be no doubt that the complex was carefully conceived. However, as will be discussed below, the same system of measurement was not used throughout. Far more important, it seems to me, are the designs of the individual buildings, their sources and functions, and the composite meaning they were meant to convey in the context of Charlemagne's political position in Europe.

The best-preserved portion of the palace is the royal chapel, which, although partially obscured by later additions, still dominates the city today. It is a complex double-shell construction, composed of a domed octagonal core with an enveloping aisle and upper gallery and enclosed within a sixteen-sided outer wall. The east end was marked by a projecting square apse (later replaced by an elegant gothic choir but its foundations are known from excavations) while to the west still stands a multistoreyed entranceway. The exterior massing of the building is simple yet bold (fig. 115). The broad, flat planes of the polygonal exterior are pierced by tiers of individual round-arched windows, corresponding to the levels of the aisle, gallery, and clerestory. A cornice with brackets caps the outermost wall, while the octagonal drum of the dome is articulated at the corners by paired pilasters with Corinthian capitals, now badly eroded. The only other ornament, according to contemporary literary sources and later medieval representations, was a golden orb perched atop the dome and others at the angles of its drum.

The central octagonal space dominates the interior, defined as it is by eight massive piers that rise to form superimposed arches, squat at the ground level and attenuated above (fig. 116). The horizontal stratification of the elevation is stressed by a heavy cornice immediately above the lower arcade and superimposed pairs of columns that fill the main arches of the gallery above. The predominant impression is one of compression and lift, created by the lateral splaying of the piers and the tall proportions of the upper storey, which together lead the eye to the eight-sided cloister (or domical) vault. The extreme height of the gallery's interior elevation is achieved by means of rampant, transverse barrel vaults that rise at an angle of some 23 degrees from the top of the outer wall to the base of the dome (fig. 117). In the gallery passage itself, however, these stilted vaults are masked by heavy diaphragm arches that divide the corridor into clear rectangular and triangular bays. The ground-level ambulatory in contrast is low and dark, covered by an intricate sequence of groin vaults. The complexity and diversity of the interior vaulting, aspects of the chapel rarely noted, are without precedent in early medieval architecture.

The resplendent interior decoration that one sees today is not Carolingian but the result of a radical restoration of the building that took place over the course of the nineteenth and early twentieth centuries after late Baroque stucco work had been stripped from the walls.[22] The original appearance of the interior has been a topic of much debate, but the argument put forth by some that the masonry was intended to be left exposed has little merit.[23] We know, for example, that the outside of the building was covered in a thin coat of red plaster and that the inside of the dome was decorated in mosaic. Remains of multicolored marble plaques have also been found in the floor of the tribune. It is inconceivable, therefore, that the interior walls between the dome mosaic and the *opus sectile* floor would have been left bare. In fact, in a famous letter of 787, Pope Hadrian I gave Charlemagne permission to transport "mosaic, marbles, and other materials from floors and walls" from Rome and Ravenna for use in his palace.[24] As will be discussed below, a similar interest in marble revetment was shown in Rome around the year 800, when Pope Leo III had the walls of a dining hall at the Lateran palace decorated with "sheets of marble" (*lamminis marmoreis*).[25] In sum, although the mosaic decoration and marble

115 and 116 *(following pages)* Aachen, royal chapel, exterior view and interior view.

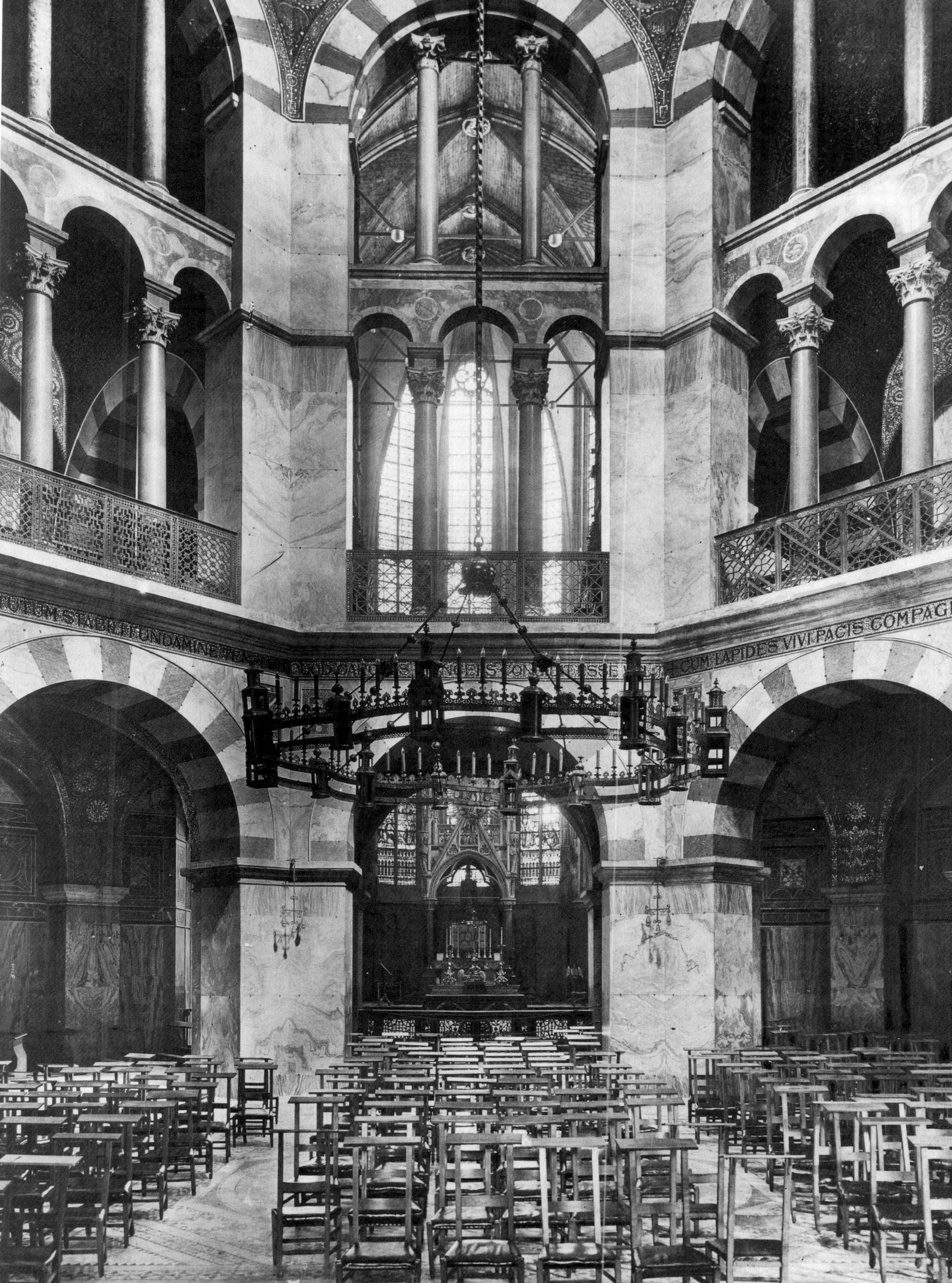

STABILI FUNDAMINE
CUM LAPIDES VIVI PACIS

117 Aachen, royal chapel, axonometric section.

revetment at Aachen are modern, they provide an accurate impression of the reflective brilliance and color that formed an integral part of the original design.

The importation of ancient *spolia* over long distances for the decoration of the royal chapel at Aachen was more than a practical matter. In spite of Einhard's statement that Charlemagne had marble columns brought to Aachen from Rome and Ravenna because "he was unable to find them anywhere else,"[26] ample supplies of similar materials must have been available from former Roman centers in the region such as Trier and neighboring Cologne, if not from among the ancient ruins of Aachen itself. The choice of *spolia* from Rome and Ravenna must be seen, therefore, as a political gesture intended to reinforce Charlemagne's claim as the heir to the rulers of Christian antiquity, making this *translatio artium* analogous to the *translatio imperii*.[27]

At the same time, ancient materials were not only reused but they were also closely studied and their techniques revived. The vast majority of the marble capitals in the gallery, for example, were, like the accompanying columns, *spolia*; however, a few were clearly carved on the spot.[28] Their Carolingian date is evident by their close resemblance to the pilaster capitals embedded in the exterior wall of the drum of the dome: in spite of the poorly preserved condition of the latter, one can still see that the general composition, the deep grooves of the running drill, and other unusual details such as a central acanthus bloom on a tall, slender stalk, are the same. In other words, they must be the work of the same team of sculptors. The Carolingian capitals on the interior are also recognizable by their elongated, almost conical, form, and the thick projection of their foliage. Still, they are remarkably accurate copies of Roman Corinthian capitals with a far greater sense of naturalism than the presumably slightly earlier capitals on the Lorsch gateway.

The extraordinarily high quality of craftsmanship at Aachen is perhaps best seen in the bronze fittings—railings and doors—that also decorate the chapel.[29] They too were produced locally, as proven by the fragments of casting moulds that were found on the site. Although unquestionably the products of the same workshop, the eight bronze railings of the gallery may be divided into three discernible groups, beginning with those that emphasize flat abstract patterns, not unlike eighth-century Frankish brooches, and ending with those that incorporate a delicate rendering of such classicizing details as vine scrolls, fluted pilasters, and Corinthian capitals (fig. 118). Such a sequence suggests a gradual process of assimilation

118 Aachen, royal chapel, detail of bronze railings.

119 Aachen, royal chapel, detail of bronze doors.

of the vocabulary of ancient ornament over several years of study and experimentation. A similar process is evident in the four sets of bronze doors, each valve divided into panels with classicizing moldings and boldly projecting lion-headed door knockers. The largest of the doors, now set within a Baroque vestibule, served the main entrance to the chapel. Particularly striking are the two ferocious lion's heads with swirling manes and glaring eyes with incised pupils, surrounded by a roundel border of acanthus leaves (fig. 119). No image better represents the stunning achievement of the artists at Aachen. While clearly inspired by ancient works, such models seem to have served only as a point of departure for no exact comparison has been found for the expressive power of this detail. In a comprehensive study of the bronzework at Aachen, published in 1965, Wolfgang Braunfels estimated that roughly ten years would have been needed to complete both the railings and the doors.[30] Based on his subtle stylistic analysis, Braunfels assigned four of the railings to before 796, the three sets of smaller doors to roughly 796–98, the largest door or *Wolfstür* to around 800, and the last four railings to shortly after 800. Although only approximate, such a chronology finds a striking parallel in the stylistic development of illuminated manuscripts produced at the court scriptorium, where ancient motifs were also used with increasing frequency and handled with growing confidence.[31] On the other hand, a more recent examination by Katharina Pawelec stresses similarities in the metalwork to decorative motifs of manuscripts and ivories assigned to the so-called Court School of Aachen in the early 790s.[32] The origins of the bronzeworkers and marble carvers, however, remain unknown. Presumably Frankish and foreign artists worked side by side, and certainly Italy is the most likely source for the latter. Braunfels stresses the influence of north Italy, pointing to comparative material, albeit on a much smaller scale, in Brescia, Bologna, and Pavia; one also thinks of the exquisite stucco work at Cividale, as well as the relief carving at the Tempietto del Clitunno in central Italy. Interestingly enough, these centers have one thing in common: they are Lombard, and it would not be surprising to find that after 774 Charlemagne called upon the assistance of artists from his new realm. At the same time, it is reasonable to suppose that craftsmen were imported from Rome and Ravenna along with the *spolia* that served as the models for much of this work. Pawelec, however, assumes that the artisans were largely Frankish.

Certainly foreign artists were involved with the dome mosaic, for we have little evidence of mosaic decoration in northern Europe after the sixth century. Again, what one sees today at Aachen is a nineteenth-century product (fig. 120). Stylistically it has no connection with the original decoration, but its iconography is revealed, at least in part, by drawings made before the late Baroque remodeling. An engraving from 1699 shows that the inside of the dome bore the representation of an apocalyptic vision of Christ enthroned with angels against a stellar sky approached from below by the twenty-four elders bearing crowns (fig. 121). The accuracy of this engraving was verified by the discovery in 1870 of portions of the original underpaintings of several of the bearded elders at the base of the dome.[33] Previously thought to represent only a preparatory stage, this layer is now considered to have been a bona fide fresco that was replaced sometime later in the ninth century by a mosaic of the same design and subject.[34]

OMNIA CONVE

121 Aachen, royal chapel. 1699 engraving of dome mosaic (G. Ciampini, *Vetera Monumenta*, Rome).

Although the authenticity of the representation of Christ has been questioned, there seems, in fact, little reason to doubt that this regal scene is original; only details of the throne may have resulted from later modifications.[35] With this in mind, it is important to note that this image of Christ, be it in fresco or mosaic, was in the eastern section of the dome above the main altar and directly opposite the site of the king's throne in the gallery. Doubts about the Carolingian date of the throne have been recently discounted by a detailed scientific analysis.[36] Moreover, the richly colored *opus sectile* floor underneath, which is certainly original, demonstrates that this area was of special significance. Important, too, is the fact that the bronze screen in front of the throne is unique in having a small gate in the center that could be opened to give an unobstructed view of the interior of the chapel. From this vantage point, Charlemagne could look down to the altar in the apse and up to the image of Christ, his heavenly counterpart, in the dome (fig. 122). At the same time, the clergy and congregation looked up to their king, "crowned by God," sitting enthroned between earth and heaven. Thus, the luxurious materials and decorative details of the chapel

122 Aachen, royal chapel, section.

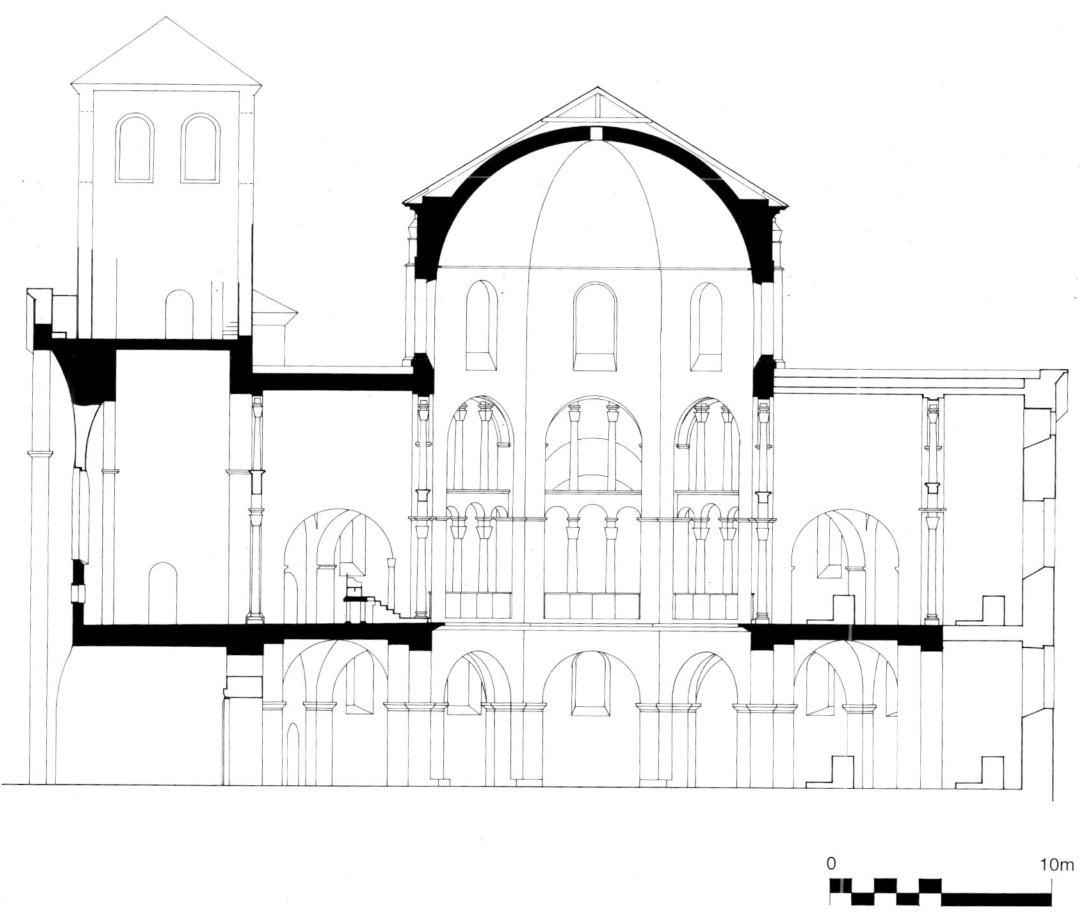

120 *(facing page)* Aachen, royal chapel, view of dome mosaic.

were meant to evoke the splendors of late antiquity, and to create a setting that reflected the king's relationship to God and his people.

The centralized design of the church, always rare in the West, also harked back to the building traditions of the Early Christian past. Numerous models have been proposed, including buildings sponsored by Constantine, such as the Holy Sepulchre in Jerusalem, known from the account by Alculf, and the Golden Octagon at Antioch, described by Eusebius, together with various churches in Constantinople, especially, SS. Sergius and Bacchus and Hagia Sophia, both built by Justinian and extolled by Procopius. Even the Dome of the Rock in Jerusalem, often associated at the time with the Temple of Solomon, is frequently cited. The dedication of the church to the Virgin Mary also calls to mind the Pantheon (S. Maria Rotunda) in Rome, the Mausoleum of Theodoric in Ravenna, which was converted into a church honoring the Virgin by the early eighth century, and even Wilfrid's rotunda at Hexham. Another important eighth-century precedent, and one no doubt known to Charlemagne, was S. Sophia in Benevento, built in imitation of the great church in Constantinople. Closer at hand, St. Gereon in Cologne (fig. 38) may have been influential given the fact that the first archchaplain of Aachen, Hildebold, was also the archbishop of Cologne. Any or all of these examples, as well as several others, may have played a role in the formulation of the building at Aachen.[37] Yet by far the closest comparison, and the one most often cited, remains S. Vitale in Ravenna. The plan and elevation of the two buildings are strikingly similar and surely the fact that Ravenna was the source for much of the building material was not coincidental. We know, for example, that Charlemagne visited there at least three times, beginning in 787. The city, after all, had until recently been the seat of Byzantine rule in the West and S. Vitale offered a firsthand impression of the splendors of distant Constantinople. Indeed, the church must have held a special appeal because of its imperial connotations, made explicit by the mosaic representation of Justinian in the lower zone of the apse. To be sure, the portrait of the emperor is not labeled, and it has been suggested that it may have been mistaken for an image of Theodoric. But the name of the archbishop, Maximianus, is there in bold letters for all to see, and the dates of his reign and his association with Justinian must have been well known.[38] Carolingian builders, then, found in S. Vitale an eloquent symbol of Christian antiquity.

Even so, the Early Christian model was not copied literally but transformed into a distinctly new and medieval form. The subtle interplay between curvilinear and angular patterns that produces such a dynamic tension in the design of S. Vitale was replaced by a far more ponderous and rectilinear approach. The billowing exedrae, for example, framed by razor-sharp, precariously thin prismatic piers become at Aachen flat screens sustained by massive, broad supports. In place of the undulating and free-flowing interior at S. Vitale, that at Aachen is contained and clearly defined through the compartmentalization of space, seen most emphatically in the heavy diaphragm arches that span the gallery corridor. The scheme seems to be based on a square module of fourteen Carolingian feet (or two seven-foot rods) that radiates from the central octagon and determines the shape of the apse. Thus the subtle irregularities of the Ravennate church have been replaced by a strict grid-like attitude toward planning that is, after all, characteristic of the layout of the palace as a whole.

The construction techniques of the two buildings are also very different. S. Vitale's brick-and-mortar masonry was translated at Aachen into the local idiom of rough-hewn stones and quoining. If anything, the Carolingian building is structurally more daring than its Early Christian counterpart in its extensive use of masonry vaulting. The only areas of S. Vitale that were originally vaulted were the dome, the choir, and the apse (the aisle vaults are eleventh-century or later), and even then they were constructed not of brick or stone but of light-weight, ceramic tubes. Inter-estingly enough, the rampant barrel vaults of the gallery at Aachen represent a change in design in the course of construction, for they do not bond with the surrounding walls; presumably a lean-to timber roof was originally planned when the vaults were substituted, perhaps because they were believed to reinforce the central dome, whether or not they actually do so. An afterthought, too, was the towering entranceway, which is bonded with the adjoining outer walls only at the second-storey level (fig. 123). This so-called westwork was an entirely new element in church architecture. It provided not only access to the gallery, as did the two stunted cylindrical towers flanking the entrance at S. Vitale, but it also added a monumental vertical accent to the facade of the church—in place of a low narthex—marking the position of the king's throne by a great arch, with a place at its summit for the hanging of bells. Such features serve to demonstrate the experimental nature of Charlemagne's chapel. A reverence for precedent did not restrict the creative talents of the Carolingian builders; instead, they were able to formulate something totally new out of the lessons of the past.

Again, like S. Vitale and many other major early Christian churches, the royal chapel was preceded by an atrium, but it, too, possessed its own distinctive characteristics. The area still serves as a forecourt to the church, but its perimeter has been built over by rowhouses, leaving only scant traces of the original arrangement. Nevertheless, sufficient remains of the foundations and rising walls have

123 *(facing page)* Aachen, royal chapel, exterior view of west facade.

124 Aachen, royal chapel, reconstruction drawing of atrium.

been found embedded in later masonry to permit a general reconstruction (fig. 124). Long and narrow, the atrium was flanked to the north and south by a solid wall from which projected two monumental exedrae, each one presenting a great curved recess approximately 6 m wide and 10 m high, articulated on the inside by superimposed rows of small, shallow niches and presumably covered by a semidome. In an apparent second phase, a row of rectangular piers with paired columns in front of each conch was added, forming a covered outer corridor with its floor raised 50 cm above the level of the open courtyard (17 × 36 m). Fragments of original masonry in the northeast corner of the forecourt show that the piers were capped by imposts above which extended thin, vertical pilasters and broad arches with subtly carved architraves, while the more closely spaced columns sustained smaller arches of alternating stone and brick voussoirs. The fact that the remains of columns were found only in front of the exedrae and that the framing piers were more widely spaced at this point than elsewhere suggests that this second phase was meant to complement the first and not replace it, as generally assumed.

The reconstruction of the elevation is even more problematic. There is no evidence that the atrium was surmounted by a second storey, as has been previously proposed, except in the northeast corner where it joined the two-storey walkway that was further linked to the audience hall to the north. Here an upper level passageway was needed to connect the tribune of the westwork to the second storey of the walkway; hence the round-arched window in the east wall (the two in the north wall are modern). Elsewhere, the pilasters presumably buttressed screen walls, perhaps fenestrated, which masked the upper halves of the exedrae and their vaults. The remains of a water channel running diagonally across the courtyard indicates that a fountain stood at its center, perhaps surmounted by the bronze pinecone, with spout holes at the tips of its scales, that now stands in the vestibule of the church. Such an arrangement would have resembled the fountain or *cantharus* in the center of the atrium of St. Peter's basilica in Rome.[39]

Be that as it may, the design of the atrium at Aachen was most unusual. It was not a traditional quadriporticus, that is a courtyard surrounded by colonnaded walkways on all four sides. In fact, there was no corridor at all adjoining the west facade of the church, which left the single doorway at ground level completely isolated from the surrounding atrium. In other words, the flanking corridors of the courtyard were not meant to lead to the church, and furthermore, the exedrae were major obstructions in the first phase and perhaps in the second phase as well, if my reconstruction is correct. Thus, the atrium was never designed as a traditional instrument of passage but as a place of assembly, a showplace, if you will, where onlookers could be relegated to the slightly elevated porticoes in order to observe ceremonial processions or other gatherings in front of the church. Indeed, elaborate rituals, often with distinct liturgical overtones, are known to have become an increasingly important aspect of life at Charlemagne's court. Occasions such as the annual gathering of nobles, the reception of foreign ambassadors, the daily assembly for morning prayer, and other public affairs were carefully staged events whereby the ruler appeared before a select audience to display his power and prestige and receive adulation.[40] The atrium of the royal chapel seems especially well suited for these activities.

The stage-like quality of the atrium was accentuated by the exedrae. It may be more than mere coincidence that elaborate depictions of imaginary architectural backdrops with columnar screens and monumental niches appeared around the same time in the decoration of luxurious manuscripts produced at Aachen (fig. 125). This fanciful use of architectural scenery in the so-called Soissons Gospels, for instance, has been likened to the ancient *scenae frons* or theater set that formed such an integral part of the illusionism of Roman wall painting that lived on in various ways in Early Christian and Byzantine art. It is generally assumed that the Carolingian artists were inspired by examples of late antique or Byzantine book illumination,[41] but the presence of the exedrae in the atrium at Aachen cannot be accounted for so easily. To be sure, monumental niches were common features in Roman architecture, and examples can be found as part of courtyards connected with many different building types, such as the Baths of Constantine in Trier. Yet their placement to either side of the main axis of the atrium is more unusual. This arrangement, however, resembles the layout of the imperial fora of Augustus and Trajan in Rome (fig. 126). Such a reference at Aachen would not be surprising. The forum of Trajan is prominently mentioned in early medieval guidebooks to the city, and it was singled out as a miraculous structure in the late eighth century by Paul the Deacon, who was for a time a prominent member of Charlemagne's court.[42] The forum of Augustus, moreover, was praised in Suetonius's biography of the emperor, which in turn served as the model for Einhard's life of Charlemagne. Only foundations are left of the exedrae in Trajan's forum (like Aachen, there were four altogether if one counts the two at either end of the basilica), but those of the Augustan forum are well preserved, lined along the inside by rows of shallow niches. We know that these niches held portraits of the historical and mythological ancestors of the Emperor Augustus, including Aeneas, Romulus and Remus, and other great figures of Rome's past.[43] This gallery of "great men," also mentioned by Suetonius, was no doubt one of the models for the decorative program in the audience hall of Charlemagne's palace at Ingelheim. Is it not possible that the niches in the exedrae of the atrium at Aachen bore similar images, painted or in mosaic (tesserae have been found in the area), of Constantine, Theodosius, Charles Martel, Pippin III, and Charlemagne, and perhaps even the emperors Augustus or

125 Gospels of Saint-Médard of Soissons (Paris, Bibliothèque Nationale, Lat. 8850, fol. 1v).

126 Rome, imperial fora, plan.

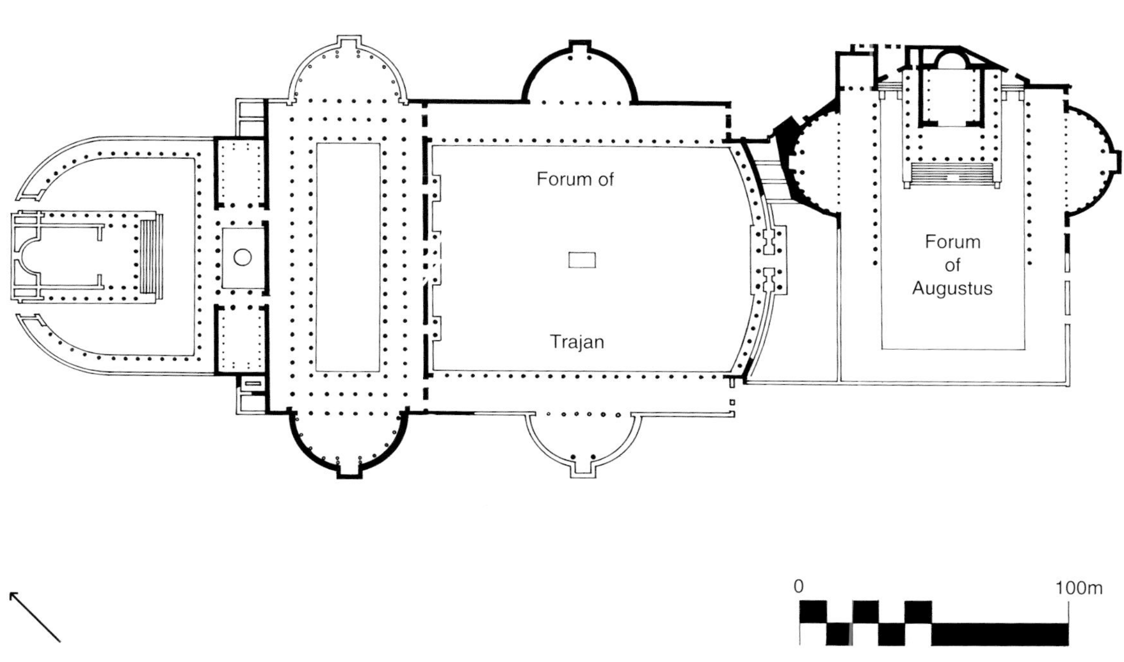

Trajan?[44] In this way, the secular theme of the exedrae would have echoed that of the westwork with its own exterior conch, and together they epitomize the union of Church and State that seems to have been the basic motivation behind the design of the chapel complex as a whole.

The two rectangular buildings set on a north–south axis to either side of the east end of the church were of similar dimensions (15 × 23 m). The structure to the north, however, was divided into nave and aisles by brick supports in the shape of columns, while the building to the south seems to have been aisleless. Each was preceded by a two-storey narthex and terminated by a small apse flanked by square side rooms; those of the north building may have contained stairs leading to galleries over each of the aisles. The function of the two structures is unknown, although they were clearly related to that of the chapel to which they were connected on two levels by short corridors joined to the narthexes. It has been conjectured that the northern building served as a dressing-room for the emperor or a treasury for liturgical objects and that the corresponding building to the south was reserved for the clergy or for synods. In any event, their importance was signaled by the original placement of two of the sets of bronze doors in the entrances to the chapel gallery.

The audience hall to the north seems at first glance to be simply a somewhat larger version of the aula at Ingelheim (47.42 × 20.76 m, as opposed to 38.20 × 14.50 m). At Aachen, however, a secondary apse was added to the middle of the north and south walls, transforming an aisleless basilica into another familiar feature of Roman domestic architecture, namely the triclinium or triconchos. Such trilobed structures have been found in association with numerous ancient villas, where they served both as elaborate reception rooms and as dining halls. The design seems to have originated in the Latin West whence it spread to the eastern Mediterranean. Indeed, it continued to be used in the East from the fourth century A.D. on in the imperial palace in Constantinople and even in early Islamic building, such as the eighth-century palace at Mschatta. In the Latin West, however, the triconch seems to have gone out of fashion by the sixth century.[45] One of the last documented examples before the Carolingian period formed part of the so-called palace of Theodoric in Ravenna (fig. 127). Although the attribution to Theodoric has not been proven conclusively, it seems likely since we know that Theodoric had a palace in the immediate vicinity, adjoining the church of S. Apollinare Nuovo.[46] If so, this comparison may be significant, given the fact that columns and decorative marbles were brought to Aachen from a palace in Ravenna. It is also worth noting that the triclinium at Ravenna stood next to an aisleless basilica with projecting cubicles flanking the apse. One could easily imagine that

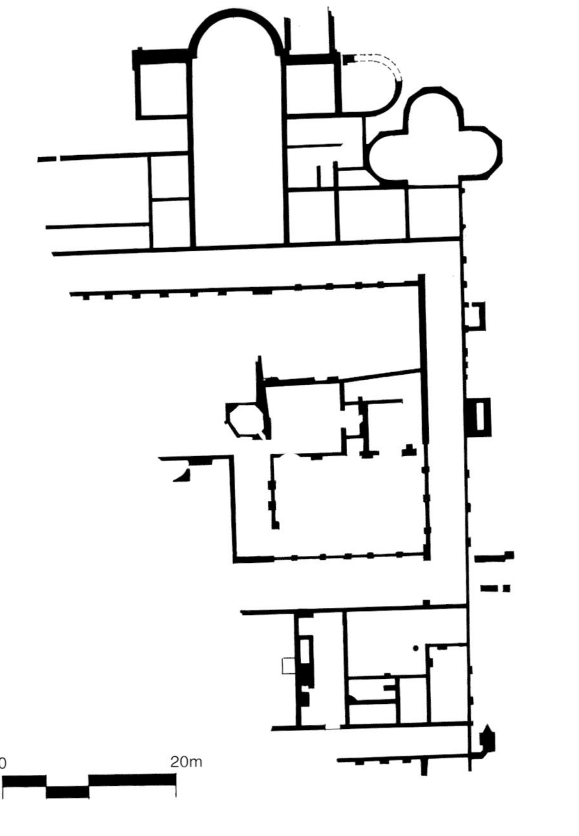

127 Ravenna, palace of Theodoric, plan.

such an arrangement could have inspired the conflation of the two distinct building types—longitudinal hall and triconch—found at Aachen, thereby creating a hybrid structure which, in turn, reveals its derivative nature. Moreover, as will be discussed below, triclinia were being built by the popes in Rome in the second half of the eighth century for the first time in centuries. The fact that the unit of measure used for the audience hall seems to have been the Roman, as opposed to the Carolingian, foot may indicate that the masons, too, came from Rome.

If the plan of the aula points to Rome, Ravenna, and possibly even Constantinople, the elevation was inspired by a different, though closely related, source. The remains of thick wall pilasters spaced at wide intervals along the north and south sides of the aula show that the exterior elevation was articulated by a series of blind arches framing one or more rows of windows (fig. 128). Such an arrangement can only have been inspired by Constantine's basilica at Trier. The reasons for such a reference are self-evident. Charlemagne, again, was the new Constantine, and Trier had been the latter's capital before he marched on Rome. Fifteen years later, Constantine founded the new Rome of

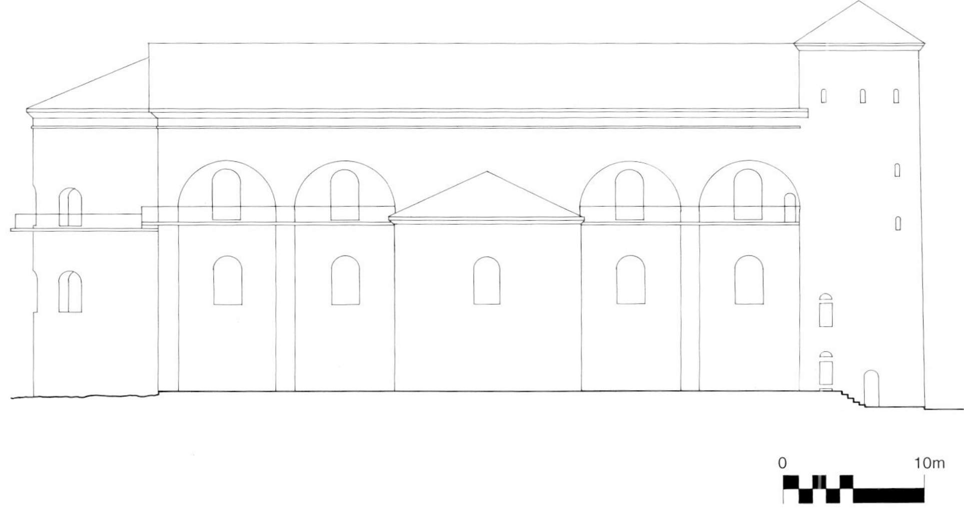

128 Aachen, audience hall, reconstruction of exterior.

Constantinople, an act commemorated in the wall paintings of the audience hall at Ingelheim. Thus the simple design of one building could resound with multiple associations. It would seem therefore that the three audience halls at Paderborn, Ingelheim, and Aachen reflect the evolution of Charlemagne from Germanic king to Roman ruler. The only intrusion was at the east end, where a massive stairtower, still largely preserved, provided access to interior and exterior catwalks for easy maintenance of the roof and windows.

The royal chapel and the audience hall, the ecclesiastical and secular foci of the palace, were linked by a long narrow passageway with two storeys, barrel-vaulted on the ground floor with mere slits for windows and timber-roofed above with broadly spaced tripartite windows looking out onto the western range of the complex. This connecting portico was intersected at a perpendicular angle in the middle by a monumental gatehouse (29.57 × 15.10m, or 100 × 51 Roman feet). Details of the elevation of the gatehouse remain uncertain but the thickness of the foundations indicates that it was vaulted in some manner, and remains of stairs in the two western corners show that it, like the corridor, was two-storeyed. The ultimate source for this arrangement was most likely the imperial palace in Constantinople where the famous Chalke or bronze gate, built by Justinian and described by Procopius, led to a covered passage that connected the palace to the south gallery of Hagia Sophia.[47] Closer at hand, the gateway to the exarch's palace in Ravenna was modeled after the Chalke in Constantinople and was referred to in the ninth century as "Ad Calchi."[48] And by the middle of the eighth century, Pope Zacharias in Rome erected a similar entrance tower with a bronze gate leading to an elevated corridor, known as the *macrona*, which linked various parts of the Lateran palace.[49] Once again, the primary models for the portico and gateway seem to have come from Constantinople, Rome, and Ravenna.

Such references were not coincidental, for the design of Charlemagne's palace was not merely utilitarian in nature but it was intended to symbolize his rule. Such an attitude toward palace building was not new. Indeed, it too, like the architectural forms themselves, harked back to the precepts of late antiquity. Three centuries earlier, in fact, Theodoric had referred to his palaces as "the pleasures of our rule, the decorous face of our authority, the honored testimony of our reign." Charlemagne and his circle no doubt agreed with such sentiments, and they must have been familiar with these very words, recorded as they are in the *Variae* of Theodoric's adviser, Cassiodorus, whose works were frequently copied in the Carolingian period.[50] Moreover, Charlemagne's high esteem for Theodoric was made manifest by the transportation of a bronze equestrian statue of the Ostrogothic king from Ravenna to Aachen, an event that took place in 801 after Charlemagne had admired the statue during a brief stopover in Ravenna on his way north from his imperial coronation in Rome.[51]

Aachen was also acclaimed as the new Rome, which was the same term used in the fourth century A.D. to describe Constantinople. And like Constantine and other great rulers of antiquity, Charlemagne was seen as the founder of a city. To be sure, Aachen was tiny in comparison to the capitals of antiquity, and it could only be considered a city in the context of the drastically reduced state of urban settlement in the early Middle Ages. Still, construction on such a scale had not been seen in western Europe since the reign of Justinian, and the palace complex equaled in size that of Theodoric in Ravenna and Piazza Armerina in Sicily. Indeed, Charlemagne's supervision of the construction of Aachen was described in heroic terms by an anonymous court poet around the year 800.

> The pious Charles stands on an exalted place, pointing to each location, and disposing of the lofty walls of the Rome to come. Here he orders the forum and also the sacred senate. . . . Crowds of workmen bustle about: some cut suitable stones into rigid columns and erect high arches, while others struggle manually to roll the stones in place. Some excavate the harbor, and others lay deep foundations for the theater and enclose the atrium with high domed vaults. Nearby, others labor to uncover hot springs, opening up channels to the steaming bath waters . . . Here others strive with great effort to build a luxurious temple for the Everlasting Lord; this sacred dwelling soars to the stars with its polished walls.

These words do not merely praise the architectural patronage of Charlemagne; they place his actions within the context of an established literary form that was perfectly suited to the antiquarian pretensions of the Carolingian court. For while certain details, such as the hot springs, the atrium with high vaults, and the temple or church with polished walls, formed part of the palace complex, others did not. Aachen, as far as we know, was not encircled by fortification walls in the eighth or ninth century, nor did it have a theater; and, as an inland settlement, it certainly did not possess a harbor. Instead, these features, together with the basic syntax of the Latin text, were taken directly from a passage in Virgil's *Aeneid* (1:430–436), where Aeneas observes the construction of Carthage. The *Aeneid*, of course, celebrates the origin of the Roman nation through the legendary exploits of Aeneas, the mythical ancestor of the first emperor, Augustus. The forum and senate, in turn, refer to Rome, and more specifically to Augustus, who built the forum bearing his name and the neighboring senate house. Through the artifice of poetry and the emulation of the great epic of Roman antiquity, Charlemagne is presented in the guise of Aeneas and Augustus, founding a new nation and a new empire, and overseeing the construction of its capital: the image of Aachen is thus merged with that of Carthage and Rome.[52]

The sophisticated and erudite mind-set inherent in this poem, written within the confines of Charlemagne's court and certainly meant to be heard by the ruler, provides a striking parallel, it seems to me, to the mental attitude behind the design of the palace.[53] Like the use of literary topoi, the revival of specific architectural forms—the centrally planned church, the atrium with exedrae, the audience hall in the form of a triclinium, the two-storeyed walkway, and the monumental gatehouse—expressed the aspirations of the new Carolingian dynasty by their clear references to ancient monuments in Rome, Ravenna, Trier, and Constantinople, monuments associated with the emperors Constantine, Justinian, Trajan, and Augustus, and the Germanic king, Theodoric. The multiple associations of the palace merged to provide tangible evidence for the Frankish ruler's claim as their legitimate heir. Charlemagne and Aachen were therefore synonymous, and the palace, to paraphrase Theodoric, was the honored testimony of his reign.

It is worth stressing that ancient models were not used indiscriminately but were chosen with great care. Particular emphasis, not surprisingly, was given to Christian rulers (Constantine, Justinian, and Theodoric), for Charlemagne's domain was after all a Christian one. His authority, according to Alcuin in a famous letter of 799, was both political and spiritual in the sense that he was God's chosen instrument for the salvation of the *populus christianus*. But this did not mean that all the pagan emperors were to be purposefully excluded. Augustus in particular was seen as an integral part of Christian history. He was the first emperor and the ruler at the time of Christ's birth. Similarly, the fourth Eclogue of Virgil, written to extoll the birth of Augustus and the glories of his reign, had been reinterpreted since the time of Augustine as referring to the coming of Christ.

A similar allusion to Rome's pre-Christian past may be found on coins minted at the palace late in Charlemagne's reign (fig. 129). On one side is the portrait of Charlemagne, shown in profile with all the trappings of a Roman ruler—the laurel wreath of victory, the diadem of the emperor, and the cloak and armor of a Roman general—encircled by the Latin inscription KAROLUS IMP(erator) AUG(ustus); only the mustache hints at his Germanic origin. The reverse side bears the schematic rendering of a building, composed of a stepped podium and four columns supporting a pediment, enframing a simple cross. The inscription reads: XPISTIANA RELIGIO; the first two letters, the chi and rho, of course, are derived from the Greek monogram for Christ. This coin type bears no resemblance to contemporary Byzantine issues; instead, it is a conflation of different late antique models. The portrait is derived from a standard type common from the reigns of Trajan to Constantine. Surely, the allusion to the latter cannot be coincidental. The architectural image on the reverse side, however, corresponds to coins of the late third and early fourth centuries where one finds a representation of the temple of Jupiter. On the Carolingian coin, the basic architectural elements of the pagan temple have been retained, albeit with four rather than six columns, but the image of the statue of the pagan deity has been replaced by

129 Silver coin with head of Charlemagne (front) and building facade (back).

a cross. In other words, the symbol of the state religion of pagan Rome has been transformed into a symbol of Christianity.[54] In similar terms, Charlemagne was seen by his contemporaries as the culmination of a long tradition and his capital was to epitomize the *renovatio imperii romani*, to use a phrase current at the time.

These imperial connotations do not mean that Charlemagne foresaw the events of Christmas Day 800 already in the 780s, when construction of the palace at Aachen began. To be sure, it may well be that the portico and second phase of the atrium, both of which seem to use the Roman as opposed to the Carolingian foot, were constructed after 800, but even so, their location, if not their specific form, had been determined from the onset, as indicated by the uniform grid that seems to underlie the entire layout. The imperial coronation, in fact, changed very little; it endowed Charlemagne with no new territory and no new clearly defined powers. Rather it seems to have been an act instigated by the pope, looking to solidify his own position in Rome through the support of the most powerful ruler in Europe. In the end, it was a symbolic gesture, which served to confirm in title what had been recognized as a political reality for some time. The palace complex at Aachen, therefore, should be seen as a unified whole, built about the armature of architectural forms derived from late antiquity, whereby the lessons of the past were carefully and selectively studied to provide the image of a new political order. Yet it is important to stress that these models, as obvious as they are, were not merely copied but transformed. Proportions were altered, disparate elements were combined, and new features, such as the westwork, were introduced. Indeed, the major contribution of the Carolingian *renovatio* to the development of medieval architecture was not so much its studied antiquarianism as its creative assimilation of ancient precedents on a new and monumental scale. At the opposite end of the empire, the city of Rome, the source of inspiration for much of the activity at Aachen, experienced a Renaissance of its own. Sponsored by a series of popes beginning in the middle of the eighth century, the Roman revival was conditioned by a particularly papal view of the past and its significance for the current political situation in Europe. Not surprisingly, the initial focus of the movement was the Lateran palace, which had served as the official residence of the bishop of Rome since the reign of Constantine. Before the middle of the eighth century, there are no records of major additions or alterations to the palace complex; presumably the original buildings that formed part of the imperial villa donated to the Church by Constantine had proven to be sufficient for the needs of the popes over the intervening centuries. In the later eighth and early ninth centuries, however, the papal residence was radically transformed.

The general tone of the work for the next fifty years was set by Pope Zacharias (741–52), the same pontiff who gave his blessing to the coup d'état of Charlemagne's father, Pippin III. Zacharias's structures are no longer preserved, since the Lateran palace was destroyed and rebuilt at the end of the sixteenth century, but the *Liber Pontificalis* states that he enlarged the papal residence by adding a triclinium and a monumental entrance-tower.[55] Both buildings found their source not in the Latin West but in Byzantium. As already noted, the triconch dining hall lived on only in the Greek East, having been abandoned in the West since the sixth century, and was a common feature of the imperial

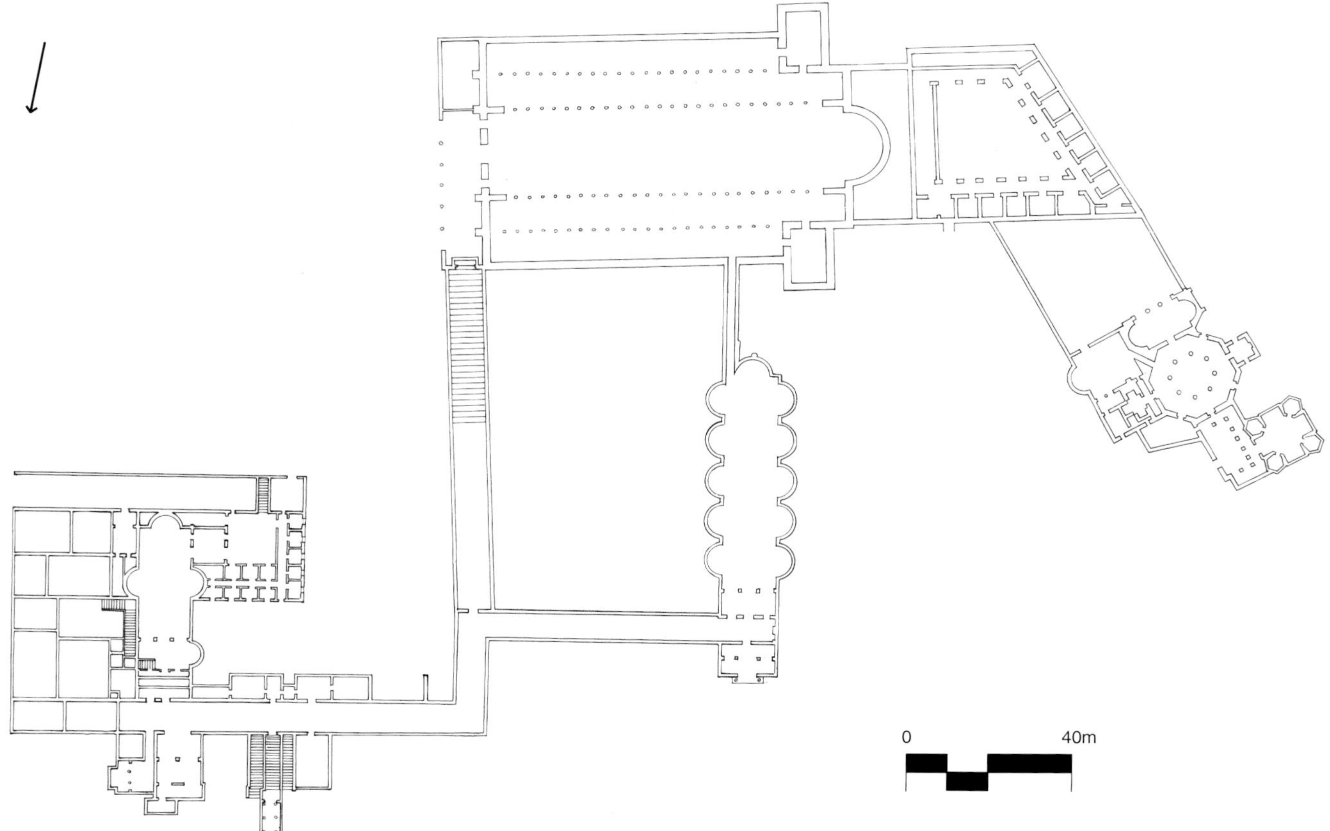

130 Rome, Lateran palace, plan.

palace in Constantinople. The towered entrance, too, with its bronze doors and portrait of Christ, was no doubt built in imitation of the famous "Chalke" or bronze gate to the emperor's palace in the Byzantine capital.[56] It is also worth noting that identical features, a triclinium and gateway called "Ad Calchi," formed part of the exarch's palace in Ravenna. The adoption of architectural forms associated with Byzantine rule, whether in Constantinople or Ravenna, must have been deliberate, for it coincided with a major change in papal political policy. Although the papacy had been gradually loosening its political ties with Byzantium since the late seventh century, it was Pope Zacharias, himself a Greek, who declared that the Duchy of Rome and the exarchate, both vestiges of imperial rule since the days of Justinian, were part of a new political entity, a republic, under the jurisdiction of St. Peter and his successor, the bishop of Rome. Such a move allowed Zacharias to act as the head of an independent state in his dealings with the hostile Lombards.[57] Moreover, it was the protection of the lands of St. Peter, stretching from Rome to Ravenna, and the recognition of this papal patrimony that formed the basis of the subsequent alliance with the Franks. Thus, under Zacharias the Lateran palace became a symbol of the new political status of the pope.

The political symbolism of the Lateran palace became even more explicit during the reign of Leo III. Although our knowledge of Zacharias's building activities is limited to a few brief written sources, the Leonine structures are better known, thanks to a variety of records made prior to the demolition of the medieval palace in 1589.[58] Plans, sketches, painted views, and literary descriptions combine to provide a reliable, albeit approximate, idea of the overall design and decoration. Leo III built two triclinia at the Lateran (fig. 130).[59] The first, a triconch described by the *Liber Pontificalis* as "larger than any other triclinia," measured 26 m long and 12.50 m wide. Entered through a screen of porphyry and white columns, the interior was sheathed with marble and the main apse decorated with mosaic, while the side apses were painted. The main apse and its mosaic were left standing at the end of the sixteenth century and thoroughly restored in 1625. In the early eighteenth century, the entire apse and its decoration were transferred and rebuilt in a new location across from the facade of the Lateran basilica. What remains of the apse mosaic today is but a copy of the original; nevertheless, although the style of the mosaic has been greatly altered, the main elements of the figural composition have been retained, as verified by views made before 1625 (fig. 131).[60]

The conch of the apse depicts the Mission of the Apostles, that is Christ commanding his eleven disciples to convert "all the people," as described in Matthew 28: 19–20. Christ stands in the center atop a hillock from which spring the four rivers of paradise, surrounded by the apostles with Peter singled out by his agitated pose and cruciform staff. Clearly the message concerns the role of the Roman Church as the primary instrument of Christ's teaching and of the spreading of the faith. The position of the papacy in this scheme is further defined by the two groups of figures on the wall of the arch surrounding the apse. On the right, St. Peter enthroned bestows upon the kneeling figure of Leo the pallium, a stole that symbolized his episcopal office, and upon Charlemagne a banner, symbol of his position as protector of Rome (fig. 132). The corresponding figures on the left had already been lost by 1625, but as restored they represent Christ seated handing the keys of Heaven to St. Peter and a banner to

132 Rome, Lateran palace, detail of triclinium mosaic depicting Charlemagne and Pope Leo III.

131 Rome, Latern palace, view of triclinium before 1625, detail (N. Alemanni, *De Lateranensibus parietinis*, Rome, 1625, pl. II).

133 Rome, Lateran palace, hypothetical reconstruction of interior of banqueting hall with eleven apses.

Constantine. We do not know the basis for this composition and the figure of Pope Sylvester I may originally have been in the place of St. Peter, but presumably Constantine was included, not only as the logical antetype for Charlemagne, but as the donor of the Lateran palace and patron of the adjoining basilica.

Charlemagne, however, is labelled as king (*rex*), and not emperor (*imperator*), indicating that the triclinium was completed before the imperial coronation in 800. The design of the banqueting hall and its decoration, therefore, was meant to express the papal view of the Roman Church as destined to convert the world to Christ, founded on the primacy of Peter, and protected by the military might of the ideal secular rule: Constantine/ Charlemagne. In doing so, the first aula of Leo III gave visual expression to the precepts of the Donation of the Constantine, which states that the Lateran palace "surpasses and takes precedence over all other palaces in the world."[61]

Soon after the events of Christmas Day 800, Leo sponsored the construction of a second triclinium of even more grandiose dimensions. Located on a second floor and connected to the rest of the palace by a long corridor, this banqueting hall was 68 m long and over 15 m wide, and articulated by eleven apses, five along either side and one at the end, each fitted with semicircular dining tables and curved couches so that one could dine in the antique manner, that is reclining rather than sitting up (figs. 130 and 133). At the north end, opposite the main apse and projecting from a towerlike vestibule, stood a balcony or benediction loggia, supported by columns, where the pope could appear before crowds assembled in the open area or *campo* along the palace's southern flank. As with the earlier triclinium, the interior of this banqueting hall was adorned with multicolored marble revetment and paving, mosaics, and frescoes; it even had a porphyry fountain in the center. The details of the figural decoration remain uncertain; the *Liber Pontificalis* states only that the ten side apses depicted "scenes of the apostles preaching to the people," without making any reference to the mosaic in the main apse. Records made before the building's destruction in 1589 are also vague, but they suggest that either the Virgin or Christ was shown in the center of the main apse, flanked by six saints with Peter and Paul presumably among them.

Although questions remain about the figural decoration, the political meaning of the design of the building seems clear enough. No triclinium of comparable size or multi-apsed design is known to have existed in the West, be it in Rome, Ravenna, or elsewhere in Europe; only the imperial palace in Constantinople provided a suitable model in the Hall of the Nineteen Couches, so named because of its grand array of dining niches. This hall vanished in the wake of the Turkish conquest of the city in 1453, but it is described in a number of written sources. These references date only from the tenth century and later, but there is good reason to believe that the great hall was built centuries before. Indeed, a similar banqueting hall, with seven instead of nineteen apses and dateable to the fifth or sixth century, was uncovered in the 1960s in Istanbul near the ruins of the ancient hippodrome and the site of the former imperial palace (fig. 134).[62] The desire to rival the imperial palace in Constantinople had been an aim of papal building in the Lateran palace since the middle of the eighth century, but Leo's hall of eleven couches proclaimed in no uncertain terms the pope's new role as the custodian of imperial authority in the west, as proclaimed in the Donation of Constantine and exercised at Charlemagne's coronation.

The contemporary building campaigns at Charlemagne's palace at Aachen and the Lateran palace in Rome represent, therefore, two sides of the same coin. For Charlemagne, his capital was the new or second Rome, rivalling both the city of the pope and the other 'new Rome' on the Bosphorus, Constantinople, expressing his position as the new Constantine, the father of Europe (*pater Europae*), and, after 800, the emperor of the Romans. At the Lateran palace in Rome, on the other hand, the pope reaffirmed the

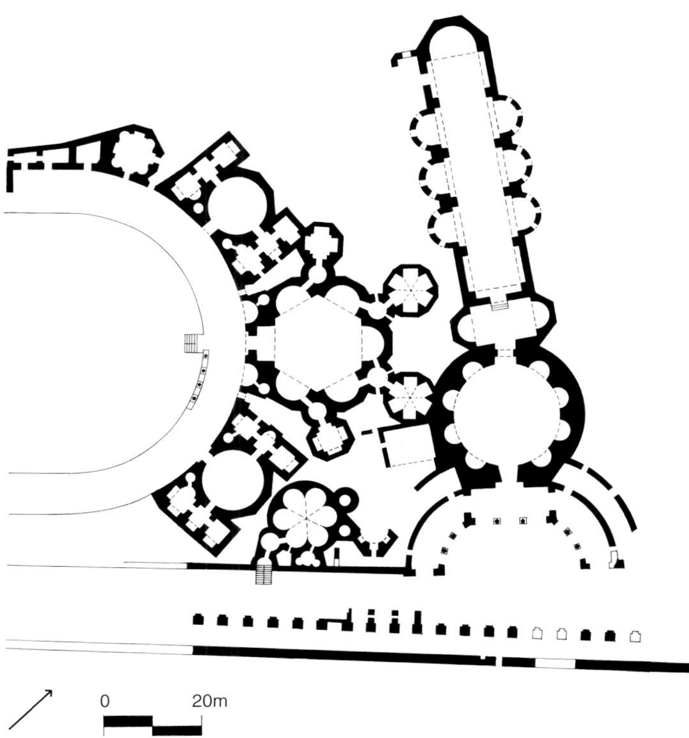

134 Constantinople (Istanbul), early Byzantine banqueting hall, plan.

supremacy of the Church of Peter, as formulated in the Donation of Constantine, displacing the authority of the Byzantine emperor. The notions of the Frankish ruler and the pope were both reciprocal and divergent. They were reciprocal in that part, if not all, of the Aachen palace was referred to as "the Lateran," in a gesture of homage to the See of Peter.[63] It may also be that Charlemagne's audience hall, with its three apses, was inspired by the pre-800 triclinia of Zacharias and Leo. If so, the Carolingian *aula* was much larger than either and included in its exterior elevation monumental blind arcading that was derived from Constantine's audience hall in Trier. Certainly, much of the marble revetment and paving, columns and capitals came from Rome, and so too must have come the artists to decorate the dome of the royal chapel. Even the equestrian statue of Theodoric, brought from Ravenna and set up near the entrance to the Aachen complex, may have been meant to imitate the original position of the famous bronze equestrian statue of Marcus Aurelius, thought in the Middle Ages to depict Constantine, near the Lateran palace before it was moved to the Capitoline Hill in the early sixteenth century.

The papacy, on the other hand, sought models for the Lateran palace in the sprawling imperial palace in Constantinople. Thus, while Aachen turned primarily to Rome, Ravenna, and Trier, papal Rome was more concerned with rivalling symbols of Byzantine rule, first in Ravenna and then in Constantinople. Charlemagne's independence from papal political concepts was made manifest by his decision in 806 to divide the empire among his three sons, and then in 813, after two of his sons had died, to bestow the imperial title upon his sole surviving heir, Louis, in a ceremony at Aachen without any participation of the pope. At the same time, Pope Leo III and his successors continued to believe that the transferal of imperial authority rested solely with the occupant of the throne of Peter. But these were problems for the future. In the years just before and after the year 800, the palaces of Charlemagne and Pope Leo III reflected the roles of Aachen and Rome as the capitals of a new political entity in Europe.

CHAPTER 7

Private Patronage and Personal Taste

The term *palatium*, or palace, in the early Middle Ages encompassed more than an architectural setting. To quote a famed contemporary authority on Carolingian politics, Hincmar of Reims, "a royal palace is defined by the intellect of its inhabitants and not by the lifeless walls of buildings or enclosures."[1] Although written in the middle of the ninth century, this statement was meant to evoke the renown of Charlemagne's court. Already by the 780s, while the complex at Aachen was still under construction, the Frankish king had gathered about him many of the leading scholars of Europe.[2] There was Alcuin from England, Theodulf from Spain, and from Italy, Paul the Deacon and Peter of Pisa, to name but the most prominent members of an elite circle. Angilbert, the sole Frank, was joined later by other compatriots, like Einhard. Today, such a gathering of minds would be called a "think-tank," but in the context of a still-itinerant court of the late eighth century, these men formed a loose confederation, bound by their devotion to ancient learning and to their patron.

They were well aware of the uniqueness of their time, which they unhesitatingly referred to as a *renovatio*.[3] Among their extensive writings in poetry and prose are examples of artifice, wit, and even satire, reflecting both the sincere comradery and intense personal rivalry engendered by such an auspicious atmosphere.[4] They self-consciously referred to one another by classical and biblical pseudonyms: Alcuin, for example, was Flaccus, better known as Horace; Theodulf was Pindar; Angilbert was Homer; and Charlemagne was David, the king, prophet, and poet of the Old Testament. Coming from diverse backgrounds and differing in age, these men contributed their individual talents to the task of reshaping the cultural landscape of Europe under the leadership of its most Christian ruler. "The old man," Peter of Pisa instructed Charlemagne in grammar. Alcuin, a renowned teacher, was placed in charge of the court school, and later in life produced a revised version of the Vulgate Bible. Theodulf, too, was a noted biblical scholar, specializing in patristic commentaries and, above all, the Old Testament; this particular expertise made him the ideal candidate to formulate the official response of Charlemagne to the recent restoration of icons in Byzantium. Einhard, a newcomer to the court in the 790s, oversaw the king's works. Through their inspiration and guidance, as well as that of their pupils, these members of Charlemagne's court helped to bring about the remarkable flowering of the arts, based on the imitation, emulation, and sometimes reinterpretation of antiquity, which has already been noted in the examination of the palace complex at Aachen. In other words, they were the founders of what has come to be known as the Carolingian Renaissance.

By 800, however, most, if not all, of these men had left the court: Angilbert to serve as lay abbot of St. Riquier at Centula, Alcuin to preside over the abbey of St. Martin at Tours, and Theodulf to become the bishop of Orléans and the abbot of Fleury and other monasteries in the Loire region. The Italians returned to their homeland, while only Einhard, the youngest of the group, remained to the end of Charlemagne's reign. What is of particular interest to this study is the fact that upon retirement from court, if not from public life, three of these men—Angilbert, Theodulf, and Einhard—became important patrons of architecture in their own right. Angilbert will be discussed in the next chapter on the development of monastic architecture. Here the focus will be on the latter two, Theodulf and Einhard, who in their buildings expressed strikingly different and very personal attitudes toward the cultural phenomenon of which they were so much a part.

We know relatively little about Theodulf's personal history. A Visigoth, he was born around 750 in northern Spain, perhaps in or near Saragossa.[5] He seems to have come to Francia by way of Septimania as a refugee from the Arab backlash to Charlemagne's failed military campaigns south of the Pyrénées. In any event, Theodulf was active at the Frankish court by 791 when he began work on the famous theological treatise commonly known as the

135 *(facing page)* Germigny-des-Prés, chapel, view of exterior after restoration, looking west.

136 Germigny-des-Prés, chapel, view of interior after restoration, looking east.

Libri Carolini but originally entitled *Opus Caroli regis contra synodum* (henceforth cited as *Opus Caroli*).[6] In 796, he composed a eulogy to his patron, entitled *Ad Carolum Regem*, in celebration of the recent victory over the Avars.[7] Within two to three years, he was in charge of the diocese of Orléans and was also serving as a *missus dominicus*, or judicial representative of the king. In 800, he participated in the trial of Pope Leo III in Rome and was presumably on hand for the imperial coronation. But in 818, he was accused of conspiring against Charlemagne's son and heir, Louis the Pious; he was deposed from office and exiled to a monastery in Angers, where he died around 826.

During his tenure as bishop and abbot, that is from approximately 798 to 818, Theodulf built a sumptuous villa at Germigny-des-Prés, a short distance from Orléans and very near the abbey of Saint-Benoît-sur-Loire, also known as Fleury. Theodulf was a connoisseur of art and he took pride in the decoration of his palace, as evidenced by his description in verse of the wall paintings of several of its rooms, representing the seasons, the liberal arts, and a map of the world.[8] Today, the only visible remnant of the complex is its justly famous chapel or oratory, but even this is but a shadow of the original structure (figs. 135 and 136).[9] Partially damaged by fire at the end of the ninth century and subsequently modified many times, the chapel was disastrously restored in the middle of the nineteenth century. Beginning in the 1840s, portions of the building were ineptly repaired until in 1867 it was decided to return the building to its "primitive" state. In truth, by 1879, virtually the entire edifice had been rebuilt, and much of its once lavish decoration, as described in early medieval sources, was lost.[10] The original marble floor, it seems, had long disappeared and had been replaced by a new pavement at a slightly higher level, while miscellaneous fragments of sculpture, both in stone and stucco, were carted off to a local museum. Only a mosaic in the main apse was retained, albeit heavily restored. Fortunately, a series of drawings, watercolors, and written records, made before the "repair" work began and in the course of the next four decades, help to verify the authenticity of the basic features of the building in spite of the recent date of much of the fabric. In 1930, moreover, limited excavations unearthed traces of important elements of the plan.[11] Using this information, one can analyze the design and decoration of Theodulf's chapel, at least in general terms.

The interior is composed of two concentric squares, the outer one measuring just under 9 m on each side, excluding the thickness of the walls, and the inner one measuring approximately 3 m per side as defined by four masonry piers supporting a lantern tower (fig. 137).[12] The interior is further divided by a series of arches, linking the piers and outer walls, into nine distinct compartments, roofed in different ways. In addition to the central tower, which was presumably covered by a timber frame, the rectangular bays along the cross axes were barrel vaulted to a height of around 9 m, while square units in the corners seem to have originally been domed at a slightly lower level. This gridlike arrangement was broken along the perimeter by a number of apses of varying shapes and sizes: three to the east and one on each of the remaining sides. It has been suggested that all but the three horseshoe-shaped eastern apses were later additions, but there is as yet no firm evidence to support this conjecture.[13] The foundation of a

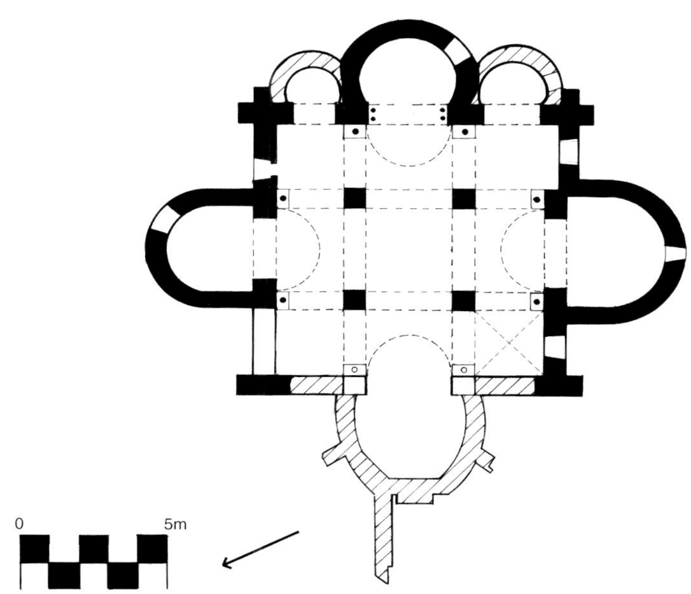

137 Germigny-des-Prés, chapel, plan.

138 Germigny-des-Prés, chapel, axonometric reconstruction.

wall projecting from the western apse indicates the presence of a vestibule.

In three-dimensional terms, the building is a compact cube (just under 9 m on each side), punctuated by an inscribed, equal-armed cross, and broken laterally by the ring of apses and vertically by the central tower (fig. 138). Before 1867, this tower bore an additional storey, which may or may not have been original; the shape of the upper windows, as recorded in nineteenth-century views, suggests a later medieval date. Nonetheless, whether of one storey or two, the tower's primary purpose was to provide light for the otherwise dark interior through round-arched windows set just above the crossing. Diaphragm arches framing the central bay were, in turn, pierced by triple-arched openings with paired colonnettes in order to allow the light to penetrate the surrounding bays in a manner vaguely reminiscent, albeit on a much smaller scale, of the upper halves of the gallery-level arches inside Charlemagne's chapel at Aachen. The general nature of the masonry—coarse rubble for the walls and cut stone for the piers and arches—was also similar to that at Aachen. Another "local" feature was the placement of colonnettes within the pilasters along the inner face of the outer walls, which can be compared to the use of applied orders in the vaulted crypt of St. Laurent at Grenoble from around 800.[14] Both monuments, in turn, belong to a tradition that can be traced back to the sixth century in Gaul at St. Pierre in Vienne (fig. 45). Frankish workmanship is also indicated by the relatively crude capitals of the colonnettes and what little stucco decoration has been preserved.[15] Thus the masons were indigenous, but this still does not explain the unusual character of the overall design.

The statement in a late-tenth-century source that the chapel at Germigny was modelled after Charlemagne's chapel at Aachen is generally discounted because, aside from the random features already noted, there seems to be little to link the two buildings directly.[16] Most scholars, instead, have emphasized the "byzantinizing" quality of the plan, because the cross-in-square, or quincunx as it is sometimes called, was commonly used for middle and late Byzantine churches.[17] Although a Greek source for the chapel at Germigny would be intriguing, for reasons that will be discussed below, such a connection remains questionable. A few examples of churches in the Greek East with "experimental" cross-in-square plans may well date to the late eighth or early ninth century, but the vast majority were constructed long after Germigny (most are from the tenth century or later). More important, the elevations of these Byzantine churches are dominated by a dome, not a tower. Rather than a direct relationship between Germigny and the Byzantine sphere, a common source seems more likely. Quincunx structures, for example, are known to have existed in ancient Roman times, as witness the so-called praetorium of an army camp at Musmiye in present-day Syria. Erected between A.D. 164 and 169, this small, square building with an apse at one end was divided into nine bays by four slender columns. Whether it originally served a religious or secular purpose, the structure was converted into a Christian church with little alteration sometime before 450.[18] The history of the cross-in-square plan in Byzantium

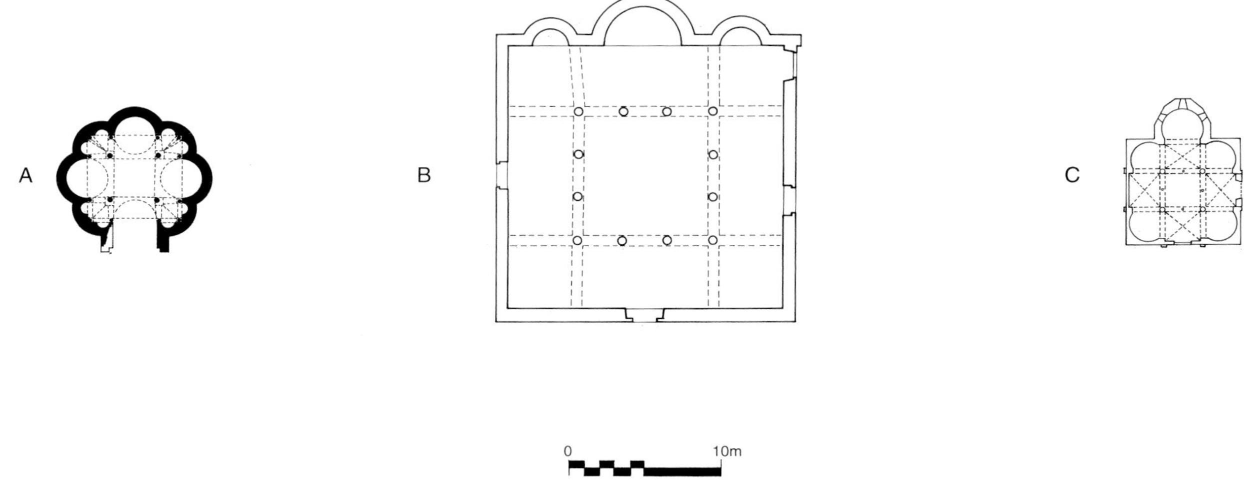

139 Comparative plans: A Milan, S. Satiro; B Cassino, S. Maria delle Cinque Torri; C Tarrasa, S. Miguel.

during the intervening years of the fifth to the tenth centuries remains obscure. Frequently cited churches in Armenia of central plan from this period seem too remote to have played a major role in the development of this type in either the Greek East or the Latin West.

More relevant for an understanding of Theodulf's chapel are three early examples of the cross-in-square plan in the western Mediterranean. S. Satiro in Milan, the one that resembles Germigny-des-Prés most closely, was built two generations later as a private chapel for Archbishop Anspert (868–81) and a small group of monks (fig. 139).[19] Now attached to Bramante's famous church of S. Maria, the exterior of S. Satiro was radically altered in the fifteenth century, but the interior retains the original cross-in-square design, centered about four monolithic columns and a lantern tower. Like Theodulf's chapel, the bays of the cross arms are barrel vaulted, while the corner compartments seem to have been covered by groin or quadrant vaults rather than domes. In spite of a difference in the proportions of the bays and the central supports, the designs of the two buildings are strikingly similar. There may even have been a direct influence from Theodulf's building on the chapel in Milan, because Anspert was an intimate of Charles the Bald, a grandson of Charlemagne and ruler of France at a time when Germigny had been declared a royal palace.[20] Be that as it may, an earlier version of the cross-in-square plan had already appeared in South Italy at S. Maria delle Cinque Torri, built for Abbot Theodemar of Montecassino (778–97) in the neighboring town of Cassino. Totally destroyed in World War II, the church can be reconstructed from prewar records and a recent archaeological study (fig. 139).[21] Although timber-roofed throughout and subdivided by twelve columns instead of only four supports, the Cassino church was composed of nine distinct bays centered about a lantern tower. It also shared with Germigny the use of triple eastern apses. Here an influence on Theodulf's chapel is possible because Montecassino had long enjoyed close contacts with the Frankish court. It was to Montecassino that Carloman, brother of Pippin III, retired in 747, and it was there, fifty years later, that Paul the Deacon lived after leaving Aachen. Abbot Theodemar, moreover, was himself from northern Gaul, and in 787 he received a letter of privilege from Charlemagne, the same year he provided the king with an "authentic" copy of the Rule of St. Benedict.[22] Theodulf, as abbot of Fleury, the most important monastery dedicated to St. Benedict north of the Alps, must have been in contact with Montecassino and may well have visited the abbey during his visit to Rome in 800.[23] Even so, Germigny is far from a direct copy of the Cassino church. At best, it is a much reduced version with extensive vaulting in place of wooden roofs and piers instead of columns. In short, S. Maria delle Cinque Torri can have served as only a partial model for the design of Theodulf's building.

The third and final example of a cross-in-square plan in the early medieval West, San Miguel at Tarrasa in the Spanish province of Catalonia is related to a decidedly different type of Early Christian structure (fig. 139).[24] Square on the outside and articulated on the inside by corner niches, the small building was originally constructed in the seventh century as a baptistery, following the variations on the octagonal formula so popular in the Mediterranean world throughout the Early Christian period. In the late ninth or early tenth century, the building was extensively remodelled, at which time a horseshoe-shaped apse was added to the east and the interior was divided into nine bays with groin vaults on the cross axes, quadrant vaults in the corners, and a central lantern tower supported by eight reused columns. The late date of this remodeling, indicated by the style of the accompanying wall paintings as well as the difference in function excludes San Miguel from having played a role in the design of Germigny. Only the distinctive horseshoe shape of the eastern apse brings out the likely Spanish background for the eastern apses of Theodulf's chapel; a fact that would not be surprising given Theodulf's Visigothic origin. These three examples of the cross-in-square design, therefore, do not in themselves provide specific models for Theodulf's chapel, but they do illustrate the fact that the cross-in-square plan was known in the West in the early Middle Ages.

The last two buildings, it should be noted, were influenced in varying ways by Early Christian precedents. San Miguel at Tarrasa was built first as a baptistery. S. Maria at Cassino, in turn, was a revival of an earlier church type represented by the east end of the cathedral at Trier, as rebuilt under the Emperor Gratian around 380, and S. Lorenzo in Milan, also from the late fourth century, with five towers (four in the corners and one in the center), hence the name *delle cinque torri*.[25] One should also not forget the widespread tradition of small, cruciform, vaulted chapels, with flat-ended cross arms and a low, central tower, seen in Italy in the early fifth century at the so-called Mausoleum of Galla Placidia in Ravenna, and in Visigothic Spain in the late seventh century at Sta. Comba de Banda and San Fructuoso near Braga (figs. 39 and 40), the last example differing only by the insertion of horseshoe-shaped apses in three of its cross arms. Against this background, the quincunx plan with its inscribed cross could be seen as a logical opening up and expansion of the cruciform design, using a minimum of supports, in order to provide sufficient space for the performance of church services and the presence of a select audience. Certainly, this was a prime reason for its adoption in the Byzantine sphere, where the intimate scale of the cross-in-square church was ideally suited to the needs of private residences and small monastic communities. Thus, in the broadest possible sense, the chapel at Germigny-des-Prés forms part of a long tradition, the roots of which go back to the Early Christian period, if not earlier. Small in scale, whether cruciform, polygonal, or rectilinear, such private chapels were invariably centered about a square crossing, surmounted by a lantern tower or dome. Recalling the tenth-century comparison between Germigny and Aachen, it may well be that their function as palace chapels, together with their centralized plans, may have been sufficient in the minds of medieval writers to suggest a common bond, regardless of the obvious differences in size and other details. Even so, specific models for Theodulf's chapel remain elusive.

Yet there is a more specific and personal level of meaning to be appreciated here, the key to which is provided by the unusual mosaic decoration in the main eastern apse (fig. 140). Although it was, like the rest of the building, heavily restored and in part reset when the apse was rebuilt in the 1860s, most details of the scene and its general iconography have been retained. The mosaic inscription at the base of the apse proclaims Theodulf's patronage and the subject: the Ark of the Covenant.[26] Like the mosaicists at Aachen, those working at Germigny probably came from Rome or perhaps Montecassino, where the art of mosaic also flourished, but the representation of the ark was, as far as is known, unique in monumental church decoration at the time.[27] The reason for its appearance at Germigny can only be explained by the aforementioned *Opus Caroli*, which Theodulf authored.[28] At the Second Council of Nicaea in 787, the Greek church reinstated the use of religious images after decades of iconoclasm. Although this turn of events was generally welcomed by the papacy, the Frankish court saw the change in a more negative and political light. Using a poor Latin translation of the acts of the council provided by Pope Hadrian I, Theodulf was assigned the task of refuting the new Byzantine policy. And he did so in the most virulent terms.

Theodulf was not an iconoclast. Indeed, he recognized the value of representing religious subject matter as a means of instruction and for inspiring acts of piety, an attitude very much in keeping with the earlier pronouncements of Pope Gregory the Great and other authorities in the Latin West. The Greeks, however, were in error, according to Theodulf, because they equated the representation of a holy subject with its prototype. That is to say, they placed manmade images on a par with divine beings, which was idolatrous. Works of art could be admired for the quality of their workmanship or the value of their materials, but they remained the mundane products of man not of God. The only exception to this truth is the Ark of the Covenant as built by Moses at the command of God (Exodus 24:10–22, 37:1–9). The *Opus Caroli* goes on to interpret the ark as a prefiguration of Christ and the Church: the two tablets it contained signify the Old and New Testaments, and the figures of the two cherubim with their wings spread over the chest represent the full wisdom contained in both parts of the Bible. The Acts of the Second Council of Nicaea, on the other hand, cite the precedent of the cherubim as justification for the placement of images of Christ and the Virgin in the apse of a church, overshadowing the altar. But at Germigny, it is the image of the ark itself that has been placed there. To quote Paul Meyvaert, "The Germigny mosaic can be considered his (Theodulf's) most authentic signature to the *Libri Carolini* (i.e., *Opus Caroli*)."[29]

140 Germigny-des-Prés, chapel, apse mosaic.

The composition in the apse, however, does not represent the ark as it stood in the tabernacle of Moses. The two larger angels shown flanking the chest and the two smaller cherubim of Moses were added by King Solomon in a way so that their wings touched one another as well as the opposite walls of the inner shrine, or Holy of Holies, of the temple in Jerusalem (1 Kings 6:23–28). By implication, therefore, the architectural setting of this image alludes to the Temple of Solomon. The Solomonic interpretation of a church was not unusual; in fact, it had been a literary *topos* since Early Christian times.[30] But it had taken on added meaning in the atmosphere of the Carolingian court. As we have seen, Charlemagne was often referred to as the new David, and by extension it is not surprising to find that Theodulf and others compared him to Solomon. Alcuin even went so far as to refer to the royal chapel at Aachen as the "temple of Solomon."[31] Here we have yet another link between the chapels of Theodulf and Charlemagne. Once again, this analogy need not be taken too far, but in the case of Germigny-des-Prés a concerted effort seems to have been made to emulate the biblical prototype as much as possible.

According to a later ninth- or early-tenth-century source, the chapel was not dedicated to the Virgin Mary, as was the principal altar at Aachen, or to some other saint, but to "God, Creator and Savior of All Things." In addition, an inscription in silver letters, once visible inside the base of the tower, proclaimed that the building was consecrated simply "in the honor of God."[32] The mosaic inscription still preserved in the apse immediately below the image of the ark, moreover, refers to the chapel as the *oraculum*, the same term used for Solomon's Holy of Holies both in the Old Testament and in the *Opus Caroli*. André Grabar was the first to notice that the painted stucco

141 Germigny-des-Prés, chapel, detail of apse decoration, palmettes, nineteenth-century watercolor, partial reconstruction.

rosettes and other floral patterns, together with rinceaux and smaller cherubim in mosaic, which are recorded as having surrounded the apse composition at Germigny before it was restored, seem to echo the "cherubim, palms, and open flowers" that covered the walls of the sanctuary in Jerusalem (1 Kings 6:29).[33] Particularly striking were stylized palmettes, depicted in mosaic within the blind arcade at the bottom of the main apse, for this motif is otherwise unknown in the West (fig. 141). It was, however, a common feature of Sasanian and early Islamic art, as seen for example in the mosaic decoration of the Dome of the Rock in Jerusalem from the late seventh century.[34] Theodulf was presumably familiar with the motif from luxurious *objets d'art* in metal, ivory, and silk, which he is known to have collected and admired. In fact, he inserted pieces of Near Eastern textiles between the pages of his Bibles.[35] None of the fifty odd fragments that survive from his collection depict this particular type of palmette, but it seems reasonable to suppose that he was well acquainted with this strictly oriental motif nonetheless and that he consciously selected it in order to add a rich and exotic air to his chapel, in keeping with its Solomonic connotations. One can even go so far as to suggest that the design of the chapel itself was inspired by Solomon's *oraculum*.

Once again, it would have been the biblical text that served as the point of reference, for the Holy of Holies is described as a cube, "20 cubits long and 20 cubits wide and 20 cubits high" (1 Kings 6:20). It is quite plausible that not only the cubic form but also the size of Germigny represent a direct translation of these dimensions. To be sure, medieval systems of measurement, as well as their ancient and biblical counterparts, are notoriously difficult to calculate precisely. The cubit, moreover, was a widespread unit of measure in the ancient Near East, derived either from the length of a man's arm from the elbow to the tip of the middle finger or from six hand-widths, and accordingly its exact length varied from region to region and from age to age; however, the most common measurement for the cubit in late antiquity and the early Middle Ages seems to have been 1.5 Roman feet (or .445 m).[36] This, for example, was the unit of measurement used at Montecassino in the late eighth and early ninth centuries.[37] It is therefore significant to note that, when multiplied by the biblical number 20, the .445-meter-cubit produces 8.90 m, which is remarkably close to the principal dimension of Germigny-des-Prés. One can well imagine that to Theodulf and his retinue, the chapel, in both design and decoration, seemed to resonate with associations to the Solomonic shrine and its relevance for the Christian faith. Thus the uniqueness of the building can be attributed to the personal predilections of its patron, a man of sophisticated tastes, who was highly educated and well travelled, but above all one who was steeped in the mysteries of the Old Testament and very much aware of the power of art to mold men's minds and their religious beliefs. In spite of the ravages of time, Germigny-des-Prés stands as a monument to Theodulf's particular genius.

Einhard was also a man of great learning and many talents. Scholar, poet, councilor, statesman, and artist, he, more than any other member of Charlemagne's court, seems to have epitomized the modern concept of a "Renaissance man." To his contemporaries, Einhard's intellectual prowess and boundless energy seemed all the more striking in contrast to his abnormally small size. Theodulf in jest, for example, compared Einhard to an ant, "scurrying back and forth at a ceaseless pace, laden with books and the burden of many responsibilities," to which he hastened to add, "this small house is inhabited by a great guest." Alcuin, in turn, likened him to the pupil of a man's eye, which, in spite of its smallness, is "master of the body's life and will."[38]

Born around 770, Einhard received his early training at the great abbey of Fulda, where he had been sent by his parents as a boy of ten or eleven. Although he never took holy orders or monastic vows, Einhard felt a deep allegiance to the abbey throughout his life, and it was probably here that he was instilled with a keen admiration for the cultural and spiritual legacy of Rome. Fulda had been founded in 744 by a disciple of the Anglo-Saxon missionary, Wynfrid, who, taking the name of the Roman martyr Boniface, had been commissioned by the papal see to convert the heathens along the easternmost fringes of the Frankish kingdom. When Boniface died at the hands of the barbarous Frisians in 754, his body was laid to rest at Fulda, and beginning in 790, Einhard was able to witness the initial stages of the construction of a new and much larger abbey church to house the tomb of the martyred missionary. In the course of the second half of the eighth century, Fulda developed into one of the leading monastic centers in Francia, and the close ties with both England and Rome meant that its library was exceptionally well stocked with the writings of ancient authors.[39] It was also sometime in the 780s that Charlemagne sent a famous letter to bishops and abbots, including Abbot Baugulf of Fulda, announcing his zeal for monastic education in order to produce "soldiers of the Church," who, "inwardly devout and outwardly learned," would have a better understanding of sacred scriptures.[40] Thus, through his affiliation with Fulda, Einhard should be seen as a product of the Carolingian Renaissance as well as one of its major contributors.

In any event, it was Baugulf who recognized Einhard's special talents and sent him to Aachen for further training around 794. Initially he was one of Alcuin's students, but he so distinguished himself that soon he became a personal adviser to the king. Upon his retirement to Tours in 796, Alcuin had apparently wanted Einhard to succeed him as head of the palace school, but in recognition of his expertise in artistic matters, he was instead appointed "director of the royal works of the palace at Aachen."[41] His pseudonym at court was Beseleel, referring to the maker of the Arc of the Covenant in the Old Testament, who had been "filled with the spirit of God in wisdom and knowledge, and in the skill of devising all manner of works of art" (Exodus 31:1–4). Although Odo of Metz is mentioned in one late ninth-century source as the "master" (*magister*) or construction supervisor of the royal chapel at Aachen, we may assume that from at least 796 on Einhard played a major role in the design and decoration of all aspects of the palace complex.[42] Einhard may also have been the author of the early ninth-century *Aachen Epic*, which, as noted in the last chapter, compared the Frankish capital to Rome and Charlemagne to Aeneas.[43] One is therefore tempted to attribute to Einhard many of the palace's most explicit references to classical models.

The most specific example of Einhard's antiquarian taste and his general attitude toward art is a reliquary he designed for the monastery of St. Servatius at Maastricht, where he served as lay abbot. The reliquary itself has been lost but a detailed drawing from the seventeenth century makes it easy to visualize (fig. 142).[44] Standing about 38 cm high and constructed of wood overlaid with hammered silver, it seems at first to have been an amazingly accurate rendering in miniature of an ancient Roman triumphal arch. Rather than a copy of a specific model, however, Einhard's reliquary has been shown to be a conflation of several sources, both Christian and pagan, in various media. Like the Arch of Titus in the Roman forum, for example, it was composed of a single arch with a high attic

142 Einhard reliquary for his abbey at Maastricht, drawing (Paris, Bibliothèque Nationale, Fr. 10440, fol. 45).

bearing an inscription in clear, capital letters, in this case proclaiming Einhard's authorship, but like the arches of Septimus Severus and Constantine it was covered with figural decoration. Yet the specific renderings of the figures, including the four evangelists and their symbols, military saints, angels, seated apostles, and scenes from the New Testament, were derived from more recent models. The inscription also makes clear that the arch was intended to serve as the base for a cross, "the trophy of eternal victory." Thus, Einhard was able to instill the traditional form of an ancient Roman monument of triumph with a new and specifically Christian meaning.

When the drawing of the reliquary was made the cross had already disappeared, but its square pedestal, perched atop the arch, was recorded as having been covered with abstract linear patterns that were virtually identical to one of the sets of bronze railing inside the royal chapel at Aachen, which further confirms Einhard's involvement with completion of the palace. Still, the best-documented examples of Einhard's involvement in architecture are the churches he had built on his private estates at present-day Steinbach and Seligenstadt. He acquired both properties in 815 as a gift from Louis the Pious; one near Michlinstadt (now Michelstadt) in the wooded mountains of the Odenwald, some 60 km east of Lorsch, and the other at Mülenheim, 50 km due north, on the banks of the Main River.[45] The churches at these two locations, however, are strikingly different in design, which can only be explained by an examination of the circumstances under which they were built. This background is provided by Einhard's own extraordinarily detailed account of the translation of the relics of SS. Marcellinus and Peter from Rome first to Steinbach and then to Seligenstadt.[46]

While still busy with affairs at court, Einhard tells us in his *translatio* that he often thought about retiring to the quiet and solitude of Steinbach, where he had built living quarters and a church for a small monastic community. By 827, as the church was nearing completion, however, he began to worry about its dedication. At Aachen, he met a deacon by the name of Deusdona, newly arrived from Rome, whom he invited to dine at his house. During the meal, according to Einhard, they discussed the recent translation of the body of St. Sebastian from Rome to St. Medard at Soissons, and the neglected tombs of other martyrs which still lay in the cemeteries outside the ancient capital. "Then, the talk turning to the dedication of our new church," Einhard continues, "I began to ask him by what means I could bring it about that some bit of the true relics of the saints, who lie in rest at Rome, could be obtained by me."[47] Deusdona was at first reluctant to respond, but upon further coaxing he agreed to send back with one of Einhard's men relics he had at home in Rome. A few days later, Deusdona, together with Einhard's representative, Ratleic, set out on their journey. They stopped first at Soissons, where the abbot of St. Medard, Hilduin, who was also the archchaplain of the palace at Aachen, requested relics from Deusdona as well and sent one of his priests to join the venture to Rome.

What follows in the *translatio* is a fascinating, but involved, tale of intrigue, deception, and perseverance. Here it need only be noted that, although Deusdona proved to be unreliable, Ratleic ultimately succeeded in stealing in the dark of night the remains of saints Marcellinus and Peter from their burial place outside Rome, and was able to return to Steinbach with his prize, being careful to avoid papal emissaries en route to Aachen along the way. The remains of the saints were then placed in a casket near the high altar of the newly completed church. Only later did Einhard discover that a portion of the remains of Marcellinus had, unbeknownst to Ratleic, been separated and taken to Hilduin at Soissons by the priest from St. Medard; they were eventually returned. We might be shocked by the blatantly surreptitious nature of the translation, but to Einhard and his colleagues the saints themselves had shown their approval of the undertaking by having guided Ratleic in a dream to their tomb along the Via Labicana.[48] The historical authenticity of the theft, if not the accompanying supernatural events, is substantiated by Einhard's description of the burial chamber as having been underground and separate from the funerary basilica of SS. Marcellinus and Peter itself, which corresponds to the arrangement uncovered by excavations of the site several decades ago.[49]

But the story does not end here, for again through a series of visions, the saints made it known that they were not pleased with their new resting place and that they wished to be taken elsewhere; exactly where, they did not specify. Einhard at first hesitated and debated in his mind "with great anxiety" what he should do next, but the visions continued, afflicting more and more of those who prayed by the saints' remains. Finally, Einhard resolved to take the matter in hand, and in spite of the threat of torrential rains set out early one morning with a convoy bearing the relics of the saints. The next day, January 16, 828, the holy treasure was placed in a new shrine in the apse of a small church at Einhard's other estate at Mülenheim, which came to be called Seligenstadt, "the city of the blessed." The church soon proved to be too small to accommodate the growing number of pilgrims who flocked to the shrine, and so over the next decade, Einhard devoted his energies toward raising funds for and overseeing the construction of a new and much larger church, which was presumably completed before his death in or around 840.

Einhard's first church at Steinbach stands today as a sad yet majestic ruin which has been partially rebuilt and restored over the past century (figs. 143–145). Substantial portions of the rising walls, especially of the east end and the nave, are preserved and the plan is clear.[50] Relatively short and squat in outline, the nave measures 12.30 m long and 7.30 m wide, and almost 15 m wide if the side aisles are included. Instead of columns, the nave and aisles were divided by a series of masonry piers supporting six extremely narrow (1.35 m) arches, now walled up; above each arch is a single round-arched clerestory window. The east end is divided into three distinct areas composed of a central extension of the nave with a broad apse, flanked by dwarf transept arms, each approximately 5 m square in plan with a smaller apse. The tripartite arrangement of the east end corresponds to the intersections of the intricate network of barrel-vaulted corridors of the crypt below, originally reached by flights of stairs in the north and south aisles. The central passageway of the crypt terminates in a cruciform chamber below the main apse and extends west below the middle of the nave, where it ends with two arcosolia facing one another; some have postulated that these two recesses were intended to serve as the burial places for Einhard and his wife Imma, but this is only speculation. Foundations at the west end of the church indicate the presence of a central vestibule, flanked by smaller rectangular rooms.

The masonry of the best-preserved sections of the church is of roughly hewn stones with ample mortar; in the crypt the stonework is enhanced by the occasional insertion of bricks. It is, however, in certain details that one is able to appreciate the influence of Einhard's artistic skill and sensibilities. Particular care, for example, was taken in the construction of the piers of the nave, which are composed of brick evidently manufactured for the purpose because of their uniform dimensions. The fine brick masonry, moreover, was framed top and bottom by delicately carved bases and moldings in red sandstone, now badly damaged but still elegant in their profile. Also striking are the pair of round windows, or oculi, that frame the main apse and resemble spotlights when filled with the morning sun. In addition, traces of plaster here and there indicate that the interior was once brightly painted; in fact, the outline of an illusionistic cornice, interspersed with sprightly birds, is still faintly visible immediately above the clerestory windows and just below the modern roof line. Thus, in spite of its rather decrepit state, one can well imagine that when newly completed this boxy little church, with its elaborate network of crypts, must have shone with light and color.

143 Steinbach, Einhard's church, view of exterior, looking northwest.

Of particular importance for us is the fact that at the time it was built (between 815 and 827), Einhard's church at Steinbach was very much up-to-date. Both its plan and its dimensions followed closely the abbey church at Inden (now Kornelimünster) near Aachen, established in 814 by Benedict of Aniane, who was a confidant of Louis the Pious and head of the monastic reform movement (fig. 146).[51] Particularly distinctive in both cases are the masonry piers of the relatively short nave, the segregated dwarf transept arms and triple apses at the east end, and the square entrance vestibule to the west. The corridor crypt at Steinbach, however, found no parallel at Kornelimünster but resembled instead the elaborate crypt at Saint-Médard at Soissons, which had been designed to receive the relics of St. Sebastian in 826 (fig. 147). Although the crypt of Soissons seems to have been extensively remodelled in the eleventh century, recent excavations indicate that its basic outline of intersecting corridors, designed perhaps to imitate the passageways of the Roman catacombs, goes back to the abbacy of Hilduin.[52] Not surprisingly, therefore, at Steinbach Einhard seems to have skillfully combined the most recent developments in ecclesiastical architecture connected with both monastic reform and the cult of relics, but it is also important to note that in doing so he was imitating buildings that were patronized by two major figures at court, which suggests an element of personal rivalry. Certainly, the *translatio* makes it clear that Hilduin's acquisition of the body of St. Sebastian inspired Einhard's desire for Roman relics for his church at Steinbach.

The church at Seligenstadt to which the relics of Marcellinus and Peter were moved, having continued in use to the present day, is also well preserved and was recently stripped of its later Baroque decoration.[53] In contrast to Steinbach, however, Seligenstadt is considerably larger, its nave measuring 33.16 m long and with the aisles 20 m wide (fig. 148). Even more important, it took on the form, albeit on a reduced scale, of Old St. Peter's in Rome, with its projecting transept, and single apse housing an annular crypt. Also like the Early Christian basilica, the church at Seligenstadt was originally approached through

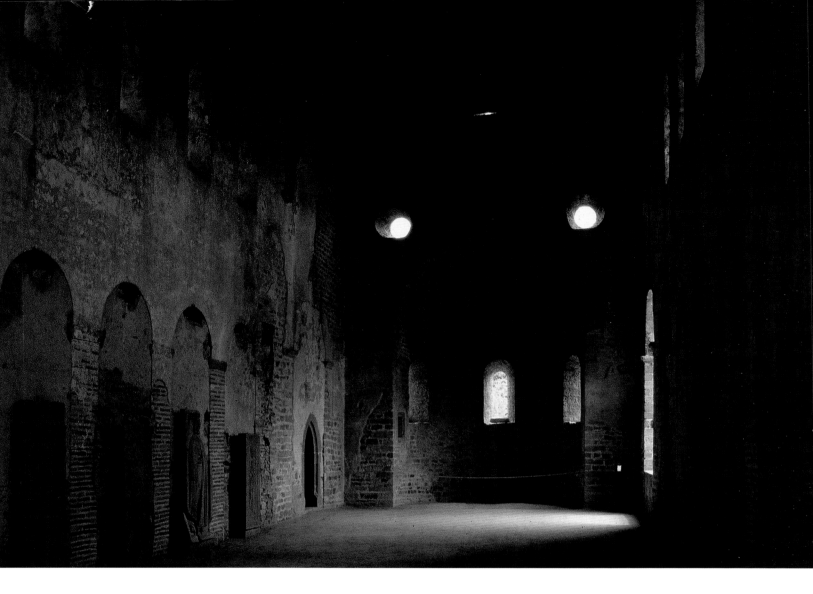

144 and 145 Steinbach, Einhard's church, view of interior, looking east and plan.

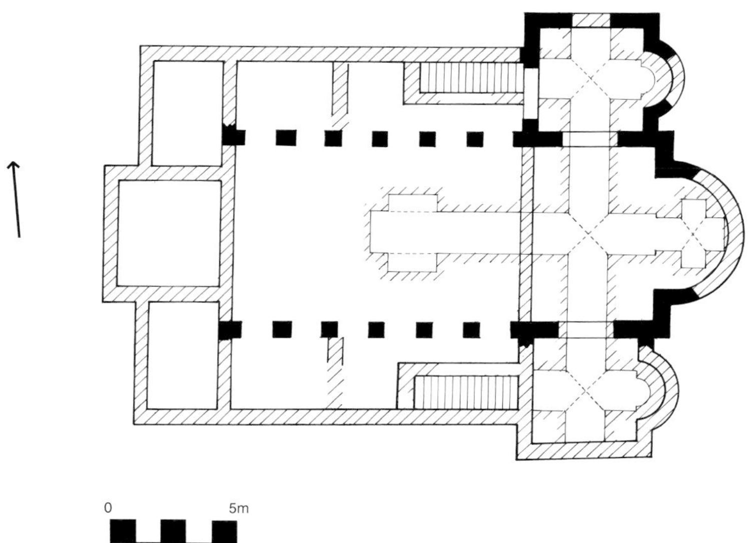

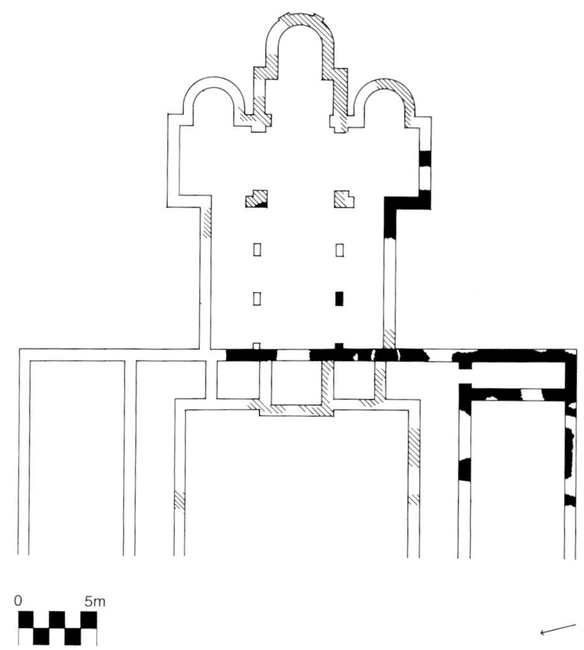

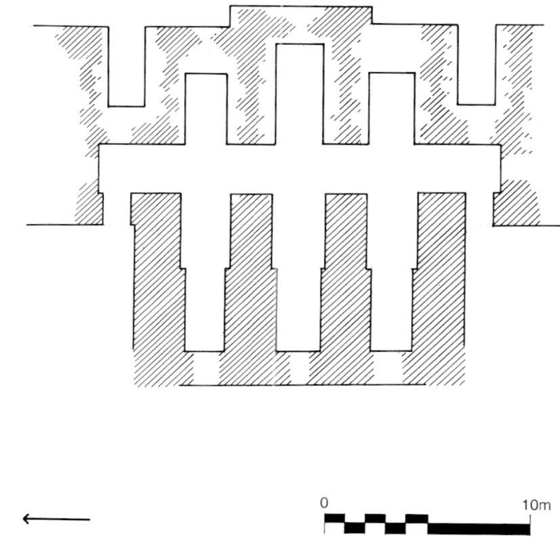

147 Soissons, abbey church of Saint-Médard, plan of crypt.

146 Kornelimünster (Inden), abbey church, plan.

an atrium. The only non-Roman element of the entire complex was the continued use of brick piers dividing the nave and aisles, but here the arches are twice as wide in keeping with the increased size of the overall design.

The resemblance to the Petrine church can not be coincidental, for it follows a tradition of reviving the Early Christian T-shaped basilica that goes back, as we have seen, to the abbey church of Saint-Denis from the beginning of Charlemagne's reign. Moreover, the new abbey church at Fulda, which Einhard had seen initiated in his youth, was further enlarged between 802 and 817 by the addition of a western apse and projecting transept to mark the tomb of Boniface. In both cases, the design of the churches represented an attempt to equate, or at least associate, the local martyrs—St. Denis, "the apostle of the Gauls," and St. Boniface, "the apostle of the Germans"—with St. Peter in Rome.[54] At Seligenstadt, on the other hand, the relics were of martyrs from Rome, and so it

148 Seligenstadt, church of SS. Marcellinus and Peter, plan.

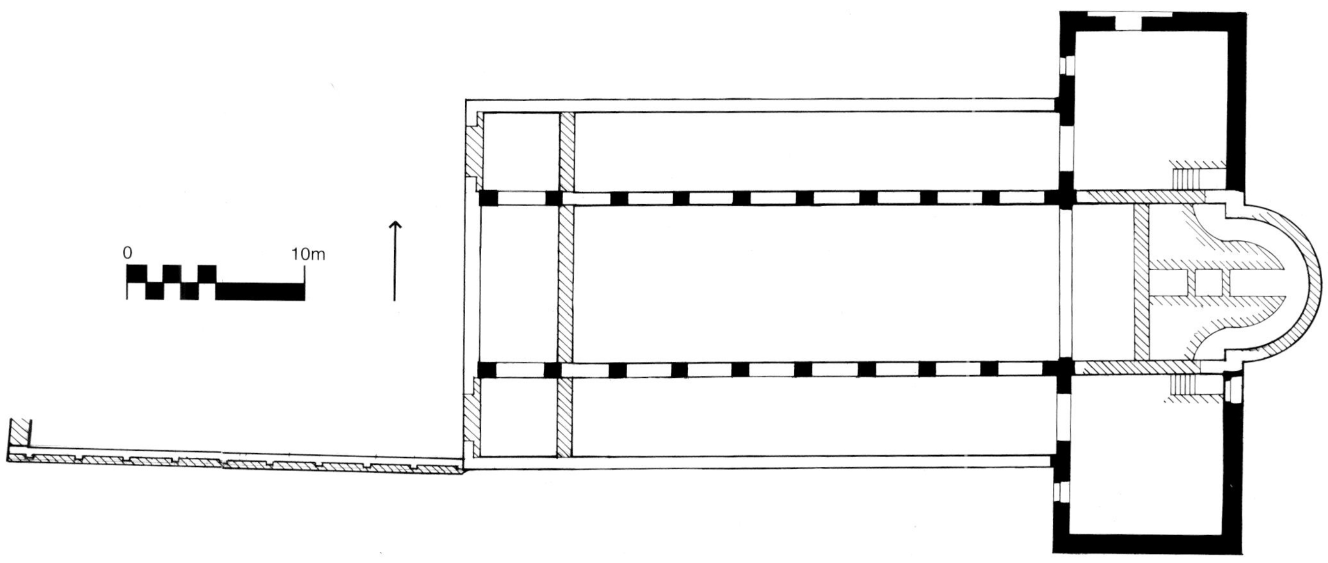

seemed only fitting that they should "feel at home" in a Roman church. In other words, at St. Denis, Fulda, and Seligenstadt, the design of the churches expressed a deep-seated sense of propriety, whereby the architectural setting was meant to symbolize simultaneously the venerated status of the relics and their close affiliation with Rome.

Einhard also viewed his acquisition of the relics and their disposition at Seligenstadt in a distinctly political light. The construction of the church between 830 and 840 coincided with a period of turmoil for the empire, resulting from a series of revolts against Louis the Pious, which were led by his sons and various factions of disgruntled nobles. Already in 828, the year in which the bodies of Marcellinus and Peter were transferred to Seligenstadt, the emperor had broken the 817 accord of succession for his three elder sons by apportioning part of the empire to a fourth son, Charles the Bald, born in 823. Einhard, who had served as the tutor of the eldest son, Lothar, tried in vain to warn Louis of impending rebellion, but his words went unheeded. In 830, frustrated with his position at court, Einhard petitioned the emperor to be relieved of his duties so that he could return to Seligenstadt in order to "dwell in peace and tranquility near the tombs of the blessed martyrs of Christ." At the same time, he did not hesitate to ask Louis for help in completing the church and monastery, because, as he reminded the emperor, "Marcellinus and Peter, who through the grace of God abandoned Rome, came to Francia for the glory and protection of your realm."[55]

Louis the Pious, however, was apparently slow to respond to this request, so that in 834, Einhard had to appeal to the abbot of St. Wandrille for assistance in roofing the basilica.[56] Still, Einhard continued to offer the emperor his advice, backed now by the authority of his patron saints. He even relates how on two separate occasions he handed Louis "little books" (*libelli*), containing divine admonitions heard by those who had prayed by the tombs at Seligenstadt. In one instance, a girl possessed by a devil spoke ominous words in Latin about "the crimes daily committed by the Frankish people and their rulers . . . for which they will be made to suffer."[57] The abundant correspondence preserved from the last years of his life shows that Einhard became increasingly despondent about the rapidly changing course of events around him, and he seems to have looked back with increasing nostalgia to the harmony and spirit of an earlier age. It was probably around this time that he wrote his biography of Charlemagne, modelled after Suetonius', *Life of the Caesars*, wherein Frankish valor, Roman virtue, and religious faith combine in the father of Louis the Pious to provide a paradigm for the Christian ruler.[58] It is also during this period that Einhard designed the reliquary arch for St. Servatius at Maastricht and, of course, wrote his *translatio* of the relics of SS. Marcellinus and Peter. As Hans Belting and Josef Fleckenstein have shown, the classicizing prose style and historical purpose of Einhard's *Vita* of Charlemagne and the supernaturally charged atmosphere and abiding faith of his *translatio* are not mutually exclusive as one might think but are in fact complementary, reflecting the author's disillusionment in the current state of the empire and his reliance on ancient precedent for guidance.[59] In this sense, the distinctly Roman form of the basilica at Seligenstadt represents a conscious rejection of the style of church building prevalent during the first decade and a half of Louis's reign and a return to the ideals of the first flowering of the Carolingian Renaissance. In other words, Seligenstadt expresses in the most intimate and tangible terms Einhard's steadfast admiration for Roman antiquity. In fact, one could go so far as to say that, in spite of its late date, the church of SS. Marcellinus and Peter is the last monument of the age of Charlemagne.

Taken together, the architectural patronage of Theodulf and Einhard represents, on a very personal level, the richness and diversity of the Carolingian era. The resultant buildings could not be more different; the centrally planned chapel at Germigny-des-Prés, inspired by the inner sanctuary of Solomon's Temple in Jerusalem, proclaims Theodulf's belief in the supremacy of Old Testament authority for the formulation of religious art and architecture, while the T-shaped basilica at Seligenstadt, modelled after Old St. Peter's in Rome, expresses Einhard's faith in the traditions of the Roman Church to provide the most appropriate setting for his precious relics. And yet in spite of their apparent differences, the attitudes of both men reflect their common experience at Charlemagne's court where the same dichotomy of reference, the Bible and Rome, had been such a potent force, making the Frankish ruler at one and the same time the personification of the Old Testament kings David and Solomon, and the Roman emperors Augustus and Constantine. Thus religion and politics were inextricably linked in the minds of both men. For Theodulf, Germigny-des-Prés reaffirmed in tangible form his anti-Byzantine stance toward the cult of images in the *Opus Caroli*, while for Einhard, the church at Seligenstadt gave new meaning to his belief in the power of Roman relics, and thereby the legacy of Rome itself, to bolster the faltering fortunes of the Frankish empire.

The building activities of Theodulf and Einhard should also be viewed in the context of contemporary developments in Rome. Both men were no doubt well acquainted with the general course of events in the papal city, for as we have seen the courts of Charlemagne and the popes enjoyed intimate contact, resulting in reciprocal

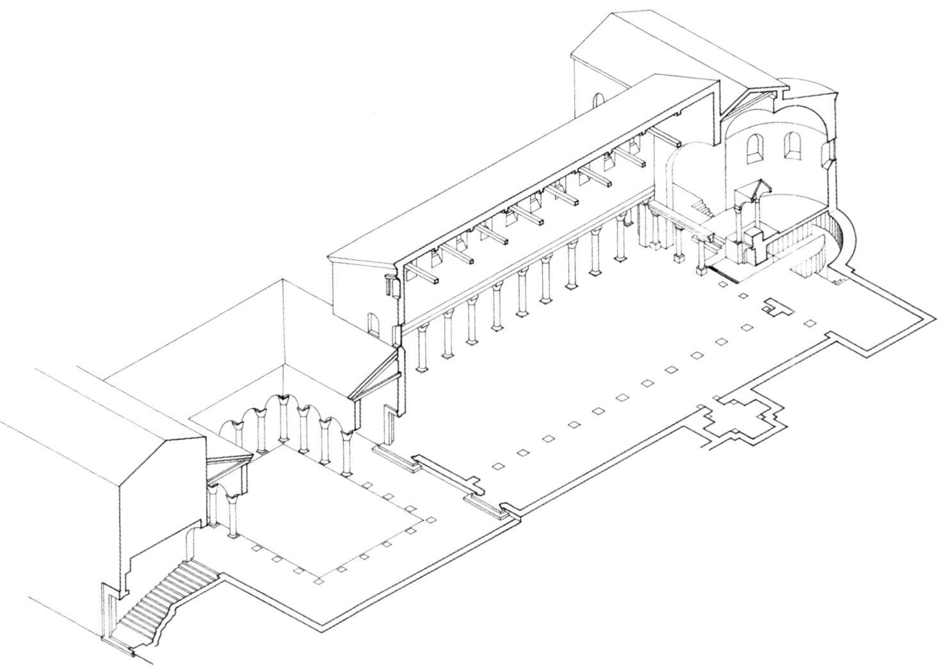

149 Rome, S. Prassede, axonometric reconstruction.

influence. Still, the decidedly antiquarian nature of ecclesiastical architecture in the Carolingian era, although inspired in large part by the Early Christian monuments of Rome, found its initial impetus north of the Alps, as exemplified by the abbey church of Saint-Denis (768–75). Indeed, it was not until the construction of S. Prassede at the beginning of the reign of Pope Paschal I (817–24) that Rome saw a full-scale copy of the plan of St. Peter's with projecting transept and atrium in the manner of the Frankish churches at Saint-Denis, Fulda, and Seligenstadt (fig. 149).[60] Under his immediate predecessors, Leo III and Stephen IV, Paschal had been responsible for the care of foreign pilgrims to the Vatican shrine and as pope he became a champion of the cult of relics.[61] It is therefore not surprising to find that S. Prassede was also built with an annular crypt, another hallmark of the Petrine basilica, to receive the remains of St. Praxedis (Prassede in Italian) and numerous other Roman martyrs transferred from the neglected cemeteries of the countryside to the relative safety of the city.[62] Moreover, contemporary legend held that Praxedis and her sister, Pudentiana, had been disciples of both St. Peter and St. Paul.[63] In this way the church was designed to celebrate Rome's glorious past through the new setting for her precious relics, reflecting a sense of propriety similar to that shown by Einhard a few years later at Seligenstadt. It seems likely, in turn, that in constructing his church in the 830s, Einhard adopted an architectural formula that he knew was current in the city of Rome at the time. Such a reference could only have served to strengthen the *romanitas* of the building, making Seligenstadt, with its relics of the Roman saints Marcellinus and Peter, literally a "city of the blessed," a miniature Rome if you will, on Frankish soil. Paschal, on the other hand, seems also to have promoted the revival of Early Christian architecture in order to underscore his fervent belief in the sovereignty of the Papal State and its independence from Frankish rule, as defined in a treaty of 817 with Louis the Pious.[64] Thus, although Paschal and Einhard were united in their admiration for the Vatican basilica and their devotion to the cult of relics, they used similar forms to express strikingly different political points of view. Seen in this light, Seligenstadt represented Einhard's adherence to the original precepts of Charlemagne's *renovatio* in the North, whereas for Paschal S. Prassede announced a distinctly Roman renaissance, based on the supremacy of the church of Rome and the authority of the pope as the successor to Peter.

The churches of SS. Marcellinus and Peter at Seligenstadt and S. Prassede in Rome are strikingly similar in both design and scale (the nave of the former, for instance, is 33 m long, while that of the latter is 36 m in length), yet they differ markedly in construction due to the building traditions of their respective regions. Seligenstadt, like all Frankish buildings of the period, is constructed primarily of rough-hewn stone blocks in thick mortar, while S. Prassede is composed solely of brick, reviving a Roman

150 Rome, S. Prassede, apse mosaic.

technique from Early Christian times as opposed to the irregular mixture of stone and brick used during the intervening centuries. This rebirth of building in brick in Rome helps, in turn, to explain Einhard's use of all-brick piers at both Steinbach and Seligenstadt. Admittedly, he may have been forced to use masonry supports in place of columns due to the scarcity of ancient *spolia* in the area and his inability to obtain them elsewhere, but even so, the bricks in each case are remarkably uniform, meaning they were custom-made. In so doing, Einhard turned these otherwise mundane features into something conspicuously Roman, although when finished the piers were presumably plastered over and painted.

In Rome, where there was no such shortage of ancient building material, the nave of S. Prassede displays an array of carefully matched columns and architraves in an arrangement reminiscent, albeit on a smaller scale, of the Constantinian basilicas of the Lateran and St. Peter's.[65] Late antique, too, was the extensive use of monumental mosaic decoration, a technique revived, as we saw in chapter six, at the papal palace during the reign of Paschal's predecessor Leo III, but employed here on an even vaster scale. At S. Prassede, the apse, its framing arch, and the triumphal arch dividing nave and transept are all covered with figural mosaics that resemble, not only in technique but also in composition, the monumental art of Rome's Early Christian basilicas. In fact, a case can be made for a direct relationship between the apse mosaic of S. Prassede and that of the sixth-century church of SS. Cosmas and Damian in the Roman Forum (fig. 150).[66] Both represent the Second Coming of Christ: the Savior standing among a colorful array of clouds at sunrise, flanked by Peter and Paul, who introduce a pair of titular saints. To the far left in each case stands the papal patron, Felix IV (526–30) and Paschal I respectively, the latter singled out by a square halo to signify that he is still living. Below the main scene of the apse are two superimposed narrow zones, one with a parade of twelve sheep, symbols of the apostles, flanking the sacrificial lamb, and the other bearing a monumental inscription of gold letters against a dark blue background. To be sure, the style of the Carolingian mosaic seems stiff and awkward in comparison to the fluid movement and weighty forms of its late antique counterpart; nonetheless, the iconographic details are so similar that a direct link must be assumed. This particular apse mosaic must have been selected as a model because, unlike the schemes of other Early Christian churches, it provided a composition incorporating paired siblings—the brothers Cosmas and Damian—as titular saints, which could easily be adapted to celebrate the venerable sisters Praxedis and Pudentiana. Like SS. Cosmas and Damian, too, the arch framing the apse depicts the apocalyptic Lamb surrounded by angels and Evangelist symbols and worshipped by the Twenty-four Elders from the Book of Revelation. The primary purpose, of course, regardless of the specific model, was to evoke through the medium of mosaic the splendor of the past to enhance the present. The arch leading into the transept bears the image of the blessed welcomed within the glistening walls of the heavenly

Jerusalem. The holy retinue, led again by the sister saints and the apostles Peter and Paul, involves a multitude of figures, including those whose relics were buried in the crypt, spread over two registers. Unlike the decoration of the apse area, however, this scheme lacks a known prototype. It may instead have been created to give visual expression to the antiphons that were sung during the procession of relics at the dedication of the church. The text of one such antiphon reads: "March forth saints of God,/ Enter the city of the Lord,/ This new church was built for you." This unique image occupies the same location as the triumphant inscription of Constantine "victor" on the arch of the transept at St. Peter's, discussed in chapter one. It is also worth noting that Paschal's biography in the *Liber Pontificalis* is the first documented instance of the use of the term "triumphal arch" (*arcus triumphalis*) to describe this feature in church architecture.[67] Similarly, the interior walls of the transept were originally covered by vivid frescoes, now fragmentary, depicting scene after scene of the torture and execution of the selfsame and other martyrs.[68] In fact, one could see the transept itself as a hall celebrating the cults of relics. Thus, the design and decoration of S. Prassede were coordinated to glorify the devotion of the saints, to celebrate the munificence of the patron, and, in so doing, to proclaim the rebirth of Rome.

Not surprisingly, the church exhibits elements of Byzantine art as well, for, although it housed Roman relics, S. Prassede was built to serve a community of Greek monks.[69] The mosaic decoration of the small, groin-vaulted chapel dedicated to S. Zeno that adjoins the basilica's right aisle has a particularly strong eastern character. Indeed, Richard Krautheimer has gone so far as to call the S. Zeno chapel "the most outstanding example of Byzantine influence on Rome within the Carolingian

151 Rome, S. Prassede, view of interior of S. Zeno chapel.

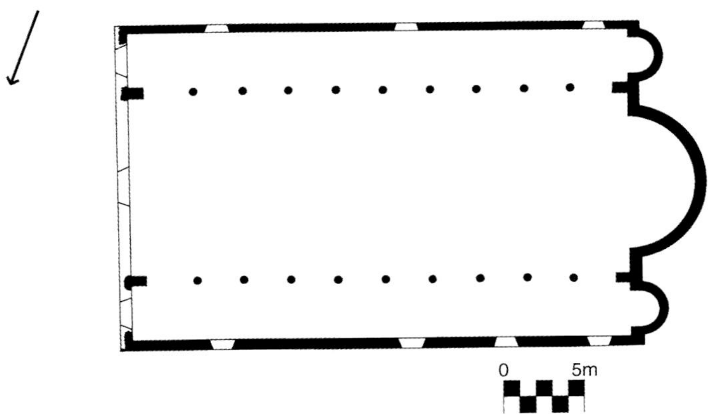

152 Rome, S. Maria in Domnica, plan.

Renascence."[70] Certainly the medallion portrait of Christ at the apex of the vault, supported by caryatid angels and followed by subordinate figures of saints, seems to foreshadow the hierarchy of images in the decorative schemes of later, Middle Byzantine churches (fig. 151). A Byzantine model also seems to lie behind the representation of Christ's Harrowing of Hell, for it is among the earliest examples of this scene in the Latin West.[71] Other motifs, such as the apostles Peter and Paul gesturing toward an empty throne, are decidedly Roman in origin and refer to the chapel's papal patronage. The reuse of ancient architectural sculpture to frame the entrance to the chapel and the presence of an inlay marble and porphyry pavement also represent local practice.

The reasons for this synthesis of Greek and Roman features are varied and complex. As has already been noted, under Pope Leo III, if not earlier, art and architecture in Rome had consciously incorporated Byzantine elements, especially those associated with Constantinople. Paschal, moreover, had ample opportunity to become well acquainted with various themes in Byzantine art through his close contacts with Greek monks, many of whom had fled the East after the reinstatement of iconoclasm in 815.[72] It is clear that Paschal, like Theodulf before him, was greatly concerned about the religious implications of Byzantine art, although their personal attitudes toward it could not have been more different.

This dichotomy is seen best at another of Paschal's churches, S. Maria in Domnica. Although contemporary with S. Prassede and similar to it in size, S. Maria in Domnica presents a strikingly different design, for it lacks a continuous transept and is terminated instead by three apses, a small one at the end of each aisle and, in the center, a broad curved niche spanning the full breadth of the nave (fig. 152). Always rare in Rome, this triple-apse arrangement was common in both North and South Italy, having been imported centuries before from the Greek East. It is also questionable whether the main apse originally contained an annular crypt.[73] As if to reinforce the non-Roman aspect of the church, the monumental mosaic in the main apse presents the Virgin Mary, dressed in a Byzantine manner wearing a simple dark blue robe or *maphorion* in place of the crown and regal attire of the traditional Roman formula of *Maria regina* (fig. 153).[74] Indeed, this image of the Virgin enthroned with the Christ child on her lap bears a striking resemblance to the apse mosaic of Hagia Sophia in Constantinople, which is generally thought to represent one of the first images set up in Byzantium after the return of icon worship in 843. One study, however, has suggested that this mosaic may in fact date back to the interlude in iconoclasm that took place during the decade and a half just before and after the year 800. According to this hypothesis, the mosaic visible today was covered up when the second wave of iconoclasm swept the Byzantine Empire in 815—the decisive synod was held in Hagia Sophia—and not uncovered until modern times.[75] In either case, the image of the Virgin and Child was used to celebrate the repeal of iconoclasm in the Byzantine capital. Could it be that the mosaic of S. Maria in Domnica represents a personal rebuke on the part of Paschal I of the Byzantine ban on religious imagery? He was, after all, a vehement opponent of the revival of iconoclasm in the Greek East. During the first year of his reign, he turned away legates who had been sent by the patriarch in Constantinople to convey the proclamations of the iconoclastic synod. Papal messages of protest to two successive, iconoclastic emperors, first Leo V and then Michael II, came to naught. In the latter instance, Paschal's envoy was none other than the exiled Greek monk Methodios, who as patriarch twenty-two years later would be instrumental in the ultimate repeal of iconoclasm. All the while Paschal was encouraged in his efforts to promote the use of sacred art by letters from the renowned Greek iconodule Theodore of Studios.[76]

In view of these circumstances, the apse mosaic of S. Maria in Domnica seems particularly poignant, appearing as it does in the guise of a monumental icon. The votive nature of this image is made explicit by the figure of Paschal shown kneeling at the feet of the Virgin, his arms outstretched in order to touch delicately Mary's right slipper. This gesture of supplication, or *proskynesis*, is a mirror image of the portrayal of an earlier pontiff, the Greek Pope John VII (705–7), renowned for his promotion of the cult of the Virgin, as it appears in the nearly life-size, painted panel of S. Maria in Trastevere.[77] Surely the similarity in this

153 Rome, S. Maria in Domnica, apse mosaic.

detail to such a prominent icon cannot be coincidental; the reference to the tradition of papal allegiance to the cult and imagery of the Virgin must be intentional. Indeed, it seems especially formulated for a local audience, combining visual symbols of eastern and western Christianity, to protest Byzantine iconoclasm and promote the orthodoxy of Rome. The pope is also depicted as a participant in a celestial vision. The single angels flanking the Virgin in the Trastevere panel have been multiplied to serve as a heavenly host attending the holy mother and child and acknowledging the miracle of Christ's incarnation and the status of Mary as the "Mother of God" and the "Queen of Heaven."[78]

It is safe to say that this monumental, mosaic icon would have appalled the author of the *Opus Caroli*, for it condones, indeed exalts, the very attitude toward religious imagery that Theodulf so harshly condemns. The papacy, after all, never embraced the pronouncements of the *Opus Caroli*, and even in the North they seem to have had little impact outside of Theodulf's immediate circle.[79] And yet, the message of Paschal's art is equally anti-Byzantine, albeit for the opposite reasons. Whereas Theodulf protests the reinstatement of the veneration of images in Byzantium at the end of the eighth century, Paschal condemns with equal fervor the reappearance of iconoclasm in the East a generation later. Moreover, at S. Prassede the pope combines a wealth of religious imagery with an abundance of corporeal relics to bolster this position.[80] Nonetheless, when taken together, S. Prassede and S. Maria in Domnica, not unlike the churches at Germigny-des-Prés and Seligenstadt, represent two major themes in the development of Carolingian architecture and its ornament, that is the influence of Byzantium and of Early Christian Rome. One might question referring to the patronage of Paschal I as "private," but the unique qualities of these two churches certainly reflect his individual taste and very personal concerns. In fact, the last line of the grand apse inscription at S. Prassede poignantly explains that Paschal carried out the project "trusting that he would thereby merit access to the gates of heaven."[81]

S. Prassede and S. Maria in Domnica were but the two most prominent of his architectural undertakings. Indeed,

154 Rome, SS. Quattro Coronati, gate tower.

Paschal restored or rebuilt close to a dozen other churches during his seven-year reign, including that of S. Cecilia, whose relics were discovered in a cemetery outside the city as the result of a vision he had experienced before the tomb of Peter.[82] Not surprisingly, this church, too, was designed with an annular crypt, although without a transept, and an apse mosaic that followed in cruder fashion the program of S. Prassede.[83] Significant patronage of church building continued under Paschal's successors as well, although at a less frantic pace, employing basically the same architectural features. The design of S. Maria in Domnica remained unique, but during the pontificates of Gregory IV (827–44) and Leo IV (847–55), annular crypts formed part of new construction at S. Marco and of SS. Quattro Coronati, and the T-shaped basilica, also with an annular crypt, reappeared under Leo IV at S. Stefano degli Abissini, situated at the Vatican just a few yards from St. Peter's itself.[84] The first half of the ninth century, then, saw a flurry of building activity.[85] Yet by its very nature, this "building boom" exerted only limited influence outside the papal capital. It was largely an introspective process whereby Rome drew upon its own traditions with little regard for architectural developments in other parts of Europe. An exception is the massive tower rising above the main gate to the entrance courtyard at SS. Quattro Coronati; without comparison in Rome, it seems instead to exhibit a more northern character, the precise nature of which will be explored in the next chapter (fig. 154).

The three great patrons of architecture examined here—Theodulf, Einhard, and Pope Paschal I—were primarily concerned with incorporating into the design and ornament of their churches ancient precedents, be they biblical, Roman, or Byzantine, in order to respond to what they perceived to be the pressing concerns of their day. In so doing, their efforts exemplify the richness and diversity of the Carolingian Renaissance on a more personal level. The attitudes of Theodulf and Einhard were shaped by, and had helped to shape, the cultural and political atmosphere of Charlemagne's court at Aachen, while Paschal, a native Roman, viewed the world from a distinctly papal perspective. Their individual tastes varied, but each man viewed architecture as a vehicle for expressing profound religious and political beliefs that can still be appreciated today. At the same time, one cannot ignore the inherent conservatism of these buildings. Elsewhere, by contrast, architectural innovations were taking place, especially within monasteries, that would have a more lasting impact on the history of medieval building. Next to nothing is known about the layout of the subsidiary structures of the religious communities sponsored by Einhard at Steinbach and Seligenstadt or by Paschal in Rome, but in many other locations there is considerable evidence of sophisticated planning and construction on a vast scale, the results of which forever changed the landscape of Europe. To understand this phenomenon, we must go back to the very roots of monasticism itself.

CHAPTER 8

The Monastic Realm: Ideal and Reality

> If it can be done, the monastery should be so established that all the necessary things, such as water, mill, garden and various workshops, may be within the enclosure, so that there is no necessity for the monks to go about outside of it, since that is not at all profitable for their souls.[1]

In this famous passage from his Rule, Benedict of Nursia, better known as St. Benedict, envisions the monastery as an economically self-sufficient entity that protects its inhabitants from the turmoil and temptations of the outside world. Monasticism, for Benedict, is a communal effort, whereby individual salvation is attained through stability, obedience, and the strictures of an ordered life of work and prayer. At various other points in his text, Benedict mentions, among other things, the need for a place of common prayer (an oratory), a dining hall (refectory) and kitchen, one or more dormitories, and guest facilities; yet nowhere does he specify the design or arrangement of these or any other buildings.[2] His Rule, after all, is a code of behavior, not an architectural treatise; the physical reality of the monastery could take whatever form addressed the needs of the community and its spiritual ideals.

When it was written in the early sixth century, Benedict's was only one of many such monastic rules in the Christian world. It was remarkable, however, for its simplicity, brevity, and keen understanding of the strengths and weaknesses of human nature. These qualities of moderation and common sense made it particularly appealing, and its influence gradually spread. Still, it was not until the age of Charlemagne that this "little rule for beginners," as Benedict called it, became the universal guide to monastic life in western Europe. Not surprisingly, it was during this same time that the basic form of the medieval abbey was established. But this was the result of a long and complex process.

Monasticism was yet another legacy of late antiquity. Its origins go back to the last decades of the third century A.D., when Anthony of Egypt (251–356) withdrew from a crowded village along the banks of the River Nile in order to seek salvation in the barren wastes of the surrounding countryside. Anthony followed the examples of John the Baptist and Christ himself by living alone in the desert. Indeed, the term monk comes from the Greek word *monos*, meaning "one who lives alone." Monks, then, were initially hermits who led an austere life sheltered only by natural caves or overhanging rocks. Any man-made dwellings were of the most primitive kind, usually built of mud-brick, and isolated from one another. Yet the notoriety of St. Anthony and other so-called Desert Fathers attracted many followers who would encamp in the vicinity of the holy man, seeking his advice and blessing, eventually forming a loose aggregate of buildings known as a laura. In such a setting, hermits would meet occasionally, often weekly, for common services and meals under the guidance of a saintly elder, but otherwise their existence remained a solitary one.

Another Egyptian, Pachomius (286–346), was a former soldier and recent convert to Christianity who saw the need for an alternative form of monasticism. Although he lived for a time as a hermit and continued to admire the goals of asceticism, Pachomius came to realize that only a select few possessed the will and discipline to follow such a path. He therefore established monastic communities or coenobia (from the Greek words *koinos*, meaning common, and *bios*, life), based on a more formally regulated way of life. There is no physical evidence for the precise layout of Pachomian monasteries but his rule makes clear that they were strictly ordered. Cut off from the outside world by a wall, the monks lived in groups of twenty to thirty, sometimes segregated according to their trades—shoemakers, bakers, weavers, carpenters, and so on. Each group or "house" had its own superior and gathered in a common meeting room, about which individual cells were arranged in some fashion. The coenobium consisted of many such nuclei under the leadership of a "father," in Greek *abbas* (hence the term abbot). In addition, there was a modest church, a refectory with a kitchen, and separate guest facilities. Initial success was limited, but soon the followers of Pachomius grew into the hundreds. Indeed, his first monastery, established in the abandoned village of Tabennesi, is said to have eventually contained 2,500 souls, so that its population came to equal that of the small town whose site it occupied.[3] In the course of the fourth century, Egypt and neighboring Palestine became the centers of a rapidly growing monastic movement that provided several models for the rest of Christendom, ranging from the isolated hermitage to the thriving coenobium, and numerous variations in between.

Through various means, including rules, biographies, and transcribed "sayings" of the Desert Fathers, as well as firsthand observations by foreign visitors, the spirit of Near Eastern monasticism in its divergent forms spread to western Europe. By the early fifth century, men like Honoratus at Lérins in southern France achieved a compromise between the eremetical and communal life by allowing elder monks to live in individual cells away from the coenobium proper. But nothing illustrates the inherent dichotomy of early monasticism better than the life of St. Benedict himself. Born in the central Italian town of Nursia around 480, Benedict was sent by his parents to Rome to be educated. Repulsed by what he considered to be the decadence of the city in the afterglow of antiquity, he withdrew to a cave in the Appennine mountains near Subiaco to lead the life of a hermit. After three years of physical deprivation and spiritual struggle he came to realize the value of the communal life for those seeking his help, and he set out to establish a series of monasteries. It was at his last foundation, Montecassino, that he wrote his Rule, combining the wisdom of his own experience with that of many earlier sources, in the years shortly before his death around 550. There is, unfortunately, no evidence for the arrangement of Benedict's monasteries other than the aforementioned comments in his Rule. Although considered today to be the father of western monasticism, Benedict achieved no particular celebrity in his lifetime. In the late sixth century, Montecassino was sacked by the Lombards and the monks fled to the safety of Rome. It was there that the Rule came to the attention of Pope Gregory the Great (590–604), who in writing an account of Benedict's life and miracles in his *Dialogues* elevated the status of the saint and his teachings. In addition, it was Gregory who sent a delegation of Benedictine monks, led by Augustine, to convert the English to Christianity.

Yet monasticism was already well established in the British Isles. As discussed in chapter four, it flourished in Ireland long before the arrival of the Augustinian mission at Canterbury. Converted to Christianity in the fifth century, while Britain was succumbing to the heathen Anglo-Saxons, Ireland became the setting for a rich monastic culture. In emulation of their Egyptian forebears, Irish monks spoke of seeking their salvation "in the desert," in spite of the island's rainswept landscape, and their lives were often austere in the extreme. Although a strong eremetical tendency was always evident in Irish monasticism, coenobitic communities thrived as well. In a land without cities or towns, bishops and priests lived in monasteries alongside monks and abbots so that the administrative hierarchy of the Church and the religious life of the entire society was inextricably linked with monasticism. Religious communities varied greatly in size, but they all followed the indigenous form of prehistoric ring forts, defined by earthen ramparts or dry-stone enclosure walls, either built anew or in some cases merely taken over and adapted to monastic use (fig. 69). Individual structures, whether dwellings or workshops, consisted of primitive round huts, built in wood or stone depending upon the availability of materials; only the chapel was rectangular. Interspersed among these buildings lay gardens and cemeteries to serve the needs of both the living and the dead. The general layout of the Irish monastery was far from haphazard and has been shown to be remarkably consistent: at its core stood the chapel and the tomb of the founder with a cross-slab about which were arrayed at a short distance the domestic buildings. To be sure, the regularity of this scheme varied according to the topography of each site. On the dramatically remote and rugged island of Skellig Michael, off the southwestern coast, the beehive cells were perched on terraces and surrounded by an undulating enclosure wall, while on the flatter terrain of Nendrum, in northeastern Ireland, the arrangement was far more uniform and allowed for controlled expansion through a series of concentric rings.[4] Still, regardless of the setting, the ideal form of the Irish monastery was circular and was delineated as such around 800 in a small Irish Gospel book known as the Book of Mulling (fig. 155). Here one finds the faint outline of two concentric, compass-drawn circles and an array of crosses with labels bearing dedications to Christ, the Holy Spirit, the four evangelists, and prophets. Rather than the actual plan of a specific site, this highly abstract rendering should be seen as a symbol of a monastic enclave with its protective crosses, serving an apotropaic function at the end of the sacred text.[5]

Monastic planning in England, however, followed a very different course, perhaps in part because of the influence of ancient Roman building. Along the Saxon shore to the southeast, for example, abandoned Roman forts at Bradwell-on-the-Sea in Essex and Reculver in Kent are known to have been used in the seventh century as the sites for monasteries, although whether this affected the

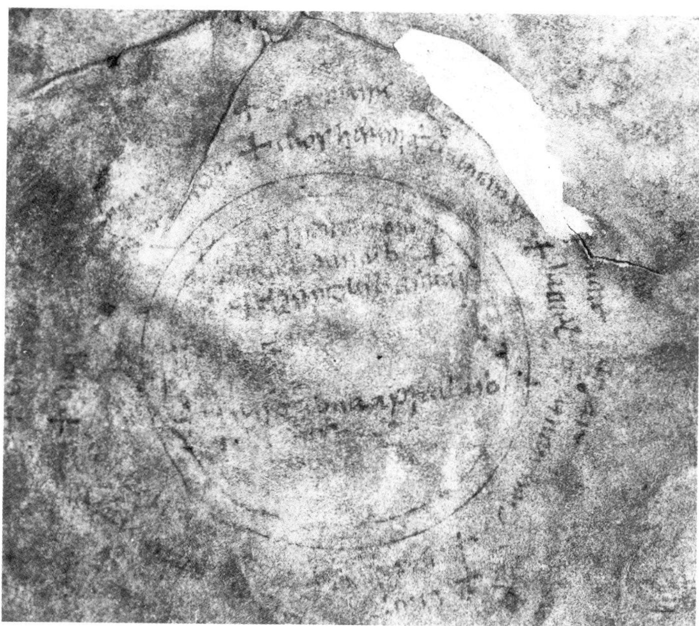

155 Schematic rendering of an Irish monastery, ca. 800. Colophon drawing from Book of Mulling (Dublin, Trinity College Library, MS 60, fol. 94v).

internal arrangement of their conventual buildings has yet to be determined.[6] In any event, we have already seen that at the abbey of SS. Peter and Paul at Canterbury three churches were aligned along a single axis, and that at Jarrow, where subsidiary structures have also been uncovered, the buildings were set up in two parallel rows with the monks' cemetery in between (figs. 64 and 85). Similarly, at the abbey of Whitby in Northumbria, founded in 657, excavations in the 1940s uncovered rows of small rectangular buildings divided by paved walkways.[7] And at Monkwearmouth a covered walk (3.35 m wide and over 30 m long) was discovered, set at a right angle to the church of St. Peter, constructed of limestone with a mortared floor and perhaps glazed windows (fig. 78). Taken together, these examples indicate that the layout of early Anglo-Saxon monasteries followed a rectilinear approach toward planning that was markedly different from the circular arrangement of the Irish monastery. Such an attitude was in keeping both with native building traditions, based on the Germanic long hall, and with earlier Roman settlement patterns. It should be remembered, too, that the churches at Canterbury were built of reused Roman brick and that for his Northumbrian monasteries Benedict Biscop found it necessary to import masons from Gaul in order to construct churches in stone in what Bede called "the Roman manner."

On the continent the legacy of the Roman past was even more pervasive. As early as the 360s, another renowned soldier-turned-hermit, St. Martin, is said to have set up a small monastic settlement in the ruins of a Roman villa at Ligugé near Poitiers. Martin was not a promoter of the coenobitical life. He seems instead to have followed the precedent of St. Anthony, who sought temporary refuge in an abandoned Roman fort before venturing into the wilderness of the Egyptian desert. Indeed, according to Martin's biographer, Sulpicius Severus, the saint established a second monastery at Marmoutier, on the banks of the Loire River near Tours, where he lived "in desert solitude" in a cell built of wood while most of his followers fashioned shelters out of the rock of an adjacent mountain.[8] Still, the use of Roman ruins was one of obvious convenience. Such remains studded the landscape and afforded immediate shelter and, if fortified, a ready-made enclosure wall, for those who in increasing numbers wished to follow a monastic existence. It seems inevitable that with time ancient Roman architecture should have come to influence the design of monasteries in more profound ways.

Unfortunately, there is as yet little archaeological evidence about the physical development of monastic sites in Merovingian Gaul, and one must glean what one can from frustratingly few and often vague literary references. The abbey of Jumièges, for example, founded by St. Philibert around 650 near the Seine River west of Rouen, may well have been founded within the towered fortification walls of an ancient Roman military camp or *castrum*, although this has not been confirmed on the site. Nonetheless, the *Vita* of St. Philibert, written by the early eighth century, tells us that the fortified enclosure of the monastery was "square in shape," which in turn suggests that the various internal structures mentioned, such as a church "in the shape of a cross," several chapels, and a two-storied building (290 ft long × 50 ft wide) with dormitory above and cellar and refectory below were laid out in a rectilinear manner. There is also a reference to "stone arches" surrounding the complex, but their exact arrangement is unknown.[9] In Lombard Italy, on the other hand, information from documentary sources has been confirmed by recent excavations to show that the abbey of Farfa was founded around 700 within the remains of an abandoned Roman villa or farmhouse and that the ancient atrium of this complex may have continued to serve as the entrance courtyard to the monastery throughout much of the Middle Ages. Similar work at the contemporary monastery of S. Vincenzo al Volturno, not far from Montecassino, has demonstrated that it, too, was established in the early eighth century on the site of a late Roman villa. It was under similar circumstances that many early monasteries were established throughout Europe.[10] It is within this context of the transition from the ancient to the medieval world that one must

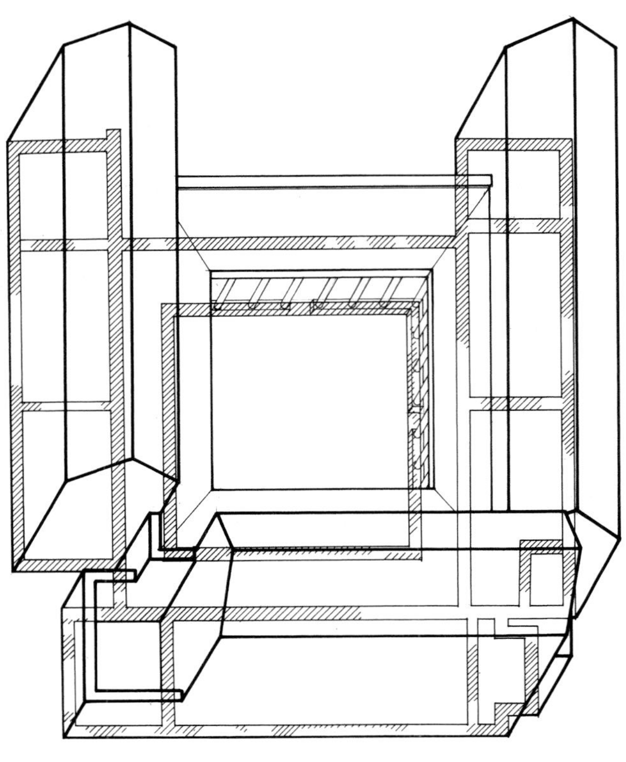

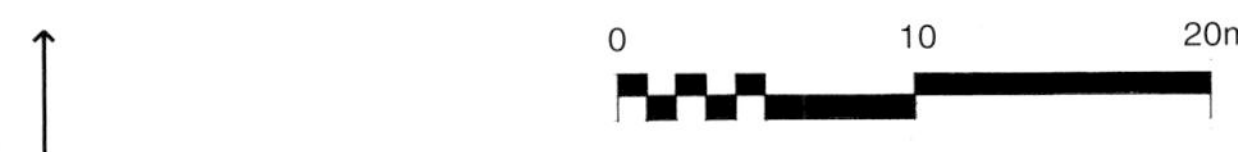

156 Lorsch, plan and axonometric reconstuction of first monastery (so-called Altenmünster), 765–74.

seek the origins of one of the most familiar features of monastic architecture, the cloister.

A case in point is the founding of the first abbey at Lorsch. In the early 760s, Chrodegang, the archbishop of Metz and an influential member of the Frankish court, was given a tract of land, then an island in the Weschnitz River (a tributary of the Rhine), by a local countess and her son in order to establish a monastery dedicated to St. Peter. Burdened with the chores of episcopal duties, Chrodegang placed his brother Gundeland in charge of the new establishment along with sixteen monks. The excavations of Friedrich Behn in 1932–33 demonstrated that the site (known as *Laurissa* or *Lauresham*, present-day Lorsch) was first occupied by a Frankish villa with buildings arranged along three sides of an open courtyard in the manner of an ancient Roman villa rustica.[11] This complex was easily adapted by the new monastic community to provide a church with a rectangular apse along the southern side of the court, while along the east and west sides two oblong buildings served as a dormitory and a cellar (fig. 156). Such an arrangement for a monastery was not without precedent. Indeed, a strikingly similar design, built in wood, seems to have already been used at the island monastery of Reichenau-Mittelzell on the Bodensee soon after it was founded in 724. During the second half of the eighth century, the complex was rebuilt in stone with a church—long, narrow, aisleless, and with a rectangular apse—that closely resembles that of Lorsch (fig. 157).[12] Only three sides of the inner courtyard at Reichenau have as yet been uncovered, but if the fourth side of the portico existed, as most likely it did, Reichenau, together with Lorsch, would provide the first archaeologically documented examples of a fully developed monastic cloister. That is to say, the main buildings of the monastery were connected by a square, covered walkway, measuring in both cases approximately 25 m on each side. Initially, the term *claustrum*, from which the word "cloister" is derived, had been used by Benedict and others to refer to the monastic enclosure as a whole, but now it began to be used in a narrower sense to mean a covered walk surrounding a square or rectangular space that connected the church, dormitory, and refectory, thereby circumscribing the monk's daily routine.[13] The form of the cloister at Lorsch was determined by the courtyard of the earlier villa, but its applicability to the goals of communal life must have been recognized long before if it was used at Reichenau some forty years earlier. Indeed, the origins of the monastic cloister may go back further still into the seventh or even the sixth century. The cloister need not have been "invented" at a specific time and place; rather it should be seen in a more general sense as a feature that resulted from the symbiotic relationship between the sites of Roman settlements, be they military or domestic, and monasteries in the early Middle Ages. For our purposes it is most important to note that by the

157 Reichenau-Mittelzell, plan of abbey church and cloister as rebuilt in stone, second half of the eighth century.

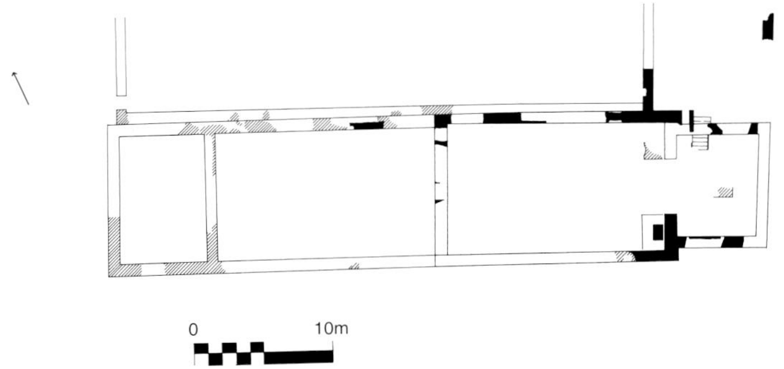

eighth century the cloister was an established feature of monastic planning, at least in eastern Francia. When the rapidly growing monastic community at Lorsch was moved ten years later to a larger site on a nearby hillock, as discussed in chapter five, a cloister (33 m square or 100 Carolingian feet) was constructed of wood, but this time along the southern flank of the new church in order to take advantage of the added comfort of greater exposure to the sun. The cloister was then rebuilt in stone by Abbot Richbod (784–804) (fig. 96). The adoption of the cloister at Reichenau and the two abbeys at Lorsch came at a particularly auspicious time, for monastic architecture was about to enter a new and monumental phase under the aegis of Charlemagne.

In the course of the seventh and eighth centuries, monasteries were increasingly supported by the landed aristocracy. Donations of land and riches were believed to assure personal salvation and to serve as a penance for past sins; monks in turn prayed for the souls of prominent benefactors. And the sons of nobles were educated with increasing frequency in monastic schools. Secular rulers aided the growth of monasticism for political reasons as well. Charles Martel and his sons Carloman and Pippin, for example, subsidized the missionary work and monastic foundations of the Anglo-Saxon Boniface and his followers, because such activity was perceived to be a stabilizing force along the eastern frontier of Francia. Yet no previous ruler recognized the potential of monasticism for achieving political and cultural aims more fully than Charlemagne. Monasteries were an essential component of his program for a cultural *renovatio*, above all as instruments of education and repositories of learning. Not surprisingly, the leading scholars of his court retired to monasteries from which they continued to influence the policies of the king. Many establishments such as Saint-Denis and Lorsch were designated royal abbeys and thereby became recipients of the king's largesse. The age of Charlemagne was therefore a period of expansion and experimentation in monastic architecture on a previously unheard of scale as seen most clearly at the two major centers of Centula and Fulda.

The history of the abbey at Centula began modestly enough. Its patron saint, St. Riquier (or Richarius), was one of many hermits in northern Gaul in the seventh century who followed the example of St. Martin and the Desert Fathers. After his death in 645, the saint's body was taken from his forest hermitage to the village of *Centulum* and a monastery bearing his name was founded. Little else is known about the abbey until the arrival around 790 of Angilbert, friend and advisor to Charlemagne, who was installed by the king as lay abbot of Saint-Riquier. With direct financial support from Charlemagne a new monastic complex was built over the next ten years. On January 1, 799, the main abbey church was dedicated to the Savior and St. Riquier, and in the spring of 800, Charlemagne spent Easter at the abbey to celebrate the completion of the grand enterprise. Angilbert belonged to the elite circle of scholars at the Frankish court and was noted especially for his ability as a poet, thus earning him the pseudonym of Homer. With such a patron, one would expect the new abbey of Saint-Riquier to reflect the burgeoning ideals of the Carolingian Renaissance. Angilbert's monastery, however, has not survived and its reconstruction depends upon a variety of sources (documentary, pictorial, and archaeological), each limited in its own way. But when taken together they provide at least a general picture of the late-eighth-century abbey.

The main documentary evidence consists of two works—the so-called *Libellus* and *Institutio*—which have long been attributed to Angilbert himself. It is not surprising that this Carolingian scholar should have taken pains to record his rebuilding of the abbey, but these texts are preserved only in much later forms. The *Libellus*, for example, was incorporated into the Chronicle of Centula (*Chronicon Centulense*), written in 1088 by Hariulf, a monk at Saint-Riquier. Another version of the *Libellus* together with the only known copy of the *Institutio* are found in a late-twelfth-century manuscript now in the Vatican Library. Some additional information comes from the *Life of Angilbert* written by an abbot of the abbey in the early twelfth century. These sources were taken at more or less face value by historians of architecture until 1976, when a detailed study by David Parsons brought this assumption into question. One need not accept all of Parsons's arguments to recognize that significant discrepancies exist among the texts and that some sections contain embellishments by the later medieval authors.[14] Not only is the reliability of the texts in dispute but also certain terms and passages are open to varied interpretations. Thus, the written sources must be treated with considerable caution.

The pictorial evidence comes from the first printed editions of Hariulf's chronicle, which were produced in the seventeenth century. In 1612, two different, but closely related, engravings were made to serve as frontispieces for the folio and quarto editions of Paul Petau's *De Nithardo* (Paris, 1613). Both images are derived from the same miniature in a medieval copy of the chronicle, now lost, and show a bird's-eye view of the monastery (fig. 158). The two engravings are virtually identical, but the smaller quarto version reveals somewhat less detail and exhibits looser draughtmanship over all. A third engraving, published in Jean Mabillon's *Acta Sanctorum*, vol. 4, pt. 1 (Paris, 1677), seems to be derived from the same miniature, but it is of less value because the buildings have been rendered according to linear perspective, thereby totally distorting the

ECCLESIAR AB ANGILBERTO APVD CENTVLAM AN DCCXCIX
CONSTRVCTARVM E SCRIPTO CODICE
EKMATEION
S. RICHARIVS
S. BENEDICTVS
S. MARIA
HÆC S. BENED ECCLA
SVPER RIPAM FLVVIOLI
SCARDVONIS SITA
CVRA·P·
1612

impression of the medieval original. All three engravings show a monumental abbey church with projecting transepts at both east and west ends above which rise multi-storeyed, cylindrical towers. In addition, they represent two smaller churches, one labelled S. Benedictus and the other S. Maria, connected to the main abbey church by porticoed walkways laid out in the shape of a trapezoid. Like the texts, these engravings have been used uncritically in the past to reconstruct Angilbert's monastery, but at best they are many times removed from the Carolingian period. In fact, the medieval image cannot have been formulated much before the time of Hariulf's chronicle because it shows an outer crypt, built under Abbot Gervin I (1045–75), projecting from the east end of the main church. Other parts of the same church and much of the rest of the abbey were substantially rebuilt under Abbot Gervin II between 1075 and 1096.[15] Thus one cannot assume that these engravings represent any part of Angilbert's monastery without corresponding evidence from at least one other source, and even then it must be kept in mind that medieval renderings of architecture are in general notoriously schematic in nature.

The archaeological record is equally problematic. Excavations and other investigations at Saint-Riquier have been carried out intermittently by Honoré Bernard since 1959.[16] This work has been limited, however, by the fact that a sizable Gothic church occupies the former site of the Carolingian abbey church, and that later town walls and other urban construction encroached extensively upon the surrounding area. Nonetheless, Bernard seems to have been able to ascertain some important features of Angilbert's monastery.

What, then, is one to make of this diverse information? Let us begin with the layout of the monastery, for here the various sources of evidence seem to agree most fully. The *Libellus*, for example, refers to three abbey churches: the smallest dedicated to St. Benedict, lying to the east; the next in size in honor of the Virgin and the Apostles, situated to the south; and the main church of Saint-Riquier, located to the north. It also states that the three churches were connected by roofed corridors, which were laid out in the form of a triangle. The number, position, and dedication of the churches, as well as the arrangement of the connecting porticoes, correspond to that shown in the engravings. Bernard, moreover, uncovered the foundations of a centrally planned structure some 300 m south of the gothic church that must belong to the church of the Virgin (fig. 159). Instead of being round, however, the plan consists of an internal hexagon (7.50 m in diameter) circumscribed by a twelve-sided external wall without any absidioles except for a single rectangular apse projecting to the east, which was added in the eleventh century. He also uncovered traces of a shallow western porch, but the box-like nave shown in the engravings he found belonged to the eleventh-century rebuilding. Thus in its original state the plan of the church of the Virgin at Centula bore a striking resemblance to that of the palatine chapel in Aachen, which no doubt reflected Angilbert's close ties with the court and suggests that he built this church in imitation, at half the size, of Charlemagne's new edifice.

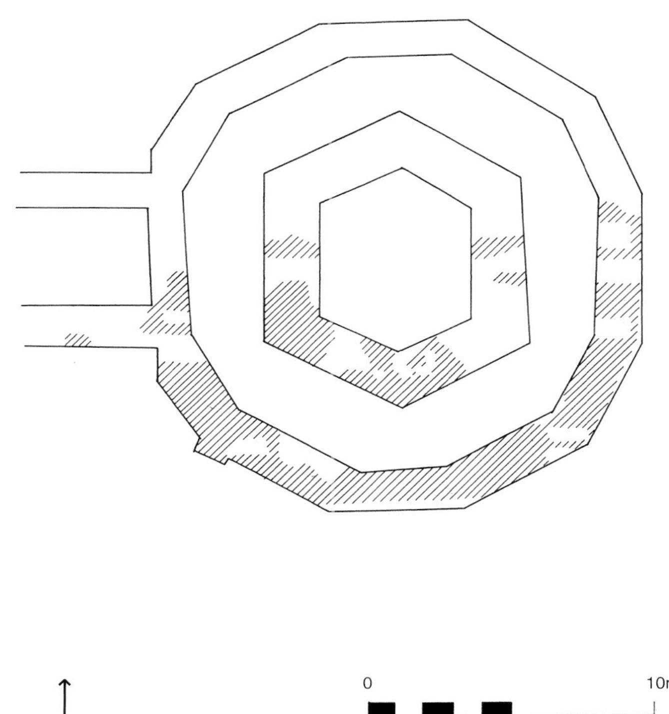

159 Centula (Saint-Riquier), plan of the church of the Virgin and Apostles.

The considerable distance between the main abbey church and that of the Virgin indicates the vast scale of the Carolingian complex, and shows that it was far larger than one would assume from the engravings (fig. 160). The site of the church of St. Benedict and the path of the connecting corridors were not available for excavation, but immediately to the south of the present Gothic church, Bernard found the remains of a rectangular courtyard (approximately 45 × 40 m) that presumably served as the cloister.[17] Assuming its identification and late-eighth-century date are correct, the appearance of a cloister at Saint-Riquier would correspond to the near contemporary developments at the second abbey of Lorsch, where the cloister exhibited basically the same dimensions (40 m square). It is worth noting, however, that a rectilinear cloister does not appear in the engravings of St. Riquier, nor is it mentioned by Angilbert, who instead uses the term *claustrum* to refer either to the

158 *(facing page)* Centula (Saint-Riquier), bird's-eye view of the medieval abbey, engraving, 1612.

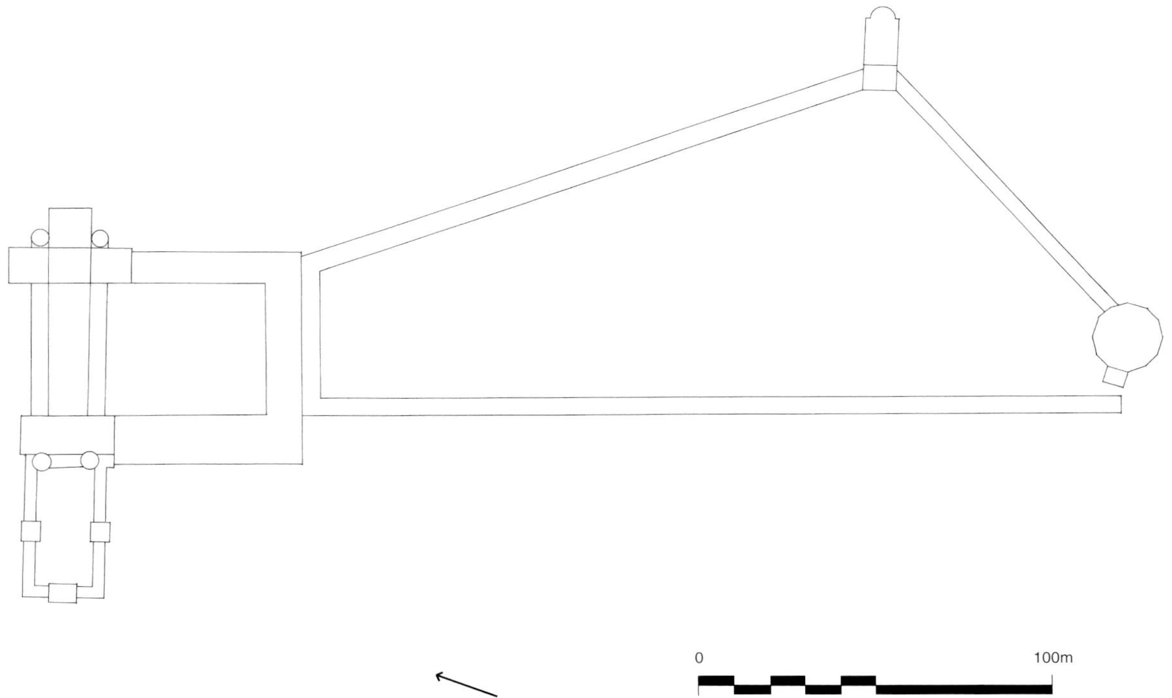

160 Centula (Saint-Riquier), general layout of the abbey in the late eighth century.

monastery as a whole or to the triangular courtyard. Yet Angilbert seems little interested in recording the more mundane activities associated with a cloister. He makes no reference to a dormitory, refectory, or cellar as one would expect to find surrounding a cloister. He stresses instead the churches, their altars and dedications, and the performance of the liturgy. Thus he points out that the triangular courtyard symbolizes the Trinity and that the surrounding porticoes were used for grand processions to the three churches in inclement weather. In other words, the absence of specific reference to a cloister in the *Libellus* is not particularly surprising. Similarly, the lost medieval miniature from which the engravings are derived was presumably created to celebrate the impressive nature of the sacred buildings and not to document the entire monastic layout. This attitude differs greatly from the more modest and strictly utilitarian concept of Benedict of Nursia. The Carolingian monastery was still self-sufficient, but it was now supported by a vast network of territorial holdings and royal patronage. Architecturally the monastery had become above all else an elaborate stage for the *opus Dei* (literally "the work of God"), a term originally used by St. Benedict to mean the performance of the daily office of psalms and lessons and on Sunday the celebration of the eucharist.[18] But by the late eighth century the liturgical life of a major monastery in the Frankish realm had been transformed through the Rome-inspired reforms of Chrodegang and others into a series of elaborate processions that involved multiple churches and altars and lengthy services and daily masses that occupied most of the waking hours of the monks.[19] This preoccupation with the liturgy is especially evident in the design of the main abbey church.

In spite of the valiant efforts of past scholars to reconstruct the church of Saint-Riquier in great detail based on the documentary and pictorial evidence, there is in fact precious little one can say with any certainty. Once again, Bernard's probings have helped to clarify the matter to some extent (fig. 161). First of all, the present church seems to correspond roughly in size to its Carolingian predecessor, meaning that Angilbert's building was approximately 80 m in length, making it considerably larger than the abbey churches at both Lorsch and Saint-Denis. To the east, Bernard found traces of a projecting transept which corresponds to the details of the engravings. He was also able to confirm the presence of a second transept at the west end of the church but one that was considerably shorter and broader than its counterpart in the east rather than identical in shape, as shown in the engravings. The use of two transepts is best explained by the dual dedication of the church, as stated in the *Libellus*, to both St. Riquier and the Savior. Angilbert also indicates that the altar to St. Riquier stood in the apse at the east end of the church, while the altar of the Savior stood near the western entrance. Inside the present Gothic facade, Bernard claims to have found vestiges of two spiral staircases, referred to by Angilbert as *cochlea*, that originally led to some form of gallery, used at various times by monks, clergy, one of several choirs, and even laity. Such a gallery and part-time choir loft must have extended over much of the western entrance, because the area directly below it was referred to as a crypt, meaning, in this case, a covered space on the ground floor. The altar to the Savior apparently stood in the gallery above. In its broad outlines, the church of Saint-Riquier incorporates several of the most recent developments of Carolingian architecture. The spiral stairs and western gallery suggest a variation on the westwork of the contemporary palatine chapel at Aachen, while the projecting transept was first used north of the Alps at Saint-Denis (768–75). Beyond these generalizations, however, the reconstruction of the abbey church becomes much more hypothetical.

The widths of the nave and aisles are not known, nor has the shape of the main apse been conclusively determined; it may have been semicircular as at Saint-Denis or, as Bernard prefers, it may have been flat-ended as seems to have been the case at Lorsch. One could well expect lantern towers to have risen over the center of one or both of the transepts, as may have been true at Saint-Denis, and indeed the term *turris* is used by Angilbert in reference to the area around the two principal altars, but their size and shape remain uncertain. For the sake of structural stability, it seems most likely that such towers, if built of stone, would have been square rather than round as shown in the engravings; for the same reason, a multi-tiered profile also seems doubtful, unless the topmost storeys were constructed of wood.[20] Bernard, on the other hand, has proposed for these areas a very complicated double-shell, polygonal design, octagonal at the core and sixteen-sided on the exterior, based on the discovery of what he interprets as the foundations of an angular pier near the supposed southeast juncture of the nave and western transept. Moreover, the possible remnants of the foundations of a smaller support (whether column or square pier is not known) within the crossing have led him to conjecture that the entire area, including the transept arms, was vaulted and supported an upper storey. According to this scheme, the aforementioned gallery would have extended throughout the entire western end of the church, while the eastern crossing would have remained open with galleries in the flanking transept arms.[21] Such a reconstruction, however, must be viewed with extreme caution. The findings are still very preliminary and have yet to be documented fully. It is hard to imagine how a vast upper floor could have been sustained across both a polygonal crossing and a projecting transept at the west end of the church. Indeed, no comparable arrangement in the entire history of medieval architecture comes to mind; the palatine chapel at

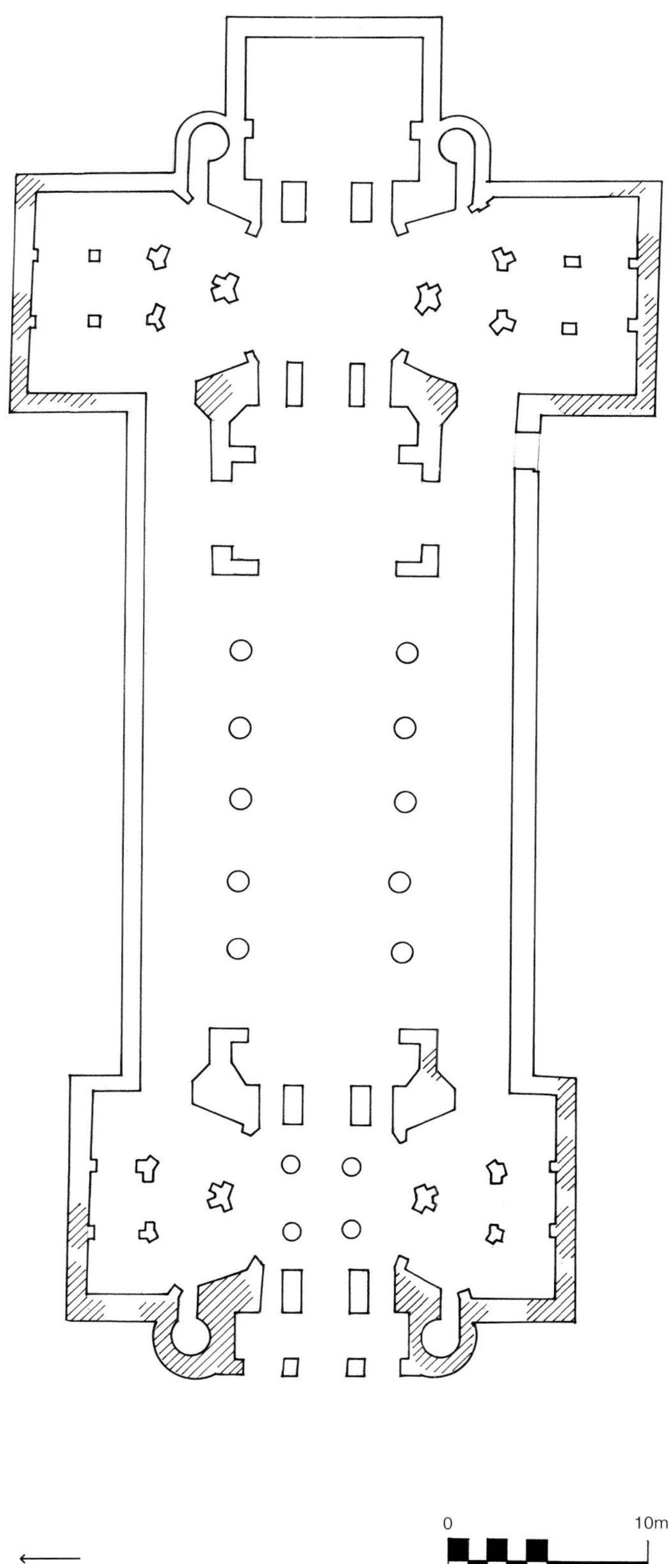

161 Centula (Saint-Riquier), plan of the church of St. Richarius, built 790–99.

Aachen, which Bernard cites as a model for Saint-Riquier, has a gallery surrounding an open, octagonal core and it lacks a transept. Beyond dispute is the fact that the *Libellus* lists nine subsidiary altars and their relics in the church. Although their exact location is not given, it is clear that they were distributed throughout the length and breadth of the building. Their very presence represents a radical departure from the liturgical arrangements of an Early Christian basilica. Instead of a unified interior space with a single altar in the apse as its primary focus, the church at Saint-Riquier was a veritable warehouse of altars, which served as stations for the monastery's elaborate liturgy.[22]

According to the *Institutio*, the church was preceded at the west end by a *paradisus*, a term used in the late eighth century to describe the atrium of Old St. Peter's in Rome.[23] Thus, it must be referring to an entrance courtyard. This would further explain the reference to three gates (*portae*) to the *paradisus* which the *Libellus* states were situated to the north, west, and south. Each gate, moreover, contained an altar dedicated to one of three archangels (Michael, Gabriel, and Raphael), presumably in an upper storey much like the gateway to the atrium at Old St. Peter's and the Lorsch *Torhalle*. A later example would be the tower gate to the atrium of SS. Quattro Coronati in Rome (847–55), cited in the previous chapter (fig. 154). The use of an atrium, like that of a transept, would be another reference to Rome. Angilbert also boasts that by order of Charlemagne luxurious materials such as marble columns, revetment, and floor paving were imported from Rome to decorate his church and the setting of Roman relics.[24]

Thus, although many details of the monastery remain to be determined, it clearly reflected the architectural currents of its day through the imitation of models both in Rome and Aachen and through the use of features that had already appeared in the abbey churches of Saint-Denis and Lorsch. Indeed, there is little doubt that in terms of both size and complexity the abbey of Saint-Riquier at Centula was one of the great architectural achievements of the Carolingian age.

The next major example of this new and monumental phase in Carolingian monastic architecture is the abbey of Fulda, located some 350 km due east of Centula in the modern German state of Hessen. Limited excavations of the site, now occupied by an early eighteenth-century cathedral complex, have been carried out intermittently by various investigators since the beginning of the twentieth century, so that we have a far more detailed archaeological record than at Saint-Riquier, although it too is far from complete. Numerous written accounts from the ninth and tenth century complement our knowledge of the monastery's architectural development. The monastery was founded in 744 by Sturmi, a disciple of St. Boniface, within the remains of an abandoned fortified settlement on a promontory overlooking the Fulda River. The archaeological record provides the following sequence of events.[25] The site had been occupied by a Frankish version of a Roman villa rustica, composed of three separate units, that was destroyed in a Saxon raid around 700. Although some of the rooms of this complex may have been used by the monks for temporary shelter, the plan of the villa did not influence the layout of the abbey as was the case at Lorsch in the 760s; instead, the church, dedicated to the Savior in 751, was set up along a strict east–west axis, that diverged significantly from the alignment of the earlier villa. Although the fragmentary nature of the remains precludes a detailed reconstruction of Sturmi's church, it seems to have been a large, single-aisled basilica, measuring over 30 m long and 20 m wide with an eastern apse 11 m in diameter. Such a design, in contrast to the aisleless, rectangular-apsed churches at the contemporary abbeys of Reichenau and Lorsch, is best explained as an influence from Italy, where Sturmi travelled soon after Fulda was founded in order to gather advice and information about regulations for monastic life.[26] The same region—Rome in particular—continued to serve as a source of inspiration for building on the site, especially after 754, when the abbey church received the body of St. Boniface, recently murdered by heathens in Frisia, and Fulda became renowned as the resting place of the great martyr. In 791, Sturmi's successor Baugulf initiated a complete rebuilding of the abbey church on a much larger scale with an apse at the east end 15 m wide, preceded by a nave 63.30 m long and 16.70 m wide, flanked by single aisles 8.35 m wide (fig. 162). Eleven years later, while the new abbey church was still under construction, Baugulf was succeeded as abbot by Ratgar, who added a western transept (77 m long and 17 m wide) and apse, the same width as its counterpart to the east, to serve as a new and monumental setting for the tomb of Boniface, which had previously stood in the nave. In accordance with the new directional emphasis of the church, an atrium was built at the east end of the church, measuring some 25 m square. In the center of the eastern range of the atrium stood a rectangular gatehouse flanked by massive square stairtowers.

In spite of modifications in later centuries (the atrium rebuilt with a new gatehouse, a small tower set atop the center of the transept, and cylindrical stair turrets built to either side of the eastern apse), the Carolingian abbey church stood little changed until it was replaced between 1704 and 1712 by the present cathedral. Representations of the sixteenth and seventeenth centuries indicate that the eastern and western walls of the transept arms were pierced by three round-arched windows and that the clerestory of the nave bore eleven such windows on either side. Only

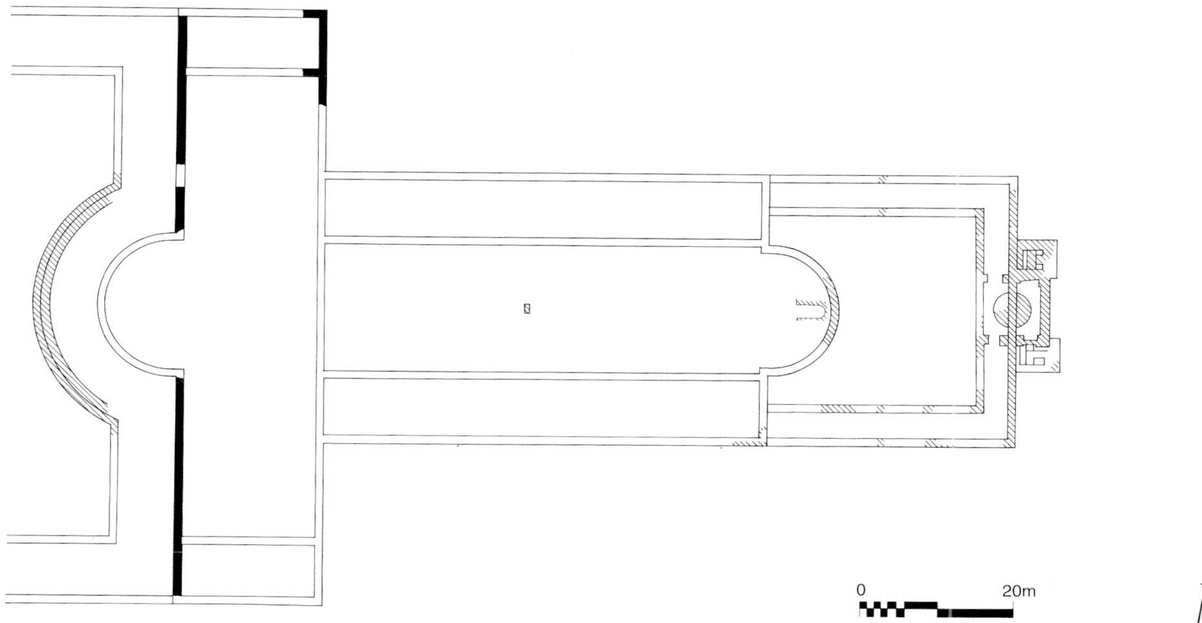

162 Fulda, plan of abbey church, late eighth to early ninth century.

five windows are shown in the aisle walls but others may have been walled up to allow for later buttresses, which are also clearly visible. This pictorial evidence together with the archaeological information demonstrate the overall simplicity and monumentality of the building.

The Roman inspiration of this design is unquestionable. The size and proportions of the transept, and its placement at the west end of the church, can only be explained as a direct reference to Old St. Peter's in Rome. Even the presence of screen walls at the ends of the transept is otherwise found only in the Vatican basilica. Thus, the abbey church at Fulda is a prime example of the Carolingian revival of Early Christian architecture, as first proposed by Richard Krautheimer in a now famous article of 1942.[27] Admittedly, Roman features were characteristic of Carolingian architecture since the building of Saint-Denis (768–75), but no church north of the Alps had previously attempted to rival the great basilicas of Rome in both form and scale. The reference to Rome seems particularly appropriate for Fulda because it was in Rome that Boniface had been inspired, with the blessing of the pope, to undertake his evangelizing mission in the German regions of the Frankish kingdom, whereupon he had changed his original Anglo-Saxon name, Wynfrid, to that of the Roman saint, Boniface. Krautheimer, therefore, is surely correct in seeing the motivation behind the design of the abbey church at Fulda as a desire to equate, or at least associate, the martyred St. Boniface, who became known as the apostle of the Germans, with St. Peter, the apostle of the Romans.

The abbey church at Fulda, of course, differs from its model in the use of two opposing apses, but this too seems to have been motivated by a desire to emulate Rome. Indeed, the placement of an altar, and concomittantly its apse, at the west end of the church was described by an eye-witness, the monk and scholar Candidus, as "following Roman custom" (*more Romano*).[28] The first known example of a double-apse scheme in Carolingian architecture is Saint-Maurice d'Agaune, in present-day Switzerland, where a western apse was added around 787 to a traditionally oriented small basilica, built ten or so years earlier.[29] Between 790 and 800, a second apse was built at the west end of the Merovingian cathedral in Cologne, a structure that must have been familiar to the abbot of Fulda (fig. 163). At Saint-Maurice the western apse housed an annular crypt which can only have been inspired by Old St. Peter's, while at Cologne the western apse housed a new altar dedicated to the apostle Peter, in contrast to its earlier apse in the east dedicated to the Virgin.[30] There may also have been liturgical reasons for employing a double-apse scheme. In the 780s, the Ordo Romanus, a description of the stational masses for the basilicas of Rome, began to be used as a model for the reform of the Frankish liturgy. As Carol Heitz has pointed out, one section of this Roman Mass book in particular has profound architectural implications when it states that the pope, after kissing the gospel-book and the altar, "approaches his throne (in the apse) and stands facing east."[31] These instructions conformed perfectly to the arrangement at the Roman basilicas of the

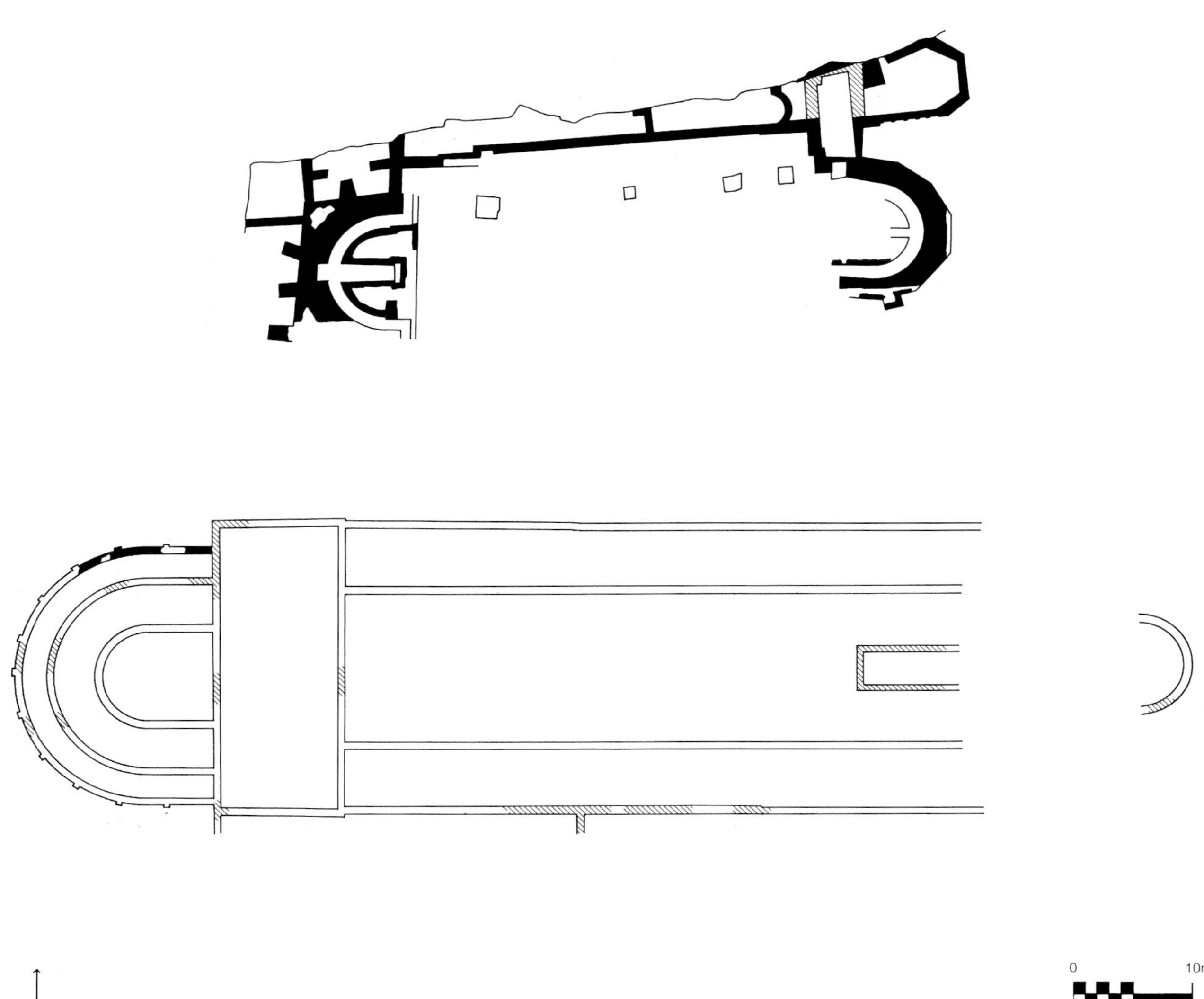

163 (above) Saint-Maurice d'Agaune, plan of abbey church, late eighth century; (below) Cologne, cathedral, ca. 800.

Lateran and St. Peter's where the apse and papal throne were at the west end of the church, but they could not be followed literally in a church with an eastern apse, as was the norm elsewhere in Europe. Thus Heitz suggests that western apses were built at Saint-Maurice, Cologne, and Fulda to comply with Roman practice. In doing so, however, it should be noted that these western apses were added to already standing structures, which indicates a piecemeal approach toward architecture that was contrary to the more uniform nature of Early Christian churches. Even at Fulda the two phases of the abbey church were considered by contemporaries to be distinct not only in time but also in terminology so that one end of the church was known as the eastern sanctuary (*templum orientale*) and the other as the western sanctuary (*templum occidentale*). As one source explains, Ratgar, "joining the western sanctuary with the other, . . . made one church."[32]

Such an ambitious project, however, was not achieved without a price. In 812, the monks of Fulda wrote to Charlemagne complaining of the "enormous and superfluous buildings . . . by which the brethren are unduly tired and the serfs are ruined." They urged instead that "all things should be done in moderation and with discretion."[33] The aged emperor did not respond to their plea, but in 817, the monks wrote again, this time to Charlemagne's son and heir, Louis the Pious, who intervened to have Ratgar deposed as abbot. A year later, the brethren were allowed to choose a successor from among their ranks, Eigil, who saw that the church was brought swiftly to completion. The floor was paved, altars decorated, and two hall crypts were installed below the main apses to receive a variety of relics; and on November 1, 819, the church was consecrated at which time the remains of St. Boniface were placed in a sarcophagus behind the altar of the western apse.[34] Not long thereafter, according to Eigil's ninth-century *Vita*, the abbot called the monastic community together to discuss the location of the new cloister. Should it be built to the south of the abbey church, they were asked, following the previous arrangement? Or should the new cloister be placed to the west of the church "according to Roman custom" (*more Romano*)? The latter proposal was adopted, "because of the vicinity of the martyr's relics (those of St. Boniface) that rested in that part of the basilica (i.e., the western apse)."[35] This episode provides a unique insight into the formulation of the arrangement of the monastery. In the wake of Ratgar's removal, Eigil went out of his way to reach a consensus before embarking on the construction of a new cloister. Still, the desire to emulate Rome remained strong.

Unfortunately, the site of the new cloister has only been partially excavated so that its full dimensions are not known. Nonetheless, between 1910 and 1918, Joseph Vonderau uncovered remains of two curved walls, built one against the other, that circumscribed the western apse at a distance of approximately 5 m, and a projecting spur wall more than one meter long to either side.[36] Thus at the point where the cloister walkway met the apse it was adapted to echo the curvature of the apse. Presumably the outer wall of the cloister walk formed a square that was contiguous with the ends of the western transept. If so, this would have created a cloister (77 × 77 m) many times larger than that of Lorsch or Saint-Riquier, which seems contrary to the earlier complaints about "enormous and superfluous buildings." Moreover, the meaning of the term "according to Roman custom" with reference to the cloister is not immediately clear. If Eigil and his monks were thinking of the atria of Early Christian basilicas in Rome, as one would assume, that of Old St. Peter's stood not at the west end of the church but at the east. Several small monasteries—S. Stefano degli Abissini among them—were situated behind the western apse and transept of the Vatican basilica, but there is no evidence that they possessed cloisters or that they were in any way enclosed within a courtyard. Among Rome's hallowed basilicas only St. Paul's-outside-the-Walls, with its apse in the east, had its atrium to the west, and here another small monastery dedicated to St. Stephen is described in an eighth-century source as having stood *in atrio beati apostoli Pauli*.[37] Still, in the case of the cloister at Fulda, as opposed to the abbey church, the notion of "Roman custom" seems to have been less precise. It was the western location and the proximity of the martyr's tomb, and not a specific architectural model, that the monks associated with Rome.

The dramatic increase in the scale of monastic architecture seems to have been widespread. Recent excavations at the aforementioned abbey of S. Vincenzo al Volturno in south Italy have revealed the remains of a monumental church, 100 m long, built it seems in the early years of the ninth century.[38] Influence from Rome, especially St. Peter's, is seen in the presence of an atrium at the entrance and an annular crypt in the central apse, while the use of three apses to terminate the building is best understood as a regional characteristic, found also at Montecassino and S. Sofia in Benevento (figs. 139 and 60). Reminiscent of Centula is the 100-meter-long corridor that connected this new and larger abbey church with the monastery's older core, including a refectory, built on the site of an ancient Roman villa. Whether S. Vincenzo ever possessed a square cloister has yet to be determined.

The abbey churches at Fulda and S. Vincenzo al Volturno marked the culmination in size and Roman influence of monastic architecture under Charlemagne, for the accession to the throne of Louis the Pious (814–40) heralded a new and very different era. Louis was a sober and intensely religious man, earning him the later epithet "the Pious." Although an accomplished soldier and a lover of the hunt, he had a decidedly different view of imperial rule, based less on military might and charismatic leadership and concerned more with spiritual matters, such as the uniformity of religious observance. As "Emperor and Majesty by will of Divine Providence," he saw himself above all as a servant of the Church. Indeed, he banished from Aachen several of Charlemagne's advisers and the more free-living members of the court, such as his infamous sisters and their lovers, and surrounded himself instead with members of the clergy. He became known as "a friend of monks," and felt strongly about the need to reform the monasteries of his realm. That his attitude toward monasticism differed significantly from that of his father has already been noted with reference to Fulda, where he advised Eigil "to stop this superfluous work of erecting structures of inordinate size and to reduce the monastery's building program to normal proportions."[39] Moreover, in 816 and 817, he presided over two synods at Aachen that were assembled to discuss and legislate regulations for the proper workings of monasteries in the Carolingian Empire.[40] It was at this time that the Rule of St. Benedict was proclaimed as the universal guide to monasticism, replacing the mixed rules that had been the norm until that time. The monks at Fulda were well aware of Louis's inclinations, for they mention the 816 synod in their petition.[41] Thus they appealed to him in 817 with the full expectation that he would intervene on their behalf.

Louis was guided in his program of monastic reform by Benedict of Aniane, the son of a Visigothic nobleman from Theodulf's homeland of Septimania.[42] Originally named Witiza, Benedict of Aniane had as a youth served at the Frankish court and distinguished himself in combat during Charlemagne's campaign in Lombardy in 774. After a brush with death, however, he entered a monastery near Dijon in

780 and took the name of the author of the famous Rule. In order to follow the spirit of Benedictine monasticism more closely, he established a monastic community on his ancestral property at Aniane and by the early 800s was renowned as a founder and reformer of some twenty-five monasteries in southern France. While king of Aquitaine, Louis came to admire Benedict's work and in 814 he summoned him to the imperial court. Benedict first was given the abbey of Maursmünster in Alsace, but soon after he moved to Inden (now Kornelimünster), a short distance from Aachen, where with the emperor's generous support he constructed a new monastery, consecrated in 817, which was to serve as a model for the reform movement. It was here that the theologically minded emperor expressed the desire to retreat for cherished moments of solitude and it was here that he wished to be buried. Thus the building of the abbey at Kornelimünster was a very personal undertaking for both Louis the Pious and Benedict of Aniane, making its design of particular importance for an understanding of the development of monastic architecture in the ninth century.

Fortunately, excavations carried out by Leo Hugot between 1959 and 1963 were able to determine the design of the abbey church in considerable detail (fig. 146).[43] The nave was short and broad (14.30 m long × 4.36 m), flanked by even shorter single aisles divided from the nave by two rectangular piers. At the west end stood a compact block made up of a central projecting porch framed by two squarish rooms. The nave continued uninterrupted to a rectangular fore-choir and a horseshoe-shaped apse, while dwarf transept arms each with a semi-circular apse were segregated from the aisles and the eastern third of the nave by L-shaped piers supporting arches, so that the east end presented a staggered triple-apse arrangement. There was no allowance for a crypt. As Werner Jacobsen has pointed out, both in size and in design, the church at Kornelimünster can only be interpreted as a conscious rejection of the grandiose schemes of earlier abbey churches such as Fulda and Centula.[44] To paraphrase the aforementioned petition from the monks of Fulda, there is nothing "enormous" or "superfluous" about this building. Nor does it bear any sign of Roman influence. As noted in chapter seven, the use of triple apses was always foreign to Rome and when it did appear, as at S. Maria in Domnica, the apses were never arranged in a staggered fashion or formed part of segregated dwarf transepts. The immediate source for the design at Kornelimünster came from Benedict's first monastery at Aniane, after which it was used again at Maursmünster. The horseshoe-shaped apse also points to Benedict's homeland.[45]

The diminutive size of the abbey church was meant to serve only a limited number of monks, set by Benedict at thirty, as opposed to several hundred brethren said to have resided at Fulda and Centula. Also in contrast to earlier developments, the cloister was not located to the side of the church but adjoining the west facade. Although this may at first seem to imitate the atria associated with some Roman basilicas, its location may have been intended instead to reflect Benedict's increased emphasis on hospitality to guests, especially to other monks come to study the ways of reform.[46] Moreover, without a cache of relics, Kornelimünster was not a major center of lay pilgrimage, thus there was no need to separate the cloister from the entrance courtyard as was the case at Fulda, Centula, and the second abbey at Lorsch.

Kornelimünster, as the home of Benedict of Aniane, served as a model for the development of monastic architecture during the early years of Louis's reign. In the previous chapter, it was noted that Einhard, for example, while still an active member of the imperial court, followed its design, save for the crypt, in his abbey church at Steinbach. Following Benedict's death in 821, however, the initial fervor of monastic reform began to subside and was replaced by a more tempered approach, promoted by prominent churchmen, such as Adalhard of Corbie and Haito of Basel, who had lived to serve both Charlemagne and Louis the Pious. Einhard, as we have seen, abandoned his church at Steinbach after he obtained the relics of SS. Marcellinus and Peter in 827, and between 830 and 840, used at Seligenstadt the Roman formula of the T-shaped basilica popular in the days of Charlemagne. Similarly, in 836, the cathedral of Paderborn, adjoining Charlemagne's palace, was enlarged at the west end by a continuous transept and an apse housing an annular crypt to receive the body of St. Liborius, which was translated with the permission of Louis the Pious from Le Mans.[47] It should be noted that in both cases the use of Roman architectural features was prompted by the acquisition of relics, a cult practice that was conspicuously missing at Kornelimünster. At the abbey of Hersfeld, on the other hand, a new church was built between 831 and 850 that followed the triple-apse and segregated transept design of Kornelimünster, although at more than twice the size (overall length of 53.30 m at Hersfeld versus 26.03 m at Kornelimünster).[48] Here the design of Benedict of Aniane's model church seems to have been combined with the inordinate scale of the church of the neighboring abbey of Fulda, whose abbot Hrabanus Maurus helped to lay the groundstone at Hersfeld. Thus, the later 820s and 830s saw not so much a wholesale return to the architectural precepts of an earlier age as a process of assimilation and compromise whereby elements of both Roman influence and recent monastic reform could be combined to suit the needs of a given situation. Such an attitude helps to explain the seemingly contradictory qualities of the unique document from this period known as the Plan of St. Gall.

Preserved in the library of the former monastery of St. Gall in Switzerland as Stiftsbibliothek, Ms. 1092 is a large sheet of vellum (77 × 112 cm) made up of five separate pieces of calfskin stitched together (figs. 164 and 165). On the smooth side of this unwieldy sheet is the detailed plan of a monastic complex, drawn in red ink and accompanied by legends in brown ink explaining the function of each building. The Plan is dominated by the abbey church, a large single-aisled basilica with two opposing apses, a projecting transept to the east, and a western entrance in the form of a semicircular atrium from which project two cylindrical towers. Small square rooms on either side of the eastern choir are identified by their inscriptions as, on the right, a sacristy and vestry, and, on the left, a scriptorium and library. Attached to the south side of the church is a square cloister walk, surrounded by a dormitory, refectory, and cellar. Along the church's northern flank are shown several freestanding structures: an abbot's house, a school, and a guest house for distinguished visitors. At the top, or east end, of the Plan, from left to right (or north to south), are found a physician's house and herbal garden, a combined infirmary and novitiate, a cemetery, a vegetable garden and gardener's house, and circular enclosures for chickens and geese, and a house for the fowlkeeper. Workrooms, such as a granary, bakery, brew house, a mill and mortar, as well as houses for coopers and wheelwrights, are set along the right or southern edge of the Plan; while toward the bottom, or west, can be found a guest house and kitchen for paupers and pilgrims, and stalls and pens for various farm animals. In short, the Plan of St. Gall provides the architectural setting for all the activities necessary for the successful functioning of a prosperous Benedictine abbey. The only feature left out is an enclosure wall, presumably because it was deemed ubiquitous and not in need of specific delineation.

The general provenance of the Plan is well attested. At the top, or east end, of the sheet is a note addressed to Abbot Gozbertus, who ruled St. Gall from 816 to 836 and initiated a rebuilding of the monastery in 830. It is clear that the Plan was meant to represent the abbey of St. Gall, because a crypt at the east end of the church is labelled to show that it was designed to house the tomb of the monastery's founder, Gallus, who died around 630 and was a disciple of the Irish missionary Columbanus. In addition, a detailed analysis of the note and inscriptions by the eminent palaeographer Bernard Bischoff has shown that they were written by two distinct individuals in the scriptorium of the abbey of Reichenau-Mittelzell in the first half of the ninth century, which suggests the Plan was also drawn there.[49] More precise information about the circumstances under which the Plan was produced is harder to ascertain.

The Plan of St. Gall has been the subject of intense scholarly research for over a century, culminating in two comprehensive studies published in 1979 and 1992, respectively: the first is a lavishly illustrated three-volume work by Walter Horn, an historian of architecture, and Ernest Born, an architect, which investigates virtually every aspect of the document, while the second, by Werner Jacobsen, is an extremely detailed analysis, which focuses on the production of the Plan and the design of the abbey church.[50] Yet, in spite of the seeming exhaustive nature of these two publications, they come to strikingly different conclusions. Horn, following the lead of several earlier scholars, believes that the Plan of St. Gall was traced around 820 from a master plan drawn up at the Aachen Synods of 816 and 817 concerned with monastic reform. According to this interpretation, the Plan is a pristine and uniform visual expression of an ideal of monastic life. Jacobsen, on the other hand, concludes that the Plan is a unique document, with many ad hoc alterations, which was drawn up on the spot around 830 in response to a plea from the abbot of St. Gall. How could there be such a fundamental disagreement?

Horn's argument begins with the interpretation of the note to Gozbert, which he translates as follows:

> For thee, my sweetest son Gozbertus, have I drawn this briefly annotated copy of the layout of the monastic buildings, with which you may exercise your ingenuity and recognize my devotion, whereby I trust you do not find me slow to satisfy your wishes. Do not imagine that I have undertaken this task supposing you to stand in need of our instruction, but rather believe that out of love of God and in the friendly zeal of brotherhood I have depicted this for you alone to scrutinize. Farewell in Christ, always mindful of us, Amen.[51]

Although this translation conveys the general sense of the message in a very readable form, it should not be taken literally in every detail. All agree that the note indicates that the Plan was sent at the request of Gozbert and that it was intended to serve as a guide to be used at his discretion in the rebuilding of his abbey. It is the precise meaning of the opening phrase ("Haec tibi . . . de posicione officinarum paucis exemplata direxi . . .") that has been challenged. Paul Meyvaert, for example, in a review of Horn's book, prefers: ". . . these brief indications for the arrangement of the various monastic buildings, which I send you, in copied form . . . ," while Adalbert de Vogüé, in a detailed philological study of the note, proposes instead: "I send you . . . this view of the disposition of buildings, summarily indicated. . . ."[52] The point being contested

164 and 165 *(following pages)* Plan of St. Gall, ca. 830 and transcription.

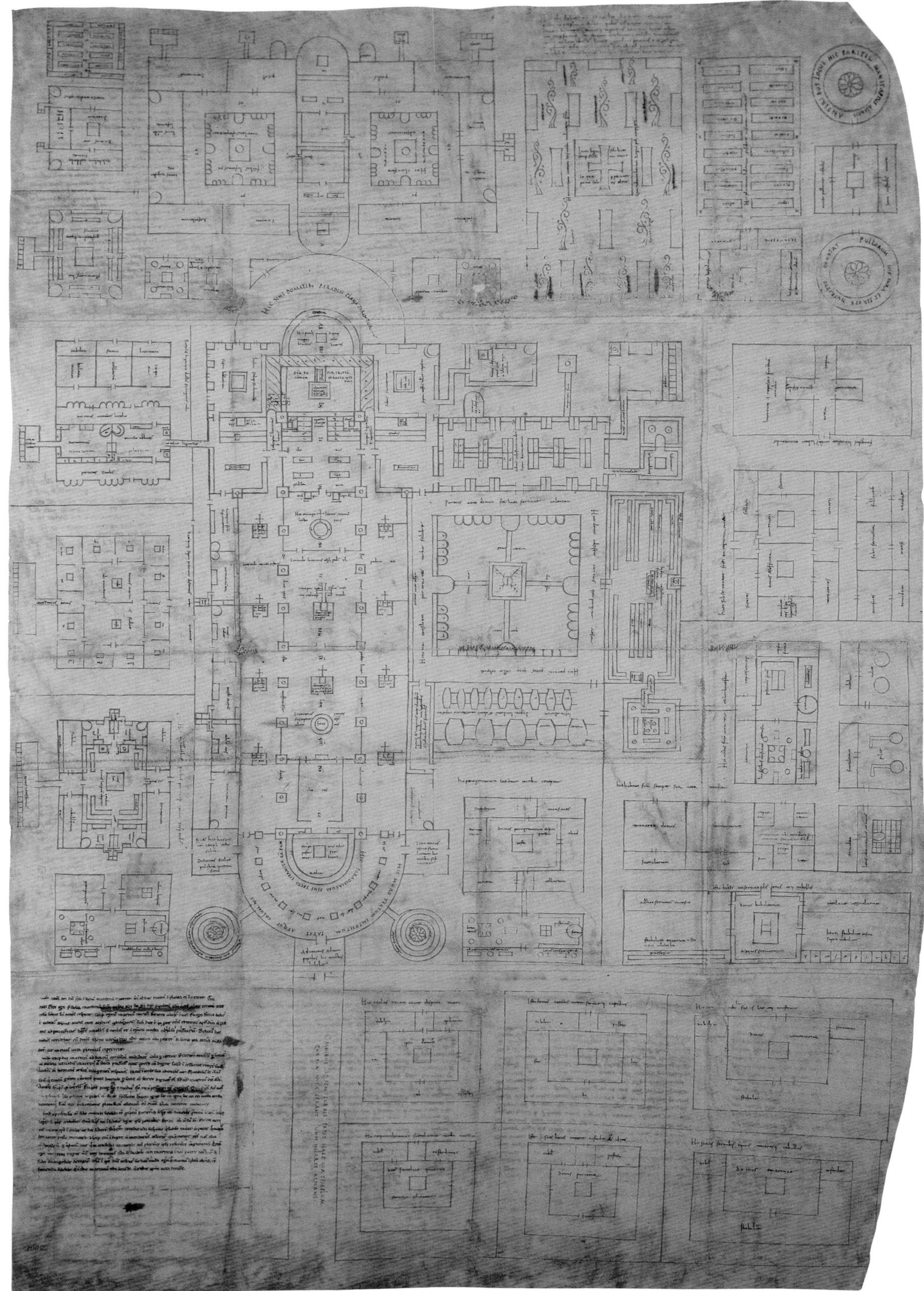

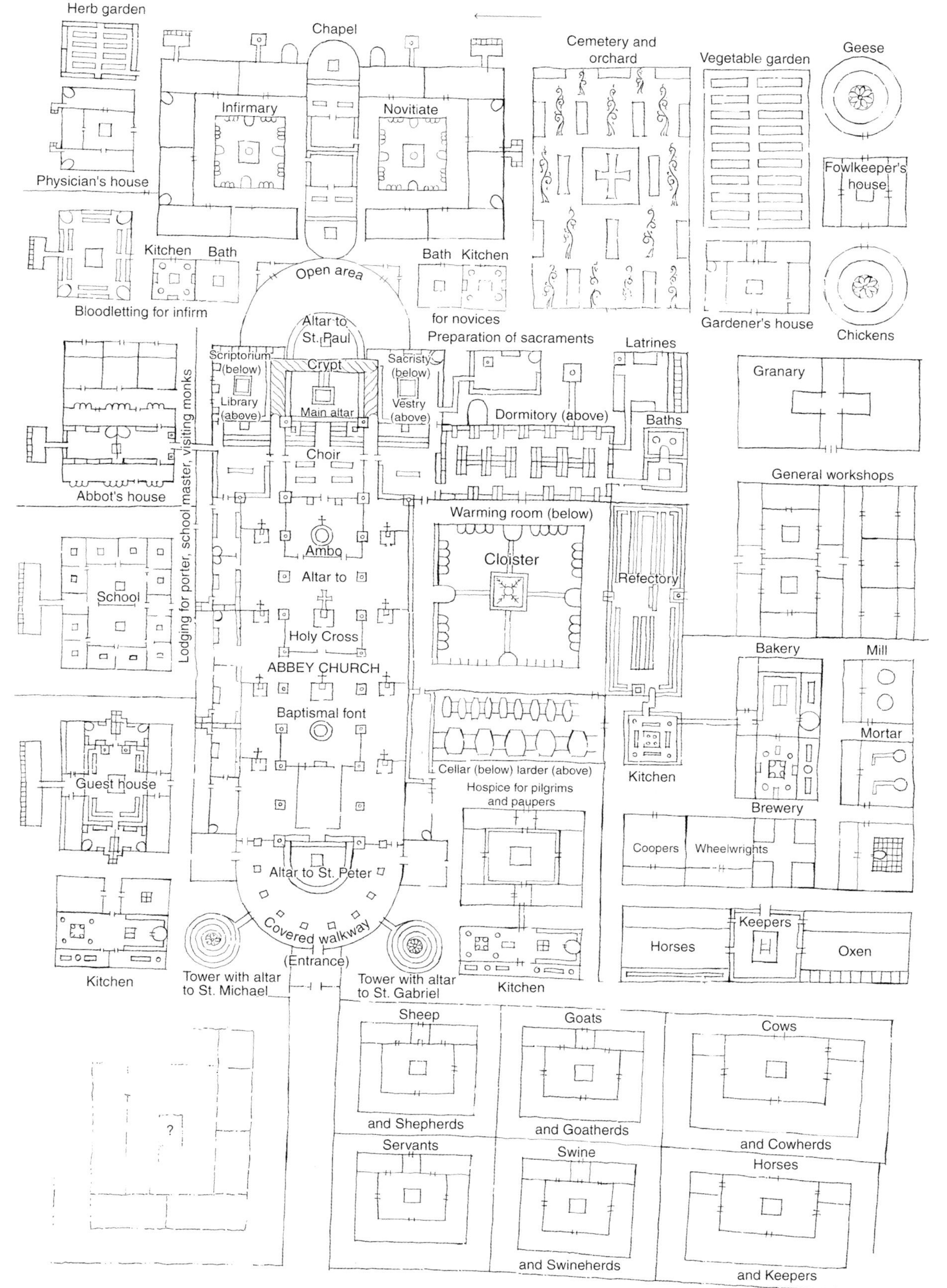
Herb garden
Chapel
Cemetery and orchard
Vegetable garden
Geese
Infirmary
Novitiate
Fowlkeeper's house
Physician's house
Kitchen
Bath
Bath
Kitchen
Open area
Bloodletting for infirm
for novices
Gardener's house
Chickens
Altar to St. Paul
Preparation of sacraments
Latrines
Scriptorium (below)
Crypt
Sacristy (below)
Granary
Library (above)
Main altar
Vestry (above)
Dormitory (above)
Baths
Lodging for porter, school master, visiting monks
Choir
Abbot's house
General workshops
Warming room (below)
Ambo
Cloister
Altar to
Refectory
School
Holy Cross
ABBEY CHURCH
Bakery
Mill
Baptismal font
Mortar
Guest house
Kitchen
Cellar (below) larder (above)
Hospice for pilgrims and paupers
Brewery
Coopers
Wheelwrights
Altar to St. Peter
Keepers
Horses
Oxen
Covered walkway
(Entrance)
Kitchen
Tower with altar to St. Michael
Tower with altar to St. Gabriel
Kitchen
Sheep
Goats
Cows
?
and Shepherds
and Goatherds
and Cowherds
Servants
Swine
Horses
and Swineherds
and Keepers

here is whether the term *exemplata* (from the Latin verb *exemplare*, meaning "to copy" or "to offer as an example") should be used as evidence that the Plan was copied from an earlier prototype.[53]

Moreover, a close physical examination of the Plan tends to contradict Horn's view. Jacobsen, expanding upon two short articles of 1978 and 1980 by Norbert Stachura, presents irrefutable evidence of numerous alterations to the Plan in the process of its production, before, during and after inking.[54] At the west end of the church, for example, Stachura was the first to find three sets of semicircles with separate center points along the same axis that indicate a process of experimentation before the final form of the apse and atrium was reached. Elsewhere lines have been erased and redrawn in different configurations. Such a procedure agrees with Bischoff's observations of corrections in some of the legends and his detection of an improvisational character in their wording, suggesting that the inscriptions were composed at Reichenau and not transcribed from an earlier source. This does not mean, however, that there may not have been preparatory drawings of some kind. The fluidity of the line and the lack of preparatory markings on other parts of the Plan indicate that some sections, at least, were worked out beforehand and then transferred in some manner to the vellum sheet. Thus the creation of the Plan of St. Gall seems to have been a complex process, part trial-and-error and part copy, but certainly not the result of tracing alone.

This brings into question another of Horn's theses: that the Plan exhibits a uniform system of measurement. A basic module for the church of 40 feet seems obvious because it is the labelled width of the nave and corresponds to the dimensions of the square crossing, but a grid of 40-foot squares does not easily accommodate the rest of the church or the cloister. To suppose, as Horn does, that every element of the drawing, no matter the size or importance, complies with this grid and its successively halved subdivisions of 20, 10, 5, and finally 2½ Carolingian feet seems extreme. According to this scheme, for example, the beds in the dormitory would be 7½ feet long! Several scholars have argued for the use of other methods, such as the square root of two and triangulation, for various parts of the Plan.[55] Jacobsen, in turn, suggests that different scales of measurement were used for different parts of the Plan.

But even so, there are inconsistencies in the labelled measurements themselves, especially within the abbey church. Based on the 40-foot width of the nave, the intercolumniations (two per bay) should be 20 feet, but they are inscribed 12 feet; and instead of 300 feet, as one would calculate from the width of the nave, the length of the nave is given as 200 feet. Horn explains these contradictions as reflections of a conflict between conservative and liberal factions at the Aachen Synods. He conjectures that the church was initially drawn, in accordance with a 40-foot grid, to be 300 feet long but that, soon after, its length was written as 200 feet as a concession to those at the synods who called for a more moderate scale in monastic architecture. Jacobsen believes that the shorter inscribed length relates to an earlier phase in the Plan when the abbey church was initially drawn as considerably shorter than its final form.

In any case, a direct connection between the Plan of St. Gall and the Synods at Aachen seems tenuous at best. Although there do seem to have been competing factions within the assembly of bishops and abbots, it was apparently the hardliners who lost out to more moderate views, which is the reverse of the sequence used by Horn to explain the discrepancies in the inscribed measurements of the church on the Plan.[56] Moreover, the various accounts of the two synods make no reference to a master plan nor do they show any particular concern for the layout of a monastery.[57] The goal of monastic reform under Louis the Pious was to establish uniformity of observance and a code of behavior based on the Rule of St. Benedict, and like the Rule, the synods of 816 and 817 were concerned with the ordering of monastic life and not with dictating architectural forms. The structural ramifications of their promulgations can only be inferred and even then they are few in number. In the final resolutions of 817, known as the *Monastic Capitulary*, for example, allowances are made for a separate abbot's residence, occasional bathing by the monks, and workshops within the monastery which do agree with features on the Plan, but this does not prove a cause-and-effect relationship because these same items are already mentioned in the Rule of St. Benedict.[58] On the other hand, one feature prominently mentioned in the *Monastic Capitulary*, a jail for recalcitrant monks, is found neither in the Rule nor on the Plan.[59] Furthermore, if the Plan of St. Gall was the tracing of an original drawing formulated at the Aachen Synods, one would expect it to reflect the outlook of Benedict of Aniane, who was the guiding spirit of the proceedings. Yet, as Jacobsen has pointed out, the large size (even at 200 feet in length) and double-apse design of the church on the Plan could not be more different from the diminutive abbey churches, with three eastern apses, at Kornelimünster and other sites associated with the father of monastic reform. The Plan of St. Gall returns instead to the design of churches built during the reign of Charlemagne, such as the abbey church at Fulda and the cathedral of Cologne. This does not mean, however, that the Aachen Synods played no role whatsoever in the formulation of the Plan of St. Gall; on the contrary, the *Monastic Capitulary* was distributed throughout the Carolingian empire and would certainly have been on the mind of anyone contemplating the rebuilding of an abbey in the 820s.

The identity of the author or sender of the Plan, who goes unnamed in the note to Gozbert, is also disputed. The salutation "my sweetest son" suggests that he was Gozbertus's superior, such as a bishop, and not another abbot. The individual most often proposed has been Haito, a leading churchman of his day, who was abbot of Reichenau-Mittelzell between 803 and 823 and bishop of Basel between 806 to 823. He also demonstrated a decided interest in architecture by sponsoring the building of new churches at both sites. In addition, Haito was an active participant at the Aachen synods, and wrote a commentary on the preliminary resolutions of 816, many of which he found unduly harsh and helped to soften in the decrees of the final gathering a year later. Jacobsen, however, has questioned Haito's involvement with the Plan, because he believes that it must have been drawn up around 830 when Haito had already resigned his offices of bishop and abbot and had retired to Reichenau.[60] His dating is based in part on the fact that a subsidiary altar in the Plan's abbey church is dedicated to St. Sebastian, whose body was transferred from Rome to Soissons in 826; Jacobsen believes therefore that relics for such an altar would not have been available at St. Gall before this date. But relics of St. Sebastian are known to have been used in connection with altar dedications north of the Alps long before then, as witness the abbey churches of both Saint-Riquier (799) and Fulda (819).[61] Nevertheless, Haito lived until 836 and, even after his retirement, remained involved in architectural matters, as shown by his patronage of a ciborium over the high altar at the cathedral in Basel.[62] And as Gozbertus's elder by several years and as a former bishop, he may well have seen fit to address the abbot of St. Gall as "my son." Jacobsen proposes, instead, that Erlebald, abbot of Reichenau from 823 to 838, was the main patron behind the Plan and that Reginbert, the head of the Reichenau scriptorium, was in charge of its production. In support of this contention, Jacobsen believes that his close examination of the Plan reveals that the abbey church was initially drawn to resemble the church of Reichenau-Mittelzell: a squat basilica with a square crossing from which projected to the north and south the arms of a segregated transept and to the east a square choir terminated by two horseshoe-shaped apses set side by side, while a continuous transept, added perhaps around 830, stood at the west end of the nave. Be that as it may, the fact remains that in its present form the abbey church bears little resemblance to the Reichenau church or, for that matter, to Haito's cathedral at Basel, which lacked a transept and was terminated at the east end by a single broad apse (fig. 166).[63] The latter did have cylindrical towers at its west end, like the church on the Plan, but they were integrated into the west facade instead of being detached, suggesting that they were used to gain access either to galleries above the aisles, which would be a highly unusual feature at this time, or, more likely, to the upper storey of a western tribune or westwork. In the end, while both Haito and Erlebald are likely candidates, the actual author of the Plan of St. Gall has yet to be determined.

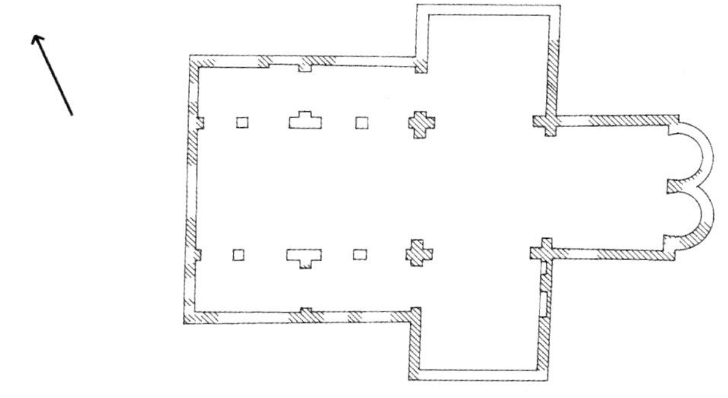

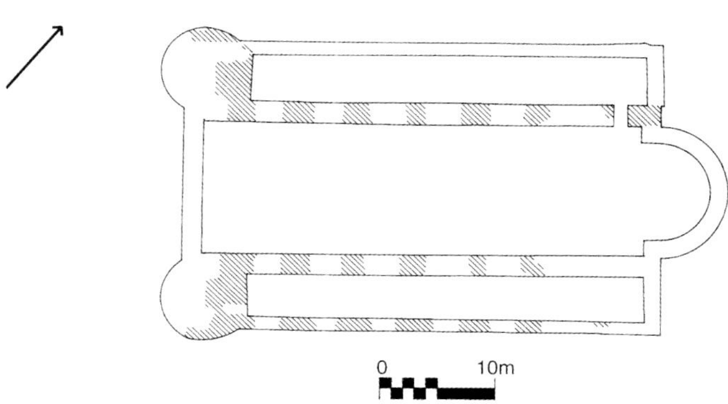

166 Churches sponsored by Haito between 816 and 822: (above) Reichenau-Mittelzell, plan of abbey church; (below) Basel cathedral, schematic plan.

No doubt specialists will continue to have much to say about the Plan of St. Gall, but for the purposes of this study, it seems best simply to accept the document for what it purports to be, that is a plan to advise Gozbertus in his rebuilding of the abbey around 830. As the note states, it was drawn up for him "alone to scrutinize." It is therefore not a blueprint for actual construction, hence the lack of dimensional consistency, but a guide for consideration. In other words, it represents an ideal, one could say utopian, scheme. When considered from this perspective, the Plan becomes an eloquent, visual elaboration of the modest description of a monastery by Benedict of Nursia, quoted at the beginning of this chapter, designed to suit the needs of a prosperous Carolingian abbey. Indeed, it is a veritable lexicon of the architectural forms and terminology available to a building patron in the 820s. As such, it represents a synthesis of over sixty years of experience, experimentation, and development in monastic architecture, going back to the first abbey at Lorsch.

The growth in the importance of the *opus Dei* for the life of the Benedictine monk in the Carolingian period is shown by the inordinate size of the church with its two apses (each labelled *exedra*) and seventeen altars. The reverence for Rome is seen not only in the opposing position of the apses but in the dedication of their altars: in the west to St. Peter and in the east to St. Paul, which corresponds to the direction of the apses in the Roman basilicas honoring the same two apostles (the apse of Old St. Peter's was in the west and that of St. Paul-outside-the-Walls was in the east). In contrast to these Early Christian basilicas, however, the internal space of the nave and aisles is not only defined by rows of columns but is broken up by the many subsidiary altars and the barriers, presumably low screens, that surround them.[64] What could only be inferred from the lists of altars and relics for the abbey church of Saint-Riquier is here given visual documentation. The cult of relics is acknowledged by the dedications of the altars, which show a notable preponderance of Roman saints or those especially associated with Rome (in addition to Peter and Paul, there are Agatha, Agnes, Andrew, Cecilia, Lawrence, Lucia, and Sebastian), and, not surprisingly, of monastic fathers (Benedict, Columban, and Martin). The crypt is reserved for the abbey's founder, St. Gallus; it is not an annular crypt, as one might expect, but a vaulted angular passageway, reminiscent of Steinbach, that leads to a rectangular recess containing the sarcophagus of the saint. Above, in the center of the raised presbytery (the square area between the crossing and the eastern apse, in this case reached via two flights of stairs) is shown the outline of the main altar dedicated to both St. Gall and the Virgin Mary. In the center of the nave is an altar dedicated to the Savior and to the Holy Cross, which seems to mark the division between the areas in the church accessible to the laity and those reserved exclusively for the monks. The crossing, to the east, therefore, is labelled "choir for the psalmodists" (*chorus psallentium*) and provided with benches for the monks, whereas in the nave, to the west between the altar of the Holy Cross and the altar of St. Peter, is the circular outline of a font, presumably for the baptism of infants of lay parents associated with the abbey. It should be noted that the practice of adult baptism had long been abandoned by the ninth century and that the celebration of the rite was no longer the sole prerogative of a bishop. Thus, there was no need for the construction of freestanding baptisteries as was common in the Early Christian period; fonts set within churches were now sufficient.[65] The Plan of St. Gall further indicates that visitors to the church are meant to enter through the curved atrium surrounding the western apse. Here, as at Cologne cathedral around 800, the semicircular portico has been adopted in order to provide a simple yet efficient entryway to a double-apsed church, taking up far less space than the traditional rectilinear atrium used at Fulda. But the inclusion of the two freestanding, cylindrical towers on the Plan of St. Gall reminds one of the similar features attached to the curved facade of the royal palace at Ingelheim and gives the entrance a fortified air. Indeed, not only do the two towers on the Plan contain altars at their summit dedicated to the archangels Michael and Gabriel, appropriate patrons for such an elevated location (no height is given), but the inscription in one of them states that the towers are there "for looking all around" (*ad universa super inspicienda*).[66] In other words, they are lookout towers with altars dedicated to the two archangels to serve as heavenly protectors of the entrance to the church and monastery. On the inside of the atrium the narrow open space between the corridor and the outer wall of the apse is referred to by its inscription as a "paradise" (*paradisus*), the same term used to designate the atria of Saint-Riquier at Centula and Old St. Peter's in Rome. A similar "paradise" surrounds the eastern apse; however, here it is not defined by a portico but by a simple curved wall like that found outside the western apse at Fulda, although not in connection with the cloister.

The rendering of the cloister on the Plan of St. Gall is of particular significance because it represents what would become the norm for the rest of the Middle Ages. Unlike Fulda and Kornelimünster where the cloister was situated at the west end of the church, on the Plan it is placed to the south and measures, according to the 40-foot module, approximately 100 feet square, which corresponds to the size and location of the cloister at the second abbey of Lorsch. The square open court is surrounded by arched porticos, drawn in elevation and labelled *arcus*, that link two-storeyed structures on three sides: to the east is shown a dormitory with seventy-seven beds on the upper floor, while below, according to the inscription, is a heated room where the monks can find temporary relief from the cold during winter months; to the south is shown the refectory on the ground floor with long tables, benches, and a lectern, while on the floor above, so the inscription states, is the vestiary; to the west is shown the cellar with five large and nine smaller barrels, while on the upper floor is a storeroom. In the southwest corner one sees the outline of the monks' kitchen attached to the refectory by a short corridor, and to the southeast two small buildings, one for laundry and bathing, and the other for privies, the former connected to the warming room and the latter, for obvious reasons, to the dormitory. One recognizes immediately the inherent logic and practicality of the cloister as it had evolved since the early eighth century and is shown here in its fully developed form. It is first and foremost an enclosure within an enclosure, at once serving the immediate needs of the monks and isolating them from other activities taking place inside the monastic compound.

Buildings designed to accommodate subsidiary functions are located along the periphery of the Plan, surrounding the core of the church and cloister. To the right, or south, are the workshops of artisans and craftsmen as well as quarters for animals and their attendants. Flanking the western entrance are matching guest facilities, for paupers on the right and distinguished visitors on the left. The latter is followed along the left, or north, side by the outer school, where sons of nobility are taught, and the house of the abbot, who serves as the personal host for important visitors. The top, or east end, of the Plan is an intermediary zone between this outer "service" area and the claustral core, containing buildings to facilitate the beginning, maintenance, and end of monastic life, for here are found, from left to right, the house of the physician, accommodations for novices and for the sick, and a cemetery. The infirmary and novitiate are combined into one complex yet are also kept separate. They are both centered about a double-apsed, aisleless church, which is divided in the middle by a wall in order to create two distinct chapels. To the right is the cloister for the novices with a single entrance into the eastern chapel and to the left the cloister for the sick with a single doorway into the western chapel. These imitations of the main church and cloister in miniature were presumably designed to help the novices prepare for their new calling and to afford the sick and dying familiar surroundings in their time of need.

The major structural features of the abbey church, cloister, novitiate, and infirmary—their apses, columns, and arches—indicate that they were meant to be built of stone, whereas the workrooms, guest facilities, and other "service" buildings, lacking such features, were designed, one assumes, to be built of wood, making them important sources for the development of vernacular architecture in the period. The Plan provides little information about the elevation of these wooden structures, but their internal spatial organization is meticulously delineated and when studied with care offers interesting insights into aspects of private life and social mores in the early Middle Ages. In the building for distinguished guests, for example, the entire retinue of servants and their masters gather in a large rectangular dining hall with a central hearth, an arrangement that is rooted in the centuries-old tradition of

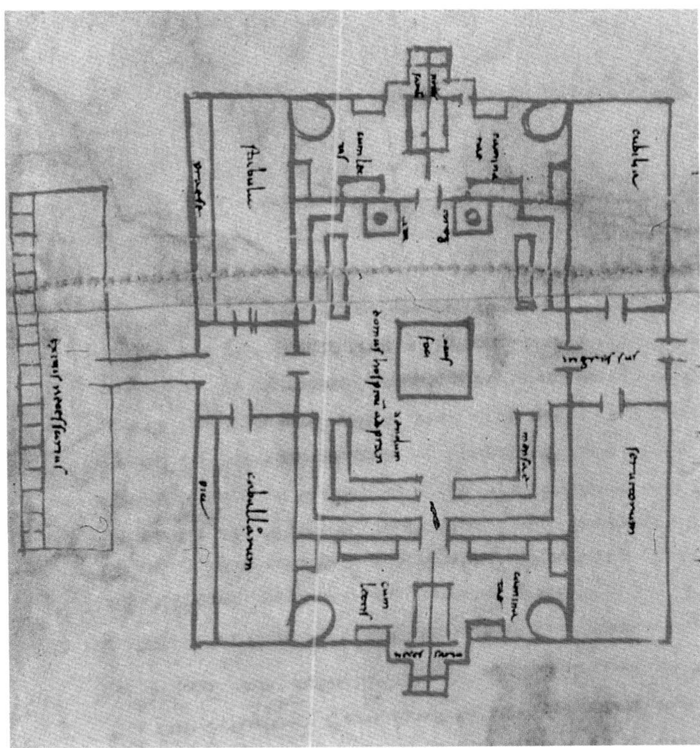

167 Plan of St. Gall, detail, building for distinguished guests.

Germanic timbered houses (fig. 167). The nobility, however, can retire to two pairs of suites just off the short ends of the main hall, each containing two beds, two benches, a fireplace, and an individual toilet. The servants, on the other hand, make do with two common sleeping rooms, flanking (and thus guarding) the entrance vestibule on the longer south side, while their privies (a row of eighteen seats) are located in a shed at the opposite end of the building just beyond the two horse stables. Still, the abundance of privies signifies an unusually high regard for convenience and hygiene, and represents a luxury for its day that is found elsewhere on the Plan; they appear in connection with the monks's dormitory, the outer school, the abbot's house, the novitiate and infirmary but not the house for paupers and pilgrims nor the accommodations for craftsmen and serfs. Servants and horses were, of course, prized possessions of the nobility and prominent symbols of their elevated social status. Interestingly enough, servants and horses are here allotted the same amount of space, which suggests that they were considered to be of equal value. If anything, the horses seem particularly cherished because access to the stables is gained only by passing through the main hall. Although this means that the horses would have to be led through the common dining hall, it is also an effective deterrent against thievery. Thus what might seem at first to be an awkward arrangement, to say the least, is in

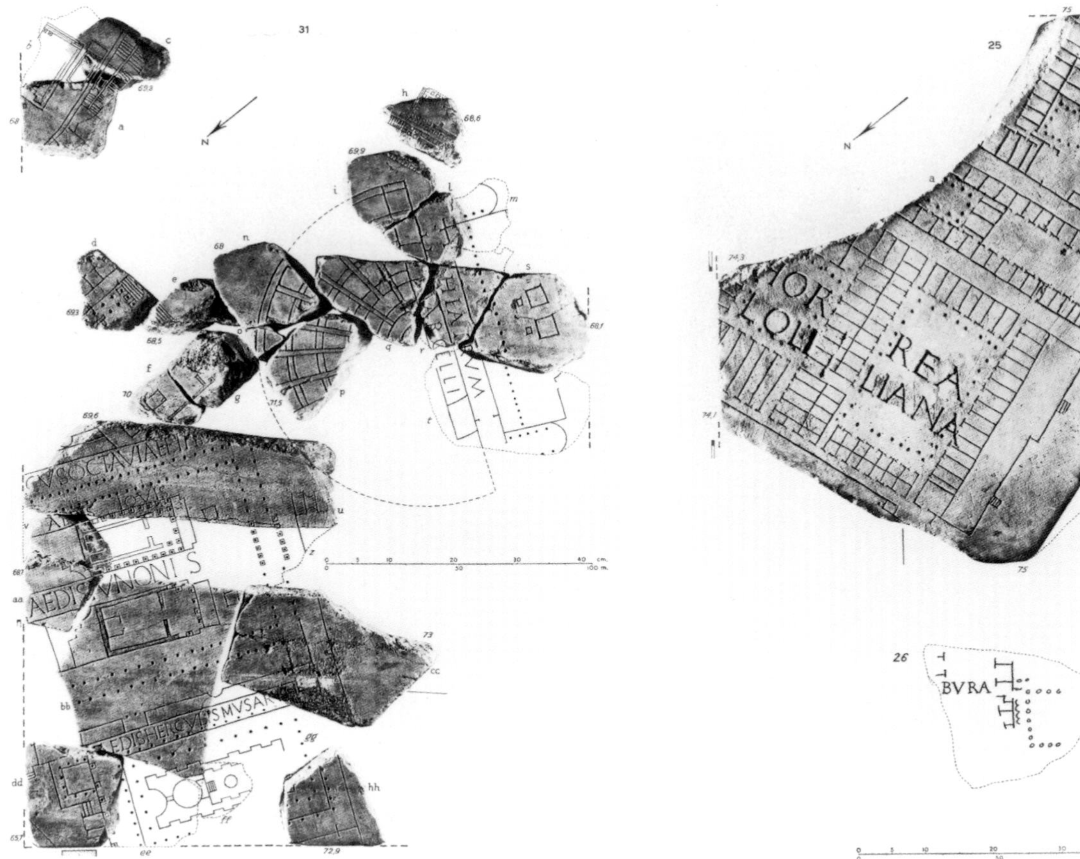

168 and 169 *Forma Urbis Romae*, early third century A.D., fragments.

fact a sound security measure. Single entrances are also characteristic of the quarters for other animals on the Plan.

If the general layout of the Plan of St. Gall is the outgrowth of the long history of the development of monastic architecture, as outlined in this chapter, its orderliness and regularity have even deeper roots. Similar outline drawings with explanatory titles are found in Carolingian copies of Adomnan's *De locis sanctis* (discussed in chapter four, fig. 75), including one manuscript assigned to the scriptorium of Reichenau in the middle of the ninth century, but the precise manner in which the buildings on the Plan are rendered corresponds even more closely to details of the preserved fragments of the monumental stone map of the city of Rome, known as the *Forma urbis Romae*, which was etched during the reign of the Emperor Septimius Severus between A.D. 205 and 208 (figs. 168 and 169). Here one finds the same predominant use of single lines to define buildings, with occasional double lines reserved for certain conspicuous features (such as the cella of a temple on the map and the apse of a church on the Plan), while the arches of aqueducts are shown in elevation, not unlike the arcades of the cloister. The taut network of parallel and perpendicular axes of individual buildings and building groups, reminiscent of the arrangement of Charlemagne's palace at Aachen, also goes back ultimately to what has been termed "the drawing-board mentality" of ancient Roman town planning.[67] Although the *Forma urbis* may no longer have been on view in the Roman forum as late as the ninth century, there were readily available sources of information about ancient Roman design and planning techniques in literary form. Surely it cannot be mere coincidence that the architectural treatise of Vitruvius and other ancient guides to surveying and construction by a variety of authors were extensively copied in the Carolingian period. Indeed, Vitruvius's *De architectura* and the *Mappae clavicula*, a construction handbook, are both listed in a catalogue of books at Reichenau dated 822. We do not know if these two manuscripts were illustrated for they are no longer extant, but two copies of the compilation of ancient Roman surveying manuals known as the *Corpus Agrimensores* are preserved from the first half of the ninth century (both have been assigned to the court scriptorium at Aachen) and they contain numerous diagrams and orthogonal layouts that resemble closely the network

Primum constituemus decumanum maximum & kardinem maximum & abeis strigas & scamna cludemus.

170 *Corpus Agrimensores*, Carolingian copy, second quarter of the ninth century, detail (Biblioteca Apostolica Vaticana, Pal. lat. 1564, fol. 107v.).

of perpendicular axes on the Plan (fig. 170).[68] In an age largely devoid of major urban development, aside from Aachen, the Benedictine monastery afforded an opportunity for the application of such large-scale planning. Indeed, one could say that the abbey of St. Gall is presented in the manner of a small Roman town or military camp, designed in this case to serve the *opus Dei* and the "army of Christ," to use Benedict's own term for a monastic community.[69] In general, then, the organization and visual clarity of the Plan of St. Gall can be attributed to the two great movements of the Carolingian period, the cultural Renaissance and monastic reform, fusing, if you will, the spirit of St. Benedict with that of Roman town planning.

The ideal nature of the Plan is underscored by the fact that its rectangular format was ill-suited to the irregular, almost trapezoidal, nature of the site bordering the Steinach River. Thus, from the onset, Gozbert had to "exercise his ingenuity" in order to adopt the Plan's recommendations. That Gozbert did in fact follow such a course has been confirmed by limited excavations carried out by Hans Rudolf Sennhauser between 1964 and 1966.[70] This investigation was restricted to the area of the Carolingian abbey church, now occupied by an eighteenth-century Baroque successor, and only preliminary reports of the results have as yet appeared in print; nonetheless, the basic outline of Gozbert's church has been recovered, which demonstrates significant elements of both agreement and divergence from the Plan.

The foundations uncovered by Sennhauser reveal a boxy, rectangular design devoid of the explicitly Roman elements of a projecting transept and a western apse (fig. 171). In fact, there is no indication of a semicircular apse at either end of the building; instead, it seems to have been terminated in the east by a flat wall. Sennhauser did, however, find the remains of a crypt similar to that on the Plan but with its longitudinal corridors extended westward almost half the length of the church. This represented a considerable improvement on the Plan's arrangement because the crypt was now accessible from the aisles, meaning that lay visitors did not have to traverse the area reserved for the monks, as was the case in the drawing, in order to approach the tomb of St. Gall. Another innovation was the introduction of a hall crypt at the apex of the angular passage with a narrow shaft projecting westward that held the saint's sarcophagus. On the other hand, the overall size of the church corresponds to the dimensions inscribed on the Plan: the nave is approximately 40 feet wide and the aisles 20 feet wide; and the total length is around 200 feet as written and not 300 feet as drawn. A transverse foundation wall roughly in the middle of the church indicates that the western aisles and the eastern presbytery and choir area were divided, perhaps by solid

171 St. Gall, plan of abbey church built by Abbot Gosbert, 830–36.

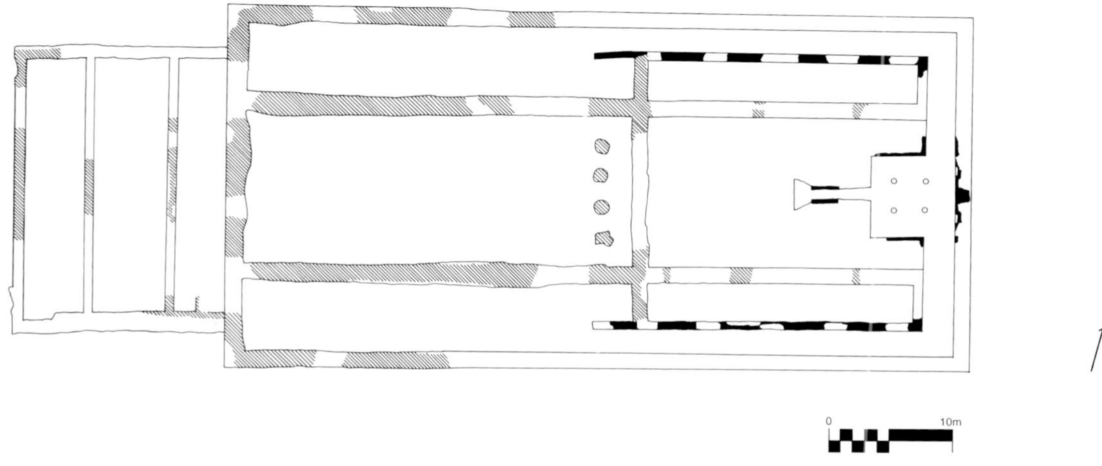

walls, while a row of four foundations at the head of the nave suggests the presence of a masonry screen. Thus, Gozbert segregated the areas used exclusively by the monks from those accessible to the laity far more emphatically than had been done on the Plan, and at the same time greatly increased the eastern sanctuary at the expense of the western nave and aisles. Fragmentary foundations in the main altar area suggest that it was subdivided in some way. The use of columns, in combination with piers, is suggested by a large composite capital (90 cm high × 60 cm wide) found reused in the foundations of the late Gothic choir, which replaced the east end of the church between 1439 and 1483. The nave of the Carolingian church, however, remained standing with little alteration until the total rebuilding of the abbey church in the eighteenth century.

Gozbert, therefore, clearly used the Plan to his advantage; he followed some of its features, modified others, rejected others still, and introduced new elements in order to create a church that suited the needs of his abbey. To be sure, he may have been influenced in this process by regional developments. The cathedral of the neighboring city of Constance, for example, had a similarly designed east end, flat with a hall crypt reached by long angular corridors, which has been ascribed to the ninth century in general.[71] More precisely dated is the abbey church at Reichenau-Mittelzell built under Haito between 806 and 816 where, as at St. Gall, the nave comprised only half the length of the entire structure (fig. 166). It seems only natural that Gozbert should have taken note of important local precedents. But in so doing, he formulated his own design. By the standards of its day, the abbey church was large yet in form it was exceedingly simple. The primary concern seems to have been one of function, enabling Gozbert to pick and choose those elements that best served the needs of the monastic community. Thus the reality of the abbey church at St. Gall differed significantly from the ideal of the Plan.

There is no archaeological evidence concerning the rest of the monastery's layout. An eleventh-century history of the abbey indicates that at that time, and presumably earlier, the cloister stood along the southern flank of the abbey church as it does today, albeit in a totally rebuilt form. The same source also makes reference to the monks' dormitory situated on an upper level and accessible from the church, much in the manner of the Plan, but unlike it the scriptorium was clearly situated in the cloister. No reference is made to the refectory or cellar.[72]

Although information about the complex built under Gozbert is extremely limited, enough is known to demonstrate that the Plan was not closely followed. The Plan of St. Gall was therefore not a paradigm; at least Gozbert did not consider it so. For us, nonetheless, it may serve as a symbol of the level of sophistication that monastic planning attained in the Carolingian age. The size, complexity, and order represent a ninth-century interpretation of St. Benedict's ideal, and the triumph of coenobitic monasticism in western Europe. The Plan of St. Gall, however, does not mark the end of this development. Abbey churches would continue to be built in a variety of shapes and sizes, and contingent structures would be arranged depending upon the requirements of individual sites and local customs. But the tight integration of abbey church and cloister at the core of the monastic complex, as exemplified by the Plan of St. Gall after a century of development, would ultimately prevail and remain the standard throughout the Middle Ages.

It seems somehow fitting that in the late twelfth century an unknown monk at the monastery of St. Gall took the Plan and transcribed on its back the text of a *Life of St. Martin*, the man who in the late fourth century had been among the first to lead the life of a hermit in northern Europe. As the scribe neared the end of his task, he ran out of room and turned the sheet over; in the lower left-hand corner he completed the text but only after having scraped off the outline of a building, the precise design and function of which remain unknown. Fortunately, the rest of the Plan was left untouched. In fact, the addition of the new text aided its preservation, for the parchment was then folded upon itself several times in order to create a book-size volume that could be easily stored.[73] In this form it sat on a shelf of the monastery's library attracting little notice until the seventeenth century when it began to become the focus of scholarly attention. Thus, through this anonymous act of preservation the Plan of St. Gall serves as a guide once again, but this time for all those interested in the history of monastic architecture in the early Middle Ages.

CHAPTER 9

The Innovations of Later Carolingian Architecture

On a snowy day in February 842, two of the three surviving sons of Louis the Pious—Charles the Bald and Louis the German—met at Strasbourg to formalize a new alliance. The previous summer their combined forces had soundly defeated the army of their eldest brother, Lothar, at the bloody Battle of Fontenoy. Now the two victors stood before their assembled cohorts to swear fealty to one another, each employing the vernacular of his own constituency: Louis in Old High German and Charles in Old French.[1] These oaths are among the first records of these two great European languages, and their use at Strasbourg, together with the political ramifications of the event, has often been cited to demonstrate the growing fragmentation of the Carolingian empire in the middle of the ninth century.

Louis the Pious had died in 840 after a decade of discord, during which time various factions of nobles and clergy backed one or the other of the emperor's sons against his father. Time and again, Louis had tried to resolve the conflict by promising to have the empire divided upon his death and by naming Lothar co-emperor, but fraternal rivalry remained and immediately after their father's demise the brothers quarreled more fiercely than ever. The pact at Strasbourg, however, proved to be a turning point. With Charles and Louis united against him, Lothar agreed to compromise and a year later accepted the tripartite division of Europe in the Treaty of Verdun: Louis was given jurisdiction over the regions east of the Rhine, excluding Frisia but including the areas around Speyer, Worms, and Mainz on the river's west bank; the western kingdom, formerly Neustrasia, plus Aquitaine, went to Charles; while Lothar retained the imperial title, resided at Aachen, and ruled over the middle kingdom that stretched from the North Sea to the Mediterranean, including northern and central Italy.[2] The empire, therefore, lived on in name, but Charlemagne's unification of Europe was no longer a reality, a fact much lamented by contemporaries. "The race of the Franks, by Christ's grace exalted to the heights of empire now brought low in the dust," bemoaned Florus of Lyons in a poem from the time: ". . . the fragments of a kingdom replace a realm."[3]

In spite of the Verdun agreement in 843, intense rivalry and armed conflict among the three siblings and their descendants continued largely unabated for the rest of the century. Internal political strife was further aggravated by external attacks. Beginning in the 840s, Vikings regularly plundered settlements along the northern and western coasts of present-day France, occasionally sailing up the Seine and Loire rivers to wreak further havoc. At about the same time in the western Mediterranean, Muslims from north Africa overran Sicily and much of southern Italy. In 846, a sizable force landed at Ostia and proceeded to Rome. The city lay safe behind its late antique fortification walls, but the two great extramural basilicas of St. Peter's and St. Paul's were sacked. Aghast, the pope appealed to the emperor, Lothar, for help, but the damage was done. Although some protection was soon afforded the Vatican area by the construction of an impressive ring of masonry, of which portions still stand, Carolingian power in Italy, as in the rest of Europe, was clearly on the wane.[4] And yet from the perspective of the history of art, the decades immediately following the death of Louis the Pious can be seen as one of the most creative periods in the entire Middle Ages. Indeed, the richness of artistic production during this time has long been recognized.[5] A similar phenomenon in architecture, however, has received comparatively little notice.

The dramatic developments in church building can be gauged immediately by turning to one of the major enterprises of the period, the abbey church at Corvey in Saxony on the Weser River, as consecrated in 885. Although the Carolingian structure is only partially preserved, the plan has been revealed through excavations (fig. 172).[6] In size, it compares closely to that of the abbey church on the Plan of St. Gall. The main differences are the notable enlargement and elaborate articulation of both ends of the church

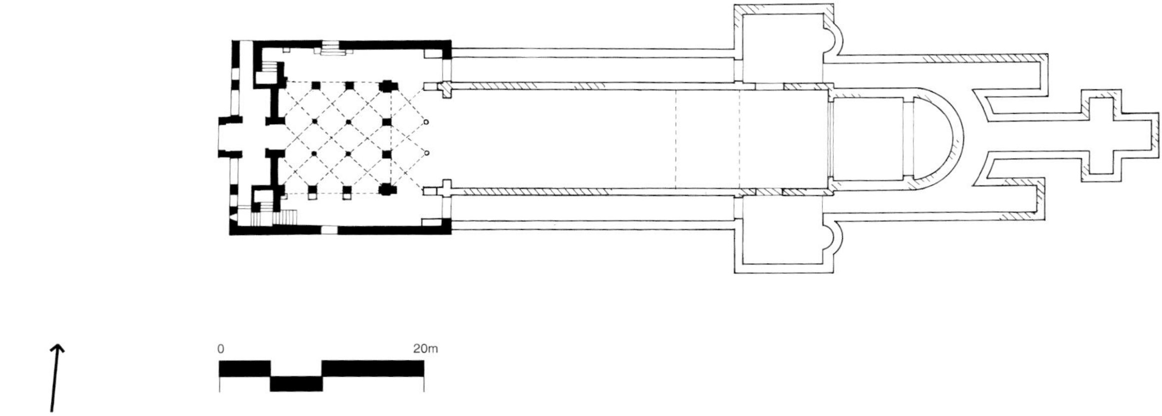

172 Corvey, plan of abbey church, late ninth century.

at Corvey. To the east a series of straight and curved passageways enveloped the main apse and extended an additional 18 m to culminate in a cruciform chapel, while to the west a massive nineteen-meter-square block, the only portion standing above ground today, forms a multistoreyed unit, centered on the ground floor about a square core of groin vaults resting on massive piers and sturdy columns. The extremities of the church at Corvey represent prime examples of the outer crypt and westwork, features which had their origins decades earlier but which reached a zenith of sophistication and importance in the later ninth century (fig. 173). In order to understand this development it is best at this point to discuss the two features separately, beginning with the outer crypt.

The Outer Crypt

The first documented example of the extension of a crypt beyond the confines of an apse is at Saint-Denis, where in 832 Abbot Hilduin dedicated a chapel attached to the apex of the east end of the abbey church. In a letter from around the same time, Hilduin describes the new structure as a "crypt (*criptam*) before the feet (*ante pedes*) of the most holy martyrs," referring to its location adjacent to the eighth-century annular crypt with the remains of St. Denis and his companions Rusticus and Eleutherius. Hilduin goes on to state that his new chapel, too, contained many relics, although their exact nature is not specified, and that it was dedicated to the Virgin Mary, the apostles, John the Baptist, and all the saints and martyrs.[7] This construction project was among Hilduin's first acts upon his return from exile at the abbey of Corvey, where he had been sent because of his complicity in the 829/30 revolt against Louis the Pious. A year later the emperor pardoned Hilduin and allowed

173 Corvey, abbey church, exterior view looking north, reconstruction, late ninth century.

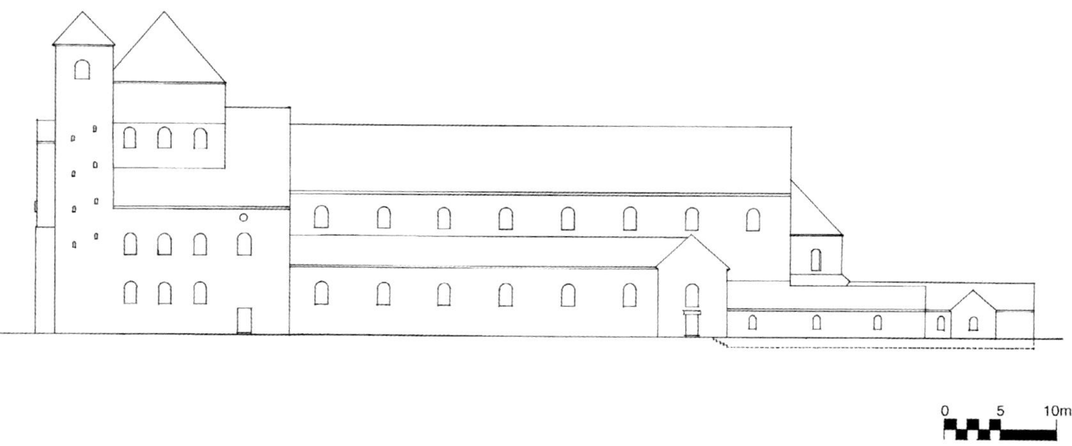

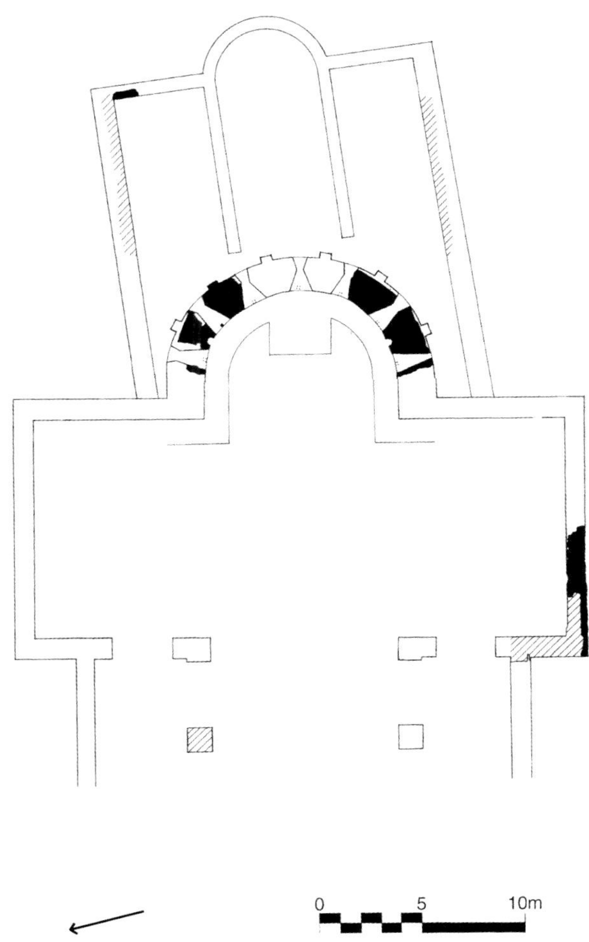

174 Saint-Denis, plan of abbey church with Hilduin's chapel, 832.

him to return as abbot to Saint-Denis, although he never again held the coveted title of archchaplain of the royal palace as he had before the rebellion. Not only were the monarch and abbot reconciled in 831 but they immediately set out together to reform the royal abbey of Saint-Denis by reinstating the Rule of St. Benedict, which had recently fallen into disuse, and by stressing anew the performance of the *opus Dei* in accordance with both Roman and Benedictine prescriptions. In the same aforementioned letter, Hilduin makes it clear that the new chapel played a crucial role in this process:

> And by common assent, we have established that eight monks of this holy community, following one another by turns, should execute all the time in this (chapel) the day and night Office in the Roman manner (*more Romano*), and that they . . . should celebrate together the established Offices and antiphons . . . with daily diligence.[8]

Roman influence, however, did not end here. The day chosen for the chapel's consecration, All Saints on November 1, was not simply appropriate to the building's dedication but it was also a feast which had only recently been introduced north of the Alps at the instigation of Pope Gregory IV (827–40).[9] And like the annular crypt before it, the design of Hilduin's chapel followed Roman models as well. Although only small portions of the foundations of this structure remain, the rest having been replaced or subsumed by the twelfth-century rebuilding of the crypt, careful studies by Sumner Crosby and, more recently, by Michaël Wyss have shown that it was a partially subterranean chamber approximately 15 m wide, subdivided into a nave and aisles of equal width, and that it projected some 10 m beyond the apse, diverging from the central axis of the church by some 5 degrees to the north (fig. 174). Presumably the nave of the chapel ended with a small apse, but that cannot be proven.[10] In any case, the model for the design and location of this chapel *ante pedes* was clearly Old St. Peter's, where a similar structure protruded in like fashion from the apse as is well attested by plans and literary descriptions from the fifteenth and sixteenth centuries (fig. 175). To be sure, the Vatican example

175 Rome, Old St. Peter's, detail of plan of Tiberio Alfarano showing apse and mausoleum of Sextus Probus.

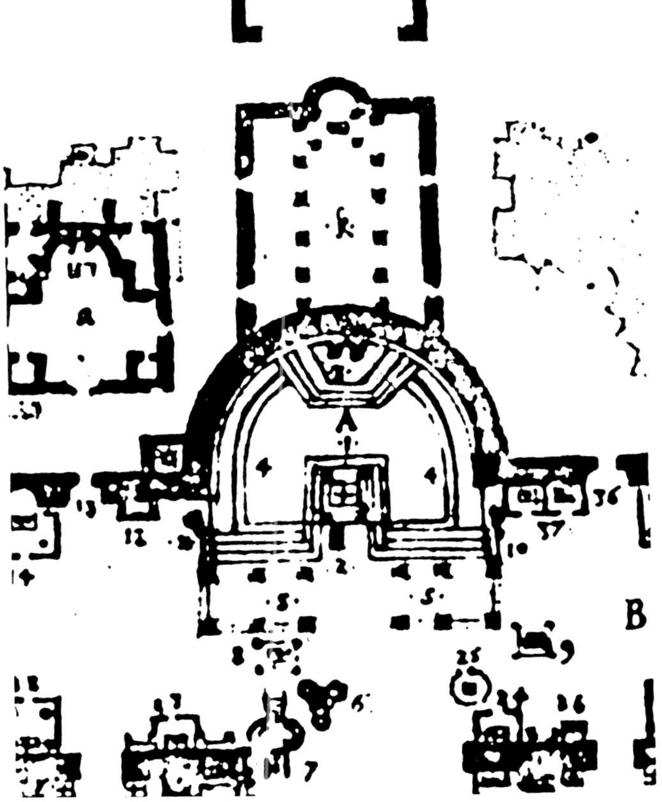

176 Rome, hall crypt of S. Maria in Cosmedin, late eighth century.

was built originally around A.D. 400 as a private mausoleum for a prominent Roman (Sextus Probus) and its precise function in the early Middle Ages is unknown, but the correspondence to the arrangement at Saint-Denis is so striking that it can hardly be coincidental. Moreover, the Probus mausoleum is known to have served as the prototype for a crypt in Rome in the late eighth century: the aisled, apsidal chamber below the main altar at S. Maria in Cosmedin built by Pope Hadrian I to receive relics brought into the city from the outlying catacombs (fig. 176).[11] Indeed, this well-preserved crypt gives one a good idea of what the interior of Hilduin's chapel probably looked like. S. Maria in Cosmedin may already have served as the model for the long-destroyed hall crypts installed below the eastern and western apses at Fulda in 819, mentioned in the previous chapter.[12] In any case, whether or not he was acquainted with the crypts at Fulda, Hilduin certainly knew both S. Maria in Cosmedin and the Vatican complex from his visit to Rome on behalf of Louis the Pious in 824.[13] The Marian connotations of the one and the apostolic associations of the other offered Hilduin an appropriate means by which to celebrate at his abbey a period of renewal, based upon a resurgence of imperial support and Roman influence not seen since the days of Charlemagne.

Once established north of the Alps, this more elaborate crypt scheme soon spread. In 836, Hilduin sent relics of St. Vitus to the abbey of Corvey, where he had been temporarily exiled six years earlier. From its founding in 822 by monks from Corbie in Picardy, Corvey (or "New Corbie") prospered under the protection of Louis the Pious and was served initially, according to recent excavations, by an aisled basilica some 30 m long and 17 m wide with a broad square eastern apse, housing an angular, vaulted crypt similar in design to that on the Plan of St. Gall. The original crypt arrangement was presumably built to contain the remains of St. Stephen, an early gift of the emperor, but it was most likely the arrival of new relics from Saint-Denis that prompted the addition of an aisleless, apsed hall extending some five meters beyond the apse; the entire complex was consecrated in 844 (fig. 177).[14] Although more simplified and angular in form, the crypt arrangement at Corvey was clearly meant to emulate that of Saint-Denis, a notion conveyed through the person of Hilduin and the relics of St. Vitus.

In the 840s, documentary sources and detailed archaeological information show that the same scheme was adopted under somewhat different circumstances for the abbey church at Werden, located in the Ruhr River valley between Corvey to the east and Saint-Denis to the west. The first church, dedicated to the Savior and the Virgin Mary, was established at the end of the eighth century by St. Liudger, who, upon his death in 819, was buried just outside the eastern apse. Abbot Altfried (840–49), nephew and biographer of the founder, arranged to have the east end of the church rebuilt and enlarged so that Liudger's

177 Corvey, plan of first abbey church, 822–44.

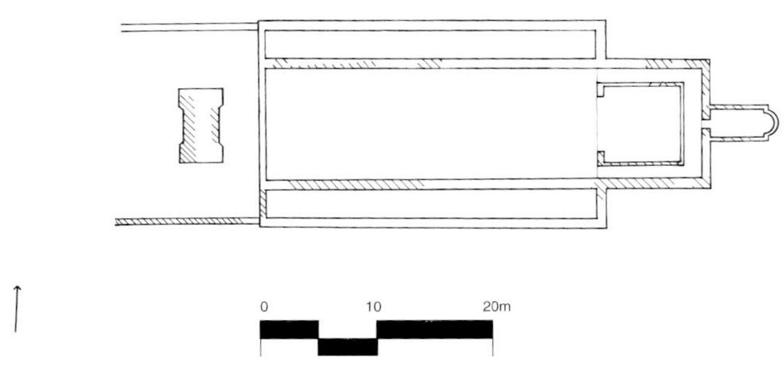

tomb stood at the center of an annular crypt below the main altar. An aisleless hall was attached to the apex of the apse in order to provide, according to Altfried in the saint's *Vita*, an honored place for the burial of Liudger's immediate successors as abbot, including Altfried himself (fig. 178).[15]

As the crypts at Corvey and Werden were being built, a somewhat different solution to a similar problem was being formulated in western Francia not far from the mouth of the Loire River. In 814, monks from the island monastery of Noirmoutier, founded a century and a half earlier by St. Philibert, established a new community at Déas near the lake of Grandlieu.[16] In 836, the church at Déas received the precious relics of the seventh-century monastic father Philibert after the mother house had suffered repeatedly from Viking attacks, thus giving the name Saint-Philibert-de-Grandlieu to the burgeoning abbey. In 847, this site, too, was sacked by the Vikings and nine years later it was abandoned altogether, the monks taking the bones of their patron with them as they headed further inland. Sometime in the early eleventh century the nave of the church at Déas was rebuilt and numerous repairs followed over the centuries so that the church today is a patchwork of various periods, restored and covered by a modern roof. Although the building has been the focus of limited excavations and the subject of several studies since the late nineteenth century, its full history is far from resolved. A new investigation, now under way, will no doubt clarify many issues. Nonetheless, the basic stages of the structure's development seem clear enough, especially when taken in conjunction with contemporary written records.[17]

The first church, complete by 819, was constructed "in the shape of a cross" (*in modum crucis*), according to the contemporary chronicler Ermentarius, and the earliest preserved masonry seems to belong to a segregated transept with a partial crossing, defined by broad arches on all sides except the one facing the nave, much in the manner of Kornelimünster from precisely the same time (fig. 146). And like the model church of Benedict of Aniane, the arms of the transept at Déas probably ended in small eastern apses.[18] A link with Kornelimünster is all the more likely since Benedict of Aniane and Arnulf, the abbot of Noirmoutier, are known to have worked closely together to promote monastic reform during the very years the first church at Déas was being built.[19] But the arrival of the remains of St. Philibert in 836 prompted a drastic remodeling of the east end of the church, which Ermentarius states was "greatly extended" (*copiose extenso*).[20] A careful study of the fabric of the church suggests that the remodeling process came in two stages. First, a polygonal apse was enveloped by a narrow corridor that led to a small rectangular room, designed most likely to receive the relics of St.

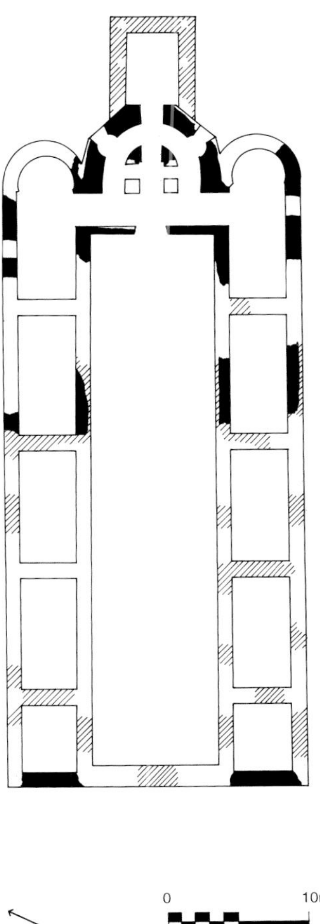

178 Werden, plan of abbey church, ca. 850.

Philibert, which in turn projected outward some 3 m from the apex of the east end. In the next and final stage, presumably the one mentioned by Ermentarius, the polygonal apse was replaced by an ample square choir and new semicircular apse below which the sarcophagus of St. Philibert was placed. Access to the relics may have been from the west either directly through a doorway below the main altar or via narrow side corridors. The entire east end of the church was also enlarged by a series of passageways punctuated by an array of small apses, creating a symmetrically staggered arrangement or *apse échelon* to use the modern French term (fig. 179). Access to St. Philibert's relics was now from the east, protected within a narrow cross-shaped chamber below the elevated floor of the main apse. In this way, the simple efficiency of the annular crypt was "greatly extended," to quote Ermentarius, offering the visitor a sequence of subsidiary altars along the path to the patron's tomb. This complex was equally striking from the outside as the novel network of passageways and apsidioles embraced the more traditional forms of the transept, choir, and main apse (fig. 180). The design not only facilitated the

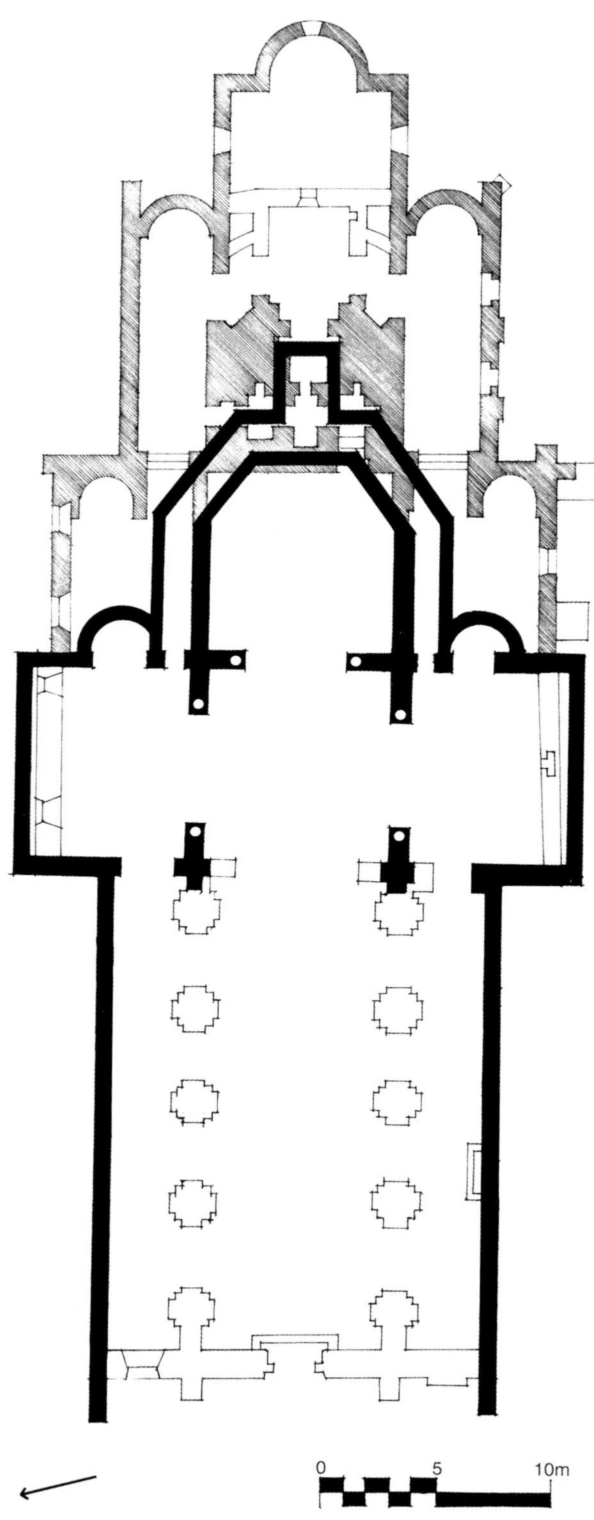

179 Saint-Philibert-de-Grandlieu (Déas), plan indicating various phases: black, in or before 836; hatching, 836–47; clear, post-ninth century.

progress of pilgrims to the saint's tomb, but, if the comments of Hilduin at Saint-Denis can be taken as a guide, it also enhanced the continuous celebration of the divine offices by the monastic community itself. Indeed, a direct influence from Saint-Denis is suggested by the fact that Ermentarius dedicated his account of Saint-Philibert-de-Grandlieu to Hilduin.[21] Thus, it seems that similar concerns about the cult of relics and the liturgy combined with specific historical circumstances bring about at Déas the earliest preserved example of the full-fledged outer crypt.

The next major development can be seen in Burgundy at the abbey church of Saint-Germain at Auxerre. Since the sixth century, the tomb of the renowned Early Christian bishop, St. Germain, had been venerated in a grand basilican complex built under the patronage of Queen Clothilde, the wife of Clovis, outside the walled town of Auxerre. Relatively little is known about this structure, but an extensive remodeling of the east end of the church in the middle of the ninth century was vividly recounted by Heiric, master of the abbey's school and a noted scholar of his day.[22] The new construction was initiated in 841, by Count Conrad I, the lay abbot of Saint-Germain and uncle of Charles the Bald, as an act of gratitude for the saint's intervention in restoring his sight. While Conrad was away from the abbey, as was often the case, the progress of the work was overseen by his wife, Adelaide. Heiric reports that she consulted the most renowned and experienced masons of the day, who drew up plans and even made a wax model of the design.[23] Careful preparations were necessary because the new complex involved a strikingly novel concept of two superimposed levels of vaulted chambers and passageways referred to in more than one medieval source as "upper and lower crypts" (*cryptae superiores et subteriores*).[24]

180 Saint-Philibert-de-Grandlieu (Déas), schematic reconstruction of exterior view of east end, 836–47.

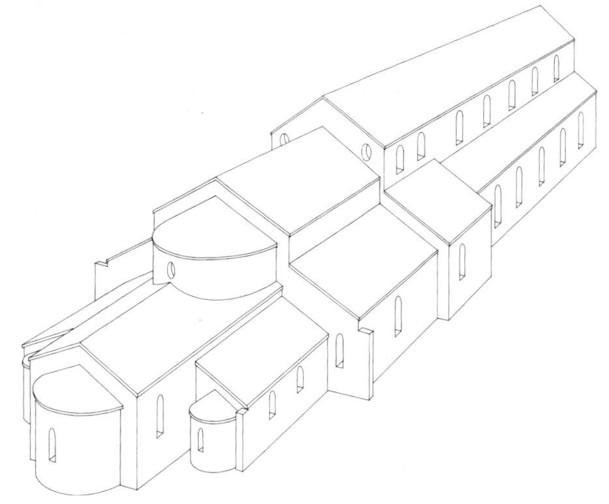

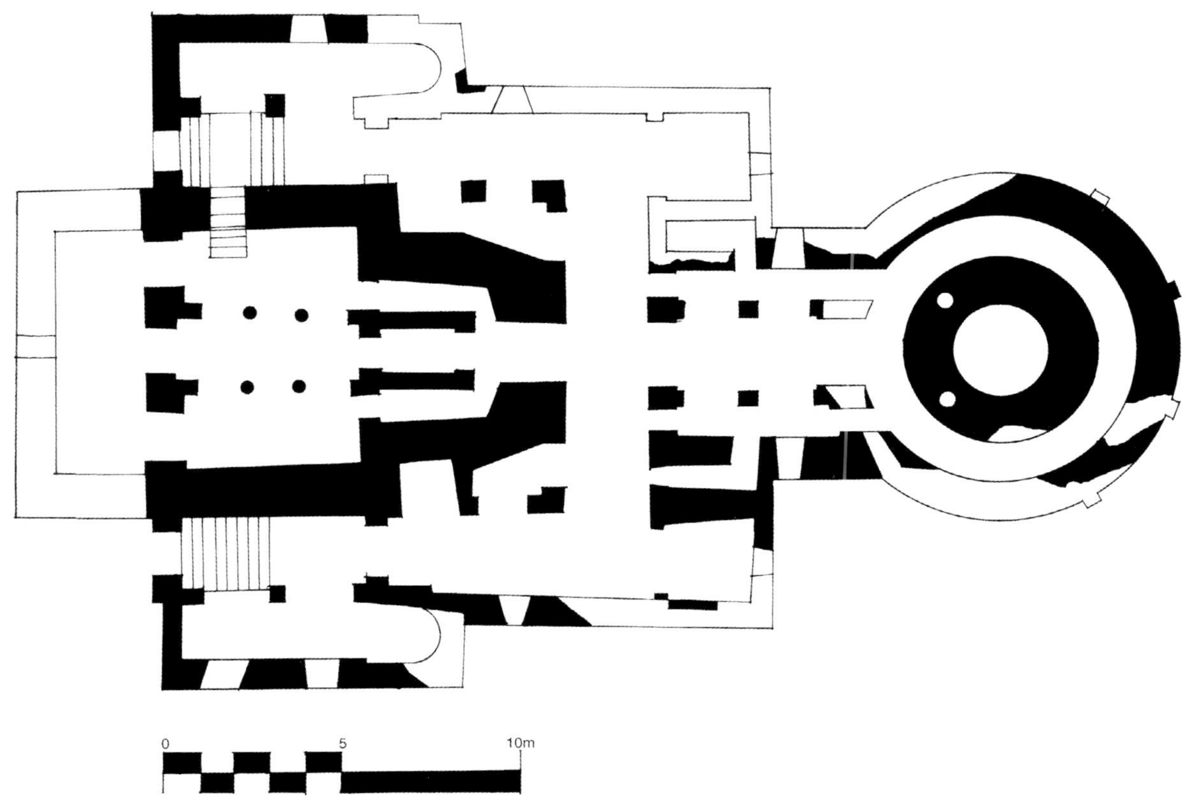

181 Auxerre, Saint-Germain, plan of crypt; solid black indicates Carolingian remains, 841–59.

Not surprisingly, such a daring project took time to complete. In 857 enough of the "lower crypt" was finished to allow for the burial of Bishop Heribald, and on Epiphany (January 6) 859, the body of St. Germain was ceremoniously placed in the new confessio in the presence of Charles the Bald.[25] The final consecration followed six years later with separate ceremonies for each level.

Most of the church was rebuilt during the eleventh to thirteenth centuries, with the upper crypt totally dismantled in the process, but the basic plan and much of the fabric of the lower crypt is preserved from the middle of the ninth century (fig. 181).[26] At its core is a hall (roughly 7m wide × 15m long) subdivided into nave and aisles by two pairs of columns and capitals with wooden architraves supporting three barrel vaults (fig. 182). To the east, the tomb of the saint is still preserved today below a small rectangular chamber, while at the west end of the hall was an extension, now gone, which, according to Heiric, provided a fenestella for visitors to view the saint's resting place from the nave of the old church. Flanking this confessio are groin-vaulted corridors, divided into a width of two bays by hexagonal piers. These corridors continue and narrow to the east fusing into a central triple-aisled projection, in line with the confessio, that leads to a circular chapel dating from the Gothic period but with traces of earlier Carolingian masonry still visible at crypt level and large portions of the original foundations preserved below.

The outer crypt at Auxerre must have presented originally a staggered array of subsidiary chapels much in the manner of Saint-Philibert-de-Grandlieu, the main difference being the central hall and the end rotunda. The popular notion that the basilica-like confessio at Auxerre had been incorporated unchanged from the earlier Merovingian shrine has been conclusively disproven by a recent scientific study that established a mid-ninth-century date for the great wooden beams. Instead, the confessio seems to have followed the basic outline of an earlier, aisleless funerary chapel, containing the saint's tomb, which was then substantially rebuilt and subdivided in the ninth century. Heiric simply refers to the construction project as an "enlargement" of the old church.[27] In short, the entire crypt complex preserved today is without doubt Carolingian. It seems likely therefore that the concept of the hall crypt, whether inspired by the Frankish churches of Saint-Denis and Fulda or the Roman churches of S. Maria in Cosmedin and Old St. Peter's, was combined here

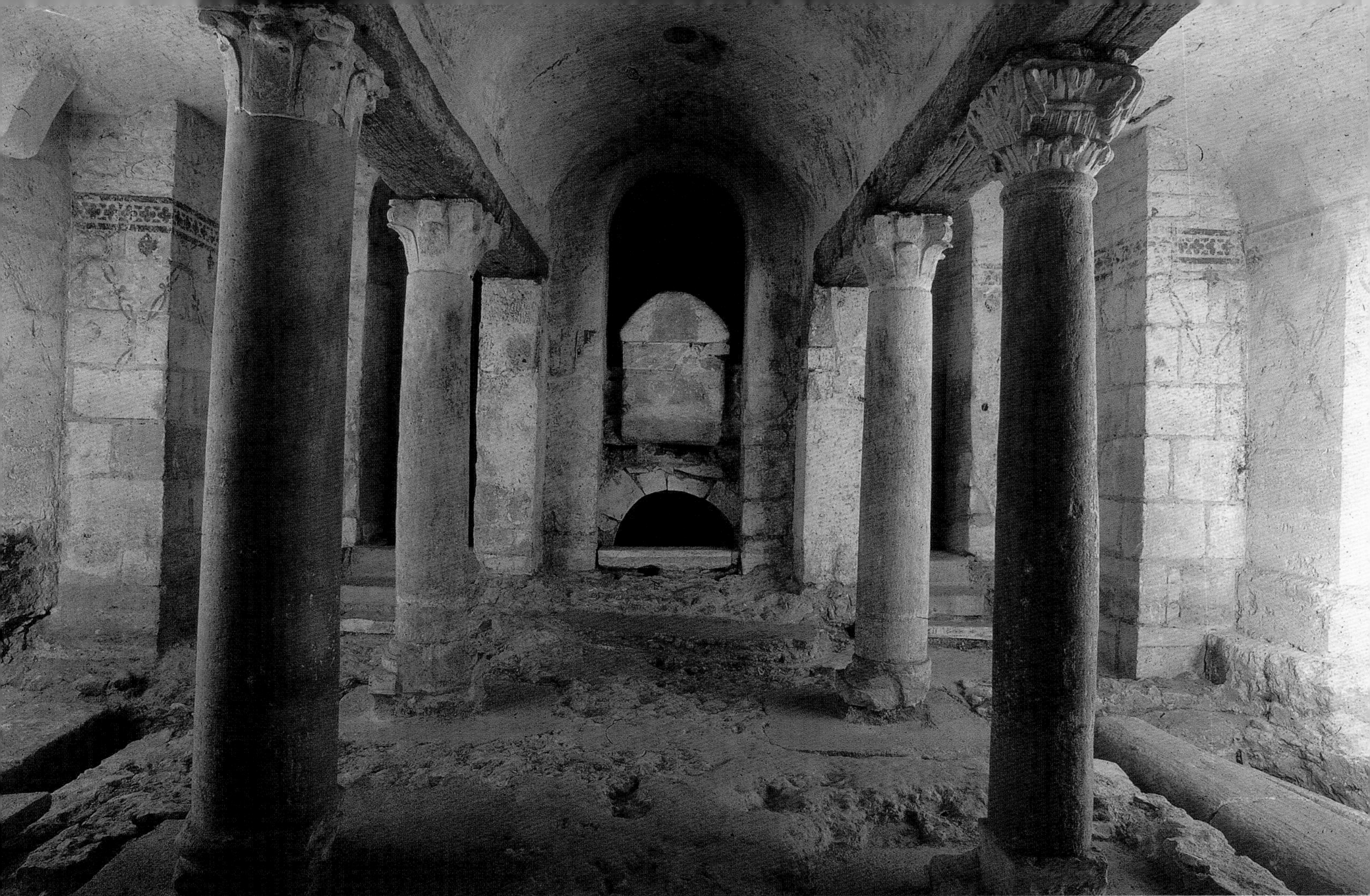

182 Auxerre, Saint-Germain, crypt, view of confessio looking east.

with the new *apse échelon* scheme as found at Grandlieu in order to provide an elaborate setting for the tomb of the great leader of the early church in Gaul. The design also presented an ecclesiastical hierarchy with the tomb of the bishop, St. Germain, at the center and the corridors and apsidioles to either side serving as chapels to the two most famous deacons of the faith, St. Stephen (on the left or north), the first Christian martyr, and to St. Lawrence (on the right or south), the first martyr of Rome. The chapels further east were dedicated in turn to two prominent fathers of Western monasticism, St. Benedict and St. Martin, while the rotunda at the apex of the complex was most likely built in honor of the Virgin Mary; at least that was the dedication of the later Gothic chapel above.[28]

Saint-Germain at Auxerre also demonstrates that such outer crypts were far from drab in spite of their semi-underground location. The original splendor of the interior can be gleaned from remnants of its once-luxurious decoration, including wall paintings, architectural sculpture, and marble paving. In the north corridor, the best-preserved frescoes depict illusionistic architectural ornament and scenes from the life and passion of St. Stephen; in the south corridor are traces of a matching St. Lawrence cycle; and in the cubicles flanking the eastern end of the confessio are paired images of rigidly standing bishops. Elaborately carved ionic capitals stand atop hexagonal piers in the side corridors, while various types of acanthus capitals are found in the confessio (figs. 183 and 184). The sparkling *opus sectile* pavement of various colored marbles in striking geometric patterns at the eastern threshold of the confessio is now thought to date from the eleventh century but may have replaced an earlier, similar flooring.[29] Clearly, no effort or expense was spared to glorify the tomb of Auxerre's great churchman, St. Germain, but there was more to it than that.

The burial of Bishop Heribald in the chapel of St. Stephen in the north corridor points out yet another factor behind the development of the outer crypt, that is the desire of individuals to be laid to rest as close as possible to the site of holy relics, or *sepultura ad sanctos*, to use the medieval term.[30] As already indicated, the area immediately

183 Auxerre, Saint-Germain, outer crypt, view of chapel of St. Stephen.

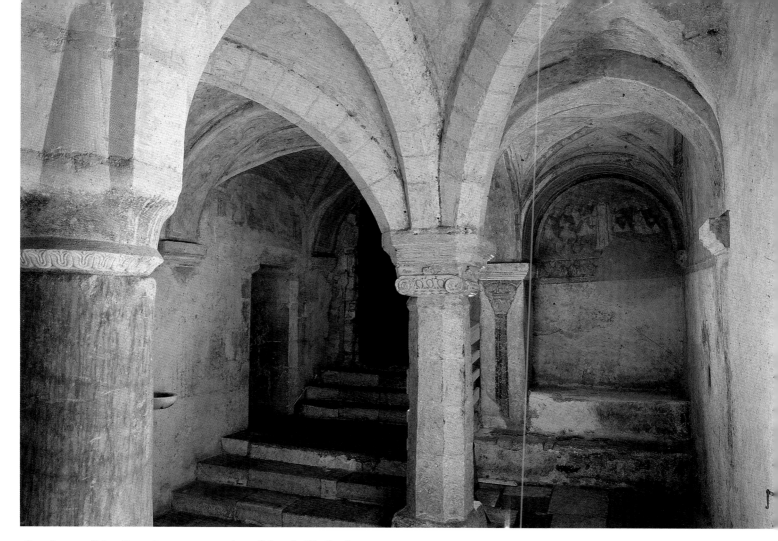

outside the main apse of a church had long been a favorite location for burial, from the Probus mausoleum at Old St. Peter's in Rome in the late fourth century to the hall crypt of the abbey church at Werden in the 840s, and it continued to be so, hence the placement of a tomb chapel for Louis the German adjoining the east end of the abbey church at Lorsch after his death in 876 (fig. 96).[31]

Not just the crown of the apse was sacrosanct however. On the Plan of St. Gall the entire ground just outside the eastern apse is circumscribed by a perimeter wall and labelled *paradisus*, or "paradise."[32] This portion of the Plan, admittedly, bears no indication of tombs, but the exact same area was used at the monastery of Fulda for the burial of abbots by, most likely, the middle of the ninth century. Moreover, the space around the apse was covered by a portico forming one side of an open courtyard, serving as a cloister.[33] It seems reasonable to assume that outer

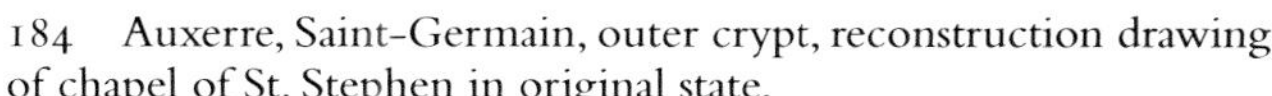

184 Auxerre, Saint-Germain, outer crypt, reconstruction drawing of chapel of St. Stephen in original state.

crypts, which covered the same terrain even more effectively, were similarly intended, at least in part, to offer prominent individuals, churchmen mostly, an elaborate and secure setting for entombment near the remains of their patron saints.

At the same time, the age-old practice of burial inside churches was looked upon with increased disfavor as naves, aisles, and apses became cluttered with graves. Already in 819, a synod at Aachen forbade it altogether, although a council at Mainz four years later specified various exceptions to the ban.[34] This dramatic change in attitude need not have been the sole, or even the primary, cause behind the development of the outer crypt, as has been claimed, but it must have underscored the need for such a feature.[35] Heiric, in fact, tells us that in the early 860s the bodies of several bishops of Auxerre, long buried in the old basilica, were transferred to the new crypt and arranged about the tomb of St. Germain, forming what to him resembled a "celestial court" (*coeli regia*). Subsequent bishops, it seems, were buried in the crypt's outer corridors, following the example of Heribald.[36] The crypt complex at Auxerre is therefore best understood as a response to several competing, if related, forces: the desire to enrich the tomb of St. Germain; the concomitant desire for burial near the saint's remains; and the need to follow new restrictions on church burial.

These factors help to explain the inclusion of the rotunda at the apex of the Auxerre crypt as well. It, too, may have been inspired by Fulda, where in the early 820s a freestanding circular chapel, dedicated to St. Michael, was built in the middle of the monastic cemetery. Although entirely rebuilt at ground level in the eleventh century, the original crypt is preserved with an annular barrel vault and a single central support in the form of a simple ionic capital atop a massive columnar pier. It was here that Fulda's abbot, Eigil—sponsor of the hall crypts of the main church, the adjacent cloister, and now the funerary chapel—was buried in 822.[37] Thus, the designers of the outer crypt at Saint-Germain seem to have taken the most recent architectural developments, associated with burial and the cult of relics (the hall crypt, the *apse échelon*, and the rotunda), and fused them into one grand scheme. It is worth noting that this process did not necessarily involve increased access to the relics by laity. On the contrary, the primary motivation behind the construction of the outer crypt at Auxerre seems to have been to satisfy the wishes of the church elite and monastic community to create a protected and elaborate setting for the tomb of their founder and his successors.[38]

The abbey church at Auxerre, in turn, provided the model for the rebuilding of Saint-Pierre at neighboring Flavigny.[39] In 860, a year after he appeared at Auxerre, Charles the Bald named another Eigil, the abbot of Prüm, situated midway between Aachen and Trier, to head the monastery at Flavigny.[40] Between 864 and 866, Eigil obtained the relics of a local martyr, St. Regina, for a newly constructed crypt at his abbey church. The central hall, of which the apse and four columns are well preserved; the surrounding corridors with paired chapels; and the terminating rotunda, replaced by a polygonal structure in the thirteenth century, were repeated from Auxerre, albeit in a far more simplified form (fig. 185). And again, the crypt was duplicated at an upper level, the doorways to which are still preserved, creating a two-storey system. In 878, seven altars, distributed over both levels, were consecrated, according to at least one account, by Pope John VIII along with several local bishops. The use of superimposed levels at Auxerre and Flavigny, it would seem, represented an effort both to integrate the outer crypt more fully with the interior of the church and to increase the number of subsidiary altars and places of burial.

In 870, the east end of the abbey church at Corvey burned necessitating a rebuilding that resulted in the crypt complex noted at the beginning of this chapter.[41] The area previously occupied by the simple square apse now served as a crossing flanked, to the north and south, by apsed transept arms and extended eastward by a deep choir and semicircular apse. Similarly, the annular crypt was superseded by an outer crypt with an *apse échelon* arrangement, if one includes the apsidioles to either side of the crossing, which culminated in a cruciform chapel instead of the now familiar rotunda. Although the arrangement at Corvey displays similarities to the examples in western Francia just cited, the immediate model was closer at hand: the newly built cathedral at nearby Halberstadt, consecrated in 859.[42] Here one finds the same cruciform termination but without the flanking chapels (fig. 186). On the other hand, the outer crypt of the neighboring cathedral at Hildesheim, begun in 859 and consecrated in 872, included side chapels, albeit round-ended, but linked up at its easternmost point with an earlier and originally freestanding rotunda (fig. 187).[43] Thus in Saxony, between 859 and 872, we have three examples of the same basic outer crypt scheme with only slight variations. At Corvey and Halberstadt, the archaeological evidence, although limited, suggests that their outer crypts, unlike those in Burgundy, did not have an upper storey. At Hildesheim, however, remains of doorways to the outer crypt on two different levels, the lower pair in the east wall of the transept and the upper pair reached by a set of stairs from the raised apse floor, demonstrate that the arrangement here was in fact two-storeyed. Moreover, traces of original masonry show that the lower passage was vaulted while the upper one was timber-roofed.[44]

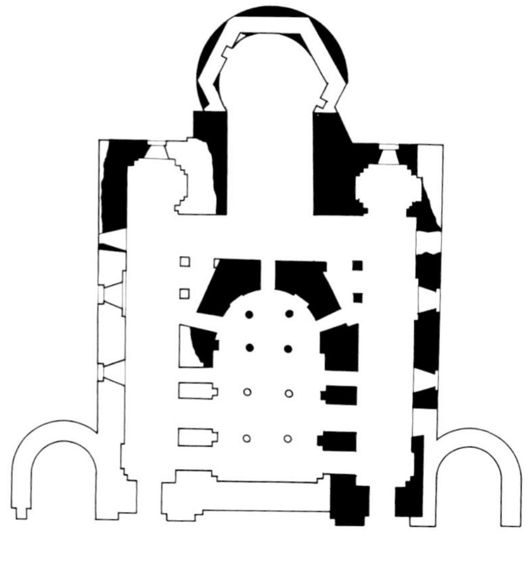

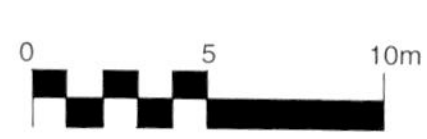

185 Flavigny, abbey church of Saint-Pierre, plan of east end, ca. 864–78.

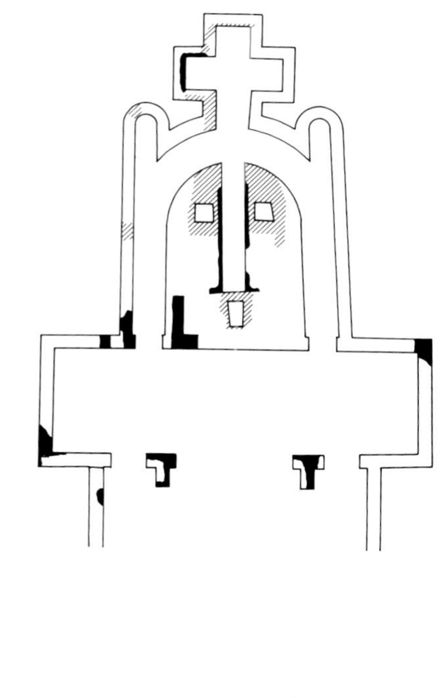

186 Halberstadt, plan of cathedral, 859.

187 Hildesheim, reconstruction drawing of east end of cathedral, 872.

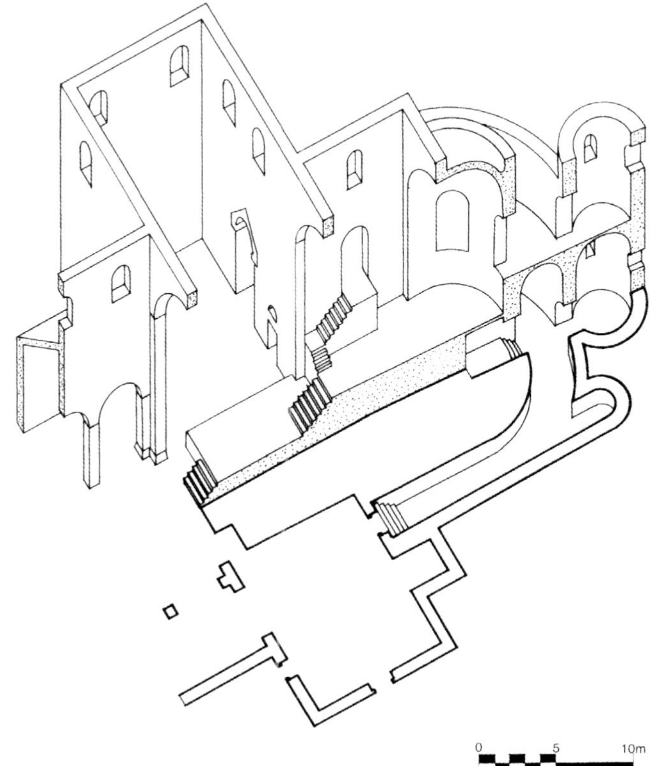

The sequence of dates and similarity in plans of these outer crypts suggest a connection between the two regions.[45] If so, such a connection did not result from some amorphous process of stylistic influence but grew out of human experience and personal contact. Heiric of Auxerre and Eigil of Flavigny, for example, were both students of Lupus of Ferrières, one of the luminaries of Carolingian scholarship. Lupus, in turn, was trained at Fulda and maintained close correspondence with its illustrious abbot, Rabanus Maurus. And Bishop Heribald, buried in the crypt at Saint-Germain in 857, was a relative of Lupus. The bishop of Hildesheim, Altfried, who oversaw the construction of his cathedral's outer crypt, had spent his youth at Corvey; he was also a friend of Christianus, the bishop of Auxerre who consecrated the crypt at Saint-Germain in 865.[46] These relationships, of course, do not in themselves explain the spread of the outer crypt, but they do indicate that, in spite of the political fragmentation of Europe in the later ninth century, there were ample means for the wide transmission of ideas affecting the development of ecclesiastical architecture. In this way, the new crypt at Corvey can be seen as the product of a broad phenomenon that developed over several decades.

The Westwork

The term westwork (from the German, *Westwerk*) was first coined in the late nineteenth century and was soon used to describe the monumental western complex of the abbey church at Corvey.[47] Since that time, the Corvey westwork has served as a paradigm for defining a generic building type, composed of stair towers flanking the western entrance of a church and leading to an interior gallery or tribune, which has come to be considered one of the most important innovations of Carolingian architecture. Shortly before the First World War, for example, Wilhelm Effmann used Corvey as the model for envisioning a westwork at the great abbey church of Saint-Riquier at Centula.[48] The hauntingly stark reconstructions of Effmann's publication have greatly influenced our notions of the power and majesty of this seemingly quintessential Carolingian architectural feature. And yet, as discussed in the previous chapter, the exact nature of a monumental westwork at Saint-Riquier is far from certain. Indeed, in spite of the efforts of numerous scholars since Effmann's time, the origins and function of the westwork are still poorly understood.

There are various reasons for this. Few westworks are preserved and several of those commonly cited by scholars (at Gandersheim, Hildesheim, Minden, and Werden, among others) are not Carolingian at all but date to the tenth century or later.[49] Others are extremely problematic both as to date and reconstruction.[50] Thus, only a very small number of examples from the Carolingian period can be cited with any confidence and even then questions remain. Moreover, a cursory glance at their plans makes it immediately apparent that we are not dealing with a uniform type, but with a long development of considerable diversity (fig 188). They also seem to fall roughly into four chronological categories: 1. the abbey churches at Saint-Denis and Lorsch, both dedicated within a year of each other (775 and 774, respectively), although the west end of the former was enlarged soon after; 2. Saint-Riquier at Centula and the royal chapel at Aachen from the 790s; 3. the cathedral of Reims and Saint-Germain at Auxerre from the second quarter to the middle of the ninth century; and 4. the cathedral at Halberstadt and the abbey church at Corvey, both in Saxony from the second half of the ninth century. Not surprisingly, these groupings exhibit some similarities in plan as well. One must keep in mind, however, that of these eight examples, only two, Aachen and Corvey, are preserved above ground, which means that for the rest any reconstruction of the elevation must remain extremely hypothetical.

Since the first four examples have already been discussed at some length in previous chapters, a brief review of the evidence will suffice here. According to the most recent analysis, the scant remains of the foundations of the west end of the abbey church at Saint-Denis indicate several stages of development before the construction of the present Gothic church. The relatively simple, tripartite narthex of the structure dedicated in 775 was doubled in size a few years later, including the addition of a polygonal structure at its core, in order, most likely, to enlarge the tomb of Pippin to accommodate his wife, who died in 783. Sometime later, probably in the eleventh century and certainly well before the work of Abbot Suger in the twelfth, the west end seems to have been substantially rebuilt along the same lines as before except for the removal of the postulated tomb structure in the center. The "narrow hall squeezed in on either side by twin towers neither high nor very sturdy," described by Suger, may therefore refer to this later phase, but even so the configuration presumably resembled the Carolingian structure in its basic elements.[51] Suger, admittedly, makes no reference either to a gallery or to stairs by which to reach it, but I suspect that the present Gothic facade has just such an upper level, because, although highly unusual for France in the twelfth century, it was intended to emulate the western gallery of its predecessor. Such a reference to the past would be very much in keeping with Suger's expressed desire to harmonize his additions with the remains of the old building.[52] The remains at Lorsch are equally enigmatic. Here we have only the outline of a rectilinear facade with a central protruding block. The thickness of the foundations in comparison to those of the nave, aisles, and atrium indicate that this area supported a multistoreyed structure with vaulting, which could have easily included the upper level and stair towers of a westwork. Certainly the west facade of the church was imposing, for in the eleventh century it was referred to as a "fortress."

At Saint-Riquier, limited excavations have confirmed the presence of a western transept and spiral stairs flanking the main entrance. These stairs must have led to an inner gallery designed to accommodate a monastic choir and, on important feast days, lay visitors, as mentioned in various medieval sources; it also housed an altar dedicated to the Savior. The exact size of this gallery is not known, but it seems unlikely that it would have extended into the crossing if Bernard's recent proposal of an octagonal design is correct. Such an arrangement would be highly unusual, if not unique. Similar plans, as at Aachen, invariably have an open central core. The main entrance at Aachen has the essential elements of a westwork, but it is also, admittedly, a special case because the complex is not attached to a basilica but to a centrally planned church with an enveloping interior gallery. In other words, the stair towers could be seen as essential to the chapel's unusual design without any

188 *(facing page)* Comparative plans of Carolingian westworks.

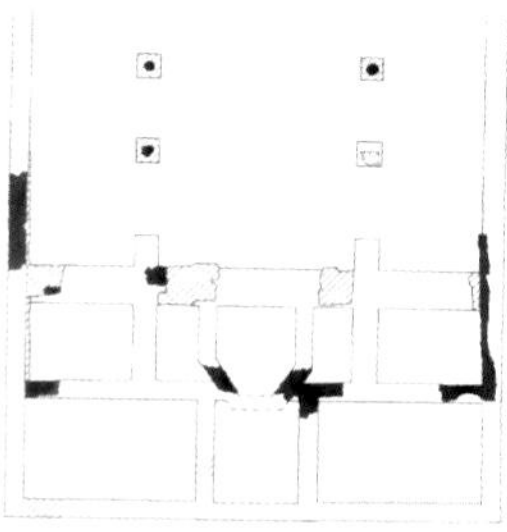
SAINT-DENIS, dedicated 775 (enlarged 783?)

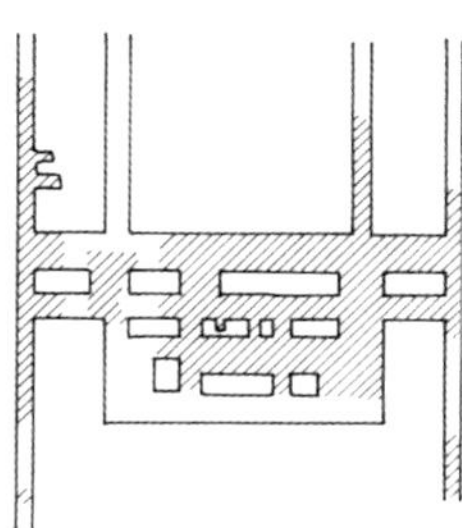
LORSCH, ded. 774

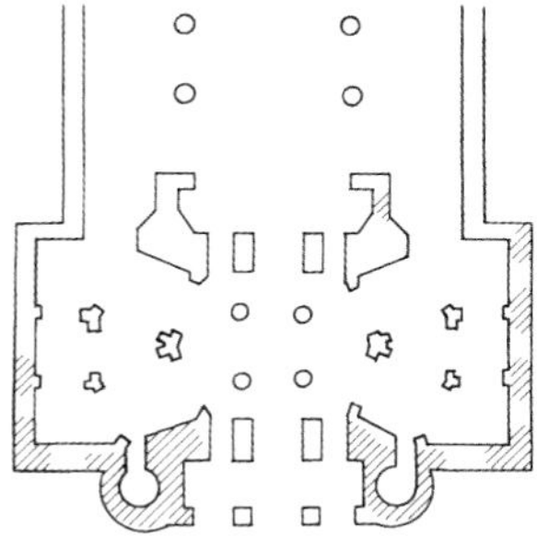
CENTULA (Saint-Riquier), ded. 799

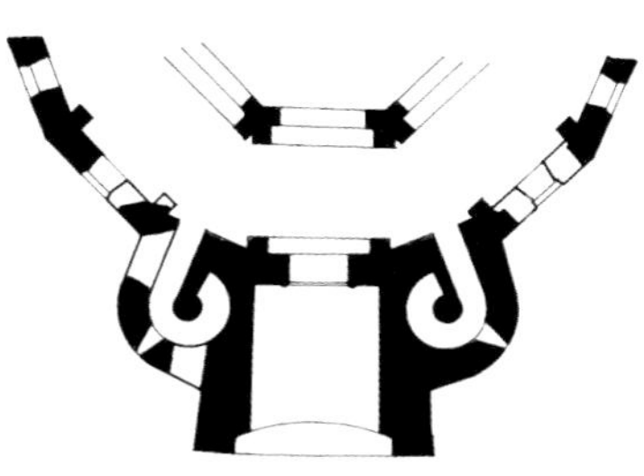
AACHEN, Royal Chapel, 790s

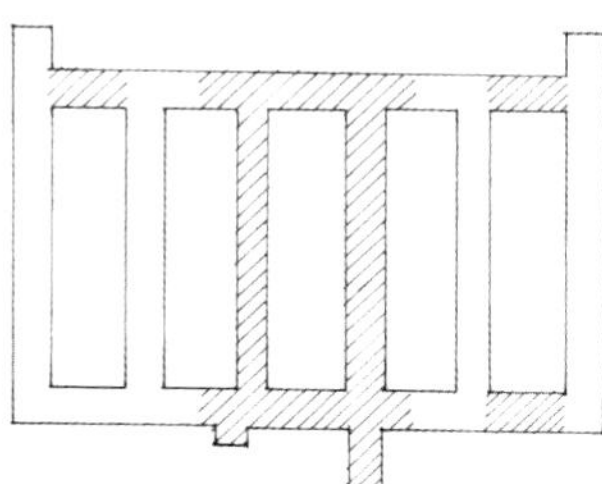
REIMS, Cathedral, 816–862

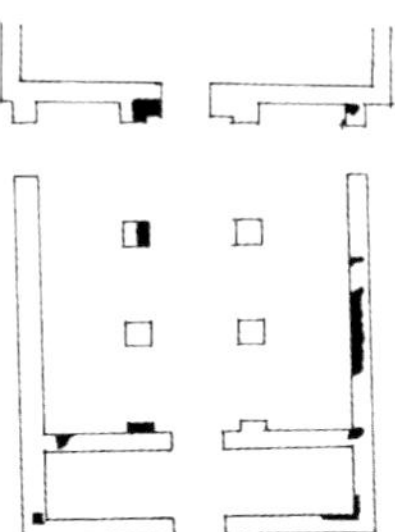
AUXERRE, Saint-Germain, mid-ninth century

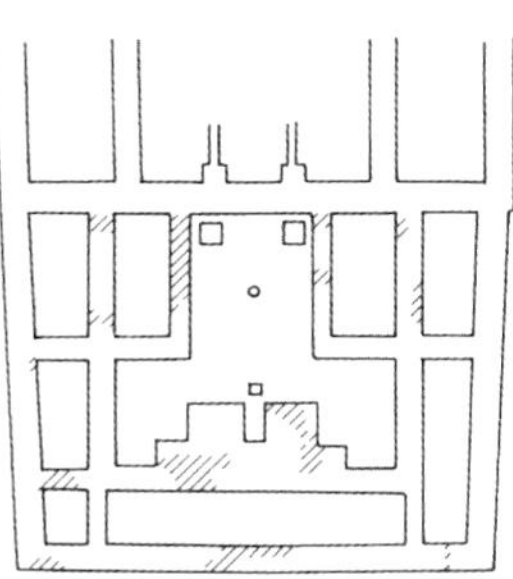
HALBERSTADT, Cathedral, ded. 859

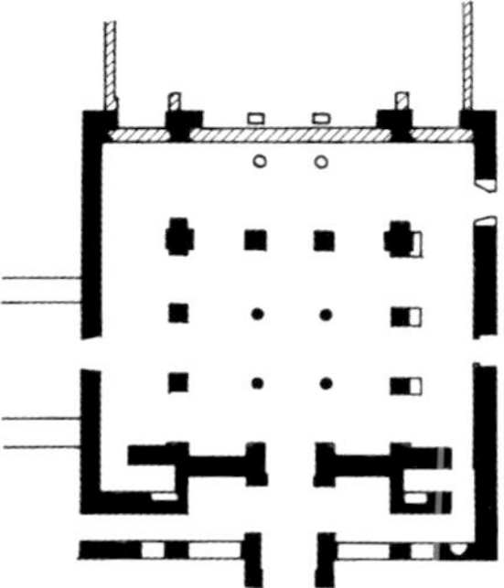
CORVEY, Abbey Church, 873–885

reference to a westwork. Note, for example, the presence of a pair of spiral stairs leading to the gallery of the similarly configured church of S. Vitale in Ravenna (fig. 20). Still, unlike the Ravennate church, the cylindrical stair towers at Aachen are combined with a conspicuously prominent, rectangular entrance vestibule. An almost identical arrangement, at least in plan, has been recently uncovered at the west end of the basilican layout of Rouen cathedral, albeit on a somewhat smaller scale, and dated to the late eighth or early ninth century.[53] It seems reasonable, therefore, to include Aachen in this discussion, since it possesses the best-preserved example of a westwork design that could be applied to a church of a very different type.

A recent reexamination of earlier excavations at the cathedral of Reims has affirmed the likelihood of a westwork, described, upon its destruction in 976, as a "vaulted structure" (*arcuatum opus*) and attributed, along with the rest of the church, to the patronage of archbishop Ebbo (816–35) by a recorded inscription that once appeared on the west facade; construction work may have continued until the dedication of the entire building in 863. The partial remains of foundations of the western complex indicate a rectangular block (14 × 24.50 m) divided into five equal aisles.[54] At Saint-Germain at Auxerre, excavations in the 1990s revealed that a western atrium, of the late sixth or early seventh century, was converted in the middle of the ninth century into a rectangular structure (16.5 × 15 m) divided by two rows of roughly square stone piers, which supported, most likely, the wooden floor of a second storey.[55] The westwork at Halberstadt is a very complicated matter.[56] It seems to have been part of the new cathedral complex consecrated in 859, but, rather than forming a uniform block, it incorporated a previously freestanding funerary chapel, built three decades earlier. There does not seem to have been a vaulted entryway in the manner of Corvey, nor is there any specific evidence for a tribune or stair towers. It is questionable whether the example at Halberstadt should be considered a westwork at all. Thus, the compact, cubic design of the westwork at Corvey seems to have been unique rather than typical, more a paradox than a paradigm.

In terms of plan alone, Saint-Denis and Lorsch could be seen as representing an early, experimental phase in the development of the westwork, characterized by a narrow alignment of towers and a central protruding unit. Similarly, Centula and Aachen seem to be closely connected; both have cylindrical stair towers, which, aside from Rouen, are conspicuously absent elsewhere, and they may have resembled one another in other ways as well. In fact, Centula's excavator Bernard has gone so far as to suggest that the western crossing at Saint-Riquier was modelled after the design of the chapel at Aachen. Certainly, an affinity between the two sites would not be surprising in view of their contemporaneity and the close relationship between the patrons, Angilbert and Charlemagne. The structures at Reims and Auxerre are both rectangular in plan, but where the former is notable for its breadth and was vaulted, the other is narrow and axial and was probably timber roofed. And finally, the block-like configuration at Halberstadt is usually compared to neighboring Corvey, but their elevations may have been very different.

If the formal development of the westwork seems unclear, even less is known about its function. At Saint-Denis, the polygonal structure probably marked the tomb of Pippin and his wife, but we have no information for Lorsch. At Centula, the tribune served several important liturgical functions, including that of a choir loft and the site of an altar, while at Aachen it housed the throne of Charlemagne. The westwork at Reims, according to a later medieval source, contained both a baptismal font and an altar to the Savior, while at Auxerre we have by 865 the reference to the consecration of an oratory of John the Baptist "in the western part of the basilica," which may have corresponded to part of the west end.[57] The western complex at Halberstadt seems to have been primarily funerary in nature. Thus, aside from serving as a main entrance, the westworks just cited seem to have shared little else in common. Nonetheless, several elaborate theories have been devised over the years to explain both the form and function of the Carolingian westwork in general. Only some of the most prominent can be cited here.[58]

Effmann, noting the presence of the laity in the Saint-Riquier gallery, saw the westwork as a kind of parish church within a monastic enclave, serving in particular as a site for baptism. Alois Fuchs, first in 1929 and again in 1950, stressed the example of Aachen to propose that the westwork was an "imperial complex" (*Kaiserkirche*), set aside for visits by the ruler and his immediate entourage and meant to symbolize the symbiotic relationship between church and state in the Carolingian era.[59] Ernst Gall, in 1954, adamantly disagreed and pointed out that, aside from Aachen, the presence of a throne in Carolingian westworks was unsubstantiated.[60] He proposed instead that the westwork's primary purpose was as a western choir for monks. Edmund Stengel, on the other hand, accepted the thesis of Fuchs in an article published in 1956, but he suggested further that the fortress-like character of the westwork indicated that it also served a defensive role as a lookout and battlement in response to the rising threat of Viking attacks.[61] In 1963, Carol Heitz returned to the example of Centula to emphasize the importance of the westwork in the Easter liturgy and to propose that it was meant to be understood as a copy, in medieval terms, of the Holy Sepulchre in Jerusalem. A few years later,

Friedrich Möbius presented a Marxist interpretation whereby the design and location of the westwork was seen to reflect emergent feudalism, characterized by the juxtaposition of church and state and the stratification of society, both political and economic, with the ruler above and the ruled below.[62] Although these summaries do not do justice to the subtleties of each argument, it is fair to say that none of these theories has proven to be fully satisfactory. Some, such as that of Möbius, are overly simplistic, while others, such as those of Fuchs and Gall, may apply to one or more examples but not to all. Indeed, the search for a single cause or purpose behind the appearance of the westwork in the Carolingian era seems futile. Instead of looking for a unifying theory, one should recognize the diversity of the monuments and their settings and acknowledge the creativity of Carolingian builders in their willingness to experiment with a variety of forms, thus transforming and enriching early medieval architecture, in order to meet a variety of needs. One German scholar has gone so far as to suggest the abandonment of the term westwork altogether, but that seems extreme.[63] As long as one acknowledges that the terminology is a modern construct, it is useful, nonetheless, to have a convenient label to recognize the novel elaboration of the west end of churches in the Carolingian era. At the same time, each example should be examined on its own terms without the influence of preconceived notions, and the westwork at Corvey is no exception.

The monumental entrance to the abbey church at Corvey is, without question, one of the most impressive structures to have come down to us from the early Middle Ages (fig. 189). In spite of some later modifications and extensive restoration work after the Second World War, the original building stands largely intact and thus provides a telling example of the simple grandeur of Carolingian architecture.[64] The facade is flat but for a central porch that protrudes about 1.5 m and rises four storeys (ca. 20 m high) to a modest gable; the towers are also flush with the rest of the facade. The elaborate arched openings of the upper two storeys of the central block and the flanking bell towers are easily recognized as Romanesque and no doubt belong to a recorded restoration in the middle of the twelfth century; the steeply peaked crowns of the towers, on the other hand, were added in the late sixteenth century. The central block is further emphasized by three great arches at the ground floor and two ranges of three round-arched windows, which, as we shall see, provide light for interior floor divisions. The stairs of the flanking towers, in turn, are lit by a staggered array of slit windows. Arches at the base of each tower provided further access to the stairs and the main entrance. Two other arched openings in the tower bases, which seem to levitate midway between the first and second storeys, are thought to have been built to connect to the upper storeys of an adjoining atrium, the foundations of which have been found extending westward. Behind the central porch, a lantern tower rose another 4 m in order to provide additional light for the westwork's interior (fig. 190). It remains uncertain whether the flanking stair towers were taller or approximately equal in height to the lantern tower; nor is it known whether or not they held bells. Still, they were conspicuous enough to prompt a late ninth-century chronicler at the abbey to refer to the entire complex as simply "the three towers."[65]

The nature of the structure's masonry, which is readily apparent today on the exterior, is rough-hewn with ashlars reserved for the piers framing the archway at the base of the central porch. The reddish-brown hue of the local sandstone, now so striking, was originally hidden by a uniform layer of white plaster. There was also no figural sculpture, only an inscribed sandstone plaque (1.68 × .84 m), visible still, in the middle of the porch immediately below the uppermost window; the meaning of the plaque's text will be discussed below. The statue niche in the gable is a later addition, replacing an oculus.

The block-like quality of the exterior is modified somewhat on the interior by a series of vertical and horizontal divisions. The ground floor is entered through a single central door which leads directly into the square core of the building (11 × 11 m) composed of nine groin-vaulted compartments (ca. 5 m high). The vaults are supported in the center by four stout columns with elegantly carved capitals and high impost blocks and along the periphery by rectilinear piers of finely cut ashlars (figs. 188 and 191). The side corridors to the north and south were originally timber-roofed, although they are now also vaulted. To the east was a single-bayed intermediary space between the multistoreyed westwork and the nave and aisles of the church proper; this area was greatly altered when the body of the church to the east was dismantled in the late seventeenth century. The stairs in the northwest and southwest corners of the westwork lead to an upper floor, the central area of which stands immediately above the vaulted square core at ground level and is similarly circumscribed by arcades with cut stone piers (fig. 192). Above is an additional storey with a series of arched openings; in the center of the west wall is a single large arch, whereas the rest are considerably smaller and further subdivided by central colonnettes. The latter have been restored, based upon the fragmentary traces of the springings of the innermost arches. Originally, this whole area was surmounted by the lantern tower and thus it once possessed an additional stratum of clerestory windows, which allowed light to flood the now dim interior. Just above the clerestory windows there

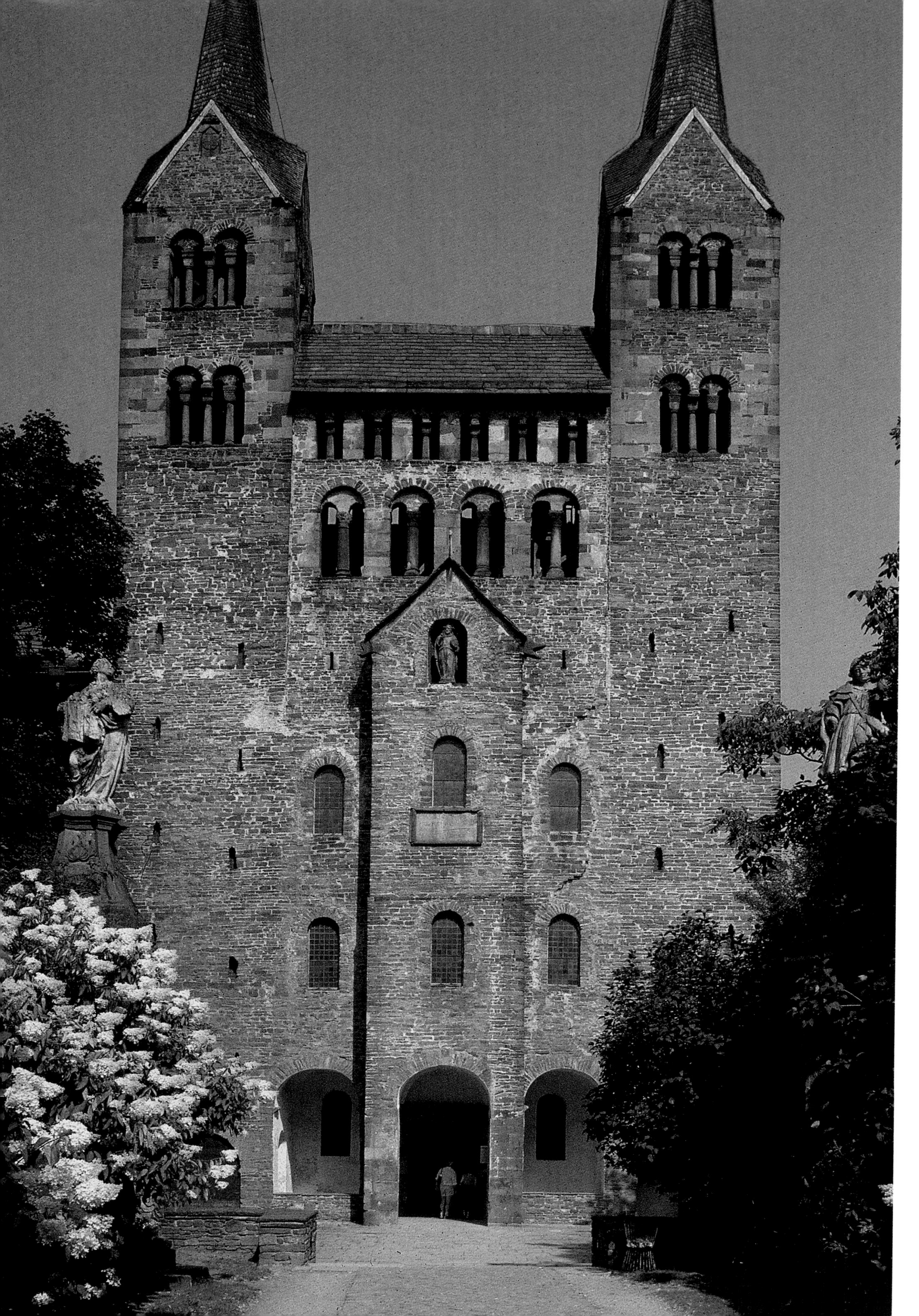

would have been a flat, wooden ceiling, while just below there seems to have been a wooden catwalk. Although vaulting is now preserved only along the west side, the corridors to the north and south were also groin-vaulted in order to sustain a gallery behind the arched openings of the second storey. From the gallery, one could originally look into the nave of the church through a screen wall of tiered arches that rose from the floor of the upper level to the base of the lantern tower (fig. 193).

The seeming austerity of this interior is deceptive, for traces of fresco decoration demonstrate that, as we have seen with the outer crypts, the walls were once ablaze with color. This is best seen in the upper floor where vestiges of acanthus rinceaux and geometric meanders were found in the soffits of the arches of the arcade and the gallery openings. Moreover, the jambs of the latter were found to have been painted with illusionistic colonnettes mimicking the real ones standing in their midst (fig. 194). As recently as 1992, traces of individual life-size, standing figures in stucco were found in the spandrels, directly above the massive rectilinear piers, of the arches of the upper floor. Although too fragmentary to reconstruct with any precision, they are reminiscent of the monumental painted stucco reliefs of S. Maria in Valle in Cividale from almost a century earlier. Even more startling was the discovery in 1954 of figural ornament at the base of the vaults of the western corridor, which, although very poorly preserved, is recognizable as an episode from Homer's *Odyssey* (fig. 195).[66] The ancient Greek hero Ulysses, with shield and spear in hand, is shown combating the mythical sea monster Scylla, recognizable by

191 Corvey, abbey church, westwork, interior view of ground floor.

190 Corvey, abbey church, reconstruction of exterior of Carolingian westwork, 885.

189 *(facing page)* Corvey, abbey church, facade of westwork.

192 Corvey, abbey church, westwork, interior view of upper level and tribune looking northwest.

193 Corvey, abbey church, section looking north, ca. 885.

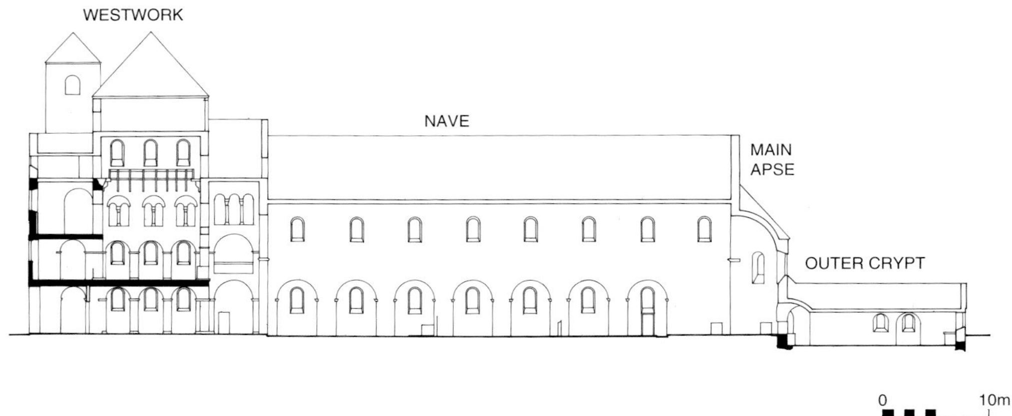

a long coiled tail and barking dogs about her waist, who gestures with her right arm and grasps a fallen sailor to her side with the other. Subsequent investigations revealed faint but discernible traces of other related figures. Immediately to the right of the Scylla, a Siren, with the head and torso of a woman and the lower body of a bird, stood playing a harp. In the same general vicinity were various marine motifs, including dolphins, other fantastic sea creatures, and small ships with a single mast and sail. Although the remains of the decoration are frustratingly fragmentary, it is clear, nonetheless, that colorful wall paintings joined monumental stucco figures and fine architectural sculpture to enliven the interior of this monumental complex, and illuminated perhaps by windows of colored glass. The central wooden ceiling may also have been brightly painted.

Although the structure at Corvey has long been at the center of the debate concerning the function and meaning of the Carolingian westwork, a rather lax use of terminology has, unfortunately, tended to cloud the issue. The vaulted ground floor of the Corvey westwork, for example, is often referred to as a "crypt," but this is based on the assumption that the structure imitates Centula and has no confirmation in any medieval sources connected with Corvey. Similarly, the upper storey is known as the "choir of St. John" (*Johanneschor*), but it was not so designated until 1481, when an altar dedicated to John the Baptist was first mentioned. We have no information about any earlier altars that may have stood in the westwork. Other suppositions should be treated with equal caution. There is, for example, no evidence that a throne was ever placed behind the large arch of the west gallery, as Fuchs and others have suggested to support the interpretation of the westwork as a *Kaiserkirche*.[67] Nor is there any clear evidence to support Heitz's view that the westworks were meant to imitate the Holy Sepulchre in Jerusalem.

If the various theories about westworks are put aside, the undisputed evidence concerning Corvey may be summarized as follows:

1. At the time the westwork was built, its defining characteristic was considered to be the presence of the three towers, so that the entire complex was referred to as simply the *tres turres*.
2. The text of the facade plaque, inscribed in bold capital letters, reads: CIVITATEM ISTAM TU CIRCUMDA D(omi)NE/ ET ANGELI TUI CUSTODIANT MUROS EIUS, which may be translated as "You, Lord, surround this city/ And your angels guard its walls."
3. Figural decoration in the west end of the upper floor contained a scene of Ulysses combatting Scylla with a Siren nearby.

194 Corvey, abbey church, westwork, reconstruction of wall paintings in upper level tribune.

195 Corvey, abbey church, westwork, upper level, remains of fresco with Ulysses, Scylla and a Sirene.

4. Rows of the Latin letters *a* through *g*, in various sequences and in a late-ninth- or early-tenth-century hand, were found scratched into the plaster covering the western face of the jambs of the arched openings of the western gallery of the upper floor. Worth noting, too, these graffiti were found at various levels, ranging in height from approximately one to two meters, above what appears to have been a low wooden platform in the center of the gallery.[68]

5. Recent excavations, not yet fully published, indicate a complex sequence of events. The present westwork replaced the eastern half of an atrium (34.50 m long × 28 m wide), filled with graves. Within this earlier courtyard were also uncovered the foundations of a freestanding structure (6.10 × 3.20 m), which stood 3.10 m in front of the original church (fig. 177); the general location and dimensions of this enigmatic monument suggest a triumphal arch or gateway in the manner of the Lorsch *Torhalle*. A new atrium of two storeys, indicated by the aforementioned openings in the upper portions of the west facade, was then built adjoining the westwork and extending further west; its length remains undetermined.[69]

With these items in mind, a more coherent picture of the circumstances surrounding the construction of the Corvey westwork begins to emerge. Originally, the abbey church at Corvey had a simple atrium, used in part for burial, and containing a freestanding arch, probably meant to symbolize the monastery's imperial status. Not only was the abbey generously patronized by Louis the Pious, but in 833 it was given the rare privilege of minting its own coins in the emperor's name.[70] The arch may have been built to commemorate this event, while construction of the first outer crypt served the gift of the relics of St. Vitus in 836. This also seems to be about the time when the facade inscription plaque was first carved.[71] Around 870, the abbey church was damaged by fire and subsequently repaired and enlarged with the new and more elaborate outer crypt, discussed earlier. This rebuilding campaign at the east end of the church presumably led to a desire or need to remodel the west end as well. In any case, construction of the present westwork was initiated soon after completion of the outer crypt and work continued for eight years until its dedication in 885.

It seems reasonable to assume that the westwork took over most, if not all, of the functions of the atrium and arch it replaced. If so, it would have served as a place of assembly for both monks and laity, as a possible site for occasional burial, and, in lieu of the triumphal arch, as a symbol of imperial status. The three towers of the westwork were no doubt meant to be not only functional but also visually impressive. Although the plaque inscription seems to have been carved before the westwork was constructed, its placement in the center of the facade suggests that the monumentality of the archways and towers was intended to evoke a city gate in keeping with the reference to the monastery as a *civitas*. Indeed, already in the middle of the ninth century, when the facade plaque was produced, a biography of Corvey's co-founder and second abbot, Wala, equated the monastery with Augustine's City of God.[72] Similarly, the prominence of features in triads throughout the westwork—on the outside: towers, windows, and archways; and on the inside: 3 × 3 central bays in the ground floor, and triple arcades on each side of the upper and lower levels—imply that a trinitarian symbolism may have played a role in the design.

The precise meaning of the painted figural decoration is less speculative. The notion of the mysterious and dangerous sea as a symbol of the troublesome world through which every individual must navigate was a common theme in patristic exegesis. Likewise, the presence of Homeric references should not be taken simply as evidence for the continuation of the Carolingian Renaissance into the late ninth century. Since Early Christian times, Ulysses had been interpreted as a virtuous man of faith, a prototype for Christ, who, as at Corvey, combated evil in the form of mythological monsters, such as the Scylla. Another scene, now lost, must have represented the Christ-like Ulysses in his ship, a symbol of the Church, and bound to the mast, a symbol of the cross, so to resist the seductive song of the Sirens.[73] Whether the westwork contained an altar dedicated to Christ is not known, but it is quite possible. Certainly, the westwork must have contained one or more subsidiary altars. But the depiction of Ulysses, which is virtually unknown in medieval church decoration, has, I suspect, even more specific ties to the function of the westwork at Corvey. In monastic circles the Sirens and their alluring singing came to personify the temptations of the flesh, shunned by those following the claustral way of life. An anonymous monastic poet in the ninth century expressed this concept most succinctly when he wrote: "The sweet Sirens . . . Disturb my song with a song/ And hinder my singing with theirs."[74] This notion of the power of song has a particular relevance for the Corvey westwork.

The graffiti, discovered in the western gallery of the upper level, appear to be examples of a kind of music notation in which letters of the alphabet are used in sequence to represent the pitches of a scale or gamut. This type of notation was revived by music theorists who were active around the year 900, on the basis of classical models, particularly the *De Musica* of Boethius.[75] There is also evidence for letter notations being used for chant and other vocal music.[76] The most likely interpretation of the Corvey graffiti is that they were used to train beginning singers. The notably low position of some of them, in fact, suggests they were meant to be visible to boys. The absence of a text underneath the musical signs does not present a problem. The melodies notated may have been purely pedagogical exercises rather than liturgical melodies. And although the Corvey letters have not been identified with any known melodies of Gregorian chant, wordless tunes certainly had a place in the liturgical repertory. Some chanted portions of the early medieval Mass, the Alleluia in particular, were amplified by long melodic embellishments or melismas which were meant to represent the sounds of angels in paradise. Notker Balbulus ("the Stammerer," ca. 840–912) cites this practice in the preface to his "Book of Hymns" (*Liber hymnorum*), when he recalls that as a youth he had to sing "very long melodies" which were difficult to remember.[77] That a letter notation used by music theorists might have been employed to teach such melodies is very plausible, and the Corvey graffiti would thus be an indication that the primary purpose of this space within the complex was singing.

Surely the placement of the Homeric scene in the corridor directly below this area cannot be accidental. The heavenly voices of the choir, soaring above the image of the profane singing of the Sirens, signified the triumph of the purity of monastic life over worldly sin. One cannot help but recall, also, the facade inscription and its reference to God's angels, who guard the walls of the monastic city. Centuries later, the western tribune still seems to have fulfilled the same function, for a chronicle of the abbey, written at the end of the sixteenth century, specifically mentions a *chorus angelicus* of children "high up under the towers."[78] Fortunately, this account was written before the rest of the Carolingian church was dismantled at the end of the seventeenth century and it is thus able to describe two adult choirs situated elsewhere in the church: a main choir (*chorus supremus*) near the high altar and a lesser choir (*chorus infimus*) in the outer crypt. The chronicle goes on to explain how these choirs were able to coordinate their singing in spite of their separate locations. Not only did the angelic choir have a clear view of the church from its perch high up in the westwork, but the choir in the crypt could be both seen and heard through a window in the main apse (fig. 193).[79] Although the reliability of this source for the early Middle Ages is questionable, it does help us imagine how the disparate parts of the church—westwork, basilica proper, and outer crypt—could be united by the sights and sounds of the liturgy. The situation must have been little different in the ninth century.

It seems reasonable to assume that the Corvey complex comprised a multiplicity of meanings, involving many, if not all, of the connotations proposed by various scholars for westworks in general, including imperial patronage, a city gate, celestial symbolism, and a meeting place for laity and clergy. Even so, these associations, however likely, remain difficult to prove conclusively. On the other hand, the one clearly demonstrated function of at least part of the westwork was as a choir loft. This would seem to connect Corvey with Saint-Riquier at Centula, as described by Angilbert more than two generations earlier; yet important differences between the two structures should also be noted. Corvey lacks the western transept at Centula and has square stair towers instead of round ones. And, if Bernard's most recent reconstruction is to be believed, the westwork at Saint-Riquier had an octagonal core, which, to my mind, could not have sustained internal upper storeys as found at Corvey. Had there been a direct link between the two abbeys, one would expect it to have become manifest when the church at Corvey was first built in the 820s and 830s instead of a half century later. But this was not the case. The Corvey westwork may have been influenced by Centula, but, if so, it was far from a slavish copy. The elaborate west end of the church at Corvey, therefore, should not be viewed primarily as a holdover from an earlier age but as a unique creation in its own right. Carolingian westworks were not uniform in either design or function; instead, they developed in different ways in different places in response to increasingly elaborate liturgical needs, among other uses, over the course of the ninth century.

A similar process of inspiration and transformation can be seen at work at the cathedral of Cologne as rebuilt in the middle of the ninth century and dedicated in 870 (fig. 196).[80] Again, only the foundations are preserved but careful excavations have revealed the full extent of the plan. The grand scale and use of counter apses to east and west were taken over from the cathedral's earlier scheme, dating back to the reign of Charlemagne (fig. 163). This time, however, much greater emphasis was given to symmetry and order. Not only were there two main apses but two annular crypts. There were two transepts as well, and thus two square crossings. In addition, the two main apses were complemented by subsidiary apses in the eastern sides of the arms of each of the transepts. Perhaps most important, the overall dimensions of plan were multiples of a square module, produced by the two crossings, which was a method hinted at in the Plan of St. Gall but used here far more consistently throughout the design.[81] The westwork at Corvey, too, may have been inspired by the past, but, like Cologne cathedral, it went far beyond mere imitation.

The outer crypt and the westwork at Corvey both exemplify the creativity of building in the later ninth century, a creativity prompted in large part by the continued elaboration of the liturgy and the concomitant multiplication of altars. But Corvey proved to be among the last major monuments of Carolingian architecture. Indeed, by the time the westwork was complete, the Carolingian empire was on the verge of collapse. Viking attacks, which

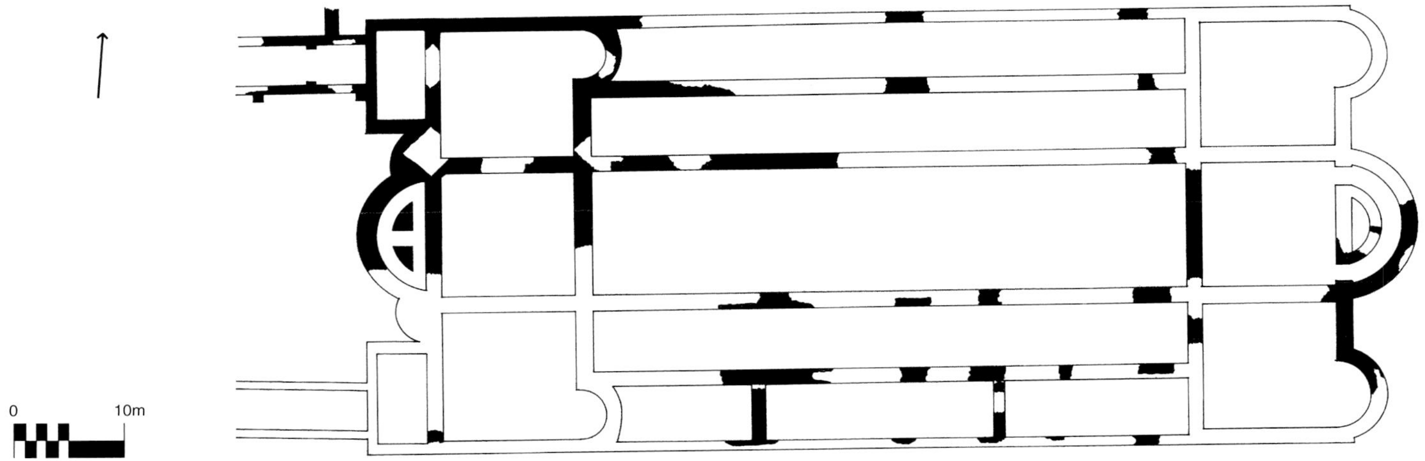

196 Cologne, plan of cathedral, ca. 870.

had continued largely unabated throughout the second half of the ninth century, penetrated ever deeper into Frankish territory. In 885, the very year in which the Corvey westwork was dedicated, the city of Paris was besieged by the Vikings and eventually set aflame. By the early 880s many of the great abbeys in northwestern Europe, including Centula and Corbie, had been abandoned, while monasteries in Italy, including Farfa, S. Vincenzo al Volturno, and Montecassino, were ransacked by the Saracens. In the wake of such disasters and the rising power of regional magnates, the emperor, Charles the Fat, was deposed in 887. Thereafter, the growing fragmentation of Europe, noted at the beginning of this chapter, became a reality: Aquitaine, Provence, Burgundy, Italy, east Francia, and west Francia were now each separate kingdoms. And just as Viking attacks began to subside, a new wave of invaders arrived from the east, the Magyars, who wreaked havoc as far as the Rhine and into Burgundy. It is no exaggeration to say that by the year 900 western Europe was at a nadir in its history. The era of great architectural projects was over, but the achievements of Carolingian architecture would not be forgotten. Indeed, they formed the basis for new building when Europe began to emerge from its troubles as a new millennium approached.

CHAPTER 10

Epilogue: The Architectural Contribution of the Early Middle Ages

The preceding chapters have tried to demonstrate some of the most significant aspects of early medieval architecture together with its richness and diversity. We have seen that during the period from the middle of the sixth through the ninth centuries church architecture was profoundly changed. In response to the rapid growth of the cult of relics, crypts of different kinds were devised to receive the bodies of saints and to unite their cherished remains with the main altar. Over time the church evolved into a repository of many relics housed within a multiplicity of subsidiary altars, which, in turn, prompted the reconfiguration of interior space. Simultaneously, the newly Christianized peoples of western Europe transformed the relative simplicity and uniformity of the Early Christian basilican design into an array of shapes, sizes, and decorative textures. The Franks, Lombards, Visigoths, and Anglo-Saxons attempted in various ways to emulate Roman techniques in design and construction, in keeping with the desire to legitimize their rule and new-found faith, but in the process they also introduced decorative qualities derived from indigenous traditions quite distinct from late antique aesthetics. The so-called Carolingian Renaissance, therefore, marked a shift in degree rather than kind. Under Charlemagne architectural projects exhibited a more accurate specificity in references to ancient, primarily Christian, models and were carried out on an ambitious scale, at such sites as Aachen, Centula, and Fulda, not seen since the reign of Justinian. These antiquarian tendencies could also be manifested on a more intimate level in buildings like those sponsored by Theodulf, Einhard, and Pope Paschal I. But the well-known revival of Early Christian forms was only one facet of Carolingian architecture. Indeed, in my view, its most creative phase came well after the death of Charlemagne in 814 with the development of monumental westworks and elaborate outer crypt schemes, which meant that the structural ideal of a church came to include towering entryways and almost labyrinthian eastern complexes, often with multiple storeys, surrounding the main altar. Many of the most elaborate buildings of the Carolingian era rose within monastic centers that served as laboratories for architectural experiments and thereupon established long-lived paradigms such as the rectilinear cloister. These achievements alone make the period deserving of study, but, in order to appreciate the lasting effect of early medieval architecture more fully, it will be necessary to survey briefly the influence on later building.

A major resurgence of church building soon after the year 1000 was reported by the Benedictine monk and chronicler Rodulfus Glaber, writing some thirty years later, in a famous and oft-quoted passage:

> Just before the third year after the millennium, throughout the whole world, but most especially in Italy and Gaul, men began to reconstruct churches, although for the most part the existing ones were properly built and not in the least unworthy. But it seemed as though each Christian community were aiming to surpass all others in the splendor of construction. It was as if the whole world were shaking itself free, shrugging off the burden of the past, and cladding itself everywhere in a white mantle of churches.[1]

Although there was considerable building activity at the time, the process had, in truth, begun much earlier. Glaber, after all, was concerned more with metaphor than historical fact. Stephen Nichols, for example, proposed some years ago that Glaber appropriated the image of white garments from biblical accounts of Christ's Transfiguration in order to complement his own account of the "reconstruction" of the faith in the early eleventh century.[2] Moreover, the prominence of the number three, and elsewhere eight, nine, and thirty-three, indicates the mystical symbolism behind much of Glaber's chronology. Already in the first decades of the tenth century, major abbeys, which had been abandoned a generation before, were reestablished while others, such as Gorze near Trier, were reformed and with the newly founded community at Cluny in Burgundy became themselves important centers of widespread monastic reform. The universality of Carolingian rule had long vanished, but by the middle of the tenth century a new dynasty, the Ottonians, ruled the Holy Roman Empire, now confined to German-speaking lands and Italy, and by the century's end another new dynasty, the Capetians, ruled France. The Vikings (or Norsemen) were subdued from 911 in exchange for being granted jurisdiction over land surrounding the mouth of the Seine, a region later known as Normandy, and the advance of the Magyars from the east was halted in a decisive battle near Augsburg in 955. The tenth century also offered clear signs of a dramatic growth in population and trade, as well as agricultural and urban development. These and other factors provided the background for a renewal of major construction projects.[3]

What is important for this study, however, is not the quantity of building but the nature of its design in relation to the recent past. In the few pages that follow only a brief overview of this phenomenon can be offered; a more complete analysis is beyond the scope of this book and will have to await another study. Nonetheless, the impact of the Carolingian era can be recognized most readily in two ways: first, by the direct imitation of specific buildings and second, by the continuation and elaboration of particular architectural features that had become prominent in the course of the ninth century.

The first category is best illustrated by a series of churches that emulated Charlemagne's chapel at Aachen (fig. 197).[4] The earliest of these, St. Donatius at Bruges from around 960, was also the closest in plan, if not in size, to its prototype. Although no longer standing, its foundations, uncovered in 1955, confirm later medieval references to the church as a copy of Aachen. With an octagonal core, 8.9 m in diameter (a third smaller than Aachen), defined by eight angular piers with a square apse to the east and a massive block to the west, the model for the design is obvious and reasons for such a blatant reference are not difficult to find. Flanders was among the first territorial principalities to emerge autonomously from the fragmentation of the Frankish kingdom and its counts, such as Arnulf I (918–64), consciously modelled their rule after that of the Carolingians with Bruges as a primary residence. Clearly, the church of St. Donatius was a manifestation of that outlook. In similar fashion centrally planned churches in Liège (St. John the Evangelist) and Muizen (St. Lambert) were sponsored around 1000 by Bishop Notker of Liège (972–1008). Under Notker, Liège and its cathedral school became one of the leading intellectual centers of Europe, and the church of St. John is recorded as having served as the renowned bishop's place of burial. Rebuilt in the eighteenth century along its original lines, so it seems, the church was virtually identical in size to the chapel of nearby Aachen, a town which Notker is known to have visited. Thus the reference to the esteemed prototype could be explained by Aachen's association with the promotion of learning and with the fact that the chapel was the site of Charlemagne's tomb.[5] The church at Muizen, on the other hand, was much smaller, as revealed by excavations, and seems to have been built to serve a chapter of canons installed by Notger on the northern edge of his diocese, perhaps as a symbol of episcopal authority. It should be noted that Lambert, to whom the church at Muizen was dedicated, was also the patron saint of Liège.

The next examples, at Nijmegen and Groningen, date to the second quarter of the eleventh century, and were sponsored by Salian rulers, successors to the Ottonian dynasty, and their supporters in a conscious effort to appropriate the architectural forms of Charlemagne's chapel, which since 936 had become the official site of the coronation of the king of the Germans (or east Franks). Less obvious, aside from sharing the same primary dedication, are the reasons for the imitation of Aachen at the extremely well preserved conventual church of St. Mary at Ottmarsheim (in Alsace), dedicated by Leo IX in 1049. Slightly later sources attribute its foundation to Rudolf of Altenburg, an imperial advisor and prominent member of the Hapsburg family, and the design may have been intended to reflect his elite status.[6] Even so, the subtleties of the model have been reduced to an austere octagon both inside and out with cubic capitals and simple moldings with none of the antiquarian flair so pervasive at Aachen (fig. 198.). In this case, the interior gallery was not used by lay nobility as at Charlemagne's chapel but ultimately by nuns to observe the celebration of mass below. Far more unusual was the arrangement at another convent, the church of SS. Cosmas and Damian at Essen, where the Aachen plan and elevation were sliced in half and used to form the west end of a basilican church (fig. 199). The gallery, reached by means of spiral stairs similar to those at Aachen, must have been reserved for nuns as at Ottmarsheim, but in this case the political implications of the architectural reference seem particularly clear. After all, the patron, Abbess Theophanou, was a prominent member of the imperial house, whose rulers, beginning with Otto I, were crowned at Aachen. Indeed, the inscription on her gravestone proclaimed her lineage as: "daughter of Mathilde, daughter of Emperor Otto II."[7] Such imitations of Aachen, although impressive, were relatively few in number and thus limited in influence.

Far more significant was the transformation of the traditional basilican scheme inherited from late antiquity. The basic formula of nave, aisles, apse, and often a transept remained but features first introduced during the Carolingian era were now firmly established as well. Recent

197 *(facing page)* Comparative plans of churches imitating Charlemagne's chapel at Aachen.

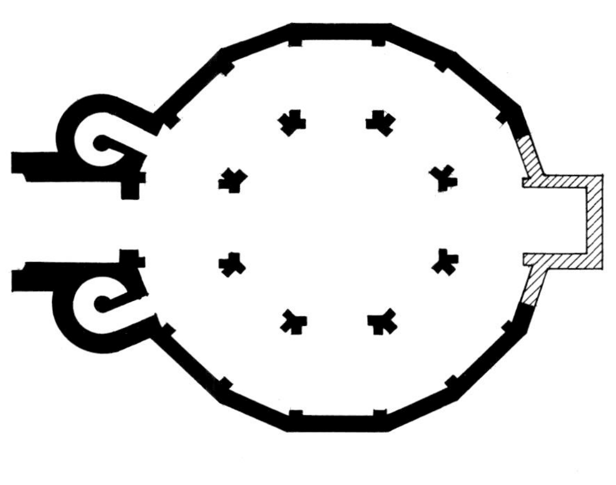

AACHEN

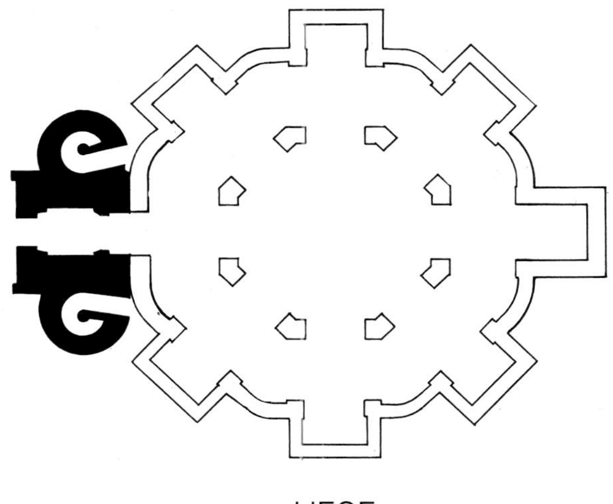

LIEGE

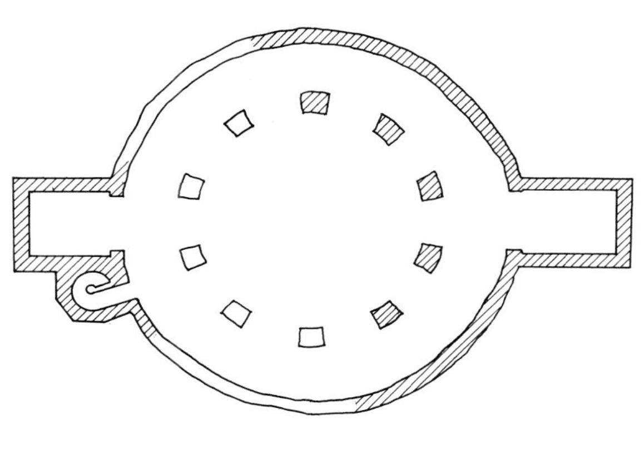

GRONINGEN

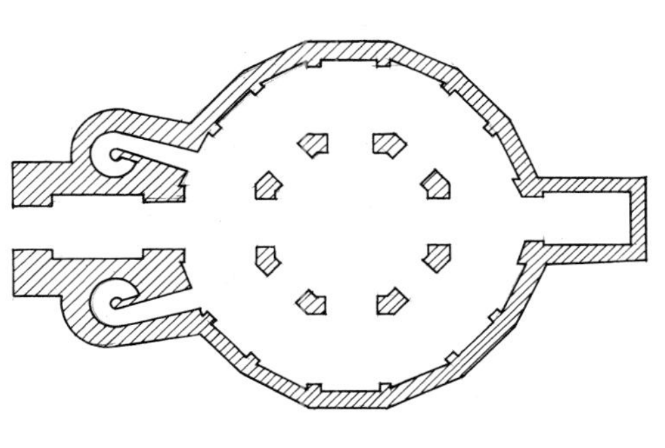

BRUGES

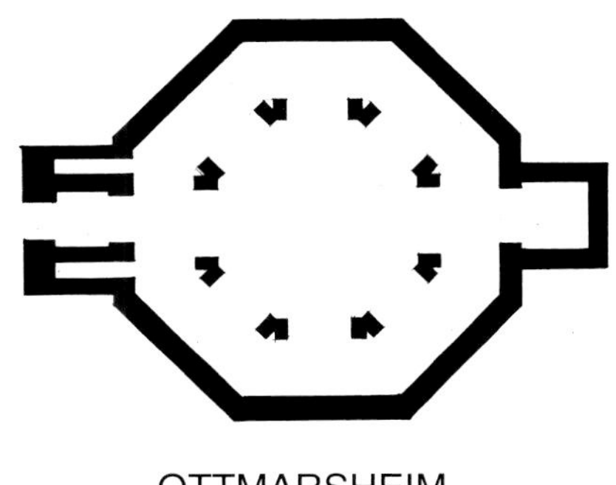

OTTMARSHEIM

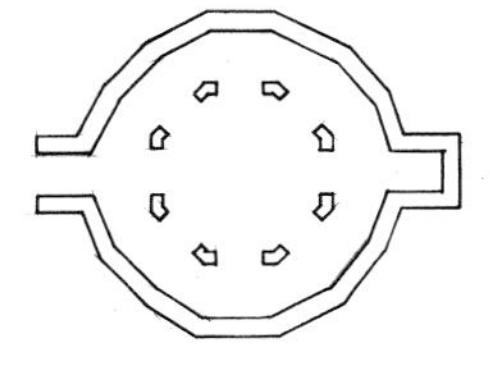

NIJMEGEN

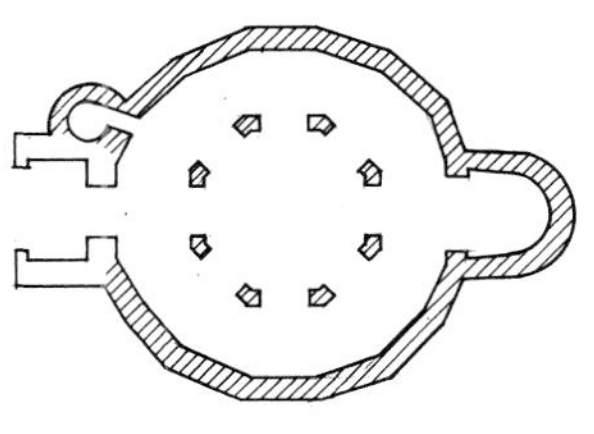

MUIZEN

198 Ottmarsheim, Convent Church of St. Mary, interior view.

excavations, for example, have shown that the symmetry of opposing apses, even if one is square, and double transepts, together with the square modular scheme, first seen at Cologne cathedral at the end of the ninth century, reappeared a century later in the layout of the cathedral of Liège (fig. 200).[8] This was another building patronized by Bishop Notker but here the reference was perhaps a homage not only to the Carolingian past but also to Cologne's current role as the center of the grand archdiocese of which Liège was a part. Soon after came the better known and far better preserved, if much rebuilt, example of the abbey church of St. Michael's at Hildesheim, sponsored by Bishop Bernward (993–1022), friend and advisor to Emperor Otto III, and dedicated in 1033.[9] At Hildesheim one can see that the square schematism of the plan was based upon the module of the eastern and western crossings and repeated in the nave by an alternating system of supports composed of rectilinear piers and paired columns (fig. 201). It is interesting to note that the first use of such an alternating system seems to have been at Cologne cathedral where paired columns and piers were used to separate inner aisles from new outer aisles, which were added in the middle of the tenth century.[10] Another link with Cologne is the fact that Bernward turned to that city to choose the first abbot to head St. Michael's, a man by the name of Goderamus. Moreover, in the new abbot's possession at Hildesheim was a rare copy of the ancient architectural treatise of Vitruvius which, based on paleographical evidence, we know had been copied in Cologne (or at least by a scribe trained in that city) some two centuries earlier. How Goderamus acquired the manuscript, we do not know, but he was certainly proud enough to have such a precious book in his possession to proclaim his ownership by writing his name in its margin.[11] One cannot help but wonder if the layout of the abbey church at Hildesheim could have been inspired, at least in part, by Vitruvius' call in Book III of *De architectura* for symmetry and proportion in planning temples based on a "fixed module" using the ideal geometric figures of the circle and square, which circumscribe the body of a man with his arms and legs outspread.[12] After all, it has already been suggested elsewhere that the Vitruvian treatise helped to determine the proportions of the columns, capitals, and bases of the Hildesheim nave, and that an addendum to this particular manuscript (by a different ninth-century hand), which deals with the casting of bronze and other metalworking techniques, may have played a role in the creation of the church's famous bronze doors and column.[13] Moreover, in spite of the fact that Vitruvius is, of course, referring in this passage about the circle and square to the design of pagan temples, the notion that geometric forms could bear a symbolic significance would be very much in accordance with Christian precepts. In the first quarter of the ninth century, for example, Eigil, the abbot of Fulda, explained that "the circle, which has no end, . . . reflects the sacredness of the Church."[14] For Vitruvius, the circle and square are inherently interconnected in their relation to the human form, and, in the Judeo-Christian tradition, man was created in the image of God. Thus the circle and square could be seen as symbols of God. Could the same manuscript of *De architectura,* or the one from which it was copied, have played a role in the design of the cathedral of Cologne in the late ninth century as well? Be that as it may, it should be noted that at Hildesheim the series of square units defined by rectilinear piers along the nave also delineated important liturgical space. Limited excavations carried out after the devastation of World War II uncovered the footings of the baptismal font in the western third of the nave and the foundations of the altar of the Holy Cross, together with

199 *(facing page)* Essen, Convent Church of SS. Cosmas and Damian, interior view looking west.

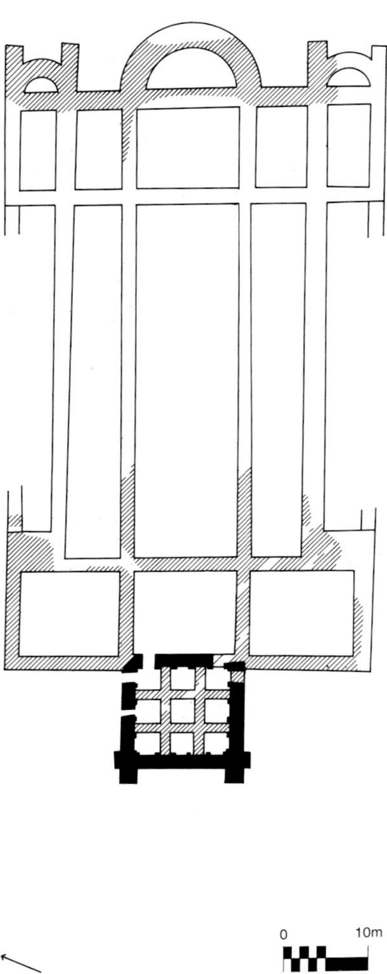

200 Liège, plan of cathedral, ca. 1000.

201 Hildesheim, St. Michael, abbey church, plan.

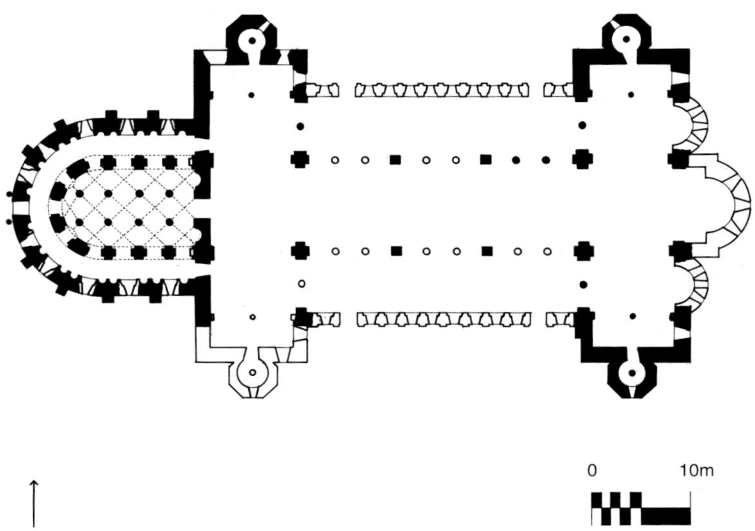

that of the bronze column, in the eastern third.[15] One could therefore say that the baptismal font and proliferation of altars represented on the Plan of St. Gall were given a fuller architectural expression at Hildesheim. No longer merely cordoned off by altar railings, the sacred precincts were now reflected in the very fabric of the church itself through its alternating pattern of supports. In place of the regular cadence of columns or piers there is a rhythmic compartmentalization of space through the A-B-B-A (pier, column, column, pier) pattern of supports. It is also reflected throughout the design of the church from the largest to the smallest features, from the square crossing towers on the outside to the cubic capitals on the inside (fig. 202). This consistent articulation of interior space would ultimately lead to the regular spatial compartmentalization known as the bay system, a concept which played a vital role in the development of Romanesque and Gothic architecture.

Equally important was the emphasis placed upon the eastern and western ends of basilican churches following the pattern of later Carolingian buildings. The western complex at Essen, cited above, was a unique example. Far more significant was the elaboration of the Carolingian westwork as seen at Corvey, but even here the configurations were highly varied. The general development has already been traced by Hans Erich Kubach and Albert Verbeek in their monumental study of the Romanesque churches of the Rhine and Maas river valleys and, more recently, in two articles by Uwe Lobbedey, so that only a few points need be reiterated here.[16] None of the many examples follows Corvey exactly (fig. 203). The closest, and also the earliest (consecrated in 943), was the westwork of

202 Hildesheim, St. Michael, abbey church, exterior view.

the monastic church at Werden which followed the same cubic design with a central core surrounded by narrow, vaulted corridors on several levels, the main difference being that, unlike Corvey, the central space seems to have been open without any floor divisions. At the cathedral of Minden, on the other hand, dedicated a few years later (952), a series of massive parallel foundations indicate the presence of vaulting on the ground floor and a second storey in the central area affronting the nave. The stair towers, however, jutted dramatically forward from the facade instead of being flush as at Corvey. Still, it must have retained the clear impression of three towers essential to the definition of the westwork. The best-preserved tenth-century example of this formulation is the abbey church of St. Pantaleon in Cologne.[17] The monastic community was founded in the 960s by Bruno, the archbishop of Cologne and brother of Emperor Otto II, but the present, monumental westwork, replacing an earlier, more compact one, is generally considered to have been built through the patronage of the Empress Theophanou between 984 and her death in 991.[18] In fact, Theophanou was buried there. In any case, as at Werden, and unlike Minden, the space below the central tower is without floor divisions. The enveloping multilevel spaces, however, are not continuous but form part of semi-independent projecting units: north and south arms of a transept and a western entryway. On the exterior, soaring stair towers are nestled into the junctures of transept and entrance with their geometric progression from square to octagon to circle providing a bold accent to the traditional three-tower formula of the Carolingian westwork (fig. 204). In spite of their significant differences, in both plan and elevation, these tenth-century

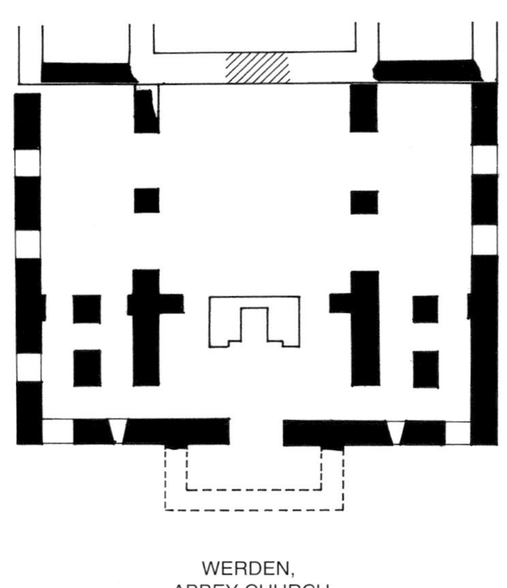

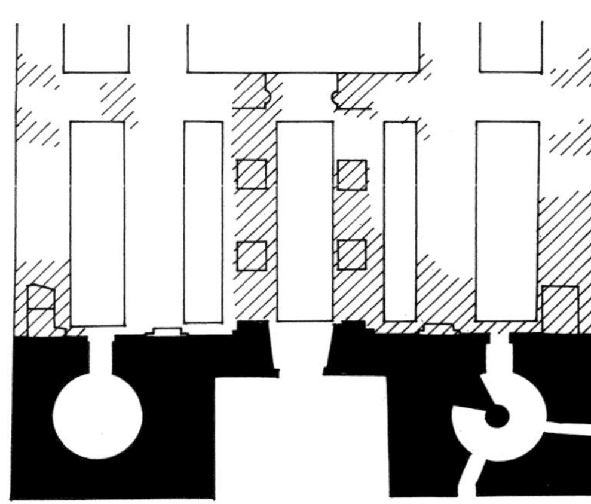

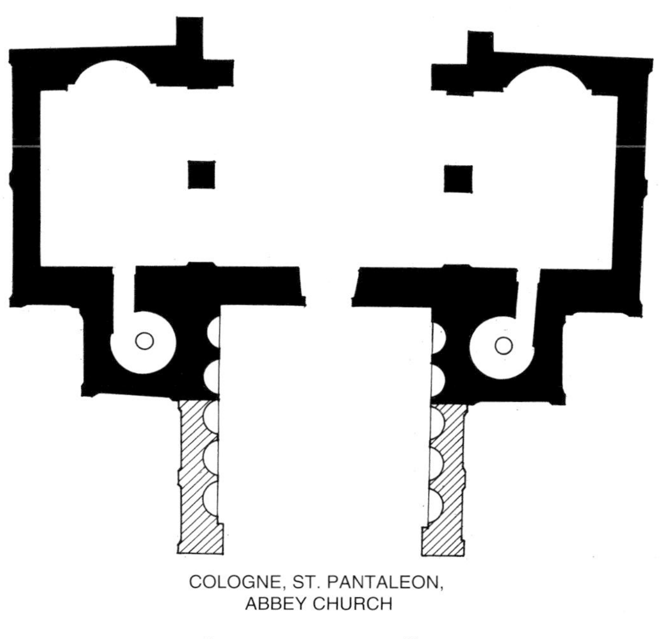

203 *(above)* Comparative plans of tenth-century westworks.

204 *(facing page)* Cologne, St. Pantaleon, abbey church, exterior view of westwork.

205 Saint-Denis, abbey church, axonometric reconstruction of twelfth-century western entrance.

westworks reflect a common process of consolidating and refining Carolingian precedents. At St. Pantaleon in Cologne, especially, there is, in comparison to Corvey, a greater sophistication in the dramatic clarity of massing between the central tower and subsidiary stair towers. There is also a sense of experimentation in the geometric play in the storeys of the flanking towers as they change in shape as they ascend from rectilinear to octagonal to cylindrical, which adds to their soaring quality.

The true two-tower facade without a central tower of any kind, which played such an important role in the development of later Romanesque and Gothic churches, had its origins, it seems, later in the eleventh century. But even so, Carolingian architecture played a vital role. At the abbey church of Saint-Denis as rebuilt under Abbot Suger in the second quarter of the twelfth century, a structure which is generally acknowledged to be the first Gothic church, the grand western entrance with its two towers and interior upper level was probably inspired, even if indirectly, by its Carolingian predecessor, as discussed in chapters five and nine (fig. 205). Such a reference to the past would be very much in keeping with Suger's aforementioned desire to harmonize the old parts of the church with the new.[19]

Elaborate east ends, too, reemerged as a major feature in the course of the tenth century as a legacy of the Carolingian past. Most Ottonian churches, beginning with St. Cyriakus at Gernrode around 960, possessed hall crypts, derived from earlier formulations as at Fulda, on the Plan of St. Gall, and the confessio at Saint-Germain at Auxerre. St. Michael's at Hildesheim is unique among Ottonian churches in combining, in this case at the west end, an extensive hall crypt, to receive the tomb of Bishop Bernward, with the curved passage of an annular crypt. But, again, a precedent, with a more angular arrangement, is found on the Plan of St. Gall.[20] On the other hand, two-storeyed outer crypts with angular passageways and projecting axial semi-subterranean chambers became an important, if not exclusive, feature of the churches associated with the Gorze reforms. In general, hall crypts and annular crypts in seemingly endless configurations flourished throughout Europe, including England and Italy, and provided a testing ground for many types of vaulting that would become important for later medieval developments.[21] The staggered or *en échelon* sequence of apses without crypts would be a hallmark of the late-tenth-century church at Cluny (dedicated 981), inspired most likely by churches of Benedict of Aniane (such as Kornelimünster, fig. 146), whose earlier reforms were revived at the great Burgundian abbey.[22]

Especially important for the later history of Romanesque and Gothic architecture was the development of the scheme commonly referred to as an ambulatory with radiating chapels. It consists of an uninterrupted semicircular passage about the main apse from which protrude, in radial fashion, a series of small chapels. The arrangement at St. Martin at Tours is now generally assigned to the later eleventh century, which makes the cathedral of Clermont-Ferrand in central France the first known example, probably dating to the late tenth century, as indicated by foundations in the crypt (fig. 206).[23] Here the chapels, at least in the crypt, were flat-ended and apparently five in number. A similar arrangement at the Burgundian abbey church of Saint-Philibert at Tournus is far better preserved both below and above ground (fig. 203). Below, a vaulted, curved passage encircles a grand hall crypt with two rows of slender columns, while above, the apse and ambulatory are separated by an elegant columnar screen. A recent study by Jacques Henriet has shown convincingly that the east

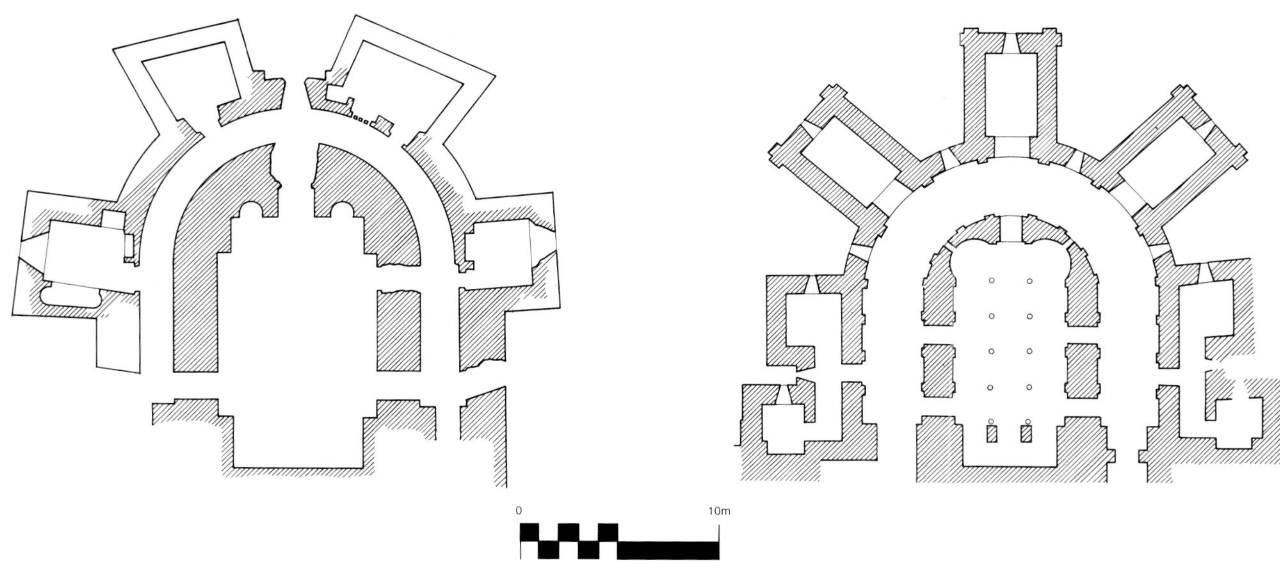

206 Comparative plans of crypts supporting an ambulatory with radiating chapels: (left) Clermont-Ferrand, cathedral; (right) Tournus, Saint-Philibert, abbey church.

end of Saint-Philibert was built after a major fire of 1008 and not earlier as previously thought.[24] It is worth noting, too, that Tournus became in 875 the ultimate resting place for the remains of St. Philibert after they were removed from Grandlieu in 858 in the face of Viking raids. Thus from the very beginning, the church of Tournus, through its primary relic, was connected with the Carolingian legacy of the outer crypt and may have been built with one in the late ninth century, although all physical traces of it have long vanished. Even so, according to documentary evidence the present east end at Saint-Philibert replaced an earlier, tenth-century arrangement, which was destroyed in the 1008 fire and was composed of what were described at the time as "upper" and "lower" chapels.[25] What we have now at Tournus, therefore, is presumably a conscious imitation of earlier precedents by having two levels to its "crypt"; the main change seems to be that the upper storey is now on the same level as the rest of the church. Thus, although at Clermont-Ferrand only the foundations in the crypt are preserved, the eleventh-century church at Tournus demonstrates that the scheme of ambulatory and radiating chapels is the direct outgrowth of the Carolingian tradition of the two-storey outer crypt in Burgundy, as seen at Auxerre and Flavigny.

A similar two-level solution (crypt below and ambulatory above), with three deep-apsed chapels, was adopted by Bishop Fulbert for the east end of Chartres Cathedral as rebuilt after a disastrous fire in 1020 (fig. 207).[26] This design formed part of Fulbert's effort to promote the cathedral as a major pilgrimage site because it possessed the purported tunic worn by the Virgin Mary at the Nativity. This birthing chemise, according to legend, had been a gift of Charles the Bald after he had received it from the Byzantine emperor.[27] Chartres, among the most admired of all Gothic cathedrals, provides an outstanding example of the long-term architectural influence of the early Middle Ages. At the core of the Chartrain crypt today are clear remnants of the Carolingian crypt built soon after the Viking devastation of 858 in order to house the newly arrived relic from King Charles. The arrangement of these remains indicates the original presence of a hall crypt with arched openings to an outer corridor which most likely formed part of a more elaborate outer crypt system. Be that as it may, the Carolingian crypt was subsequently enveloped by the foundations of Fulbert's church, which supported the arrangement of ambulatory and radiating chapels above. This eleventh-century crypt, in turn, was used as the foundations for the east end of the present church following another devastating fire in 1194 and in so doing helped to determine the unusual character of the east end of the present Gothic church with its undulating sequence of subsidiary, radial chapels. At Chartres, the

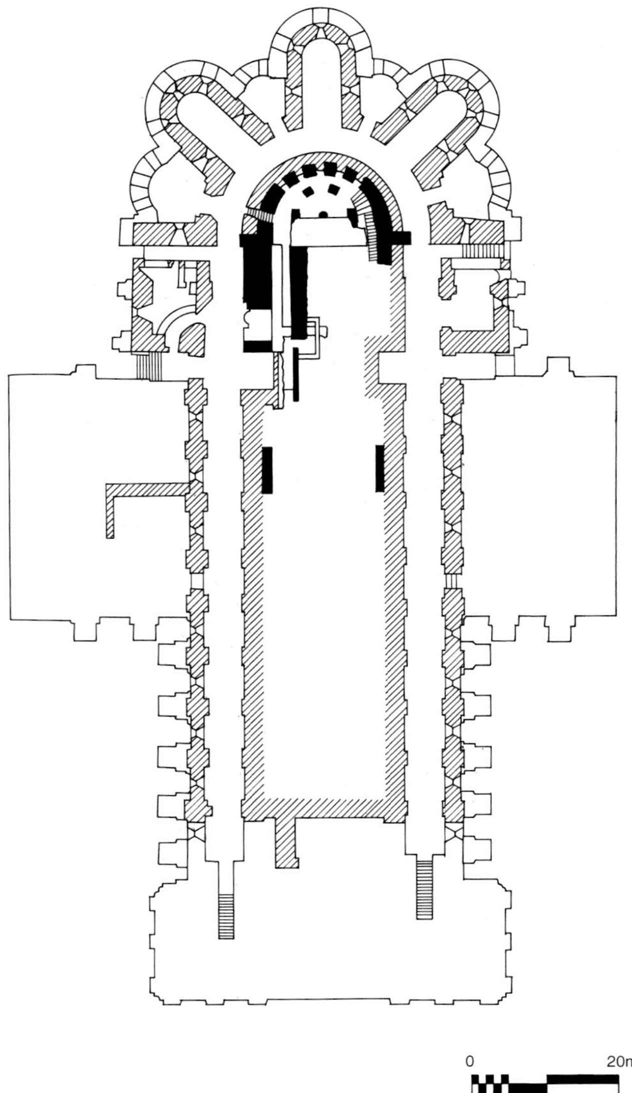

207 Chartres, cathedral, composite plan showing various phases of construction: black, ninth century; hatching, eleventh century; clear, twelfth century.

architectural contribution of the early Middle Ages remains hidden from view but it is profound nonetheless. The same may be said about the development of medieval architecture as a whole.

Many other examples could be shown to exemplify this point but none more telling than the plan of St. Philibert at Tournus (fig. 208).[28] A comparison with the relative simplicity of the basilican plans of St. Peter's and St. Paul's in Rome, cited in chapter one (fig. 3), shows how far we have come. The basic elements of nave, aisles, transept, and curved apse are all still there, but far more complex forms are manifest at Tournus, especially at the eastern and western extremities. The arrangement of the east end has

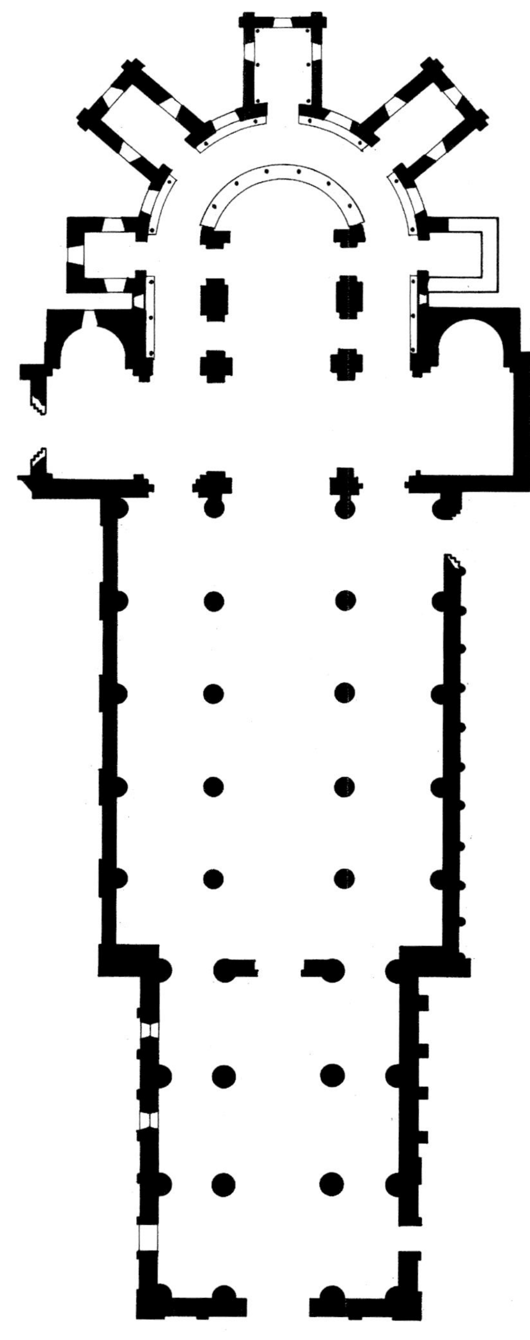

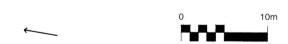

208 Tournus, Saint-Philibert, abbey church, plan.

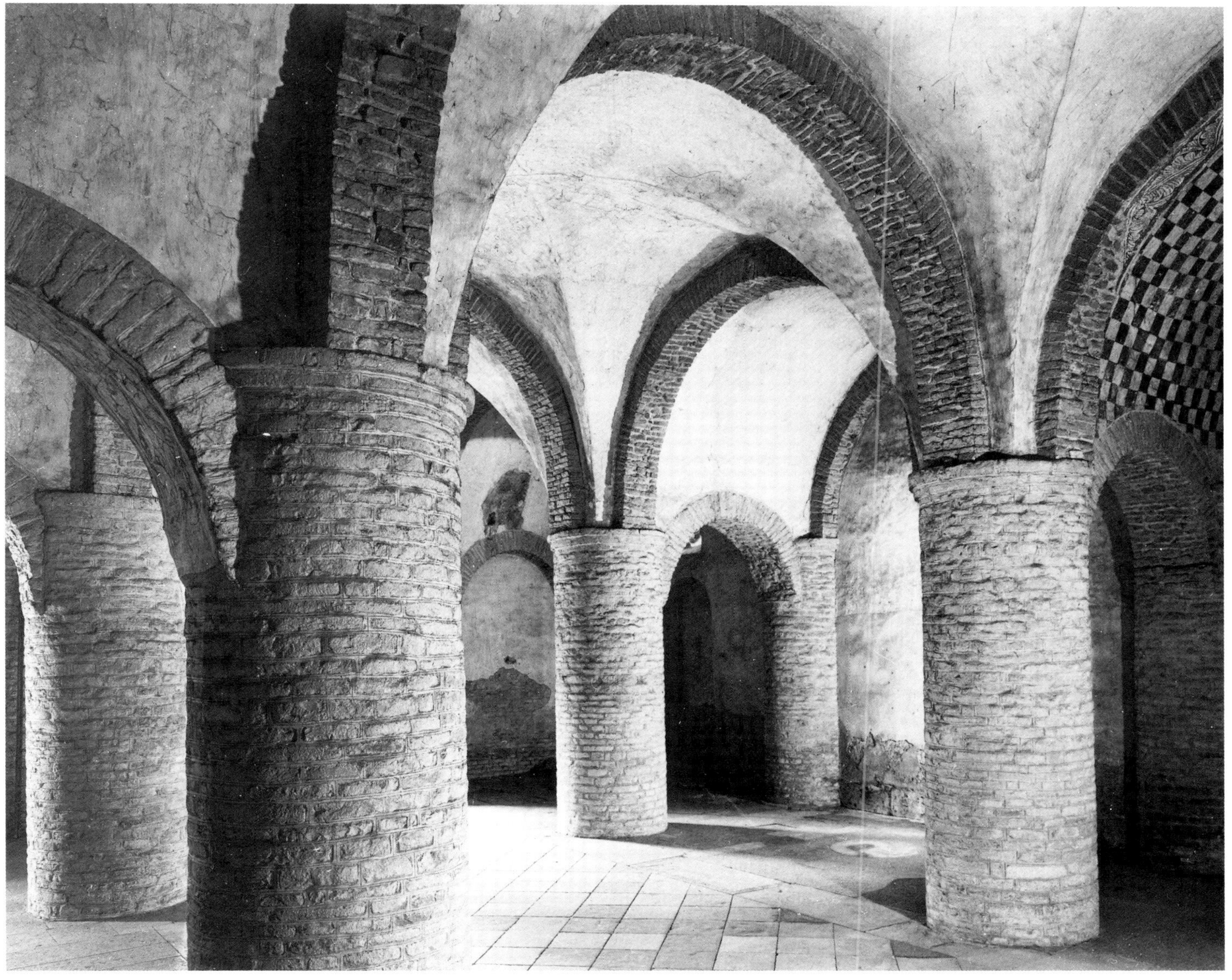

209 Tournus, Saint-Philibert, abbey church, interior view, ground floor of western entrance.

already been discussed as an important stage in the development of the scheme of ambulatory and radiating chapels. But at the west end, there is a blocky unit, perhaps planned soon after 1008 but not built until a full generation later, that is derived in form, if not necessarily in function, from the tradition of the Carolingian westwork.[29] The main difference in plan is the strong longitudinal axis at Tournus, more like a miniature basilica, without the square centrality of the westwork at Corvey. Divided into two floors supported by massive cylindrical piers, the interior offers a tour de force of vaulting types (fig. 209). The groin vaults in the central bays of the ground floor are reminiscent of the westwork at Corvey (fig. 191), but at Tournus the side aisles display transverse barrel vaults while above is a central, axial barrel vault framed by half barrel (or quadrant) vaults. On the exterior are two stair towers, flush with the facade and both originally stunted as the one on the right (or south) (fig. 210). Conspicuously absent is any hint of a central or third tower essential to the Carolingian formula. New, too, is the exuberant display of pilaster strips and raked corbel tables. Although traditionally seen as purely decorative elements derived ultimately from the exterior blind arcades of Early Christian and Carolingian churches in north Italy and Switzerland, these features are now believed to play an essential structural role whereby the complex articulation of the exterior wall surface helps

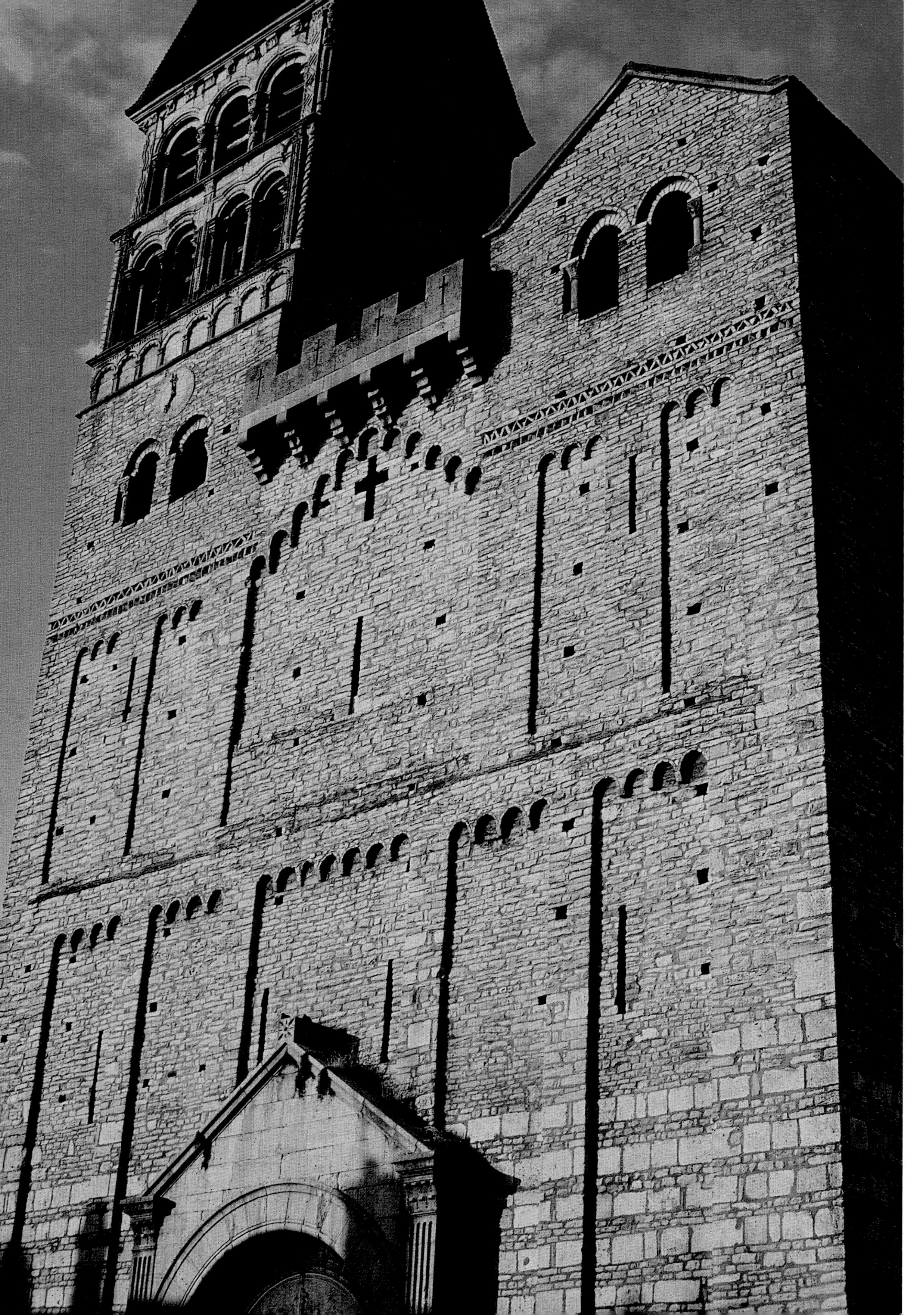

to stabilize interior vaulting.[30] Thus, like the east end, the western complex at Tournus is an innovative variant of earlier developments. With the nave in its present form completed in the mid-eleventh century, the elaborate but rather awkward assemblage of features at Tournus demonstrates that we are at a point of transition between the early Middle Ages and what would come to be termed "Romanesque."

During the period between the sixth and tenth centuries the architectural legacy of late antiquity was dramatically transformed. It should not be construed, however, that Early Christian architecture was in any way lacking in originality; on the contrary, it provided the basic vocabulary of forms for all subsequent church building throughout the Middle Ages and beyond by establishing the essential characteristics of the basilican and centrally planned schemes in an array of permutations. Moreover, the great Christian, and in some cases pagan, monuments of Rome and other late antique centers would continue to exert influence, but the innovations of the subsequent several centuries had steered developments along new paths in response to a variety of needs, including, among others, those related to the cult of relics, liturgical changes, political considerations, and aesthetic preferences. Monumental, often towered, western entryways, increasingly compartmentalized interiors, ever more elaborate east ends, and continued exploration of the potentials of vaulting, all inherited from the recent past, would become the hallmarks of the future. Indeed, with the start of a new millennium, ecclesiastical architecture in western Europe, as exemplified by Saint-Philibert at Tournus, was on a new footing.

In many ways, therefore, Rodulfus Glaber was right to extol the accomplishments of the early eleventh century. It was indeed the beginning of a new age. Earlier in the twentieth century, the great historian of medieval art and architecture Henri Focillon referred to the eleventh century as an age of "experiments" during which time the way was prepared for many of the most famous monuments of the High Middle Ages, including the present cathedral of Chartres.[31] I fully concur. Nonetheless, I hope that this study has served to demonstrate that these achievements would not have been possible without the architectural contribution of the early Middle Ages.

 (facing page) Tournus, St. Philibert, abbey church, exterior view of west facade

NOTES

Chapter 1: The Legacy of Late Antiquity

1 See, among other studies, George Ostrogorsky, *History of the Byzantine State,* rev. ed. (New Brunswick, New Jersey, 1969), 68–79, and, more recently, John Moorhead, *The Roman Empire Divided, 400–700* (London, 2001), 125–55.

2 Richard Hodges and David Whitehouse, *Mohammed, Charlemagne and the Origins of Europe* (London, 1983), 46; P. Allen, "The 'Justinianic' Plague," *Byzantion* 49 (1979), 5–20; and Michael McCormick, *Origins of the European Economy: Communications and Commerce A.D. 300–900* (Cambridge, 2001), 38–41.

3 Bryan Ward-Perkins, *From Classical Antiquity to the Middle Ages: Urban and Public Building in Northern and Central Italy, A.D. 300–850* (Oxford, 1984), 14ff.

4 Jean-Charles Picard, "Conscience urbaine et culte des saints. De Milan sous Liutprand à Vérone sous Pépin 1er d'Italie," *Hagiographie cultures et sociétés IVe–XIIe siècles* (Paris, 1981), 455–69.

5 Richard Krautheimer, *Early Christian and Byzantine Architecture,* 4th rev. ed. with Slobodan Curcic (Harmondsworth, 1986).

6 L. Michael White, *The Social Origins of Christian Architecture,* 2 vols. (Valley Forge, Pennsylvania, 1996), passim.

7 Various laws were issued in the course of the fourth century restricting pagan practices, but it was not until 391 that Emperor Theodosius I officially banned access to all shrines and temples. See Garth Fowden, "Polytheist religion and philosophy," *The Cambridge Ancient History,* vol. 13; *The Late Empire, A.D. 337–425,* ed. Averil Cameron and Peter Garnsey (Cambridge, 1998), 548ff.; and Stephen Williams and Gerard Friell, *Theodosius: The Empire at Bay* (New Haven and London, 1994), 119ff.

8 Richard Krautheimer, "The Constantinian Basilica," *Dumbarton Oaks Papers* 21 (1967), 151–40; and J. B. Ward-Perkins, "Constantine and the Origins of the Christian Basilica," *Papers of the British School at Rome* 22 (1954), 69–90. For a review and discussion of the various opinions about the origin and meaning of the basilica for Christian use see: Dale Kinney, "The Church Basilica," *Acta ad archaeologiam et artium historiam pertinentia* 15 (2001), 115–35.

9 J. B. Ward-Perkins, *Roman Imperial Architecture,* 2nd ed. (New Haven and London, 1994), 442ff., and *Trier. Kaiserresidenz und Bischofssitz. Die Stadt in spätantiker und frühchristlicher Zeit* (Mainz, 1984), 139–58.

10 Richard Krautheimer, et al., *Corpus Basilicarum Christianarum Romae,* 5 vols. (Vatican City, 1937–77), 5:1–92; and Sible de Blaauw, *Cultus et Decor. Liturgia e architettura nella Roma tardoantico e medievale,* 2 vols., Studi e testi 355 (Vatican City, 1994), 1:109–29.

11 Krautheimer, *Corpus,* 5:165ff.; and Blaauw, *Cultus et Decor,* 2:451–92. See also Jocelyn Toynbee and J. B. Ward-Perkins, *The Shrine of St. Peter and the Vatican Excavations* (London, 1956), and Achim Arbeiter, *Alt-St. Peter in Geschichte und Wissenschaft* (Berlin, 1988).

12 Beat Brenk, "Spolia from Constantine to Charlemagne: Aesthetics versus Ideology," *Dumbarton Oaks Papers* 41 (1987), 103–9; Joseph Alchermes, "*Spolia* in Roman Cities of the Late Empire: Legislative Rationales and Architectural Reuse," *Dumbarton Oaks Papers* 48 (1994), 167–78; Bryan Ward-Perkins, "Re-using the Architectural Legacy of the Past, *entre idéologie et pragmatisme,*" *The Idea and Ideal of the Town between Late Antiquity and the Early Middle Ages,* ed. G. P. Brogiolo and B. Ward-Perkins, *The Transformation of the Roman World,* vol. 4 (Leiden, 1999), 225–33. For a somewhat different view see Dale Kinney, " 'Spolia. Damnatio' and 'Renovatio Memoriae'," *Memoirs of the American Academy in Rome* 42 (1997), 117–48.

13 "QUOD DUCE TE MUNDUS SURREXIT IN ASTRA TRIUMPHANS / HANC CONSTANTINUS VICTOR TIBI CONDIDIT AULUM." Krautheimer, *Corpus,* 5:172. For a more detailed discussion of the context of this inscription see idem, "The Building Inscriptions and the Dates of Construction of Old St. Peter's: A Reconsideration," *Römisches Jahrbuch der Bibliotheca Hertziana,* 25 (1989), 7ff.

14 Krautheimer, *Corpus,* 1:12ff., 2:1ff., 2:191ff., 4:99ff. For SS. Marcellinus and Peter see also Jean Guyon, *Le cimetière aux deux lauriers: Recherches sur les catacombes romaines* (Rome, 1987), 207–63. Herman Geertman, "The Builders of Basilica Maior in Rome," *Festoen* (Groningen, 1976), 277ff., assigns the grand funerary basilica of S. Lorenzo to the reign of Pope Sixtus III (432–40). For the original dedication and function of S. Sebastiano see chapter two, note 3.

15 Krautheimer, *Early Christian,* 48–50, and Jochen Zink, "Der Baugeschichte des Trierer Domes von den Anfängen im 4. Jahrhundert bis zur letzten Restaurierung," *Der Trierer Dom,* ed. Franz Ronig (Neuss, 1980), 18ff.

16 For the cathedral in Antioch see Krautheimer, *Early Christian,* 76ff., and Friedrich W. Deichmann, "Das Oktogon von Antiocheia," *Byzantinische Zeitschrift* 65 (1972), 40ff; and for the Minerva Medica in Rome see J. B. Ward-Perkins, *Roman Imperial,* 433ff., and Richard Krautheimer, "Success and Failure in Late Antique Church Planning," *The Age of Spirituality,* ed. Kurt Weitzmann (New York, 1980), 121–39.

17 For a general discussion of Constantinian churches in the Holy Lands see Krautheimer, *Early Christian,* 59ff. with additional bibliography. The most detailed archaeological analysis of the Holy Sepulchre in Jerusalem remains Virgilio C. Corbo, *Il Santo Sepulcro di Gerusaleme,* 3 vols. (Jerusalem, 1981). For a

more general, and somewhat less reliable, summary see Charles Coüasnon, *The Holy Sepulchre in Jerusalem* (London, 1974). The description of Eusebius appears in *Vita Constantini,* 3:33–9, and is translated in Cyril Mango, *The Art of the Byzantine Empire, 312–1453* (Englewood Cliffs, New Jersey, 1972), 12–13.

18 Ward-Perkins, *Roman Imperial,* 454ff.; Richard Krautheimer, *Three Christian Capitals: Topography and Politics* (Berkeley, 1983), 70.

19 The letter to the bishop of Jerusalem is in *Vita Constantini,* 3:31–2, translated in Mango, *The Art of the Byzantine Empire,* 12. For the Pantheon, imperial mausolea in Rome, and the Anastasis Rotunda see Ward-Perkins, *Roman Imperial,* 424ff., and Krautheimer, *Early Christian,* 74.

20 Krautheimer, *Three Christian Capitals,* 41ff. See also Cyril Mango, *Le développement urbain de Constantinople IVe–VIIe siècles* (Paris, 1985).

21 For the attribution to Constantine see Krautheimer, *Three Christian Capitals,* 50ff., and idem, "On Constantine's Church of the Apostles in Constantinople," *Studies in Early Christian, Medieval, and Renaissance Art* (New York, 1969), 27–34. For the attribution to Constantius see Cyril Mango, "Constantine's Mausoleum and the Translation of Relics," *Byzantinische Zeitschrift* 83 (1990), 51–62.

22 Krautheimer, *Early Christian,* 67, and R. Biering and H. von Hesberg, "Zur Bau- und Kultgeschichte von St. Andreas apud S. Petrum," *Römischer Quartalschrift für christliche Altertumskunde und Kirchengeschichte* 82 (1987), 145–82.

23 Krautheimer, *Corpus,* 4:144ff., and more recently Hugo Brandenburg, *Die Kirche S. Stefano Rotondo in Rom: Bautypologie und Architektursymbolik in der spätantiken und frühchristlichen Architektur,* Hans-Lietzmann-Vorlesungen (Berlin, 1998). For S. Maria Maggiore and S. Sabina see Krautheimer, *Corpus,* 3:1ff. and 4:72ff.

24 Krautheimer, *Corpus,* 5:93ff. and idem, "Intorno all fondazione di San Paolo fuori le mura," *Rendiconti della pontificia accademia romana di archeologia,* 53–4 (1980–81, 1981–82), 207ff.

25 Krautheimer, *Early Christian,* 85ff., and Zink, "Die Baugeschichte," *Der Trierer Dom,* 24ff.

26 The bibliography of S. Lorenzo in Milan is extensive. G. Chierici and C. Cecchelli, *La basilica di San Lorenzo maggiore in Milano* (Milan, 1951), remains standard and posits a late-fourth-century date, as does Krautheimer, *Three Christian Capitals,* 81–89 with additional bibliography. Enrico Cattaneo is among the most recent to prefer a date in the early fifth century, *La basilica di San Lorenzo in Milano,* ed. G.A. dell'Acqua (Milan, 1985), 18–20. The dating controversy is summarized by Neil B. McLynn, *Ambrose of Milan* (Berkely, 1994), 176ff. Useful surveys of church building in late antique Milan are Dale Kinney, "Le chiese paleocristiane di Mediolanum," *Milano, una capitale da Ambrogio ai Carolingi,* ed. Carlo Bertelli (Milan, 1987), 48–79; and Francoise Monfrin, " À propos de Milan chrétien: Siège épiscopal et topographie chrétienne IVe–VIe siècles," *Cahiers archéologiques,* 39 (1991), 7–46.

27 Dale Kinney, " 'Capella Regina': S. Aquilino in Milan," *Marsyas* 15 (1970–71), 13–35.

28 For the life and career of Ambrose see McLynn, *Ambrose,* passim. For the churches he founded see, among others: Krautheimer, *Three Christian Capitals,* 77ff.; Kinney, "Le chiese," 65ff.; and Monfrin, "A propos," 22ff., 28ff., 32ff.

29 Suzanne Lewis, "The Latin Iconography of the Single-Naved Cruciform Basilica Apostolorum in Milan," *Art Bulletin* 51 (1969), 205–19; idem, "Function and Symbolic Form in the Basilica Apostolorum at Milan," *JSAH* 28 (1969), 83–98.

30 Krautheimer, *Early Christian,* 82ff., and G. Traversi, *Architettura paleocristiana milanese* (Milan, 1964), 111ff.

31 Krautheimer, *Early Christian,* 179, 481 n. 25; and Paolo Verzone, "Le chiese cimiteriali a struttura molteplice nell'Italia settentrionale," *Arte del primo millennio,* Atti del II° convegno per lo studio dell'arte dell'alto medio evo, ed. E. Arslan (Turin, 1950), 28–41.

32 M. Mirabella Roberti, "La cattedrale antica di Milano e il suo battistero," *Arte Lombarda* 8 (1963), 77ff.; Krautheimer, *Three Christian Capitals,* 74ff.; and Kinney, "Le chiese," 48ff.

33 *De sacramentis,* 3.1.4, and 3.2: "in baptismate, quoniam simultudo mortis est . . ." For an English translation see Roy J. Deferrari, *Saint Ambrose, Theological and Dogmatic Works,* Fathers of the Church 44 (Washington, D.C., 1963). For the "rediscovery of the writings of St. Paul for making the theology of baptism" in the later fourth and early fifth centuries see Hugh Riley, *Christian Initiation,* Studies in Antiquity 17 (Washington, D.C., 1974), 213ff. For a discussion of the connection between the writings of Ambrose and the design and function of Early Christian baptisteries within a more political context see Annabel Jane Wharton, "Ritual and Reconstructed Meaning: The Neonian Baptistery in Ravenna," *Art Bulletin* 69 (1987), 358–75; and idem, *Refiguring the Post Classical City* (Cambridge, 1995), 114ff.

34 "Octachorum sanctos templum surrexit in usus / octagonus fons est munere dignus eo / Hoc numero decuit sacri baptismalis aulam / surgere, quo populis vera salus rediit. . . ." *DACL* 1, col. 1386. The English translation is taken from Spiro Kostof, *The Orthodox Baptistery of Ravenna* (New Haven, 1965), 50. For the symbolic meaning of the octagon see ibid., 51, and Richard Krautheimer, "Introduction to an 'Iconography of Medieval Architecture,' " *Journal of the Warburg and Courtauld Institutes* 5 (1942), 1–33, reprinted with a postscript in idem, *Studies,* 115–50, esp. 131ff.

35 Friedrich W. Deichmann, *Ravenna. Haupstadt des spätantiken Abendlandes,* 6 vols. (Wiesbaden, 1958–89), 2 pt. 1, 25–7.

36 ". . . luce resurgentis Christi, qui claustra resoluit /mortis et e tumulis suscitat examines / confessosque reos maculoso crimine solvens / fontis puriflui diluit inriguo." For an analysis of the theological meaning of this passage see Peter Cramer, *Baptism and Change in the Early Middle Ages c. 200–c. 1150* (Cambridge, 1990), 270ff.

37 Krautheimer, *Early Christian,* 176ff., G. De Angelis d'Ossat, "Origine e fortuna dei battisteri ambrosiani," *Arte Lombarda* 14 (1969), 1ff.; Sebastian Ristow, *Frühchristliche Baptisterien,* Jahrbuch für Antike und Christentum Ergänzungsband 27 (Münster, 1998), esp. 68–81; and Jean Guyon, *Les premiers bapitisteres des Gaules (IVe–VIIIe siécles)* (Rome, 2000).

38 Giovanni Pelliccioni, *Le nuove scoperte sugli origini del battistero lateranense,* Memorie della pontificia accademia romana di archeologia 12 (Vatican City, 1973), believes the original, Constantinian bapistery was cylindrical; whereas Krautheimer, *Early Christian,* 468–69, n. 47, argues that, from the beginning, the baptistery was octagonal above ground while resting on circular foundations. For a review of the debate see Blaauw, *Cultus et Decor,* 1:129–36. For a summary of current opinion see Olof Brandt, "Il battistero lateranense dell'Imperatore Costantino e l'architettura contemporanea: Come si crea un'architettura battesimale cristiana?" *Acta Hyperborea* 8 (2001), 117–44. For a discussion of the significance of the inscription see the classic study by Paul Underwood, "The Fountain of Life in Manuscripts of the Gospels," *Dumbarton Oaks Papers* 5 (1950), 53ff.

39 Deichmann, *Ravenna,* remains the most complete study of the subject.

40 Kostof, *The Orthodox Baptistery,* passim; and Deichmann, *Ravenna,* 2 pt. 1:1ff.

41 Ernst Kitzinger, *Byzantine Art in the Making* (Cambridge, Massachusetts, 1977), 58f. and fig. 103.

42 Deichmann, *Ravenna*, 2 pt. 1: 61ff.; Krautheimer, *Early Christian*, 181ff.; and Gillian Mackie, *Early Christian Chapels in the West: Decoration, Function and Patronage* (Toronto, 2003), 172–94.

43 Mark J. Johnson, "On the Burial Places of the Theodosian Dynasty," *Byzantion* 61 (1991), 336ff.

44 Kitzinger, *Byzantine Art*, 53ff. and figs. 93–5. Mackie, op. cit., believes the chapel was dedicated to St. Vincent.

45 Deichmann, *Ravenna*, 1:93ff, and 2 pt. 1:91ff. See also Janet Charlotte Smith, "Form and Function of the Side Chambers of Fifth- and Sixth-Century Churches in Ravenna," *JSAH* (49, 1990), 181–204.

46 B. Ward-Perkins, *From Classical Antiquity*, passim; Mark J. Johnson, "Toward a History of Theodoric's Building Program," *Dumbarton Oaks Papers* 42 (1988), 73–96; and John Morehead, *Theodoric in Italy* (Oxford, 1992), 142ff.

47 Deichmann, *Ravenna*, 2 pt. 1:125ff., and Kitzinger, *Byzantine Art*, 62.

48 Deichmann, *Ravenna*, 1:226ff., 2 pt. 1:45ff., and Krautheimer, *Early Christian*, 232ff.

49 Deichmann, *Ravenna*, 1:257ff., 2 pt. 1:234ff., and Krautheimer, *Early Christian*, 277ff.

50 Eusebius, *Vita Constantini*, 3:29ff.; Prudentius, *Peristephanon*, 12:29–31; and Procopius, *De aedificiis*, 1:1:23ff. For English translations see Caecilia Davis-Weyer, *Early Medieval Art 300–1150* (Englewood Cliffs, New Jersey, 1971), 14; and Cyril Mango, *The Art of the Byzantine Empire*, 13, 74.

51 Roland Günter, *Wand, Fenster und Licht in der Trierer Palastaula und in spätantiken Bauten* (Bonn, 1968); Konrad Onasch, *Lichthöhle und Sternenhaus: Licht und Materie im spätantik-christlichen und frühbyzantinischen Sakralbau* (Basel, 1973); and Dominic James, *God and Gold in Late Antiquity* (Cambridge, 1998), 74–5, 145ff. For the relation between language and aesthetics see Michael Roberts, *The Jeweled Style: Poetry and Poetics in Late Antiquity* (Ithaca and London, 1989), esp. 66ff. For the letter of Constantine see Eusebius Vita Constantini 3.31, translated in Mango, *The Art of the Byzantine Empire*, 12.

Chapter 2: The Roman Response to the Cult of Relics

1 Ep. 4.30. (*A Select Library of Nicene and Post-Nicene Fathers of the Church*, 2nd ser. Grand Rapids, Michigan, 1976, 12:154–55. The Latin text can be found in *Gregorii I Papae Registrum Epistolarum, MGH Epist*, ed. P. Ewald and L. M. Hartmann, Berlin, 1887; reprint 1957, 1:263–66.)

2 Peter Brown, *The Cult of the Saints* (Chicago, 1981), 10.

3 The church of S. Sebastiano, originally dedicated to the Holy Apostles, may be seen as an exception to this general rule in that its design, with a U-shaped ambulatory and no transept, fits the first building type even though it was constructed in an open-air cemetery over a spot associated with the veneration of SS. Peter and Paul. However, two factors suggest that this was a unique situation. 1) The building may pre-date the other basilicas in Rome associated with specific saints and thus may represent an early, experimental stage of development, and 2) the church did not mark the tombs of the apostles but rather a small loggia where a festival commemorating Peter and Paul had been celebrated as early as A.D. 258. For a detailed analysis of S. Sebastiano see Krautheimer, *Corpus*, 4:99–147. For a general discussion of these churches as a group, see Krautheimer, *Rome*, 24–8 and 336–37 with further bibliography.

4 For a detailed discussion of the function of these churches as covered cemeteries see Richard Krautheimer, "Mensa-Coemeterium-Martyrium," *Cahiers archéologiques* 11 (1960) 15–40, reprinted in idem, *Studies*, 35–58. Krautheimer prefers to apply the term *coemeterium* only to the first building type, i.e., S. Lorenzo, S. Agnese, and SS. Marcellinus and Peter, and not to the *basilicae ad corpus*, i.e., St. Peter's and St. Paul's. And yet both groups of churches are known to have been filled with tombs in the Early Christian period. It seems to me that the deciding factor in the choice of design was not so much one of function as one of topography, that is, whether or not the venerated tomb was at ground level and thus available to be incorporated into the body of the church. Friedrich W. Deichmann, on the other hand, stresses, more than Krautheimer, that these buildings functioned as sites for regular church services in addition to their use for burial. Yet in so doing, he fails to explain the reason for placing these churches in cemeteries in the first place and for the wealth of graves they contained. See idem, "Märtyrerbasilika, Martyrion, Memoria and Altargrab," *Römische Mitteilungen* 77 (1970) 144–69, reprinted in idem, *Rom, Ravenna, Konstantinopel, Naher Osten* (Wiesbaden, 1982), 375–401.

5 Krautheimer, "Mensa-Coemetrium-Martyrium," *Studies*, 46–49.

6 For a discussion of pilgrimage in Rome in the early Middle Ages see Peter Llewellyn, *Rome in the Dark Ages* (New York, 1971), 173–98, and Krautheimer, *Rome*, 80–83. The two earliest guide books, *Notitia Ecclesiarum Urbis Romae* and *De Locis Sanctorum Martyrum quae sunt foris Civitate Roma*, both dating from shortly before A.D. 641, are published in Roberto Valentini and Giuseppe Zucchetti, *Codice topografico della città di Roma*, Fonti per la storia d'Italia, 4 vols. (Rome, 1942), 2:67–131.

7 Glanville Downey, *A History of Antioch in Syria* (Princeton, 1961), 364, 387, 415–16. The body of St. Babylos was moved first ca. A.D. 351 to Daphne by order of the caesar Gallus. The remains of the saint were moved two more times before finally being placed in the crossing of a cruciform church built in his honor between 380 and 381. See also G. Downey, "The Shrines of St. Babylos at Antioch and Daphne," *Antioch on the Orontes*, ed. R. Stilwell (Princeton, 1938), 2:45–48.

8 Richard Krautheimer, *Three Christian Capitals*, 80 and 146 n. 23.

9 Ibid.

10 Ibid., 80 and 146 n. 22. See also Suzanne Lewis, "Function and Symbolic Form," 83ff.

11 Ambrose, Ep. 22.10. For the Latin text of this letter together with an English translation see Arthur Kingsley Porter, *Lombard Architecture*, 3 vols. (New Haven, 1917), 2:539–40.

12 Ernst Dassmann, "Ambrosius und die Märtyrer," *Jahrbuch für Antike und Christentum* 18 (1975), 49–68; Brown, *Cult of Saints*, 37; Krautheimer, *Capitals*, 79 and 145 n. 17.

13 Same as note 1 above.

14 John M. McCulloh, "The Cult of Relics in the Letters and 'Dialogues' of Pope Gregory the Great: A Lexicographical Study," *Traditio* 32 (1976), 145–84, and idem, "From Antiquity to the Middle Ages: Continuity and Change in Papal Relic Policy from the 6th to the 8th Century," *Pietas: Festschrift für Bernhard Kötting*, ed. E. Dassmann and K. Suso Frank, Jahrbuch für Antike und Christentum, Ergänzungsband 8 (1980), 313–24.

15 Deichmann, "Märtyrerbasilika," *Rom*, 393–94.

16 *Contra Vigilantium*, cap. 8 (Migne, *PL*, vol. 23, col. 346): ". . . male fecit ergo, Romanus episcopus, qui super mortuorum hominum Petri et Pauli, secundum nos ossa veneranda, secundum te vilem pulvisculum, offert Domino sacrificia, et tumulos eorum Christi arbitratur altaria?"

17 Krautheimer, *Corpus*, 5:259; Otto Nussbaum, *Der Standort des Liturgen am christlichen Atlar vor dem Jahre 1000*, 2 vols.

(Bonn, 1965), 1:228–29; and De Blaauw, *Cultus et Decor*, 2:503ff.

18 Louis Reekmans, "Les cryptes des martyrs romains. Etat de la recherche," *Atti del IX congresso internazionale di archeologia cristiana*, 2 vols. (Vatican City, 1978), 1:275–302. See also Deichmann, "Märtyrerbasilika," *Rome*, 383–84 n. 46.

19 Margarete Weidemann, *Kulturgeschichte der Merowingerzeit nach den Werken Gregors von Tours*, 2 vols. (Mainz, 1982), 2:143–44, provides all references to *cryptae* in the writings of Gregory of Tours. See also May Vieillard-Troiekouroff, *Les monuments religieux de la Gaule d'après les oeuvres de Gregoire de Tours* (Paris, 1976), especially 394–96, and John Crook, *The Architectural Setting of the Cult of Saints in the Early Christian West c. 300–1200* (Oxford, 2000), 48–61.

20 *Liber in gloria martyrum*, 49: "Hic (Irenaeus) in cripta basilicae beati Johannis sub altari (*sic*) est sepultus." W. Seston and C. Perrat, "Une basilique funéraire païenne à Lyon d'après une inscription inédite," *Revue des études anciennes* 49 (1947) 139–59; A. Audin and C. Perrat, "Fouilles exécutées dans la crypte de Saint-Irénée en 1956 et 1957," *Bulletin monumental* 117 (1959), 109–18; Vieillard-Troiekouroff, *Les monuments religieux*, 143–45.

21 *Liber in gloria martyrum*, 33: "Huius enim altaris in posita in altum pulpita locatum habetur, cuius pars inferior in modum criptae ostio clauditur." See Weidemann, *Kulturgeschichte der Merowingerzeit*, 2:144, Vieillard-Troiekouroff, *Les monuments religieux*, 55–56, and Crook, *The Architectural Setting*, 57.

22 Werner Jacobsen, "Saints' Tombs in Frankish Church Architecture," *Speculum* 72 (1997), 1107–43.

23 Noël Duval, *Les églises africaines a deux absides. Recherches archéologiques sur la liturgie chrétienne en Afrique du Nord*, 2 vols. (Paris, 1973), 2:1–9, 69–73, 301–55. For the cult of relics in North Africa see Yvette Duval, *Loca Sanctorum Africae: Le culte des martyrs en Afrique du IVe au VIIe siècle*, Collection de l'école française de Rome, 2 vols. (Paris, 1982). For a general discussion of crypts in Early Christian churches in North Africa see Krautheimer, *Early Christian Architecture*, 200–01. See also Deichmann, "Märtyrerbasilika," *Rom*, 395–96.

24 W. Kleiss, "Neue Befunde zur Chalkopratenkirche in Istanbul," *Akten des VII. Internationalen Kongress für christliche Archäologie*, Trier, 5–11 September 1965 (Vatican City and Berlin, 1969), 587–94, esp. 589–90, pls. CCXCIX–CCCIV; Thomas F. Mathews, *The Early Churches of Constantinople: Architecture and Liturgy* (University Park and London, 1971), 19–33, esp. 26–27, 32–33.

25 G. and M. Sotiriou, *Hi basiliki tou Hagiou Dimitriou tis Thessalonikis* (Athens, 1952); R. F. Hoddinott, *Early Byzantine Churches in Macedonia and Southern Serbia* (London, 1963), 128–34. The evidence for the date of this construction in the second half of the fifth century is discussed by Krautheimer, *Early Christian Architecture*, 132–35, 500 n. 132, and more recently, Beat Brenk, "Zum Baukonzept von Hagios Demetrios in Thessaloniki," *Boreas* 17 (1994), 27–38.

26 See especially Hoddinott, *Early Byzantine Churches*, 134–37 and fig. 64.

27 Hoddinott, *Early Byzantine Churches*, 161–64; Ernst Kitzinger, "The Early Christian Town of Stobi," *Dumbarton Oaks Papers* 3 (1946), 93–98; James R. Wiseman, "Archaeology and History at Stobi, Macedonia," *Rome and the Provinces: Studies in the Transformation of Art and Architecture in the Mediterranean World*, ed. Charles McClendon (New Haven, 1986), 43f., figs. 52–53; and Carolyn S. Snively, "Apsidal Crypts in Macedonia: Possible Places of Pilgrimage," *Akten des XII. Internationalen Kongresses für Christliche Archäologie*, Jahrbuch für Antike und Christentum Ergänzungsband 20, 1 (1995), 2 vols., 2:1179–84.

28 The following discussion of S. Lorenzo fuori-le-mura is derived from the detailed analysis in Krautheimer, *Corpus*, 2:1–144.

29 "Demovit dominus tenebras ut luce creata / His quondam latebris sic modo fulgor inest / Angustos aditus venerabile corpus habebat / Huc ubi nunc populum largior aula capit." Krautheimer, *Corpus*, 2:10. The inscription seen today was set in 1860 and is derived from transcriptions found in several early medieval manuscripts (i.e., the syllogai of Tours, Lorsch IV, and Würzburg). Its original location in the church is unknown, but as the dedicatory inscription it must have occupied a prominent place such as the apse, which was destroyed in the thirteenth century.

30 Documentary evidence for the construction of these churches is lacking; however, Krautheimer dates them to the late sixth century on the basis of the similarity of their masonry to that of the Pelagian basilica of S. Lorenzo. For S. Ermete see Krautheimer, *Corpus*, 1:195–208; for SS. Nereo ed Achilleo on the Via Ardeatina see Krautheimer, *Corpus*, 3:128–34.

31 The bibliography on Gregory the Great is extensive and cannot be cited fully here. Suffice it to mention the study by F. Homes Dudden, *Gregory the Great: His Place in History and Thought*, 2 vols. (London, 1905), which, though very much out of date, still remains basic. More recent studies include: Jeffrey Richards, *Consul of God: The Life and Times of Gregory the Great* (London, 1980); Joan Petersen, *The 'Dialogues' of Gregory the Great and Their Late Antique Cultural Background*, Pontifical Institute of Medieval Studies, Studies and Texts 69 (Toronto, 1984); and Carole Straw, *Gregory the Great: Perfection in Imperfection* (Berkeley and London, 1988), each with additional bibliography. Extremely informative discussions of the city of Rome in the time of Gregory the Great are found in Llewellyn, *Rome*, 78–108, and Krautheimer, *Rome*, 59–87.

32 *LP*, 1:312: ". . . fecit ut super corpus beati Petri missae celebrarentur."

33 Krautheimer, *Corpus*, 5:259–61; Toynbee and Ward Perkins, *The Shrine*, 215; and Sible de Blaauw, "Die Krypta in Stadtrömischen Kirchen: Abbild eines Pilgerziels," *Akten des XII. Internationalen Kongresses*, 1:559–67.

34 Gregory of Tours, *Liber in gloria martyrum*, 1.28, found in Migne, *PL*, vol. 71, col. 728ff. The English translation comes from Llewellyn, *Rome*, 175.

35 Some modern commentators on Gregory of Tours' description of St. Peter's have suggested that he was, in fact, describing the arrangement of an altar tomb and annular crypt, which would mean that it existed prior to Gregory the Great's pontificate (see, for example, Krautheimer, *Rome*, 86), but this is clearly not the case. As I mentioned above, Gregory of Tours was very familiar with crypts in association with the tombs of saints in churches in Gaul. Indeed, he uses the term *cripta* several times in his writings (see note 19 above); it seems highly unlikely, therefore, that he would have failed to mention such an important feature at St. Peter's had it been in existence at the time of his writing. It should be noted, however, that Gregory of Tours never visited Rome; his information was derived from the firsthand observations of a deacon, Agiulf, who visited Rome in 588. See Blaauw, *Cultus et Decor*, 2:530–34.

36 Apollonj-Ghetti, "Esplorazioni," 175.

37 *LP*, 1:310: ". . . fecit ut super corpus beati Petri missas celebrantur; item et in ecclesiam beati Pauli . . . eadem fecit."

38 Krautheimer, *Corpus*, 5:93–164, esp. 134–35, 163, and most recently, Francesco Tolotti, "Le confessioni succedutesi sul sepolchro di S. Paolo," *Rivista di archeologia cristiana*, 59 (1983) 87–149, esp. 87–103.

39 "Sub confessione . . . sunt due porte nunc murate, per quas

iter erat per cemeterium in quo iacent multa milia martyrum; supra quod est altare putei: et est super illum pavimentum tessellatum, a leva are maxime et chori: est clausum cemeterium illud" (Biblioteca Apostolica Vaticana lat. 6780). Quoted by Tolotti, "Le confessioni succedutesi," 100. The mosaic pavement, mentioned by Panvinio as lying above the underground cemetery, is shown in two of his drawings accompanying this text as a narrow band stretching almost the full length of the south arm of the transept. For Panvinio, the directional indication, "to the left of the high altar," is determined by facing the nave, i.e., west. See ibid., 101, fig. 6, and Krautheimer, *Corpus*, 5:129, 134–35, fig. 125 a,b.

40 Tolotti, "Le confessioni succedutesi," 96, fig. 4, 102–3.

41 "Sed et ego . . . ad sacratissimum corpus sancti Pauli apostoli meliorare volui, et quia necesse erat, ut iuxta sepulcrum eiusmodi effodiri altius debuisset. . . ." For the source of the letter see note 1 above. See also Krautheimer, *Corpus*, 5:99.

42 For Gregory's sojourn in Constantinople see Dudden, *Gregory the Great*, 1:123–56, and Richards, *Consul of God*, 37–40. See also Claude Dagens, "Gregoire le Grand et le monde oriental," *Rivista di storia e letturatura religiosa* 17 (1981), 243–52.

43 *LP*, 1:317. See also Krautheimer, *Rome*, 72, 90; Mirella Colucci, *Bonifacio IV (609–15): Momenti e questioni di un pontificio* (Rome, 1976), 25–36. For the later date of 613, see Herman Gertman, *More Veterum* (Groningen, 1975), 226.

44 Krautheimer, *Corpus*, 1:14ff., provides detailed archaeological information but parts of the *basilica ad corpus* are incorrectly attributed to Constantine. The church is now universally assigned to Honorius I. See Krautheimer, "Mensa-Coemeterium-Martyrium," *Studies*, 36 and idem, *Rome*, 85.

45 Krautheimer, *Corpus*, 3:153–74, and Crook, *The Architectural Setting*, 80–83. In this case, the saint's body may have been moved into the crypt for the adjoining catacomb. If so, the Gregorian stricture against translating relics was already breaking down, prompted perhaps by the growing importance of the annular crypt as an architectural device to promote the cult of relics.

46 See note 6 above.

47 Krautheimer, *Corpus*, 1:156ff.; B. M. Apollonj Ghetti, *S. Crisogono*, Le chiese illustrate, 92 (Rome, 1966), 39ff. Crook (*The Architectural Setting*, 85) thinks the crypt may be later, but the rather crude nature of the masonry supports the traditional, early-eighth-century date. See Robert Coates-Stephens, "Dark Age Architecture in Rome," *Papers of the British School at Rome*, 65 (1997), 223.

48 *LP*, 1:417: ". . . concessas sibi columnas VI onichinas volutiles ab Eutychio exarcho . . . statuit erga presbiterium ante confessionem tres a dextris et tres a sinistris iuxta alias antiquas sex filopares."

49 Krautheimer, *Rome*, 90. For references to the translation of relics by Eastern popes see *LP*, 1:310, 331, 334, 330, 332, 360.

50 Nicole Herrmann-Mascard, *Les reliques des saints. Formation coutumière d'un droit* (Paris, 1975), 50–53.

51 *LP*, 1:455, 464.

52 Herrmann-Mascard, *Les reliques*, 51–52; *LP*, 1:511, 2:12–13, 29, 59.

53 Krautheimer, *Rome*, 123.

54 Friedrich Prinz, "Stadtrömisch-italische Märtyrreliquien und fränkischer Reichsadel im Maas-Moselraum," *Historisches Jahrbuch* 87 (1967), 1–25, and Julia Smith, "Old Saints, New Cults: Rome Relics in Carolingian Francia," *Early Medieval Rome and the Christian West: Essays in Honour of Donald A. Bullough*, ed. J. Smith (Leiden, 2000), 317–39.

55 Franz Alto Bauer, "La frammentazione liturgica nella chiesa romana del primo medioevo," *Rivista di archeologia cristiana* 75 (1999), 384–446, provides an excellent discussion of the development of chapels and secondary altars, in addition to crypts, in Roman churches during the early Middle Ages.

Chapter 3: Romanitas *and the Barbarian West*

1 Among the many historical studies, J. M. Wallace-Hadrill, *The Barbarian West 400–1000*, rev. 3rd ed. (London, 1967, rep. Oxford, 1988), remains a classic. Malcolm Todd, *The Early Germans* (Oxford, 1992), provides a more anthropological and archaeological approach. See also: Judith Herrin, *The Formation of Christendom* (Princeton, 1987); Klaus Randsborg, *The First Millennium* A.D. *in Europe and the Mediterranean: An Archaeological Essay* (Cambridge, 1991); Leslie Webster and Michelle Brown, eds., *The Transformation of the Roman World* A.D. *400–900* (London, 1997); P. S. Barnwell, *Kings, Courtiers and Imperium: The Barbarian West, 565–725* (London, 1997); and Walter Pohl, ed., *Kingdoms of the Empire: The Integration of Barbarians in Late Antiquity* (Leiden, 1997). For a summary of the debate about the nature of urban life in the early Middle Ages see Bryan Ward-Perkins, "Urban Continuity?" *Towns in Transition: Urban Evolution in Late Antiquity and the Early Middle Ages*, ed. N. Christie and S. T. Loseby (Aldershot, England, 1996), 4–17; and Nancy Gauthier, "From the Ancient City to the Medieval Town: Continuity and Change in the Early Middle Ages," *The World of Gregory of Tours*, ed. Kathleen Mitchell and Ian Wood (Leiden, 2002), 47–66. For economic developments see McCormick, *Origins*, 27–119.

2 Bernhard Salin, *Die altgermanische Tierornamentik* (Stockholm, 1935); Jean Hubert et al., *Europe of the Invasions* (New York, 1969), 209–86; Peter Lasko, *The Kingdom of the Franks* (London, 1971); and more recently *From Attila to Charlemagne: Arts of the Early Medieval Period in The Metropolitan Museum of Art*, ed. Katharine R. Brown et al. (New York, 2000).

3 Todd, *The Early Germans*, 62ff.; Walter Sage, "Frühmittelalterlicher Holzbau," *Karl der Grosse*, 4 vols. (Düsseldorf, 1965), 3:573–90. For a broad and richly illustrated overview see Walter Horn and Ernest Born, *The Plan of St. Gall*, 3 vols. (Berkeley and Los Angeles, 1979), 2:23–77.

4 Richard Fletcher, *The Barbarian Conversion from Paganism to Christianity* (Berkeley and Los Angeles, 1997) provides a survey of the subject.

5 See most recently: Maurice Scellès, "Toulouse: Église Notre-Dame La Daurade," *Les premiers monuments chrètiens de la France*, 3 vols. (Paris, 1995–98), 2:190–96 with additional bibliography. Helen Woodruff, "The Iconography and Date of the Mosaics of La Daurade," *Art Bulletin* 13 (1931), 80–104, remains basic. See also Gillian Mackie, "La Daurade: A Royal Mausoleum," *Cahiers archéologiques* 42 (1994), 17–34, and idem, *Early Christian Chapels*.

6 *VK*, 147–48; *VK, Nbd*, 219–21. Gregory of Tours, *Liber in gloria martyrum*, cap. 61. For an English translation see *Gregory of Tours: Glory of the Martyrs*, trans. and introduction Raymond Van Dam (Liverpool, 1988), 85.

7 Scellès, "Toulouse: Eglise Notre-Dame," *Les premiers monuments*, 2:190. Gregory of Tours, *Historia Francorum*, VII:10.

8 Richard Krautheimer, "Sancta Maria Rotunda," *Studies in Early Christian, Medieval, and Renaissance Art* (New York, 1969), 107–14.

9 E. A. Thompson, *The Goths of Spain* (Oxford, 1969); A. Ferreiro, *The Visigoths in Gaul and Spain* A.D. *418–711: A Bibliography* (Leiden, 1988); and Roger Collins, *Early Medieval Spain*, 2nd ed. (London, 1995), and idem, *Visigothic Spain 409–711* (Oxford, 2004).

10 J. Fontaine, *Isidore de Séville et la culture classique dans l'Espagne visigothique* (Paris, 1959). For brief discussions see Pierre Riché,

Education and Culture in the Barbarian West, trans. J. J. Contreni (Columbia, South Carolina, 1978), 255ff., and Herrin, *The Formation*, 233ff.

11 Thilo Ulbert, *Frühchristliche Basiliken mit Doppelapsiden auf der iberischen Halbinsel: Studien zur Architektur- und Liturgiegeschichte* (Berlin, 1978); Stephanie J. Maloney, "Early Christian Double-apsed Churches in Iberia. Some Considerations," *Art History* 3 (1980), 129–43; and Noël Duval, "Les relations entre l'Afrique et l'Espagne dans le domaine liturgique: Existe-t-il une explication commune pour le 'contre-absides' et 'contre-choeurs'?" *Rivista di archeologia cristiana* 76 (2000), 429–76.

12 Theodor Hauschild, "Westgotische Quaderbauten des 7. Jahrhunderts auf der iberischen Halbinsel," *Madrider Mitteilungen* 13 (1972), 270–85; Karen Kingsley, "Visigothic Architecture in Spain and Portugal: A Study of Masonry, Documents, and Form," Ph.D. diss., University of California at Berkeley, 1980; Helmut Schlunk and Theodor Hauschild, *Die Denkmäler der frühchristlichen und westgotischen Zeit* (Mainz, 1978); and Achim Arbeiter, "Die Anfänge der Quaderarchitektur im westgotenzeitlichen Hispanien," *Innovation in der Spätantike*, ed. Beat Brenk (Wiesbaden, 1996), 11–44.

13 Karl Friedrich Stroheker, "Das spanische Westgotenriech und Byzanz," *Bonner Jahrbücher* 163 (1963), 252–74; J. N. Hillgarth, "Coins and Chronicles: Propaganda in Sixth-Century Spain and the Byzantine Background," *Historia* 15 (1966), 483–508 reprinted in idem, *Visigothic Spain, Byzantium and the Irish* (London, 1985), II:483ff.; Michael McCormick, *Eternal Victory: Triumphal Rulership in Late Antiquity* (Cambridge and Paris, 1986), 297–327; and Pablo C. Diaz and M. R. Valverde, "The Theoretical Strength and Practical Weakness of the Visigothic Monarchy of Toledo," *Rituals of Power from Late Antiquity to the Early Middle Ages*, ed. Frans Theuws and Janet L. Nelson, *The Transformation of the Roman World*, vol. 8 (Leiden, 2000), 59–93.

14 Reccared was the first to assume this title. Wallace-Hadrill, *The Barbarian West*, 122, and Diaz and Valverde, "The Theoretical Strength," 76. On the other hand, Andrew Gillett, "Was Ethnicity Politicized in the Earliest Medieval Kingdoms?" *On Barbarian Identity: Critical Approaches to Ethnicity in the Early Middle Ages* (Turnhout, 2002), 116, points out that the name *Flavius* was in common usage in late antiquity and thus, although clearly Roman, did not necessarily carry imperial connotations.

15 For Isidore see *Conquerors and Chroniclers of Early Medieval Spain*, trans. and introduction by Kenneth B. Wolf, 2nd ed. (Liverpool, 1999), 12 and 79ff. For the Byzantine perspective see Ostrogorsky, *History of the Byzantine State*, 28ff.

16 The quote comes from Wallace-Hadrill, *The Barbarian West*, 129. For the full Latin inscription and a detailed architectural analysis see Schlunk and Hauschild, *Die Denkmäler*, 204–9, pls. 102–9. See also Kingsley, "Visigothic Architecture," 22–27, 119–23. Roger Collins, *Visigothic Spain*, 186–96, cautions that the chronology ofVisigothic churches remains problematic.

17 *Alahan: An Early Christian Monastery in Southern Turkey*, ed. Mary Gough (Toronto, 1985), 30ff., 102ff. and figs. 48–49. For Frankish Gaul see, for example, the apse in the plan of St. Martin at Angers, seventh century: Hubert et al., *Europe*, 307 fig. 348.

18 Schlunk and Hauschild, *Die Denkmäler*, 209–11, pls. 110–13; Kingsley, "Visigothic Architecture," 57–75.

19 Jerrilyn Dodds, *Architecture and Ideology in Early Medieval Spain* (University Park, 1990), 18–19.

20 Kingsley, "Visigothic Architecture," 69–70, believes that only the two capitals of the west arm are ancient and that the others, along with their imposts, are to be dated to the first half of the eleventh century.

21 Schlunk and Hauschild, *Die Denkmäler*, 218–27, pls. 120–3, 126–38; and Kingsley, "Visigothic Architecture," 34–49.

22 Dodds, *Architecture and Ideology*, 16–26, describes and discusses the liturgical divisions within these churches, but her conclusion that they represent a "largely unconscious" desire on the part of the Hispano-Roman clergy to assert their hegemony over the Visigothic, and formerly Arian, ruling elite remains questionable. Increased compartmentalization of interior space was not unique to churches in Spain; in fact, it was a general characteristic of the period. For a fine overview of architecture and liturgy in the early Middle Ages see Sible De Blaauw, "Architecture and Liturgy in Late Antiquity and the Middle Ages," *Archiv für Liturgiewissenschaft* 33 (1991), 1ff., with extremely valuable advice about methodology at the end, 31–34. See most recently Cristina Godoy Fernandez, *Arqueologia y liturgia. Iglesias hispanicas (siglos IV–VIII)* (Barcelona, 1995).

23 André Grabar, "Le rayonnement de l'art sassanide dans le monde chrétien," *La Persia nel medioevo*, Accademia nazionale dei Lincei, Quaderni 160 (Rome, 1971), 679–707; Prudence Harper, *The Royal Hunter. Art of the Sasanian Empire* (New York, 1978); and Martin Harrison, *A Temple for Byzantium* (Austin, Texas, 1989), 122ff.

24 Schlunk and Hauschild, *Die Denkmäler*, 227–28, pl. 133b identify the belt buckle as a Byzantine import, whereas it is believed to be a Visigothic imitation by Gisela Ripoll Lopez, *Toreutica de la Betica (siglos VI y VII D.C.)* (Barcelona, 1998), 89 fig. 11.2, 92 and 104–5.

25 Kingsley, "Visigothic Architecture," 47ff., and Jean-Marie Hoppe, "L'église espagnole visigothique de San Pedro de la Nave (El Campillo—Zamora): Un programme iconographique de la fin du VIIe siècle," *Annales d'histoire de l'art et d'archeologie* 9 (1987), 59–81. For Early Christian precedents see Achim Arbeiter, "Frühe hispanische Darstellungen des Daniel in der Löwengrube," *Boreas* 17 (1994), 5–12. For a roughly contemporary Visigothic belt buckle with felines strikingly similar to those in the Daniel relief see *The Art of Medieval Spain A.D. 500–1200*, The Metropolitan Museum of Art (New York, 1993), 67–68, no. 27.

26 *Alahan*, ed. Gough, passim.

27 Schlunk and Hauschild, *Die Denkmäler*, 230–34, pls. 141–6; *The Art of Medieval Spain*, 49–50.

28 Lasko, *The Kingdom*, 25–32; Edward James, *The Franks* (Oxford, 1988), 59–62; and more recently *Die Franken—Wegbereiter Europas*, exhib. cat. Reiss-Museum Mannheim, 2 vols. (Mainz, 1997), 1:173–82. Birgit Arrhenius suggests much of the garnet cloisonné in Childeric's tomb originated as panels manufactured in Constantinople that were dispersed among Germanic allies of the empire in northern Europe: "Garnet Jewelry of the Fifth and Sixth Centuries," *From Attila to Charlemagne*, 215–16. The treasure was first published in Jean-Jacques Chifflet, *Anastasius Childerici I, Francorum regis, sine Thesaurus sepulchris Tonaci Neruisrum* (Antwerp, 1655). For a summary and analysis of Childeric's career see James, *The Franks*, 64–77, and Eugen Ewig, *Die Merowinger und das Frankenreich*, 2nd rev. ed. (Stuttgart, 1993) 14–17.

29 Gregory of Tours, *Historiae Francorum* (henceforth *HF*), II.38. For an English translation see *Gregory of Tours: History of the Franks*, trans. and introduction by Lewis Thorpe (Harmondsworth, 1974), 154. See also McCormick, *Eternal Victory*, 335–37, and Steven Fanning, "Clovis Augustus and Merovingian *Imitatio Imperii*," *The World of Gregory of Tours*, 321–36.

30 Gregory of Tours, *HF*, II.14; *Gregory of Tours*, Thorpe, 130. For analyses see Weidemann, *Kulturgeschichte der Merowingerzeit*, 2:145–51; Vieillard-Troiekouroff, *Les monuments religieux*,

311–24; and Luce Pietri, "Tours: Basilique Saint-Martin," *Les premiers monuments*, 2:106–10.

31 Gregory of Tours, *HF*, II.43; *Gregory of Tours*, Thorpe, 158; and James, *Franks*, 158.

32 Gregory of Tours, *HF*, II.31; and *Gregory of Tours*, Thorpe, 144.

33 Monique Jannet-Vallat et al., "Vienne: Eglise Saint-Pierre," *Les premiers monuments*, 1:254–66, and Jean Hubert, "La basilique de Martin le Confesseur," *Arts et vie sociale de la fin du monde antique au Moyen Age* (Geneva, 1977), 297–303.

34 Paul-Albert Février, "Poitiers: Baptistère Saint-Jean," *Les premiers monuments*, 2:290–301, summarizes and supersedes earlier studies. The current program of detailed archaeological investigations and restoration will no doubt clarify many issues. For a preliminary report see Brigitte Boissavit-Camus et al., "Archéologie et restauration des monuments. Instaurer de véritables 'études archéologiques préalables'," *Bulletin monumental* 161 (2003), 199–201, 213f.

35 Hubert et al., *Europe*, 38–48, 170 fig. 181, and Lasko, *The Kingdom*, 104, fig. 101.

36 Denise Fossard, "Les chapitaux de marbre du VIIe siècle en Gaule: Style et evolution," *Cahiers archéologiques* 2 (1947), 69–85.

37 Hubert et al., *Europe*, 40, 47, fig. 54.

38 Xavier Barral I Altet et al., "Poitiers: Chapelle funéraire dite 'hypogée des Dunes'," *Les premiers monuments*, 2:302–9 with earlier bibliography. See also Crook, *The Architectural Setting*, 61–62.

39 For Frankish metalwork and manuscripts see Lasko, *The Kingdom*, esp. 55–62 and 106ff., and Hubert et al., *Europe*, 165ff. For the Hornhausen relief see K. Böhner, "Die Reliefplatten von Hornhausen," *Jahrbuch des Römisch-Germanischen Zentralmuseums* 23/24 (1976/77), 89ff. Ernst Kitzinger, "Interlace and Icons: Form and Function in Early Insular Art," *The Age of Migrating Ideas: Early Medieval Art in Northern Britain and Ireland*, ed. R. Michael Spearman and John Higgitt (Edinburgh, 1993), 6, proposes an apotropaic function for the relief.

40 Marquise de Maillé, *Les cryptes de Jouarre* (Paris, 1971) and more recently Gilbert-Robert Delahaye and Patrick Perin, "Jouarre: Eglise funéraire Saint-Paul," *Les premiers monuments*, 3:188–97. For the sculpture see also Lasko, *The Kingdom*, 99–102. For a new interpretation see Claude de Mecquenem, "Les cryptes de Jouarre (Seine-et-Marne). Des indices pour une nouvelle chronologie," *Archéologie médiévale* 32 (2002), 1–29.

41 For Le Mans see Stephen Johnson, *Late Roman Fortifications* (Totowa, New Jersey, 1983), 38–41, 89–91, pls. 1–3. For discussion of *opus reticulatum* see James C. Anderson, Jr., *Roman Architecture and Society* (Baltimore and London, 1997), 145–51. For its absence in Roman Gaul see Ward-Perkins, *Roman Imperial*, 223.

42 Barbara A. Watkinson, "Lorsch, Jouarre et l'appareil décoratif du Val de Loire," *Cahiers de civilisation médiévale* 33 (1990), 49–63.

43 Delahaye and Perin, "Jouarre," 196. On the other hand, de Mecquenem, "Les cryptes," 20–21, prefers to assign the west wall to a period between the late tenth and middle eleventh centuries, but the similarity to these later examples is far from exact.

44 Among the most recent general studies are: Neil Christie, *The Lombards* (Oxford, 1995); Paolo Delogu, "Il regno longobardo," *Longobardi e bizantini*, P. Delogu et al., Storia d'Italia, vol. 1 (Turin, 1980); idem, "Lombard and Carolingian Italy," and T. S. Brown, "Byzantine Italy c. 680–876," both in *The New Cambridge Medieval History c. 700–c. 900*, ed. Rosamond McKitterick (Cambridge, 1995), 290–310 and 320–48; *I Longobardi*, ed. Gian Carlo Menis (Milan, 1990); *Il futuro dei Longobardi: L'Italia e la construzione dell'Europa di Carlo Magno*, ed. Carlo Bertelli and Gian Pietro Brogiolo (Milan and Brescia, 2000); and Chris Wickham, *Early Medieval Italy: Central Power and Local Society 400–1000* (Ann Arbor, 1989).

45 Stefano Gasparri, "Kingship Rituals and Ideology in Lombard Italy," *Rituals of Power*, 107.

46 See especially McCormick, *Eternal Victory*, 289–93, with additional bibliography. For illustrations and brief commentary see also *I Longobardi*, 96, and Hubert et al., *Europe*, 247–48, figs. 271–72. For the *missorium* of Theodosius see Kitzinger, *Byzantine Art*, 31–33, figs. 57–59.

47 Gasparri, "Kingship Rituals," 106–7. The primary source is Paul the Deacon's *Historia Longobardorum* (henceforth *HL*) 5.30, written at the end of the eighth century. The standard English translation is *Paul the Deacon, History of the Lombards*, trans. William D. Foulke (Philadelphia, 1905) reprinted several times since then.

48 Bryan Ward-Perkins, *From Classical Antiquity*, 166–72, 179–99; Cristina La Rocca, "Public Buildings and urban change in northern Italy in the early medieval period," *The City in Late Antiquity*, ed. John Rich (London, 1992), 161–80; and Gian Pietro Brogiolo, "Ideas of the Town in Italy during the Transition from Antiquity to the Middle Ages," *The Idea and Ideal of the Town between Late Antiquity and the Early Middle Ages*, ed. G. P. Brogiolo and Bryan Ward-Perkins, *The Transformation of the Roman World*, vol. 4 (Leiden, 1999), 99–126. Chris Wickham, "Aristocratic Power in Eighth Century Lombard Italy," *After Rome's Fall: Narrators and Sources in Early Medieval History*, Essays Presented to Walter Goffart, ed. A. C. Murray (Toronto, 1998), 159–60, stresses the limited nature of the maintenance of the urban fabric. See now Gian Pietro Brogiolo, *La città nell'alto medioevo italiano: Archeologia e storia* (Rome, 1998).

49 *HL*, 4.21. See Bryan Ward-Perkins, *From Classical Antiquity*, passim, for Lombard patronage of this church and others, especially in Pavia.

50 *HL*, 4.34. For the plan and section of this church see *Il futuro dei Longobardi*, 240–43, figs. 141–42, 248 ns. 262–63.

51 The most recent and complete study is Judson Emerick, *The Tempietto del Clitunno near Spoleto*, 2 vols. (University Park, Pennsylvania, 1998). Carola Jäggi, *San Salvatore in Spoleto* (Wiesbaden, 1998), 149ff., also makes important contributions to our understanding of the building.

52 Pliny the Younger, *Epistolae*, 8.8. For an English translation see *Pliny, Letters and Panegyricus*, trans. Betty Radice, vol. 2, Loeb Classical Library (Cambridge, Massachusetts, 1969), 23–27.

53 Emerick, *The Tempietto*, 1:423–25, offers a detailed discussion of the procedures, strengths, and limitations of this analysis. It should be noted that Emerick prefers to leave the issue of date open and suggests several possible scenarios for its contruction, from the late seventh to the ninth centuries. Ibid., 1:347–422. Nevertheless, for the reasons stated here, I agree with Jäggi that the Tempietto dates to the early 700s.

54 Emerick, *The Tempietto*, 1:295–345 and 2:figs. 146–50, 213–14. For color plates of these frescoes see *I dipinti murali e l'edicola marmorea del Tempietto sul Clitunno*, ed. Giordana Benazzi (Todi, 1985). For the Mt. Sinai icons and frescoes of S. Maria Antiqua in Rome see Kitzinger, *Byzantine Art*, 116–22, figs. 216–17, 221, and P. J. Nordhagen, *The Frescoes of John VII (A.D. 705–707) in A. Maria Antiqua in Rome*, Institutum Romanum Norvegiae, Acta ad archaeologiam et artium historiam petinentia 3 (Rome, 1968). For Rome in general during this time see Krautheimer, *Rome*, 89ff. Among others, however, Thomas F. X. Noble, *The Republic of St. Peter: The Birth of the Papal State*

680–825 (Philadelphia, 1984), 185–88, discounts the notion of Byzantine dominance during this period.

55 Delogu, "Il regno longobardo," 99–101; idem, "Lombard and Carolingian Italy," 294; and Brown "Byzantine Italy," 322–23.

56 *Il Regesto di Farfa*, ed. Ignazio Giorgio and Ugo Balzani, Bibliotheca della società romana di storia patria, 5 vols., 1883–1914, 22–25, docs. 1 and 2. These letters are also reprinted in Charles B. McClendon, *The Imperial Abbey of Farfa: Architectural Currents in the Early Middle Ages* (New Haven, 1987), 125–28. See also Emerick, *The Tempietto*, 1:372–75.

57 The most recent and detailed study with earlier bibliography is Jäggi, *San Salvatore*.

58 Hubert et al., *Europe*, 39.

59 Jäggi, *San Salvatore*, 84ff.

60 The so-called "fondo Tullio" church at Aquielia, probably from the sixth century, may have had a square crossing with a dome of light material above as cited in Paolo Verzone, *The Art of Europe: The Dark Ages from Theodoric to Charlemagne*, trans. Pamela Waley (New York, 1968), 78, fig. 36, and 80. I wish to thank James Morganstern for pointing this out to me.

61 Among the most important studies of S. Sofia are Hans Belting, "Studien zum beneventanischen Hof in 8. Jahrhundert," *Dumbarton Oaks Papers* 16 (1962), 141–93; *Il futuro dei Longobardi*, 368–69; M. Rotili, *Benevento romana e longobarda. L'immagine urbana* (Naples, 1986), 184–201; and A. Rusconi, "La chiesa di S. Sofia di Benevento," *Corso di cultura sull'arte Ravennate e Bizantina* 14 (1967), 339–59.

62 "Arichis igitur princeps illustris, perfecta iam sancte Sophie basilica, quam ad exemplar illius condidit Justiniane. . . ." *Translatio sancti Mercurii, MGH Scriptores rerum Langobardicarum et Italicarum saec VI–IX*, ed. G. Waitz (Hannover, 1878, repr. 1964), 576–77.

63 See the classic study of this notion: Krautheimer, "Introduction to an 'Iconography'." See also Eugene W. Kleinbauer, "Pre-Carolingian Concepts of Architectural Planning," *The Medieval Mediterranean Cross Cultural Contacts*, ed. M. J. Chiat and K. L. Reyerson (Minnesota, 1988), 67–79.

64 For the writings of Arculf see *Adamnani de locis sanctis* 3.3. For an English translation with Latin text see *Adamnan's "De Locis Sanctis*," ed. D. Meehan, Scriptores Latini Hiberniae, 3 (Dublin, 1958), 108–9, and for Procopius, *De aedificis*, 1:1:23ff. For an English translation with the original Greek text see *Procopius VII, Buildings*, trans. H. B. Dewing and G. Downey (Cambridge, Massachusetts, 1940), 13ff. For the English translation alone see Mango, *Art of the Byzantine Empire*, 72ff. The circumstances and importance of the account of Arculf's travels are discussed further in the next chapter.

65 Paul the Deacon, *Historia Romana*, 16.11. See *Pauli Diaconi Historia Romana*, ed. Amedeo Crivellucci, Fonti per la storia d'Italia 51 (1914), 231ff. Noted also by Janet Nelson, "Making a Difference in Eighth-Century Politics: The Daughters of Desiderius," *After Rome's Fall*, 177.

66 Ottorino Bertolini, "Carlomagno e Benevento," *Karl der Grosse*, 4 vols. (Düsseldorf, 1965), 1:609–71; Stefano Gasparri, *I duchi longobardi*, Istituto storico italiano per il medio evo, Studi storici 109 (Rome, 1978), 98–100; and more recently Roger Collins, *Charlemagne* (Toronto, 1998), 60–64, 70–72.

67 John Mitchell, "Artistic Patronage and Cultural Strategies in Lombard Italy," *Towns and their Territories between Late Antiquity and the Early Middle Ages*, ed. G. P. Brogiolo et al., The Transformation of the Roman World, volume 9 (Leiden, 2000), 361–70.

68 Werner Jacobsen, "San Salvatore in Brescia," *Studien zur mittelalterlichen Kunst 800–1250*, Festschrift für Florentine Mütherich zum 70. Geburtstag (Munich, 1985), 75–80, proposes a ninth-century date, while Gian Pietro Brogiolo and others assign the church to the middle of the eighth century: see, with additional bibliography, *L'Èta altomedievale: longobardi e carolingi, San Salvatore* (Brescia, 1999), esp. 84ff.

69 Pietro and Ornella Rugo, *Il tempietto longobardo di Cividale del Friuli* (Pordenone, 1990). The most detailed study, which proposes a date before 774, remains Hans Peter L'Orange and Hjalmar Torp, *Il tempietto longobardo di Cividale*, Acta ad archaeologium et artium historiam pertinentia 7, 3 vols. (Rome 1977–79).

Chapter 4: The Christianization of Anglo-Saxon England

1 Kevin Crossley-Holland, trans., and Bruce Mitchell, ed., *The Battle of Maldon and Other Old English Poems*, London, 1965, 69.

2 *Historia ecclesiastica gentis Anglorum* (henceforth cited as *HE*) was finished by Bede in 731 while a monk, scholar, and teacher at the abbey of Jarrow in Northumbria. The standard edition of Bede's historical writings is Charles Plummer, ed., *Venerabilis Baedae Opera Historica*, 2 vols. (Oxford, 1896; reprinted 1969). A reliable edition of the Latin text, together with an excellent English translation, can be found in Bertram Colgrave and R.A.B. Mynors, eds., *Bede's Ecclesiastical History of the English People* (Oxford, 1969).

3 David M. Wilson, "Introduction," *The Archaeology of Anglo-Saxon England*, ed. David M. Wilson (Cambridge, 1976), 7–8. For a somewhat different view, stressing the continuity between Roman Britain and Anglo-Saxon England, see in the same volume the essay by Martin Biddle, "Towns," 99–150, esp. 103–12.

4 Rosemary Cramp, "'Beowulf' and Archaeology," *Medieval Archaeology* 1 (1957), 68–77, and idem, "The Hall in Beowulf and Archaeology," *Heroic Poetry in the Anglo-Saxon Period: Studies in Honor of Jess B. Bessinger, Jr.*, ed. J. Damico and J. Leyerle, Studies in Medieval Culture 32 (Kalamazoo, Michigan, 1993), 331–46. For the remains of a series of impressive long halls found at the Anglo-Saxon royal villa at Yeavering, see Brian Hope-Taylor, *Yeavering: An Anglo-British Centre of early Northumbria*, Department of the Environment, Archaeological Reports No. 7 (London, 1977), passim.

5 For two excellent surveys of this question see Peter V. Addyman, "The Anglo-Saxon House: A New Review," *Anglo-Saxon England* 1 (1972), 273–307, and Philip Rahtz, "Buildings and rural settlements," *Archaeology of Anglo-Saxon England*, 49–98. For a more recent survey see Philip Dixon, "Secular Architecture," *The Making of England: Anglo-Saxon Art and Culture AD 600–900*, ed. Leslie Webster and Janet Backhouse (London and Toronto, 1991), 67–70, and Martin Welch, *Discovering Anglo-Saxon England* (University Park, Pennsylvania, 1992), 14–53.

6 *HE*, 2.1.

7 Nicholas Brooks, *The Early History of the Church of Canterbury* (Leicester, 1984), 4; and Richard Gameson, "Augustine of Canterbury: Context and Achievement," *St Augustine and the Conversion of England*, ed. Richard Gameson (Stroud, 1999), 10–12. These letters of introduction are mentioned in *Greg. Ep.* 6.50–54.

8 *HE*, 1.25–26.

9 Frank Jenkins, "St. Martin's Church at Canterbury: A Survey of the Earliest Structural Features," *Medieval Archaeology* 9 (1965), 11–15, and Jonathan Rady, "Excavations at St. Martin's Hill, Canterbury, 1984–85," *Archaeologia Cantiana* 104 (1987), 123–30, where it is suggested that the building may have originated as part of a Roman villa instead of a church, as previously supposed.

10 *HE*, 1.26.

11 Ibid., 1.33.

12 Kevin Blockley, Margaret Sparks, and Tim Tatton-Brown, *Canterbury Cathedral Nave: Archaeology, History and Architecture* (Canterbury, 1997), esp. 12–14, 95–100. These limited findings suggest that it was not a Roman church, as Bede reports, but a new structure reusing Roman material. Yet such a small area was explored that it is impossible to know whether this actually represents the building Bede is referring to. For words of caution see Nicholas Brooks, "Canterbury, Rome and the Construction of English Identity," *Early Medieval Rome*, 230–32.

13 William St. J. Hope, "Recent discoveries in the abbey church of St. Austin of Canterbury," *Archaeologia* 66 (1914–15), 377–400, reprinted in *Archaeologia Cantiana* 32 (1917), 1–26. For a general discussion of the site see Harold M. and Joan Taylor, *Anglo-Saxon Architecture*, 2 vols. (Cambridge, 1965) 1:134–43, 1:145–48.

14 In addition to the studies cited in the preceding note see the detailed report by A. D. Saunders, "Excavations in the Church of St Augustine's Abbey, Canterbury: 1955–58," *Medieval Archaeology* 22 (1978), 25–63.

15 *HE*, 1.33, 2.3. The English translation is taken from Leo Sherley-Price, *Bede: A History of the English Church and People*, revised by R. E. Latham (Harmondsworth, 1968), 91–92, 104. See also Colgrave and Mynors, *Bede's Ecclesiatical History*, 115, 143–44.

16 The chronicle in question is Gocelin's *Book of the translation of St. Augustine the apostle of the English and his followers* (British Library Cotton MS. Vesp. Bxx), written about 1097. Extracts are quoted and translated by Hope, "Recent discoveries," *Archaeologia*, 377ff., and the evidence is summarized by Taylor and Taylor, *Anglo-Saxon Architecture*, 1:138–39.

17 *HE*, 2.5.

18 See my discussion of funerary basilicas on the outskirts of Rome in chapter two. The first archbishop of Canterbury known to have been buried in the grounds of the cathedral was Cuthbert (740–60) at a time when the ancient ban against burial within the city limits was being relaxed in Rome itself. See Brooks, "The ecclesiastical topography," *European Towns, their archaeology and early history*, ed. M.W. Barley (London, 1977), 491, and idem, *Church of Canterbury*, 51.

19 *HE*, 2.6.

20 The following analysis is based upon the summary of the excavations directed by F. Jenkins as reported by Leslie Webster and John Cherry in *Medieval Archaeology* 20 (1976), 163–64.

21 Richard Gem, "The Anglo-Saxon and Norman churches," *St Augustine's Abbey*, ed. R. Gem (London, 1997), 101–4, and Eric Cambridge, "The Architecture of the Augustinian Mission," *St Augustine*, 213–14.

22 *HE*, 3.29.

23 For a discussion of this letter and its historical context see N. Brooks, *Church of Canterbury*, 68–70. It is worth noting that Gregory the Great displayed particular reverence for St. Pancras in a sermon on the saint's feast day (Migne, *PL*, 76, col. 1204). In 594, he also donated the pre-Honorian church of St. Pancras in Rome to a group of Benedictine monks (*MGH Epist*, 1:252f.). See also Krautheimer, *Corpus*, 3:155. It is therefore not surprising that relics of the saint should appear in England during this time. I wish to thank Alan Thacker for advice in this matter.

24 Mario Salmi, "Nuovi reperti alto medievali 'intra Tevere et Arno,'" *Commentari* 21 (1970) 7–11, and idem, "Architettura longobarda o architetturra preromanica?" *Atti del convegno sul tema: La civiltà dei longobardi in Europa*, Accademia Nazionale dei Lincei (Rome, 1974), 271–72, 273 fig. 2. Eric Fernie, *The Architecture of the Anglo-Saxons* (London, 1984), 46, cites other examples in the Italian Tyrol and Switzerland.

25 *HE*, 4.18. See also C. Silva-Tarouca, "Giovanni 'archcantor' di S. Pietro a Roma," *Atti della Pontificia Accademia Romana di Archeologia*, Memorie, 3d ser. 1 (1923) 163ff. See also note 64 below.

26 *HE*, 1.29.

27 For a discussion of the reliability of Alfarano's plan and text, entitled *De Basilicae Vaticanae antiquissima et nova structura* and written between 1570 and 1582, see Krautheimer, *Corpus*, 5:208–12, 218–19. For information about the church of St. Martin in particular see Paola Réfice, "'Habitatio Sancti Petri': Glosse ad alcune fonti su S. Martino in Vaticano," *Arte medievale* Ser. 2, vol. 4 (1990), 13–16.

28 The remains of a small apsed building with side alcoves excavated at Silchester in the late nineteenth century have sometimes been cited as evidence for a Romano-British source for the porticus churches at Canterbury, but several factors make this derivation unlikely. First of all, the building is miniscule, only 8.91 m long by 3.05 m wide, making it almost half the size of the church of SS. Peter and Paul at Canterbury. Second, while the building at Silchester may well have served as a church, this has not been conclusively proven. Third, while it was built sometime in the late third or early fourth century, there is no indication that the building was still intact in the sixth and seventh centuries. And fourth, as Bede tells us (*HE* 2.2, 2.4, 5.22), Augustine's relations with the British Church are known to have been anything but friendly, making a Romano-British source for the churches at Canterbury highly unlikely. For the building at Silchester see S. S. Frere, "The Silchester Church: The Excavation by Sir Ian Richmond in 1961," *Archaeologia* 105 (1975), 277–302. Both Fernie (*The Architecture* 43–46) and Cambridge ("The Architecture," 216–25) argue, not always for the same reasons, that the building traditions of Italy exerted a strong influence at Canterbury.

29 *HE*, 2.5, 2.20. For a general discussion of the difficulties facing the see of Canterbury in these early years see N. Brooks, *Church of Canterbury*, 63–67.

30 Walter Horn, "On the Origins of the Medieval Cloister," *Gesta* 12 (1973), 23–33, and Edward R. Norman and J. K. S. St. Joseph, *The Early Development of Irish Society: The Evidence of Aerial Photography* (Cambridge, 1969), 90–121, provide very useful surveys, with additional bibliographical references, of early monastic architecture in Ireland. See also Nancy Edwards, *The Archaeology of Early Medieval Ireland* (London, 1990), 6–33, 99–131, and Lisa M. Bitel, *Isle of Saints. Monastic Settlement and Christian Community in Early Ireland* (Ithaca and London, 1990), 17–82. For historical background see T. M. Charles-Edwards, *Early Christian Ireland* (Cambridge, 2000), 182–281.

31 Finbar McCormick, "Iona: The Archaeology of the Early Monastery," *Studies in the Cult of Saint Columba*, ed. Cormac Bourke (Dublin, 1997), 46 fig. 1, 49–51.

32 *HE*, 3.25.

33 James F. Kenney, *The Sources for the Early History of Ireland: Ecclesiastical* (New York, 1929; reprinted ed., Dublin, 1979) 210–17, and, more recently, Charles-Edwards, *Early Christian Ireland*, 405–11, describe the various methods used for determining the date of Easter, together with differences between the traditions of the Irish and Roman Churches.

34 *HE*, 3.25.

35 W. J. Moore, "The Saxon Pilgrims to Rome and the Schola Saxonum," Ph.D. diss., University of Fribourg, Switzerland, 1937; Rosemary Cramp, "The Anglo-Saxons and Rome,"

Transactions of the Architectural and Archaeological Society of Durham and Northumberland, n.s. 3 (1974), 27–38; and Janet Nelson, "Viaggiatori, pellegrini e vie commerciali," *Il futuro dei Longobardi: Saggi*, eds. C. Bertelli and G. P. Brogiolo (Milan, 2000), 163–71.

36 Bertram Colgrave, text, trans., and notes, *The Life of Bishop Wilfrid by Eddius Stephanus* (Cambridge, 1927) provides an excellent English translation, together with the Latin text. Another English translation of Eddius' text is found in *The Age of Bede*, D. H. Farmer, ed., and J. F. Webb, trans. (Harmondsworth, 1983).

37 Eddius, *Life of Wilfrid*, chap. 5.

38 Ibid., chaps. 14, 47.

39 *HE*, 2.1.

40 Richard Bailey, "St. Wilfrid, Ripon and Hexham," *Studies in Insular Art and Archaeology*, ed. Catherine Karkov and Robert Farrell, American Early Medieval Studies (Oxford, Ohio, 1991), 17–22, cites various comparisons, some rather far-fetched. On the other hand, Crook, *The Architectural Setting*, 91–93, stresses the similarity of Wilfrid's crypts to the passageways and vaulted chambers of the Roman catacombs.

41 Richard N. Bailey, "The Anglo-Saxon Church at Hexham," *Archaeologia Aeliana*, 5th ser. 4 (1976) 47–67, and idem, "St. Wilfrid, Ripon and Hexham," *Studies*, 3–25. See also idem and Deirdre O'Sullivan, "Excavations over St. Wilfrid's Crypt at Hexham, 1978," *Archaeologia Aeliana*, 5th ser. 7 (1979), 145–58; Eric Cambridge, "C. C. Hodges and the Nave of Hexham Abbey," *Archaeologia Aeliana*, 5th ser. 7 (1979), 159–68; and idem, Alan Williams, a.o., "Hexham Abbey: A review of recent work and its implications," *Archaeologia Aeliana*, 5th ser. 23 (1995), 51–138, esp. 73–80.

42 Eddius, *Life of Wilfrid*, chap. 22: "Nam in Aegustaldesae, . . . domum Domino in honorem sancti Andreae apostoli fabrefactam fundavit: cuius profunditatem in terra cum domibus mire politis lapidibus fundatam et super terram multiplicem domum columnis variis et porticibus multis suffultam mirabileque longitudine et altitudine murorum ornatam et variis liniarum anfractibus viarum, aliquando sursum, aliquando deorsum per cocleas circumductam, non est meae parvitatis hoc sermone explicare, quod sanctus pontifex noster, a spiritu Dei doctus, opera facere excogitavit, neque enim ullam domum aliam citra Alpes montes talem aedificatam audivimus."

43 G. Baldwin Brown, *The Arts of Early England*, 7 vols. (London, 1903–37), vol. 2, *Anglo-Saxon Architecture*, revised and enlarged (1929), 152–56, provides excerpts of this text, both in Latin and in English translation, compared with that of Eddius. For the full Latin text of Prior Richard's *Historia ecclesiae Haugustaldensis* see James Raine, *The Priory of Hexham*, 2 vols. (Edinburgh, 1864–65), 1:8–105, esp. 11–13. For these and other primary texts related to Wilfrid's church at Hexham see also Otto Lehmann-Brockhaus, *Lateinische Schriftquellen zur Kunst in England, Wales und Schottland vom Jahre 901 bis zum Jahre 1307*, 5 vols. (Munich, 1955–60), 1:557–66 nos. 2093–120. Prior Richard describes the columns as *quadratis*, meaning literally "squared," which has led some scholars to suggest that the church at Hexham had masonry piers instead of columns; however, in the next sentence he refers to the "capitals of the columns," which in a pre-Romanesque church could only mean that the nave walls rested on cylindrical shafts. In this context, therefore, *quadratis* would seem to refer to the solidity or robust nature of the columns. It may be that Prior Richard was using this term to indicate that the columns were squat or stout in comparison to what he was used to seeing in churches built in his own time.

44 Raine, *Hexham*, 1:12.

45 Eddius, *Life of Wilfrid*, chap. 63.

46 For the Probus mausoleum at St. Peter's see Richard Krautheimer, "The Crypt of Sta. Maria in Cosmedin and the Mausoleum of Probus Anicius," *Essays in Memory of Karl Lehmann, Marsyas*, Supplement 1 (Locust Valley, New York, 1964), 171–75.

47 The predominant building material employed in Rome in the early Middle Ages was reused ancient brick. It is true, however, that in the late sixth and early seventh centuries brick was often combined with locally quarried tufa to form a so-called *opus mixtum*, but these small blocks of volcanic material are very different in character from the massive sandstone blocks found at Hexham. See G. Bertelli, A. G. Guidobaldi, and P. R. Spagnoletti, "Stutture murarie degli edifici religiosi di Rome dal VI al IX secolo," *Rivista dell'istituto nazionale d'archeologia e storia dell'arte*, n.s. 23–24 (1976–77), 95–172, and T. L. Heries, *Paries* (Amsterdam, 1982).

48 Eddius, *Life of Wilfrid*, chap. 12.

49 Aelred of Rievaulx, *De sanctis ecclesiae Haugustaldensis, et eorum miraculis libellus* (Raine, *Hexham* 1:175), writing in the twelfth century states that Wilfrid acquired masons from "across the sea" (*transmarinis*). William of Malmesbury, on the other hand, writing about the same time, says that the masons came from Rome (Lehmann-Brockhaus, *Lateinische Schriftquellen*, 1:561 no. 2106), but I think Gaul is a more likely source for the reasons stated above. See also Eric Fletcher, "The influence of Merovingian Gaul on Northumbria in the seventh century," *Medieval Archaeology* 24 (1980) 69–86, esp. 82, where a strong case is presented for the importance of Gaul for Northumbrian architecture in this early period; however, in doing so, this study underestimates the influence of Rome.

50 Janet Backhouse, *The Lindisfarne Gospels* (Oxford and Ithaca, New York, 1981), 31, fig. 18, illustrates Anglo-Saxon writing implements, including several stylae and a carved bone writing tablet, found during excavations at Whitby in the 1920s.

51 *Adamnani de locis sanctis* 2.2. For an English translation see *Adamnan's "De Locis Sanctis,"* ed. Meehan, 43. See also John Wilkinson, *Jerusalem Pilgrims before the Crusades* (Jerusalem, 1977), 191–97 and pls. 1–6. Kenney, *Sources for the Early History of Ireland*, 285–86, provides a list of medieval copies of the text together with more modern editions. For discussion of the plan of the Holy Sepulchre in early Christian times see chapter one.

52 Eddius, *Life of Wilfrid*, chap. 56.

53 ". . . in modum turris erecta, et fere rotunda, a quatuor partibus totidem porticus habens. . . ." Raine, *Hexham*, 1:14.

54 ". . . ecclesiam in honore beatissimae virginis Mariae opere rotundo, quam quatuor porticus, quatuor respicientes mundi climata, ambiebant." Ibid., 1:183.

55 For a detailed study of this building see Hugo Brandenburg, "La chiesa di S. Stefano Rotondo a Roma. Nuove ricerche e risultati: Un rapporto preliminare," *Rivista di archeologia cristiana* 68 (1992), 201–32, and Krautheimer, *Corpus*, 4:199–240. See also idem, "Success and Failure in Late Antique Church Planning," *Age of Spirituality*, 121–40.

56 Eddius, *Life of Wilfrid*, chap. 55.

57 Guglielmo De Angelis D'Ossat, "La chiesa di S. Angelo di Perugia," *Corsi di cultura sull'arte ravennate e bizantina* 13 (1966), 105–11; D. Viviani, "Tempio di S. Angelo in Perugia," *Bolletino d'Arte* 5 (1911), 28–32; and Donatella Scortecci, "Riflessioni sulla cronologia del tempio perugino di San Michele Arcangelo," *Rivista di archeologia cristiana* 67 (1991), 405–28. A detailed study of this interesting building is very much needed.

58 Eddius, *Life of Wilfrid*, chap. 63.

59 For a detailed study of S. Maria Maggiore see Krautheimer, *Corpus*, 5:1–60, and De Blaauw, *Cultus et Decor*, 1:336–447. See also R. Krautheimer, "The Architecture of Sixtus III: A Fifth-Century Renascence?" *Essays in Honor of Erwin Panofsky* (New York, 1961), 291–302, reprinted in idem, *Studies*, 181–96.

60 *HE*, 2.4.

61 Richard Krautheimer, "Sancta Maria Rotunda," *Arte del primo millenio*, Atti del II° convegno per lo studio dell'arte dell'alto medioevo (Turin, 1953), 23–27, reprinted in idem, *Studies*, 107–14. For the significance of the Pantheon for the cult of the Virgin in Rome see Sible de Blaauw, "Das Pantheon als christlicher Tempel," *Boreas* 17 (1994), 13–26.

62 Lehmann-Brockhaus, *Lateinische Schriftquellen*, 1:562 n. 2106.

63 For an overview of this material see, among others, David Wilson, *Anglo-Saxon Art* (London and Woodstock, New York, 1984), 29–91; Carol Neuman de Vegvar, *The Northumbrian Renaissance: A Study in the Transmission of Style* (Selingsgrove, Pennsylvania, 1987); *The Making of England*, 108–56; and *Northumbria's Golden Age*, ed. Jane Hawkes and S. Mills (Stroud, 1999).

64 *Historia Abbatum* (henceforth *HA*) in Plummer *Opera Historica*, 1:364–87. An English translation is found in *The Age of Bede*, trans. D. H. Farmer, 185–208. Additional information is provided by a work of the same title by an anonymous author (i.e., *Historia Abbatum auctore Anonymo*, henceforth *HAA*) found in Plummer, *Opera Historica*, 1:388–404.

65 *HA*, chap. 4.

66 *HA*, chap. 5.

67 Ibid.

68 Ibid., chap. 6, and *HAA*, chap. 10.

69 Paul Meyvaert, "Bede and the church paintings at Wearmouth-Jarrow," *Anglo-Saxon England* 8 (1979), 63–77, provides a penetrating analysis of Biscop's journeys to Rome and the goods he brought back to Northumbria. See also Richard Gem, "Documentary References to Anglo-Saxon Painted Architecture," *Early Medieval Wall Painting and Painted Sculpture in England*, ed. Sharon Cather, David Park, and Paul Williamson, British Archaeological Reports, British Series 216 (Oxford, 1990), 1–5; and Kitzinger, "Interlace and Icons," *The Age of Migrating Ideas*, 6–8.

70 For a detailed analysis of the church see Taylor and Taylor, *Anglo-Saxon Architecture*, I, 432–46. Summaries of the excavations are provided by the project's director, Rosemary Cramp, in various sources including "Excavations at the Saxon Monastic Sites of Wearmouth and Jarrow, Co. Durham: an Interim Report," *Medieval Archaeology* 13 (1969) 21–66; "Monkwearmouth Church," *Archaeological Journal* 133 (1976) 230–37; and "Monkwearmouth and Jarrow in their Continental Context," *"Churches Built in Ancient Times": Recent Studies in Early Christian Archaeology*, ed. Kenneth Painter (London, 1994), 279–294. The final excavation report has been announced and is eagerly awaited.

71 *HA*, chap. 21.

72 For a detailed description of these and other baluster shafts at Wearmouth see *Corpus of Anglo-Saxon Stone Sculpture*, ed. and general introduction by Rosemary Cramp, vol. 1 (Oxford, 1984), pt. 1:19, 23–27, 128–29.

73 Carol Heitz, "Poitiers: Foyer d'art chrétien du IVe au Xe siècles," *Archéologia* 113 (1977), 21, and Lucien Musset, "L'église d'Evrecy (Calvados) et ses sculptures préromanes," *Bulletin de la Société des Antiquaires de Normandie* 53 (1955–56), 116–68, fig. 2. For the date of the founding of Nouaillé (*Nobiliacum*) see L. Levillain, "Les origines du monastère de Nouaillé," *Bibliothèque de l'Ecole des Chartes* 71 (1910), 278.

74 *HA*, chap. 4.

75 Paul Meyvaert, "Bede the Scholar," *Famulus Christi: Essays in Commemoration of the Thirteenth Centenary of the Birth of the Venerable Bede*, ed. Gerald Bonner (London, 1976), 47, 64 n. 30, reprinted in P. Meyvaert, *Benedict, Gregory, Bede and Others* (London, 1977) with the same pagination, and Peter Hunter Blair, *Northumbria in the Days of Bede* (London, 1977), 123.

76 For a summary of opinions concerning this manuscript together with additional bibliography see J. J. G. Alexander, *Insular Manuscripts 6th to the 9th Century* (London, 1978), 30–32.

77 Rupert Bruce-Mitford, *The Sutton Hoo Ship Burial: A Handbook*, 3rd ed. (London, 1979), 84–92. The ship burial and its date are discussed in greater detail in idem et al., *The Sutton Hoo Ship-Burial*, 3 vols. (London, 1975–83), 1:578–607. See also the general study by George Speake, *Anglo-Saxon Animal Art and Its Germanic Background* (Oxford, 1980).

78 Kitzinger, "Icons and Interlace," 4–6. It is worth noting that in the mid-eighth century the Anglo-Saxon missionary Boniface complained in a letter to England about serpents along the borders of vestments as symbols of evil. *Die Briefe des heiligen Bonifatius und Lullus, MGH Epistolae Selectae*, ed. Michael Tange, 5 vols. (1916–52), 1:170 no. 78.

79 *HA*, chap. 7.

80 The date is provided by the dedicatory inscription that is still preserved and can be seen, reset in the eighteenth century, over the chancel arch of the present church. See John Higgitt, "The Dedication Inscription at Jarrow and Its Context," *The Antiquaries Journal* 59 (1979), 343–74.

81 Taylor and Taylor, *Anglo-Saxon Architecture*, 1:338–49; Cramp, "Excavations at Wearmouth and Jarrow," 42–45; idem, "St. Paul's Church, Jarrow," *The Archaeological Study of Churches*, ed. Peter Addyman and Richard Morris, The Council for British Archaeology, Research Report 13 (London, 1976), 28–35; idem, "Jarrow Church," *Archaeological Journal* 133 (1976), 220–28; idem, "Monastic Sites," *Archaeology of Anglo-Saxon England*, 234–41; idem, *The Bede Monastery Museum* (Jarrow, 1980), passim; "Monkwearmouth and Jarrow," *"Churches Built,"* passim.

82 This suggestion was first made by Baldwin Brown, *Arts of Early England*, 2:140, who compares the imposts at Escomb to a gateway of the Roman fort at Chesters. See also Taylor and Taylor, *Anglo-Saxon Architecture*, 1:236–37.

83 Michael Pocock and Hazel Wheeler, "Excavations at Escomb Church, County Durham, 1968," *Journal of the British Archaeological Association*, 3rd ser., 34 (1971), 9–29.

84 Rosemary Cramp, "Window Glass from the Monastic Site of Jarrow," *Journal of Glass Studies* 17 (1975), 88–96; and idem and J. Cronyn, "Anglo-Saxon Polychrome Plaster and other Materials from the Excavations of Monkwearmouth and Jarrow: An Interim Report," *Early Medieval Wall Painting*, 17–27, and more recently Cramp, "Window Glass from the British Isles 7th–10th century," *Il colore nel medioevo: Arte simbolo tenica. La vetrata in occidente dal IV all'XI secolo*, Atti delle giornate di studi, Lucca 23–25 settembre 1999, eds. Francesca Dell'Acqua and Romano Silva (Lucca, 2001), 67–85.

85 Pocock and Wheeler, "Excavations at Escomb Church," 26–28, with a report on these glass fragments by Rosemary Cramp.

86 *HA*, chap. 9. See also Meyvaert, "Bede and the church paintings," 66ff.

87 *HE*, 1.12.

88 Colgrave, *Bede's Ecclesiastical History*, 44 n. 2. For further discussion of possible Anglo-Saxon associations with stone masonry see: Tyler Bell, "Churches on Roman Buildings: Christian Associations and Roman Masonry in Anglo-Saxon England," *Medieval Archaeology* 42 (1998), 1–18; and Jane Hawkes, "*Iuxta Morem Romanorum*: Stone and Sculpture in Anglo-Saxon

England," *Anglo-Saxon Styles*, ed. Catherine E. Karkov and George Hardin Brown (Albany, New York, 2003), 69–100.

89 For examples in Gaul see Cramp, "Window Glass," 94–95. For Rome see David Whitehouse, "Window glass between the first and the eighth centuries," and Marina Del Nunzio, "La produzione di vetri da finestra tra tarda antichità e medioevo: La situatione romana," *Il colore nel medioevo*, 31–65, along with other studies in the same volume about related material at other sites.

90 *HE*, 1.25.

91 Ernst Kitzinger, "The Cult of Images in the Age before Iconoclasm," *Dumbarton Oaks Papers* 8 (1954), 83–150, and idem, "On Some Icons of the Seventh Century," *Late Classical and Medieval Studies in Honor of A. M. Friend, Jr.*, ed. K. Weitzman et al. (Princeton, 1955) 132–50, both reprinted in idem, *The Art of Byzantium and the Medieval West*, ed. W. Eugene Kleinbauer (Bloomington, 1976), 90–156, 233–55. For icons in general see Kurt Weitzmann, *The Icon* (New York, 1978).

92 Cramp, "Window Glass," 95.

93 B. Hope-Taylor, *Yeavering*, passim. For a similar development on the continent see Günter P. Fehring, "Die Stellung des frühmittelalterlichen Holzkirchenbaues in der Architekturgeschichte," *Jahrbuch des Römisch-Germanischen Zentral Museums Mainz* 14 (1967), 179–97, and Charles Bonnet, "Les églises en bois du haut Moyen-Age d'après les recherches archéologiques," *Grégoire de Tours et l'espace gaulois*, Actes du congrès international, 3–5 November 1994 (Tours, 1997), 217–36. Dixon, "Secular Architecture," 67, suggests that in Anglo-Saxon England the simple, aisleless, rectangular hall may have been derived from Romano-British predecessors. Even so, it was very much part of an indigenous building tradition by the time of the construction of Wearmouth and Jarrow.

94 *HA*, chap. 11.

95 *HA*, chap. 17.

96 Cramp, "Excavations at Wearmouth and Jarrow," 45–52; idem, "Jarrow Church," 224–25; idem, "Monastic sites," 236–39; idem, *Monastery Museum*, 8–10.

97 Rupert Bruce-Mitford, "The Art of the 'Codex Amiatinus,'" *Journal of the British Archaeological Association* 32 (1969), 1–25, and Alexander, *Insular Manuscript*, 32–35. See also M. B. Parkes, *The Scriptorium of Wearmouth-Jarrow*, Jarrow Lecture (Jarrow, 1982).

98 See the classic study by Wilhelm Levison, *England and the Continent in the Eighth Century* (Oxford, 1946).

99 G. N. Garmonsway, ed. and trans., *The Anglo-Saxon Chronicle* (London, 1953), 56–57.

100 *Annals of Ulster, otherwise Annals of Senat, A Chronicle of Irish Affairs from A.D. 431 to A.D. 1540*, ed. William M. Hennessy (Dublin, 1887), 801 and 805. The *Annals of Ulster* ere by one year in the entries for the period through the tenth century; thus, the events of 802 and 806 are listed under 801 and 805. Even so, some monks remained on the island as late as the middle of the ninth century. See Ian Fisher, "The monastery of Iona in the eighth century," *The Book of Kells*, ed. Felicity O'Mahony, Proceedings of a Conference at Trinity College, Dublin, 6–9 September 1992 (Aldershot, 1994), 47.

Chapter 5: Symbols of the New Alliance

1 ". . . de regibus in Francia, qui illis temporibus non habentes regalem potestatem, si bene fuisset an non." *Fredegarii continuatio*, 32, *MGH SS, rer. Mer.*, 2:182. Also quoted and discussed in Léon Levillain, "L'avènement de la dynastie carolingienne et les origines de l'état pontifical (749–57)," *Bibliothèque e l'école des chartes* 94 (1933), 227ff., and *Handbook of Church History*, eds. Hubert Jedin and John Dolan, 10 vols. (London, 1965–80), 3:17–18.

2 J. M. Wallace-Hadrill, *The Frankish Church* (Oxford, 1983), 167, and T. F. X. Noble, *The Republic of St. Peter*, 65–71.

3 Wallace-Hadrill, *The Frankish Church*, 169. It is still unclear as to whether or not the emperor played any role in these proceedings. For a discussion of this issue see *Handbook of Church History*, 3:22 n. 2, with references to further literature, and Noble, *The Republic*, 278ff.

4 The best edition of the text is *Constitutum Constantini*, ed. Horst Fuhrmann, *MGH, Fontes iuris germanici antiqui*, N.S. 10 (Hannover, 1968). For a summary of the diverse opinions concerning the date and significance of the Donation see Noble, *The Republic*, 134–37.

5 Wallace-Hadrill, *The Frankish Church*, 163.

6 *MGH, DD Karol.*, 1:38–40.

7 Ibid., 1:133.

8 The references to the dedication of an altar by Pope Stephen II come in a letter, dated 835, from Charlemagne's son, Louis the Pious, to Abbot Hilduin of Saint-Denis and in a contemporary note by Hilduin himself. See *MGH, Epist.*, 5:326; Migne, *PL*, 107:3.

9 Bernhard Bischoff, "Eine Beschreibung der Basilika von Saint-Denis aus dem Jahre 799," *Kunstchronik*, 34 (1981), 97–103; Alain J. Stoclet, "La 'Descriptio Basilicae Sancti Dyonisii': Premiers Commentaires," *Journal des Savants* (1980), 104–17.

10 See Werner Jacobsen, "Saint-Denis im neuem Licht: Consequenzen der neuentdeckten Baubeschreibung aus dem Jahre 799," *Kunstchronik* 36 (1983), 301–8, for a more detailed discussion of the dating of the church.

11 An edition of the Latin text, together with an excellent English translation, is found in *Abbot Suger on the Abbey Church of St.-Denis and Its Art Treasures*, ed., trans., and annot. Erwin Panofsky, 2nd ed. Gerda Panofsky (Princeton, 1979).

12 The work of Viollet-le-Duc and others in the nineteenth century is summarized by Sumner Crosby in *The Abbey of St.-Denis, 475–1122* (New Haven, 1942), 8–12, 97 passim. For Crosby's excavations undertaken during the period from 1946 to 1948 see idem, "Fouilles exécutées récemment dans la basilique de Saint-Denis," *Bulletin Monumental* 105 (1947) 167–81, and idem, "Excavations in the Abbey Church of St.-Denis 1948: The Façade of Fulrad's Church," *Proceedings of the American Philosophical Society* 93 (1949), 347–61; and for the excavations from 1967 to 1969 see idem, "Excavations at Saint Denis—July 1967," *Gesta* 7 (1968), 48–50, and idem, "A Carolingian Pavement at Saint-Denis: A Preliminary Report," *Gesta* 9 (1970), 42–45. Jules Formigé presents his findings in *L'abbaye royale de Saint-Denis: Recherches nouvelles* (Paris, 1960); this volume contains useful information concerning the Carolingian church but Formigé erroneously dates the building to the reign of Dagobert in the early seventh century. Moreover, his reconstructions of the pre-Gothic phases of the church must be treated with extreme caution. For a more reliable treatment of Formigé's findings see May Vieillard-Troiekouroff, "L'architecture en France du temps de Charlemagne," *Karl der Grosse*, 4 vols. (Düsseldorf, 1965), 3:336–55; however, all previous studies of the Carolingian abbey church of Saint-Denis were superseded by Sumner Crosby, *The Royal Abbey of Saint-Denis from Its Beginning to the Death of Suger, 475–1151*, ed. and completed by Pamela Blum (New Haven, 1987). Werner Jacobsen, "Die Abteikirche von Saint-Denis als kunstgeschichtliches Problem," *La Neustrie*, Beihefte der Francia 16:2 (1989), 151–84, was written before Crosby's 1987 volume appeared. For an overview see now Michaël Wyss et al., *Atlas historique de Saint-Denis: Des origines au XVIIIe siècle*, (Paris, 1996), 32ff.

13 Werner Jacobsen, "Spolien in der karolingischen Architektur," *Antike Spolien in der Architektur des Mittelalters und der Reniassance*, ed. Joachim Poeschke (Munich, 1996), 158.

14 Suger, *De Administratione*, Chap. XXXIV (*Abbot Suger*, ed. and trans. Panofsky, 2nd ed. 73). For an analysis of the relief sculpture and its possible connection with Italy see: Miljenko Jurokovic, "Quelques reflections sur la basilique carolingienne de Saint-Denis: Une oeuvre d'esprit paléochrétien," *L'abbé Suger, le manifeste gothique de Saint-Denis et la pensée victorine*, Colloque organisé à la Fondation Singer-Polignac le mardi 21 novembre 2000, ed. Dominique Poirel (Turnhout, 2001), 37–57.

15 Crosby, *The Abbey of St.-Denis*, figs. 9–11.

16 *De Consecratione*, Chap. 2 (*Abbot Suger*, ed. Panofsky, 2nd ed., 89).

17 Suger, *De Administratione*, Chap. 15 (*Abbot Suger*, ed. and trans. Erwin Panofsky, 2nd ed., 45).

18 Werner Jacobsen and Michaël Wyss, "Saint-Denis: Essai sur la genèse du massif occidental," *Avant-nefs et espaces d'accueil dans l'église entre le IVe et le XIIe siècle*, Published under the direction of Christian Sapin (Auxerre, 2002), 76–87.

19 "Basilicae fabrica completa, impositaque turri, in quia signa, ut moris est, penderent," in *Miracula sancti Dionysii*, 1.15 (cited by Crosby, *The Abbey of St.-Denis*, 153 n. 91). Abbot Hilduin (814–40) further states that the main altar was "beneath the big bells" (*subtus campanas, . . . ante altare*). See *Ex Hilduini abbatis libro de S. Dionysio*, *MGH, SS*, vol. 15, pt. 1:2.

20 The complete text of the description can be found in Bischoff, "Eine Beschreibung," 99–100, and Stoclet, "La 'Descriptio,'" 104–5.

21 Louis Reeksmans, "Le dévelopment topographique de la région du Vatican a la fin de l'antiquité et au debut du moyen âge (300–850)," *Mélanges d'archéologie et d'historie de l'art offerts au Professeur Jacques Lavalleye* (Louvain, 1970), 218.

22 *LP*, 1:455, 464.

23 Jean Hubert, "Le mausolée royal de Saint-Denis et le mausolée impérial de Saint-Pierre de Rome," *Bulletin de la Société nationale des Antiquaires de France* (1961), 24–26.

24 Pope Paul I, Ep. 24 (*MGH, Ep.* 3:529). See also Riché, *Education and Culture in the Barbarian West*, 443, and *The Cambridge History of Later Greek and Early Medieval Philosophy*, ed. A. H. Armstrong (Cambridge, 1970), 518.

25 Herrmann-Mascard, *Les reliques*, 59.

26 Klaus Derstroff, "Der Heilige Nazarius: Zur Person und Verehrung des Lorscher Patrons," *Laurissa Jubilans: Festschrift zur 1200—Jahrfeier von Lorsch, 1964* (Mainz, 1964), 77–90. See also my remarks concerning St. Ambrose and St. Nazarius in chapters one and two.

27 A funerary inscription, dated A.D. 404, found outside Rome along the Via Aurelia refers to a private burial "in basilica sanctorum Nasari et Naboris." The veneration of S. Nazarius in Rome in the early fifth century is confirmed further by a contemporary martyrology. See A. Silvagni, "La topographia cimiteriale della via Aurelia," *Rivista di archeologia cristiana* 9 (1932), 105. On the other hand, Julia Smith, "Old Saints, New Cults," 321 n. 17, assumes the relics came from Milan.

28 For an excellent summary of the findings of these excavations, together with an extensive bibliography, see *VK*, 179–81; and *VK, Nbd*, 251–53. The most complete report of Behn's excavations is Friedrich Behn, *Die karolingische Klosterkirche von Lorsch an der Bergstrasse nach Ausgrabungen von 1927–1928 und 1932–1933* (Berlin and Leipzig, 1934).

29 *Codex Laureshamensis*, ed. Karl Glöckner, 2 vols. (Darmstadt, 1929), 1:404: "repentino ac miserablili incendio tota laureshamensis ecclesia conflagravit . . . Primo castellum mirabili dolatura fabrefactum, in quo signa ecclesiae dependebant, . . . dehinc totam superiorem fabricam, turres quoque cum porticibus flamma vitrix obtinuit."

30 Uwe Süssenbach, *Die Stadtmauer des römischen Köln* (Cologne, 1981), esp. 86–90.

31 For a detailed review of previous scholarship on the Lorsch gateway see Günther Binding, "Die karolingische Königshalle," *Die Reichsabtei Lorsch*, ed. Friedrich Knöpp, 2 vols. (Darmstadt, 1973 and 1977), 2:273–97. Kerstin Merkel, "Die Antikenrezeption der sogenannten Lorscher Torhalle," *Kunst in Hessen und am Mittelrhein* 32/33 (1993), 23–42, suggests that the upper storey served as a library.

32 Richard Krautheimer, "The Carolingian Revival of Early Christian Architecture," *The Art Bulletin* 24 (1942), 1–38, reprinted with a postscript in idem, *Studies*, 203–56.

33 Eugen Ewig, "Das Bild Constantins des Grossen in den ersten Jahrhunderten des abendländischen Mittelalters," *Spätantikes und Fränkisches Gallien: Gesammelte Schriften (1952–1973)*, ed. Hartmut Atsma, 2 vols. (Munich, 1976), 1:98–104.

34 See, for example, Richard Krautheimer, "Introduction to an 'Iconography of Medieval Architecture,'" *Studies*, 115–50.

35 The best discussions of the gatehouse are found in Krautheimer, *Corpus*, 5:268–70, passim, and Blaauw, *Cultus et Decor*, 2:525–27, passim. A detailed study of the gatehouse together with its possible influence on the Lorsch gateway is found in Werner Meyer-Barkhausen, "Die frühmittelalterlichen Vorbäuten am Atrium von Alt St. Peter in Rom, zweitürmige Atrien, Westwerke und Karolingisch-Ottonische Königskapellen," *Wallraf-Richartz-Jahrbuch* 20 (1958), 7–40; nevertheless, I do not agree with the proposed reconstruction of the original appearance of the gatehouse and adjoining buildings. I also find it unlikely that a monumental bell tower stood next to the gatehouse in the early Middle Ages; with Krautheimer (*Corpus*, 5:175), I believe that the tower for three bells said to have been built *super basilicam* by Pope Stephen II (752–57) (see *LP* 1:454) refers to a wooden structure built atop the roof of the basilica. Meyer-Barkhausen is certainly correct (p. 12), however, in assigning the campanile visible to the right of the gatehouse in the sixteenth-century drawing by Martin van Heemskerck (see fig. 5.16) to the later Middle Ages.

36 *LP*, 1:465.

37 *LP*, 1:465. For a detailed study of this mosaic see Hans Belting, "Das Fassadenmosaik des Atriums von Alt St. Peter in Rom," *Wallraf-Richartz-Jahrbuch* 23 (1961), 37–54.

38 Krautheimer, *Corpus*, 5:269; Blaauw, *Cultus et Decor*, 2:734.

39 Ernest Nash, *Pictorial Dictionary of Ancient Rome*, 2 vols. (New York, 1961–62), 1:450, fig. 547; and, most recently, James E. Packer, *The Forum of Trajan in Rome*, 3 vols. (Berkeley, 1997), 1:85–95, 415–16. There was, in fact, one main, central arch and, detached from it, two smaller, lateral arches.

40 *LP* 1:514. "Idem vero sacratissimus praesul portas aereas majores mire magnitudinis decoratas, studiose a civitate Perusine eas deducens, in basilica beati Petri apostoli ad turrem compte erexit."

41 Josef Fleckenstein, "Erinnerung an Karl den Grossen: Zur Torhalle von Lorsch und zum Kaisertum Karls," *Geschichtsblätter für den Kreis Bergstrasse* 7 (1974), 15–28, reprinted in *Beiträge zur Geschichte des Klosters Lorsch* (Lorsch, 1980), 63–78. Roswitha Zeilinger-Büchler expands upon Fleckenstein's thesis in "Kunstgeschichtliche Betrachtungen zur Datierung der Lorscher Königshalle," also found in *Beiträge zur Geschichte des Klosters Lorsch*, 79–91.

42 Anonymous Valesianus, *Pars posterior*, cap. 65–70 (*MGH, Auct. antiq.*, 9:324). This chronicle was written ca. 575; see Deichmann, *Ravenna*, 1:42.

43 See A.H.M. Jones, "The Constitutional Position of Odoacer and Theodoric," *Journal of Roman Studies* 52 (1962), 128, where an inscription by Caecina Mavortius Basilius Decius is discussed which refers to Theodoric as "d.n. gloriosissimus atque rex . . . victor ac triumfator semper Augustus."

44 Ewig, "Das Bild Constantins des Grossen," 98.

45 Werner Jacobsen, "Die Lorscher Torhalle. Zum Problem ihrer Datierung und Deutung. Mit einem Katalog der bauplastischen Fragmente als Anhang," *Jahrbuch des Zentralinstituts für Kunstgeschichte* 1 (1985), 9–75.

46 Ruth Meyer, *Frühmittelalterliche Kapitelle und Kämpfer in Deutschland*, 2 vols. (Berlin, 1997), 1:214–55, 530–34, 573–76.

47 Meyer, *Frühmittelalterliche Kapitelle*, 1:9–39, 563–64. See also Felix Kreusch, "Im Louvre wiedergefundene Kapitelle und Bronzebasen aus der Pfalzkirche Karls des Grossen zu Aachen," *Cahiers archéologiques* 18 (1968), 71–98, see esp. 72–77, and idem, "Zwei im Louvre wiedergefundene Kapitelle aus Karls des Grossen Pfalzkirche zu Aachen," *Bonner Jahrbücher* 171 (1971), 407–15.

48 *Annales regni Francorum 741–829*, ed. F. Kurze, *MGH*, *Scriptores rerum Germanicarum* (Hanover, 1895), 774.

49 *Codex Laureshamensis*, 1:282.

50 *Codex Laureshamensis*, 1:288: ". . . vir planae dilectus deo et hominibus, simplex et sapiens, atque tam in divinis quam in secularibus disciplinis adprime eruditus." In a letter dated 791/2 (*MGH, Ep. kar.* 2:38), Alcuin reprimands his former pupil for an overzealous love for the writings of Virgil. See also Friedrich Knöpp, "Richbod (Erz-) Bischof von Trier 791(?)-804," *Die Reichsabtei*, 1:247–51.

51 *Codex Laureshamensis*, 1:288–89: "Qui statim in primordio destructis ligneis domibus in quibus fratres eatenus c[om]manebant, in aquilonali videlicet parte, claustrum muris circumdans ad meridianam partem uti nunc videtur transtulit, dormitorium quoque cum ecclesia triplici fecit, cancellos circa requiem beati Nazarii ex auro argentoque mirifice vestiens, pavimentum etiam coram altari vario stratum marmore sublimavit." For a general discussion of the reappearance of such pavements in the eighth and ninth centuries see Charles McClendon, "The Revival of *Opus Sectile* Pavements in Rome and the Vicinity in the Carolingian Period," *PBSR*, 48 (1980), 157–64.

52 Florentine Mütherich and Joachim E. Gaehde, *Carolingian Painting* (New York, 1970), 10. For a color reproduction of the portrait of Christ with a brief commentary see ibid., 32–33, pl. 1. The fundamental study of the manuscript remains that of Wilhelm Koehler in *Die Karolingische Miniaturen II: Die Hofschule Karls des Grossen* (Berlin, 1958), 25ff. and pls. 1b–3b. See also Florentine Mütherich, "Die Buchmalerei am Hofe Karls des Grossen," *Karl der Grosse*, 3:12–15, passim.

Chapter 6: Aachen and Rome: The Poles of an Empire

1 *LP*, 2:7; similar words are recorded in the Royal Frankish Annals (*Annales Regni Francorum*, a. 801, *MGH SS, rer. Germ.*, 112). For a brilliant discussion of this acclamation see Ernst H. Kantorowicz, *Laudes Regiae: A Study in Liturgical Acclamations and Medieval Ruler Worship* (Berkeley and Los Angeles, 1946), passim.

2 Albrecht Mann, "Grossbauten vorkarlischer Zeit und aus der Epoche von Karl dem Grossen bis zu Lothar I," *Karl der Grosse*, 3:320–21. The terms royal villa (*villa regalis*) and palace (*palatium*) were used interchangeably in documents of the period and the same will be done so here. See Du Cange, *Glossarum mediae et infimae latinitatis;* Barbara Fois *Il "Capitulare de Villis"* (Milan, 1981), 31; and Günther Binding, *Deutsche Königspfalzen: von Karl dem Grossen bis Friedrich II. (765–1240)* (Darmstadt, 1996), 21ff.

3 See also Werner Jacobsen, "Die Pfalzkonzeptionen Karls des Grossen," *Karl der Grosse als vielberufener Vorfahr*, ed. Lieselotte E. Saurma-Jeltsch (1994), 23–48; and Uwe Lobbedey, "Carolingian Royal Palaces: The State of Research from an Architectural Historian's Viewpoint," *Court Culture in the Early Middle Ages: The Proceedings of the First Alcuin Conference*, ed. Catherine Cubitt (Turnhout, 2003), 129–53.

4 Manfred Balzer, "Paderborn als karolingischer Pfalzort," *Deutsche Königspfalzen*, 3 vols. (Göttingen, 1963–79), 3:9–85.

5 No final report of the excavations has as yet been published. For a detailed summary of the findings see Wilhelm Winkelmann, "'Est locus insignis, quo Patra et Lippis fluetant.' Uber die Ausgrabungen in den karolingischen und ottonischen Königspfalzen in Paderborn," *Chateau Gaillard. Etudes de castellologie médiévale*, Actes du Ve colloque international tenu a Hindsgaul, Danemark, 1–6 Septembre 1970 (Caen, 1972), 203–16. See also Balzer, "Paderborn." More recent summaries are provided by Binding, *Deutsche Königspfalzen,* 123ff., and Sveva Gai, "Die Pfalz Karls des Grossen in Paderborn," *799. Kunst und Kultur der Karolingerziet: Beiträge zum Katalog der Ausstellung* (henceforth *799. KKK: Beiträge*), ed. Christoph Stiegemann and Matthias Wemhoff (Mainz, 1999), 183–96.

6 Walter Sage, "Frühmittelalterlicher Holzbau," *Karl der Grosse*, 3:573–90, esp. 585–87 and fig. 5, and Wilhelm Winkelmann, "Die Ausgrabungen der frühmittelalterlichen Siedlung bei Warendorf," *Neue Ausgrabungen in Deutschland* (Berlin, 1958), 492–516.

7 John Percival, *The Roman Villa* (Berkeley and Los Angeles, 1976), 83–87.

8 There is as yet no final report of the excavations carried out at Ingelheim between 1960 and 1970. The following discussion is based upon the preliminary reports and analyses found in Uta Wengenroth-Weimann, *Die Grabungen an der Königspfalz zu Nieder-Ingelheim in den Jahren 1960–1970*, Beiträge zur Ingelheimer Geschichte, vol. 23, Historischer Verein (Ingelheim, 1973); Konrad Weidemann, "Die Königpfalz in Ingelheim," *Ingelheim am Rhein 774–1974. Geschichte und Gegenwart* (Ingelheim, 1974), 37–56; idem, "Ausgrabungen in der karolingischen Pfalz Ingelheim," *Ausgrabungen in Deutschland*, 4 vols. (Mainz, 1975), 2:437–46; and W. Sage, "Die Ausgrabungen in der Pfalz zu Ingelheim am Rhein 1960–1970," *Francia* 4 (1976), 141–60. Recent summaries are found in Binding, *Deutsche Königspfalzen*, 99–113, and Holger Grewe, "Die Konigspfalz zu Ingelheim am Rhein," *799. KKK: Beiträge*, 142–51.

9 For a general discussion of Piazza Armerina and other villas in the late Roman world see R.J.A. Wilson, *Piazza Armerina* (London, 1983), 73–85. In addition, see the following analyses of individual sites: for Piazza Armerina, J. B. Ward-Perkins, *Roman Imperial Architecture*, 460–64 with further bibliography; for Montmaurin, G. Fouet, *La villa gallo-romane de Montmaurin, Haute-Garonne*, 20e Supplément a *Gallia* (Paris, 1969); and for Teting, Albert Grenier, *Habitations gauloises et villas latines dans la Cité des Médiomatrices* (Paris, 1906), 159–74, plan 1. A similar curved wall was uncovered before World War I on the site of another Frankish palace at Samoussy, but the archaeological evidence remains too limited to offer a reliable reconstruction. See Georg Weise, *Zwei fränkische Königspfalzen. Bericht über die an den Pfalzen zu Quierzy und Samoussy vorgenommenen Grabungen* (Tübingen, 1923).

10 Süssenbach, *Die Stadtmauer . . . Köln*, 91–93, and in general, Luigi Crema, *L'architettura romana* (Turin, 1959), 620–24.

11. Sven Schütte, "Uberlegungen zu architektonischen Vorbildern

der Pfalz Ingelheim und Aachen," *Krönungen: Könige in Aachen—Geschichte und Mythos*, ed. Mario Kramp, 2 vols. (Mainz, 2000), 1:204–5.

12 Ward-Perkins, *Imperial Roman Architecture*, 430 and fig. 292.

13 The so-called Einsiedeln Itinerary from the late eighth or early ninth century lists the Baths of Constantine as *thermae* but it also refers to the Baths of Trajan as a *palatium*: Valentini and Zucchetti, *Codice topografico*, 2:192 and 196.

14 Pliny the Younger, *Epistola* 27 (to Gallus); Sidonius Apollinaris, *Carmina* 22 (the villa of Burgus). The *Letters* of the younger Pliny and the *Poems* of Sidonius are recorded in early catalogues of books at the monastery of Fulda: M. L. W. Laistner, *Thought and Letters in Western Europe A.D. 500 to 900* (Ithaca, 1966), 232; and P. Lehmann, "Fulda und die antike Literatur," *Aus Fuldas Geistesleben* (Fulda, 1928), 9–23.

15 Poeta Saxo, *Vita Caroli Magni*, *MGH*, *Poetae lat.*, 4:65. In truth, remains of columns, bases, and capitals found on the site are from a geological source north of the Alps. Nonetheless, they are ancient Roman spolia or accomplished Carolingian copies. See *799. Kunst und Kultur der Karolingerziet* (henceforth *799. KKK*), exh. cat., ed. Christoph Stiegemann and Matthias Wemhoff, 2 vols. (Mainz, 1999), 1:100–3.

16 *MGH*, *Poetae Latini Aevi Carolini* II (Berlin: 1884), 63–66; English translation in Caecelia Davis-Weyer, *Early Medieval Art 300–1150: Sources and Documents* (Englewood Cliffs, New Jersey, 1971), 84–88. See also Walter Lammers, "Ein karolingisches Bildprogram in der Aula Regia von Ingelheim," *Festschrift für Hermann Heimpel* (Göttingen, 1972), 226–89. The reliability of this source has been questioned, but, even if it involves considerable "poetic license," it reveals the Carolingian desire to connect Frankish rule with traditions of the ancient past.

17 Eugen Ewig, "Résidence et capitale pendant le haut moyen age," *Spätantikes und frankisches Gallien*, 2 vols. (Zurich and Munich, 1976–79), 1:394–99.

18 Einhard, *Vita Karoli*, cap. 22.

19 The building chronology of the palace at Aachen remains a topic of debate and opinions vary in the sources cited in the following note. In general, there are two camps of thought, those who assign most of the construction to the 790s, citing among other sources Alcuin's reference in a letter dated to 798 (*MGH*, *Epist.*, 4:244) to the interior columns in the chapel, and those who prefer a decade earlier, citing the dendrochonological analysis of a beam used to anchor the upper portions of the chapel. In the latter instance, Ernst Hollstein, *Mitteleuropäische Eichenchronologigie*, Trier dendrochronologische Forschungen zur Archäologie und Kunstgeschichte (Mainz, 1980), 44–45, estimates that the tree for the beam was cut in 776 +/− 10 years. Neither position is conclusive. Obviously, Alcuin's reference is only a *terminus ante*, while Hollstein based his opinion on a single sample, which was far from ideal. He readily acknowledges the presence of extensive larva damage and records that it possessed only 56 rings, a number insufficient to support any firm conclusions. Three samples from the western tower of the audience hall were also severely damaged but contained more rings. Here Hollstein ascertains that the "most likely" cutting date was 798 +/− 6 years. I wish to acknowledge the expert advice of Peter Ian Kuniholm of Cornell University on the matter of the dendrochronological evidence. A reexamination of the material in Trier has also brought into question the reliability of the dendrochronological evidence for the royal chapel. See Mattias Exner, "Review: *799. Kunst und Kultur der Karolingerzeit. Karl der Grosse und Papst Leo III. in Paderborn*," *Kunstchronik*, 53 (2003), 250.

20 The literature on the palace at Aachen is immense and growing; an extensive bibliography up to 1989 may be found in *VK*, 17–18, and *VK*, *Nbd*, 15–16. More recently see especially Ludwig Falkenstein, "Charlemagne et Aix-la-Chapelle," *Byzantion* 61 (1991), 231–89; Jacobsen, "Die Pfalzkonzeptionen"; Binding, *Deutsche Königspfalzen*, 72–98; idem, "Die Aachener Pfalz Karls des Grossen as archäologisch-baugeschichtliches Problem," *Zeitschrift für Archäologie des Mittelalters*, 25/25 (1997/98), 63–85; and Matthias Untermann, "'Opera mirabili constructa.' Die Aachen 'Residence' Karls des Grossen," *799. KKK: Beiträge*, 152–64. The monograph by Ernst G. Grimme, *Der Dom zu Aachen: Architektur und Ausstattung* (Aachen, 1994), could be more discerning.

21 Leo Hugot, "Die Pfalz Karls des Grossen in Aachen," *Karl der Grosse*, 3:542–43; however, for a discussion of the difficulties in determining medieval units of measure in general and the Carolingian foot in particular see Eric Fernie, "Historical Metrology and Architectural History," *Art History* 1 (1978), 383–99.

22 Hans Belting, "Das Aachener Münster im 19. Jahrhundert. Zur ersten Krise des Denkmal-Konzepts," *Wallraf-Richartz Jahrbuch* 45 (1984) 257–90.

23 For a summary of the debate not long after the restoration was completed see Paul Clemen, *Die Romanischen Wandmalereien der Rheinlande*, 2 vols. (Düsseldorf, 1905–16), 2:39–53.

24 *MGH: Epistolae III*, *Merowingici et Karolini aevi*, 1:614. Some have suggested that this letter refers to work at Ingelheim, but this seems unlikely. See note 15 above.

25 *LP* 2:3–4.

26 Einhard, *Vita Karoli*, 26.

27 Beat Brenk, "Spolia from Constantine to Charlemagne," 109; and Jacobsen, "Spolien," *Antike Spolien*, 157ff.

28 For the most complete analysis of the Carolingian capitals at Aachen see Meyer, *Frühmittelalterliche Kapitelle*, 1:9–39. See also Kreusch, "Im Louvre wiedergefundene Kapitelle," and idem, "Zwei im Louvre wiedergefundene Kapitelle."

29 The following remarks are based largely upon the detailed analysis by Wolfgang Braunfels, "Karls des Grossen Bronzewerkstatt," *Karl der Grosse*, 3:168–202.

30 Ibid., 196.

31 The best summaries of this development are Mütherich, "Die Buchmalerei," *Karl der Grosse*, 3:9–53; and idem, "Carolingian art: Manuscripts," *The Dictionary of Art*, 26 vols. (London, 1996), 5:800–5.

32 Katharina Pawelec, *Aachener Bronzegitter. Studien zur karolingischen Ornamentik um 800* (Cologne, 1990).

33 Paul Clemen, *Die Romanische Wandmalereien*, 1:plates 1–2, and 2:59.

34 Ulrike Wehling, *Die Mosaiken im Aachener Münster und ihre Vorstufen* (Cologne, 1995).

35 Hermann Schnitzler, "Das Kuppelmosaik der Aachener Pfalzkappelle," *Aachener Kunstblätter* 29 (1957), 69–78, suggested that the enthroned Christ was added in the twelfth century to replace what was originally the sacrificial lamb. Citing the absence of depictions of Christ in human form in manuscripts believed to have been produced at Aachen between roughly 795 and 810, Schnitzler saw the use of the lamb as a reflection of the iconoclastic tone of the so-called *Libri Carolini*, cited at a synod of Frankfurt in 794. These arguments were effectively countered by Hubert Schrade und Wolgang Grape, who point out that there is no clear evidence that representations of Christ were in fact banned in Carolingian art during this period, and that the statements of the *Libri Carolini* must be seen in the context of a running debate with Byzantium over the worship of icons, which had recently been restored in the East. Hubert Schrade, "Zum Kuppelmosaik der Pfalzkapelle und zum Theodorich-Denkmal in Aachen," *Aachener*

Kunstblätter 30 (1965), 25–37; and Wolfgang Grape, "Karolingische Kunst und Ikonoklasmus," *Aachener Kunstblätter* 45 (1974), 49–58. The Carolingian synod did not ban the representation of Christ and other holy figures but rather the adoration of such images; possible discrepancies in the details of Christ's throne in the mosaic are to be seen as the result of the Romanesque restoration. Our understanding of the *Libri Carolini*, moreover, has been greatly enhanced by the subsequent studies of Ann Freeman now conveniently collected in idem, *Theodulf of Orléans: Charlemagne's Spokesman against the Second Council of Nicaea* (Aldershot, Hampshire, 2003). The next chapter contains a discussion of Theodulf and his career in connection with the *Libri Carolini*.

36 Sven Schütte, "Der Aachener Thron," *Krönungen*, 1:213–22.

37 For a detailed survey of the problem see Günter Bandmann, "Die Vorbilder der Aachener Pfalzkapelle," *Karl der Grosse*, 3:424–62.

38 The ninth-century chronicler Agnellus, in his history of the bishops of Ravenna (*Liber pontificalis ecclesiae Ravennatis*, cap. 165) records that Charlemagne visited the city in 787. He may have been there earlier as well but the relevant portions of the chronicle are lost. The 801 visit is discussed below. For the possible confusion of Justinian for Theodoric see Brenk, "Spolia," 108, and Otto Demus, *Byzantine Art and the West* (New York, 1970), 68–69. Agnellus (cap 77: Max. 26), however, gives special mention to the image of Maximianus in S. Vitale and notes that it is accompanied by mosaic portraits of the emperor and empress. Although he does not name the latter two individuals, Agnellus recognizes their imperial status and does not confuse them with Theodoric or members of his court. See Claudia Nauerth, *Agnellus von Ravenna. Untersuchungen zur archäologischen Methode des ravennatischen Chronisten* (Munich, 1974), 21–22.

39 Krautheimer, *Early Christian*, 57, and Margaret Finch, "The Cantharus and Pigna at Old St. Peter's," *Gesta* 30 (1991), 16–26.

40 M. McCormick, *Eternal Victory*, 362–87; and Walter Schlesinger, "Beobachtungen zur Geschichte und Gestalt der Aachener Pfalz in der Zeit Karls des Grossen," *Studien zur europäischen Vor- und Frühgeschichte* (Neumünster, 1968), 258–81, esp. 280f. For a reference to the clergy waiting in the atrium for Charlemagne see Notker's *De Carolo Magno* 1:31. One is also reminded of a later event. In 936, Otto I appeared on a temporary throne set up in the atrium to an assembly of nobles before entering the royal chapel for the coronation ceremony. Widukind of Corvey, *Res gestae Saxonicae*, *MGH SS, rer. Germ.*, 60:63–64.

41 Albert Boeckler, "Formgeschichtliche Studien zur Ada gruppe", *Abhandlung der Bayerischen Akademie der Wissenschaften, Phil. Hist. Klasse*, n.s. 42 (1956), 8–16. See also Mütherich and Gaehde, *Carolingian Painting*, 39, pl. 4.

42 It is mentioned no less than three times in the late-eighth-century Einsiedeln Itinerary (Valentini and Zucchetti, *Codice topografico*, 2:177, 185, 195). Paul the Deacon, in his life of Gregory the Great (chapter 27 in Migne, *PL* 75, cols. 56–57), refers to the Forum of Trajan as "quod opere mirifico constat esse exstructum."

43. Paul Zanker, *Forum Augustum* (Tübingen, n.d.), 14ff. Zanker suggests a similar display of earlier emperors and important relatives in the atrium exedrae of Trajan's Forum: idem, "Das Trajansforum in Rom," *Archaeologische Anzeiger* 85 (1970), 517–19. See also Packer, *The Forum of Trajan*, 1:96–111.

44 For the argument that the emperor Augustus was also portrayed in the aula at Ingelheim, see Walther Lammers, "Ein karolingisches Bildprogramm," *Festschrift . . . Heimpel*, 265–68. Trajan, too, was viewed with great admiration at the time. Again, Paul the Deacon depicts no less an authority than Pope Gregory the Great praying at the tomb of St. Peter for the salvation of Trajan's soul because of the emperor's acts of kindness and justice (*Vita Sancti Gregorii Magni*, 27 in Migne, *PL* 75, cols. 56–57).

45 Irving Lavin, "The House of the Lord: Aspects of the Role of Palace Triclinia in the Architecture of Late Antiquity and the Early Middle Ages," *Art Bulletin* 44 (1962), 1–27.

46 The results of excavations of the site in 1908–14 were only partially published: Gherardo Ghirardini, "Gli scavi del Palazzo di Teodorico a Ravenna," *Monumenti antichi*, Reale accademia dei Lincei 24 (1916), cols. 738–838. For a summary of the archaeological and literary evidence for the identification of this complex as the palace of Theodoric see Mark J. Johnson, "Toward a History of Theoderic's Building Program," 80–92. See also Deichmann, *Ravenna: Kommentar*, vol. 2, pt. 3:58–70.

47 Cyril Mango, *The Brazen House: A Study of the Vestibule of the Imperial Palace in Constantinople* (Copenhagen, 1959), 88–89.

48 B. Ward-Perkins, *From Classical Antiquity to the Middle Ages*, 162.

49 Krautheimer, *Rome*, 120–22.

50 Cassiodorus, *Variae*, 7.5. The *Variae*, for example, are listed in a ninth-century library inventory of the abbey at Lorsch. See M. Manitius, *Geschichte der lateinischen Literatur des Mittelalters*, 2 vols. (Munich, 1959), 1:41, and Brenk, "Spolia," 108 n. 24.

51 For Charlemagne's attitude toward Theodoric: Heinz Löwe, "Von Theoderich dem Grossen zu Karl dem Grossen," *Von Cassiodor zu Dante* (Berlin and New York, 1973) 70–74. For the equestrian statue of Theodorich: Hartmut Hoffmann, "Die Aachener Theoderichstatue," *Das erste Jahrtausend. Kultur und Kunst im werdenden Abendland an Rhein und Ruhr*, ed. Victor H. Elbern, 2 vols. (Düsseldorf, 1962), 1:318ff; and for additional bibliography, Johnson, "Theoderic's Building Program," 87 n. 142.

52 Otto Zwierlein, "Karolus Magnus—alter Aeneas," *Literatur und Sprache im europäischen Mittelalter* (Darmstadt, 1973), 44–52; D. Schaller, "Das Aachener Epos für Karl den Kaiser," *Frühmittelalterliche Studien* 10 (1976), 165–67.

53 For a general discussion of Charlemagne, his elite circle of poets, and their cultural milieu at court see Peter Godman, *Poetry of the Carolingian Renaissance* (Norman, Oklahoma, 1985), esp. 9–33.

54 Jean Lafaurie, "Les monnaies impériales de Charlemagne," *Comptes rendus de l'academie des inscriptions et belles-lettres*, January–March, 1978, 154–72, and Bernd Kluge, "Nomen imperatoris und Christiana Religio: Das Kaisertum Karls des Grossen und Ludwigs des Frommen im Licht der numismatischen Quellen," *799. KKK: Beiträge*, 82–87.

55 *LP*, 1:432.

56 Krautheimer, *Rome*, 120–22.

57 Thomas F. X. Noble, *The Republic of St. Peter*, 51–57, passim.

58 The main studies of the medieval palace at the Lateran remain C. Rohault de Fleury, *Le Latran au Moyen-Age* (Paris, 1877), and Ph. Lauer, *Le Palais de Latran* (Paris, 1911). A useful summary of the evidence is provided by Krautheimer, *Rome*, 114–22, and more recently by Ingo Herklotz, "Der Campus Lateranensis im Mittelalter," *Römisches Jahrbuch für Kunstgeschichte* 22 (1985), 1–44. Pertinent excerpts from the *Liber Pontificalis* are found in Ward-Perkins, *From Classical Antiquity*, 256–57. See also Manfred Luchterhandt, "Päpstlicher Palastbau und höfisches Zeremoniell unter Leo III," *799. KKK: Beiträge*, 109–22; and John Osborne, "Papal Court Culture under the Pontificate of Zacharias (A.D. 741–52)," *Court Culture*, 223–34.

59 Leo III also built a triclinium at the Vatican next to St. Peter's basilica about which relatively little is known. See Katherina

Steinke, *Die mittelalterlichen Vatikan Paläste und ihre Kapellen* (Vatican City, 1984), 27–30.

60 See Caecilia Davis-Weyer, "Die Mosaiken Leos III. und die Anfänge der karolingischen Renaissance in Rom," *Zeitschrift für Kunstgeschichte* 29 (1966), 111–32; Hans Belting, "Die beiden Palastaulen Leos III. im Lateran und die Enstehung einer päpstlichen Programmkunst," *Frühmittelalterliche Studien* 12 (1978), 55–83; and Manfred Luchterhandt, "*Famulus Petri*—Karl der Grosse in den römischen Mosaikbildern Leos III," *799. KKK: Beiträge*, 55–70.

61 *Constitutum Constantini*, cap. 14, *MGH*, *Fontes iuris germanici antiqui*, X, ed. Horst Fuhrmann (Hannover, 1968), 87.

62 Richard Krautheimer, "Die Decanneacubita in Konstantinopel. Ein kleiner Beitrag zur Frage Rom und Byzanz," *Tortulae. Römische Quartalschrift*, Supplement 30, 1966, 195–99; and ibid., *Early Christian*, 71, 347–50. Paolo Verzone attempts to identify this excavated triclinium as the famous Hall of the Nineteen couches in "La distruzione dei palazzi imperiali di Roma e di Ravenna e la ristrutturazione del palazzo lateranense nel IX secolo nei rapporti con quello di Costantinopoli," *Roma e l'éta carolingia*, Atti delle giornate di studio, 3–8 Maggio 1976, Istituto nazionale di archeologia e storia dell'arte (Rome, 1976), 39–54; I remain unconvinced.

63 Schlesinger, "Beobachtungen zur Geschichte," *Studien*, 258ff.; and Ludwig Falkenstein, *Der 'Lateran' der karolingischen Pfalz zu Aachen* (Cologne, 1966), passim.

Chapter 7: Private Patronage and Personal Taste

1 In a synodal letter to Louis the German dated November 858 Hincmar wrote: "Palatium . . . regis dicitur propter rationabiles homines inhabitantes, et non propter parietes insensibiles sive macerias." *MGH, Capitularia regum francorum*, 2:431. For a discussion of the meaning of *palatium* in the early Middle Ages see Wilhelm A. Diepenbach, "'Palatium' in spätrömischen und fränkischen Zeit," Diss. Hessischen Ludwigs-Universität (Giessen, 1921), and Pierre Riché, "Les représentations du palais dans les textes littéraires du haut moyen age," *Francia* 4 (1976), 161–71.

2 For this phenomenon and the preceding phase see Donald Bullough, "'Aula Renovata': the Carolingian Court before the Aachen Palace," *Carolingian Renewal: Sources and Heritage* (Manchester, England, 1991), 123–60.

3 A. Guerreau-Jalabert, "La 'Renaissance carolingienne'; modèles culturels, usages linguistiques et, structures sociales," *Bibliotheque de l'école des chartes* 39 (1981) 5–35.

4 For a brilliant introduction to the subject with English translations of selected works see Godman, *Poetry*. See also idem, *Poets and Emperors: Frankish Politics and Carolingian Poetry* (Oxford, 1987), 38–92.

5 For Theodulf's origins see Ann Freeman, "Theodulf of Orleans: A Visigoth at Charlemagne's Court," *L'Europe héritière de l'Espagne wisigothique*, Colloque international du C.N.R.S. tenu à la Fondation Singer-Polignac, Paris, 14–16 May 1990 (Madrid, 1992), 185–94, reprinted in idem, *Theodulf of Orléans*, VIII:185–94.

6 *Opus Caroli regis contra synodum (Libri Carolini)*, ed. A. Freeman with P. Meyvaert, *MGH, Concilia*, II, Supplementum, I (Hannover, 1998). The introduction in German of this volume is reprinted in its original English in Ann Freeman, *Theodulf of Orléans*, I:1–123.

7 Godman, *Poetry*, 150–63.

8 *MGH, Poetae latini*, 1:544–48 and 1:554–56. For Theodulf's interest in art see Ann Freeman, "Theodulf of Orléans and the *Libri Carolini*," *Speculum* 32 (1957), 695–703. Ms. Freeman, however, believes that the map of the world was carved into the surface of a wooden table. See also idem, "Scripture and Images in the *Libri Carolini*," *Testo e immagine nell'alto medioevo*, Settimane di studio del centro italiano di studi sull'alto medioevo, 41 (1994), 163–88. Both articles are reprinted in idem, *Theodulf of Orléans*, II:695–703 and VII:163–88.

9 The most complete study of the building remains that of Jean Hubert, "Germigny-des-Prés," *Congrès archéologique de France*, 93 (1930), 534–68. A new, thorough investigation is sorely needed. The date 806 often assigned to the chapel is erroneously based on an inscription from the nineteenth century; however, a second inscription, providing the day and month of dedication (*Tertio nonas januarias dedicatio huius ecclesiae*), has been shown to date from the ninth or tenth century. See J. Soyer, "Les inscription gravées sur les piliers de l'église carolingienne de Germigny-des-Prés sont-elles anthentiques?" *Bulletin archéologique* (1923), 197–216.

10 The *Catalogus abbatum floriacensium*, from the later ninth or early tenth century, describes the decoration of the chapel as follows: ". . . floribus gipseis atque musivo eius venustavit interiora, pavimentum quoque marmoreo depinxit emblemate. . . ." See *MGH, SS*, 15:500–1, also cited by Hubert, "Germigny-des-Prés," 536 n. 3. For a review of the nineteenth-century restoration and an analysis of what little original decoration is left see Anne-Orange Poilpré, "Le décor de l'oratoire de Germigny-des-Prés: L'authentique et le restauré," *Cahiers de civilisation médiévale Xe–XIIe siècles*, 41 (1998), 281–98.

11 The post-medieval history of the building and the results of the excavations are summarized by Hubert, "Germigny-des-Prés," passim.

12 Precise measurements of the building have never been published either before the rebuilding of the nineteenth century or after. The dimensions used in this discussion are derived from a plan and elevation drawing executed in 1841, before any restoration work, but first published by Hubert, "Germigny-des-Prés," 543 fig. 5, 548 fig. 7.

13 A. Khatchatrian, "Notes sur l'architecture de l'église de Germigny-des-Prés," *Cahiers archéologiques* 7 (1954), 161–69.

14 Carol Heitz, *L'architecture religieuse carolingienne. Les formes et leurs fonctions* (Paris, 1980), 38–40, fig. 27.

15 M. Vieillard-Troiekouroff, "Tables de canons et stucs carolingiens. Le decor architectural et aniconique des bibles de Theodulphe et celui de Germigny-des-Prés," *Stucchi e mosaici altomedioevali*, Atti dell'ottavo congresso di studi sull'arte dell' alto medioevo (Milan, 1962), 154–78.

16 *Miracula sancti Maximi abbatis Miciancensis*: "Theodulf igitur episcopus inter cetera suorum operum basilicam miri operis, instar videlicet eius quae Aquis est constituta, aedificavit in villa quae dicitur Germiniacus." This statement seems to be derived from the more general comment in the earlier *Catalogus abbatum floriacensium*: "Emulatus itaque in hoc facto Magnum Karolum, qui ea tempestate Aquisgrani palatio tanti decoris edificaverat ecclesiam ut in omni Gallia nullam habeat similem." Hubert, "Germigny-des-Prés," 536 n. 3.

17 For a general discussion of this building type see Krautheimer, *Early Christian*, 340–44; Dorothea Lange, "Theorien zur Entstehung des byzantinischen Kreuzkuppelkirche," *Architectura* 16 (1986), 93–113; and Robert Ousterhout, *Master Builders of ByzantiumArchitectura* (Princeton, 1999), 15–19.

18 Stephen Hill, "The 'Praetorium' of Musmiye," *Dumbarton Oaks Papers* 29 (1975), 347–49.

19 Gino Chierici, *La chiesa di S. Satiro a Milano* (Milan, 1942), and more recently Carlo Perogalli, "Analisi critica dell'architettura del sacello di San Satiro," *San Satiro*, ed. Ambrogio Palestra and Carlo Perogalli (Milan, 1980), 155–90 with additional bibliography.

20 Hubert, "Germigny-des-Prés," 537.

21 Angelo Pantoni, "Santa Maria delle Cinque Torri di Cassino: Risultati e problemi," *Rivista di archeologia cristiana*, 51 (1975), 243–80; A. Venditti, *Architettura bizantine nell'Italia meridionale*, 2 vols. (Naples, 1967), 1:591–97; E. Scaccia Scarafoni, "La chiesa cassinese detta 'Santa Maria delle Cinque Torri,'" *Rivista di archeologia cristiana*, 22 (1946), 139–89.

22 Theodemar is referred to as being from the same country as the Frisian saint Liudger: *Vita Sancti Liudgeri, MGH, SS*, 2:410 n. 5. Concerning the copy of the Rule of St. Benedict see Theodemar's letter to Charlemagne, *MGH, Epist.*, 4:510, and *Corpus consuetudinum monasticarum*, ed. Kassius Hallinger, 12 vols. (Siegburg, 1963–), 1:159–60. Hallinger prefers to date the letter to the early ninth century.

23 For the close connections between Fleury and Montecassino see Wallace-Hadrill, *Frankish Church*, 355–57. Both abbeys claimed to possess the bones of St. Benedict. For Paul the Deacon's role in the dispute see Paul Meyvaert, "Peter the Deacon and the Tomb of Saint Benedict," *Revue Bénédictine*, 65 (1955), 3–70, reprinted in idem, *Benedict, Gregory, Bede and Others* (London, 1977). For Theodulf's trip to Rome see Ann Freeman and Paul Meyvaert, "The Meaning of Theodulf's Apse Mosaic at Germigny-des-Prés," *Gesta*, 40 (2001), 125–26.

24 Pedro De Palol, *Early Medieval Art in Spain* (New York, n.d.), 46, 475, ill. 49.

25 Charles B. McClendon, "The Church of S. Maria di Tremiti and Its Significance for the History of Romanesque Architecture," *Journal of the Society of Architectural Historians* 43 (1984), 13–14.

26 ORACULUM SANCTUM ET CHERUBIM HIC ASPICE SPECTANS/ET TESTAMENTI EN MICAT ARCHA DEI/HEC CERNENS PRECIBUSQUE STUDENS PULSARE TONANTEM/THEODULFUM VOTIS IUNGITO QUESO TUIS. Also recorded in *Catalogum abbatum floriacensium, MGH, SS*, 15:500–1, and Hubert, "Germigny-des-Prés," 536 n. 3.

27 Peter Bloch, "Das Apsismosaik von Germigny-des-Prés, Karl der Grosse und der Alte Bund," *Karl der Grosse*, 3:234–61.

28 For a useful summary of the evidence and its relationship to the Germigny mosaic with additional bibliography see Paul Meyvaert, "The Authorship of the Libri Carolini," *Revue Bénédictine*, 89 (1979), 29–57, and more recently Freeman and Meyveart, "The Meaning of Theodulf's Apse Mosaic," 125–39.

29 Meyvaert, "The Authorship," 56.

30 Bloch, "Das Apsismosaik," 257 n. 82, and idem, "Der Kirchenbau als neuer Tempel," *Monumenta Judaica, 2000 Jahre Geschichte und Kultur der Juden am Rhein* (Cologne, 1963), 756 ff. See also Stanley Ferber, "The Temple of Solomon in Early Christian and Byzantine Art," *The Temple of Solomon*, ed. Joseph Gutmann (Missoula, Montana, 1976), 21–46, and Martin Harrison, *A Temple for Byzantium*, 137ff.

31 Bloch, "Das Apsismosaik," 259. Theodulf, *Ad Carolum Regem*: Godman, *Poetry*, 150f. Alcuin: *MGH, Epist.*, 4:235.

32 "Porro in matherio turris, de qua signa pendebant, huiusmodi inseruit versus argenteo colore expressos: HAEC IN HONORE DEI THEODULFUS TEMPLA SACRAVI. . . . At vero Theodulfus, aulam a se constructam omnium conditori ac salvatori rerum Deo consecrans. . . ." *Catalogus abbatum floriacensium, MGH, SS*, 15:500–1, and Hubert, "Germigny-des-Prés," 536 n. 3. For the more common dedicatory formula to Christ or to the Savior in the early Middle Ages see Adolf Ostendorf, "Das Salvator-Patrocinium, seine Aufgänge und seine Ausbreitung im mittelalterlichen Deutschland," *Westfälische Zeitschrift*, 100 (1950), 357–76. For Theodulf's comments about the oneness of God and the Son of God, the second Person of the Trinity, as both creator and savior see Freeman and Meyvaert, "The Meaning of Theodulf's Apse Mosaic," 133ff.

33 André Grabar, "Les mosaiques de Germigny-des-Prés," *Cahiers archéologiques*, 7 (1954), 171–83. See also M. Vieillard-Troiekouroff, "Nouvelles études sur les mosaiques de Germigny-des-Prés," "*Cahiers archéologiques*, 17 (1967), 103–12.

34 Grabar, "Les mosaiques," 180ff.

35 R. Pfister, "Les tissus de la Bible de Théodulf," *Coptic Studies in Honor of Walter Ewig Crum* (Boston, 1951), 501ff.

36 For the historical background and variations of the cubit see Fernie, "Historical Metrology," esp. 383–91. For a discussion of the "standard" .445-meter-cubit see Harrison, *A Temple for Byzantium*, 137f.

37 This, at least, is the unit of measure used by Leo of Ostia in his eleventh-century chronicle of Montecassino to describe the church of S. Salvatore built by Abbot Gisulf (797–817). See Angelo Pantoni, *Le vicende della basilica di Montecassino*, Miscellanea Cassinese 36 (Montecassino, 1973), 149, and Giovanni Carbonara, *Iussu Desiderii. Montecassino e l'architettura campano-abruzzese nell'undicesimo secolo* (Rome, 1979), 79, ns. 17–19.

38 Theodulf, *Ad Carolum Regem*: Godman, *Poetry*, 458–59, and *MGH, Poetae latini*, 1:487. Alcuin: carmen no. 30, *MGH, Poetae latini*, 1:248.

39 Laistner, *Thought and Letters*, 232, and Lehmann, "Fulda und die antike Literature," *Geistesleben*, 9–23.

40 "Epistola de litteris colendis," *MGH, Capitaularia*, 1:78f.; an English translation appears in Laistner, *Thought and Letters*, 196–97. For a likely date between 781 and 791 see Rosamond McKitterick, *The Frankish Kingdoms under the Carolingians, 751–987* (London and New York, 1983), 145. It has been shown that the copy received at Fulda was originally addressed to Angilram of Metz, the Charlemagne court chaplain, and not to Baugulf, as previously assumed. See Thomas Martin, "Bemerkungen zur 'Epistola de litteris colendis,'" *Archiv für Diplomatik* 31 (1985), 227–72.

41 Alcuin: carmen 26, *MGH, Poetae latini*, 1:245. "Gesta abbatum Fontanellensium," *MGH, SS*, 2:296f, under Abbot Ansegis (823–33): "exactor operum regalium in Aquisgrani palatio sub Einhardo abbate, viro undecumque doctissimo, a domno rege constitutus est." See also Josef Fleckenstein, "Einhard, seine Gründung und sein Vermächtnis in Seligenstadt," *Das Einhardkreuz*, ed. Karl Hauck, Abhandlungen der Akademie der Wissenschaften in Göttingen, Phil. Hist. Kl. 87 (1974), 99 n. 18 and 101 n. 28, and more recently Günther Binding, "'Multis arte fuit utilis' Einhard als Organisator am Aachener Hof und als Bauherr in Steinbach und Seligenstadt," *Mittellateinisches Jahrbuch* 30 (1995), 30–36.

42 "Infra capella scriptum: Insignem hanc dignitatis aulam Karolus caesar magnus instituit, egregius Odo magister explevit, Metensi fotus in urbe quiescit." (Inside the chapel was written: This great hall was established by the emperor Charles; the distinguished master Odo, who is buried in the city of Metz, carried out [the project].) The text of this purported inscription is inserted in section 31 of a late-ninth-century copy of Einhard's *Life of Charlemagne* in the Austrian National Library in Vienna: Codice bibliothecae Caesares Vindobonensis 969 (Theol. 354), fol. 55v. Odo is otherwise unknown. See Günther Binding, "Zur Ikonologie der Aachener Pfalzkapelle nach den Schriftquellen," *Mönchtum—Kirche—Herrschaft 750–1000*, ed. Dieter R. Bauer et al. (Sigmaringen, 1998), 198–99.

43 Schaller, "Das Aachener Epos," passim, and Godman, *Poetry*, 22.

44 The following remarks are based on the article by Hans Belting, "Der Einhardbogen," *Zeitschrift für Kunstgeschichte* 36

(1973) 93–121, and the collected essays by a variety of specialists in *Das Einhardkreuz*, ed. Hauck, and *Einhard: Studien zu Leben und Werk*, ed. Hermann Schefers (Darmstadt, 1997).

45 *MGH, SS*, 21:359.

46 "Translatio et miracula sanctorum Marcellini et Petri auctore Einhardo," *MGH, SS* 15:239–64. For English translations see *The History of the Translation of the Blessed Martyrs of Christ Marcellinus and Peter*, trans. Barrett Wendell (Cambridge, Mass., 1926); and *Charlemagne's Courtier: The Complete Einhard*, ed. and trans. Paul Edward Dutton (Ontario, 1998), 69–130.

47 "Translatio," *MGH, SS*, 15:240; *The History*, trans. Wendell, 6; and *Charlemagne's Courtier*, 70.

48 Fleckenstein, "Einhard," 110; Krautheimer, *Corpus*, 2:191–204. Excavations of 1956 first published by F. W. Deichmann and A. Tschira, "Das Mausoleum der Kaiserin Helena und die Basilika der heiligen Marcellinus und Petrus an der Via Labicana vor Rom," *Jahrbuch des deutschen archäologischen Instituts* 72 (1957), 44ff., and reprinted in Deichmann, *Rom, Ravenna*, 305–74.

49 Hermann Schefers, "Einhards römische Reliquien: Zur Bedeutung der Reliquientranslation Einhards von 827/828," *Archiv für hessische Geschichte und Altertumskunde*, N.S. 48 (1990), 279–92; Fleckenstein, "Einhard," 111; Hermann-Mascard, *Les reliques*, 375. See also Patrick Geary, *Furta Sacra: Thefts of Relics in the Central Middle Ages* (Princeton, 1978), passim.

50 Thomas Ludwig, Otto Müller, and Irmgard Widdra-Spiess, *Die Einhards-Basilika in Steinbach bei Michelstadt im Odenwald* (Mainz, 1996). For a more concise description and historical summary with extensive bibliography see *VK*, 320–22, and *VK, Nbd*, 399.

51 Leo Hugot, *Kornelimünster*, Rheinische Ausgraben 2, Beihefte der Bonner Jahrbücher 26 (1968). See also Werner Jacobsen, "Benedikt von Aniane und die Architektur unter Ludwig dem Frommen zwischen 814 und 830," *Riforma religiosa e arti nell'epoca carolingia*, ed. Alfred Schmid, Atti del XXIV congresso internazionale di storia dell'arte (Bologna, 1983), 15–22; and Binding, " 'Multis arte fuit utilis'," 43–44.

52 For a summary of the results of the limited excavations see *La Neustrie: Les pays au nord de la Loire de Dagobert à Charles le Chauve (VIIe–IXe siècles)*, ed. Patrick Périn and L.-C. Feffer (Paris, 1985), 169–75. Crook, *The Architectural Setting*, 109–16 provides a useful discussion of the evidence with further bibliography.

53 *VK*, 309–11. Dendrochonological analysis has shown that timber from two wood samples was originally cut in 833 and 835. See *VK, Nbd*, 382–83.

54 Krautheimer, "Carolingian Revival," *Studies*, 206–12.

55 Einharti Epistola n. 10, *MGH, Epist* 5:113f.

56 Einhardi Epistola n. 36, *MGH, Epist* 5:128.

57 "Translatio," *MGH, SS*, 15:254; *The History*, trans. Wendell, 67–66; *Charlemagne's Courtier*, 104; and Eleanor Shipley Duckett, *Carolingian Portraits: A Study in the Ninth Century* (Ann Arbor, 1969), 84.

58 The date of composition of Einhard's *Vita Caroli* is still much debated, but the general consensus seems to be the mid-820s to ca. 830. See, for example, the discussion in *Charlemagne's Courtier*, xviii–xx, and Bullough, " 'Aula Renovata,' " 147 n. 2.

59 Belting, "Der Einhardsbogen," 114f.; Fleckenstein, "Einhard," 116–21.

60 Krautheimer, *Rome*, 123–39; idem, "Carolingian Revival," *Studies*, 203ff. For a detailed architectural analysis of S. Prassede see: idem, *Corpus*, 3:232–59. Although Popes Hadrian I and Leo III had been generous patrons of church building, the Petrine formula of the T-shaped basilica was not used during their reigns. See Franz Alto Bauer, "Die Bau- and Stiftungspolitik der Päpste Hadrian I. (772–95) und Leo III. (795–816)," *799. KKK: Beiträge*, 514–28.

61 *LP*, 2:52.

62 *LP*, 2:64: ". . . multa corpora sanctorum dirutis in cimiteriis iacentia . . . deportans recondidit." An inscription in the church, now believed to be original, claims that the remains of a total of 2,300 (!) saints were translated. See Ursula Nilgen, "Die grosse Relinquieninschrift von Santa Prassede," *Römische Quartalschrift* 69 (1974), 7–29.

63 Richard Lipsius, *Die Apokryphen Apostelgeschichte und Apostellegenden*, 2 vols. (Braunschweig, 1887), 2:418–19; *Bibliotheca Sanctorum*, 12 vols. (Rome, 1961–69), 10:col. 1064. The father of Praxedis and Pudentiana was identified as a certain Pudens, mentioned by St. Paul (2 Tm 4.21).

64 Adalheid Hahn, "Das Hludowicianum," *Archiv für Diplomatik* 21 (1975), 15–135, provides the most detailed study of this document. See also Noble, *The Republic of St. Peter*, 148–53, 299–308, and the comments by Raymond Davis, trans., *The Lives of the Ninth-Century Popes (Liber Pontificalis)* (Liverpool, 1995), 1–4. For a discussion of this material from a somewhat different perspective see my article "Louis the Pious, Rome and Constantinople," *Architectural Studies in Memory of Richard Krautheimer* (Mainz, 1997), 103–6. For Paschal's artistic patronage in general see Erik Thuno, *Image and Relic: Mediating the Sacred in Early Medieval Rome* (Rome, 2002).

65 At S. Prassede a screen of six ornamental columns at the head of the nave in front of the transept's triumphal arch imitated the arrangement in front of the apse at St. Peter's (fig. 2.7). See Judson J. Emerick, "Focusing on the Celebrant: The Column Display inside Santa Prassede," *Papers of the Netherlands Institute in Rome (Mededelingen van het Nederlands Instituut te Rome)*, Historical Studies 59 (2000), 127–9.

66 P. J. Nordhagen, "Un problema di carattere iconografico e tecnico a S. Prassede," *Roma e l'età carolingia*, 159–66; and Rotraut Wisskirchen, *Das Mosaikprogram von S. Prassede in Rome: Ikonographie und Ikonologie* (Jahrbuch für Antike und Christentum 17), Münster, 1990, 29ff.

67 The text of the antiphon reads: "Ambulante sanct dei, ingredimini in civitatem domini; hedificatum est enim vobis ecclesiam novam. . . ." See Joseph Dyer, "Prologomena to a History of Music and Liturgy at Rome in the Middle Ages," *Essays on Medieval Music in Honor of David G Hughes*, ed. G. M. Hughes (Cambridge, Massachusetts; 1995), 94–99. Thomas D. Kozachek, "The Repertory of Chant for Dedicating Churches in the Middle Ages: Music, Liturgy, and Ritual," Ph.D. diss. (Harvard University, 1995), 252, shows that these antiphons probably predate the reign of Paschal. The suggestion by Marchita B. Mauck, "The Mosaic of the Triumphal Arch of S. Prassede: A Liturgical Interpretation," *Speculum* 62 (1987), 813–28, that the mosaic relates to an antiphon for the funeral liturgy seems less likely. For the use of the term *arcus triumphalis* see: Krautheimer, "Carolingian Revival," *Studies*, 233.

68 Guglielmo Matthiae, *Pittura romana del medioevo*, 2 vols. (Rome, 1965–66), 1:218–19 and figs. 141–42; and J. Wilpert, *Die Römischen Mosaiken und Malereien der kirchlichen Bauten von IV bis XIII Jahrhunderts*, 4 vols. (Freiburg, 1916), 4:pls. 202–4.

69 *LP*, 2:54. See also Jean-Marie Sansterre, *Les moines grecs et orientaux à Rome aux époques byzantine et carolingienne (milieu du VIe s.–du IXe s.)*, 2 vols. (Brussels, 1983), 38f.

70 Krautheimer, *Rome*, 128. See also Beat Brenk, "Zum Bildprogramm der Zenokapelle in Rom," *Archivo Espanol de Arqueologia* 45–47 (1972–74), 213–21; and Gillian Mackie, "The Zeno Chapel: A Prayer for Salvation," *PBSR* 57 (1989), 172–99.

71 Caecilia Davis-Weyer, "Die ältesten Darstellungen der Hadesfahrt Christi, Das Evangelium Nikodemi und ein Mosaik der Zeno-Kappelle," *Roma e l'éta carolingia*, 183–94, and

Anna Kartsonis, *Anastasis: The Making of an Image* (Princeton, 1986), 88–96.

72 Sansterre, *Les moines grecs*, 1:42f. In a letter to Pope Paschal I, the fervent opponent to iconoclasm, the Greek abbot Theodore of Studios, described Rome as "a city of refuge." *PG*, 99, col. 1156. For further remarks concerning Paschal's contacts with Byzantine iconodules see below.

73 Krautheimer, *Corpus*, 2:308–21; idem, *Rome*, 105, 122; and de Blaauw, "Die Krypte," 564.

74 Franz Rademacher, *Die Regina Angelorum in der Kunst des Mittelalters*, Die Kunstdenkmäler des Rheinlandes, Beiheft 17 (Düsseldorf, 1972), passim; Marian Lawrence, "Maria Regina," *Art Bulletin* 7 (1925), 150–61; and Ursula Nilgen, "Maria Regina—ein Politischer Kultusbild?" *Römisches Jahrbuch für Kunstgeschichte* 19 (1981), 1–33. For this apse mosaic in general see Guglielmo Matthiae, *Mosaici medioevali delle chiese di Roma*, 2 vols. (Rome, 1967), 1:235ff. To appreciate the unique qualities of this composition in comparison to other apse mosaics in Rome see: Christa Belting-Ihm, "Theophanic Images of Divine Majesty in Early Medieval Italian Church Decoration," *Italian Church Decoration of the Early Middle Ages and Early Renaissance*, ed. William Tronzo (Bologna, 1989), 43–59; and Rotraut Wisskirchen, "Santa Maria in Domnica. überlegungen zur frühesten apsidialen Darstellung der thronenden Maria in Rom," *Aachenener Kunstblätter*, 61 (1995–97), 381–93.

75 Nicholas Oikonomides, "Some Remarks on the Apse Mosaic of St. Sophia," *Dumbarton Oaks Papers* 39 (1985), 111–15. For a rebuttal of this thesis see Elizabeth James and Ruth Webb, "'To Understand Ultimate Things and Enter Secret Place': Ekphrasis and Art in Byzantium," *Art History* 14 (1991), 1–17, esp. 12–13.

76 Sansterre, *Les moines grecs*, 1:42–45, 128–31, and V. Grumel, "Les relations politico-religieuses entre Byzance et Rome sous le règne de Léon V l'Arménien," *Revue des études byzantines* 18 (1960), 19–44. For Paschal's letter to Leo V see G. Mercati, *Note di litteratura biblica e cristiana antica*, Studi e testi 5 (Rome, 1901), 227–35. The art historical significance of Paschal's contacts with participants in the iconoclastic upheaval has not to my knowledge been adequately explored. It is mentioned in passing by Hélène Ahrweiler, "The Geography of the Iconoclast Reform," and Robin Cormack, "The Arts during the Age of Iconoclasm," both in *Iconoclasm*, ed. Anthony Bryer and Judith Herrin (Birmingham, 1977), 24 and 44. It is also discussed briefly by Thuno, *Image and Relic*, 131–40. Emile Mâle in *The Early Churches of Rome*, trans. D. Buxton (Chicago, 1960), 85–88, considers the decoration of S. Maria in Domnica in the general context of iconoclasm without pursuing the full implications of this relationship.

77 Carlo Bertelli, *La Madonna di Santa Maria in Trastevere* (Rome, 1961), passim.

78 Rademacher, *Regina Angelorum*, 21 n. 34, and Leo Scheffczyk, *Das Mariengeheimnis in Frömmigkeit und Lehre der Karolingerzeit*, Erfuhrter Theologische Studien 5 (Leipzig, 1959), passim. For further comments on the importance of images of Mary for the opposition in Rome to Byzantine iconoclasm see John Osborne, "Images of the Mother of God in Early Medieval Rome," *Icon and Word: The Power of Images in Byzantium*, Studies presented to Robin Cormack, ed. Anthony Eastmond and Liz James (Aldershot, 2003), 146.

79 Ann Freeman, "Carolingian Orthodoxy and the Fate of the *Libri Carolini*," *Viator* 16 (1985), 65–108.

80 Since the reign of Hadrian I, the papacy had linked the use of religious imagery to the cult of relics in its condemnation of iconoclasm. See David F. Appleby, "Holy relic and holy image: Saints' relics in the western controversy over images in the eighth and ninth centuries," *Word and Image* 8 (1992), 342 n. 49. See also Thuno, *Image and Relic*, passim, esp. 151ff.

81 EMICAT AULA PIAE VARIIS DECORATA METALLIS/ PRAXEDIS D(omi)NO SUPER AETHRA PLACENTIS HONORE/PONTIFICIS SUMMI STUDIO PASCHALIS ALUMNI/SEDIS APOSTOLICAE PASSIM QUI CORPORA CONDENS/PLURIMA S(an)C(T)ORUM SUBTER HAEC MOENIA PONIT/FRETUS UT HIS LIMEN MEREATUR ADIRE POLORUM. *LP* 2:63 n.10.

82 *LP*, 2:56. For a discussion of the discovery and translation see Thomas Connolly, *Mourning into Joy: Music, Raphael, and Saint Cecilia* (New Haven and London, 1994), 37ff.

83 Krautheimer, *Rome*, fig. 98, passim, and idem, *Corpus*, 1:93–112.

84 Krautheimer, *Rome*, passim; idem, "Carolingian Revival," *Studies*, 203ff.; idem, *Corpus*, 2:216–47, 4:1–36, 4:178–98; and de Blaauw, "Die Krypta," 565, 567.

85 For the political and economic background to the architectural transformation of Rome in general during this period see Thomas F. X. Noble, "Paradoxes and Possibilities in the Sources for Roman Society in the Early Middle Ages," *Early Medieval Rome and the Christian West: Essays in Honour of Donald A. Bullough*, ed. J. Smith (Leiden, 2000), 55–83, and idem, "Topography, Celebration, and Power: The Making of Papal Rome in the Eighth and Ninth Centuries," *Topographies of Power in the Early Middle Ages*, ed. Mayke De Jong and Frans Theuws with Carine van Rhijn (Leiden, 2001), 45–91.

Chapter 8: The Monastic Realm: Ideal and Reality

1 *Sancti Benedicti Regula Monachorum*, chapt. 66. Authoritative English translations of the entire text are *The Rule of St Benedict in Latin and English*, ed. and trans. Abbot Justin McCann (London, 1972), and *The Rule of St. Benedict in Latin and English with Notes*, ed. Timothy Fry, O.S.B., et al. (Collegeville, Minn., 1980).

2 *S. Benedicti Regula*, chaps. 22, 35, 38, 41, 52, and 53.

3 For a survey of early monastic architecture in Egypt and elsewhere in the Near East see Horn, "On the Origins," 13–18, and Ossa Raymond Sowers, "Medieval Monastic Planning: Its Origins in the Christian East and Later Developments in the Western Europe," Ph.D. diss., Columbia University, 1951, 41ff. For Pachomius in particular see Philip Rousseau, *Pachomius: The Making of a Community in Fourth-Century Egypt* (Berkeley and London, 1985). The survey by Wolfgang Braunfels, *Monasteries of Western Europe* (London, 1972), 9–46, provides a general discussion of early developments in monastic architecture.

4 See chapter 4 note 30. In addition see: for the Irish monastic layout in general, Michael Herity, "The Layout of Irish early Christian monasteries," *Irland und Europa*, ed. P. N. Chatain and Michael Richter (Stuttgart, 1984), 105–15, and Leo Swan, "Monastic Proto-Towns in Early Medieval Ireland: The Evidence of Aerial Photography, Plan Analysis and Survey," *The Comparative History of Urban Origins in non-Roman Europe*, ed. H. B. Clarke and A. Simms, British Archaeological Reports International Series 255, 2 vols. (Oxford, 1985), 1:77–102; for Skellig Michael, Liam de Paor, "A Survey of Sceilig Mhichil," *Journal of the Royal Society of Antiquaries of Ireland* 85 (1955), 174–87; for Nendrum, H. C. Lawlor, *The Monastery of St. Mochaoi of Nendrum* (Belfast, 1925); and for the reuse of ring forts as monasteries, Charles Thomas, *The Early Christian Archaeology of North Britain* (London and Oxford, 1971), 32–35.

5 Lawrence Nees, "The Colophon Drawing in the Book of Mulling: A Supposed Irish Monastery Plan and the Tradition

of Terminal Illustrations in Early Medieval Manuscripts," *Cambridge Medieval Celtic Studies* 5 (1983), 67–91.

6 S. E. Rigold, "'Litus Romanus'—The Shore Forts as Mission Stations," *The Saxon Shore*, ed. D. E. Johnson, Council for British Archaeology, Research Report 18 (London, 1977), 70–75.

7 Charles Peers and C. A. Ralegh Radford, "The Saxon Monastery at Whitby," *Archaeologia* 89, 1943, 27–88.

8 For the early settlements of St. Martin see Edward James, "Archaeology and the Merovingian Monastery," *Columbanus and Merovingian Monasticism*, ed. H. B. Clarke and Mary Brennan, British Archaeological Reports, International Series 113 (Oxford, 1981), 36 and 49 ns. 9–11. For the *Life of St. Martin* see *Sulpice Sévère: Vie de Saint Martin*, ed. and trans. Jacques Fontaine, 2 vols. (Paris, 1967–69).

9 See Horn, "The Origins," 34–35, and James, "Archaeology and the Merovingian Monastery," 38–40, for an analysis of this text and alternative reconstructions.

10 Charles B. McClendon, *The Imperial Abbey of Farfa*, 62–64; Richard Hodges, *Light in the Dark Ages: The Rise and Fall of San Vincenzo al Volturno* (Ithaca, New York, 1997), 43ff. with additional bibliography. In general see Percival, *The Roman Villa*, 176–78, and idem, "Villas and Monasteries in Late Roman Gaul," *Journal of Ecclesiastical History* 48 (1997), 1–21.

11 Behn, *Die karolingische Klosterkirche von Lorsch*, passim. For subsequent literature see *VK*, 181–82, and *VK, Nbd*, 251–53. For recent discussions of monastic planning from somewhat different perspectives see: Beat Brenk, "Benedetto e il problema dell'architettura monastica prima dell'anno mille," *L'Europa e l'arte italiana*, ed. Max Seidel (Venice, 2000), 16–39, and three essays by Werner Jacobsen, "Die Anfänge des abendländischen Kreuzgangs," Jean-Pierre Caillet, "Atrium, péristyle et cloître: Des réalités si diverses?" and Rolf Legler, "Der abendländische Kreuzgang: Erfindung oder Tradition?" in *Der mittelalterlicher Kreuzgang*, ed. Peter K. Klein (Regensbeurg, 2004), 37–79.

12 Alfons Zettler, *Die frühen Klosterbauten Reichenau* (Sigmaringen, 1988), passim.

13 Paul Meyvaert, "The Medieval Monastic Claustrum," *Gesta* 12 (1973), 53–54.

14 David Parsons, "The Pre-Romanesque Church of St-Riquier: The Documentary Evidence," *Journal of the British Archaeological Association* 129 (1976), 21–51. For a refutation of Parsons's conclusions see Susan A. Rabe, *Faith, Art, and Politics at Saint-Riquier: The Symbolic Vision of Angilbert* (Philadelphia, 1995), 12–20. The detailed reconstructions of the abbey church in Georges Durand, "Saint-Riquier," *La Picardie historique et monumentale* (Amiens and Paris, 1907–11), 4:133–358, and Wilhelm Effmann, *Centula: Saint-Riquier. Eine Untersuchung zur Geschichte der kirchlichen Baukunst in der Karolingerzeit* (Münster, 1912), have until recently been considered standard. The best edition of the Chronicle of Centula is Ferdinand Lot, *Hariulf: Chronique de l'Abbaye de Saint-Riquier (Ve siècle-1104)* (Paris, 1894). See also Migne, *PL*, 174, col. 1213ff. The text of the *Institutio* from the Vatican manuscript (Reg. lat. 235) is found in *Corpus Consuetudinum Monasticarum*, ed. Kassius Hallinger, 1:284ff.

15 Parsons, "The Pre-Romanesque Church," 23 and n. 12. See also H. M. Taylor, "Tenth-Century Church Building in England and on the Continent," *Tenth-Century Studies*, ed. David Parsons (London, 1975), 238 n. 8.

16 Only preliminary reports have thus far appeared, including: Honoré Bernard, "D'Hariulphe à Effmann, à la lumière des récentes fouilles de Saint-Riquier," *Actes du 95e congrès national des société savantes, Reims 1970*, Section d'archéologie et d'histoire de l'art (Paris, 1974), 220–35; idem, "Un site prestigieux du monde-carolingien, Saint-Riquier. Peut-on connaitre la grande basilique d'Angilbert?" *Cahiers archeologique de Picardie* 5 (1978), 241–54; idem, "Saint-Riquier: une restitution nouvelle de la Basilique d''Angilbert," *Revue du Nord* 71 (1989), 307–61; and idem, "Saint-Riquier. Fouilles et découvertes récentes," *Avant-nefs*, 88–107.

17 First reported by Heitz, *L'architecture religieuse carolingienne*, 238 n. 7, who quotes a letter from Bernard dated August 31, 1979. See now Honoré Bernard, "L'abbaye de Saint-Riquier. Evolution des batiments monastiques du IXe au XVIIIe siècle," *Sous la règle de Saint Benoit. Structures monastiques et sociétés en France du moyen age à l'époque moderne*, Abbaye bénédictine Sainte-Marie de Paris 23–25 Octobre 1980 (Geneva, 1982), 518–23.

18 *S. Benedicti Regula*, chaps. 43–47 and 52. See also C. Butler, *Benedictine Monachism* (London, 1919).

19 Angelus A. Häussling, *Mönchskonvent und Eucharistifeier. Eine Studie über die Messe in der abendländischen Klosterliturgie des frühen Mittelalters und zur Geschichte der Messhäufigkeit*, Liturgiewissenschaftliche Quellen und Forschungen 58 (Münster, 1973), passim, esp. 54ff.; Cyrille Vogel, "La réforme liturgique sous Charlemagne," *Karl der Grosse*, 2:217–32; and *Corpus Consuetudinum*, ed. Hallinger, 1:159–60.

20 For a discussion of this issue see Virginia Jansen, "Round or Square? The Axial Towers of the Abbey Church of Saint-Riquier," *Gesta* 21 (1982), 83ff.

21 For Bernard's most recent interpretation see "Saint-Riquier: Fouilles et découvertes récentes," 91ff.

22 Edgar Lehmann, "Die Anordnung der Altäre in der karolingischen Klosterkirche zu Centula," *Karl der Grosse*, 3:374–83; Carol Heitz, "Architecture et liturgie processionnelle à l'époque préromane," *Revue de l'art*, 24 (1974), 30–47; and Rabe, *Faith, Art, and Politics*, 117–20. Subsidiary altars and chapels began to appear in Roman churches in the course of the early Middle Ages, but they were not as evenly distributed throughout the interior as seems to have been the case at Saint-Riquier. For Rome in general and Old St. Peter's in particular see Bauer, "La frammentazione liturgica," 398ff.

23 Jean-Charles Picard, "Les origines du mot *paradisus*—parvis," *Mélanges de l'école française de Rome: Moyen-Age—Temps Modernes* 83 (1971), 158–86.

24 Lot, *Hariulf*, 53. This reference comes in Book 2 of the Chronicle of Centula, which is derived from Angilbert's *Libellus*.

25 For a review of the material in English with additional bibliography see David Parsons, "Sites and Monuments of the Anglo-Saxon Mission in Central Germany," *Archaeological Journal* 140 (1983), 280–321, esp. 288–91, 295–306, 312–16. See also *VK*, 84–87, and *VK, Nbd*, 132–33.

26 Vita Sturmi abbatis auctore Eigilo, *Die Vita Sturmi des Eigil von Fulda*, ed. Pius Engelbert (Marburg, 1968), 91–95, 146–47. Sturmi travelled to monasteries in Tuscany and Rome in 747, and spent a year at Montecassino. Between 744 and his return from Italy, there may, in fact, have been a temporary church along the same axis, without aisles and with a square apse, but the evidence is too fragmentary to be conclusive. For a review of the controversy see Parsons, "Sites and Monuments," 300–3.

27 Krautheimer, "The Carolingian Revival," *Studies*, 209–12.

28 Candidus de vita Aeigili (metrica), *MGH, Poetae latini*, 2:111.

29 *VK*, 297–99.

30 Arnold Wolff, *Vorbericht über die Ergebnisse der Kölner Domgrabung 1946–1983. Dargestellt nach den Veröffentlichungen von Otto Doppelfeld und Willy Weyres*, Forschungsberichte des Landes Nordrhein-Westfalen, Nr. 3000, Fachgruppe Geisteswissenschaften (Opladen, 1983), 42–46, and Willy

Weyres, *Die vorgotischen Bischofskirchen in Köln*, Studien zum Kölner Dom 1, ed. Arnold Wolff (Cologne, 1987), 88–100.

31 *Les Ordines Romani du haut moyen age*, ed. M. Andrieu, 3 vols. (Louvain, 1948–51), 2:83: "Et surgens pontifex osculat evangelia et altare et accedit ad sedem suam et stat ad orientem." See Carol Heitz, "Nouvelles interprétations de l'art carolingienne," *Revue de l'art*, 1–2 (1968), 107, and idem, "More Romano: Problèmes d'architecture et liturgie carolingiennes," *Roma e l'età carolingia*, 28–29. For a detailed discussion of the transmission and revisions of the so-called *Hadrianum*, the sacramentary sent to Charlemagne by Pope Hadrian I between 784 and 791, see Rosamond McKitterick, *The Frankish Church*, 130ff.

32 Catalogus abbatum fuldensium, *MGH, SS*, 13:272: "Ratgar, sapiens architectus, occidentale templum . . . mira arte et immensa magnitudine alteri copulans, unam fecit ecclesiam." This source was written in the tenth century.

33 "Supplex libellus monachorum," *Corpus consuetudinum*, 1:324: "Ut aedificia immensa atque superflua et cetera inutilia opera omittantur, quibus fratres ultra modum fatigantur et familiae foris dispereunt, sed omnia iuxta mensuram et discretionem fiant. Fratribus quoque secundum regulam certis horis vacare lectioni liceat et item certis operari."

34 Daniel J. Sheerin, "The Church Dedication 'Ordo' used at Fulda, 1 Nov., 819," *Revue Bénédictine* 92 (1982), 305–16.

35 Vita Eigilis fuldensis, *MGH, SS*, 15:231: "Tamen claustrum monasterii ex modo construere cogitavit. Vocantur ad consilium fratres. Quaesitum est, in quo loco aedificatis claustris congruentes potuisset aptari. Quidam dederunt consilium, contra partem meridianam basilicae iuxta morem prioris, quidam autem romano more contra plagam occidentalem satius poni, confirmant, propter vicinitatem martyris, qui in ea basilicae parte quiescit."

36 Joseph Vonderau, "Die Ausgrabungen am Dome zu Fulda in den Jahren 1908–1913," *Sechszehnte Veröffentlichung des Fuldaer Geschichtsvereins* (1919), 5–36.

37 Jean-Charles Picard, "Le quadriportique de Saint-Paul-hors-les-murs à Rome," *Mélanges d'archéologie et d'histoire de l'école française de Rome: Antiquité* 87 (1975), 395.

38 Hodges, *Light in the Dark Ages*, 77–117; Richard Hodges and John Mitchell, *The Basilica of Abbot Joshua at San Vincenzo al Volturno* (Abbey of Monte Cassino, 1996).

39 Vita Eigilis fuldensis, *MGH, SS*, 15:228: "Immensa vero aedificia, pater, et opera non necessaria, quibus familiae foris et intus fratrum congregatio fatigatur, exhinc penitus ad mensuram dimitte."

40 Thomas F. X. Noble, "The Monastic Ideal as a Model for Empire: The Case of Louis the Pious," *Revue Bénédictine* 86 (1976), 235–50, with references to earlier bibliography. Above all, see also Joseph Semmler, "Reichsidee und kirchliche Gesetzgebung," *Zeitschrift für Kirchengeschichte* 71 (1960), 37–65.

41 Joseph Semmler, "Studien zum Supplex Libellus und zur anianischen Reform in Fulda," *Zeitschrift für Kirchengeschichte* 69 (1958), 268–98.

42 P. Schmitz, "L'influence de Saint Benoit d'Aniane dans l'histoire de l'Ordre de Saint Benoit," *Il monachesimo nell'alto medioveo a la formazione della civiltà occidentale*, Settimane di studio del centro italiano di studi sull'alto medioevo 4 (1957), 401–15, and Josef Narberhaus, *Benedikt von Aniane. Werk und Persönlichkeit* (Münster, 1930). For an account of Benedict's life see: Ardonis vita Benedicti abbatis Anianensis et Indensis, *MGH, SS*, 15:198–220. For an English translation see: *Soldiers of Christ: Saints and Saints' Lives from Late Antiquity and the Early Middle Ages*, ed. Thomas F. X. Noble and Thomas Head (University Park, 1995), 213–54.

43 Leo Hugot, *Kornelimünster*, passim.

44 Jacobsen, "Benedikt von Aniane," 15–22.

45 Werner Jacobsen, "Gab es die karolingische 'Renaissance' in der Baukunst?" *Zeitschrift für Kunstgeschichte* 51 (1988), 336–37.

46 Semmler, "Studien zum Supplex Libellus," 282–83.

47 U. Lobbedey, *Die Ausgrabungen im Dom zu Paderborn 1978/80 und 1983*, Denkmalpflege und Forschung in Westfalen 11, 4 vols. (Bonn, 1986), 1:20–34, 143–58.

48 Günther Binding, "Die karolingisch-salische Klosterkirche Hersfeld," *Aachener Kunstblätter* 41 (1971), 189–200.

49 Bernhard Bischoff, "Die Entstehung des Klosterplanes in paläographischer Sicht," *Studien zum St. Galler Klosterplan* (St. Gallen, 1962), 67–78.

50 Horn and Born, *The Plan of St. Gall*, and Werner Jacobsen, *Der Klosterplan von St. Gallen und die karolingische Architectur* (Berlin, 1992). For a review of the previous literature see Horn and Born, op. cit., 1:2–7, and Jacobsen, op. cit., 15–34. See also Jacobsen, "Altere und neuere Forschungen um den St. Galler Klosterplan," *Unsere Kunstdenkmäler* 34 (1983), 134–51.

51 Horn and Born, *The Plan of St. Gall*, 3:16. Haec tibi dulcissime fili cozb(er)te de posicione officinarum paucis examplata direxi, quibus sollertiam exerceas tuam, meamq(ue) devotione(m) utcumq(ue) cognoscas, qua tuae bonae voluntati satisfacere me segnem non inveniri confido. Ne suspiceris autem me haec ideo elaborasse, quod vos putemus n(ost)ris indigere magisteriis, sed potius ob amore(m) dei tibi soli p(er) scrutinanda pinxisse amicabili fr(ater)nitatis intuitu crede. Vale in Chr(ist)o semp(er) memor n(ost)ri ame(n).

52 Paul Meyvaert, review of Horn and Born, *The Plan of St. Gall*, in *University Publishing* (Summer, 1980), 18–19, and Adalbert de Vogüé, "Le Plan de Saint-Gall, copie d'un document officiel? Une lecture de la lettre à Gozbert," *Revue Bénédictine* 94 (1984), 295–314, esp. 301. See also Lawrence Nees, "The Plan of St. Gall and the Theory of the Program of Carolingian Art," *Gesta* 25 (1986), 1–8.

53 Certainly *exemplata*, as a past participle, cannot be combined with the preposition *haec* to mean "this copy" as one finds in Horn's translation; rather it must refer to the fact that the plan was "copied" (Meyvaert, op. cit.) or, if combined with *paucis* (meaning "briefly"), "summarily indicated" (de Vogüé, op. cit.)

54 Jacobsen, *Der Klosterplan*, 35–106; Norbert Stachura, "Der Plan von St. Gallen—ein Original?" *Architectura* 8 (1978), 184–86, and idem, "Der Westabschluss der Klosterkirche und seine Varianten," *Architectura* 10 (1980), 33–37.

55 Eric Fernie, "The Proportions of the St. Gall Plan," *Art Bulletin* 40 (1978), 583–89; Albrecht Kottmann, "Neue Thesen zum St. Galler Klosterplan," *Das Münster: Zeitschrift für christliche Kunst und Kunstwissenschaft* (1978), 277–79. See also David Parson, "Consistency and the St. Gallen plan: a review article," *Archaeological Journal* 138 (1981), 259–65.

56 Joseph Semmler, "Die Beschlüsse des Aachener Konzils im Jahre 816," *Zeitschrift für Kirchengeschichte* 74 (1963), 15–82.

57 The legislation from these two synods, in various compilations, are found in *Corpus Consuetudinum Monasticarum*, 1:423–582.

58 The text of the *Monastic Capitulary* under the title "Regula Sancti Benedicti Anianensis" may be found in *Corpus Consuetudinum Monasticarum*, 1:500–36.

59 Edward A. Segal, "The Plan of Saint Gall and the Monastic Reform Councils of 816 and 817," *Cuyahoga Review* 1 (1983), 57–71.

60 Jacobsen, review of Horn and Born, *The Plan of St. Gall* in *Kunstchronik* 35 (1982), 93, and idem, "Altere und neuere Forschungen," 144–45, following the conclusion reached earlier by Iso Müller, "Die Altar-Tituli des Klosterplanes," *Studien zum St. Galler Klosterplan*, 129–76.

61 For Saint-Riquier see Lot, *Hariulf*, 59, and Parsons, "The Pre-Romanesque Church of St-Riquier," 35; and for Fulda see Hrabanus Maurus's "Denotatio dedicationis ecclesiae," *MGH, Poetae latini aevi carolini*, 2:206. Abbot Eigil also dedicated a church at Lüder in 820 to the Virgin Mary, St. Peter, and St. Sebastian: *MGH, SS* 15:1287.

62 Christian Wilsdorf, "L'éveque Haito reconstructeur de la cathédrale de Bale (Premier quart du IXe siècle): Deux textes retrouvés," *Bulletin Monumental* 133 (1975), 175–81.

63 For Reichenau-Mittelzell see Wolfgang Erdmann and A. Zettler, "Zur karolingischen und ottonischen Baugeschichte des Marienmünsters zu Reichenau-Mittelzell," *Die Abtei Reichenau. Neue Beiträge zur Geschichte und Kultur des Inselklosters*, ed. H. Mauer (Signaringen, 1974), 501–9; and for Basel see Hans Rudolf Sennhauser, "Das Münster des Abtes Gozbert (816–37) und seine Ausmalung unter Hartmut (Proabbas 841, Abt 872–83)," *Unsere Kunstdenkmäler* 34 (1983), 155, and *VK, Nbd*, 44–46.

64 During the eighth and ninth centuries, secondary altars in Old St. Peter's in Rome, for example, were concentrated in the transept. No altars were located in the center of the nave or aisles as indicated on the Plan of St. Gall. See Bauer, "La frammentazione liturgica," esp. fig. 24, p. 436, and Blaauw, *Cultus et Decor*, 2:fig. 25.

65 J.D.C. Fisher, *Christian Initiation: Baptism in the Medieval West* (London, 1965), 47–77.

66 For the tradition of dedicating altars in elevated locations to archangels see Paolo Verzone, "Les églises du haut moyen-age et le culte des anges," *L'art mosan* (Paris, 1953), 71–80; Jean Vallery-Radot, "Notes sur les chapelles hautes dédiées à St. Michael," *Bulletin Monumentale* 93 (1929), 453–78; and Claire Etienne-Steiner, "Le culte des archanges et sa place dans l'église pre-romane et romane entre Loire et Rhin," Ph.D. diss., Université de Paris IX–Nanterre, 1990.

67 For color reproductions of the plans from the Reichenau copy of Adomnan's text (Zürich, Zentralbibliothek, Codex Rhenaugensis 73) see Horn and Born, *The Plan of St. Gall*, 1:54–56, figs. 41–44. Illustrations in other ninth-century copies are found in Wilkinson, *Jerusalem Pilgrims*, 191–97. For the *Forma Urbis Romae* see Horn and Born, *The Plan of St. Gall*, 1:57ff., and Gianfilippo Carettoni et al., *La pianta marmorea di Roma antica*, 2 vols. (Rome, 1960). The phrase "drawing-board mentality" was coined by Peter von Blanckenhagen in "The Imperial Fora," *JSAH* 13 (1954), 21–26. For general studies of Roman town planning see J. B. Ward-Perkins, *Cities of Ancient Greece and Italy: Planning in Classical Antiquity* (New York, 1972), and F. Castagnoli, *Orthogonal Town Planning in Antiquity* (Cambridge, Mass., and London, 1972).

68 Paul Lehmann, *Mittelalterliche Bibliothekskataloge Deutschlands und der Schweiz*, Vol. 1, *Die Bistumer Konstanz und Chur* (Munich, 1918), 247. See also Karl-August Wirth, "Bemerkungen zum Nachleben Vitruv im 9. und 10. Jahrhundert und zu dem Schlettstädter Vitruv-Codex," *Kunstchronik* 20 (1967), 281–91; Carol Heitz, "Vitruve et l'architecture du haut moyen age," *La cultura antica nell'occidente latino dal VII al'XI secolo*, Settimane di studio del centro italiano di studi sull'alto medioevo 22, 2 vols. (1975), 2:725–52; and Carol H. Krinsky, "Seventy-Eight Vitruvius Manuscripts," *Journal of the Warburg and Courtauld Institutes* 30 (1967), 36–70. For a discussion of the *Mappae clavicula* in general see V. Mortet, "Un formulaire du VIIIe siècle pour les fondations d'édifices et de ponts d'après des sources d'origine antique," *Bulletin Monumentale* 71 (1907), 442–65. For Carolingian copies of the *Corpus Agrimensores* (Vatican Library, Palatinus latinus 1564, and Florence, Laurentian Library, Plut. XXIX codex 32) see Bernhard Bischoff, "Die Hofbibliothek unter Ludwig dem Frommen," *Medieval Learning and Literature. Essays presented to Richard William Hunt*, ed. J.J.G. Alexander and M. T. Gibson (Oxford, 1976), 3–22; Florentine Mütherich, "Der karolingische Argimensorem-Codex in Rom," *Aachener Kunstblätter* 45 (1974), 59–74; and Oswald A. W. Dilke, *The Roman Land Surveyors* (New York, 1971), 129f.

69 For military terminology in the Rule of St. Benedict see the prologue and chapters 2 and 61. For the vocabulary of military life in monastic literature in general see A. von Harnack, *Militia Christi* (Tübingen, 1905), 28f. See also Horn and Born, *The Plan of St. Gall*, 1:114–17.

70 Interim reports of the excavations appear in Horn, *The Plan of St. Gall*, 2:258–359, and Jacobsen, *Der Klosterplan*, 176–85. See also Sennhauser, "Das Münster des Abtes Gozbert," 152–55; and idem, "St. Gallen: Zum Verhältnis von Klosterplan und Gozbertbau," *Hortus Artium Medievalium* 8 (2002), 49–55.

71 Peter Eggenberger and Werner Stöckli, "Die Krypta im Münster Unsere Lieben Frau zu Konstanz," *Schriften des Vereins für Geschichte des Bodensees und seiner Umgebung* 95 (1977), 1–18. See also in the same volume Wolfgang Erdmann and Alfons Zettler, "Zur Archäologie des Konstanzer Münsterhügels," esp. 110–29. The monastery of St. Gall belonged to the diocese of Constance, although it enjoyed episcopal immunity from 818 when it was designated an imperial abbey by Louis the Pious.

72 Horn and Born, *The Plan of St. Gall*, 1:261–62 and 2:327ff.

73 For a description of this process, with diagrams, see ibid., 1:1–2, 4–5.

Chapter 9: The Innovations of Later Carolingian Architecture

1 A description of this event and the text of the oaths is found in the eyewitness account by Nithard, *De dissensionibus filiorum Ludowici Pii*, 3:5, published in several editions including *MGH, SrG*, 3rd ed. E. Müller (Hannover and Leipzig, 1907), and *Les classiques de l'histoire de France au moyen age*, vol. 7, ed. P. Lauer (Paris, 1926). For an English translation with commentary and additional bibliography see *Carolingian Chronicles*, trans. Bernhard W. Scholtz (Ann Arbor, 1970), 161ff. Linguistic analyses of the oaths are provided by J. Knight Bostock, *A Handbook on Old High German Literature*, 2nd ed. (Oxford, 1976), 187–89, and Ferdinand Brunot, *Histoire de la langue française des origines a nos jours*, vol. 1 (Paris, 1906, repr. 1966), 143–45.

2 McKitterick, *Frankish Kingdoms*, 169ff., provides a discussion of this period with additional bibliography. See also Janet L. Nelson, "The Reign of Charles the Bald: A Survey," *Charles the Bald: Court and Kingdom*, ed. Margaret T. Gibson and J. L. Nelson, 2nd rev. ed. (Hampshire, 1990), 1–22.

3 "Lament on the division of the empire," in Godman, *Poetry*, 265ff.

4 For the Muslims (or Saracens) in Italy in the ninth century see Peter Partner, *The Lands of St Peter* (Berkeley and Los Angeles, 1972), 50–67. For a general discussion of the Vatican fortification walls, known as the Leonine Wall for Pope Leo IV (847–55), see Krautheimer, *Rome*, 117–20. A detailed analysis is found in Sheila Gibson and Bryan Ward-Perkins, "The Surviving Remains of the Leonine Wall," *PBSR* 47 (1979), 30–57, and 51 (1983), 222–39.

5 See, for example, Mütherich and Gaehde, *Carolingian Painting*, 13ff.; Hubert et al., *Carolingian Renaissance* (New York, 1970), passim; and W. Koehler and F. Mütherich, *Die Karolingische Miniaturen V: Die Hofschule Karls des Kahlens* (Berlin, 1982). Florentine Mütherich, "Carolingian art, 3: Manuscripts," 5:802–5, provides a useful summary.

6 For a summary of the archaeological and historical evidence see *VK*, 55–57, and *VK, Nbd*, 81–84.

7 "Idcirco ego . . . criptam ante pedes sanctissimorum martyrum nostrorum ad laudem et gloriam nominis Domini, in honore sanctae et intemeratae semperque virginis genetricis Dei Mariae omniumque sanctorum aedificavi, in qua multa pretiosissima sanctorum pignora auxiliante Domino collocavi." Crosby, *Royal Abbey*, 473 n. 16, and Dom M. Félibien, *Histoire de l'abbaye de Saint-Denis en France* (Paris, 1706), Pièce justicative, pt. 1, p. lvi, no. lxxv. Excerpts also in Migne, *PL*, 106:11. The letter is usually dated to 833.

8 "Communi etiam voto statuimus ut octo ex monachis hujus sanctae congregationis succedentes sibi per vices; omni tempore in ea tam diurnum quam nocturnum more Romano officium faciant et constituta officia vel antiph . . . (*lacuna*) . . . cotidiana assiduitate concelebrent." Félibien, *Histoire de l'abbaye*, Pièce justicative, pt. 1, p. lvi, no. lxxv; Migne, *PL*, 106:11. The English translation comes from Anne Walters Robertson, *The Service-Books of the Royal Abbey of Saint-Denis* (Oxford, 1991), 224, with an accompanying discussion of the liturgical implications of Hilduin's chapel.

9 Walther Lipphardt, *Der Karolingische Tonar von Metz*, Liturgiewissenschaftliche Quellen und Forschungen 43 (Münster, 1965), 64 n. 320, 180–81.

10 Crosby, *Royal Abbey*, 87–94; and Wyss, *Atlas historique* 33–34, 44–45.

11 Richard Krautheimer, "The Crypt of Santa Maria in Cosmedin," 171–75; and idem, *Rome: Profile of a City, 1312–1307* (Princeton, 1980), 113. The statement by Carol Heitz (*L'architecture religieuse*, 165) that the Probus mausoleum at St. Peter's was dedicated to the Virgin is without foundation.

12 The only vestige is the apex of the two-meter wide apse of the eastern crypt. *VK*, 84–87; *VK, Nbd*, 133. Textual sources, however, describe the crypts as divided by columns supporting arches or vaults. See, for example, *Vita Eiglili abbatis, MGH, SS*, 15, Pt. 1:229, n. 5: ". . . Arcubus atque interpositis hinc inde columnis/Binas magnifice erexit pulcro ordine cryptas."

13 Johannes Fried, "Ludwig der Fromme, das Papsttum und die fränkische Kirche," *Charlemagne's Heir*, ed. Peter Godman and Roger Collins (Oxford, 1990), 258f.

14 This initial crypt arrangement at Corvey was revealed during excavations undertaken in the mid-1970s and published by Uwe Lobbedey, "Neue Grabungsergebnisse zur Baugeschichte der Corveyer Abtei-Kirche," *Architectura* 8 (1978), 28–38. A very brief summary is found in idem, *Westphalie romane* (La Pierre-Qui-Vire, 1999), 222. See also *799. KKK*, 2:560–61. Lobbedey believes that the angular crypt corridor and the projecting apse hall were built at the same time, in part, because they share a common layer of painted plaster. Yet their masonry does not bond and there is a difference in floor levels between the two of more than half a meter, which suggests that the subterranean hall was an afterthought. Moreover, considerable time elapsed between the promise of relics from Saint-Denis and their actual arrival. After his reinstatement in 831, Hilduin sought the approval of the emperor, the bishop of Paris, and local nobles before allowing the abbot of Corvey and his entourage to escort the relics of St. Vitus to their new home. See Anne Van Landschoot, "La translation des reliques de saint Vit de l'abbaye de Sanit-Denis à celle de Corvey en 836," *Revue belge de philosophie et d'histoire*, 74 (1996), 593–632. Thus, the crypt extension could have been built in anticipation of this event as well as after the fact.

15 *VK*, 368–71; *VK, Nbd*, 453–54. For Altfried's narrative see "Vita sancti Liudgeri," *MGH, SS*, 2:414ff.

16 Ermentarius, a monk at Noirmoutier, recounts the early history of the monastery in his mid-ninth-century work "Translationes et miracula sancti Filiberti," *Acta Sanctorum*, ed. J. Carnadet, 69 vols. (Paris, 1863–1940), August t.4, 38:81–95.

17 Excavations were carried out in the late ninteenth century: below the choir in 1896, Léon Maitre, "Une église carolingienne à Saint-Philibert-de-Grandlieu," *Bulletin Monumental* 63 (1898), 127–65; and a more extensive investigation in 1898, Camille de La Croix, *Etude sur l'ancienne église de Saint-Philibert-de-Grandlieu (Loire-Inférieure), d'après des fouilles, des sondages et des chartes* (Poitiers, 1905). For an excellent critique of de La Croix's work see Robert de Lasteyrie, "L'église de Saint-Philibert-de-Grandlieu," *Mémoires de l'"Académie des Inscriptions et Belles-Lettres* 37 (1910), 1–82. The most recent detailed study is Pierre Lebouteux, "L'église de Saint-Philibert-de-Grandlieu," *Bulletin Archéologique du Comité des travaux historiques et scientifiques*, n.s. 1–2 (1965–66), 49–107. For a preliminary summary of current investigations see Boissant-Camus et al., "Archéologie et restauration des monuments," 215–16.

18 In a letter dated 819, Louis the Pious referred to the "new monastery" (*novum monasterium*) at Déas as already built (*aedificasse*), thus the first church was presumably finished by that time. Migne, *PL*, 104:1089. The formal resemblance to Kornelimünster was first pointed out by Werner Jacobsen in "Benedict von Aniane," *Riforma religiosa*, 16.

19 Around 817, for example, Benedict of Aniane and Arnulf of Noirmoutier were sent by Louis the Pious to the abbey of Saint-Denis in order to promote the observance of the Rule of St. Benedict. Otto G. Oexle, *Forschungen zu Monastischen und Geistlichen Gemeinschaften im Westfränkischen Bereich*, Münstersche Mittelalter-Schriften 31 (Munich, 1978), 113f., and Josef Semmler, "Benedictus II: Una regula—una consuetudo," *Benedictine Culture 750–1050*, ed. W. Lourdaux and D. Verhelst (Leuven, 1983), 24.

20 "Interdum venerandum sepulcrum cum sacratissimo pignore de scala deponitur, et in dextro cornu ecclesiae, quae (sicut diximus) in modum crucis constructa est, collocatur, atque in sinistro latere ecclesiae scala ipsa appenditur. Non enim ad sepulturam capiendam fundamenta ipsius ecclesiae apprime jacta fuerant; sed postea a praedicto Hilbodo venerabili abbate, pariete primae frontis disjecto, et quidquid altitudinis est crucis funditus everso atque copiose extenso, locus sepulturae mirifice est transvolutus, tribus perinde absidis circumcirca adjectis. Haec de ecclesiae adjectione dicta sint." "Translationes," *Acta Sanctorum*, 38:84–85.

21 *Acta sanctorum*, 38:68.

22 "Miracula sancti Germani," in Migne, *PL*, 124:1207–70. A French translation of pertinent sections can be found in *Saint-Germain d'Auxerre: Intellectuels et artistes dans l'Europe carolingienne IXe–XIe siècle*, exh. cat. (Auxerre, 1990), 97–101. By his own account, Heiric entered the abbey at the age of seven in 848, and the text was completed around 873. See *Saint-Germain d'Auxerre*, 37–40, and Joachim Wollasch, "Zu den persönlichen Notizen des Heiricus von S. Germain d'Auxerre," *Deutsches Archiv für Erforschung des Mittelalters* 15 (1959), 211–26, esp. 214, and R. Quadri, "Del nuovo su Eirico di Auxerre," *Studi Medievali* 23 (1992), 217–28.

23 "Ad artifices talium experientissimos res confertur: horum industria ad loci opportunitatem accedente, concepti operis examplar conficitur, et quasi quodam praeludio futurae moles magnitudinis ceris brevibus informatur. . . ." Migne, *PL*, 124:1249–50.

24 Jean Hubert, "'Cryptae inferiores' et 'cryptae superiores' dans l'architecture religieuse de l'époque carolingienne," *Mélanges d'histoire du moyen age dédiés à la mémoire de Louis Halphen* (Paris, 1951), 351–57.

25 For the political ramifications of the king's participation in this event see Janet Nelson, *Charles the Bald* (London and New York, 1992), 189–90.

26 The basic study of the Carolingian phase of the church by René Louis, *Autessiodurum Christianum: Les églises d'Auxerre des origines au XIe siècle* (Paris, 1952) has been superseded by Christian Sapin, *Archéologie et architecture d'un site monastique, Ve–XXe siècles. 10 ans de recherches à l'abbaye Saint-Germain d'Auxerre* (Auxerre, 2000). Two earlier studies provide preliminary summaries of this detailed reexamination of the site: Christian Sapin, *La Bourgogne préromane* (Paris, 1986), 41–63; and *Saint-Germain d'Auxerre*, passim.

27 Dendrochronological analyses of samples from the wooden architraves of the confessio show that the timber was cut sometime between 820 and 855. *Saint-Germain d'Auxerre*, 115. Heiric refers to the new construction project with the phrase *amplificata eadem basilica*. See the analysis of his text by Jean-Charles Picard in op. cit., 105–8, esp. 107, and Migne, *PL*, 124:1253. For the various phases of the funerary chapel, details of which are still highly conjectural, see Sapin, *Archéologie et architecture*, 225ff.

28 Christian Sapin, "L'origine des rotondes mariales des IXe–XIe siècles et le cas de Saint-Germain-d'Auxerre," *Marie, le culte de la Vierge dans la société médiévale*, ed. Dominique Iogna-Prat et al. (Paris, 1996), 295–312.

29 For the wall paintings uncovered in 1927, Louis, *Autessiodurum Christianum*, 69–85, and Hubert et al., *Carolingian Renaissance*, 5–11, figs. 5–8, have both been superseded by Christian Sapin, *Peindre à Auxerre au Moyen Age, IXe–XIVe siècles* (Auxerre, 1999). For the capitals: Sapin, *La Bourgogne*, 192–97, who, contrary to Louis and others, believes that all four capitals in the confessio were carved in the middle of the ninth century and that none are reused from Late Roman or Merovingian times. All three elements of decoration are discussed and amply illustrated in *Saint-Germain d'Auxerre*, 122ff., and Sapin, *Archéologie et architecture*, 269–89, 436–37.

30 Bernhard Kötting, *Der frühchristliche Reliquienkult und die Bestattung im Kirchengebäude* (Cologne and Oplanden, 1965), 24–28, and idem, "Die Tradition der Grabkirche," *Memoria. Der geschichtliche Zeugniswert des liturgischen Gedenkens im Mittelalter*, ed. Karl Schmid and Joachim Wollasch (Munich, 1984), 69–78, esp. 74–76.

31 The chapel was referred to as the *ecclesia varia* because of its once colorfully painted geometric decoration and richly carved architectural sculpture. The floor level originally lay some 4 m below that of the main church. See *VK*, 181; and *VK, Nbd*, 252.

32 Picard, "Les origines du mot *paradisus*," 158–86; Horn and Born, *The Plan of St. Gall*, 1:204–6.

33 Joseph Vonderau, "Die Ausgrabungen am Dome zu Fulda," 5–36.

34 Kötting, *Der frühchristliche Reliquienkult*, 33–35; idem, "Grabkirche," 77–78; and more recently, Christian Sapin, "Dans l'église ou hors l'église, quel choix pour l'inhumé?" *Archéologie du cimetière chrétien*, Actes du 2e colloque A.R.C.H.E.A. (Tours, 1996), 65–78.

35 See, for example, Albert Verbeek, "Die Aussenkrypta. Werden einer Bauform des frühen Mittelalters," *Zeitschrift für Kunstgeschichte* 13 (1950), 7–38.

36 Migne, *PL*, 117:1262–63. It seems unlikely that the bodies of the translated bishops were actually arranged in the symmetrical manner described by Heiric, which suggests that the configuration outlined in the text was more symbolic than real. See *Saint-Germain d'Auxerre*, 100–1, 107–8, and 158; and Sapin, *Archéologie et architecture*, 290–92.

37 *VK*, 87–89; *VK, Nbd*, 133; and Otfried Ellger, *Die Michaelskirche zu Fulda als Zeugnis der Totensorge* (Fulda, 1989). The design of the chapel seems to have been inspired by the Anastasis rotunda of the Holy Sepulchre in Jerusalem (Krautheimer, "An 'Introduction'," *Studies*, 117ff.) in spite of Ellger's remarks to the contrary (*Die Michaelskirche*, 20ff.).

38 Cynthia Hahn, "Seeing and Believing: The Construction of Sanctity in Early-Medieval Saints' Shrines," *Speculum* 72 (1997), 1079–106, esp. 1101ff.

39 The most detailed study is provided by Sapin, *La Bourgogne*, 81–111. For a summary see idem, "Saint-Pierre de Flavigny, l'ancienne abbatiale et ses cryptes," *Congrès archéologique de France* 144 (1986), 97–109, and, more recently, idem, "La crypte de Flavigny, 'un reliquaire' pour sainte Reine?" *Reine au Mont Auxois. Le culte et le pèlerinage de sainte Reine des origines à nos jours*, ed. Philippe Boutry and Dominique Julia (Paris, 1997), 81–94.

40 For the historical background see Sapin, *La Bourgogne*, 81–85, based in part upon the ninth-century anonymous account "Translatio et Miracula S. Reginae," *Acta Sanctorum*, ed. Carnalet, Sept. t. 3, 43:40–43, and with commentary and French translation by J. Marilier in *Alésia: Textes littéraires antiques*, ed. J. Le Gal et al. (Paris, 1973), 147–59.

41 "870. Basilica ictu tonitrui fulmine percussa ad orientem exarsit." "Annales Corbeienses," *Bibliotheca rerum Germanicarum*, ed. P. Jaffé, 6 vols. (Berlin, 1864), 1:33. The following analysis is based upon the results of the excavations published by U. Lobbedey, "Neue Grabungsergebnisse," op. cit., and summarized in idem, *Westphalie romane*, 224.

42 *VK*, 105–6; *VK, Nbd*, 160–63.

43 *VK*, 116–18; *VK, Nbd*, 181–83.

44 For the most recent and complete review of the evidence see Werner Jacobsen and Uwe Lobbedey with Andrea Kleine-Tebbe, "Der Hildesheimer Dom zur Zeit Bernwards," *Bernward von Hildesheim und das Zeitalter der Ottonen*, ed. Michael Brandt and A. Eggebrecht, 2 vols. (Hildesheim, 1993), 1:299–311, esp. 301–6 and 2:464–66.

45 See the excellent study of this issue by Hilde Claussen, "Spätkarolingische Umgangskrypten im Sächsischen Gebiet," *Karolingische und Ottonische Kunst*, Forschungen zur Kunstgeschichte und Christlichen Archäologie 3 (Wiesbaden, 1957), 118–40. Claussen, however, wrote before the latest excavations at Corvey.

46 See the discussion by Christian Sapin in *Saint-Germain d'Auxerre*, 206–8, 229–32.

47 See, for example, J. B. Nordhoff, "Corvei und die westfälisch-sächische Früharchitektur," *Repertorium für Kunstwissenschaft* 11 (1888), 147–65. Nordhoff had first applied the term in 1873 to the west end of the cathedral at Minden. For further discussion see Dagmar von Schönfeld de Reyes, *Westwerkprobleme. Zur Bedeutung der Westwerke in der kunsthistorischen Forschung* (Weimar, 1999), 10ff. There is no exact equivalent in French. Among the terms commonly used in French literature are: *antéglise, avant-nef, église-porche*, and *massif occidental*.

48 Effmann, *Centula*, passim.

49 Sapin, *Archéologie et architecture*, believes that the later vaulted westwork replaced an earlier timber-roofed, Carolingian structure. The other examples are discussed in the next chapter.

50 See, for example, the controversy over the abbey church at Hersfeld in *VK*, 113–15, *VK Nbd*, 179.

51 *De Consecratione*, chap. 2 (*Abbot Suger*, ed. Panofsky, 2nd ed., 89). For a discussion of Saint-Denis see chapter five above.

52 Throughout his writings, Suger is clearly concerned with the problem of harmonizing (*adaptare et coaequare*) his new work (*opus novum*) with that of the old basilica (*opus antiquum*), the core of which he thought had been built by King Dagobert in the seventh century while he attributed much of the west end to Charlemagne. He went so far as to have a mosaic, even

though the technique was "contrary to modern custom," placed in the tympanum above a set of Carolingian bronze doors, which were reused in a side portal of the new west facade. *De Administratione*, chap. 27 (*Abbot Suger*, ed. Panofsky, 47 and passim).

53 Jacques Le Maho, "Tours et entrées occidentales des églises de la basse vallée de la Seine (IXe–XIIe siècle)," *Avant-nefs*, 281–82.

54 Sylvie Balcon and Walter Berry, "Le massif occidental de la cathédral de Reims," *Avant-nefs*, 108–26. The destruction of a "vaulted structure" in 976 at the entrance of Reims cathedral, containing both a baptismal font and an altar to the Savior, is recorded by later eleventh- and twelfth-century chroniclers, but no date for its original construction is given. See "Flodoardi Annalium Additamentum," and "Richeri historiarum," *MGH SS*, 3:407 and 613. The inscription is recorded in the tenth-century "Historia Remensis Ecclesiae," *MGH SS*, 13:467. Foundations of a monumental entranceway were partially uncovered after World War I but these excavations were never fully published: Henri Deneux, *Dix ans de fouilles dans la cathédrale de Reims (1919–30)*, Conférence donnée à la Société des amis du vieux Reims le 1er juin 1946 (Reims, n.d.). The assumption by H. Reinhardt (*La cathédrale de Reims*, Paris, 1963, 40ff.) that Reims cathedral possessed a westwork identical to the one at Centula is no longer tenable.

55 Sapin, *Archéologie et architecture*, esp. 84–90.

56 *VK*, 105–6; *VK Nbd*, 160–63.

57 "In occidentali parte eiusdem basilicae consecratio oratorii sancti Johannis Baptistae." Sapin, *Archéologie et architecture*, 73 n. 3 and 89. The primary source is a late ninth- or early-tenth-century addition to the Martyrology of Ado, an archbishop of Vienne (ca. 800–75). See *Le martyrologe d'Adon*, ed. Jacque Dubois and Genevive Renaud (Paris, 1984), 165.

58 For a more detailed discussion see: Schönfeld de Reyes, *Westwerkprobleme*, 19–75. General reviews of many of these theories are also found in Dieter Grossmann, "Zum Stand der Westwerkforschung," *Wallraf-Richartz Jahrbuch* 19 (1957), 255–64, and Friedrich Möbius, *Westwerkstudien* (Jena, 1968), 9–22, with extensive bibliography.

59 Alois Fuchs, *Die karolingische Westwerke und andere Fragen der karolingischen Baukunst* (Paderborn, 1929); idem, "Enstehung und Zweckbestimmung der Westwerke," *Westfälische Zeitschrift* 100 (1950), 227–78; idem, "Zum Problem der Westwerke," *Karolingische und Ottonische Kunst* (Wiesbaden, 1957), 109–17.

60 Ernst Gall, "Westwerkfragen," *Kunstchronik* 7 (1954), 274–76; idem, "Zur Frage der 'Westwerke,'" *Jahrbuch des Römisch-Germanischen Zentralmuseum* 1 (1954), 245–52.

61 Edmund Stengel, "Über Ursprung, Zweck und Bedeutung der karlingischen Westwerke," *Festschrift Adolf Hofmeister*, ed. Ursula Scheil (Halle, 1955), 283–311.

62 Carol Heitz, *Recherches sur les rapports entre architecture et liturgie à l'époque carolingienne* (Paris, 1963); and Möbius, *Westwerkstudien*.

63 Schönfeld de Reyes, *Westwerkprobleme*, 110–13. Moreover, other, more general, substitute terms, like *Westbau*, have no satisfactory equivalent in English.

64 A new, detailed study of Corvey is promised by Uwe Lobbedey and Hilde Claussen. A preliminary summary may be found in *Westphalie romane*, 217–29. See also *799. KKK*, 2:567–70. For now, the most reliable and detailed analysis and reconstruction of the Corvey westwork remains Felix Kreusch, *Beobachtungen an der Westanlage der Klosterkirche zu Corvey*, Beihefte der Bonner Jahrbücher, vol. 9 (Cologne and Graz, 1963). The following discussion is based largely on this account.

65 "873. Hoc anno fundamenta trium Turrium posita in corbeia nova. . . ." and "885. Dedicatio Trium TURRIUM." from the annals of Corvey. See Philippus Jaffé, *Bibliotheca rerum Germanicarum*, 6 vols. (Berlin, 1864), 1:33–34; and Joseph Prinz, ed., *Die Corveyer Annalen*, Abhandlungen zur Corveyer Geschichtsschreibung 7 (Münster, 1982), 106–7.

66 Hilde Claussen, "Karolingische Stuckfiguren im Corveyer Westwerk. Vorzeichnungen und Stuckfragmente," *Kunstchronik* 48 (1995), 521–34. For the fresco decoration see idem, "Odysseus und Herkules in der karolingischen Kunst. I. Odysseus und 'das grausige Meer in dieser Welt': Zur ikonographischen Tradition der karolingischen Wandmalerei in Corvey," *Iconologia sacra. Mythos, Bildkunst und Dichtung in der Religions- und Sozialgeschichte Alteuropas*, ed. Hagen Keller and Nikolaus Staubach (Berlin, 1994), 341–82; and *Saint-Germain d'Auxerre*, 244–53.

67 This issue is treated in detail by Kreusch, *Beobachtungen*, 60–63. The abbey was frequently visited by kings and emperors during the tenth and eleventh centuries, but the first and only recorded visit by a ruler in the ninth century is that of Arnulf, king of east Francia, in 889. See Prinz, *Die Corveyer Annalen*, 23.

68 Ibid., 49–51, figs. 26–30.

69 Uwe Lobbedey, "Corvey (Grabungsnotiz)," *Westfalen* 61 (1983), 230; *VK, Nbd*, 83; and *Westphalie romane*, 222.

70 Simon Coupland, "Money and coinage under Louis the Pious," *Francia* 17 (1990), 39.

71 Renate Neumüllers-Klauser, "Die Westwerktafel der Kirche Corvey," *Westfalen* 67 (1989), 127–38; and *799. KKK*, 2:570–71.

72 See David Ganz, *Corbie in the Carolingian Renaissance* (Sigmaringen, 1990), 114 and 123, where the pertinent passage of Paschasius Radbert's *Epitaphium Arsenii* is quoted and discussed.

73 Claussen, "Odysseus und Herkules," passim. See also *Saint-Germain d'Auxerre*, 251; and George M. A. Hanfmann, "The Scylla of Corvey and Her Ancestors," *Dumbarton Oaks Papers* 41 (1987), 249–60. For a general study of Ulysses (or Odysseus) in Christian theology see Hugo Rahner, *Griechische Mythen in christlicher Deutung* (Zurich, 1957), translated by Brian Bradshaw as *Greek Myths and Christian Mystery* (London, 1963), 328–86.

74 "Sirenae quoque dulces . . . Carmen carmine laedunt/Cantu cantibus obstant." *MGH Poetae Latini*, 4:244 and Rahner, *Greek Myths*, 369. This reference may explain in part the next appearance of sirens, this time with fish tails, in cycles painted in the twelfth and thirteenth centuries in or near the choirs of churches. See Claussen, "Odysseus und Herkules," 373ff.

75 David Hiley, *Western Plainchant: A Handbook* (Oxford, 1995), 386–88. In Kreusch, *Beobachtungen*, 52–53, Heinrich Freistedt concluded that the letters should be interpreted in such a way that "a" is set to the modern pitch "c" with a half step occuring between "c" and "d" (the modern "e" and "f"). Such a notation is used in a chart in *De Harmonica Institutione* by Hucbald of St. Amand (d. 930), although he also uses other types of letter notations. See Alma Colk Santosuosso, *Letter Notations in the Middle Ages* (Ottawa, 1989), 11–17, and the English translation in *Hucbald, Guido, and John on Music: Three Musical Treatises*, trans. Warren Babb, ed. Clause V. Palisca (New Haven, 1978), 24. Because Hucbald used this type of notation in the course of a discussion of musical instruments, Freistedt supposed that the Corvey graffiti were meant not for singers but for players of string instruments or the organ. There is, however, no evidence that string instruments were used for liturgical purposes in early medieval churches and the pipe organ is attested in the Carolingian period for court ceremonial and musical peda-

gogy rather than liturgical performance. Moreover, the earliest example of written music for organ dates to the fourteenth century. See Peter Williams, *A New History of the Organ from the Greek to the Present Day* (London, 1980), 34–37; and Willi Apel, *The History of Keyboard Music to 1700*, trans. and rev. Hans Tischler (Bloomington, 1972), 224–32. I wish to thank Margot Fassler, Susan Boynton, and especially Peter Jeffrey for helping me to formulate these remarks.

76 The type of letter notation used in the Corvey graffiti (wherein "a" = modern "c") also occurs in one of the manuscripts of the Winchester troper. See Adreas Holschneider, "Die instrumentalen Tonbuchstaben im Winchester Troper," *Festschrift Georg von Dadelsen zum 60. Geburtstag* (Neunhausen-Stuttgart, 1978), 155–66.

77 Willi Apel, *Gregorian Chant* (Bloomington, 1958), 443; Richard L. Crocker, *The Early Medieval Sequence* (Berkeley and Los Angeles, 1972), 1ff. with an English translation of Notker's preface; and Margot Fassler, *Gothic Song* (Cambridge, 1993), 30–43.

78 ". . . Chorus angelicus sub turribus in der höhe. . . ." Johannes Letzner, *Corbeische Chronica* (Hamburg, 1590, repr. Hildesheim, 1604). Quoted in full in Kreusch, *Beobachtungen*, 55–56.

79 Ibid., 55ff., with further discussion. For a somewhat different interpretation of this same source, see Hermann Busen, "Kloster und Klosterkirche zu Corvey," *Kunst und Kultur im Weserraum*, 2 vols. (Münster, 1967), 1:35ff. Busen agrees that the angelic choir was in the western gallery, but he would place the *chorus supremus* immediately below near an altar to St. Vitus in the upper level of the westwork and the *chorus infimus* in the apse at the east end of the church. Nevertheless, Letzner's chronicle must be treated with caution. See Prinz, *Die Corveyer Annalen*, 92–93, concerning its many historical inaccuracies. Hans Klinge, "Johannes Letzner: Ein niedersächsischer Chronist des 16. Jahrhunderts," *Niedersächsisches Jahrbuch für Landesgeschichte* 24 (1952), 36–97, offers a more positive assessment.

80 *VK, Nbd*, 214ff. with extensive bibliography and discussion of differing opinions about chronology. For further support of the later ninth-century date see Georg Hauser, "Abschied von Hildebold-Dom. Die Bauzeit des alten Domes aus archäologischer Sicht," *Kölner Domblatt*, 56 (1991), 209–28.

81 Arnold Wolff, "Mass und Zahl am Alten Dom zu Köln," *Baukunst des Mittelalters in Europa. Hans Erich Kubach zum 75. Geburtstag*, ed. Franz J. Much (Stuttgart, 1988), 97–106.

Chapter 10: Epilogue: The Architectural Contribution of the Early Middle Ages

1 Rodulfus Glaber, *Historiarum Libri Quinque*, 3.4.13. For an excellent English translation and commentary see: *Rodulfus Glaber: The Five Books of Histories*, ed. and trans. John France (Oxford, 1989).

2 Stephen G. Nichols, Jr., *Romanesque Signs: Early Medieval Narrative and Iconography* (New Haven, 1983), 7, 15–17, and 30. See also and Thomas Head and Richard Landes, *The Peace of God* (Ithaca, 1992), 11–12. For a recent and revisionist discussion of the "terrors of the year 1000" see: Richard Landes, *Relics, Apocalypse, and the Deceits of History: Ademar of Chabannes, 989–1034* (Cambridge, Mass., 1995), 17ff., 287ff.

3 See the collected essays in *The White Mantle of Churches: Architecture, Liturgy, and Art around the Millennium*, ed. Nigel Hiscock (Turnhout, 2003).

4 Albert Verbeek, "Zentralbauten in der Nachfolge der Aachener Pfalzkapelle," *Das erste Jahrhundert* 2 vols. (Düsseldorf, 1964), 2:898–947; idem, "Die architektonische Nachfolge der Aachener Pfalzkapelle," *Karl der Grosse*, 4:113–56; W. Eugene Kleinbauer, "Charlemagne's Palace Chapel at Aachen and Its Copies," *Gesta* 4 (1965), 1–11; and, more recently, Jenny H. Shaffer, "Recreating the Past: Aachen and the Problem of the architectural 'Copy'," Ph.D. diss., Columbia University, 1992.

5 The precise location of Charlemagne's tomb within the chapel is still much disputed. See Helmut Beumann, "Grab und Thron Karls des Grossen zu Aachen," *Karl der Grosse*, 4:9–38, and reprinted in *Wissenschaft vom Mittelalter: Ausgewählte Aufsätze* (Cologne and Vienna, 1972), 347–76.

6 R. Guild and S. Braun, "La datation de l'abbatiale d'Ottmarsheim," *Revue d'Alsace* 124 (1998), 23–34, and S. Braun, "Avant-Nefs en Alsace aux Xie–XIIe siècles," *Avant-nefs*, 152–54. By 1065, Ottmarsheim was a conventual church, but its original purpose remains unknown.

7 Walter Zimmermann, "Das Grab der äbtissin Theophanu von Essen, " *Bonner Jahrbücher* 152 (1952), 226–27. See also Wolfgang Braunfels, "Die Kirchenbauten der Ottonenäbtissinnen," *Beiträge zur Kunst des Mittelalters: Festschrift für Hans Wentzel* (Berlin, 1975), 33–40.

8 *VK*, 184–85, and *VK, Nbd*, 253–55.

9 The main study remains Hartwig Beseler and Hans Roggenkamp, *Die Michaelskirche in Hildesheim* (Berlin, 1954). See also *VK*, 119–21, *VK, Nbd*, 183–84, and most recently *Bernward von Hildesheim und as Zeitalter der Ottonen*, exhibition catalogue, 2 vols. (Hildesheim and Mainz, 1993), 1:369–82. For a recent discussion of the church's relationship to Ottonian architecture as a whole see Werner Jacobsen, Uwe Lobbedey, and Dethard von Winterfeld, "Ottonische Baukunst," *Otto der Grosse: Magdeburg und Europa*, ed. Matthias Puhle, exhibition catalogue, Kunsthistorisches Museum Magdeburg 27 August—2 December 2001, 2 vols. (Mainz, 2001), 1:251–82.

10 *VK, Nbd*, 214–15.

11 Beseler/Roggenkamp, *Hildesheim*, 147–48, and *Bernward von Hildesheim*, 1:530–5311.

12 Vitruvius, *De Architectura*, 3.1.1–4.

13 Beseler/Roggenkamp, *Hildesheim*, 147–50, and *Bernward von Hildesheim*, 1:531.

14 "Circulus vero ecclesiae, qui nullo fine terminatur, . . . id est divina sacramenta. . . ." *Vita Eigilis abbatis, MGH, SS*, 15, pt. 1: 231. For other considerations of the possible relationship between church planning and geometry in the Middle Ages see Nigel Hiscock, *The Wise Master Builder: Platonic Geometry in Plans of Medieval Abbeys and Cathedrals* (Aldershot, Hampshire, 2000).

15 See the excavation plan of Joseph Bohland reproduced in Francis Tschan, *Saint Bernward of Hildesheim*, 3 vols. (Fort Wayne, Indiana, 1942–52), fig. 8, 402–3.

16 Hans Erich Kubach and Albert Verbeek, *Romanische Baukunst an Rhein und Maas*, 4 vols. (Berlin, 1976–89), 4:132–47; Uwe Lobbedey, "Der Beitrag von Corvey zur Geschichte der Westbauten und Westwerke," *Hortus Artium Medievalium* 8 (2002), 83–98; and idem, "Les Westwerke de l'époque ottonienne en Allemagne du Nord," *Avant-nefs*, 67–75.

17 Kubach and Verbeek, *Romanische Baukunst*, 4:134ff., *VK*, 151–53, and *VK, Nbd*, 225–27.

18 Lobbedey, "Les Westwerke," 72, suggests that the westwork at St. Pantaleon in Cologne may date as late as 1030.

19 *De Consecratione*, 2:15–16. "In carrying out such plans my first thought was for the concordance and harmony of the ancient and the new work." *Abbot Suger on the Abbey Church of St.-Denis*, ed., trans., and annotated by E. Panofsky, 91.

20 Uwe Lobbeday, "Ottonische Krypten: Bermerkungen zum Forschungsstand an Hand ausgewählte Beispiele," *Herrschaftrepräsentation im Ottonischen Sachsen*, ed. Gerd Althoff and Ernst Schubert (Sigmaringen, 1998), 77–102.

21 Taylor, *Anglo-Saxon Architecture*, 3: 1014–17, and Mariaclotilde Magni, "Cryptes du haut Moyen Age en Italie: problèmes de typologie du IXe jusqu'au début du XIe siècle," *Cahiers archéologiques* 28 (1979), 41–85.

22 Kenneth John Conant, *Carolingian and Romanesque Architecture 800–1200*, repr. 2nd rev. ed. (Harmondsworth, 1979), 148. Heitz, *L'architecture religieuse*, 194, compares the plan of Cluny II to that of Flavigny but the absence of an underground crypt at Cluny is striking. For the influence of the reforms of Benedict of Aniane see, among others, C. H. Lawrence, *Medieval Monasticism*, 2nd ed. (London, 1989), 87, and McKitterick, *The Frankish Kingdoms*, 279ff. with additional bibliography.

23 Charles Lelong, "La date du déambulatoire de Saint-Martin de Tours," *Bulletin monumental* 131 (1973), 298–309; and Jacques Henriet, "Saint-Philibert de Tournus: Histoire—Critique d'authenticité—étude archéologique du chevet (1009–19)," *Bulletin monumental* 148 (1990), 267–68. Henriet offers some modifications to his chronology in "Saint-Philibert de Tournus. Les campagnes de construction du XIe siècle," *Saint-Philibert de Tournus: Histoire, Archéologie, Art*, Actes du colloque du Centre international d'etudes romanes, Tournus, 15–19 July 1994 (Tournus, 1995), 177–203. See also in the same volume the article by Christian Sapin, "Saint-Philibert et les débuts de l'architecture romane en Bourgogne," 215–30.

24 Henriet, "Saint-Philibert," 229–316.

25 Ibid., 237. "monasterii superioris oratorium" and "inferius oratorium." For a discussion of the translation of the relics of St. Philibert from Grandlieu to Tournus and their relationship to the local saint, Valerian, see Dominique Iogna-Prat, "Un texte hagiographique épineux: La 'translation sancti Valeriani'," *Saint-Philibert*, 27–40.

26 Harry H. Hilberry, "The Cathedral at Chartres in 1030," *Speculum* 34 (1959), 561–72, is useful but out of date. See most recently Xavier Barral I Altet, "Chartres: Cathédrale," *Les premiers monuments chrétiens de la France*, Vol. 2, Sud-Ouest et Centre (Paris, 1996), 92, with additional bibliography.

27 The relic is first mentioned in 911 when it is recorded as having been used to protect the city against a Viking attack: *Historia Francorum Senonensis*, and Hugh of Fleury *Modernorum regum Francorum acuts*, *MGH, SS*, 13:365 and 380.

28 Jacques Henriet, "Saint-Philibert de Tournus. L'oeuvre du second maitre: La galilée et la nef," *Bulletin monumental* 150 (1992), 101–64.

29 Kristina Krüger, "Tournus et la fonction des Galilées en Bourgogne," *Avant-nefs*, 414–23, and idem, "Architecture and Liturgical Practice: The Cluniac *galilaea*," *White Mantle of Churches*, 139–59, distinguishes the west end of St. Philibert at Tournus from Carolingian westworks because, unlike the latter, the upper storey does not open onto the nave; instead it is closed off from the rest of the church and originally had a small central apse. The term *galilaea* was first used in reference to the west end of the abbey church at Cluny (so called Cluny II), which seems to have had a similar arrangement, in the early-eleventh-century Cluniac customary known as the *Liber tramitis*. The primary function of the upper storey of the Galilee seems to have been to serve as the site for the celebration of masses for the dead. For a discussion of the Carolingian westwork as a direct antecedent to the Burgundian Galilee see Carol Heitz, "A propos de quelques "Galilées" bourguignonnes," *Saint-Philibert*, 253–72. See also Christian Sapin, "D'Auxerre à Cluny, Le dossier archéologique des premières avant-nefs et galilées," *Avant-nefs*, 398–413.

30 C. Edson Armi, "The Corbel Table," *Gesta* 39 (2000), 89–116; and idem, "Orders and Continuous Orders in First Romanesque Architecture," *JSAH* 34 (1975), 173–88.

31 Henri Focillon, *The Art of the West in the Middle Ages*, ed. and intro. Jean Bony, 2 vols., 2nd ed. (London, 1969), 17ff., where chapter one is entitled "The Great Experiments: The Eleventh Century."

BIBLBIOGRAPHY

Addyman, Peter V., "The Anglo-Saxon House: A New Review," *Anglo-Saxon England* 1 (1972), 273–307.

Ahrweiler, Hélène, "The Geography of the Iconoclast Reform," *Iconoclasm*, ed. Anthony Bryer and Judith Herrin (Birmingham, 1977), 21–28.

Alchermes, Joseph, "*Spolia* in Roman Cities of the Late Empire: Legislative Rationales and Architectural Reuse," *Dumbarton Oaks Papers* 48 (1994), 167–78.

Alexander, J. J. G., *Insular Manuscripts 6th to the 9th Century* (London, 1978).

Allen, P. "The 'Justinianic' Plague," *Byzantion* 49 (1979), 5–20.

Anderson Jr., James C., *Roman Architecture and Society* (Baltimore and London, 1997).

Andrieu, M., ed., *Les Ordines Romani du haut moyen age*, 3 vols. (Louvain, 1948–51).

Apel, Willi, *The History of Keyboard Music to 1700*, trans. and rev. Hans Tischler (Bloomington, 1972).

Apollonj Ghetti, B. M., *S. Crisogono*, Le chiese illustrate, 92 (Rome, 1966).

——, A. Ferrua, E. Josi, and E. Kirschbaum, *Esplorazioni sotto la confessione di San Pietro in Vaticano eseguite negli anni 1940–1949*, 2 vols. (Vatican City, 1951).

Appleby, David F., "Holy Relic and Holy Image: Saints' Relics in the Western Controversy over Images in the Eighth and Ninth Centuries," *Word and Image*, 8 (1992), 333–43.

Arbeiter, Achim, *Alt-St.Peter in Geschichte und Wissenschaft* (Berlin, 1988).

——, "Die Anfänge der Quaderarchitektur im westgotenzeitlichen Hispanien," *Innovation in der Spätantike*, ed. Beat Brenk (Wiesbaden, 1996), 11–44.

——, "Frühe hispanische Darstellungen des Daniel in der Löwengrube," *Boreas* 17 (1994), 5–12.

Armi, C. Edson, "The Corbel Table," *Gesta* 39 (2000), 89–116.

——, "Orders and Continuous Orders in First Romanesque Architecture," *Journal of the Society of Architectural Historians* 34 (1975), 173–88.

The Art of Medieval Spain A.D. 500–1200, The Metropolitan Museum of Art (New York, 1993).

Audin, A., and C. Perrat, "Fouilles exécutées dans la crypte de Saint-Irénée en 1956 et 1957," *Bulletin monumental* 117 (1959) 109–18.

Backhouse, Janet, *The Lindisfarne Gospels* (Oxford and Ithaca, New York, 1981).

Bailey, Richard N., "The Anglo-Saxon Church at Hexham," *Archaeologia Aeliana*, 5th ser. 4 (1976) 47–67.

——, "St. Wilfrid, Ripon and Hexham," *Studies in Insular Art and Archaeology*, ed. Catherine Karkov and Robert Farrell, American Early Medieval Studies (Oxford, Ohio, 1991), 3–25.

Balcon, Sylvie, and Walter Berry, "Le massif occidental de la cathédral de Reims," *Avant-nefs et espaces d'accueil dans l'église entre le IVe et le XIIe siècle*, Published under the direction of Christian Sapin (Auxerre, 2002), 108–26.

Baldwin Brown, G., *The Arts of Early England*, 7 vols. (London, 1903–37), vol. 2, *Anglo-Saxon Architecture*, revised and enlarged (1929).

Balzer, Manfred, "Paderborn als karolingischer Pfalzort," *Deutsche Königspfalzen*, 3 vols. (Göttingen, 1963–79), 3:9–85.

Bandmann, Günter, "Die Vorbilder der Aachener Pfalzkapelle," *Karl der Grosse*, 4 vols. (Düsseldorf, 1965), 3:424–62.

Barnwell, P. S., *Kings, Courtiers and Imperium: The Barbarian West, 565–725* (London, 1997).

Bauer, Franz Alto, "Die Bau- and Stiftungspolitik der Päpste Hadrian I. (772–795) und Leo III. (795–816)," *799. KKK: Beiträge*, 514–28.

——, "La frammentazione liturgica nella chiesa romana del primo medioevo," *Rivista di archeologia cristiana* 75 (1999), 384–446.

Behn, Friedrich, *Die karolingische Klosterkirche von Lorsch an der Bergstrasse nach Ausgrabungen von 1927–1928 und 1932–1933* (Berlin and Leipzig, 1934).

Bell, Tyler, "Churches on Roman Buildings: Christian Associations and Roman Masonry in Anglo-Saxon England," *Medieval Archaeology* 42 (1998), 1–18.

Belting, Hans, "Das Aachener Münster im 19. Jahrhundert. Zur ersten Krise des Denkmal-Konzepts," *Wallraf-Richartz Jahrbuch* 45 (1984), 257–90.

——, "Der Einhardbogen," *Zeitschrift für Kunstgeschichte* 36 (1973), 93–121.

——, "Das Fassadenmosaik des Atriums von Alt St. Peter in Rom," *Wallraf-Richartz-Jahrbuch* 23 (1961), 37–54.

——, "Die beiden Palastaulen Leos III. im Lateran und die Enstehung einer päpstlichen Programmkunst," *Frühmittelalterliche Studien* 12 (1978), 55–83.

——, "Studien zum beneventanischen Hof in 8. Jahrhundert," *Dumbarton Oaks Papers* 16 (1962), 141–93.

Belting-Ihm, Christa, "Theophanic Images of Divine Majesty in Early Medieval Italian Church Decoration," *Italian Church*

Decoration of the Early Middle Ages and Early Renaissance, ed. William Tronzo (Bologna, 1989), 43–59.

Benazzi, Giordana, ed., *I dipinti murali e l'edicola marmorea del Tempietto sul Clitunno* (Todi, 1985).

Bernard, Honoré, "L'abbaye de Saint-Riquier. Evolution des bâtiments monastiques du IXe au XVIIIe siècle," *Sous la règle de Saint Benoit. Structures monastiques et sociétés en France du moyen age à l'époque moderne*, Abbaye bénédictine Sainte-Marie de Paris 23–25 Octobre 1980 (Geneva, 1982), 518–23.

——, "D'Hariulphe à Effmann, à la lumière des récentes fouilles de Saint-Riquier," *Actes du 95e congrés national des société savantes, Reims 1970*, Section d'archéologie et d'histoire de l'art (Paris, 1974), 220–35.

——, "Un site prestigieux du monde-carolingien, Saint-Riquier. Peut-on connaitre la grande basilique d'Angilbert?" *Cahiers archeologique de Picardie* 5 (1978), 241–54.

——, "Saint-Riquier. Fouilles et découvertes récentes," *Avant-nefs et espaces d'accueil dans l'église entre le IVe et le XIIe siècle*, Published under the direction of Christian Sapin (Auxerre, 2002), 88–107.

——, "Saint-Riquier: Une restitution nouvelle de la Basilique d'Angilbert," *Revue du Nord* 71 (1989), 307–61.

Bernward von Hildesheim und as Zeitalter der Ottonen, exhibition catalogue, 2 vols. (Hildesheim and Mainz, 1993).

Bertelli, Carlo, *La Madonna di Santa Maria in Trastevere* (Rome, 1961).

——, and Gian Pietro Brogiolo, eds., *Il futuro dei Longobardi: L'Italia e la construzione dell'Europa di Carlo Magno* (Milan and Brescia, 2000).

Bertelli, G., A. G. Guidobaldi, and P. R. Spagnoletti, "Stutture murarie degli edifici religiosi di Rome dal VI al IX secolo," *Rivista dell'istituto nazionale d'archeologia e storia dell'arte*, n.s. 23–24 (1976–77), 95–172.

Bertolini, Ottorino, "Carlomagno e Benevento," *Karl der Grosse*, 4 vols. (Düsseldorf, 1965), 1:609–71.

Beseler, Hartwig, and Hans Roggenkamp, *Die Michaelskirche in Hildesheim* (Berlin, 1954).

Beumann, Helmut, "Grab und Thron Karls des Grossen zu Aachen," *Karl der Grosse*, 4 vols. (Düsseldorf, 1965), 4:9–38, and reprinted in *Wissenschaft vom Mittelalter: Ausgewählte Aufsätze*, (Cologne and Vienna, 1972), 347–76.

Biddle, Martin, "Towns," *The Archaeology of Anglo-Saxon England*, ed. David M. Wilson (Cambridge, 1976), 99–150.

Biering, R., and H. von Hesberg, "Zur Bau- und Kultgeschichte von St. Andreas apud S. Petrum," *Römischer Quartalschrift für christliche Altertumskunde und Kirchengeschichte* 82 (1987), 145–82.

Binding, Günther, "Die Aachener Pfalz Karls des Grossen as archäologisch-baugeschichtliches Problem," *Zeitschrift für Archäologie des Mittelalters*, 25/25 (1997/98), 63–85.

——, *Deutsche Königspfalzen: Von Karl dem Grossen bis Friedrich II. (765–1240)*, (Darmstadt, 1996).

——, "Zur Ikonologie der Aachener Pfalzkapelle nach den Schriftquellen," *Mönchtum—Kirche—Herrschaft 750–1000*, ed. Dieter R. Bauer et al. (Sigmaringen, 1998), 187–211.

——, "Die karolingische Königshalle," *Die Reichsabtei Lorsch*, ed. Friedrich Knöpp, 2 vols. (Darmstadt, 1973 and 1977), 2:273–97.

——, "Die karolingisch-salische Klosterkirche Hersfeld," *Aachener Kunstblätter* 41 (1971), 189–200.

——, "'Multis arte fuit utilis' Einhard als Organisator am Aachener Hof und als Bauherr in Steinbach und Seligenstadt," *Mittellateinisches Jahrbuch* 30 (1995), 30–36.

Bischoff, Bernhard, "Eine Beschreibung der Basilika von Saint-Denis aus dem Jahre 799," *Kunstchronik* 34 (1981), 97–103.

——, "Die Entstehung des Klosterplanes in paläographischer Sicht," *Studien zum St. Galler Klosterplan* (St. Gallen, 1962), 67–78.

——, "Die Hofbibliothek unter Ludwig dem Frommen," *Medieval Learning and Literature. Essays presented to Richard William Hunt*, ed. J.J.G. Alexander and M. T. Gibson (Oxford, 1976), 3–22.

Bitel, Lisa M., *Isle of Saints. Monastic Settlement and Christian Community in Early Ireland* (Ithaca and London, 1990).

Blaauw, Sible de, "L'altare nelle chiese di Rome come centro di culto e della committenza papale," *Roma nell'alto medioevo*, Settimane di studio del centro italiano di studi sull' alto medioevo, 2 vols., 47 (2001), 2:969–89.

——, "Architecture and Liturgy in Late Antiquity and the Middle Ages," *Archiv für Liturgiewissenschaft* 33 (1991), 1–34.

——, *Cultus et Decor. Liturgia e architettura nella Roma tardoantico e medievale*, 2 vols., Studi e testi 355 (Vatican City, 1994).

——, "Die Krypta in Stadtrömischen Kirchen: Abbild eines Pilgerziels," *Akten des XII. Internationalen Kongresses*, 1:559–67.

——, "Das Pantheon als christlicher Tempel," *Boreas* 17 (1994), 13–26.

——, and Giorgio Filippi, "San Paolo fuori le mura; la disposizione liturgica fino a Gregorio Magno," *Papers of the Netherlands Institute in Rome (Mededelingen van het Nederlands Instituut te Rome)*, Historical Studies 59 (2000), 5–25.

Blair, Peter Hunter, *Northumbria in the Days of Bede* (London, 1977).

Peter Bloch, "Das Apsismosaik von Germigny-des-Prés, Karl der Grosse und der Alte Bund," *Karl der Grosse*, 4 vols. (Düsseldorf, 1965), 3:234–61.

——, "Der Kirchenbau als neuer Tempel," *Monumenta Judaica, 2000 Jahre Geschichte und Kultur der Juden am Rhein* (Cologne, 1963), 756 ff.

Blockley, Kevin, Margaret Sparks, and Tim Tatton-Brown, *Canterbury Cathedral Nave: Archaeology, History and Architecture* (Canterbury, 1997).

Boeckler, Albert, "Formgeschichtliche Studien zur Ada gruppe," *Abhandlung der Bayerischen Akademie der Wissenschaften, Phil. Hist. Klasse*, n.s. 42 (1956), 8–16.

Böhner, K., "Die Reliefplatten von Hornhausen," *Jahrbuch des Römisch-Germanischen Zentralmuseums* 23/24 (1976/77), 89 ff.

Boissavit-Camus, Brigitte, a.o., "Archéologie et restauration des monuments. Instaurer de véritables 'études archéologiques préalables'," *Bulletin monumental* 161 (2003), 195–222.

Bonnet, Charles, "Les églises en bois du haut Moyen-Age d'après les recherches archéologiques," *Grégoire de Tours et l'espace gaulois*, Actes du congrès international, 3–5 November 1994 (Tours, 1997), 217–36.

Brandenburg, Hugo, "La chiesa di S. Stefano Rotondo a Roma. Nuove ricerche e risultati: un rapporto preliminare," *Rivista di archeologia cristiana* 68 (1992), 201–32.

——, *Die Kirche S. Stefano Rotondo in Rom: Bautypologie und Architektursymbolik in der spätantiken und frühchristlichen Architektur*, Hans-Lietzmann-Vorlesungen (Berlin, 1998).

Brandt, Olof, "Il battistero lateranense dell'imperatore Costantino e l'architettura contemporanea: Come si crea un'architettura battesimale cristiana?" *Acta Hyperborea* 8 (2001), 117–44.

Braun, Suzanne, "Avant-Nefs en Alsace aux XIe–XIIe siècles," *Avant-nefs et espaces d'accueil dans l'église entre le IVe et le XIIe siècle*, published under the direction of Christian Sapin (Auxerre, 2002), 152–59.

Braunfels, Wolfgang, "Karls des Grossen Bronzewerkstatt," *Karl der Grosse*, 4 vols. (Düsseldorf, 1965), 3:168–202.

——, "Die Kirchenbauten der Ottonenäbtissinnen," *Beiträge zur Kunst des Mittelalters: Festschrift für Hans Wentzel* (Berlin, 1975), 33–40.

——, *Monasteries of Western Europe* (London, 1972).

Brenk, Beat, "Zum Baukonzept von Hagios Demetrios in Thessaloniki," *Boreas* 17 (1994), 27–38.

——, "Benedetto e il problema dell'architettetura monastica prima dell'anno mille," *L'Europa e l'arte italiana*, ed. Max Seidel (Venice, 2000), 16–39.

——, "Zum Bildprogramm der Zenokapelle in Rom," *Archivo Espanol de Arqueologia* 45–47 (1972–74), 213–21.

——, "Spolia from Constantine to Charlemagne: Aesthetics versus Ideology," *Dumbarton Oaks Papers* 41 (1987), 103–9.

Brogiolo, Gian Pietro, *La città nell'alto medioevo italiano: archeologia e storia* (Rome, 1998).

——, "Ideas of the Town in Italy during the Transition from Antiquity to the Middle Ages," *The Idea and Ideal of the Town between Late Antiquity and the Early Middle Ages*, ed. G. P. Brogiolo and Bryan Ward-Perkins, *The Transformation of the Roman World*, volume 4 (Leiden, 1999), 99–126.

Brooks, Nicholas, "Canterbury, Rome and the Construction of English Identity," *Early Medieval Rome and the Christian West: Essays in Honour of Donald A. Bullough*, ed. J. Smith (Leiden, 2000), 221–47.

——, *The Early History of the Church of Canterbury* (Leicester, 1984).

——, "The Ecclesiastical Topography," *European Towns, Their Archaeology and Early History*, ed. M.W. Bailey (London, 1977), 491.

Brown, Katharine R., ed., *From Attila to Charlemagne: Arts of the Early Medieval Period in The Metropolitan Museum of Art* (New York, 2000).

Brown, Peter, *The Cult of the Saints* (Chicago, 1981).

Brown, T. S., "Byzantine Italy," *The New Cambridge Medieval History c.700–c.900*, ed. Rosamond McKitterick (Cambridge, 1995), 320–48.

Bruce-Mitford, Rupert, "The Art of the 'Codex Amiatinus,'" *Journal of the British Archaeological Association* 32 (1969), 1–25.

——, *The Sutton Hoo Ship Burial: A Handbook*, 3rd ed. (London, 1979).

——, et al., *The Sutton Hoo Ship-Burial*, 3 vols. (London, 1975–83).

Bullough, Donald, "'Aula Renovata': The Carolingian Court before the Aachen Palace," *Carolingian Renewal: Sources and Heritage* (Manchester, England, 1991), 123–60.

Busen, Hermann, "Kloster und Klosterkirche zu Corvey," *Kunst und Kultur im Weserraum*, 2 vols. (Münster, 1967), 1:35 ff.

Caillet, Jean-Pierre, "Atrium, péristyle et cloître: des réalités si diverses?" *Der mittelalterlicher Kreuzgang*, ed. Peter K. Klein (Regensbeurg, 2004), 57–65.

Cambridge, Eric, "The Architecture of the Augustinian Mission," *St Augustine and the Conversion of England*, ed. Richard Gameson Stroud, 1999), 213–14.

——, "C. C. Hodges and the Nave of Hexham Abbey," *Archaeologia Aeliana*, 5th ser. 7 (1979), 159–68.

——, Alan Williams et al., "Hexham Abbey: A Review of Recent Work and its Implications," *Archaeologia Aeliana*, 5th ser. 23 (1995), 51–138.

Carbonara, Giovanni, *Iussu Desiderii. Montecassino e l'architettura campano-abruzzese nell'undicesimo secolo* (Rome, 1979).

Carettoni, Gianfilippo, et al., *La pianta marmorea di Roma antica*, 2 vols. (Rome, 1960).

Castagnoli, F., *Orthogonal Town Planning in Antiquity* (Cambridge, Mass., and London, 1972).

Charles-Edwards, T.M., *Early Christian Ireland* (Cambridge, 2000).

Chierici, Gino, *La chiesa di S. Satiro a Milano* (Milan, 1942).

Chierici, Gino, and C. Cecchelli, *La basilica di San Lorenzo maggiore in Milano* (Milan, 1951).

Christie, Neil, *The Lombards* (Oxford, 1995).

Claussen, Hilde, "Karolingische Stuckfiguren im Corveyer Westwerk. Vorzeichnungen und Stuckfragmente," *Kunstchronik* 48 (1995), 521–34.

——, "Odyssseus und Herkules in der karolingischen Kunst. I. Odysseus und 'das grausige Meer in dieser Welt': Zur ikonographischen Tradition der karolingischen Wandmalerei in Corvey," *Iconologia sacra. Mythos, Bildkunst und Dichtung in der Religions- und Sozialgeschichte Alteuropas*, ed. Hagen Keller and Nikolaus Staubach (Berlin, 1994), 341–82.

——, "Spätkarolingische Umgangskrypten im Sächsischen Gebiet," *Karolingische und Ottonische Kunst*, Forschungen zur Kunstgeschichte und Christlichen Archäologie 3 (Wiesbaden, 1957), 118–40.

Clemen, Paul, *Die Romanischen Wandmalereien der Rheinlande*, 2 vols. (Düsseldorf, 1905–16).

Coates-Stephens, Robert, "Dark Age Architecture in Rome," *PBSR*, 65 (1997), 223.

Colgrave, Bertram, text, trans., and notes, *The Life of Bishop Wilfrid by Eddius Stephanus* (Cambridge, 1927).

——, and R.A.B. Mynors, eds., *Bede's Ecclesiastical History of the English People* (Oxford, 1969).

Collins, Roger, *Charlemagne* (Toronto, 1998).

——, *Early Medieval Spain*, 2nd ed. (London, 1995).

——, *Visigothic Spain 409–711* (Oxford, 2004).

Colucci, Mirella, *Bonifacio IV (609–615): Momenti e questioni di un pontificio* (Rome, 1976).

Conant, Kenneth John, *Carolingian and Romanesque Architecture 800–1200*, repr. 2nd rev. ed. (Harmondsworth, 1979).

Connolly, Thomas, *Mourning into Joy: Music, Raphael, and Saint Cecilia* (New Haven and London, 1994).

Corbo, Virgilio C., *Il Santo Sepulcro di Gerusaleme*, 3 vols. (Jerusalem, 1981).

Cormack, Robin, "The Arts during the Age of Iconoclasm," *Iconoclasm*, ed. Anthony Bryer and Judith Herrin (Birmingham, 1977), 35–44.

Coüasnon, Charles, *The Holy Sepulchre in Jerusalem* (London, 1974).

Coupland, Simon, "Money and coinage under Louis the Pious," *Francia* 17 (1990), 39.

Cramer, Peter, *Baptism and Change in the Early Middle Ages c.200–c.1150* (Cambridge, 1990).

Cramp, Rosemary, "The Anglo-Saxons and Rome," *Transactions of the Architectural and Archaeological Society of Durham and Northumberland*, n.s. 3 (1974), 27–38.

——, *The Bede Monastery Museum* (Jarrow, 1980).

——, "'Beowulf' and Archaeology," *Medieval Archaeology* 1 (1957), 68–77.

——, ed. and general introduction, *Corpus of Anglo-Saxon Stone Sculpture*, vol. 1 (Oxford, 1984).

——, "Excavations at the Saxon Monastic Sites of Wearmouth and Jarrow, Co. Durham: An Interim Report," *Medieval Archaeology* 13 (1969) 21–66.

——, "The Hall in Beowulf and Archaeology," *Heroic Poetry in the Anglo-Saxon Period: Studies in Honor of Jess B. Bessinger, Jr.*, ed. J. Damico and J. Leyerle, Studies Medieval Culture 32 (Kalamazoo, Michigan, 1993), 331–46.

——, "Jarrow Church," *Archaeological Journal* 133 (1976), 220–28.

——, "Monastic Sites," *Archaeology of Anglo-Saxon England*, ed. David M. Wilson (Cambridge, 1976), 234–41.

——, "Monkwearmouth and Jarrow in Their Continental Context," *'Churches Built in Ancient Times': Recent Studies in Early Christian Archaeology*, ed. Kenneth Painter (London, 1994), 279–94.

——, "Monkwearmouth Church," *Archaeological Journal* 133 (1976), 230–37.

——, "St. Paul's Church, Jarrow," *The Archaeological Study of Churches*, ed. Peter Addyman and Richard Morris, The Council for British Archaeology, Research Report 13 (London, 1976), 28–35.

——, "Window Glass from the British Isles 7th–10th century," *Il colore nel medioevo: Arte simbolo tenica. La vetrata in occidente dal IV all'XI secolo*, Atti delle giornate di studi, Lucca 23–25 settembre 1999, ed. Francesca Dell'Acqua and Romano Silva (Lucca, 2001), 67–85.

——, "Window Glass from the Monastic Site of Jarrow," *Journal of Glass Studies* 17 (1975), 88–96.

——, and J. Cronyn, "Anglo-Saxon Polychrome Plaster and Other Materials from the Excavations of Monkwearmouth and Jarrow: An Interim Report," *Early Medieval Wall Painting*, ed. Sharon Carter, David Park, and Paul Williamson, British Archaeological Report, British Series 216 (Oxford, 1990), 17–27.

Crema, Luigi, *L'architettura romana* (Turin, 1959).

Crook, John, *The Architectural Setting of the Cult of Saints in the Early Christian West c.300–1200* (Oxford, 2000).

Crosby, Sumner, *The Abbey of St.-Denis, 475–1122* (New Haven, 1942).

——, "A Carolingian Pavement at Saint-Denis: A Preliminary Report," *Gesta* 9 (1970), 42–45.

——, "Excavations at Saint Denis—July 1967," *Gesta* 7 (1968), 48–50.

——, "Excavations in the Abbey Church of St.-Denis 1948: The Façade of Fulrad's Church," *Proceedings of the American Philosophical Society* 93 (1949) 347–61.

——, "Fouilles exécutées récemment dans la basilique de Saint-Denis," *Bulletin Monumental* 105 (1947), 167–81.

——, *The Royal Abbey of Saint-Denis from Its Beginning to the Death of Suger, 475–1151*, ed. and completed by Pamela Blum (New Haven and London, 1987).

Dagens, Claude, "Gregoire le Grand et le monde oriental," *Rivista di storia e letturatura religiosa* 17 (1981), 243–52.

Dassmann, Ernst, "Ambrosius und die Märtyrer," *Jahrbuch für Antike und Christentum* 18 (1975), 49–68.

Davis, Raymond, trans. and commentary, *The Lives of the Ninth-Century Popes (Liber Pontificalis)* (Liverpool, 1995).

Davis-Weyer, Caecelia, "Die ältesten Darstellungen der Hadesfahrt Christi, Das Evangelium Nikodemi und ein Mosaik der Zeno-Kappelle," *Roma e l'éta carolingia*, Atti delle giornate di studio, 3–8 maggio 1976, Istituto nazionale di archeologia e storia dell'arte (Rome, 1976), 183–94.

——, *Early Medieval Art 300–1150: Sources and Documents* (Englewood Cliffs, N.J., 1971).

——, "Die Mosaiken Leos III. und die Anfänge der karolingischen Renaissance in Rom," *Zeitschrift für Kunstgeschichte* 29 (1966), 111–32.

De Angelis D'Ossat, Guglielmo, "La chiesa di S. Angelo di Perugia," *Corsi di cultura sull'arte ravennate e bizantina* 13 (1966), 105–11.

——, "Origine e fortuna dei battisteri ambrosiani," *Arte Lombarda* 14 (1969), 1 ff.

Deichmann, Friedrich W., "Märtyrerbasilika, Martyrion, Memoria and Altargrab," *Römische Mitteilungen* 77 (1970), 144–69, reprinted in idem, *Rom, Ravenna, Konstantinopel, Naher Osten* (Wiesbaden, 1982), 375–401.

——, "Das Oktogon von Antiocheia," *Byzantinische Zeitschrift* 65 (1972), 40 ff.

——, *Ravenna. Haupstadt des spätantiken Abendlandes*, 6 vols. (Wiesbaden, 1958–89).

——, and A. Tschira, "Das Mausoleum der Kaiserin Helena und die Basilika der heiligen Marcellinus und Petrus an der Via Labicana vor Rom," *Jahrbuch des deutschen archäologischen Instituts* 72 (1957), 44 ff., and reprinted in Deichmann, *Rom, Ravenna*, 305–74.

de La Croix, Camille, *Etude sur l'ancienne église de Saint-Philibert-de-Grandlieu (Loire-Inférieure), d'après des fouilles, des sondages et des chartes* (Poitiers, 1905).

de Lasteyrie, Robert, "L'église de Saint-Philibert-de-Grandlieu," *Mémoires de l'Académie des Inscriptions et Belles-Lettres* 37 (1910), 1–82.

Dell'Acqua, G. A., ed., *La basilica di San Lorenzo in Milano* (Milan, 1985).

Del Nunzio, Marina, "La produzione di vetri da finestra tra tarda antichità e medioevo: la situazione romana," *Il colore nel medioevo: Arte simbolo tecnica. La vetrata in occidente dal IV all'XI secolo*, Atti delle giornate di studi, Lucca 23–25 settembre 1999, ed. Francesca Dell'Acqua and Romano Silva (Lucca, 2001), 45–65.

Delogu, Paolo, "Lombard and Carolingian Italy," *The New Cambridge Medieval History c.700–c.900*, ed. Rosamond McKitterick (Cambridge, 1995), 290–319.

——, "Il regno longobardo," *Longobardi e bizantini*, ed., P. Delogu et al., Storia d'Italia, vol. 1 (Turin, 1980).

Demus, Otto, *Byzantine Art and the West* (New York, 1970).

Deneux, Henri, *Dix ans de fouilles dans la cathédrale de Reims (1919–30)*, Conférence donnée à la Société des amis du vieux Reims le 1er juin 1946 (Reims, n.d.).

De Palol, Pedro, *Early Medieval Art in Spain* (New York, n.d.).

de Paor, Liam, "A Survey of Sceilig Mhichil," *Journal of the Royal Society of Antiquaries of Ireland* 85 (1955), 174–87.

Derstroff, Klaus, "Der Heilige Nazarius: Zur Person und Verehrung des Lorscher Patrons," *Laurissa Jubilans: Festschrift zur 1200-Jahrfeier von Lorsch, 1964* (Mainz, 1964), 77–90.

de Vogüé, Adalbert, "Le Plan de Saint-Gall, copie d'un document officiel? Une lecture de la lettre à Gozbert," *Revue Bénédictine* 94 (1984), 295–314.

Diaz, Pablo C., and M. R. Valverde, "The Theoretical Strength and Practical Weakness of the Visigothic Monarchy of Toledo," *Rituals of Power from Late Antiquity to the Early Middle Ages*, ed. Frans Theuws and Janet L. Nelson, The Transformation of the Roman World, vol. 8 (Leiden, 2000), 59–93.

Diepenbach, Wilhelm A., "'Palatium' in spätrömischen und fränkischen Zeit," Diss. Hessischen Ludwigs-Universität (Giessen, 1921).

Dilke, Oswald A. W., *The Roman Land Surveyors* (New York, 1971).

Dixon, Philip, "Secular Architecture," *The Making of England: Anglo-Saxon Art and Culture A.D. 600–900*, ed. Leslie Webster and Janet Backhouse (London and Toronto, 1991), 67–70.

Dodds, Jerrilyn, *Architecture and Ideology in Early Medieval Spain* (University Park, 1990).

Downey, Glanville, *A History of Antioch in Syria* (Princeton, 1961).

——, "The Shrines of St. Babylos at Antioch and Daphne," *Antioch on the Orontes*, ed. R. Stilwell (Princeton, 1938), 2:45–48.

Duchesne, Louis, ed., Le Liber Pontificalis. Texte, introduction, et commentaireed, 2 vols. (Paris, 1886–1892); Additions et corrections, ed. Cyrille Vogel (Paris, 1957), repr. 3 vols (Paris, 1981).

Duckett, Eleanor Shipley, *Carolingian Portraits: A Study in the Ninth Century* (Ann Arbor, 1969).

Dudden, F. Homes, *Gregory the Great: His Place in History and Thought*, 2 vols. (London, 1905).

Durand, Georges, "Saint-Riquier," *La Picardie historique et monumentale* (Amiens and Paris, 1907–11), 4:133–358.

Dutton, Paul Edward, ed. and trans., *Charlemagne's Courtier: The Complete Einhard* (Ontario, 1998).

Duval, Noël, *Les églises africaines à deux absides. Recherches archéologiques sur la liturgie chrétienne en Afrique du Nord*, 2 vols. (Paris, 1973).

——, "Les relations entre l'Afrique et l'Espagne dans le domaine liturgique: Existe-t-il une explication commune pour le 'contre-absides' et 'contre-choeurs'?" *Rivista di archeologia cristiana* 76 (2000), 429–76.

Duval, Yvette, *Loca Sanctorum Africae: Le culte des martyrs en Afrique du IVe au VIIe siècle*, Collection de l'école française de Rome, 2 vols. (Paris, 1982).

Dyer, Joseph, "Prologomena to a History of Music and Liturgy at Rome in the Middle Ages," *Essays on Medieval Music in Honor of David G. Hughes*, ed. G. M. Hughes (Cambridge, Massachusetts; 1995), 87–115.

Edwards, Nancy, *The Archaeology of Early Medieval Ireland* (London, 1990).

Effmann, Wilhelm, *Centula: Saint-Riquier. Eine Untersuchung zur Geschichte der kirchlichen Baukunst in der Karolingerzeit* (Münster, 1912).

Eggenberger, Peter, and Werner Stöckli, "Die Krypta im Münster Unsere Lieben Frau zu Konstanz," *Schriften des Vereins für Geschichte des Bodensees und seiner Umgebung* 95 (1977), 1–18.

Ellger, Otfried, *Die Michaelskirche zu Fulda als Zeugnis der Totensorge* (Fulda, 1989).

Emerick, Judson, "Focusing on the Celebrant: The Column Display inside Santa Prassede," *Papers of the Netherlands Institute in Rome (Mededelingen van het Nederlands Instituut te Rome)*, Historical Studies 59 (2000), 127–59.

——, *The Tempietto del Clitunno near Spoleto*, 2 vols., (University Park, Pennsylvania, 1998).

Erdmann, Wolgang, and A. Zettler, "Zur Archäologie des Konstanzer Münsterhügels," *Schriften des Vereins für Geschichte des Bodensees und seiner Umgebung* 95 (1977), 110–29.

——, "Zur karolingischen und ottonischen Baugeschichte des Marienmünsters zu Reichenau-Mittelzell," *Die Abtei Reichenau. Neue Beiträge zur Geschichte und Kultur des Inselklosters*, ed. H. Mauer (Signaringen, 1974).

L'èta altomedievale: longobardi e carolingi, San Salvatore (Brescia, 1999).

Etienne-Steiner, Claire, "Le culte des archanges et sa place dans l'église pre-romane et romane entre Loire et Rhin," Ph.D. diss., Université de Paris IX–Nanterre, 1990.

Ewig, Eugen, "Das Bild Constantins des Grossen in den ersten Jahrhunderten des abendländischen Mittelalters," *Spätantikes und Fränkisches Gallien: Gesammelte Schriften (1952–1973)*, ed. Hartmut Atsma, 2 vols. (Munich, 1976), 1:98–104.

——, *Die Merowinger und das Frankenreich*, 2nd rev. ed. (Stuttgart, 1993).

——, "Résidence et capitale pendant le haut moyen age," *Spätantikes und frankisches Gallien*, 2 vols. (Zurich and Munich, 1976–1979), 1:394–99.

Exner, Mattias, "Review: *799. Kunst und Kultur der Karolingerzeit. Karl der Grosse und Papst Leo III. in Paderborn*," *Kunstchronik*, 53 (2003), 246–57.

Falkenstein, Ludwig, "Charlemagne et Aix-la-Chapelle," *Byzantion* 61 (1991).

——, *Der 'Lateran' der karolingischen Pfalz zu Aachen* (Cologne, 1966).

Fanning, Steven, "Clovis Augustus and Merovingian *Imitatio Imperii*," *The World of Gregory of Tours*, ed. Kathleen Mitchell and Ian Wood (Leiden, 2002), 321–36.

Farmer, D. H., ed., and J. F. Webb, trans., *The Age of Bede* (Harmondsworth, 1983).

Fehring, Günter P., "Die Stellung des frühmittelalterlichen Holzkirchenbaues in der Architekturgeschichte," *Jahrbuch des Römisch-Germanischen Zentral Museums Mainz* 14 (1967), 179–97.

Félibien, Dom M., *Histoire de l'abbaye de Saint-Denis en France* (Paris, 1706).

Ferber, Stanley, "The Temple of Solomon in Early Christian and Byzantine Art," *The Temple of Solomon*, ed. Joseph Gutmann (Missoula, Montana, 1976), 21–46.

Fernie, Eric, *The Architecture of the Anglo-Saxons* (London, 1984).

——, "Historical Metrology and Architectural History," *Art History* 1 (1978), 383–99.

——, "The Proportions of the St. Gall Plan," *Art Bulletin* 40 (1978), 583–89.

Ferreiro, A., *The Visigoths in Gaul and Spain A.D. 418–711: a Bibliography* (Leiden, 1988).

Finch, Margaret, "The Cantharus and Pigna at Old St. Peter's," *Gesta* 30 (1991), 16–26.

Fisher, Ian, "The monastery of Iona in the eighth century," *The Book of Kells*, ed. Felicity O'Mahony, Proceedings of a Conference at Trinity College, Dublin, 6–9 September 1992 (Aldershot, 1994), 47.

Fisher, J.D.C., *Christian Initiation: Baptism in the Medieval West* (London, 1965).

Fleckenstein, Josef, "Einhard, seine Gründung und sein Vermächtnis in Seligenstadt," *Das Einhardkreuz*, ed. Karl Hauck, Abhandlungen der Akademie der Wissenschaften in Göttingen, Phil. Hist. Kl. 87 (1974), 96–121.

——, "Erinnerung an Karl den Grossen: Zur Torhalle von Lorsch und zum Kaisertum Karls," *Geschichtsblätter für den Kreis Bergstrasse* 7 (1974), 15–28, reprinted in *Beiträge zur Geschichte des Klosters Lorsch* (Lorsch, 1980), 63–78.

Fletcher, Eric, "The Influence of Merovingian Gaul on Northumbria in the Seventh Century," *Medieval Archaeology* 24 (1980) 69–86.

Fletcher, Richard, *The Barbarian Conversion from Paganism to Christianity* (Berkeley and Los Angeles, 1997).

Focillon, Henri, *The Art of the West in the Middle Ages*, ed. and intro. Jean Bony, 2 vols., 2nd ed. (London, 1969).

Fontaine, J., *Isidore de Séville et la culture classique dans l'Espagne visigothique* (Paris, 1959).

Formigé, Jules, *L'abbaye royale de Saint-Denis: Recherches nouvelles* (Paris, 1960).

Fossard, Denise, "Les chapitaux de marbre du VIIe siècle en Gaule: style et evolution," *Cahiers archéologiques* 2 (1947), 69–85.

Fouet, G., *La villa gallo-romane de Montmaurin, Haute-Garonne*, 20e Supplément a *Gallia* (Paris, 1969).

France, John, ed. and trans., *Rodulfus Glaber: The Five Books of Histories* (Oxford, 1989).

Die Franken—Wegbereiter Europas, exh. cat. Reiss-Museum Mannheim, 2 vols. (Mainz, 1997).

Freeman, Ann, "Carolingian Orthodoxy and the Fate of the *Libri Carolini*," *Viator* 16 (1985) 65–108, reprinted in idem, *Theodulf of Orléans: Charlemagne's Spokesman against the Second Council of Nicaea* (Aldershot, Hampshire, 2003), III:65–108.

——, "Scripture and Images in the *Libri Carolini*," *Testo e immagine nell'alto medioevo*, Settimane di studio del centro italiano di studi sull'alto medioevo, 41 (1994), 163–88, reprinted in idem, *Theodulf of Orléans: Charlemagne's Spokesman against the Second Council of Nicaea* (Aldershot, Hampshire, 2003), VII:163–88.

——, *Theodulf of Orléans: Charlemagne's Spokesman against the Second Council of Nicaea* (Aldershot, Hampshire, 2003).

——, "Theodulf of Orléans and the *Libri Carolini*," *Speculum* 32 (1957), 695–703, reprinted in idem, *Theodulf of Orléans: Charlemagne's Spokesman against the Second Council of Nicaea* (Aldershot, Hampshire, 2003), II:695–703.

——, "Theodulf of Orleans: a Visigoth at Charlemagne's Court," *L'Europe héritière de l'Espagne wisigothique*, Colloque international du C.N.R.S. tenu à la Fondation Singer-Polignac, Paris, 14–16 May 1990 (Madrid, 1992), 185–94, reprinted in idem, *Theodulf of Orléans: Charlemagne's Spokesman against the Second Council of Nicaea* (Aldershot, Hampshire, 2003), VIII:185–94.

——, and Paul Meyvaert, "The Meaning of Theodulf's Apse Mosaic at Germigny-des-Prés," *Gesta*, 40 (2001), 125–39.

Frere, S. S., "The Silchester Church: The Excavation by Sir Ian Richmond in 1961," *Archaeologia* 105 (1975), 277–302.

Fried, Johannes, "Ludwig der Fromme, das Papsttum und die fränkische Kirche," *Charlemagne's Heir*, ed. Peter Godman and Roger Collins (Oxford, 1990), 258 ff.

Fuchs, Alois, "Enstehung und Zweckbestimmung der Westwerke," *Westfälische Zeitschrift* 100 (1950), 227–78.

——, *Die karolingische Westwerke und andere Fragen der karolingischen Baukunst* (Paderborn, 1929).

——, "Zum Problem der Westwerke," *Karolingische und Ottonische Kunst* (Wiesbaden, 1957), 109–17.

Gai, Sveva, "Die Pfalz Karls des Grossen in Paderborn," *799. KKK: Beiträge*, 183–96.

Gall, Ernst, "Westwerkfragen," *Kunstchronik* 7 (1954), 274–76.

——, "Zur Frage der 'Westwerke,'" *Jahrbuch des Römisch-Germanischen Zentralmuseum* 1 (1954), 245–52.

Gameson, Richard, "Augustine of Canterbury: Context and Achievement," *St Augustine and the Conversion of England*, ed. Richard Gameson (Stroud, 1999), 1–40.

Ganz, David, *Corbie in the Carolingian Renaissance* (Sigmaringen, 1990).

Gasparri, Stefano, *I duchi longobardi*, Istituto storico italiano per il medio evo, Studi storici 109 (Rome, 1978).

——, "Kingship Rituals and Ideology in Lombard Italy," *Rituals of Power from late antiquity to the early Middle Ages*, ed. Frans Theuw and Janet Nelson (Leiden, 2000), 107.

Gauthier, Nancy, "From the Ancient City to the Medieval Town: Continuity and Change in the Early Middle Ages," *The World of Gregory of Tours*, ed. Kathleen Mitchell and Ian Wood (Leiden, 2002), 47–66.

Geary, Patrick, *Furta Sacra: Thefts of Relics in the Central Middle Ages* (Princeton, 1978).

Geertman, Herman, "The Builders of Basilica Maior in Rome," *Festoen* (Groningen, 1976), 277 ff.

——, *More Veterum: Il 'Liber Pontificalis' e gli edifici ecclesiastici di Roma nella tarda antichità e nel medioevo* (Groningen, 1975).

Gem, Richard, "The Anglo-Saxon and Norman churches," *St Augustine's Abbey*, ed. R. Gem (London, 1997), 90–107.

——, "Documentary References to Anglo-Saxon Painted Architecture," *Early Medieval Wall Painting and Painted Sculpture in England*, eds. Sharon Cather, David Park, and Paul Williamson, British Archaeological Reports, British Series 216 (Oxford, 1990), 1–5.

Ghirardini, Gherardo, "Gli scavi del Palazzo di Teodorico a Ravenna," *Monumenti antichi*, Reale accademia dei Lincei 24 (1916), cols. 738–838.

Gibson, Sheila, and Bryan Ward-Perkins, "The Surviving Remains of the Leonine Wall," *Papers of the British School at Rome*, 47 (1979), 30–57, and 51 (1983), 222–39.

Gillett, Andrew, "Was Ethnicity Politicized in the Earliest Medieval Kingdoms?" *On Barbarian Identity: Critical Approaches to Ethnicity in the Early Middle Ages* (Turnhout, 2002), 85–122.

Godman, Peter, *Poetry of the Carolingian Renaissance* (Norman, Oklahoma, 1985).

——, *Poets and Emperors: Frankish Politics and Carolingian Poetry* (Oxford, 1987).

Godoy Fernandez, Cristina, *Arqueologia y liturgia. Iglesias hispanicas (siglos IV–VIII)*, (Barcelona, 1995).

Gough, Mary, ed., *Alahan: An Early Christian Monastery in Southern Turkey* (Toronto, 1985).

Grabar, André, "Les mosaiques de Germigny-des-Prés," *Cahiers archéologiques*, 7 (1954), 171–83.

——, "Le rayonnement de l'art sassanide dans le monde chrétien," *La Persia nel medioevo*, Accademia nazionale dei Lincei, Quaderni 160 (Rome, 1971), 679–707.

Grape, Wolfgang, "Karolingische Kunst und Ikonoklasmus," *Aachener Kunstblätter* 45 (1974), 49–58.

Grenier, Albert, *Habitations gauloises et villas latines dans la Cité des Médiomatrices* (Paris, 1906).

Grewe, Holger, "Die Konigspfalz zu Ingelheim am Rhein," *799. KKK: Beiträge*, 142–51.

Grimme, Ernst G., *Der Dom zu Aachen: Architektur und Ausstattung* (Aachen, 1994).

Grossmann, Dieter, "Zum Stand der Westwerkforschung," *Wallraf-Richartz Jahrbuch* 19 (1957), 255–64.

Grumel, V., "Les relations politico-religieuses entre Byzance et Rome sous le règne de Léon V l'Arménien," *Revue des études byzantines* 18 (1960), 19–44.

Guerreau-Jalabert, A., "La 'Renaissance carolingienne'; modèles culturels, usages linguistiques, et structures sociales," *Bibliotheque de l'école des chartes* 39 (1981), 5–35.

Guidobaldi, Federico, and Alessandra Guiglia Guidobaldi, ed., *Ecclesiae Urbis*, Atti del congresso internazionale di studi sulle chiese di Roma (IV–X secolo), Roma, 4–10 settembre 2000, 3 vols. (Vatican City, 2002).

Guild, R., and S. Braun, "La datation de l'abbatiale d'Ottmarsheim," *Revue d'Alsace* 124 (1998), 23–34.

Günter, Roland, *Wand, Fenster und Licht in der Trierer Palastaula und in spätantiken Bauten* (Bonn, 1968).

Guyon, Jean, *Le cimetière aux deux lauriers: Recherches sur les catacombes romaines* (Rome, 1987).

——, *Les premiers baptistères des Gaules (IVe–VIIIe siécles)* (Rome, 2000).

Hahn, Adalheid, "Das Hludowicianum," *Archiv für Diplomatik* 21 (1975), 15–135.

Hahn, Cynthia, "Seeing and Believing: The Construction of Sanctity in Early-Medieval Saints' Shrines," *Speculum* 72 (1997), 1079–106.

Hallinger, Kassius, ed., *Corpus consuetudinum monasticarum*, 12 vols (Siegburg, 1963–).

Hanfmann, George M. A., "The Scylla of Corvey and Her Ancestors," *Dumbarton Oaks Papers* 41 (1987), 249–60.

Harrison, Martin, *A Temple for Byzantium. The Discovery and Excavation of Anicia Juliana's Palace-Church in Istanbul* (Austin, Texas, 1989).

Hauck, Karl, ed., *Das Einhardkreuz*, Abhandlungen der Akademie der Wissenschaften in Göttingen, Phil. Hist. Kl. 87 (1974).

Hauschild, Theodor, "Westgotische Quaderbauten des 7. Jahrhunderts auf der iberischen Halbinsel," *Madrider Mitteilungen* 13 (1972), 270–85.

Hauser, Georg, "Abschied von Hildebold-Dom. Die Bauzeit des alten Domes aus archäologisischer Sicht," *Kölner Domblatt*, 56 (1991), 209–28.

Häussling, Angelus A., *Mönchskonvent und Eucharistifeier. Eine Studie über die Messe in der abendländischen Klosterliturgie des frühen Mittelalters und zur Geschichte der Messhäufigkeit*, Liturgiewissenschaftliche Quellen und Forschungen 58 (Münster, 1973).

Hawkes, Jane, "*Iuxta Morem Romanorum*: Stone and Sculpture in Anglo-Saxon England," *Anglo-Saxon Styles*, ed. Catherine E. Karkov and George Hardin Brown (Albany, New York, 2003), 69–100.

——, and S. Mills, eds., *Northumbria's Golden Age* (Stroud, 1999).

Head, Thomas, and Richard Landes, *The Peace of God* (Ithaca, 1992).

Heitz, Carol, "Architecture et liturgie processionnelle à l'époque préromane," *Revue de l'art*, 24 (1974), 30–47.

——, *L'architecture religieuse carolingienne. Les formes et leurs fonctions* (Paris, 1980).

——, "More Romano: Problèmes d'architecture et liturgie carolingiennes," *Roma e l'età carolingia*, Atti delle giornate di studio, 3–8 maggio 1976, Istituto nazionale di archeologia e storia dell'arte (Rome, 1976), 27–37.

——, "Nouvelles interprétations de l'art carolingienne," *Revue de l'art*, 1–2 (1968), 107.

——, "Poitiers: Foyer d'art chretien du IVe au Xe siècle," *Archéologia* 113 (1977), 21.

——, "A propos de quelques 'Galilées' bourguignonnes," *Saint-Philibert de Tournus: Histoire, Archéologie, Art*, Actes du colloque du Centre international d'études romanes, Tournus, 15–19 July 1994 (Tournus, 1995), 253–72.

——, *Recherches sur les rapports entre architecture et liturgie à l'époque carolingienne* (Paris, 1963).

——, "Vitruve et l'architecture du haut moyen age," *La cultura antica nell'occidente latino dal VII al'XI secolo*, Settimane di studio del centro italiano di studi sull'alto medioevo 22, 2 vols. (1975), 2:725–52.

Hennessy, William M., ed., *Annals of Ulster, otherwise Annals of Senat, A Chronicle of Irish Affairs from A.D. 431 to A.D. 1540* (Dublin, 1887).

Henriet, Jacques, "Saint-Philibert de Tournus: Histoire—Critique d'authenticité—étude archéologique du chevet (1009–19)," *Bulletin monumental* 148 (1990), 267–68.

——, "Saint-Philibert de Tournus. Les campagnes de construction du XIe siècle," *Saint-Philibert de Tournus: Histoire, Archéologie, Art*, Actes du colloque du Centre international d'études romanes, Tournus, 15–19 July 1994 (Tournus, 1995), 177–203.

——, "Saint-Philibert de Tournus. L'oeuvre du second maitre: La galilée et la nef," *Bulletin monumental* 150 (1992), 101–64.

Heries, T. L., *Paries* (Amsterdam, 1982).

Herity, Michael, "The Layout of Irish early Christian monasteries," *Irland und Europa*, ed. P. N. Chatain and Michael Richter (Stuttgart, 1984), 105–15.

Herklotz, Ingo, "Der Campus Lateranensis im Mittelalter," *Römisches Jahrbuch für Kunstgeschichte* 22 (1985), 1–44.

Herrin, Judith, *The Formation of Christendom* (Princeton, 1987).

Herrmann-Mascard, Nicole, *Les reliques des saints. Formation coutumière d'un droit* (Paris, 1975).

Higgitt, John, "The Dedication Inscription at Jarrow and its Context," *The Antiquaries Journal* 59 (1979) 343–74.

Hilberry, Harry H., "The Cathedral at Chartres in 1030," *Speculum* 34 (1959), 561–72.

Hiley, David, *Western Plainchant: A Handbook* (Oxford, 1995).

Hill, Stephen, "The 'Praetorium' of Musmiye," *Dumbarton Oaks Papers* 29 (1975), 347–49.

Hillgarth, J. N. "Coins and Chronicles: Propaganda in Sixth-Century Spain and the Byzantine Background," *Historia* 15 (1966), 483–508, reprinted in idem, *Visigothic Spain, Byzantium and the Irish* (London, 1985).

Hiscock, Nigel, ed., *The White Mantle of Churches: Architecture, Liturgy, and Art around the Millennium* (Turnhout, 2003).

——, *The Wise Master Builder: Platonic Geometry in Plans of Medieval Abbeys and Cathedrals* (Aldershot, Hampshire, 2000).

Hoddinott, R. F., *Early Byzantine Churches in Macedonia and Southern Serbia* (London, 1963).

Hodges, Richard, *Light in the Dark Ages: The Rise and Fall of San Vincenzo al Volturno* (Ithaca, New York, 1997).

——, and David Whitehouse, *Mohammed, Charlemagne and the Origins of Europe* (London, 1983).

——, and John Mitchell, *The Basilica of Abbot Joshua at San Vincenzo al Volturno* (Abbey of Monte Cassino, 1996).

——, Sheila Gibson, and John Mitchell, "The Making of a Monastic City. The Architecture of San Vincenzo al Volturno in the Ninth Century," *PBSR* 65 (1997), 233–86.

Hoffmann, Theodorich: Hartmut, "Die Aachener Theoderichstatue," *Das erste Jahrtausend. Kultur und Kunst im werdenden Abendland an Rhein und Ruhr*, ed. Victor H. Elbern, 2 vols. (Düsseldorf, 1962), 1:318 ff.

Holloway, R. Ross, *Constantine and Rome* (New Haven and London, 2004).

Hollstein, Ernst, *Mitteleuropäische Eichenchronologigie*, Trier dendrochronologische Forschungen zur Archäologie und Kunstgeschichte (Mainz, 1980).

Holschneider, Adreas, "Die instrumentalen Tonbuchstaben im Winchester Troper," *Festschrift Georg von Dadelsen zum 60. Geburtstag* (Neunhausen-Stuttgart, 1978). 155–66.

Hope, William St. J., "Recent discoveries in the abbey church of St. Austin of Canterbury," *Archaeologia* 66 (1914–15), 377–400, reprinted in *Archaeologia Cantiana* 32 (1917), 1–26.

Hope-Taylor, Brian, *Yeavering: An Anglo-British Centre of early Northumbria*, Department of the Environment, Archaeological Reports No. 7 (London, 1977).

Hoppe, Jean-Marie, "L'église espagnole visigothique de San Pedro de la Nave (El Campillo—Zamora): Un programme iconographique de la fin du VIIe siècle," *Annales d'histoire de l'art et d'archeologie* 9 (1987), 59–81.

Horn, Walter, "On the Origins of the Medieval Cloister," *Gesta* 12 (1973) 13–52.

——, and Ernest Born, *The Plan of St. Gall*, 3 vols. (Berkeley and Los Angeles, 1979).

Hubert, Jean, "La basilique de Martin le Confesseur," *Arts et vie sociale de la fin du monde antique au Moyen Age* (Geneva, 1977), 297–303.

——, "'Cryptae inferiores' et 'cryptae superiores' dans l'architecture religieuse de l'époque carolingienne," *Mélanges d'histoire du moyen age dédiés à la mémoire de Louis Halphen* (Paris, 1951), 351–57.

——, "Germigny-des-Prés," *Congrès archéologique de France*, 93 (1930), 534–68.

——, "Le mausolée royal de Saint-Denis et le mausolée impérial de Saint-Pierre de Rome," *Bulletin de la Société nationale des Antiquaires de France* (1961), 24–26.

——, et al., *Carolingian Renaissance* (New York, 1970).

——, et al., *Europe of the Invasions* (New York, 1969).

Hugot, Leo, *Kornelimünster*, Rheinische Ausgraben 2, Beihefte der Bonner Jahrbücher 26 (1968).

——, "Die Pfalz Karls des Grossen in Aachen," *Karl der Grosse*, 4 vols. (Düsseldorf, 1965), 3:542–43.

Iogna-Prat, Dominque, "Un texte hagiographique épineux: La 'translation sancti Valeriani'," *Saint-Philibert de Tournus: Histoire, Archéologie, Art*, Actes du colloque du Centre international d'études romanes, Tournus, 15–19 July 1994 (Tournus, 1995), 27–40.

Jacobsen, Werner, "Die Abteikirche von Saint-Denis als kunstgeschichtliches Problem," *La Neustrie*, Beihefte der Francia 16:2 (1989), 151–84.

——, "Altere und neuere Forschungen um den St. Galler Klosterplan," *Unsere Kunstdenkmäler* 34 (1983), 134–51.

——, "Die Anfänge des abendländischen Kreuzgangs," *Der mittelalterlicher Kreuzgang*, ed. Peter K. Klein (Regensbeurg, 2004), 37–56.

——, "Benedikt von Aniane und die Architektur unter Ludwig dem frommen zwischen 814 und 830," *Riforma religiosa e arti nell'epoca carolingia*, ed. Alfred Schmid, Atti del XXIV congresso internazionale di storia dell'arte (Bologna, 1983), 15–22.

——, "Gab es die karolingische 'Renaissance' in der Baukunst?" *Zeitschrift für Kunstgeschichte* 51 (1988), 336–37.

——, *Der Klosterplan von St. Gallen und die karolingische Architectur* (Berlin, 1992).

——, "Die Lorscher Torhalle. Zum Problem ihrer Datierung und Deutung. Mit einem Katalog der bauplastischen Fragmente als Anhang," *Jahrbuch des Zentralinstituts für Kunstgeschichte* 1 (1985), 9–75.

——, "Die Pfalzkonzeptionen Karls des Grossen," *Karl der Grosse als vielberufener Vorfahr*, ed. Lieselotte E. Saurma-Jeltsch (1994), 23–48.

——, "Saint-Denis im neuem Licht: Consequenzen der neuentdeckten Baubeschreibung aus dem Jahre 799," *Kunstchronik* 36 (1983), 301–8.

——, "Saints' Tombs in Frankish Church Architecture," *Speculum* 72 (1997), 1107–43.

——, "San Salvatore in Brescia," *Studien zur mittelalterlichen Kunst 800–1250*, Festschrift für Florentine Mütherich zum 70. Geburtstag (Munich, 1985), 75–80.

——, "Spolien in der karolingischen Architektur," *Antike Spolien in der Architektur des Mittelalters und der Renaissance*, ed. Joachim Poeschke (Munich, 1996), 158.

——, Uwe Lobbedey and Dethard von Winterfeld, "Ottonische Baukunst," *Otto der Grosse: Magdeburg und Europa*, ed. Matthias Puhle, exhibition catalogue, Kunsthistorisches Museum Magdeburg 27 August—2 December 2001, 2 vols. (Mainz, 2001), 1:251–82.

——, and Uwe Lobbedey with Andrea Kleine-Tebbe, "Der Hildesheimer Dom zur Zeit Bernwards," *Bernward von Hildesheim und das Zeitalter der Ottonen*, ed. Michael Brandt and A. Eggebrecht, 2 vols. (Hildesheim, 1993), 1:299–311 and 2:464–66.

——, Leo Schaefer, and Hans Rudolf Sennhauser, *Vorromanische Kirchenbauten, Nachtragsband* (Munich, 1991).

——, and Michaël Wyss, "Saint-Denis: Essai sur la genèse du massif occidental," *Avant-nefs et espaces d'accueil dans l'église entre le IVe et le XIIe siècle*, published under the direction of Christian Sapin (Auxerre, 2002), 76–87.

Jäggi, Carola, *San Salvatore in Spoleto* (Wiesbaden, 1998).

James, Dominic, *God and Gold in Late Antiquity* (Cambridge, 1998).

James, Edward, "Archaeology and the Merovingian Monastery," *Columbanus and Merovingian Monasticism*, ed. H. B. Clarke and Mary Brennan, British Archaeological Reports, International Series 113 (Oxford, 1981), 33–55.

James, Elizabeth, and Ruth Webb, "'To Understand Ultimate Things and Enter Secret Place': Ekphrasis and Art in Byzantium," *Art History* 14 (1991), 1–17.

Jansen, Virginia, "Round or Square? The Axial Towers of the Abbey Church of Saint-Riquier," *Gesta* 21 (1982), 83ff.

Jedin, Hubert, and John Dolan, eds., *Handbook of Church History*, 10 vols. (London, 1965–80).

Jenkins, Frank, "St. Martin's Church at Canterbury: A Survey of the Earliest Structural Features," *Medieval Archaeology* 9 (1965), 11–15.

Johnson, Mark J., "On the Burial Places of the Theodosian Dynasty," *Byzantion* 61 (1991), 336ff.

——, "Toward a History of Theodoric's Building Program," *Dumbarton Oaks Papers* 42 (1988), 73–96.

Johnson, Stephen, *Late Roman Fortifications* (Totowa, New Jersey, 1983).

Jones, A.H.M,. "The Constitutional Position of Odoacer and Theodoric," *Journal of Roman Studies* 52 (1962) 128.

Jungmann, Josef A., *The Early Liturgy to the Time of Gregory the Great* (Notre Dame, Indiana, 1959).

Jurokovic, Miljenko, "Quelques reflections sur la basilique carolingienne de Saint-Denis: une oeuvre d'esprit paléochrétien," *L'abbé Suger, le manifeste gothique de Saint-Denis et la pensée victorine*, Colloque organisé à la Fondation Singer-Polignac le mardi 21 novembre 2000, ed. Dominique Poirel (Turnhout, 2001), 37–57.

Kantorowicz, Ernst H., *Laudes Regiae: A Study in Liturgical Acclamations and Medieval Ruler Worship* (Berkeley and Los Angeles, 1946).

Kartsonis, Anna, *Anastasis: The Making of an Image* (Princeton, 1986).

Khatchatrian, A., "Notes sur l'architecture de l'église de Germigny-des-Prés," *Cahiers archéologiques* 7 (1954), 161–69.

Kenney, James F., *The Sources for the Early History of Ireland: Ecclesiastical* (New York, 1929; reprinted ed., Dublin, 1979).

Kingsley, Karen, "Visigothic Architecture in Spain and Portugal: A Study of Masonry, Documents, and Form," Ph.D. diss., University of California at Berkeley, 1980.

Kinney, Dale, "'Capella Regina': S. Aquilino in Milan," *Marsyas* 15 (1970–71), 13–35.

——, "Le chiese paleocristiane di Mediolanum," *Milano, una capitale da Ambrogio ai Carolingi*, ed. Carlo Bertelli (Milan, 1987), 48–79.

——, "The Church Basilica," *Acta ad archaeologiam et artium historiam pertinentia* 15 (2001), 115–35.

——, "Roman Architectural *Spolia*," *Proceedings of the American Philosophical Society* 145 (2001), 138–50.

——, "'Spolia. Damnatio' and 'Renovatio Memoriae'," *Memoirs of the American Academy in Rome* 42 (1997), 117–48.

Kitzinger, Ernst, *Byzantine Art in the Making* (Cambridge, Massachusetts, 1977).

——, "The Cult of Images in the Age before Iconoclasm," *Dumbarton Oaks Papers* 8 (1954) 83–150, reprinted in idem, *The Art of Byzantium and the Medieval West*, ed. W. Eugene Kleinbauer, (Bloomington, 1976), 90–156.

——, "The Early Christian Town of Stobi," *Dumbarton Oaks Papers* 3 (1946), 93–98.

——, "Interlace and Icons: Form and Function in Early Insular Art," *The Age of Migrating Ideas: Early Medieval Art in Northern Britain and Ireland*, ed. R. Michael Spearman and John Higgitt (Edinburgh, 1993), 3–15.

——, "On Some Icons of the Seventh Century," *Late Classical and Medieval Studies in Honor of A. M. Friend, Jr.*, ed. K. Weitzman et al. (Princeton, 1955), 132–50, reprinted in idem, *The Art of Byzantium and the Medieval West*, ed. W. Eugene Kleinbauer, (Bloomington, 1976), 233–55.

Kleinbauer, Eugene W., "Charlemagne's Palace Chapel at Aachen and Its Copies," *Gesta* 4 (1965), 1–11.

——, "Pre-Carolingian Concepts of Architectural Planning," *The Medieval Mediterranean Cross Cultural Contacts*, ed. M. J. Chiat and K. L. Reyerson (Minnesota, 1988), 67–79.

Kleiss, W., "Neue Befunde zur Chalkopratenkirche in Istanbul," *Akten des VII. Internationalen Kongress für christliche Archäologie*, Trier, 5–11 September 1965 (Vatican City and Berlin, 1969), 587–94.

Klinge, Hans, "Johannes Letzner: Ein niedersächsischer Chronist des 16. Jahrhunderts," *Niedersächsisches Jahrbuch für Landesgeschichte* 24 (1952), 36–97.

Kluge, Bernd, "Nomen imperatoris und Christiana Religio: Das Kaisertum Karls des Grossen und Ludwigs des Frommen im Licht der numismatischen Quellen," *799. KKK: Beiträge*, 82–87.

Knöpp, Friedrich, "Richbod (Erz-) Bischof von Trier 791(?)–804," *Die Reichsabtei Lorsch*, Festschrift zum Gedenken an ihre Stiftung 764, ed. Friedrich Knöpp, 2 vols. (Darmstadt, 1973), 1:247–51.

Koehler, Wilhelm, *Die Karolingische Miniaturen II: Die Hofschule Karls des Grossen* (Berlin, 1958).

—— and F. Mütherich, *Die Karolingische Miniaturen V: Die Hofschule Karls des Kahlens* (Berlin, 1982).

Kostof, Spiro, *The Orthodox Baptistery of Ravenna* (New Haven, 1965).

Kötting, Bernhard, *Der frühchristliche Reliquienkult und die Bestattung im Kirchengebäude* (Cologne and Oplanden, 1965).

——, "Die Tradition der Grabkirche," *Memoria. Der geschichtliche Zeugniswert des liturgischen Gedenkens im Mittelalter*, ed. Karl Schmid and Joachim Wollasch (Munich, 1984), 69–78.

Kottmann, Albrecht, "Neue Thesen zum St. Galler Klosterplan," *Das Münster: Zeitschrift für christliche Kunst und Kunstwissenschaft* (1978), 277–79.

Kozachek, Thomas D., "The Repertory of Chant for Dedicating Churches in the Middle Ages: Music, Liturgy, and Ritual," Ph.D. diss. (Harvard University, 1995).

Krautheimer, Richard, "The Architecture of Sixtus III: A Fifth-Century Renascence?" *Essays in Honor of Erwin Panofsky* (New York, 1961), 291–302, reprinted in idem, *Studies*, 181–96.

——, "The Building Inscriptions and the Dates of Construction of Old St. Peter's: A Reconsideration," *Römisches Jahrbuch der Bibliotheca Hertziana*, 25 (1989), 7ff.

——, "The Carolingian Revival of Early Christian Architecture," *The Art Bulletin* 24 (1942) 1–38, reprinted with a postscript in idem, *Studies in Early Christian, Medieval, and Renaissance Art* (New York, 1969), 203–56.

——, "The Crypt of Sta. Maria in Cosmedin and the Mausoleum of Probus Anicius," *Essays in Memory of Karl Lehmann, Marsyas*, Supplement 1 (Locust Valley, New York, 1964), 171–75.

——, et al., *Corpus Basilicarum Christianarum Romae*, 5 vols. (Vatican City, 1937–77).

——, "The Constantinian Basilica," *Dumbarton Oaks Papers* 21 (1967), 151–40.

——, "Die Decanneacubita in Konstantinopel. Ein kleiner Beitrag zur Frage Rom und Byzanz," *Tortulae. Römische Quartalschrift*, Supplement 30, 1966, 195–99.

——, *Early Christian and Byzantine Architecture*, 4th rev. ed. with Slobodan Curcic (Harmondsworth, 1986).

——, "Intorno all fondazione di San Paolo fuori le mura," *Rendiconti della pontificia accademia romana di archeologia*, 53–54 (1980–81, 1981–82), 207ff.

——, "Introduction to an 'Iconography of Medieval Architecture,'" *Journal of the Warburg and Courtauld Institutes* 5 (1942), 1–33, reprinted with a postscript in idem, *Studies in Early Christian, Medieval, and Renaissance Art* (New York, 1969), 115–50.

——, "Mensa-Coemeterium-Martyrium," *Cahiers archéologiques* 11 (1960), 15–40, reprinted in idem, *Studies in Early Christian, Medieval and Renaissance Art* (New York, 1969), 35–58.

——, "On Constantine's Church of the Apostles in Constantinople," *Studies in Early Christian, Medieval, and Renaissance Art* (New York, 1969), 27–34.

——, *Rome: Profile of a City, 312–1307* (Princeton, 1980).

——, "Sancta Maria Rotunda," *Arte del primo millenio*, Atti del II° convegno per lo studio dell'arte dell'alto medioevo (Turin, 1953), 23–27, reprinted in idem, *Studies in Early Christian, Medieval, and Renaissance Art* (New York, 1969), 107–14.

——, "Success and Failure in Late Antique Church Planning," *The Age of Spirituality*, ed. Kurt Weitzmann (New York, 1980), 121–39.

——, *Three Christian Capitals: Topography and Politics* (Berkeley, 1983).

Kreusch, Felix, *Beobachtungen an der Westanlage der Klosterkirche zu Corvey*, Beihefte der Bonner Jahrbücher, vol. 9 (Cologne and Graz, 1963).

——, "Im Louvre wiedergefundene Kapitelle und Bronzebasen aus der Pfalzkirche Karls des Grossen zu Aachen," *Cahiers archéologiques* 18 (1968), 71–98.

——, "Zwei im Louvre wiedergefundene Kapitelle aus Karls des Grossen Pfalzkirche zu Aachen," *Bonner Jahrbücher* 171 (1971), 407–15.

Krinsky, Carol H., "Seventy-Eight Vitruvius Manuscripts," *Journal of the Warburg and Courtauld Institutes* 30 (1967), 36–70.

Krüger, Kristina, "Architecture and Liturgical Practice: The Cluniac *galilea*," *White Mantle of Churches: Architecture, Liturgy, and Art around the Millennium* (Turnhout, 2003), 139–59.

——, "Tournus et la fonction des Galilées en Bourgogne," *Avant-nefs et espaces d'acceuil dans l'église entre le IVe et le XIIe siècle*, published under the direction of Christian Sapin (Auxerre, 2002), 414–23.

Kubach, Hans Erich, and Albert Verbeek, *Romanische Baukunst an Rhein und Maas*, 4 vols. (Berlin, 1976–89).

Lafaurie, Jean, "Les monnaies impériales de Charlemagne," *Comptes rendus de l'académie des inscriptions et belles-lettres*, January–March, 1978, 154–72.

Laistner, M. L.W., *Thought and Letters in Western Europe A.D. 500 to 900* (Ithaca, 1966).

Lammers, Walter, "Ein karolingisches Bildprogram in der Aula Regia von Ingelheim," *Festschrift für Hermann Heimpel* (Göttingen, 1972), 226–89.

Landes, Richard, *Relics, Apocalypse, and the Deceits of History: Ademar of Chabannes, 989–1034* (Cambridge, Mass., 1995).

Landschoot, Anne Van, "La translation des reliques de saint Vit de l'abbaye de Saint-Denis à celle de Corvey en 836," *Revue belge de philosophie et d'histoire*, 74 (1996), 593–632.

Lange, Dorothea, "Theorien zur Entstehung des byzantinischen Kreuzkuppelkirche," *Architectura* 16 (1986), 93–113.

La Rocca, Cristina, "Public Buildings and Urban Change in Northern Italy in the Early Medieval Period," *The City in Late Antiquity*, ed. John Rich (London, 1992), 161–80.

Lasko, Peter, *The Kingdom of the Franks* (London, 1971).

Lauer, P., *Le Palais de Latran* (Paris, 1911).

Lavin, Irving, "The House of the Lord: Aspects of the Role of Palace Triclinia in the Architecture of Late Antiquity and the Early Middle Ages," *Art Bulletin* 44 (1962), 1–27.

Lawlor, H. C., *The Monastery of St. Mochaoi of Nendrum* (Belfast, 1925).

Lawrence, C. H., *Medieval Monasticism*, 2nd ed. (London, 1989).

Lawrence, Marian, "Maria Regina," *Art Bulletin* 7 (1925), 150–61.

Lebouteux, Pierre, "L'église de Saint-Philibert-de-Grandlieu," *Bulletin Archéologique du Comité des travaux historiques et scientifiques*, n.s. 1–2 (1965–66), 49–107.

Legler, Rolf, "Der abendländische Kreuzgang: Erfindung oder Tradition?" in *Der mittelalterlicher Kreuzgang*, ed. Peter K. Klein (Regensbeurg, 2004), 66–79.

Lehmann, Edgar, "Die Anordnung der Altäre in der karolingischen Klosterkirche zu Centula," *Karl der Grosse*, 4 vols. (Düsseldorf, 1965), 3:374–83.

Lehmann, Paul, "Fulda und die antike Literatur," *Aus Fuldas Geistesleben* (Fulda, 1928), 9–23.

——, *Mittelalterliche Bibliothekskataloge Deutschlands und der Schweiz*, Vol. 1, *Die Bistumer Konstanz und Chur* (Munich, 1918).

Lelong, Charles, "La date du déambulatoire de Saint-Martin de Tours," *Bulletin monumental* 131 (1973), 298–309.

Le Maho, Jacques, "Tours et entrées occidentales des églises de la basse vallée de la Seine (IXe–XIIe siècle)," *Avant-nefs et espaces d'accueil dans l'église entre le IVe et le XIIe siècle*, published under the direction of Christian Sapin (Auxerre, 2002), 281–95.

Levillain, Léon, "L'avènement de la dynastie carolingienne et les origines de l'état pontifical (749–57)," *Bibliothèque de l'Ècole des Chartes* 94 (1933), 227ff.

——, "Les origines du monastère de Nouaillé," *Bibliothèque de l'Ecole des Chartes* 71 (1910), 278

Levison, Wilhelm, *England and the Continent in the Eighth Century* (Oxford, 1946).

Lewis, Suzanne, "Function and Symbolic Form in the Basilica Apostolorum at Milan," *JSAH* 28 (1969), 83–98.

——, "The Latin Iconography of the Single-Naved Cruciform Basilica Apostolorum in Milan," *Art Bulletin* 51 (1969), 205–19.

Lipphardt, Walther, *Der Karolingische Tonar von Metz*, Liturgiewissenschaftliche Quellen und Forschungen 43 (Münster, 1965).

Lipsius, Richard, *Die Apokryphen Apostelgeschichte und Apostellegenden*, 2 vols. (Braunschweig, 1887).

Llewellyn, Peter, *Rome in the Dark Ages* (New York, 1971).

Lobbedey, Uwe, *Die Ausgrabungen im Dom zu Paderborn 1978/80 und 1983*, Denkmalpflege und Forschung in Westfalen 11, 4 vols. (Bonn, 1986).

——, "Der Beitrag von Corvey zur Geschichte der Westbauten und Westwerke," *Hortus Artium Medievalium* 8 (2002), 83–98.

——, "Carolingian Royal Palaces: The State of Research from an Architectural Historian's Viewpoint," *Court Culture in the Early Middle Ages: The Proceedings of the First Alcuin Conference*, ed. Catherine Cubitt (Turnhout, 2003), 129–53.

——, "Corvey, ancienne abbey bénédict, " *Westphalie romane* (La Pierre-Qui-Vire, 1999), 219–29.

——, "Corvey (Grabungsnotiz)," *Westfalen* 61 (1983), 230.

——, "Neue Grabungsergebnisse zur Baugeschichte der Corveyer Abtei-Kirche," *Architectura* 8 (1978), 28–38.

——, "Ottonische Krypten: Bermerkungen zum Forschungsstand an Hand ausgewählte Beispiele," *Herrschaftrepräsentation im Ottonischen Sachsen*, ed. Gerd Althoff and Ernst Schubert (Sigmaringen, 1998), 77–102.

——, "Les Westwerke de l'époque ottonienne en Allemagne du Nord," *Avant-nefs et espaces d'accueil dans l'église entre le IVe et le XIIe siècle*, published under the direction of Christian Sapin (Auxerre, 2002), 67–75.

L'Orange, Hans Peter, and Hjalmar Torp, *Il tempietto longobardo di Cividale*, Acta ad archaeologium et artium historiam pertinentia 7, 3 vols. (Rome 1977–79).

Lot, Ferdinand, *Hariulf: Chronique de l'Abbaye de Saint-Riquier (Ve siècle–1104)* (Paris, 1894).

Louis, René, *Autessiodurum Christianum: Les églises d'Auxerre des origines au XIe siècle* (Paris, 1952).

Löwe, Heinz, "Von Theoderich dem Grossen zu Karl dem Grossen," *Von Cassiodor zu Dante* (Berlin and New York, 1973) 70–74.

Luchterhandt, Manfred, "*Famulus Petri*—Karl der Grosse in den römischen Mosaikbildern Leos III," *799. KKK: Beiträge*, 55–70.

——, "Päpstlicher Palastbau und höfisches Zeremoniell unter Leo III," *799. KKK: Beiträge*, 109–22.

Ludwig, Thomas, Otto Müller, and Irmgard Widdra-Spiess, *Die Einhards-Basilika in Steinbach bei Michelstadt im Odenwald*, (Mainz, 1996).

Mackie, Gillian, *Early Christian Chapels in the West: Decoration, Function and Patronage* (Toronto, 2003).

——, "La Daurade: A Royal Mausoleum," *Cahiers archéologiques* 42 (1994), 17–34.

——, "The Zeno Chapel: A Prayer for Salvation," *PBSR* 57 (1989), 172–99.

Magni, Mariaclotilde, "Cryptes du haut Moyen Age en Italie: problèmes de typologie du IXe jusqu'au début du XIe siècle," *Cahiers archéologiques* 28 (1979), 41–85.

Maillé, Marquise de, *Les cryptes de Jouarre* (Paris, 1971).

Maitre, Léon, "Une église carolingienne à Saint-Philibert-de-Grandlieu," *Bulletin Monumental* 63 (1898), 127–65.

Mâle, Emile, *The Early Churches of Rome*, trans. D. Buxton (Chicago, 1960).

Maloney, Stephanie J., "Early Christian Double-apsed Churches in Iberia. Some Considerations," *Art History* 3 (1980), 129–43.

Mango, Cyril, *The Art of the Byzantine Empire 312–1453* (Englewood Cliffs, New Jersey, 1972).

——, *The Brazen House: A Study of the Vestibule of the Imperial Palace in Constantinople* (Copenhagen, 1959).

——, "Constantine's Mausoleum and the Translation of Relics," *Byzantinische Zeitschrift* 83 (1990), 51–62.

——, *Le développement urbain de Constantinople IVe–VIIe siècles* (Paris, 1985).

Manitius, M., *Geschichte der lateinischen Literatur des Mittelalters*, 2 vols. (Munich, 1959).

Mann, Albrecht, "Grossbauten vorkarlischer Zeit und aus der Epoche von Karl dem Grossen bis zu Lothar I," *Karl der Grosse*, 4 vols. (Düsseldorf, 1965), 3:320–21.

Martin, Thomas, "Bermerkungen zur 'Epistola de litteris colendis,'" *Archiv für Diplomatik* 31 (1985), 227–72.

Mathews, Thomas F., *The Early Churches of Constantinople: Architecture and Liturgy* (University Park and London, 1971).

Matthiae, Guglielmo, *Mosaici medioevali delle chiese di Roma*, 2 vols. (Rome, 1967).

——, *Pittura romana del medioevo*, 2 vols. (Rome, 1965–66).

Mauck, Marchita B., "The Mosaic of the Triumphal Arch of S. Prassede: A Liturgical Interpretation," *Speculum* 62 (1987), 813–28.

McClendon, Charles B., "The Church of S. Maria di Tremiti and Its Significance for the History of Romanesque Architecture," *Journal of the Society of Architectural Historians* 43 (1984), 9–15.

——, *The Imperial Abbey of Farfa: Architectural Currents in the Early Middle Ages* (New Haven, 1987).

——, "Louis the Pious, Rome and Constantinople," *Architectural Studies in Memory of Richard Krautheimer* (Mainz, 1997), 103–6.

——, "The Revival of *Opus Sectile* Pavements in Rome and the Vicinity in the Carolingian Period," *Papers of the British School at Rome*, 48 (1980), 157–64.

McCormick, Finbar, "Iona: The Archaeology of the Early Monastery," *Studies in the Cult of Saint Columba*, ed. Cormac Bourke (Dublin, 1997) 46–51.

McCormick, Michael, *Eternal Victory: Triumphal Rulership in Late Antiquity* (Cambridge and Paris, 1986).

——, *Origins of the European Economy: Communications and Commerce A.D. 300–900* (Cambridge, 2001).

McCulloh, John M., "The Cult of Relics in the Letters and 'Dialogues' of Pope Gregory the Great: A Lexicographical Study," *Traditio* 32 (1976), 145–84.

——, "From Antiquity to the Middle Ages: Continuity and Change in Papal Relic Policy from the 6th to the 8th Century," *Pietas: Festschrift für Bernhard Kötting*, ed. E. Dassmann and K. Suso Frank, Jahrbuch für Antike und Christentum, Ergänzungsband 8 (1980), 313–24.

McGrade, Michael, "Affirmations of Royalty: Liturgical Music in the Collegiate Church of St. Mary in Aachen, 1050–1350," Ph.D. diss., University of Chicago, 1998.

McKitterick, Rosamond, *The Frankish Kingdoms under the Carolingians, 751–987* (London and New York, 1983).

——, ed., *Carolingian Culture: Emulation and Innovation* (Cambridge, 1994).

——, ed., *The New Cambridge Medieval History c. 700–c.900* (Cambridge, 1995).

McLynn, Neil B., *Ambrose of Milan* (Berkeley, 1994).

Mecquenem, Claude de, "Les cryptes de Jouarre (Seine-et-Marne). Des indices pour une nouvelle chronologie," *Archéologie médiévale* 32 (2002), 1–29.

Menis, Gian Carlo, ed., *I Longobardi* (Milan, 1990).

Mercati, G., *Note di litteratura biblica e cristiana antica*, Studi e testi 5 (Rome, 1901).

Merkel, Kerstin, "Die Antikenrezeption der sogenannten Lorscher Torhalle," *Kunst in Hessen und am Mittelrhein* 32/33 (1993), 23–42.

Meyer, Ruth, *Frühmittelalterliche Kapitelle und Kämpfer in Deutschland*, 2 vols. (Berlin, 1997).

Meyer-Barkhausen, Werner, "Die frühmittelalterlichen Vorbäuten am Atrium von Alt St. Peter in Rom, zweitürmige Atrien, Westwerke und Karolingisch-Ottonische Königskapellen," *Wallraf-Richartz-Jahrbuch* 20 (1958), 7–40.

Meyvaert, Paul, "The Authorship of the Libri Carolini," *Revue Bénédictine*, 89 (1979), 29–57.

——, "Bede and the Church Paintings at Wearmouth-Jarrow," *Anglo-Saxon England* 8 (1979) 63–77.

——, "Bede the Scholar," *Famulus Christi: Essays in Commemoration of the Thirteenth Centenary of the Birth of the Venerable Bede*, ed. Gerald Bonner (London, 1976), 47, 64 n. 30, reprinted in P. Meyvaert, *Benedict, Gregory, Bede and Others* (London, 1977).

——, "The Medieval Monastic Claustrum," *Gesta* 12 (1973), 53–59.

——, "Peter the Deacon and the Tomb of Saint Benedict," *Revue Bénédictine*, 65 (1955), 3–70, reprinted in idem, *Benedict, Gregory, Bede and Others* (London, 1977).

——, Review of Horn and Born, *The Plan of St. Gall*, in *University Publishing* (Summer, 1980), 18–19.

Mirabella, Roberti, M., "La cattedrale antica di Milano e il suo battistero," *Arte Lombarda* 8 (1963), 77ff.

Mitchell, John, "Artistic Patronage and Cultural Strategies in Lombard Italy," *Towns and Their Territories between Late Antiquity and the Early Middle Ages*, ed. G. P. Brogiolo et al., The Transformation of the Roman World, vol. 9 (Leiden, 2000), 361–70.

——, "The Uses of *spolia* in Longobard Italy," *Antike Spolien in der Architektur des Mittelalters und der Renaissance*, ed. Joachim Poeschke (Munich, 1996), 93–107.

Möbius, Friedrich, *Westwerkstudien* (Jena, 1968).

Monfrin, Francoise, "À propos de Milan chrétien: Siège épiscopal et topographie chrétienne IVe–VIe siècles," *Cahiers archéologiques*, 39 (1991), 7–46.

Moore, W. J., "The Saxon Pilgrims to Rome and the Schola Saxonum," Ph.D. diss., University of Fribourg, Switzerland, 1937.

Moorhead, John, *The Roman Empire Divided, 400–700* (London, 2001).

——, *Theodoric in Italy* (Oxford, 1992).

Mortet, V., "Un formulaire du VIIIe siècle pour les fondations d'édifices et de ponts d'après des sources d'origine antique," *Bulletin Monumentale* 71 (1907), 442–65.

Müller, Iso, "Die Altar-Tituli des Klosterplanes," *Studien zum St. Galler Klosterplan* (St. Gallen, 1962), 129–76.

Musset, Lucien, "L'église d'Evrecy (Calvados) et ses sculptures préromanes," *Bulletin de la Société des Antiquares de Normandie* 53 (1955–56), 116–68.

Mütherich, Florentine, "Die Buchmalerei am Hofe Karls des Grossen," *Karl der Grosse*, 4 vols. (Düsseldorf, 1965), 3:12–15.

——, "Carolingian art 3: Manuscripts," *The Dictionary of Art*, 26 vols. (London, 1996), 5:800–5.

——, "Der karolingische Argimensorem-Codex in Rom," *Aachener Kunstblätter* 45 (1974), 59–74.

—— and Joachim E. Gaehde, *Carolingian Painting* (New York, 1970).

Narberhaus, Josef, *Benedikt von Aniane. Werk und Persönlichkeit* (Münster, 1930).

Nash, Ernest, *Pictorial Dictionary of Ancient Rome*, 2 vols. (New York, 1961–62).

Nauerth, Claudia, *Agnellus von Ravenna. Untersuchungen zur archäologischen Methode des ravennatischen Chronisten* (Munich, 1974).

Nees, Lawrence, "The Colophon Drawing in the Book of Mulling: A Supposed Irish Monastery Plan and the Tradition of Terminal Illustrations in Early Medieval Manuscripts," *Cambridge Medieval Celtic Studies* 5 (1983), 67–91.

——, "The Plan of St. Gall and the Theory of the Program of Carolingian Art," *Gesta*, 25 (1986), 1–8.

Nelson, Janet, "Aachen as a Place of Power," *Topographies of Power in the Early Middle Ages*, ed. Mayke De Jong and Frans Theuws with Carine van Rhijn (Leiden, 2001), 217–37.

——, *Charles the Bald* (London and New York, 1992).

——, "Making a Difference in Eighth-Century Politics: The Daughters of Desiderius," *After Rome's Fall: Narrators and Sources in early Medieval History*, Essays Presented to Walter Goffart, ed. Alexander Collander Murray (Toronto, 1998), 177.

——, "The Reign of Charles the Bald: A Survey," *Charles the Bald: Court and Kingdom*, ed. Margaret T. Gibson and J. L. Nelson, 2nd rev. ed. (Hampshire, 1990), 1–22.

——, "Viaggiatori, pellegrini e vie commerciali," *Il futuro dei Longobardi: Saggi*, ed. C. Bertelli and G. P. Brogiolo (Milan, 2000), 163–71.

Neuman de Vegvar, Carol, *The Northumbrian Renaissance: A Study in the Transmission of Style* (Selingsgrove, Pennsylvania, 1987).

Neumüllers-Klauser, Renate, "Die Westwerktafel der Kirche Corvey," *Westfalen* 67 (1989), 127–38; and *799. KKK*, 2:570–71.

Nichols, Jr., Stephen G., *Romanesque Signs: Early Medieval Narrative and Iconography* (New Haven and London, 1983).

Nilgen, Ursula, "Die grosse Relinquieninschrift von Santa Prassede," *Römische Quartalschrift* 69 (1974), 7–29.

——, "Maria Regina—ein Politischer Kultusbild?" *Römisches Jahrbuch für Kunstgeschichte* 19 (1981), 1–33.

Noble, Thomas F. X., "The Monastic Ideal as a Model for Empire: The Case of Louis the Pious," *Revue Bénédictine* 86 (1976), 235–50.

——, "Paradoxes and Possibilities in the Sources for Roman Society in the Early Middle Ages," *Early Medieval Rome and the Christian West: Essays in Honour of Donald A. Bullough*, ed. J. Smith (Leiden, 2000), 55–83.

——, *The Republic of St. Peter: The Birth of the Papal State 680–825* (Philadelphia, 1984).

——, "Topography, Celebration, and Power: The Making of Papal Rome in the Eighth and Ninth Centuries," *Topographies of Power in the Early Middle Ages*, ed. Mayke De Jong and Frans Theuws with Carine van Rhijn (Leiden, 2001), 45–91.

Noble, Thomas F. X., and Thomas Head, ed., *Soldiers of Christ: Saints and Saints' Lives from Late Antiquity and the Early Middle Ages* (University Park, 1995).

Nordhagen, P. J., *The Frescoes of John VII (A.D. 705–707) in A. Maria Antiqua in Rome*, Institutum Romanum Norvegiae, Acta ad archaeologiam et artium historiam petinentia 3 (Rome, 1968).

——, "Un problema di carattere iconografico e tecnico a S. Prassede," *Roma e l'età carolingia*, Atti delle giornate di studio, 3–8 Maggio 1976, Istituto nazionale di archeologia e storia dell'arte (Rome, 1976), 159–66.

Nordhoff, J. B., "Corvei und die westfälisch-sächische Früharchitektur," *Repertorium für Kunstwissenschaft* 11 (1888), 147–65.

Norman, Edward R., and J. K. S. St. Joseph, *The Early Development of Irish Society: The Evidence of Aerial Photography* (Cambridge, 1969).

Nussbaum, Otto, *Der Standort des Liturgen am christlichen Atlar vor dem Jahre 1000*, 2 vols. (Bonn, 1965).

Oexle, Otto G., *Forschungen zu Monastischen und Geistlichen Gemeinschaften im Westfränkischen Bereich*, Münstersche Mittelalter-Schriften 31 (Munich, 1978), 113f.

Oikonomides, Nicholas, "Some Remarks on the Apse Mosaic of St. Sophia," *Dumbarton Oaks Papers* 39 (1985), 111–15.

Onasch, Konrad, *Lichthöhle und Sternenhaus: Licht und Materie im spätantik-christlichen und frühbyzantinischen Sakralbau* (Basel, 1973).

Osborne, John, "Images of the Mother of God in Early Medieval Rome," *Icon and Word: The Power of Images in Byzantium*, Studies presented to Robin Cormack, ed. Anthony Eastmond and Liz James (Aldershot, 2003), 135–51.

——, "Papal Court Culture under the Pontificate of Zacharias (A.D. 741–52)," *Court Culture in the Early Middle Ages: The Proceedings of the First Alcuin Conference*, ed. Catherine Cubitt (Turnhout, 2003), 223–34.

Ostendorf, Adolf, "Das Salvator-Patrocinium, seine Aufgänge und seine Ausbreitung im mittelalterlichen Deutschland," *Westfälische Zeitschrift*, 100 (1950), 357–76.

Ostrogorsky, George, *History of the Byzantine State*, rev. ed. (New Brunswick, New Jersey, 1969).

Oswald, Friedrich, Leo Schaefer, and Hans Rudolf Sennhauser, *Vorromanische Kirchenbauten* (Munich, 1966–71).

Ousterhout, Robert, *Master Builders of Byzantium* (Princeton, 1999).

Packer, James E., *The Forum of Trajan in Rome*, 3 vols. (Berkeley, 1997).

Palisca, Clause V., ed., *Hucbald, Guido, and John on Music: Three Musical Treatises*, trans. Warren Babb (New Haven and London, 1978).

Panofsky, Erwin, ed., trans., and annot., *Abbot Suger on the Abbey Church of St.-Denis and Its Art Treasures*, 2d ed. Gerda Panofsky (Princeton, 1979).

Pantoni, Angelo, "Santa Maria delle Cinque Torri di Cassino: Risultati e problemi," *Rivista di archeologia cristiana*, 51 (1975), 243–80.

——, *Le vicende della basilica di Montecassino*, Miscellanea Cassinese 36 (Montecassino, 1973).

Parkes, M. B., *The Scriptorium of Wearmouth-Jarrow*, Jarrow Lecture (Jarrow, 1982).

Parsons, David, "Consistency and the St. Gallen Plan: A Review Article," *Archaeological Journal* 138 (1981), 259–65.

——, "The Pre-Romanesque Church of St-Riquier: The Documentary Evidence," *Journal of the British Archaeological Association* 129 (1976), 21–51.

——, "Sites and Monuments of the Anglo-Saxon Mission in Central Germany," *Archaeological Journal* 140 (1983), 280–321.

Partner, Peter, *The Lands of St Peter* (Berkeley and Los Angeles, 1972).

Pawelec, Katharina, *Aachener Bronzegitter. Studien zur karolingischen Ornamentik um 800* (Cologne, 1990).

Peers, Charles, and C. A. Ralegh Radford, "The Saxon Monastery at Whitby," *Archaeologia* 89 (1943), 27–88.

Pelliccioni, Giovanni, *Le nuove scoperte sugli origini del battistero lateranense*, Memorie della pontificia accademia romana di archeologia 12 (Vatican City, 1973).

Percival, John, *The Roman Villa* (Berkeley and Los Angeles, 1976).

——, "Villas and Monasteries in Late Roman Gaul," *Journal of Ecclesiastical History*, 48 (1997), 1–21.

Perin, Patrick, and L.-C. Feffer, eds., *La Neustrie: Les pays au nord de la Loire de Dagobert à Charles le Chauve (VIIe–IXe siècles)*, (Paris, 1985).

Perogalli, Carlo, "Analisi critica dell'architettura del sacello di San Satiro," *San Satiro*, ed. Ambrogio Palestra and Carlo Perogalli (Milan, 1980), 155–90.

Petersen, Joan, *The 'Dialogues' of Gregory the Great and their Late Antique Cultural Background*, Pontifical Institute of Medieval Studies, Studies and Texts 69 (Toronto, 1984).

Pfister, R., "Les tissus de la Bible de Théodulf," *Coptic Studies in Honor of Walter Ewig Crum* (Boston, 1951), 501ff.

Picard, Jean-Charles, "Conscience urbaine et culte des saints. De Milan sous Liutprand à Vérone sous Pépin 1er d'Italie," *Hagiographie cultures et sociétés IVe–XIIe siècles* (Paris, 1981).

——, "Les origines du mot *paradisus*—parvis," *Mélanges de l'école française de Rome: Moyen-Age—Temps Modernes* 83 (1971), 158–86.

——, "Le quadriportique de Saint-Paul-hors-les-murs à Rome," *Mélanges d'archéologie et d'histoire de l'école française de Rome: Antiquité* 87 (1975), 395.

Plummer, Charles, ed., *Venerabilis Baedae Opera Historica*, 2 vols. (Oxford, 1896; reprinted 1969).

Pocock, Michael, and Hazel Wheeler, "Excavations at Escomb Church, County Durham, 1968," *Journal of the British Archaeological Association*, 3rd ser., 34 (1971), 9–29.

Pohl, Walter, ed., *Kingdoms of the Empire: The Integration of Barbarians in Late Antiquity* (Leiden, 1997).

Poilpré, Anne-Orange, "Le décor de l'oratoire de Germigny-des-Prés: l'authentique et le restauré," *Cahiers de civilisation médiévale Xe–XIIe siècles*, 41 (1998), 281–98.

Porter, Arthur Kingsley, *Lombard Architecture*, 3 vols. (New Haven, 1917).

Les premiers monuments chrètiens de la France, 3 vols (Paris, 1995–98).

Prinz, Friedrich, "Stadtrömisch-italische Märtyrreliquien und fränkischer Reichsadel im Maas-Moselraum," *Historisches Jahrbuch* 87 (1967), 1–25.

Prinz, Joseph, ed., *Die Corveyer Annalen*, Abhandlungen zur Corveyer Geschichtsschreibung 7 (Münster, 1982).

Quadri, R., "Del nuovo su Eirico di Auxerre," *Studi Medievali* 23 (1992), 217–28.

Rabe, Susan A., *Faith, Art, and Politics at Saint-Riquier: The Symbolic Vision of Angilbert* (Philadelphia, 1995).

Rademacher, Franz, *Die Regina Angelorum in der Kunst des Mittelalters*, Die Kunstdenkmäler des Rheinlandes, Beiheft 17 (Düsseldorf, 1972).

Rady, Jonathan, "Excavations at St. Martin's Hill, Canterbury, 1984–85," *Archaeologia Cantiana* 104 (1987), 123–30.

Rahner, Hugo, *Griechische Mythen in christlicher Deutung* (Zurich, 1957), translated by Brian Bradshaw as *Greek Myths and Christian Mystery* (London, 1963).

Rahtz, Philip, "Buildings and Rural Settlements," *Archaeology of Anglo-Saxon England*, ed. David M. Wilson (Cambridge, 1976), 49–98.

Raine, James, *The Priory of Hexham*, 2 vols. (Edinburgh, 1864–65).

Randsborg, Klaus, *The First Millennium A.D. in Europe and the Mediterranean: An Archaeological Essay* (Cambridge, 1991).

Reekmans, Louis, "Les cryptes des martyrs romains. Etat de la recherche," *Atti del IX congresso internazionale di archeologia cristiana*, 2 vols. (Vatican City, 1978), 1:275–302.

——, "Le dévelopment topographique de la région du Vatican à la fin de l'antiquité et au debut du moyen âge (300–850)," *Mélanges d'archéologie et d'historie de l'art offerts au Professeur Jacques Lavalleye* (Louvain, 1970), 218.

Réfice, Paola, "'Habitatio Sancti Petri': Glosse ad alcune fonti su S. Martino in Vaticano," *Arte medievale* Ser. 2, vol. 4 (1990), 13–16.

Reinhardt, H., *La cathédrale de Reims* (Paris, 1963).

Rice, Eric North, "Music and Ritual in the Collegiate Church of Saint Mary in Aachen, 1300–1600," Ph.D. diss., Columbia University, 2002.

Richards, Jeffrey, *Consul of God: The Life and Times of Gregory the Great* (London, 1980).

Riché, Pierre, *Education and Culture in the Barbarian West*, trans. J. J. Contreni (Columbia, South Carolina, 1978).

——, "Les représentations du palais dans les textes littéraires du haut moyen age," *Francia* 4 (1976), 161–71.

Rigold, S. E., "'Litus Romanus'—The Shore Forts as Mission Stations," *The Saxon Shore*, ed. D. E. Johnson, Council for British Archaeology, Research Report 18 (London, 1977), 70–75.

Riley, Hugh, *Christian Initiation*, Studies in Antiquity 17 (Washington, D.C., 1974).

Ripoll Lopez, Gisela, *Toreutica de la Betica (siglos VI y VII D.C.)* (Barcelona, 1998).

Ristow, Sebastian, *Frühchristliche Baptisterien*, Jahrbuch für Antike und Christentum Ergänzungsband 27 (Münster, 1998).

Roberts, Michael, *The Jeweled Style: Poetry and Poetics in Late Antiquity* (Ithaca and London, 1989).

Robertson, Anne Walters, *The Service-Books of the Royal Abbey of Saint-Denis* (Oxford, 1991).

Rohault de Fleury, C., *Le Latran au Moyen-Age* (Paris, 1877).

Rotili, M., *Benevento romana e longobarda. L'immagine urbana* (Naples, 1986), 184–201.

Rousseau, Philip, *Pachomius: The Making of a Community in Fourth-Century Egypt* (Berkeley and London, 1985).

Rugo, Pietro, and Ornella, *Il tempietto longobardo di Cividale del Friuli* (Pordenone, 1990).

Rusconi, A., "La chiesa di S. Sofia di Benevento," *Corso di cultura sull'arte Ravennate e Bizantina* 14 (1967), 339–59.

Sage, Walter, "Die Ausgrabungen in der Pfalz zu Ingelheim am Rhein 1960–1970," *Francia* 4 (1976), 141–60.

——, "Frühmittelalterlicher Holzbau," *Karl der Grosse*, 4 vols. (Düsseldorf, 1965), 3:573–90.

Saint-Germain d'Auxerre: Intellectuels et artistes dans l'Europe carolingienne IXe–XIe siècle, exh. cat. (Auxerre, 1990).

Salin, Bernhard, *Die altgermanische Tierornamentik* (Stockholm, 1935).

Salmi, Mario, "Architettura longobarda o architettura preromanica?"

Atti del convegno sul tema: La civiltà dei longobardi in Europa, Accademia Nazionale dei Lincei (Rome, 1974), 271–73.

——, "Nuovi reperti alto medievali 'intra Tevere et Arno,'" *Commentari* 21 (1970), 7–11.

Sansterre, Jean-Marie, *Les moines grecs et orientaux à Rome aux époques byzantine et carolingienne (milieu du VIe s.–du IXe s.)*, 2 vols. (Brussels, 1983).

Santosuosso, Alma Colk, *Letter Notations in the Middle Ages* (Ottawa, 1989).

Sapin, Christian, *Archéologie et architecture d'un site monastique, Ve–XXe siècles. 10 ans de recherches à l'abbaye Saint-Germain d'Auxerre* (Auxerre, 2000).

——, D'Auxerre à Cluny, Le dossier archéologique des premières avant-nefs et galilées," *Avant-nefs et espaces d'accueil dans l'église entre le IVe et le XIIe siècle*, Published under the direction of Christian Sapin (Auxerre, 2002), 398–413.

——, *La Bourgogne préromane* (Paris, 1986).

——, "La crypte de Flavigny, 'un reliquaire' pour sainte Reine?" *Reine au Mont Auxois. Le culte et le pèlerinage de sainte Reine des origines à nos jours*, ed. Philippe Boutry and Dominique Julia (Paris, 1997), 81–94.

——, "Dans l'église ou hors l'église, quel choix pour l'inhumé?" *Archéologie du cimetire chrétien*, Actes du 2e colloque A.R.C.H.E.A. (Tours, 1996), 65–78.

——, "L'origine des rotondes mariales des IXe–XIe siècles et le cas de Saint-Germain-d'Auxerre," *Marie, le culte de la Vierge dans la société médiévale*, ed. Dominique Iogna-Prat et al. (Paris, 1996), 295–312.

——, *Peindre à Auxerre au Moyen Age, IXe–XIVe siècles* (Auxerre, 1999).

——, "Saint-Philibert et les débuts de l'architecture romane en Bourgogne," *Saint-Philibert de Tournus: Histoire, Archéologie, Art*, Actes du colloque du Centre international d'études romanes, Tournus, 15–19 July 1994 (Tournus, 1995), 215–30.

——, "Saint-Pierre de Flavigny, l'ancienne abbatiale et ses cryptes," *Congrès archéologique de France* 144 (1986), 97–109.

Saunders, A. D., "Excavations in the Church of St Augustine's Abbey, Canterbury: 1955–58," *Medieval Archaeology* 22 (1978), 25–63.

Scaccia Scarafoni, E., "La chiesa cassinese detta 'Santa Maria delle Cinque Torri,'" *Rivista di archeologia cristiana* 22 (1946), 139–89.

Schaller, D. "Das Aachener Epos für Karl den Kaiser," *Frühmittelalterliche Studien* 10 (1976), 165–67.

Schefers, Hermann, ed., *Einhard: Studien zu Leben und Werk* (Darmstadt, 1997).

Scheffczyk, Leo, *Das Mariengeheimnis in Frömmigkeit und Lehre der Karolingerzeit*, Erfuhrter Theologische Studien 5 (Leipzig, 1959).

Schieffer, Rudolf, "Charlemagne and Rome," *Early Medieval Rome and the Christian West: Essays in Honour of Donald A. Bullough*, ed. J. Smith (Leiden, 2000), 279–95.

Schlesinger, Walter, "Beobachtungen zur Geschichte und Gestalt der Aachener Pfalz in der Zeit Karls des Grossen," *Studien zur europäischen Vor- und Frühgeschichte* (Neumünster, 1968), 258–81.

——, "Einhards römische Reliquien: Zur Bedeutung der Reliquientranslation Einhards von 827/828," *Archiv für hessische Geschichte und Altertumskunde*, N.S. 48 (1990), 279–92.

Schlunk, Helmut, and Theodor Hauschild, *Die Denkmäler der frühchristlichen und westgotischen Zeit* (Mainz, 1978).

Schmitz, P., "L'influence de Saint Benoit d'Aniane dans l'histoire de l'Ordre de Saint Benoit," *Il monachesimo nell'alto medioveo a la formazione della civiltà occidentale*, Settimane de studio del centro italiano di studi sull'alto medioevo 4 (1957), 401–15.

Schnitzler, Hermann, "Das Kuppelmosaik der Aachener Pfalzkappelle," *Aachener Kunstblätter* 29 (1957), 69–78.

Schönfeld de Reyes, Dagmar von, *Westwerkprobleme. Zur Bedeutung der Westwerke in der kunsthistorischen Forschung*, (Weimar, 1999).

Schrade, Hubert, "Zum Kuppelmosaik der Pfalzkapelle und zum Theodorich-Denkmal in Aachen," *Aachener Kunstblätter* 30 (1965), 25–37.

Schütte, Sven, "Der Aachener Thron," *Krönungen: Könige in Aachen—Geschichte und Mythos*, ed. Mario Kramp, 2 vols. (Mainz, 2000), 1:213–22.

——, "Überlegungen zu architektonischen Vorbildern der Pfalz Ingelheim und Aachen," *Krönungen: Könige in Aachen—Geschichte und Mythos*, ed. Mario Kramp, 2 vols. (Mainz, 2000), 1:203–11.

Scortecci, Donatella, "Riflessioni sulla cronologia del tempio perugino di San Michele Arcangelo," *Rivista di archeologia cristiana* 67 (1991), 405–28.

Segal, Edward A., "The Plan of Saint Gall and the Monastic Reform Councils of 816 and 817," *Cuyahoga Review* 1 (1983), 57–71.

Semmler, Joseph, "Benedictus II: Una regula—una consuetudo," *Benedictine Culture 750—1050*, ed. W. Lourdaux and D. Verhelst (Leuven, 1983), 24.

——, "Die Beschlüsse des Aachener Konzils im Jahre 816," *Zeitschrift für Kirchengeschichte* 74 (1963), 15–82.

——, "Reichsidee und kirchliche Gesetzgebung," *Zeitschrift für Kirchengeschichte* 71 (1960), 37–65.

——, "Studien zum Supplex Libellus und zur anianischen Reform in Fulda," *Zeitschrift für Kirchengeschichte* 69 (1958), 268–98.

Sennhauser, Hans Rudolf, "Das Münster des Abtes Gozbert (816–37) und seine Ausmalung unter Hartmut (Proabbas 841, Abt 872–83)," *Unsere Kunstdenkmäler* 34 (1983), 152–55.

——, "St. Gallen: Zum Verhältnis von Klosterplan und Gozbertbau," *Hortus Artium Medievalium* 8 (2002), 49–55.

Seston, W., and C. Perrat, "Une basilique funéraire païenne à Lyon d'après une inscription inédite," *Revue des études anciennes* 49 (1947), 139–59.

Shaffer, Jenny H., "Recreating the Past: Aachen and the Problem of the architectural 'Copy'," Ph.D. diss., Columbia University, 1992.

Sheerin, Daniel J., "The Church Dedication 'Ordo' used at Fulda, 1 Nov., 819," *Revue Bénédictine* 92 (1982), 305–16.

Silvagni, A., "La topographia cimiteriale della via Aurelia," *Rivista di archeologia cristiana* 9 (1932) 105.

Silva-Tarouca, C., "Giovanni 'archcantor' di S. Pietro a Roma," *Atti della Pontificia Accademia Romana di Archeologia*, Memorie, 3d ser. 1 (1923), 163ff.

Smith, Julia, "Old Saints, New Cults: Rome Relics in Carolingian Francia," *Early Medieval Rome and the Christian West: Essays in Honour of Donald A. Bullough*, ed. J. Smith (Leiden, 2000), 317–39.

Snively, Carolyn S., "Apsidal Crypts in Macedonia: Possible Places of Pilgrimage," *Akten des XII. Internationalen Kongresses für Christliche Archäologie*, Jahrbuch für Antike und Christentum Ergänzungsband 20, 1 (1995) 2 vols., 2:1179–84.

Sotiriou, G. and M., *Hi basiliki tou Hagiou Dimitriou tis Thessalnikis* (Athens, 1952).

Sowers, Ossa Raymond, "Medieval Monastic Planning: Its Origins in the Christian East and Later Developments in the Western Europe," Ph.D. diss., Columbia University, 1951.

Soyer, J., "Les inscription gravées sur les piliers de l'église carolingienne de Germigny-des-Prés sont-elles anthentiques?" *Bulletin archéologique* (1923), 197–216.

Speake, George, *Anglo-Saxon Animal Art and Its Germanic Background* (Oxford, 1980).

Stachura, Norbert, "Der Plan von St. Gallen—ein Original?" *Architectura* 8 (1978), 184–86.

——, "Der Westabschluss der Klosterkirche und seine Varianten," *Architectura* 10 (1980), 33–37.

Steinke, Katherina, *Die mittelalterlichen Vatikan Paläste und ihre Kapellen* (Vatican City, 1984).

Stengel, Edmund, "Über Ursprung, Zweck und Bedeutung der karlingischen Westwerke," *Festschrift Adolf Hofmeister*, ed. Ursula Scheil (Halle, 1955), 283–311.

Stiegemann, Christoph, and Matthias Wemhoff, eds., *799 Kunst und Kultur der Karolingerzeit. Karl der Grosse und Papst Leo III. in Paderborn*, exh. cat. Paderborn 1999, 2 vols. (Mainz am Rhein, 1999).

——, *799 Kunst und Kultur der Karolingerzeit. Karl der Grosee und Papst Leo III. in Paderborn: Beiträge zum Katalog der Ausstellung*, (Mainz am Rhein, 1999).

Stoclet, Alain J., "La 'Descriptio Basilicae Sancti Dyonisii': Premiers Commentaires," *Journal des Savants* (1980), 104–17.

Straw, Carole, *Gregory the Great: Perfection in Imperfection* (Berkeley and London, 1988).

Stroheker, Karl Friedrich, "Das spanische Westgotenriech und Byzanz," *Bonner Jahrbücher* 163 (1963), 252–74.

Süssenbach, Uwe, *Die Stadtmauer des römischen Köln* (Cologne, 1981).

Swan, Leo, "Monastic Proto-Towns in Early Medieval Ireland: The Evidence of Aerial Photography, Plan Analysis and Survey," *The Comparative History of Urban Origins in non-Roman Europe*, ed. H. B. Clarke and A. Simms, British Archaeological Reports International Series 255, 2 vols. (Oxford, 1985), 1:77–102.

Taylor, Harold M., *Anglo-Saxon Architecture*, 3 vols. (Cambridge, 1978).

——, "Tenth-Century Church Building in England and on the Continent," *Tenth-Century Studies*, ed. David Parsons (London, 1975), 141–68.

—— and Joan, *Anglo-Saxon Architecture*, 2 vols. (Cambridge, 1965).

Thacker, Alan, "In Search of Saints: The English Church and the Cult of Roman Apostles and Martyrs on the Seventh and Eighth Centuries," *Early Medieval Rome and the Christian West: Essays in Honour of Donald A. Bullough*, ed. J. Smith (Leiden, 2000), 247–77.

Thomas, Charles, *The Early Christian Archaeology of North Britain* (London and Oxford, 1971).

Thompson, E. A., *The Goths of Spain* (Oxford, 1969).

Thuno, Erik, *Image and Relic: Mediating the Sacred in Early Medieval Rome* (Rome, 2002).

Todd, Malcolm, *The Early Germans* (Oxford, 1992).

Tolotti, Francesco, "Le confessioni succedutesi sul sepolchro di S. Paolo," *Rivista di archeologia cristiana*, 59 (1983), 87–149.

Toynbee, Jocelyn, and J. B. Ward-Perkins, *The Shrine of St. Peter and the Vatican Excavations* (London, 1956).

Traversi, G., *Architettura paleocristiana milanese* (Milan, 1964).

Trier. Kaiserresidenz und Bischofssitz. Die Stadt in spätantiker und frühchristlicher Zeit (Mainz, 1984).

Tschan, Francis, *Saint Bernward of Hildesheim*, 3 vols. (Fort Wayne, Indiana, 1942–52).

Ulbert, Thilo, *Frühchristliche Basiliken mit Doppelapsiden auf der iberischen Halbinsel: Studien zur Architektur- und Liturgiegeschichte* (Berlin, 1978).

Underwood, Paul, "The Fountain of Life in Manuscripts of the Gospels," *Dumbarton Oaks Papers* 5 (1950), 53ff.

Untermann, Matthias, "'Opera mirabili constructa.' Die Aachen 'Residence' Karls des Grossen," *799. KKK: Beiträge*, 152–64.

Valenzani, Riccardo Santangeli, "Residential Building in Early Medieval Rome," *Early Medieval Rome and the Christian West: Essays in Honour of Donald A. Bullough*, ed. J. Smith (Leiden, 2000), 101–12.

Vallery-Radot, Jean, "Notes sur les chapelles hautes dédiées à St. Michael," *Bulletin Monumentale* 93 (1929), 453–78.

Venditti, A., *Architettura bizantine nell'Italia meridionale*, 2 vols. (Naples, 1967), 1:591–97.

Verbeek, Albert, "Die architektonische Nachfolge der Aachener Pfalzkapelle," *Karl der* Grosse, 4 vols. (Düsseldorf, 1965), 4:113–56.

——, "Die Aussenkrypta. Werden einer Bauform des frühen Mittelalters," *Zeitschrift für Kunstgeschichte* 13 (1950), 7–38.

——, "Zentralbauten in der Nachfolge der Aachener Pfalzkapelle," *Das erste Jahrhundert*, 2 vols. (Düsseldorf, 1964), 2:898–947.

Verzone, Paolo, *The Art of Europe: The Dark Ages from Theodoric to Charlemagne*, trans. Pamela Waley (New York, 1968).

——, "Le chiese cimiteriali a struttura molteplice nell'Italia settentrionale," *Arte del primo millennio*, Atti del II° convegno per lo studio dell'arte dell'alto medio evo, ed. E. Arslan (Turin, 1950), 28–41.

——, "La distruzione dei palazzi imperiali di Roma e di Ravenna e la ristrutturazione del palazzo lateranense nel IX secolo nei rapporti con quello di Costantinopoli," *Roma e l'éta carolingia*, Atti delle giornate di studio, 3–8 Maggio 1976, Istituto nazionale di archeologia e storia dell'arte (Rome, 1976), 39–54.

——, "Les églises du haut moyen-age et le culte des anges," *L'art mosan* (Paris, 1953), 71–80.

Vieillard-Troiekouroff, May, "L'architecture en France du temps de Charlemagne," *Karl der Grosse*, 4 vols. (Düsseldorf, 1965), 3:336–55.

——, *Les monuments religieux de la Gaule d'après les oeuvres de Gregoire de Tours* (Paris, 1976).

——, "Nouvelles études sur les mosaiques de Germigny-des-Prés," *Cahiers archéologiques*, 17 (1967), 103–12.

——, "Tables de canons et stucs carolingiens. Le decor architectural et aniconique des bibles de Theodulphe et celui de Germigny-des-Prés," *Stucchi e mosaici altomedioevali*, Atti dell'ottavo congresso di studi sull'arte dell' alto medioevo (Milan, 1962), 154–78.

Viviani, D., "Tempio di S. Angelo in Perugia," *Bolletino d'Arte* 5 (1911), 28–32.

Vogel, Cyrille, "La réforme liturgique sous Charlemagne," *Karl der Grosse*, 4 vols. (Düsseldorf, 1965), 2:217–32.

von Blanckenhagen, Peter, "The Imperial Fora," *Journal of the Society of Architectural Historians* 13 (1954), 21–26.

Vonderau, Joseph, "Die Ausgrabungen am Dome zu Fulda in den Jahren 1908–1913," *Sechszehnte Veröffentlichung des Fuldaer Geschichtsvereins* (1919), 5–36.

Wallace-Hadrill, J. M., *The Barbarian West 400–1000*, rev. 3rd ed. (London, 1967, rep. Oxford, 1988).

——, *The Frankish Church* (Oxford, 1983).

Ward-Perkins, Bryan, *From Classical Antiquity to the Middle Ages: Urban and Public Building in Northern and Central Italy, A.D. 300–850* (Oxford, 1984).

——, "Re-using the Architectural Legacy of the Past, *entre idéologie et pragmatisme,*" *The Idea and Ideal of the Town between Late Antiquity and the Early Middle Ages*, ed. G. P. Brogiolo and B. Ward-Perkins, *The Transformation of the Roman World*, 4 vols. (Leiden, 1999), 225–33.

——, "Urban Continuity?" *Towns in Transition: Urban Evolution in Late Antiquity and the Early Middle Ages*, ed. N. Christie and S.T. Loseby (Aldershot, England, 1996), 4–17.

Ward-Perkins, J. B., *Cities of Ancient Greece and Italy: Planning in Classical Antiquity* (New York, 1972).

——, "Constantine and the Origins of the Christian Basilica," *Papers of the British School at Rome* 22 (1954), 69–90.

——, *Roman Imperial Architecture*, 2nd ed., (New Haven and London, 1994).

Watkinson, Barbara A., "Lorsch, Jouarre et l'appareil décoratif du Val de Loire," *Cahiers de civilisation médiévale* 33 (1990), 49–63.

Webster, Leslie, and Michelle Brown, eds., *The Transformation of the Roman World A.D. 400–900* (London, 1997).

Webster, Leslie, and John Cherry, "Kent: Canterbury, St. Pancras Church," *Medieval Archaeology* 20 (1976), 163–64.

Wehling, Ulrike, *Die Mosaiken im Aachener Münster und ihre Vorstufen* (Cologne, 1995).

Weidemann, Konrad, "Ausgrabungen in der karolingischen Pfalz Ingelheim," *Ausgrabungen in Deutschland*, 4 vols. (Mainz, 1975) 2:437–46.

——, "Die Königpfalz in Ingelheim," *Ingelheim am Rhein 774–1974. Geschichte und Gegenwart* (Ingelheim, 1974), 37–56.

Weidemann, Margarete, *Kulturgeschichte der Merowingerzeit nach den Werken Gregors von Tours*, 2 vols. (Mainz, 1982).

Weise, Georg, *Zwei fränkische Königspfalzen. Bericht über die an den Pfalzen zu Quierzy und Samoussy vorgenommenen Grabungen*, (Tübingen, 1923).

Weitzmann, Kurt, *The Icon* (New York, 1978).

Welch, Martin, *Discovering Anglo-Saxon England* (University Park, Pennsylvania, 1992).

Wengenroth-Weimann, Uta, *Die Grabungen an der Königspfalz zu Nieder-Ingelheim in den Jahren 1960–1970*, Beiträge zur Ingelheimer Geschichte, vol. 23, Historischer Verein (Ingelheim, 1973).

Weyres, Willy, *Die vorgotischen Bischofskirchen in Köln*, Studien zum Kölner Dom 1, ed. Arnold Wolff (Cologne, 1987), 88–100.

Wharton, Annabel Jane, *Refiguring the Post Classical City* (Cambridge, 1995).

——, "Ritual and Reconstructed Meaning: The Neonian Baptistery in Ravenna," *Art Bulletin* 69 (1987), 358–75.

White, L. Michael, *The Social Origins of Christian Architecture*, 2 vols. (Valley Forge, Pennsylvania, 1996).

Whitehouse, David, "Window Glass between the First and the Eighth Centuries," *Il colore nel medioevo: Arte simbolo tecnica. La vetrata in occidente dal IV all'XI secolo*, Atti delle giornate di studi, Lucca 23–25 settembre 1999, ed. Francesca Dell'Acqua and Romano Silva (Lucca, 2001), 31–44.

Wickham, Chris, "Artistocratic Power in Eighth Century Lombard Italy," *After Rome's Fall: Narrators and Sources in Early Medieval History*, Essays Presented to Walter Goffart, ed. A. C. Murray (Toronto, 1998), 159–60.

——, *Early Medieval Italy: Central Power and Local Society 400–1000* (Ann Arbor, 1989).

Wilkinson, John, *Jerusalem Pilgrims before the Crusades*, (Jerusalem, 1977).

Williams, Peter, *A New History of the Organ from the Greek to the Present Day* (London, 1980).

Williams, Stephen, and Gerard Friell, *Theodosius: The Empire at Bay* (New Haven and London, 1994).

Wilpert, J., *Die Römischen Mosaiken und Malereien der kirchlichen Bauten von IV bis XIII Jahrhunderts*, 4 vols. (Freiburg, 1916).

Wilsdorf, Christian, "L'éveque Haito reconstructeur de la cathédrale de Bale (Premier quart du IXe siècle): Deux textes retrouvés," *Bulletin Monumental* 133 (1975), 175–81.

Wilson, David M., *Anglo-Saxon Art* (London and Woodstock, New York, 1984).

——, "Introduction," *The Archaeology of Anglo-Saxon England*, ed. David M. Wilson (Cambridge, 1976), 7–8.

Wilson, R.J.A., *Piazza Armerina* (London, 1983).

Winkelmann, Wilhelm, "Die Ausgrabungen der frühmittelalterlichen Siedlung bei Warendorf," *Neue Ausgrabungen in Deutschland* (Berlin, 1958), 492–516.

——, "'Est locus insignis, quo Patra et Lippis fluetant.' Uber die Ausgrabungen in den karolingischen und ottonischen Königspfalzen in Paderborn," *Chateau Gaillard. Etudes de castellologie médiévale*, Actes du Ve colloque international tenu a Hindsgaul, Danemark, 1–6 September 1970 (Caen, 1972), 203–16.

Wirth, Karl-August, "Bemerkungen zum Nachleben Vitruv im 9. und 10. Jahrhundert und zu dem Schlettstädter Vitruv-Codex," *Kunstchronik* 20 (1967), 281–91.

Wiseman, James R., "Archaeology and History at Stobi, Macedonia," *Rome and the Provinces: Studies in the Transformation of Art and Architecture in the Mediterranean World*, ed. Charles McClendon (New Haven, 1986), 37–50.

Wisskirchen, Rotraut, *Das Mosaikprogram von S. Prassede in Rome: Ikonographie und Ikonologie* (Jahrbuch für Antike und Christentum 17), Münster, 1990, 29ff.

——, "Santa Maria in Domnica. Überlegungen zur frühesten apsidialen Darstellung der thronenden Maria in Rom," *Aachenener Kunstblätter* 61 (1995–97), 381–93.

Wolff, Arnold, "Mass und Zahl am Alten Dom zu Köln," *Baukunst des Mittelalters in Europa. Hans Erich Kubach zum 75. Geburtstag*, ed. Franz J. Much (Stuttgart, 1988), 97–106.

——, *Vorbericht über die Ergebnisse der Kölner Domgrabung 1946–1983. Dargestellt nach den Veröffentlichungen von Otto Doppelfeld und Willy Weyres*, Forschungsberichte des Landes Nordrhein-Westfalen, Nr. 3000, Fachgruppe Geisteswissenschaften (Opladen, 1983).

Wollasch, Joachim, "Zu den persönlichen Notizen des Heiricus von S. Germain d'Auxerre," *Deutsches Archiv für Erforschung des Mittelalters* 15 (1959), 211–26.

Woodruff, Helen, "The Iconography and Date of the Mosaics of La Daurade," *Art Bulletin* 13 (1931), 80–104.

Wyss, Michaël, et al., *Atlas historique de Saint-Denis: Des origines au XVIIIe siècle* (Paris, 1996).

Zanker, Paul, *Forum Augustum* (Tübingen, n.d.).

——, "Das Trajansforum in Rom," *Archaeologische Anzeiger* 85 (1970), 517–19.

Zeilinger-Büchler, Roswitha, "Kunstgeschichtliche Betrachtungen zur Datierung der Lorscher Königshalle," *Beiträge zur Geschichte des Klosters Lorsch* (Lorsch, 1980), 79–91.

Zettler, Alfons, *Die frühen Klosterbauten Reichenau* (Sigmaringen, 1988).

——, "Der St. Galler Klosterplan. Überlegungen zu seiner Herkunft und Entstehung," *Charlemagne's Heir: New Perspectives on the Reign of Louis the Pious (814–840)*, ed. Peter Godman and Roger Collins (Oxford, 1990), 655–87.

Zimmermann, Walter, "Das Grab der Äbtissin Theophanu von Essen," *Bonner Jahrbücher* 152 (1952), 226–27.

Zink, Jochen, "Der Baugeschichte des Trierer Domes von den Anfängen im 4. Jahrhundert bis zur letzten Restaurierung," *Der Trierer Dom*, ed. Franz Ronig (Neuss, 1980), 18ff.

Zwierlein, Otto, "Karolus Magnus—alter Aeneas," *Literatur und Sprache im europäischen Mittelalter* (Darmstadt, 1973), 44–52.

INDEX

Page numbers in *italics* refer to illustrations.

PHOTOGRAPHIC ACKNOWLEDGMENTS

While every effort has been made to trace copyright holders, any further information would be welcome.

Anderson / Art Resource, New York: 16, 74; Bede's World: 89, Image reproduced courtesy of the Trustees of Bede's World, Jarrow; © Biblioteca Apostolica Vaticana: 31 (from B.M. Apolloni Ghetti, et al., *Esplorazioni*, fig. 141), 49, 158, 170; Bibliothèque nationale de France, Paris: 110, 125, 129, 142; Bildarchiv d. ÖNB, Wien (Vienna): 75; George Braziller Publishers: 93, 98; Bridgeman-Giraudon / Art Resource, New York: 50, 53, 209; © Copyright The British Museum, London: 84; © Cambridge University Press, reprinted with permission: 62 from P. Addyman, "The Anglo-Saxon House: A New Review," *Anglo-Saxon England* 1 (1972), fig. 9; © Centre des monuments nationaux, Paris: 136 and 198 Cliché Arch. Phot. / Coll. MAP; 141 Coll. MAP (watercolor by Lisch); Conway Library, Courtauld Institute of Art, London: 73; Deutsches Archäologisches Institut, Madrid: 40, Neg. D-DAI-MAD-N-62 (Photo: R. Friedrich); Deutsches Archäologisches Institut, Rome: 19, Neg. 54.56; 21, Neg. 57.1876; 22, Neg. 57.1896; English Heritage.NMR, reproduced by permission: 72; Foto Marburg / Art Resource, New York: 45, 116; Fototeca Unione, AAR: 1, 7, 176; Istituto Centrale per il Catalogo e la Documentazione, Rome: 151; Erich Lessing / Art Resource, New York: 120, 199; The Metropolitan Museum of Art, The Cloisters Library and Archives, Sumner McKnight Crosby Papers: 95; Christian Sapin, reprinted with authorization: 182, 183, 184, 194; Scala / Art Resource, New York: 4, 150; Soprintendenza per i Beni Artistici e Storici di Roma, Gabinetto Fotografico: 153; Stiftsbibliothek St. Gallen: 164, 167; Matthew Tash: 41, 43, 44; Trinity College Library, The Board of Trinity College Dublin: 83, 155; Westfälisches Amt für Denkmalpflege, Münster: 191, 192; Peter Willi /Bridgeman Art Library: 140; Yale University Library, courtesy of: 168, 169; Yale University Press: 5, 6, 24 from R. Krautheimer with S. Curcic, *Early Christian and Byzantine Architecture*, 4th rev. ed., 1986 (figs. 18, 26, 27B); 205 from S. Crosby, *The Royal Abbey of Saint-Denis*, 1987 (fig. 74).